New Lights in the Valley

New Lights in the Valley

The Emergence of UAB

Tennant S. McWilliams

The University of Alabama Press

Tuscaloosa

Typeface: Stone Serif and Stone Sans

∞

The paper on which this book is printed meets the minimum requirements of
American National Standard for Information Sciences-Permanence of Paper for
Printed Library Materials, ANSI Z39.48-1984.

Library of Congress Cataloging-in-Publication Data

McWilliams, Tennant S., 1943–
    New lights in the valley : the emergence of UAB / Tennant S. McWilliams.
        p.   cm.
    Includes bibliographical references and index.
    ISBN-13: 978-0-8173-1546-7 (cloth : alk. paper)
    ISBN-10: 0-8173-1546-2
    1. University of Alabama at Birmingham—History. I. Title.
    LD59.13.M38 2007
    378.761'781—dc22
                                                                2006039822

February 12, 2009

For Susan

Contents

Preface

Only in the last half of the twentieth century did American urban history move beyond relatively narrow studies of a few venerable old cities—New York City, Boston, Chicago. And it was not until the mid-1970s that the historians Blaine Brownell, David Goldfield, and Raymond Mohl, through the collection of essays *The City in Southern History* (1977), legitimated the idea of the "urban South." Goldfield expanded on this compelling idea in *Cotton Fields and Skyscrapers* (1982).[1]

Today, from those writings and others, the urban South offers some of the most fruitful frontiers for understanding not only this section of America but many other places, too. Yet one of the highest-profile components of the urban South, as David Goldfield has suggested, remains essentially unexplored: the role of urban research universities. Such institutions are key components of life in most major urban areas. Indeed, as the post–World War II South evolved out of an era of material capital as the key to modernity (e.g., cotton and iron ore) and into a time of social capital (intellectual development and networked approaches to social change), one of the most historic components of urban life, the university, emerged as both a creator and a reflector of such modernization. Hence the theme of urban life and Southern change provides the backdrop for what in other ways is a narrative institutional history of the University of Alabama at Birmingham (UAB).[2]

To be a teacher and administrator at UAB while tackling this project, as well as joining with others (especially those of Alabama's Higher Education Partnership) to seek change in Alabama's general approach to public policy, produced some curious dynamics of perspective, not to mention time management. So close to recent elements of the story, I found myself constantly intrigued by matters of objectivity, often after consulting with others on the accuracy of my evolving viewpoints. It is an understatement that being so close to one's topic is not ideal—far from it. On the other hand, as William E. Leuchtenburg said in his 1991 presidential address to the American Historical Association (quoting Richard Hofstadter), there is really nothing new about historians struggling between "'detachment'" and the "'urgency of our political problems [playing upon] their desire to get out of history some lessons that will be of use.'" In short, with a citizen's stake in the way higher education can facilitate social progress, I have told this story as truthfully as I can. I hope what flaws remain out of my closeness to the subject are offset by my access to rich detail about something relatively atypical in historical scholarship: the daily lives of human beings as played out in an evolving society at one of its universities.[3]

Several published works treat the origins and development of the UAB medical center.[4] Hence this particular book is overtly a narrative focused on the entire institution including the medical center, for that is such a large part of the story, but also on programs and people associated with the arts and sciences, business, engineering, and teacher education as well as student life—from athletics to student activism to enrollment patterns. To get at this expanse of life in detail has been no small task, and it certainly would not have occurred without significant assistance by many, some from UAB, some not. Four physicians read the manuscript at different stages: Max Michael III, hospital director turned public health dean at UAB; James Pittman and Wayne Finley, officially retired but still deeply engaged members of the UAB community; and Clifton Meador, a faculty member in medicine at Vanderbilt University and many years before a faculty member at UAB. Pittman and Meador, old friends, differ on so much, and out of their differences I learned so much. At least two historians critiqued all or portions of the manuscript: Clarence Mohr, chair of the History Department at the University of South Alabama and coauthor of an excellent book about Tulane University; and E. Culpepper Clark, dean of the Grady College of Journalism and Mass Communication at the University of Georgia and author of the noted *Schoolhouse Door* (1993). Lengthy discussions with Professor Clark were particularly rewarding, though to all six of these individuals I remain most grateful for honest, time-consuming critiques and constant encouragement. Likewise, to the anonymous critics the University of Alabama Press asked to assess the manuscript at the many different stages of its development I will simply say thank you for such straight-talking analysis.

Then there is the matter of pivotal conversations. In addition to Professor Clark's (regarding everything in the book), I thank journalist Howell

Raines; my UAB colleague in government, Wendy Gunther-Canada; New York University's Thomas L. Bender; Harvard's E. O. Wilson; my UAB colleague in sociology, Mark LaGory; the noted urbanist Nevin Brown; the equally noted urbanist at the University of Pennsylvania, Ira Harkavy; City University of New York's Judith Stein; the University of Liverpool's Sylvia Harrop; my UAB history colleagues, Robert G. Corley and Raymond Mohl; the executive director of Alabama's Higher Education Partnership, Gordon Stone; the chief archivist for the Birmingham Public Library, James Baggett; the director of UAB's Sterne Library, Jerry W. Stephens; and the chief archivist for the State of Alabama, Edwin Bridges. Of course, a multitude of others permitted me to interview them—all vital—and these are reflected in the notes at the end of the book. Then there is Jane Williams, who applied her sharp mind, broad education, and mother lode of UAB history in critiquing the entire manuscript.

On a daily basis for more than a decade Timothy L. Pennycuff, director of the UAB Archives, guided me to materials simply off the top of his head, materials that a researcher without his assistance would have taken weeks to find. This book still would be only "an interesting idea" without him and fellow archivist Jennifer Beck. I would also like to thank Glenna Brown, Mary Beth Adams, Janice Weathers, Deborah Littleton, Priscilla Case, Jennifer Ellison, Mary Balfour Van Zant, and most particularly Charles R. Clark and Patricia S. Meginniss. In some ways they know and others they do not know how I share this book with them. My thanks also go to research assistants Gordon Harvey, Robert Maddox, Kip Hubbard, Christina Bemrich, and most recently Adam Pinson; to all the folks affiliated with The University of Alabama Press; and to the artist Sally Patricia Smith and the photographer Michael Griffin. Finally, my family, especially at home but also beyond, gave enduring and unforgettable patience while I worked for a long time to tell this story as truthfully as I could tell it.

Overture

The Spirit of the Dutchman

In the early 1960s an eclectic group gathered on Friday afternoons at a pub in Birmingham, Alabama, called the Dutchman. Located at what earlier had been known as Magnolia Point, between St. Vincent's Hospital and the emergent Medical Center of the University of Alabama (UA), it profiled bleary-eyed interns, civil rights workers, a sprinkling of liberal lawyers, "just some regulars," and select leaders of the UAB's Medical Center and Extension Center. In retrospect, the Dutchman seemed out of place in a city known for tightly controlled social and intellectual life. Nevertheless, alongside its occasional crudeness, it had a special social openness university folks found pleasing. Since its development around 1915, the Dutchman's location at Magnolia Point had been one of the few commercial and residential areas of Birmingham not rigidly segregated, and it remained that way some fifty years later. No doubt the pub and its setting conjured up for the professors fond memories of earlier times in more sophisticated cities such as Boston, New York, or Philadelphia.[1]

To be sure, the Dutchman beckoned them because of the spirited conversation normally found around the table where one of the UA Medical Center leaders, Joseph F. Volker, consistently held forth on challenging the status quo. Granted, it would be wrong to suggest that Volker evolved his thoughts at the Dutchman; his mind often functioned like a sponge, absorbing thought from all conceivable sources of both intellectual and popular culture. Yet it appears that Volker indeed used the pub as a place to test his ideas with a diverse group of change-oriented people. "This city has some big changes ahead," he posited, "and its people will need greater access to public higher education the way it has happened in New York and Chicago." Here, Volker and offbeat civic activists such as bookstore owner

Gene Crutcher framed and reframed Birmingham's future beyond the age of heavy industry and racial segregation, always seeing a public university as a critical ingredient in the new way of life. A few years later, Volker distilled these thoughts for a Newcomen Society speech titled simply, "The University and the City."[2]

How Volker got to this juncture and where he and others went afterward is in some ways the story behind the emergence of the University of Alabama at Birmingham (UAB). In these "Dutchman seminars," he captured the core social spirit and the very will to consider new thought that ultimately led to what many consider one of the most compelling stories of university development in the United States—compelling, in part, because the story involves both the heart and the mind of a city once known as the least likely place in America for such social innovation.

Indeed, such matters of heart and mind are of fundamental importance for a historian seeking to understand key elements of the emergence of UAB. Here, matters of the heart might best be understood as a vision, at first a vision of a relatively few people in a New South city. It was a vision of starting over in the development of their community a century after its founding while shackled by the reality of no models anywhere in America for a truly functioning city. It was a vision offering concrete daily application of C. Vann Woodward's otherwise metaphor of the Burden of Southern History: that out of their defeat and tragedy at least a few Southerners could learn lessons of great use not just for themselves but for America and the world.[3] By the same token, matters of the mind provided a strategy to accomplish this vision of a functioning city. Through education and new technologies citizens might acquire the basic skills and knowledge necessary to build for themselves a vibrant society of the modern era: to thrive in a new economy; to live not just longer but healthier and happier lives; to elect sophisticated politicians with social consciences; and, perhaps most poignantly, to seize control of their own individual as well as collective destinies. To be sure, by the late twentieth century not all of this had happened. Just steps in these directions, however, make for fascinating deliberation.

Before one digs beneath the surface to the inner developments of UAB, certain more outward characteristics of the institution need emphasis as reference points for the story ahead. In the late 1990s as many as 50 percent of UAB's 11,000 undergraduate students were "first-generation college students"—the first in their families to go to college. Some 60 percent were "place-bound" in metropolitan Birmingham,[4] leading one senior UAB faculty member who had emerged out of one of America's most elite social, economic, and educational backgrounds to this finely honed distillation:

> Reasonably smart middle-class kids, not to mention the real smart and real rich ones, for a long time have had and always will have a good chance at a strong college education in America. The institutions that cater *mainly* to them, then, represent no net gain for society. . . . At UAB we are in some ways the opposite. Mind you, we attract some extraordinarily smart students from Alabama and from just about everywhere else. In terms of enduring influences on society, however, through our graduates we often offer ideas, values, and life goals which are badly needed *new* influences at a time when society desperately needs fresh thought on wide-ranging issues.[5]

The accuracy of this assessment could be argued endlessly. No doubt it is more right than wrong. For certain, UAB came to offer the most striking form of socioeconomic impact a university can offer, if one of the most difficult to measure: increasing the numbers of productive and sophisticated citizens at the city, state, and national levels. Though so gradual as to be almost unnoticeable, here were crucial steps as some in Alabama sought to bring serious modernization to the state.

Given the relatively low profile of this undergraduate experience, other key steps in the emergence of UAB captured more public attention. Here was a research-oriented faculty producing scholarship and other creative accomplishments of the highest "peer-reviewed" levels. Of even greater public profile, here was a modern medical center directly adjacent to arts and sciences, business, teacher education, and engineering. Despite almost incomprehensible issues of managing these different subcultures of learning as "one complicated family," the "family" intensely pursued new interdisciplinary knowledge about genes, AIDS, cancer, DNA, Alzheimer's, and heart disease; about revitalized body parts as well as new hearts, kidneys, jaws, faces, knees, hips, and even elbows; and about a whole new approach to health care called social and behavioral medicine.[6] The institution also offered an undergraduate honors program including not just students deemed "very, very smart" by standardized test scores but, of relative uniqueness, those who, "when interviewed and despite a modest test score, reveal a fire in their guts about creating something truly new or actually helping others before thinking about themselves." Few honors students in America could study with teams of faculty so radically pushing the conventional limits of interdisciplinary thought: a historian paired with an epidemiologist, a microbiologist with an urban planner, a pulmonologist with a philosopher.[7] Here, too, was a student life program premised outwardly on new national emphases on "diversity" but perhaps even more on hard-learned "Birmingham lessons" about prejudice. Finally, certain characteristics of development are best presented quantitatively: in the late 1990s UAB had an annual budget exceeding $1.3 billion with *less* than 20 percent of those funds derived from state appropriations; 900 hospital beds serving 43,000 patients annually; 16,500 students; 16,000 employees (2,500 of whom were faculty), accounting for one in every nine jobs in Birmingham; and an urban campus of some seventy-five city blocks with an incipient tree-lined University Boulevard running through the center of campus, one of the most traveled stretches of state highway in Alabama.

Still, recent appraisals of this vigorous place were mixed. There was the positive. In 1991 the *New York Times* featured UAB for the leadership its Center for Urban Affairs director, Odessa Woolfolk, played in helping create the internationally acclaimed Birmingham Civil Rights Institute and for the university's other roles running "deep into the public life of Birmingham."[8] The next year, *U.S. News & World Report* ranked the institution the number one "up and coming" university in the United States.[9] Likewise, by 1994 the Carnegie Endowment designated it a Class I Research University, putting UAB in the same category as institutions such as the University of Pennsylvania and the University of Chicago.[10] There was also the negative. In 1994 the *Wall Street Journal* implicitly challenged the evaluation of the *New York Times,* asking if UAB was acting socially responsible in accepting $2 million from a City of Birmingham bond issue to expand the university's football program when the city's school system needed every dime it could get to attack the metropolitan area's most oppressive problem, the essential failure of the inner city's K–12 system, and when the State of Alabama did not exactly lack for football.[11]

Local views varied, too. In early 1993 a man working at a seafood restaurant on the eastern fringe of the UAB campus told a raw-oyster eater that UAB could not have been created without the support of the surrounding community; if its physical expansion "ate up" that community the "bragged about" point of "UAB economic impact is about as significant as an empty oyster shell." The very next day, however, Nadim Shunnarah, a noted restaurateur operating on the western fringe of the campus, told the same eater, his palate having moved to hummus, "Professor, 50 percent of

Fig. 1. Aerial westerly view of proto-UAB, c. 1962. In addition to striking urban renewal tracts, note the miniature golf course (lower left) where the UAB Administration Building would be located by the early 1990s. Photo courtesy of the UAB Archives; credit: Media Relations.

Fig. 2. Aerial westerly view of UAB, 2006. Photo by Michael Griffin.

my business comes from you people. *Please* keep growing." Asked when he would be willing to help raise money for an endowed professorship in international studies, the businessman replied, "Ah, Professor, soon. . . . I think it will be soon. Yes, very soon. More hummus?"[12]

If these and other appraisals varied, more important is the understanding of how they all underscored the central reality behind UAB. There is no way to separate the conventionally defined "institutional" aspects of this story from the broader currents of social change in Birmingham, Alabama, and in modern America and well beyond. Nor should this separation be sought. With the major exception of his unsophisticated assertion about the past not being part of the present and future, what the noted education critic Abraham Flexner wrote in his general study of universities, published in 1930, is still true today: "A university, like all other human institutions— like the church, like governments, like philanthropic organizations—is not outside, but inside the general social fabric of a given era. It is not something apart, something historic, that yields as little as possible to forces and influences that are more or less new. It is, on the contrary . . . an expression of the age, as well as an influence operating upon both present and future."[13]

Hence, UAB emerged out of the myriad forces of history. There were the obvious influences of science and medicine, and particularly recent interdisciplinary revolutions involving microbiology, organ transplantation, materials science, behavioral science, and computer science. There were also bittersweet and at times less obvious political, social, and economic forces of the past. Look back to the late medieval and early Renaissance eras and then forward to Europe's expansion into the Western Hemisphere. More recently, turn to the experience of the American South: an antebellum rural elite growing cotton with slaves, Civil War and Reconstruction, the industrial revolution, the Progressive Era, the Roaring Twenties, the Great Depression, the New Deal, and the post–World War II economic boom. Even more—for it was the social reform forces of the 1960s that permitted the final appearance of UAB in 1969 and motivated so much of Joe Volker's discussion at the Dutchman—look to the 1960s and to the rise and fall of Big Steel, the environmental movement, the "Sunbelt" movement, the city revitalization movement, and, most dramatically, the Southern-based civil rights movement. Look to all of these. You find more than general context. You find seminal forces of the past leading to the emergence of a new institutional life.

This story invokes several themes. If ever there were a tale where the mind and heart were intertwined in a seamless experience of past, present, and future, this is it. And if ever there were one where civic leaders consciously turned to lessons of the past as well as to rapidly breaking knowledge as ways of improving the quality of life around them, succeeding on some occasions, failing on others, this is it. Yet, narrowing the focus, the emergence of UAB together with the redevelopment of Birmingham can be seen as a story set in a particular place in America: undoubtedly, this is a Southern story. Still, because in recent times new knowledge has been so interconnected and main currents of society so globalized, the story of UAB as with any modern institution surely transcends place, section, and nation, reaching out to the dreams and experiences of a multitude of people living so far beyond the South.

New Lights in the Valley

I

Forces of a Thousand Years

Europe

Despite prescient talk at the Dutchman, UAB's story is just like any other true story: it has no precise beginning in time or place. In the name of pragmatics, therefore, let us just say it all started at 8:00 a.m. on a crisp day in the fall of 1175 when the doors of what would become the University of Bologna opened to its first seventeen students, probably nine of whom had been drinking some heavy brew for most of the previous night at a tavern across the road and making the tavern keeper wonder, if only for a fleeting moment, whether that wise-cracking bunch back in the corner was really worth his time. Soon, similar doors opened at the University of Paris, the University of Oxford, the University of Salamanca, the University of London, and the University of Vienna. Why? Because clerics and others of late medieval and early Renaissance Europe began to believe that advanced learning was useful for individuals and for society, that universities could foster this enterprise, and that cities were the place to have all of this going on—because that was where modern people increasingly sought to live as commerce came back to life after a hiatus of some five hundred years.[1] Indeed, in Lewis Mumford's classic words, unlike previous vehicles for learning such as single texts, priests, or scholars, "in the university the pursuit of knowledge was elevated in an enduring structure . . . a system of knowledge . . . more important than the thing known. In the university, the functions of cultural storage, dissemination, and interchange, and creative addition—perhaps the . . . most essential functions of the city—were adequately performed."[2]

More to the point, here was the seedbed for the complicated idea of the city and the university combined to form a constantly expanding critical mass of knowledge and social change catalyzed by a shared sense of place—not, coincidentally, the core idea behind UAB. If all of this happened gradually, it also happened incompletely. As Thomas Bender has suggested in *The University and the City* (1988), the first combinations of European universities and their cities never existed as a clearly functioning "homology," nor did these combinations exist individually as an "organic" or "unified whole." To the contrary, an urban university represented a "*semi*cloistered heterogeneity" surrounded by an "uncloistered heterogeneity." Later on, moreover, with the gradual rise of an immature if powerfully seductive belief that one of the inherent advantages of science was its translocal viewpoint, many university-based thinkers did everything *but* feel a connection with, not to mention a stake in, their surrounding city. "International disciplinary communities" became the object of their thought and adoration and the key source of their status, "local living communities" the almost irrelevant base of their operations. Given these complexities and limitations, however, and the fact that there indeed were cases of intellectual life in European cities advancing much faster than that occurring in local educational institutions, for example, in Florence, overall the mutually reinforcing connection between the city and the university took shape as Europe moved through late medieval times and into the initial years of the early modern era.[3]

Normally, what bound the city and university together were evolving commonalities of "public culture," economic development, or government—or a combination of these functioning simultaneously.[4] As Walter Ruegg explains, by the late thirteenth century "the commercial towns were well aware of the advantage of having universities which made provision for lawyers who could solve legal problems unknown to common law, as well as civil servants who could be a match for the princely authorities." Early university students tended to be attracted more to individual faculty members than to the university, which led to even greater growth of the university. In many cases city leaders "compelled" certain faculty to "take an oath" to remain with their universities for a certain number of years; over time such pledges became key elements of city codes all over Europe. Not surprisingly, cities that managed to retain excellent faculty reaped even more benefits than students spending money and faculty occasionally helping out on a problem of law or public policy. The inevitable tensions of town-and-gown in such matters as real estate and law enforcement gained acceptance as "part of it all" as "kings often found their advisors and diplomats" in the universities—faculty members with what later would be called "applied knowledge."[5]

Teaching also helped connect city and university. What the professor-preachers of 1300 taught is erroneously assumed to be entirely different from what professors teach today. Certainly people of that time had an intensely religious orientation, with faculty, curriculum, and instruction mirroring this preoccupation. From the late medieval until the early Renaissance eras, however, the pervasive spirituality was distinctly different from that of most modern Americans. To faculty and students of the late twelfth century, religion and spirituality encompassed everything in life— from theology and medicine to career planning and mathematics, from the ideal to the utilitarian. Moreover, because craft guilds reflecting the practical concerns of skilled and professional people provided the foundation for many early universities, leaving the "humanism" of "ancient literature" to development later in the Renaissance, early university faculty taught and wrote on practical matters of law, medicine, and even theology unfolding around them. Thus "service learning," too often viewed as some incredible invention of the 1990s, occurred daily as the "urban setting" melded with "scholastic thought" and faculty, students, and citizens of the city jointly tackled twelfth-century urban issues such as illness and homelessness. No wonder cities felt strongly about their universities. Theirs was a mutual stake. If he overestimates the organic oneness of the relationship, Mumford's elegant assertion still stands true: "Here was a social invention of the first order."[6]

Still, with the early modern era urban universities as well as those removed from cities began to lose their vibrancy because of the intense nationalism as well as the exciting commercialism of the time. To Thomas Bender, there even is a question as to "whether universities between, say, 1400 and 1700, may have come very close to extinction" and with their demise the end of the intellectual tradition. The rise of Spain, France, England, and Portugal, alongside the daily excitement of capitalistic business activity, the age of exploration, and the Protestant Reformation, simply eclipsed university life as important vehicles for human interaction. To be sure the era had its creative intellectuals, some of the greatest of all time; but John Locke and other innovative thinkers of the Enlightenment were usually more connected to centers of governmental or economic activity than educational institutions, inadvertently striking an all but deadly blow at the tradition of intellectuals gathering at a university in London, Paris, Madrid, or Salamanca to stimulate each other and analyze and create. Only in three unique and smaller places—Geneva, Edinburgh, and Leiden—did the spirit appear to live on and, indeed, undergo further advancement.[7] Universities such as those at Salamanca, according to the Spanish economist Jaime del Castillo, "by deferment became agents of conservatism rather than change, with remaining faculty increasingly preoccupied with their own narrowly defined intellectual and scholastic interests—interests often disconnected from the flow of life around them."[8] In *Killing the Spirit* (1990), risking overstatement about the contemporary scene, Page Smith sharpens this point: "[T]he medieval university . . . attained a brief glory, and then sank into the long twilight of scholasticism, where the original mission was forgotten, and scholarship became what it is [in the late twentieth century] . . . an end in itself, producing increasingly meaningless refinements."[9]

America

The spirit of the city and the university lost out not just in Europe but where Europe went. Toward the end of the Renaissance many people of this Old World, some of whom were educated in the old urban universities of Britain and Europe, had colonized North and South America. Those who headed south of the Rio Grande River or to the Caribbean Sea carried governmental instructions to emulate Old World universities in the New World. At places like Caracas, Lima, Havana, and Bogotá great cities emerged alongside universities. By virtue of the imperialistic national cultures responsible for them, namely those of Spain and Portugal, these institutions certainly reflected no message from Leiden, Geneva, or Edinburgh. Usually they were modeled on the University of Salamanca—the recent Salamanca experience of conservative social and intellectual thought. Those who prevailed in North America, people from England who had been given little clear plan about anything from the British government, carried the idea of city and university with even less effectiveness. In only the most nominal ways did King's College (later Columbia University) emerge with nascent New York City, Yale with New Haven, Harvard with Boston. The College of William and Mary played a part in some early visions for Williamsburg, and the University of Pennsylvania figured vaguely into Benjamin Franklin's concept of brotherly love. Overall, however, as the North American colonial period gave way to the era of the new republic, there was little interest in having universities join forces with cities for economic, political, or social reasons. If their faculties happened not to be supportive of the current intellectual and religious mind-set, these thinkers usually focused on an abstract idea of social change within some still emergent "disciplinary community," their adjacent "living community" left essentially out of mind and, to all intents and purposes, out of sight.[10]

Not only did virtually all urban-located universities of early America exhibit little connection with their surrounding communities, but as the United States continued to develop most people who were interested in higher education soon reflected the consensus that the best place to go to college was out in the woods. A growing preference for the countryside in the United States is understandable when one remembers the "Virgin Land" myths so fundamental to New World self-images of unending abundance and innocence and so comfortably antithetical to those of the Old World.[11] Myths aside, a staggering abundance of fertile land was almost free for the taking, leading many Americans to pursue life on the farm rather than in bustling port cities such as Boston, New York, Philadelphia, Charleston, Mobile, or New Orleans. Here also was a way to avoid the less palatable aspects of life in these cities whenever possible, including urban education. With the unfolding of the nineteenth century and the continued expansion of American farm and frontier life, Americans embraced an entire litany of myths portraying the city as the symbol of sin—as if eye gouging, scalping, murder, rape, disease, theft, and sudden death never happened on the rural frontier. Although geography explained this lack of sophistication, most rural Americans—meaning most Americans—nevertheless had a view of cities that educated Europeans had discarded as backward some five centuries earlier.[12] Still, out of this attitude and in emulation of colonial efforts at Athens, Georgia, Chapel Hill, North Carolina, and Princeton, New Jersey, Thomas Jefferson built the University of Virginia in 1819. He did this some 250 miles west of the port cities of Norfolk and Portsmouth, 90 miles northwest of nascent Richmond, 100 miles southwest of the nation's capital, and some 2,500 miles from the next towns to the west out on the Pacific coast. Safe! How curious that the Sage of Monticello, a man at home in all the capitals of Europe and one whom many credit with first envisioning the American public school system, went off to the crossroads of Charlottesville and far away from any concentration of democratic citizens to build his "academical village." Aside from that fact that Jefferson, like all other human beings, could be contradictory, the riddle has two answers. First, Jefferson wanted that university near *him* on a daily basis, and he would live in only *one* place: magnificent Monticello. Go there and you may understand. Second, and more central to this story, throughout the nineteenth and much of the twentieth centuries most Americans lived on the almost endless stretches of hinterland. With virtually no rails, few decent roads for horse and buggy, and the prevailing negativism about cities, it was easier for them to attend college in Charlottesville—or in Chapel Hill, North Carolina, or Athens, Georgia, or Tuscaloosa, Alabama, or Oxford, Mississippi—than it was for them to go to some "mysterious and dangerous" city along the seacoast.[13]

However pronounced North Americans' lack of sophistication about urban life, it was not monolithic. As early as the 1830s the founding of New York University (NYU) reflected an effort to improve Manhattan's middleclass sophistication in a context of religious tolerance. Unsurprisingly, this small, private exception to the North American pattern could be traced not just intellectually but biographically to Europe's surviving enclaves of urban consciousness at Geneva, Leiden, and Edinburgh.[14] In the 1840s exceptions of broader impact began to appear as industry emerged in Northeastern cities. First textiles and shoes, then precursors of steel created more commerce, more jobs, and larger cities. Boston, New York, and Philadelphia took on new vibrancy as recurring waves of European immigrants sought to fill the seemingly insatiable need for labor. Some of these new Americans, especially Germans, Swedes, and Irish, moved out to the frontier to embrace the myth of happy farm life. Others stayed in the cities where their unaddressed needs shouted for recognition, often as the emergent movement of organized labor lobbied their causes in state legislatures. When the Civil War led to an even stronger surge in industry during the 1880s and 1890s, still other immigrants arrived in Northeastern cities. Here were more Germans and Irish as well as Italians, Greeks, and Russians—Catholics, Protestants, and Jews. Now folks began to get the point. To make it beyond pathetic housing and hard labor, immigrants had to learn "American ways." Unions converted these social issues into political pressures with immigrants thus providing the single most important force behind a vibrant wave of urban education in East Coast cities. The City College of New York (CCNY) began to take shape. Temple University in Philadelphia appeared. The University of Pittsburgh took off.[15] A thousand miles inland, people on the south shore of Lake Michigan felt not just the immigrant needs but the commercial benefits of being a rail head for western cattle and attendant meatpacking businesses. They created a city, then a private university—the University of Chicago. Here emerged the prototype for virtually all urban social work programs in the nation and the careful application of applied urban research among other social scientists, especially sociologists. At a time when University of Chicago sociologists were embracing the notion of empirical data they also became overwhelmed by "the visibility of [deplorable] social conditions in their city" following the 1893–94 World's Fair. Too, some of these professors had grown up with the "moral sentiment" of Midwestern Protestantism or had received graduate training under the Progressive social reform influences radiating out of Johns Hopkins University. As they joined in passionate discussions about the need for urban reform regularly occurring at Jane Addams's Hull House near the campus, they discovered within themselves deep bonds between issues of the heart and of the mind and felt compelled to tackle "applied research" projects with teams of nonacademic reformers from the community. At least for a while some of the key faculty at the University of Chicago seemed in touch with the central truth that their "disciplinary communities" and their "living communities" had common roots and should be experienced simultaneously. They also shared lively communications with colleagues at the University of Wisconsin and a few other state universities that encouraged faculty to engage in Progressive reform in the cities and elsewhere.[16]

It is important to note that something similar was happening on the other side of the Atlantic where the notion of the urban university had taken shape. Five centuries after Leiden, Edinburgh, Salamanca, and others had first witnessed the rise of the city-university connection, in most cases only to see it dissipate in the sixteenth and seventeenth centuries, new "civic universities" (or "red brick universities") arose out of much the same social origins that led to the creation of Temple, NYU, and the University of Chicago—out of social implications of the industrial revolution. These civic universities of Britain were distinctly apart from the elitist and static-knowledge orientation of an Oxford or a University of Paris; as David R. Jones has written with overstatement about the "idle" professors, the civic universities were "different organizations . . . costs [were generally] . . . low, residence . . . [was] not originally considered desirable . . . [and] a busy professoriate [replaced] a class of idle college fellows." Just as important, the British civic universities of Manchester (est. 1851), Leeds (est. 1874), Bristol (est. 1876), Birmingham (est. 1880), Liverpool (est. 1881), Reading (est. 1892), and Sheffield (est. 1872) more often than not arose as civic leaders of their communities turned to higher education as a way of maximizing the benefits of and minimizing the social problems spawned by the new industrial economy as this social change played out in their cities. Clearly, the civic universities were premised on the same mutually reinforcing notions of city and university of earlier times. Still, even though these new British institutions evolved far more as a relatively cohesive national urban movement when compared to their approximate counterparts in the United States—Temple, NYU, Chicago—and their urban consciousness would be reasserted through Britain's "concrete universities" established a century later, they were unable to sustain this original mission with increased pressures for academic specialization and new complexities of urban life during the early to mid-twentieth century. They would give in to the "Oxbridge ideal," emphasizing knowledge as extolled by disciplinary learning communities and practiced so fervently by nineteenth- and twentieth-century life in the universities of Cambridge and Oxford. They increasingly lost focus on their local living communities.[17]

Back across the Atlantic the story was much the same, just more extreme, with the lack of a cohesive movement of cities consciously, even unconsciously, developing in concert with American universities. After 1912, when domestic Progressivism began to lose its momentum on campus and in some instances off campus, the bond between urban scholars and urban reformers, not to mention the merger of the two, lost out even more. Despite NYU, Temple, CCNY, and the University of Chicago, universities whose missions arose in part out of the needs of their respective cities during eras of intense social change, most universities in cities only *located* themselves there and did not play a vital role in the surrounding urban experience. So clearly defined in the early nineteenth century through private institutions like Harvard, Yale, Columbia, and the University of Pennsylvania, this "lack-of-a-sense-of-place" or translocal approach appeared by the second decade of the twentieth century as the dominant countervailing force to the noted scholar-reformism at Chicago, despite the fact that a valiant minority of faculty at Chicago, especially in sociology, still advocated the city as a social laboratory for scholars to understand more about the world just beyond the campus. More to the point, ultimately, the translocal perspective on higher education overpowered even the scholar-reformers in Chicago. Both public and private universities identified with international disciplinary communities, certainly including the University of Chicago, sought to serve general society and particularly people of privilege; their presidents seemed far more focused on trying to hire Nobel laureates than on studying and educating and learning from those who lived within shouting distance of urban-located campuses whether the neighbors were the unemployed poor or the working middle class—thousands upon thousands of potentially successful citizens. So, while America experienced a resurrection of the original medieval-era spirit of the university focused in part on its locale as a laboratory and a place for service, the revival swiftly faded with the nationalism and specialization that came to dominate American higher education during and after World War I.[18] In a sense, here increasingly was a U.S. version of the "Oxbridge ideal," an emphasis on legitimacy as defined by international disciplinary communities and less by local living communities—reaching perhaps greatest intensity not just at the University of Chicago but at the University of Pennsylvania and Yale.

Indeed, America not only lacked a cohesive movement uniting cities and universities but it received the opposite. At the beginning of the greatest era of city growth this nation or any other nation ever likely would experience, the late nineteenth century, the U.S. Congress implemented the Morrill Act committed to *agricultural* education and *rural* democracy. One can argue, as have many from Allan Nevins to Page Smith, that the Morrill Act fits neatly into the theme of the short-lived Progressive movement in higher education—the theme of "placing the mind in the service of society." An underdeveloped continent needed developing, and it would take skilled people to make this development happen. This is clearly the way the educators who implemented the Morrill Act in state after state viewed their roles, and within that context the Morrill Act represents a major achievement.[19] Still, there was a far larger context for the Morrill Act involving sectionalism, arrogance, greed, and modernization of the nation. Examined in this broader context, the act assumes a more complicated role, one working against many aspects of American social progress, particularly the connection of cities and universities, especially in the American South.

In 1848, at the end of the Mexican War, the U.S. government had all but completed its acquisition of the trans-Mississippi west. By 1862, with the first "Emancipation Proclamation" and key Union victories in the Civil War, Southern efforts to protect slavery in the South and extend it to the West increasingly appeared to be lost causes. Also lost, therefore, were chances for a postbellum revival of King Cotton influences in the power circles of Washington, D.C., influences so frustrating for big business interests based in New York and New England. To these Northeasterners, there was but one useful vision for post–Civil War America: their own control.

The Cornell University political economist Richard F. Bensel has given this Northeastern vision full and documented analysis in *Yankee Leviathan: The Origins of Central State Authority in America, 1859–1877* (1990). Bensel's notion of a "Leviathan" implicitly plays off images of "all powerful" and "dominating" first used in Hebrew biblical texts; later developed in the seventeenth century by the philosopher Thomas Hobbes; then again in the nineteenth century by Herman Melville in *Moby Dick* (1851); and in the twentieth century by Donald Davidson in *Nationalism and Sectionalism in the United States* (1938). From this deep well of literature, Bensel depicts an "all powerful" Northeastern-based commercial and industrial complex of the nineteenth century, a Leviathan, managed through the Republican Party, with Southerners and Westerners ultimately providing raw materials and "free labor" (earning wages that also would let them be consumers), as well as local managers equipped for local politics. Eerily, for it appeared ages before industrialism dawned upon humanity, the Book of Job (reflecting the Leviathan as dragon) captures the central character of Bensel's modern industrial-commercial behemoth: "Out of his mouth goes burning lamps, and sparks of fire leap out. Out of his nostrils goeth smoke, as out of a seething pot or caldron. His breath kindleth coals, and a flame goeth out of his mouth. . . . His heart is as firm as stone." Perhaps most important, however, alongside its greed this hard heart had fear. If the Leviathan's control failed to emerge, the dramatic physical expansion of the nation would shift the center of American power and wealth out of the Northeast, defeating the growth of Northeastern influences in all elements of American life.[20]

Hence, it was in this context of a Northeastern-controlled national economy and "central state authority" that in 1862 Senator Justin Morrill of Vermont and other New England Republicans climaxed a decade of hard lobbying and maneuvered the Morrill Act through Congress. On the surface the Morrill Act originated out of mid-1850s Illinois politics. Through land grants based on the size of a state's congressional delegation, the act offered millions of dollars of endowment to foster teaching, research, and service in public universities located in rural areas. With distinct tones of proto-populism, it emphasized agricultural and, to a lesser extent, mechanical education—two keys, it was understood, to economic modernization in late nineteenth-century America. Many westerners soon rushed to get their share of the aid. As the Civil War ended and defeated Dixie rejoined the Union, some Southern leaders remembered warnings of their antebellum predecessors on the matter of centralized national government controlled by and selfishly benefiting Northeastern industrialists. In their defeated condition, however, they soon echoed the Westerners.

Thus over the next sixty years this "national educational reform" developed natural and human resources necessary for the Yankee-industrial growth.[21] In raw terms, urges Bensel, it was through these and other national policies that Northeastern entrepreneurs now invoked economic colonization on the South and West. In another classic case of the conservative achievements of what appeared to be liberal reform, profits from

Southern and Western resources invariably went back to investors in the Northeast. Indeed, Andrew Carnegie and other capitalists made so much money from this arrangement that they had to give it away—and they gave it chiefly to universities, schools, museums, libraries, and hospitals in the Northeast. At the same time, because Southern and Western states were "encouraged" to keep corporate taxes low to "attract and keep" industry and jobs, these states had paltry public revenues to fund schools, museums, libraries, and hospitals, which their own people needed. Now called "extractive third-world economics," the same scheme simultaneously became a vital factor in American foreign policy particularly regarding Latin America and engendered worldwide cynicism about "American industrial liberalism." So brash in their newness, Westerners managed to keep the Morrill aid but otherwise began to control their social and economic destinies. So recently whipped and now "benighted," Southerners mustered little opposition; some actually supported it. Indeed, for a tiny self-styled elite of Southern lawyers and businessmen needed by Northeastern capitalists for various hired-hand chores in this scheme, the arrangement delivered so much wealth that they could afford to send their children up East for secondary and higher education, up East where opportunities for cultural and intellectual advancement received strong financial support. Tragically, almost a century passed before most Southerners, black and white, began to understand what had happened.[22]

The Leviathan's Birmingham

Birmingham, Alabama, emerged out of virtually every element of social change of the late nineteenth and early twentieth centuries. Only one event of that era in the South did *not* help create Birmingham—a Civil War battle complete with the burning of white columns. Granted, the oral tradition of at least one Alabama family includes a Thanksgiving dinner in 1958 where the grandfather seated at the head of the dining room table futilely sought to settle, once and for all, the family debate on the matter of why Birmingham started in 1871: "We knew that Yankee general [Sherman] was heading this way. I'll guarantee he would have attacked us and burned us, instead of Atlanta, if we had existed then. We did the right thing in waiting him out. Why build a city twice if you don't have to?"

On the surface the lack of sophistication of this serious statement, offered by a corporate executive trained in chemical engineering at Virginia Polytechnic Institute, elicits a chuckle then dismissal. No such "plan" could have existed at the time of the Civil War, and it is an understatement that Birmingham did indeed have to start over.[23] Still, there was in fact a clear cause-and-effect relationship between the Civil War and Birmingham's first birth, a documented "deal" of considerable sophistication. This "deal" remained essential to Northeasterners' vision for maintaining control of America and, over time, became a primary reason Birmingham had to begin rebirthing itself a century after Atlanta did.

In the years leading up to the Civil War, Alabama as a longtime bastion of King Cotton had relatively little need for anything in the deep divide of the Appalachian foothills known as Jones Valley, the area that would become Birmingham. In fact the valley had a history essentially at odds with what prevailed in so many other areas in the state. In a seminal synthesis of what would become Birmingham, "Birmingham, Alabama: The City of Perpetual Promise," the *Harper's Magazine* writer George R. Leighton, critiquing the area from the perspective of 1937 and the Great Depression, wrote this: "The word Southern implies a past, a past going back to Calhoun and slavery wealth. Birmingham has no such past: when Sherman was marching from Atlanta to the sea Birmingham did not exist. Many of the frontier towns of the West were booming before Birmingham was born, and Denver, another mineral town, had visions of grandeur while Birmingham was still a cornfield and a swamp."[24]

It was all a matter of late Paleozoic geology as well as the physical geography that sprang from it: iron ore filled the earth in Jones Valley, and cotton would not grow in iron ore. Even if it could have the valley had no navigable streams of water that could transport cotton or much of anything else. Indeed, as Leah Atkins has shown, the most prehistoric of humans who lived in the area did so, for the most part, on the fringes of Jones Valley so as to have access to the neighboring Cahaba and Warrior Rivers; and the later developing families of Creek, Choctaw, Cherokee, and Chickasaw did likewise, viewing the valley as a place to move through swiftly for hunting or as "a buffer zone between the tribes." The campfires of these transients undoubtedly were the first lights in the valley, providing in more than a metaphorical sense the ignominious beginnings of a valley that would have to struggle hard and long against the forces of nature and history before enduring and nurturing lights ultimately prevailed.[25]

In an effort to make the best of this situation, in 1815 a hard and mean man named John ("Devil") Jones and a few other white settlers came to the valley that would bear his name as a result of General Andrew Jackson's practice of paying for soldier service in the War of 1812 by awarding veterans free "land grants" in the area. Most of these veterans farmed on a subsistence level; a few found plots of ground suitable for cotton and produced it with slave labor, though never on any large scale because of the lack of transportation—navigable streams.[26] Soon their descendants and a few others, aware of what ore was doing to the economy of the Northeast, tried to develop the much maligned ground of Jones Valley into an industry. At the far western end of the valley, indeed, Moses Stroup attempted to fit in with the local labor culture by using slave labor at his Tannehill furnaces. But lack of state support for a railroad in the area, at a time when the State of Alabama was beginning to support railroads that would move cotton from plantations to textile mills and river ports, limited his success. Even by the early 1860s, when at the eastern end of Shades Valley— one mile south of Jones Valley—Wallace S. McElwain's ironworks produced desperately needed pig iron for Confederate munitions, there was no more than "a plan" for a serious railroad to connect the iron-rich central portion of Alabama with Selma, Huntsville, or other places well integrated into the agrarian economy of the state. McElwain had to use mules to haul his products down the Montevallo Road. At Montevallo, they could be loaded on a railroad moving back and forth between Selma and Talladega, a railroad designed to skirt Jones Valley. In short, throughout the antebellum era publicly funded railroads remained under the control of those seeking to move cotton to port or mill. The cotton lobby in Montgomery was not about to let state railroad subsidies encourage what they understood to be an alternative and threatening economic way of life in Jones Valley.[27] So self-defeating in wartime efforts to protect King Cotton, this irrational view of Jones Valley and the central Alabama iron district loomed as a threat to "the establishment." In fact, the idea of Jones Valley-as-threat remained ingrained in the minds of Alabamians not only as Civil War eliminated King Cotton but long afterward, influencing in subtle but powerful ways what happened to virtually every institution and person ever associated with this valley.

The era of the Civil War and Reconstruction ended with the presidential election of 1876 and its "Compromise of 1877." Through this corrupt "deal," Yankee soldiers ceased their Reconstruction occupation of Alabama and other Southern states; powerful old families of the South returned to political influence; the Ohio Republican Rutherford B. Hayes captured the White House although New York Democrat Samuel J. Tilden got more votes; and Yankee capitalists were welcomed to Alabama's potential industrial sites while an axis of rural-urban elites (soon called the Big Mules) delivered State of Alabama policies, keeping corporate taxes low and social services lower. Then in 1896 the U.S. Supreme Court implicitly legalized segregation in *Plessy v. Ferguson,* that is, in the eyes of Northeastern corporate attorneys who dominated the Court—many of whom had recently donned blue military uniforms to help eliminate slavery—segregation was not considered "wrong," which effectively guaranteed cheap labor.[28] To seal the deal, in 1901 Alabama found itself embracing a state constitution that not only legalized segregation but ensured low corporate taxes to further maximize profits for Northeastern investments. In turn, the state's constitution also guaranteed a retrogressive approach to funding social services—including health care and education—that would frustrate change in Alabama well into the twenty-first century. A few wealthy and powerful Alabamians, some Confederate veterans of high social standing, and some extensions of the old King Cotton establishment called "Bourbons" used their law firms and banks to lobby through Montgomery the essential support for this scheme, including laws restricting labor unions. As a result, Northeastern corporations sent their Alabama business to these firms. Odd "bedfellows" remains C. Vann Woodward's noted sobriquet for this mutual seduction, emphasizing that antebellum Whig interests once expressed through a national political party were now reasserting themselves. Given the bonds that can be fused out of greed and arrogance, however, this renewed union seems anything but strange.[29]

The resultant story of iron and steel in Birmingham is well known. Catalyzed by capital and railroads, the iron ore along with the coal and limestone of central Alabama delivered up an industrial complex, "a new city in an old land." Burned down by Yankee troops in 1865, McElwain's ironworks returned to operation before the end of 1866 ready for the new business environment; he soon would have nearly three thousand employees and by 1872 have the area around him incorporated as "Irondale." (Over time, the ruins of the furnace were developed as a park slightly west of Stone River Road within the city limits of neighboring Mountain Brook.)[30] Far more important, a few Mississippi and Alabama entrepreneurs—Confederate veterans James R. Powell, John T. Milner, and Samuel Tate—decided to sell pig iron manufactured in Jones Valley and to create a city to make it happen. Well attuned to this new and dominating force, McElwain closed his furnace in 1873 just as the new entrepreneurs began to build the community they would call "Birmingham," confidently naming it for the English place near where the industrial revolution may have begun. By the early 1880s, aided by the salesmanship of a "Southern carpetbagger on Wall Street," Tennessean John H. Inman, Northeastern capital poured into the city. None was more important than that channeled through the German Yankee Albert Fink, the American railroad magnate, and his special creation for Birmingham, the Louisville and Nashville Railroad, which quickly bought up 500,000 acres of mineral land around Birmingham. With freight rates rigged to advance Northeastern profits, more investments came south and still more development occurred. In 1886 many of the businesses were consolidated as Tennessee Coal and Iron (TCI) with 95 percent of all stock shares owned by investors living in New England and New York. By 1900 mergers and absentee stock deals created three others—Republic Iron and Steel, Woodward Iron Company, and Sloss-Sheffield Iron and Steel.[31]

From some perspectives all of this meant growth. In 1886 Birmingham and the surrounding Jefferson County had a population of 17,000. By 1904 this number had swollen to 76,123, and by 1910 to 132,685—a 74 percent increase in population between 1900 and 1910. In 1873 Alabama had produced a total of 11,000 tons of pig iron, twentieth in the nation. By 1900 the state produced 870,000 tons, third in the nation. Despite cholera epidemics and the Depression of 1893 virtually all of this came from Birmingham.[32] Birmingham's takeoff looked so enticing that on the night of November 2, 1907, with a distant wink from fellow New Yorker and U.S. president Theodore Roosevelt, J. Pierpont Morgan violated virtually every element of the Sherman Anti-Trust Act and bought out TCI. Morgan paid $35 million for Birmingham assets conservatively estimated to be worth $1 billion. Greed combined with a deep sense of sectional inferiority prompted the owner of the *Birmingham News*, "General" Rufus Rhoades, to praise what U.S. Steel had just swallowed: "The United States Steel Corporation practically controls the steel trade in the United States. With enlarged and improved plants it can make steel cheaper in this district than anywhere else . . . and make Birmingham . . . the largest steel manufacturing center in the universe."[33] It was the noted Northeastern journal, *Harper's,* again through George Leighton's analysis, that would put Birmingham in clearer perspective: "Of the [railroads] entering Birmingham, the Southern had been put together by Morgan in the nineties. The [Louisville and Nashville Railroad] was acquired by Morgan in 1901 by the Atlantic Coastline in a Morgan transaction. Now through Morgan the Steel Corporation had annexed the biggest property in Birmingham. In 1907 the Alabama Power Company was organized, which . . . came to rest as a subsidiary of the Commonwealth and Southern Corporation, reputedly a Morgan company. Ultimate decisions in power, transport, and industry were made at last in a distant banking house."[34] Now viewed as a key chapter in the national merger movement so instrumental in the further concentration of economic power among a few Northeastern capitalists—a movement producing Anaconda Copper, U.S. Rubber, DuPont, and Eastman Kodak—Birmingham became a gem in the informal merger empire of U.S. Steel.[35]

In all practical aspects Morgan owned Birmingham. Yet this master—this foremost personification of the Leviathan with "a flame [going] out of his mouth . . . [and] his heart as firm as stone"—never even set eyes on his chattel. Indeed, his personal life included only two Southerners. In the late 1840s, when they both attended Episcopal Academy in Cheshire, Connecticut, Morgan befriended Joseph H. ("Fight'n Joe") Wheeler, the future Confederate hero and congressman from north Alabama. Such teenage bonds reunited them in London in 1901, and thereafter, until Wheeler's death in 1906, the two saw each other periodically in New York City as Wheeler mixed with his numerous Yankee relatives and supported himself by making speeches in eastern cities with egotistical war stories and urgings that the New South could be a useful appendage (*not* partner) of the industrial Northeast. If no records remain to tell what specific influence Wheeler had on Morgan's acquisition of Birmingham, the two definitely had private, relatively unnoticed access to each other at the time just prior to Morgan's buying out TCI.[36] Likewise, Morgan had a trusted professional relationship with the Virginian Samuel Spencer. A Confederate general who beat Wheeler to New York City by some twenty-five years, Spencer worked his way up in the railroad component of Morgan's empire and finally enjoyed a reputation as the brilliant manager of one of Morgan's most lucrative holdings, the Southern Railway. Aside from contact with these two Southerners, however, and occasional vacations with fellow Northeastern millionaires on salubrious Jekyll Island off the coast of Brunswick, Georgia, Morgan, the single most powerful force in the life of Birmingham and arguably all of Alabama, never set foot in Jones Valley nor in any other part of Alabama.[37] All he cared to know about Birmingham—what Birmingham mayor David Vann later called U.S. Steel's "Banana Republic"—was "what his staff gave him on year-end ledger sheets." And when questions lingered he and those who succeeded him at U.S. Steel simply summoned the puppets from Birmingham. One-time Birmingham attorney Charles ("Chuck") Morgan, Jr., sardonically depicted this process as it played out over the succeeding century: "Birmingham's powerful men met in Pittsburgh and New York. Their view of Alabama was like their view of Venezuela, which also had iron-ore mines."[38]

Still, in deliverance of Wheeler's vision, the manipulations of Morgan's empire found striking symbolism in the lights of nighttime "runs" (pourings) of molten iron: "The molten iron . . . running a bright golden grill in the darkness . . . a fitful glow, now dim and sinking down, now ruddy and flaming up—the furnaces at Ensley and Fairfield, enclaves of the Tennessee Coal and Iron Company, property of the great absentee landlord, the United States Steel Corporation. When the landlord speaks the people listen."[39] As these lights of the industrial revolution grew brighter, so expanded the jobs, commerce, and population of Birmingham beyond any reasonable projections. In 1900 the city limits encompassed three square miles of Jones Valley and held a population of 38,400. By 1910, three years before Morgan's death led his son, J. P. Morgan, Jr., to assume control, the population takeoff combined with a "Greater Birmingham" annexation movement (reaching out to include such communities as Woodlawn and Avondale) produced a city of forty-eight square miles and 132,600 people minus, as Charles E. Connerly demonstrates, key parcels of land owned by U.S. Steel, so as to avoid the corporation's paying significant city taxes. Most blacks, however, who made up some 20 percent of the Jefferson County population in 1870 and almost 40 percent by 1916, lived in shotgun shanties in the shadow of the steel mills. And after 1901 the new state constitutional convention resulted in few if any Birmingham blacks voting. However, a few black families lived in graceful middle-class neighborhoods such as Smithfield and Titusville. Some whites also lived close to the mills in the communities of Ensley and, to the southwest, West End.[40]

Wealthier whites avoided the dirty air and the expanding population of laborers by moving to ritzy new streetcar suburbs such as Woodlawn, the Highlands, and later Forest Park. Here, sons and daughters of high-ranking officers from both sides of the recent war worked for U.S. Steel and lived side by side in white-columned ("neo-antebellum") homes, the plantation house brought to town for Yankee and Southerner alike. They golfed and dined and danced at the Country Club of Birmingham, recently moved from north Birmingham to fifty-five acres just south of new Clairmont Avenue.[41]

The wealthy sent their children to one of several local private academies and then off to Princeton, Radcliffe, or Harvard. Less wealthy whites went to the public school system; despite segregation, as Ruth LaMonte has shown, it was considered by national education agencies one of the top ten systems in America. Then they went southwest sixty miles to the University of Alabama (UA) in Tuscaloosa, or they went southeast some one hundred miles to Alabama Polytechnic Institute (now Auburn University). A few might have ridden the train ninety miles to Montgomery to the small Methodist liberal arts college, Huntingdon, or three hundred miles down to Mobile to the state's oldest continuing institution of higher learning, the Jesuits' Spring Hill College. If they wanted to be teachers and were female, they might have gone to the Alabama Girls Technical Institute at the antebellum trade intersection of Montevallo (now the University of Montevallo), some thirty miles south of Birmingham; or to Livingston State Teachers College (now the University of West Alabama) some fifty miles southwest of Tuscaloosa; or to Jacksonville State Teachers College (now Jacksonville State University) about sixty miles northeast of Birmingham adjacent to the iron-producing town of Anniston. Still other whites stayed at home in Birmingham where another Methodist college, Birmingham-Southern College, and a Baptist institution, Howard College (later Samford University), offered solid liberal arts education with chapel at least once a week.

Prohibited by state law and institutional policy from attending any of these institutions, whether private or public, Birmingham blacks attended the local Colored-Methodist-Episcopal school, Miles College, located to the west of Birmingham-Southern, or one of the five Negro colleges across the state—private Talladega College, Stillman College, and Tuskegee Institute, plus the State Agricultural and Mechanical Institute for Negroes (later Alabama A&M) and the Alabama State College for Negroes (later Alabama State).[42]

Regardless of which Alabama institution the white or black student chose, however, the student encountered "a curtain of silence" among faculty and others of an analytical outlook when it came to the less appealing elements of Birmingham's reality—its economic relationship with the Northeast, its racial problems, and its sad social services.[43] Granted, even in the early 1900s a few Birmingham citizens represented the exception: as *Harper's* Leighton wrote, "a few resolute Negroes who struggled through the restriction clauses and managed to hold on to their vote, . . . the occasional labor organizer," and three others—the lawyer A. O. Lane, the public health physician Thomas D. Parke, and the lay rabbi and general mercantilist Samuel Ullman.[44] Moreover, with the 1920s and early 1930s a few others, some from outside Birmingham, had stepped forward with robustly accurate portraits of life around them. There was the University of Alabama journalism professor Clarence Cason, from Ragland, whose *90 Degrees in the Shade* (1935) pondered why the mass of Alabamians were so out of touch with their reality. There was the Camden, Alabama, Presbyterian minister Renwick C. Kennedy. The product of a South Carolina plantation family who helped lead student dissent against his Princeton professors for being theologically and socially "too conservative," he later wrote for the *New Republic* and *Social Forces* on topics revealing the economic and racial injustices in Alabama. There was the Birmingham-Southern College literature professor James Saxon Childers, who as a student at Oberlin College and Oxford University developed a sensitivity to the racial hypocrisy of his native Birmingham and ultimately wrote a flawed but poignant novel about Birmingham race relations, *A Novel about a White Man and a Black Man in the Deep South* (1936). If critics happened to be white Protestant Southerners of prominent social standing like Kennedy and Childers, or in other ways nonthreatening, they were treated in Alabama as these two were—written off as "a bit kooky" and "a fun twist" at a social gathering. If they were not prominent white Protestant Southerners and certainly if they were black or Catholic or Jewish (Samuel Ullman being a major exception possibly because of his well-known service as a Confederate soldier), they could be brutalized by the Ku Klux Klan on secret orders from prestigious business leaders, Yankee and Southerner alike. Or they simply were fired from their employment as in the case of the Kansas City native and Harvard-educated attorney Charles Zukoski, who ultimately had to leave a high-level position with a prominent Birmingham bank for having "unacceptable social views" in his leadership of the Community Chest and other social action groups.[45]

Despite these few who aggressively sought discussion of and solutions to Alabama's problems, and a few other whites such as Donald Comer who along with Zukoski helped form the courageous but frustrated Interracial Committee, the overwhelming majority of potential critics and leaders of both the public and private sectors stayed silent, suggesting that in Birmingham what the historian Morton Sosna has called "the silent South" reached epic proportions.[46] And through this deferment emerged mighty reinforcement for U.S. Steel's greedy and hypocritical vision of modernizing the Northeast through control of places such as Birmingham.

On the other hand, the "magic" of Morgan's steel seemed unabating throughout the valley as the red hot lights of nighttime "runs" grew even brighter. In the 1920s Americans and others had an insatiable interest in automobiles and other products of iron and steel. In response, U.S. Steel and related Birmingham metals companies had Jefferson County producing more and more, and hiring more and more. Of Jefferson County's approximately 21,500 wage earners in 1920, 6,250 (29 percent) had employment with Big Steel and metals; of the 26,000 wage earners in 1928, 9,500

(36 percent) had employment in these areas. And of course these figures do not include usually dependent areas of employment such as coal, railroads, and cement. Encouraged by opportunities in both management and labor of Big Steel, still more people moved to Birmingham. In 1920 the Jefferson County population was 178,806. In 1928 it was 259,000—in eight years a 45 percent increase.[47]

Back in the 1880s, when James R. Powell proclaimed Birmingham to be "the Magic City of the world, the marvel of the South, the miracle of the continent, the dream of the hemisphere, the vision of Mankind," some said they needed to drink "a full quart of whiskey before [they could see] what Powell said was there."[48] By the late 1920s, however, there were far fewer naysayers. Even those unwilling to use the hyperbole of "the Magic City" admitted to major tangible evidence for enthusiasm about Birmingham. Skyscrapers occupied all four corners of the intersection of Twentieth Street and First Avenue North. And the city was growing southward. A Sunday afternoon automobile ride over Red Mountain and into Shades Valley revealed Robert Jemison's new garden-like suburb, Mountain Brook, bounded on the west by the fledgling community of Homewood and on the east by Club Village (now Crestline and encompassing the municipal center of Mountain Brook). The ride also could cross through worn-out dairy lands recently developed into private clubs. First there was the yet again relocated Country Club of Birmingham, developed with profits made as members sold the club on Clairmont to the City of Birmingham, forming the public Highlands Golf Club. Soon after Jemison's Mountain Brook Club appeared, complete with horse trails. Smiling down on Mountain Brook from the hill to the south, Shades Mountain, were isolated summer retreats, hunting lodges, and moonshine stills as well as the clean-air retreats at Bluff Park. On that mountain, too, rested the oxymoronic Temples of Vesta, Roman goddess of the hearth, the replicated temple home of the stockbroker and former Birmingham mayor George Ward. Indeed, this fifty-eight-foot structure, replete with house staff of white-gowned "vestal virgins" supposedly "imported from Italy," led the physician-novelist Walker Percy, whose father was a U.S. Steel attorney in Birmingham, to write one of the classic paragraphs in *The Last Gentleman* (1966). Thus the few profits from "Birmingham's chief absentee landlord," U.S. Steel, that managed, somehow, not to find their way back to Philadelphia, New York, and Boston slipped out of Jones Valley and "over the mountain" to the south—over Red Mountain, granted, Ward's scene being the extreme—to these beautiful new places with clean air and beyond the industrial lights of the valley.[49]

With the "the Magic City" being essentially a hypocritical myth, things got even worse. In October 1929, despite—or because of—all that Northeastern capitalists could do, Birmingham came to a grinding halt as Wall Street crashed and the overnight dissipation of the steel industry eliminated Birmingham's virtually sole source of employment and growth. No city in America fell more quickly into the prostration of the Great Depression than Birmingham did. Far more was involved than people like Zukoski suddenly being unable to live in a grand new home just off Robert Jemison's Shades Creek Parkway. Local steel and metals production dropped 40 percent between October 1929 and October 1930, and by October 1932 these industries were functioning 60 percent below capacity. Throughout the early and mid-1930s unemployment in the city hovered around 28 percent. While population had skyrocketed—from 178,806 in 1920 to 259,700 in 1930—steel production in 1930 was 1.2 million tons, back to what it had been in 1920. All this prompted President Franklin Roosevelt's advisors to say what the people of Birmingham knew all too well: "Birmingham was the hardest hit city in the nation."[50]

To help with unemployment, the Roosevelt administration funded numerous New Deal construction projects in Birmingham, none more yearning than the placement on top of Red Mountain of a fifty-five-foot statue of Vulcan, Roman god of the forge, made of once profitable Birmingham iron and winner of the Grand Award at the 1904 St. Louis Exposition.[51] Indeed, as if finally willed by mighty Vulcan himself, no city then came out of the Depression faster than Birmingham did. The outbreak of war in Europe in 1939 created insatiable demand for American steel. Birmingham suddenly had orders to fill. Night lights of the "runs" once again dominated the valley. In 1941, with U.S. entry into World War II and the resulting postwar economic expansion there were even more dramatic cries for steel, and Birmingham's economy shot back to its 1928 vibrancy. Steel production went from 1.2 million tons in 1930 to 2.7 million tons in 1945. With jobs rebounding population again grew. Between 1930 and 1940 Birmingham's population experienced a 19 percent loss; between 1940 and 1950 it had a 35 percent gain. In 1940 Big Steel and metals employed 5,748; in 1950 that number had risen to 31,435—a 182 percent increase in ten years.[52]

These numbers, of course, do not account for the multiplier effect of Big Steel, from general commerce and banking to law firms. Nor do they account for the resurgence of Big Steel in the postwar years as a factor in real estate and especially residential developments. In the late 1940s developers built Goldwire southwest of the city center and other middle-class neighborhoods where black veterans were allowed to buy property with low-interest veterans' loans and an income from employment in local industry, chiefly steel.[53] On a fancier scale, the same occurred in white residential neighborhoods. In the late 1940s and early 1950s Mountain Brook and Homewood experienced dramatic expansion. Just south of George Ward's temples, the neighborhood of Vestavia took off and soon became a municipality.[54] In the same way the Green Valley community—renamed Hoover by 1967—moved to infancy down along Highway 31 South. Years later Hoover would be inhabited by middle-class whites and blacks, not to mention a tantalizing mix of Hispanics, Middle Easterners, Asians, and Europeans, some new immigrants struggling to get a foothold, others steadily moving upward in the professional middle class. Indeed, by the early twenty-first century, Hoover reflected a more "diverse" population than any other in metropolitan Birmingham and was one of the fastest-growing municipalities in the state, while metropolitan Birmingham—despite its growing national image as a place with relatively typical American race relations—remained the only Southern metropolis to make the Brookings Institution's list of the twenty "most segregated metropolitan areas" in the nation. Originally, however, Hoover emerged out of that ingenious New England import from old England called "the restrictive covenant," which allowed the new community to serve the whites fleeing the people and dirty air of inner-city Birmingham. Despite the twenty-minute drive downtown to work, grandchildren of Johnny Reb and Billy Yank, grandchildren of those who owned slaves and grandchildren of those who helped free them, bonded as if there never had been a Civil War and bought early before the prices went up.[55]

In the years immediately following World War II, accordingly, life in Birmingham suggested that the colonial plan was working, at least in the South if not in the West. Despite setbacks of depressions and epidemics and the inefficiency of a racially dual system of private and public services, Birmingham's economy delivered greater profits to those in the Northeast who controlled the major investments in the city. Likewise, the population increased not just in the downtown area of mills, shops, and office buildings but out in the new suburbs. And government did its part. City, county, municipal, and state governments—white government reputedly managed behind the scenes through local lawyers and financiers retained by U.S. Steel—appeared in careful control of Birmingham's growth.

Beneath the surface, however, at least some of Birmingham's colonial elite began to worry about the modern utility of the old scheme. As Christopher Scribner has shown in *Renewing Birmingham* (2002), in the immediate post–World War II years, while the diversified commercial economy and metropolitan development of Atlanta moved the once sleepy vestige of Scarlett O'Hara into a proto-Sunbelt city, Birmingham teetered on the precipice of becoming a rust-belt city, much like Pittsburgh, and had an inner soul described by *Birmingham News* writer Irving Beiman as "civic anemia." Indeed, by the mid-1950s, when Sidney Smyer and a few other Birmingham business leaders commissioned the Southern Institute of Management for a profile of the present and future of Birmingham, the preliminary results were so devastating—socially and economically the city appeared increasingly archaic—they cancelled the study.[56] In *Industrialization and Southern Society* (1984), James Cobb broadens the portrait that Smyer rejected: "U.S. Steel long had dominated the local economy, and its executives had little interest in recruiting new industries that competed with them for labor and thereby bid up wages. . . . With its corporate and professional leaders standing silently by, Birmingham drifted from one image spoiling episode to another."[57] In short, whether compared to Atlanta, Charlotte, Dallas, or Louisville where futuristic commerce gained momentum daily, Birmingham remained paralyzed by persisting forces of the immediate post-Reconstruction era, an industrial revolution managed by entrepreneurs from up East. U.S. Steel and its hired (management-class) hands of Jones Valley showed no signs of losing control.

Yet this is precisely what happened. This change did not derive from one of the key sources of earlier progress in the Northeast, that is, from European immigrants organizing through politics to get their share of the American dream. Relatively few such immigrants came to Birmingham. Children and grandchildren of slaves living in segregation under the thumb of strong state laws hampering unions kept the wage scale too low to attract many European workers. Still, one of the vehicles for social progress first appearing in late medieval Europe then reappearing with European immigrants in the American Northeast found resurrection yet again in Birmingham where it helped lead the city into an era, at last, of controlling its own destiny. Steadily, sometimes tortuously, new lights appeared in the valley. One major source of this development was the emergence of a public urban research university.

2

Unknowing Relationships, 1936–44

The Extension Center

It was the fall of 1936. The people of Birmingham paid little attention to the appearance of something new in their city. They failed to notice because, despite Vulcan's raised arm of optimism, their minds were on the central question of whether their city and their livelihood would ever recover from the Great Depression and because this new thing was small and involved relatively few people. But even if it had touched many lives and they had noticed it, few probably would have comprehended what it could be for it was something with which they as Americans—and especially as Southerners—had had little historic experience. This new thing was the key beginning of public higher education in the city of Birmingham: the Extension Center of the University of Alabama. As stated by officials of the university in Tuscaloosa, here was an effort to be of "greater service to the commercial and industrial interests of Birmingham and vicinity."[1] Initially targeted at recovering the traditional order in the severe times of the Depression, this effort ultimately would be transformed into a beachhead for dramatic change in post-1945 Birmingham.

The notion of a Birmingham Center had evolved over three decades. As early as 1904 UA president John Abercrombie, formerly state school superintendent of Alabama, had become so impressed with the "Wisconsin Idea" of Progressive reform including "field education" and "extension service" that he had encouraged individual faculty to lecture statewide on topics ranging from arts and sciences to teacher education.[2] He preached his point by urging that UA join a new educational movement. Since the 1890s major universities had been experimenting with the overt use of higher education to bring about social and economic change, not just "knowledge" disconnected from "modern society." Many of those most responsible for the development of the German model of research-oriented doctoral education in America—people such as the historian Herbert Baxter Adams at Johns Hopkins University—took campus leadership roles in this movement. Nowhere did the idea blossom faster than at the University of Wisconsin, where the most prestigious professors urged and practiced the modified Jeffersonian ideal that education must reach *all* citizens for democracy and capitalism to work, and, just as important, that scholarly investigators must always be involved beyond the university laboratory, library, and classroom to stay in touch with the genuine complexity of reality. Essentially British in origin, here were powerful ideas for American educators of the Progressive Era that fired the imagination of many beyond the East and the Midwest and inadvertently provided a new vehicle for the expansion of land grants.[3]

In response to President Abercrombie's calling, UA's new dean of education, James J. Doster, created a lecture series in 1911 that sent groups of UA faculty throughout the state two or three times a year. By 1917, with Virginian George H. Denny serving as UA's president and World War I bringing national Progressivism to high tide, Doster tried something else that was unfolding in Wisconsin—classes offered to "extension students" through correspondence, with first efforts on behalf of vocational or "shop" teachers. When the U.S. government's *Educational Study of Alabama* (1919) found its way to the Alabama Education Commission, major developments took place as a result. The report recommended that extension education, which had long been underway at Auburn as part of its Morrill Act commitment to agricultural education, be expanded to include other types of education, especially engineering, and in cities with industry—"the keys to the future." Philosophically aligned with the land grant mission, though technically not a Morrill Act institution, UA used its considerable influence with the legislature and turned up $5,000 per year (later increased to $7,500) for UA to take on this responsibility. In October 1920 the institution implemented an "Extension Division" to include everything from correspondence courses to a lecture series to off-campus classes on topics from engineering to teaching techniques.[4]

Over the next decade UA's extension work broadened dramatically. What prompted this development, ironically, was less a bigger concept and more the pragmatics of protecting the Tuscaloosa campus following the stock market crash of 1929. Not long afterward, UA state appropriations—which had long been paltry from Alabama's nineteenth-century "low taxes" economic "plan"—became even more of a problem. The Alabama legislature joined the national movement to cut education appropriations, reducing higher education funding by some 28 percent during 1931–33. Likewise, beginning with the fall of 1933, UA's on-campus enrollments declined precipitously as students, many from Birmingham, could not afford to leave home to go to college. As if state cuts were not enough, tuition revenues now plummeted. Denny even had to borrow from the institution's highly protected Rose Bowl [Income] Fund to cover faculty payrolls, a debt he carefully repaid. Desperate for more revenue from more enrollment, UA now turned to the large place-bound population of Birmingham.[5]

In September 1932 Denny negotiated through Smith-Schultz-Hodo Realty of Birmingham to acquire a building for a Birmingham extension center that would initially serve the continuing education needs of teachers. A friend of the firm, James D. Head, had been devastated by the Depression and lost to foreclosure his family's twelve-room, two-story home located on the southwest corner of Sixth Avenue North and Twenty-Second Street. UA agreed to a $24,500 mortgage purchase from the First National Bank of Birmingham, which held the title. By the time of the sale the property had been zoned for "business," so UA rented the home as offices for four years, plowing the proceeds into renovations to make classrooms suitable for instruction.[6]

Meanwhile, the second phase of President Franklin D. Roosevelt's New Deal unfolded, which included the Works Progress Administration (WPA). This effort offered funds for higher education targeted at easing unemployment through adult education.[7] Thad Holt, a Sumterville, Alabama, native and graduate of Colorado College, ran the project in Alabama. Holt was no neophyte.[8] With a background in Birmingham radio, advertising, and civic life, during the late 1920s he had held industry-hunting jobs for the state and with the onslaught of the Depression first managed President Herbert Hoover's Reconstruction Finance (RFC) activities in the Southeast, then the Alabama Relief Administration, which continued after 1933 under Roosevelt's New Deal.[9] In this latter role he no sooner had helped Denny get Civil Works Administration (CWA) funding for a new women's dining hall at UA than he got the word from New Deal administrator Harry Hopkins to use WPA funds on urban efforts such as the Birmingham Center. Holt immediately convened a meeting in Montgomery for all college and university presidents to brief them on applications for the funds. He urged that applications be targeted at places with the greatest industrial unemployment, such as Birmingham. Robert E. Tidwell, who had served as dean of the UA extension service since 1920, delivered President Denny's message that UA would be honored to assume the Birmingham project for it already had an extension center on the drawing board. Despite protests by Birmingham-Southern College president Guy E. Snavely, Holt soon tapped UA for this and other major parts of the Alabama application, and with the aid of Alabama governor Bibb Graves lobbied the application to acceptance by Harry Hopkins.

With WPA funds for student aid and faculty salaries, development moved rapidly. Tidwell had made a trial effort at a center in several rooms of the new Jefferson County Courthouse, built in 1931 as part of President Hoover's relief program.[10] Then, on September 14, 1936, the center opened for regular classes in its renovated home on Sixth Avenue North. With the dining room housing a fifty-book library, "small classes [convened] in bedrooms . . . , large ones . . . in the living room." Tidwell asked Edward K. Austin, a UA marketing instructor, to manage the Birmingham operation that fall, giving him the august Extension Center title of "University Representative."[11] For the two semesters of 1936–37 Tidwell and Austin delivered classes Monday through Friday from 6 to 9 p.m.: six general education courses, five in "pre-law," seven in business, and five in "pre-engineering." One hundred thirty-nine students enrolled that first year. They attended under UA's announced policy by which a student would complete only freshman and sophomore work at the center and then go to the main campus in Tuscaloosa for the last two years and graduation. They paid tuition based on the formula of four dollars per semester hour; those qualifying for "relief" had aid out of the WPA allocation. Since Austin was the only full-time faculty member at the center that first year, and UA believed that "the men who are in the upper ranks of the faculty for [Tuscaloosa] campus courses cannot be assigned for extension courses," most courses had entry-level UA instructors or adjuncts hired from Birmingham-Southern College and Howard College or from local business and engineering firms; in some cases the adjuncts had credentials far superior to those of their counterparts on the Tuscaloosa campus. For career faculty in the Birmingham area, Depression-era salaries were weak at best. In 1936 a Harvard-trained literature scholar at Birmingham-Southern made $2,400 for nine months of full-time work (four or five courses per quarter) and felt fortunate to have it. Tidwell and Austin offered adjuncts $75 for the equivalent of a three-credit-hour course. They had no trouble finding teachers.[12]

They also found general growth in operations. By September 1939, as Hitler invaded Poland, 365 students had enrolled for one or more classes at the Birmingham Center. Encouraged to believe that he could sustain more than himself as a full-time faculty member, Austin obtained Tidwell's approval to add four full-time teachers that fall—Adrienne Rayl (teacher education), Quentin Dabbs (engineering), Marguerite Matlock Butler (English), and Richard Eastwood (business administration), with annual salaries averaging $2,800. He also hired a part-timer, George W. Campbell, Jr., who held a full-time faculty position at neighboring Phillips High School. Young Campbell soon moved from this part-time role in mathematics to a full-time mathematics and physics instructorship. Ultimately, Campbell would become a key administrator with UA urban centers and with what followed in Birmingham.[13]

No sooner had faculty and class offerings increased at the center than enrollment fell. Pearl Harbor and the U.S. entry into World War II in December 1941 saw some men and women head off to war instead of enrolling in college. On the other hand, Big Steel was a "strategic interest," which allowed many in Birmingham to work at U.S. Steel throughout the war years while going to college. Industrial engineering courses became particularly important and popular in conjunction with the U.S. government's Engineering, Science, and Management War Training (ESMWT) program and from local industries—most prominently Alabama Power—urging that a complete engineering degree be offered through the center.[14] After lengthy study documenting the availability of engineering laboratories and technology in local industry, a study orchestrated by Alabama Power's Thomas W. Martin, the four-year industrial engineering program became a reality in 1940 under the direction of civil engineer James M. Faircloth. Robert A. Jackson, who worked at U.S. Steel while taking courses at the Birmingham Center and who served as president of the Birmingham Center Student Council, completed the engineering program in five years and went on to become a manager with three U.S. Steel subsidiaries—Ohio Barge Line, Warrior and Gulf Navigation Company, and Birmingham-Southern Railway. Three others also completed the engineering program in Birmingham then joined the local economy: William C. Chase and William D. McCrary became mining engineers with Alabama Byproducts, and John G. Glodt became a longtime engineer at Tennessee Coal and Iron (TCI). Hence UA's original mission for the center worked. Through education, citizens helped themselves and also the established (colonial) economy.[15]

The center survived wartime with enrollment averaging around 200 students per semester. UA had a new president during these years, Raymond Ross ("Bill") Paty. Although he had no terminal degree, Paty had been an Emory University theology professor, then fellowship director for the Rosenwald Fund, before assuming the presidency of Birmingham-Southern

College. His striking successes in Birmingham led to his accepting the UA presidency in 1942. Fully apprised of the Birmingham scene, he worked with Tidwell and with Birmingham-based UA board member Hill Ferguson to bring about a series of leadership changes at the center. Rayl replaced Austin in 1943 when he headed off to war. A year later Rayl returned to the classroom full time when Paty hired Ernest A. Lowe to run the center. A proven extension service administrator at the University of Georgia and a good friend of Paty from the days he was at Emory, Lowe rapidly emerged as an influential confidant to Paty. Indeed two years later Paty asked teacher education professor Isaac J. ("Ike") Browder to manage the daily operations of the center when he made Lowe general coordinator of all UA activities in Birmingham—activities verging on something well beyond the center. For the time being Lowe continued to report to Tidwell.[16] Under Lowe and Browder the center surged into the immediate postwar years. Veterans increasingly came home with their educational benefits, and U.S. Steel ran at full capacity with the resultant job market bringing more people out of rural Alabama into Birmingham. Even by the fall of 1945, as Birmingham-Southern College led the local enrollment competition with 1,900 students and Howard College just behind, the center enrolled 800 (more than a third of whom were engineering majors) and Paty and Tidwell had to rent additional classroom space at nearby Phillips High School. This growth in enrollment and tuition easily took the place of the terminated WPA funds.[17]

Ultimately, however, Tidwell, Denny, Paty, and others found themselves limited in conceiving what could happen in Birmingham. Granted, they believed the extension service they offered Birmingham and, subsequently, Mobile, Montgomery, Dothan, Selma, Gadsden, and Huntsville helped meet important vocational needs of citizens and served UA's severe tuition-income needs. Here was a good cause, one conceived out of national Progressivism and reinforced by the New Deal. And many Birmingham leaders agreed.[18] Denny's immediate successor, the Tuscaloosa attorney Richard C. Foster, had a relative named Key Foster who was a vice president at Birmingham Trust and Savings Bank. The cousin wrote a long letter trying to make sure that UA administrators understood how much Birmingham industry valued this opportunity for "employees" to advance themselves. And one of President Foster's close friends, the Birmingham attorney Borden Burr, who did much of UA's legal work as well as much of U.S. Steel's legal work in Birmingham, took time off from supporting the Crimson Tide football team—Foster let him hold the first-down marker at many home games—to offer unrestrained advice on a whole range of university affairs including the matter of the engineering education needs of U.S. Steel, needs for center courses that could be of "immeasurable benefit to the graduates . . . in the way of securing positions here with the company."[19]

Still, beyond this assistance to the established economic order, the vision had strong if vague boundaries. In 1940 the student council of the "Bama Center," to use the label of the *Birmingham Post,* began to speak out on behalf of expanding the vision of the facility. The council consisted of Earle Kirkland, secretary; Neil Bryn, second vice president; Kenneth Haigler, first vice president; Stonewall Vinton, treasurer; and Richard A. ("Dick") Storm, Jr., president. On behalf of the council, Storm wrote President Foster that "every possible effort [should be made] to gain for the University a stronger foothold in the community of Birmingham as well as striving to build up the Center." Clearly ahead of his time on how one builds a city, it turned out that Storm was a Birmingham native and personnel manager at U.S. Steel not exactly attuned to what his upper management privately wanted out of Birmingham. (After being decorated for U.S. Navy service in World War II, Storm continued with U.S. Steel and became a major civic leader through the Exchange Club program; he died unexpectedly in 1959 just a few years before others who favored a public university in Birmingham began to prevail.)[20] Meanwhile, Tidwell held back on the center. As he advised President Foster, "We should hold in abeyance any comprehensive expansion of plant and program for the Birmingham Center."[21] Even in the spring of 1944 when over half of its enrollment and tuition income came from urban centers, UA remained focused on a land grant style mission modified by recent experiences, that is, education to meet vocational needs of the traditional local urban economy—what Tidwell called "adult education"—so long as the established role of the original campus was not seriously challenged.[22] Thus by 1944 Tidwell tentatively considered the construction of a larger, modern Birmingham Center to handle the increased enrollment, then decided against it. Worried about the center's expansion requiring use of State Building Commission funds needed for "the [Tuscaloosa] campus," William E. Pickens, Jr., UA's comptroller, reinforced Tidwell's caution: "[T]he Extension Division . . . should be kept separate from the operations of the physical plant" in Tuscaloosa.[23] Likewise, after UA had successfully courted local industry laboratories and technology for a four-year engineering program in Birmingham, by 1948 the institution had reverted to the old two-year program that required students to complete their degrees in Tuscaloosa rather than developing the Birmingham engineering program to function effectively within the Birmingham engineering scene, which soon boasted the largest collection of engineering firms in the Southeast. In theory some Birmingham business leaders dissented from this reluctance to move forward with developments in Birmingham. However, they also concurred as they continued to view the center as a place "for the education of employees"—not for themselves and not for their own children. Most felt caught between developing Birmingham and protecting the role of the Tuscaloosa campus.[24]

In this sense the UA family shared a dilemma faced by many in the post-1945 era. They were certain that high-quality, degree-granting public higher education should occur beyond the city, well removed from where most citizens lived in the new industrial age. Still, much like other Americans they were at best unsure about fully developed public higher education *in* the city. How far could extension service develop before it fostered something alien to the traditional scheme of things? There is every indication that Tidwell, Foster, Paty, board members, and numerous powerful UA alumni in Birmingham understood the dilemma.

To find a way through this unknown terrain, Tidwell sought advice from the leadership of the new National University Extension Association. He also watched closely the extension operations of major land grant universities. He wanted to know how they dealt with needs for more faculty as center enrollment increased and "campus enrollment" decreased. To move the primary faculty was unthinkable. Instead, fully aware from experiences with Birmingham-Southern that urban-located private liberal arts colleges provided a strong pool of adjuncts for university extension work, Tidwell concluded that the part-time employment of Wayne University faculty and other "activities in Detroit by the University of Michigan [based in Ann Arbor] approximate what we should be doing in Birmingham." Tidwell also suggested the bolder idea that Paty approach his counterparts at Howard College and at Birmingham-Southern about selling their current campuses and joining with UA in the creation of a Birmingham higher education center in one location "of one hundred or more acres" somewhere near the city, similar to what he had heard was developing in Toronto. In this scheme, Howard would offer half of the undergraduate programs and with no overlap Birmingham-Southern would offer the other half, UA being responsible for all "adult and continuing education." Although the tripartite vision reached the level of a site visit to Toronto in the summer of 1946, the presidents and boards of the two liberal arts colleges blocked further deliberations when it was clear that the vision would not include their own institutions as autonomous entities.[25]

In the end, as earnest citizens in a benighted region and as people pulled like all people ultimately are between revered tradition and the uncertainty of change, UA worked its way through the dilemma as best it could. In the process, several nuances of the story likely went unnoticed. UA's extension approach to Birmingham commendably helped some people get better jobs. But in being so cautious about overexpansion in Birmingham, most obviously for financial reasons, UA missed an opportunity to deliver college education to large portions of Birmingham and to help create the diversity of "white-collar" talents that might have given local citizens an incentive to become something more than a U.S. Steel town. In turn, Birmingham's colonial order continued, as did the powerful Big Steel lobby in the Alabama legislature that blocked the development of state policies necessary for higher education and other social services to receive adequate funding, including adequate funding for UA. From the opposite perspective, however, in starting extension-service education in Birmingham, in effect UA initiated a force that, over time, evolved into something powerful enough to help move Birmingham and Alabama toward autonomy and a better chance for a government sensitive to the needs of its people.

The Medical College

The educational dynamic that ultimately helped trigger big change in the life of Birmingham was something as striking as Big Steel. It was Big Medicine. In 1945 the century-old dilemma about what Alabamians would do about medical education and where they would do it was finally resolved. That year UA moved its medical education programs out of Tuscaloosa and into Birmingham. Although essentially independent from the difficult planning related to Birmingham extension activities, the decision about the medical college nevertheless evolved out of the same forces of urbanization responsible for the Extension Center, and they encountered the same ambivalence about change among UA leaders.

Nineteenth-century heritage played a powerful role in this story of modern medicine. In 1844, dissident faculty from a botanical medical school in Forsyth, Georgia, received a State of Alabama charter to found a proprietary (privately owned) herbal medical school in Wetumpka, Alabama, just north of Montgomery. The effort lasted about a year; by 1846 its faculty migrated to the Botanico-Medical College of Memphis. In 1852, the Alabama legislature agreed to charter another proprietary medical college, the Grae-fenberg Medical Institute, in the farming community of Dadeville located twenty miles north of Auburn. It failed when its owner, Philip Madison Shepherd, died in 1861.[26] Two years earlier, however, with the Civil War about to erupt, the Alabama legislature also had taken the bolder step of es-tablishing the public one-year Medical College of Alabama, at Mobile. An urban center since the mid-1700s, by the 1850s Mobile had evolved into a self-proclaimed "golden era" of prosperity and growth from exporting cot-ton grown on Black Belt plantations and brought down the Alabama River on paddle-wheel vessels to the port city's warehouses and docks. Hence as the state's primary concentration of people—which included sick folks, physicians, and private clinics—Mobile had a clear priority when it came time for Alabama to join the national movement to establish modern, public medical education.[27] No sooner had the school opened its doors, however, than the Civil War set in motion a series of developments that ultimately closed them. That revolutionizing conflict brought on not just the bombardment and occupation of Mobile; more important, it brought on the elimination of slavery and King Cotton, which undercut Mobile's economy and placed the city in deep debt.

Meanwhile, the fall of the cotton culture cut even shorter the life of an-other effort at medical education, that of Southern University founded in 1856 by Methodists in the western Black Belt center of Greensboro. South-ern's Medical Department was organized in 1872 before the final reality of King Cotton's death had hit home, and it produced six new physicians be-fore failing in 1880 due to lack of funds. Finally, in 1918, after hanging on for another three decades, Southern University moved to Birmingham and merged with the recently formed Methodist institution, Birmingham Col-lege, to create Birmingham-Southern College. Southern University's move to Birmingham was but part of a gradual shift of certain cultural institu-tions away from the old agrarian setting and toward the new iron and steel activities in the center of the state. As industry caused Birmingham's popu-lation to grow in the 1880s and 1890s, so did its numbers of sick people, physicians, and private and charity clinics. Thus, while the Medical Col-lege of Alabama struggled on, reorganizing in 1897 as the Medical Depart-ment of the University of Alabama (at Mobile), a new wave of medicine and medical education surged forward in the shadow of the steel mills 250 miles inland.[28]

The actual beginnings of Birmingham medical education had been ignominious at best. In 1896 a pathologist-turned-evangelical minister, Joseph A. B. Lovett, established Montezuma University at the eastern end of Jones Valley near Bessemer. The college operated out of a Mexican pavilion that local iron-maker Henry F. DeBardeleben had brought back as "just a souvenir" from the New Orleans Exposition. Despite continuing criticism of the Jefferson County Medical Society, Lovett and two or three others offered a program with "admission requirements" reputedly the same as those at the Mobile school. Montezuma University sent at least eight homeopathic or "eclectic" physicians out into local medical practice with documented state licenses before it burned to the ground in 1898.[29] No evidence remains to clarify the local lore that John Davis and William Davis, physician-sons of longtime Jefferson County doctor Elias Davis, led the Jefferson County Medical Society in torching the pavilion. Still, the intentional burning of Montezuma is more than comprehensible. Brawling and even point-blank gunfighting were not unknown to the society's monthly meetings as those of the Hippocratic oath competed over the money and status soon to be theirs as a result of the unfolding scientific revolution in health care.[30]

Montezuma and money aside, the medical community of Birmingham also reflected some of the more civilized outcomes of modern medicine, including a commitment to advancing research and education. Mortimer H. Jordan, born in 1844 on a farm in Elyton, then the county seat of Jefferson, fought for the Confederate army then earned a modern medical education at Miami University of Ohio, only to return to Birmingham well in time to bring new public health approaches to cholera as the fledgling city battled its way through recurring epidemics of the disease.[31] Indeed, according to the most authoritative listing for American physicians of the time, Polk's *Register,* by 1886, 60 percent of Birmingham's physicians had met the educational standards of the American Medical Association and by 1904, 79 percent were "professionalized." The city's strong patient market—in 1900 probably 75 physicians for a population of 80,000 with more people coming to the city each month—encouraged young, well-trained doctors to come to Birmingham, and they came not just from the Mobile institution but from New York University, Johns Hopkins, the University of Virginia, and fledgling Vanderbilt. Indeed, William Davis completed his education at Vanderbilt, the Kentucky School of Medicine at Louisville, Bellevue Hospital in New York City, and in surgical clinics in Vienna, Berlin, and London. Moreover, in 1900 three of these physicians were women; at least one, Mary Harris, was educated at the University of Michigan, and ten were African

American men—most educated at Meharry or Leonard medical colleges but three had completed their medical training outside the South: Herbert C. Cruickshank from the University of Vienna, Samuel S. H. Washington from Howard University, and the long revered Arthur McKinnon Brown from the University of Michigan. With segregation dictating virtually every element of Birmingham race relations, a few black doctors curiously had office clinics in the city's major buildings at First Avenue North and Twentieth Street, though none would have access to public or private hospitals for a long time. Still, Southern health care was not alone in its practice of discrimination, and whether because of this sad fact or the encouraging professional educational backgrounds of many physicians, the city's early medical practice had a tone and substance not too different from that of older Northeastern cities.[32]

As this sophistication emerged so did a solid effort to provide medical education in a seminal medical center setting. The first step was the Birmingham Medical College. Established as a proprietary venture with prominent doctors as stockholders, people such as the Davis brothers, Edward C. Bondurant, and Joseph C. LeGrande, the school began in 1894 on two floors of the old Lunsford Hotel at 211 Twenty-First Street in the center of the commercial district. The city also began to acquire hospitals—essential as pools of patients for clinical instruction. In 1899 the Sisters of Charity of St. Vincent DePaul started St. Vincent's Hospital in the inner-city area then reestablished it with better funding just north of Highland Avenue in the suburbs. Over the next twenty years many others opened: South Highlands Infirmary, west of St. Vincent's in the southern suburbs; Holy Innocents Hospital, later called Children's Hospital, adjacent to St. Vincent's; the Crippled Children's Clinic, dedicated to polio victims, in north Birmingham; Lloyd Noland Hospital on the western edge of the city in Fairfield, next to the TCI plant; Norwood Hospital, later called Carraway Methodist Hospital and located in the city's oldest suburbs just north of the main business district; and Birmingham Baptist Hospital Center, just west of the business district in the new suburb of West End.[33]

Still, the most important hospital development from the standpoint of medical education appeared closer to the central city. Back in 1888 wives of business leaders in the city organized as the United Daughters of Charity had teamed up with local TCI executive Thomas Tennessee Hillman to establish a five-story public charity hospital just six blocks south of the city on Twentieth Street: Hillman Hospital. Initial efforts had sought this development first in space rented in the Hughes Building in the central business district and then in a wooden building two miles west on a hill donated by physician-farmer Joseph R. Smith, an area already known as Smithfield and later developed as a middle-class neighborhood for blacks. Though built to be a hospital, this facility not only lacked sufficient beds to meet the city's growing needs but faced major funding problems following the Depression of 1893 and thus remained unsanitary even by hospital standards of the day. So when the Smithfield facility burned as part of a robbery in 1894, the Board of Lady Managers—a subgroup of the United Daughters of Charity— paid John S. Cox $11,400 for the northeast corner of Sixth Avenue South and Twentieth Street and began planning for a new Hillman Hospital. With Hillman increasing his original gift from interest off a $20,000 bond to the whole bond, plus $45,000 in small donations from local citizens as well as the governments of Jefferson County and the City of Birmingham committed to assist with costs for indigent patients, virtually overnight the board brought Hillman Hospital out of the ground and opened for business on July 15, 1903, as the most modern hospital in the state. It offered ninety-eight beds, two operating rooms, a pediatrics ward, four surgical wards, an ambulatory clinic, and a nurses' dormitory.[34]

To get staff physicians to treat the growing numbers of indigent patients, the board next deeded some of its property facing Sixth Avenue to the Birmingham Medical College, which immediately vacated its rented space downtown and built a new four-story educational facility. Here was a modern step: the *first* teaching hospital in the United States, at Johns Hopkins, had begun only a decade earlier. And one of the first students to enter these glistening doors in Birmingham was Hugo Black. At seventeen, the future Supreme Court justice studied medicine for one term before moving on to Tuscaloosa and law school where he did not have to encounter what so "unnerved" him, "the sight of flowing blood." Four years later, in 1907, the Hillman board gave its hospital to Jefferson County with the agreement that the county would pay off all debts, keep the name of Hillman Hospital, and use the facility exclusively for charity patients. In turn, the county signed a ninety-nine-year contract with the college that extended the reciprocity arrangement.

Something even more modern than a "teaching hospital" soon appeared. In the 1880s physicians had rented office and clinic space in buildings at the intersection of First Avenue North and Twentieth Street. However, even by 1908, as the sociologist Ferris Ritchey has shown, with the Hillman Hospital-Birmingham Medical College offering such a potential critical mass of professional health care, physicians were moving their practices south on Twentieth Street to form a loosely knit center where private practice physicians treated patients, taught part time, and did more research than most realize—especially in the field of surgery where Birmingham's accident-prone life of railroads and steel mills offered unending opportunities for "applied research." The surgery research of the Davis brothers gained recognition nationwide and appeared in articles published by the *Alabama Medical and Surgical Journal,* which they helped found. Finally, in 1910 the Davis brothers and other proprietors of the Birmingham Medical College bought out the neighboring Birmingham Dental College for a total expenditure of $1,041, added a pharmacy, and formed the new Birmingham Medical, Dental and Pharmaceutical College, though people continued to call it the Birmingham Medical College. An early twentieth-century medical center now appeared poised for development in Birmingham.[35]

To quicken the pulse, in the summer of 1914 a fight within the board of trustees of Vanderbilt University saw the Methodist Episcopal Church, South, ceasing association with Vanderbilt and looking for another college in the Southeast where it might relocate its divinity school and its general money and influence in the creation of a first-class university. Focused on an urban location, the Methodists decided to turn either to fledgling Emory College near Atlanta or to whatever Methodist college merger would occur in Birmingham, soon to be clarified as Birmingham-Southern College. The Methodists also indicated they would seek to purchase a medical school for development in the new urban complex, either the Atlanta Medical College or the more scientifically advanced, if financially unstable, Birmingham Medical College.[36] Early on the Medical College of Georgia, in Augusta, also may have crossed the Methodists' minds, but any serious thought along these lines likely was dashed by the political embroilment attendant to that institution's merger with the University of Georgia in Athens.[37]

Beneath the surface of this story flowed powerful currents of social change. Big Steel had Birmingham payrolls and powerful business leadership far ahead of their counterparts in Atlanta, a town only forty years beyond its destruction at the hands of General Sherman. Still, Atlanta already had leadership dominated by native Georgians carefully focused on rebuilding Atlanta as a modern city serving Georgians, not investors from the Northeast and particularly not a Yankee named Morgan. None of Atlanta's leadership was more significant than the Candler family; one son, Warren, was a Methodist bishop mad at Vanderbilt; another, Asa, was principal owner of the new Coca Cola, Inc. Although Methodist leaders went to Birmingham for a site visit in June 1914, a careful strategy from Atlanta, a plan built around a $500,000 incentive from the Atlanta Chamber of Commerce and one of $1,000,000 from Coca Cola, landed the deal for Emory—no doubt the first in a long series of steps permitting Atlanta's eventual eclipse of Birmingham by the late 1950s.[38]

The Methodists were serious. By 1917 they had raised an additional $2,065,000 for newly opened Emory University. Here were not just the liberal arts (incorporating faculty and programs initially developed as Emory College at Oxford, Georgia) but law and theology and a relatively well-funded medical school. By contrast, still lacking serious development, Birmingham's medical education remained poised—and only poised—for greatness, while its steel industry remained the only big-time game in town. With many of the company records and archives of U.S. Steel still closed to historians, one can either assume that in the deep South the field of medicine and of medical education as an "authoritative" social force was too incipient (but growing) in the years 1914–17 for U.S. Steel managers to have shown much interest, one way or the other, in the possibility of a new medical school appearing in its city, or that these managers saw the nascent force of professionalized medicine as it gradually claimed its share in the power elite of Northeastern cities and decided to kill the deal for its company town of Birmingham just by leaving the Methodists' card on the table. One thing, however, seems at least plausible. If U.S. Steel had wanted the Methodists' new, invigorating influence in Birmingham, an influence that even short term would have raised the wage scale in the city, U.S. Steel would have made that happen. In 1914, Coca Cola was no match for the House of Morgan.[39]

Still, competition with Atlanta did not represent the only roadblock to more medical education in Birmingham. In the early twentieth century new, expensive laboratory equipment kept appearing in American health care where it was integrated into how medical students were trained. Where there were funds to acquire these changing technologies, a medical school–hospital complex, such as Johns Hopkins, stood out as stellar. Where the funds were not available, as in Birmingham, the quality of the health care and related medical education appeared less and less modern. There also was the problem of Alabamians themselves. Indeed, the full development of medical education in Birmingham came only after competing citizens statewide joined in virtually mortal combat. As early as the 1890s physicians associated with the Jefferson County Medical Society had collided with physicians from such antebellum towns as Tuscaloosa, Montgomery, and Mobile over control of the Alabama Department of Public Health. Despite the phenomenal growth of Birmingham and its influx of well-trained physicians, Mobile and Montgomery physician Jerome Cochran stayed in tight control of the department and blocked repeated Birmingham efforts to develop a more centralized approach to epidemics and other public health issues, foreshadowing the battle ahead.[40]

In 1910 the Flexner Report sponsored by the American Medical Association and the Carnegie Foundation for the Advancement of Teaching proclaimed that Alabama's medical education understandably lacked accreditation and credibility. Whether one looked to Mobile or to Birmingham, it had weak undergraduate requirements, inadequate scientific curriculum, and fiscal instability. As a corrective, Flexner urged that private efforts in Birmingham along with the public one in Mobile be discontinued; in their place should be one modern, four-year state medical college that might make use of Hillman Hospital, though Flexner also viewed it, young as it was, as already lacking the new standards of major hospitals in the East.[41] What Flexner described as "the rival claims of competing towns" in Alabama blocked implementation of his report. Granted, in 1912 members of the Alabama legislature found themselves with a draft bill to provide state support for the Hillman Hospital–Birmingham Medical College complex as a way of addressing these issues. With the Big Steel lobby curiously silent (but absent?) in the fray, legislators aligned with Tuscaloosa, Montgomery, and Mobile—and possibly some out of Birmingham—blocked the bill as written. Instead, the legislature embraced Flexner's secondary recommendation. Short of a major new four-year institution, Alabama should develop a strong two-year school in Tuscaloosa as part of UA, with the assumption that those who completed its program would then go elsewhere to complete their medical education. Therefore, in 1915—while the Candlers carefully laid the cornerstones for a modern Atlanta unencumbered by parasitic influences based elsewhere and while Hillman lost its accreditation as a teaching hospital for being substandard—what Flexner called a "not too savory regional fight" developed in Alabama. Tuscaloosa versus Birmingham versus Mobile—where would the new two-year state medical school be located? The Birmingham Medical College incurred more debt as it sought to buy new laboratory equipment without the benefit of public funding. Its indebtedness finally grew too large and the college entered into bank receivership. UA then bought it out of receivership. When the political dust settled, it seems that the state, led at the time by Governor Charles Henderson, provided funds for President Denny to build a three-story structure in Tuscaloosa. Here, starting in 1920, would be UA's new two-year Graduate School of Basic Medical Sciences formed by the removal of the medical college from Mobile to Tuscaloosa, and by its merger with the equally removed vestiges of the Birmingham Medical College.[42]

When the dust settled there was no evidence that the Black Belt–Birmingham alliance in the legislature, the "Big Mules" so deeply committed to high steel profits through low taxes and racial segregation, had supported the Birmingham doctors. Why? There is no clear answer to this question. Granted, one logically can factor in Governor Henderson's worry about two public medical schools during a time of temporary economic downturn for Alabama. Yet, given the momentum and status of the Birmingham medical scene, why Tuscaloosa? Another plausible insight comes from Kenneth M. Ludmerer's classic, *A Time to Heal* (1999). The late nineteenth and early twentieth centuries, writes Ludmerer, saw U.S. medical education increasingly move out of proprietary status and into university settings, where medical education benefited theoretically both from greater access to new science and from focused fund-raising. Though relatively late in the national movement, the UA/Tuscaloosa development fits that national pattern. As reinforcement for what Ludmerer describes as a national pattern, however, it also is hard to ignore the relatively unique demography, economics, and politics of Alabama.[43] Most native leaders of Alabama, from Montgomery politicos to Birmingham industrialists, were only one generation beyond an antebellum state polity that had high culture centered in the Black Belt and in its urban extensions of Mobile, Montgomery, and Tuscaloosa.[44] In this context, no doubt their perceptions of where important *cultural* (as opposed to materialistic) developments occurred, developments such as a state medical school, remained dominated by tradition. Likewise, if one recalls how U.S. Steel did little, if anything, to pursue a major medical school for Birmingham back in 1914, there at least can be the wonder if in 1919–20 U.S. Steel did not feel more than comfortable about its "Big Mule" colleagues to the south keeping the state medical school away from Birmingham. Yes, a post hoc theory—only a hypothesis owing to the lack of archival access.[45]

Unproved hypotheses aside, other forces delivered some of what Flexner had urged, with political ramifications yet to be untangled. During the 1920s and 1930s UA medical students, though trained by outstanding professors such as John Bruhn, George Pack, and Charles Goss, had to try to leave the state to complete their last two years of medical school. Although all but a few went to other institutions to earn the M.D., they were at a distinct disadvantage in obtaining post-M.D. residencies; priority went to applicants who were citizens of the state where they were applying and who had benefited from a modern, integrated four-year and accredited M.D. program. It was a story played out all over Dixie. The harsh truth, according to Flexner's later reflections, was that with the exception of what was occurring at three institutions of "promise"—Vanderbilt, Tulane, and Duke; Emory was too new to make the list—no other medical schools of quality existed in the South, a section made up of thirteen states and some twenty-nine million people. All this in turn discouraged many Alabamians from even entering the program in Tuscaloosa. Instead, they sought to complete all their medical education in states with modern medical programs; when they did they sometimes did not want to return to a place where they were so desperately needed.[46] Indeed, during the Depression, Alabama had the worst physician-population ratio in the nation, and between 1922 and 1938 the total number of Alabama doctors had *declined* by over 400. As Alabama sought to achieve vital Progressive reforms in railroad regulation, education, and public health, it had a medical education program chasing doctors out of the state.[47]

Granted, in 1928 President Denny enticed the pathologist Stuart Graves to leave his post as dean of medicine at the University of Louisville and assume the same position at UA with the express purpose of building a four-year program in Tuscaloosa. The Crash of 1929 intervened. As Graves later understated, "[T]he severe economic depression . . . soon . . . blocked progress." The pressures of the Depression urged what Flexner had advised. In 1930, as Wayne Flynt has pointed out in *Poor But Proud* (1989), "Alabama had . . . a State Board of Health with only fourteen clinics to serve indigents, and health departments that operated in only fifty-two of the state's sixty-seven counties." Along with unemployment and illiteracy there was wretched health. Finally, however, in 1938, after the Depression had already bottomed out, UA's medical alumni association joined forces with the Medical Association of the State of Alabama (MASA) under the leadership of the Birmingham physician Seale Harris and set out to document, publicize, *and* politicize the need for something different in the way of health care and medical education for Alabama.[48]

A prominent former professor at the Mobile medical college, Seale Harris by the 1920s had traveled to Toronto to meet Frederick G. Banting, who recently had won the Nobel Prize for the discovery of insulin. From his consultations with Banting and his observations of Toronto patients overdosed with insulin and showing symptoms of hypoglycemia, Harris gained international attention for his description of the new disease called hyperinsulinism. Harris not only enjoyed a leadership role in the Alabama medical community, but he had a natural flair for using his reputation to court the support of Alabama's major newspaper editors and political leaders. Through "white papers" and interviews, he facilitated journalism coverage on the point that a four-year medical school connected to a major hospital was the only viable option. He was assisted by Tuscaloosa physician William D. Partlow, UA president Foster, and UA medical dean Graves. Despite this flurry of activity and press coverage, however, throughout the late 1930s he seemed to be getting nowhere.[49]

With U.S. entry into World War II in 1941, Harris, Graves, Partlow, and other medical leaders in the state thought they finally had some arguments that would succeed. When the results of Alabama's backward medical education were revealed, combined with the fact that the military draft took numerous Alabama physicians away from home, many Alabama counties suddenly had even worse health care than they had had in the depths of the Depression—many counties had no physician under the age of fifty. MASA sent press releases statewide drawing attention to this fact. At the same time, Alabamians, as part of a Southern pattern, had one of the highest rates in the nation for rejection by the military draft due to poor health. MASA also got out the word about this "travesty."[50] Granted, the problem had roots deep in Alabama's historic underfunding of all social services, not just health care, but it was undoubtedly exacerbated by doctors leaving home for the war. Regardless, here was "a pragmatic problem" that might be confronted by powerful Alabamians issuing press releases that ballyhooed the number of soldiers Alabama was sending to fight Germany and Japan. Sent nationwide and especially into Washington, D.C., such journalism and unpublished "white papers" often emanated from the Southern Council on International Relations (SCIR) based at the University of North Carolina–Chapel Hill. SCIR's most influential members included Alabama textile leader Donald Comer and the Birmingham journalist John Temple Graves, who would soon publish the often inaccurate but well-received book, *The Fighting South* (1943). Their marketing of Alabama patriotism reflected the SCIR—funded for the most part by Southern businesses—in its strategy to bring U.S. military expenditures (training bases and the purchase of war materiel) into Alabama and other Southern states. If MASA could spread the word that public health issues and the paucity of doctors were diminishing Alabama's manpower contribution to the war effort, perhaps appropriate business pressures would be applied to Montgomery to correct the situation. Despite these additional arguments coming from the war effort, however, the Alabama legislature showed little interest.[51]

Thoroughly frustrated, MASA simply ignored the lack of state action and sent out press releases in 1942 announcing that the selection of a site for a new four-year medical school would need to follow legislative appropriation. Hopson Owen Murfee, a well-educated civic activist from Prattville, Alabama, and not a physician, quickly eclipsed even Seale Harris as the shrewd political operative behind this movement. Under Murfee's influence, MASA worked quietly through county medical societies to pressure the legislature to act. The strategy: a carefully designed committee of physicians and civic leaders, representing different geographical sections of the state, began to address the incendiary question of "site selection" of "a new medical school." Letters to the editor and guest pieces in daily newspapers across the state, along with numerous addresses before civic groups, quickly moved the issue to the forefront of public discourse.[52]

Their manipulative brinkmanship worked. Whether Harris, Partlow, Murfee, and others of the medical education lobby already had reached private agreement on where *they* wanted the school to be located remains unclear. For certain, however, a genuine statewide competition and heated controversy did indeed emerge as boosters and political supporters rallied around the same old options: Birmingham, Mobile, or Tuscaloosa. Though at times unclear on locations, Murfee actually called for two schools, one for blacks, one for whites.

Still bitter about the 1920 relocation of their school from the port town to Tuscaloosa, Mobilians urged that Alabama's rich tradition of medical education needed restoration along the Gulf. To do this, they promised what Dean Graves saw as the "very fine offer" of constructing "a 300 bed hospital for patients who might be purely indigent or who might pay up to the per diem cost of maintenance of the hospital." In addition, Mobile would "allow the University of Alabama to have complete control of the hospital and to name everyone on the staff, medical and otherwise," as well as donate "an adjoining site for the building of a school of medicine."[53]

Outside consultants gave yet other plans. As if to echo Tuscaloosa's Partlow, Alan Gregg of the Rockefeller Foundation urged one four-year program in the Druid City because the school needed to be near a university and a hospital, which Tuscaloosa had, and because of the drawbacks of Birmingham. "I know of no university medical school in a large city," Gregg warned, "which . . . has not had at least one serious quarrel between the

university and the powerful and privileged professional leaders in the city."
He went further: "Unless your University is resigned to offering teaching
positions in return for support and collaboration of clinicians with few
other claims to attention, they may as well prepare themselves for a decade
of pressures and political maneuvers."[54]

To urge Birmingham, Victor Johnson of the American Medical Association critiqued Tuscaloosa from another standpoint: "The medical school
building in Tuscaloosa is old and not suited for a high grade of medical instruction at the present time. Even if it would be possible to obtain funds
to build a sufficiently large hospital and even if elaborate arrangements
could be made to gather patients from all parts of the state, it would still
be true that the preclinical departments would remain poorly housed. [By
contrast] . . . Hillman Hospital [in Birmingham and with recently upgraded
facilities] would seem to be adequate for the development of a clinical program for the medical school."[55] Years later, as director of the Mayo Foundation, Johnson recalled that he "felt very strongly . . . that the school be . . .
in Birmingham" and that Fred C. Zapfee of the Association of American
Medical Colleges concurred: "[T]he Hillman Hospital will supply all the
needed clinical material for teaching as well as pathology and the outpatient department."[56]

Several factors finally eased the statewide debate and led to a consensus
on Birmingham. First, in the mid-1930s, even before MASA geared up for
change, physicians and civic leaders in Birmingham laid plans for a badly
needed expansion of Hillman Hospital. As World War II saw Birmingham's
economy rebounding more rapidly than many could have thought and the
city's population surging forward again, Hillman's expansion became even
more critical. Even by 1938, in response to an application developed by
such leading Birmingham physicians as James S. McLester and by Jefferson County commissioner Henry W. Sweet, the WPA had awarded Jefferson County $300,000 for the construction of a five-story clinic addition
to Hillman Hospital. Yet that addition, dedicated in 1939, proved insufficient to reach the evolving goal of something major in health care in Birmingham.[57] A year later the same leaders, plus the iconoclastic Presbyterian minister-turned-entrepreneur Sterling Foster (father-in-law to newly
appointed U.S. Supreme Court justice Hugo Black), businessman James C.
Lee, Sr., Birmingham postmaster W. Cooper Green, and particularly physicians Harry Lee Jackson and James R. Garber, developed plans for a majestic sixteen-story county hospital for patients who were neither indigent nor
wealthy. With drawings by local architect Charles McCauley, the delegation

went back to the WPA offices in Washington for funds to build "Jefferson Hospital." In this application Birmingham of course had something besides an economy tied to the war effort and an expanding population; it had Alabama's striking influence in New Deal political circles—John Sparkman and Lister Hill in the Senate, Luther Patrick in the House of Representatives, and Hugo Black on the Supreme Court. And out of the aid of all these political leaders the WPA awarded Jefferson County an outright grant of $900,000 and a loan of $1,100,000. With these funds and additional monies totaling $2,250,000, construction of Jefferson Hospital began on the block directly behind Hillman facing Nineteenth Street and opened in January 1941, a month late due to infighting over staff assignments. Here were 575 patient beds as well as living quarters for nurses, interns, and residents. Moreover, as local radio stations WSGN, WAPI, and WBRC gave "live" coverage of the laying of the cornerstone and of Charles R. Skelton, who had labored on the construction project, checking in as the hospital's first patient, Sweet and Garber were developing plans to merge the boards of Jefferson Hospital with Hillman's, providing more centralized administration of this public facility.[58]

In this encouraging context, by late 1941 the Citizens Committee of Birmingham under the leadership of First National Bank of Birmingham president Oscar Wells began lobbying anybody of influence on the need for a four-year medical school in Birmingham. Wells soon raised $160,000 as "matching" money to entice the legislature to appropriate funds for the program in his city. Wells and others also extolled the strategic advantages of the Magic City. Birmingham now had two major county hospitals with at least seminal plans for centralized administration. It had a large indigent population, essential as "teaching cases" for medical education. It long had had large numbers of private practice physicians educated in the best medical schools in the United States and thus a well-developed medical culture filled with potential clinical or part-time faculty. And by the early 1940s it had a surging (if nondiversified) local economy, not just a growing population.[59]

Finally, in 1943, Harris, Partlow, and others with MASA went to the new governor, Chauncey Sparks, with "the plan": most doctors from around the state had now closed ranks and were ready to go to the legislature for funding for a four-year program in Birmingham; the state's fiscal status, moreover, was showing a surplus for educational funding—a far cry from conditions during the 1930s. To hammer home the point, Partlow and Graves stated that as ex-advocates of the Tuscaloosa site, they saw this as the best step to meet the pressing needs of Alabama. In his former role as medical dean at the University of Louisville, Graves had seen how the various dynamics of urban life could enhance a medical school. Privately, unknown certainly to most people in Tuscaloosa, he had been inclined to favor the Birmingham site all along. Now he urged that while Louisville stood as one of the South's oldest cities, and Birmingham its youngest, he saw the advantages of developing medical education in the Magic City as more important than the disadvantages. Above all, there was the economic argument. The state did not have the money to build, much less maintain, a statewide hospital for indigent-care service on the UA campus. Yet the state could afford to build a medical school given that the essential adjunct, the teaching hospital, could be provided through some other nonstate source. Sparks concurred. But he knew well the visceral feelings over where the school should be located and how the upstart urban center of Birmingham could threaten the traditional order of the state. Undoubtedly influenced by the current surplus in education funding—a function of increased sales tax revenues during the mid-1940s—Sparks now moved to *his* "plan."[60]

Governor Sparks astutely proceeded with the full appearance of rural sponsorship. He used Gordon Madison, the Tuscaloosa attorney and chairman of the Senate's Education Committee, to draft the bill. Then he turned to Thomas Jefferson Jones, a physician from the Black Belt center of Marion and chairman of the Senate's Public Health Committee, to introduce the bill in the Senate—a bill quickly labeled "The Jones Bill." At the same time he had the Jones Bill submitted to the House by George D. Norman, of Union Springs, just southeast of Montgomery, who chaired that body's Finance and Taxation Committee.[61] On June 2, 1943, a unanimous vote of both houses created a fund of $1,000,000 for the construction of a four-year state medical college to be part of the University of Alabama. It would have an annual allocation of $366,750 for maintenance and scholarships, including a $400 scholarship each year for a resident of each of the state's sixty-seven counties; a decision on the college's location would be determined by a building commission appointed by the governor working in consultation with the UA board of trustees. So as to leave nothing to chance, Sparks personally kept a tight rein on the building commission.[62]

In October 1943, the *Birmingham News,* long supportive of educational activities in Tuscaloosa, had a clear prediction: "The choice, we gather, is between Tuscaloosa and Birmingham [and] the commission should have no trouble in arriving at a decision. Birmingham has what a medical school must have. Tuscaloosa does not. This is a problem which solves itself." One member of the commission, Mobile businessman Alfred F. Delchamps, held out for a while to revive medical education in his historic town but "fell in line" at the end. On February 16, 1944, Governor Sparks announced the unanimous vote: the "Medical College of Alabama, a school of medicine of the University of Alabama," offering a modern four-year program would be developed in Birmingham as part of the Jefferson-Hillman complex.[63] As Stuart Graves wrote to a friend at Cornell University, at last "the Rubicon was crossed." Sparks considered the medical school the "greatest single development" in the legislative history of Alabama. The *Birmingham News* also applauded, then dreamed: "The end of the year may see Birmingham well on its way to becoming one of the leading Southern medical centers . . . beyond the position of Memphis, New Orleans, and Atlanta." Out of Alabama's past, understandably, here was a dream of distinctly regional limitations. Into Birmingham and Alabama's future the dream would have no choice but to expand.[64]

During 1944 several swift actions consummated Sparks's plan. First, Jefferson County began the complicated conveyance of Hillman and Jefferson hospitals to the University of Alabama with the provision that revenue from Jefferson Hospital be employed to retire $1,227,000 in outstanding bonds used to build the new facility. President Paty saw the arrangement as evidence of the "leadership of this great community" and promised that UA would always act responsibly toward the "good and permanent care of the indigent sick."[65] Second, Paty directed that the faculty and equipment of the medical college be moved from Tuscaloosa to Birmingham and be ready to function in 1945. Though devoted to this development, Dean Graves indicated he would not be making the move—he would be retiring.[66] Third, Paty reemphasized that the previous Birmingham Center director, Ernest A. Lowe, now had overarching responsibilities for administrative matters in all Birmingham affairs: Lowe's multistate experience with "field service" and knowledge of Birmingham politics would be vital for daily administration. In reality, however, it would be the medical college dean who served as senior officer on most medical matters.[67] Finally, Paty and Graves quietly wrapped up six months of hard searching for a dean in which they had used the dean of medicine at Cornell University, Joseph C. Hinsey, as a confidential sounding board. Turned down by several sitting deans—including Carlyle Jacobsen at Washington University, St. Louis, who saw the start-up tasks so filled with political pitfalls that the first dean probably would find himself a "sacrifice"—Paty proudly announced that his old friend from his Emory days, Hartselle, Alabama, native and esteemed UA alumnus Roy R.

Kracke, would soon arrive in Birmingham to serve as dean of the Medical College of Alabama.[68]

The Kracke announcement met with great approval among Alabama physicians. Many already knew his story. After a year at Alabama Polytechnic Institute (Auburn University) "playing tennis and generally goofing off," then a year as a pharmacy assistant in Guntersville, near his home, and in north Birmingham, he confronted World War I by signing on with the U.S. Navy's Hospital Corps. He attended the Naval Medical School in Washington, D.C., for advanced training in laboratory technology, then shipped out for eighteen months near Brest, France, at U.S. Naval Base Hospital No. 1. In 1919, with the war over, he returned to the Naval Medical School for a stint as a laboratory instructor. Next, he moved to Memphis to serve as laboratory technician for well-known physician William S. Krauss. Under Krauss's tutelage he reached a final conclusion on a thought he had had since wartime—he wanted to be a physician. With well-connected references, including the north Alabama populist political leader Oliver D. Street, he moved to UA in 1920 as a part-time instructor in bacteriology as well as a student. Over the next three years he completed the equivalent of two years of undergraduate courses and two years in the new medical school. In the midst of all this he also courted and married Virginia Carolyn Minter, a UA student from Birmingham.[69]

By 1925 the young couple had landed in Chicago. Supported with his "co-op" student stipend and a small quarterly income from his own recently patented invention for laboratory research, the "Kracke staining dish," he completed the final two years of medical education and, in 1928, earned his M.D. at Rush Medical School of the University of Chicago. Then the couple headed for Atlanta, where Kracke launched a longtime career as professor of pathology, bacteriology, and laboratory diagnosis in the vibrant new four-year medical school at Emory. Kracke soon enjoyed a national reputation as a hematologist and medical educator with great knowledge of leukemia. By 1941 J. P. Lippincott had published his well-written and highly regarded *Diseases of the Blood and Atlas of Hematology*. The same flowing usage of words, sentences, and grammar showed in his limited correspondence with none other than President Franklin Roosevelt, who sought communication with Kracke as a way of knowing what health care specialties were available in Georgia should the president have need while resting at Warm Springs. Despite his literary bent, however, Kracke could appear utterly consumed with science. Shades of Transylvania drifted over Atlanta— and more than a little controversy—when he extracted human livers from the morgue at Grady Memorial Hospital, then mashed them into something that looked like medicine, and fed the substance to patients with blood disorders. He could document the success of the treatment. And often when he went home he really did not. He kept cages of rabbits and rats in his backyard near Emory so that he could monitor experiments when he was not in his laboratory at the university. The children, ultimately all five of them, served as lab technicians.[70]

George Pack of the Pack Cancer Center in New York City approached Kracke in 1942 about joining his team as head of pathology. An Ohio native and Yale University medical graduate, Pack had taught Kracke in Tuscaloosa's two-year medical program before moving east in 1926. Now an international figure in cancer research and destined to be director of the Sloan Kettering Cancer Institute in New York City, Pack's star shined brighter each day. And he sought Kracke to shine alongside. Yet Kracke's daughter, Rachel Kracke Drennen, recalled that the invitation from Pack immediately became a dilemma: "He really soul-searched about this because [Dr. Pack] offered him so much money and such great latitude in his work. [Moreover,] the cultural and educational opportunities that his children would have in New York intrigued him." But he declined. He "hated to uproot us," Kracke told his daughter. "He wanted to stay in the South."[71]

Then came the offer from home. It came from his trusted friend Bill Paty. But he also was drawn to "the idea of returning to Alabama and being closer to his mother" in Hartselle and of working in a state where one of the U.S. senators—rising Progressive star John Sparkman—happened to be his childhood friend from Hartselle and his UA roommate. They might just get something done. Kracke's wife, Virginia, supported the plan, too. Granted, all members of her Birmingham family had died except one, her brother, Dr. Russell Minter. This infamous Birmingham surgeon reputedly had cut out his own appendix aided only by a shaving mirror and a quart of whiskey, and had burned down the home of a competitor before moving on to greater medical frontiers in Texas. Virginia had clear memories of the hard knocks and harder egos of medical life in Birmingham. Nevertheless, her sense of place beckoned to the excitement of her husband's building a medical school adjacent to the intersection of Twentieth Street and Eighth Avenue South. At the southeastern corner of this intersection her grandfather had established the first business in the area, Minter's Grocery, a virtual icon of neighborhood life on Birmingham's fledgling "Southside" and a place where more than one "dope," or Coca Cola, was had by a granddaughter. The great tornado of 1909 had leveled this landmark business only to leap-frog newly constructed Hillman Hospital before heading on northward into the city to render even greater destruction. Against this backdrop of vivid memories, good and bad, "the survivor hospital" and the city of Birmingham now awaited her husband.[72]

At age forty-seven Kracke now found himself in the curious position of having declined a prestigious and lucrative opportunity in a major center of science and medicine to try to build a medical school in one of the poorest states in the nation. Paty had told him his operating budget would total $1.5 million—for everything, including the hospitals. Still, to William Maloney, one of Kracke's friends from his University of Chicago days, he explained the pull of Alabama: "I finally decided that I owed it to my native state and my native school to see if I could do the job as it should be done in Alabama."[73] He addressed other implications in writing to another physician colleague, Jack Norris: "It was a question of what to devote the rest of my life . . . to continue in medical education [or] to go into a limited type of practice concentrating mainly on hematology." Clearly, he had strong feelings about the long-term implications of his juncture: "The latter would have been the easier without any questions and probably the most lucrative, but I have reached the age now to where I realize that money isn't worth a damn . . . the greatest satisfaction seems to come from some type of accomplishment, so I deliberately chose the hard way."[74] It is doubtful, however, that he anticipated just how difficult this "hard way" would be. Directly ahead lay tornados of another kind.

Kracke's arrival in Birmingham signaled a watershed. What had been attempted in the first decade of the century, the creation of a Birmingham medical center, was finally about to happen. Why had it taken so long? When Birmingham's general health care scene was ready for this development as early as 1912, when other urban areas of the nation were creating medical centers in the Progressive Era, why had Alabama delayed doing so? Because Birmingham needed the ensuing half century to evolve as a viable political and economic force that could compete with what Jonathan Weiner has called "persisting nineteenth-century centers of power" in Alabama.[75]

Big Steel played a pivotal and ironic role in this story. Between 1907 and 1929 U.S. Steel developed its influence over Birmingham and much of Alabama by embracing (while controlling) Alabama's old power structure, and early on reinforced many social and economic traditions of Alabama life. Still, U.S. Steel inadvertently provided the economic and political clout and ultimately the very population (including a large pool of poor, indigent patients) behind Birmingham's new viability—a viability that threatened the old agrarian-based power structure that U.S. Steel courted. Then, again at the hands of U.S. Steel, Birmingham surged forward in response to the sale of steel during the Roaring Twenties and World War II while the rest of the state lagged behind in recovering from the Depression. In the process, between 1907 and 1944 the distribution of political influence in the state also began to change in favor of Birmingham. If, in the midst of this transition, U.S. Steel also worked behind the scenes to oppose bringing the medical school to Birmingham—a big "if" but one interesting to ponder—the irony of U.S. Steel's role is doubled. What remains clear, however, is that by February 1944 the scales of power in Alabama had tipped just enough to allow for the medical school and Roy Kracke to move to Birmingham. And in the coming decades, as these same scales tipped again and again toward Birmingham, one ultimately would be able to look back at February 1944 as a deciding moment leading not just to the conception of a university but to the remaking of a city.

3
Conception, 1944–50
Kracke and Volker

Overnight Roy Kracke discovered exactly what the "hard way" was. To prepare for the beginning of classes to start in the summer of 1945 he moved to Birmingham without his family in late July 1944. He lived in an office above the morgue in the Hillman clinic and began working eighty-hour weeks. Cup after cup of coffee, chocolate bars of any description, and huge dishes of vanilla ice cream kept him going. He refused to slow down in September when his family moved from Atlanta to begin new life in a spacious craftsman-style home in Forest Park.[1] Quickly, he made new friends. There was Oscar Wells, who often took the Kracke children for long walks on the Highland Park golf course. Henry W. Edmonds, the engaging intellectual, fearless social reformer, and recently retired but still civically involved Presbyterian minister, was more compatible with Kracke, as they shared similar views on life in Birmingham. Indeed, after a brief time with the Third Presbyterian Church just east of Hillman Hospital (where the self-absorbed evangelist, James A. ["Brother"] Bryan, recently had preached), the new dean and his family became active members of the congregation Edmonds had built at Independent Presbyterian Church on the southern fringe of Forest Park, a place where Charles Darwin's ideas about science and evolution were not considered at odds with either God or the future of Birmingham.[2] Even so, despite the vitality of a new personal and civic life, virtually all of Kracke's time that first summer and fall was occupied with developments of a more mundane, though vital, nature—implementing the complexities of the hospital merger.

In his broadened role as general director of both medical and Extension Center affairs in Birmingham, Ernest Lowe joined Kracke in hospital discussions with Henry Sweet, attorney James Simpson, and other Jefferson County leaders in working out the final details of UA's assumption of the Jefferson-Hillman debt. They also spent long hours orchestrating a joint board for Hillman and Jefferson, which James Garber and Sweet first had conceptualized back in the spring of 1939. Two sticking points were slowing things down. First, the old Jefferson board did not want a new UA hospital complex to accept charity patients at Jefferson until UA had paid off the Jefferson construction debt. Kracke finally prevailed with his point that medical schools had to have charity patients for teaching purposes. Second, there was the issue of staff physicians. For years, doctors practicing at Hillman had been required to hold faculty appointments with the Tuscaloosa two-year program as well as have county approval. Yet Jefferson Hospital could be used by any white physician who was a member of the Jefferson County Medical Society. Back in April, before moving from Atlanta, Kracke had addressed this issue in no uncertain terms. In a letter to Jefferson County commissioner Robert H. Wharton he described this situation as "simply untenable": no quality control. By correcting the situation, however, "we can look back with pride on what we have built for the people of Jefferson County and for the State of Alabama." Thus through detailed deliberations with Wharton and the old hospital boards, Kracke ultimately prevailed in establishing clinical or adjunct faculty status as a prerequisite for all private physicians using the Jefferson-Hillman complex. This gave the new medical college control over increasing the quality of physicians using the hospital; there had been numerous criticisms in the city about the quality of doctors working in Jefferson. In turn, the increased reputation of the new complex then gave Kracke leverage in attracting more highly qualified private practice physicians of Birmingham into the clinical-faculty ranks at the college.[3]

With these issues resolved, by early 1945 Kracke's deal fell into place. Jefferson County gave UA the block including Hillman Hospital and its outpatient and nursing facilities as well as Jefferson Hospital for ninety-nine years. The county also promised to give UA $150,000 within two months to purchase additional land. As a result, UA would provide a block of land in the same area on which to construct a health department facility and promised to provide outstanding indigent care, with the county to pay "sufficient" funds to cover costs for indigent patients from Jefferson County. Though the hot political issue of funding for indigent care would resurface interminably, more than once involving the state attorney general, the basic merger agreement was now in effect with a single board for the hospital complex. John W. MacQueen, a pathologist (later psychiatrist) who had directed Hillman affairs since 1936, would run the daily activities of the new complex and report to Kracke.[4]

Kracke also pushed ahead on other matters of real estate and space. With the help of his neighbor Oscar Wells and others of the Birmingham Chamber of Commerce, Kracke accumulated sufficient donations to have his own $500,000 "development fund." To this he added an advance of $255,000 out of earmarked state funds, and with the assistance of Lowe and President Paty acquired for UA's medical college three blocks adjacent to Jefferson-Hillman. These in turn he targeted for the possible development of major projects—the Crippled Children's Clinic, the Children's Hospital, the Veterans' Hospital, and the Jefferson County Department of Public Health building. These facilities were either federal, state, county, or private. None, however, was dependent on state *educational* funds. Thus, with no additional stress on Alabama's already minimal education dollars, their eventual location on the blocks set aside by Kracke would provide more "teaching cases" for medical students and more specialized health care for patients. Here was no vision for a medical school. It was for something bigger.[5]

Simultaneously, the new dean went to work establishing an initial faculty—172 who could be ready to offer courses in 1945, no easy task with so many of America's physicians still in the military. Still, between January and October 1945 Kracke created sixteen departments for a four-year medical school, the greatest single year of organizational development in the history of what would become UAB. Granted, the basic science departments—anatomy, bacteriology and clinical pathology, biochemistry, physiology, and pharmacology—were transferred up from Tuscaloosa during a two-week break between terms, with the Tuscaloosa faculty making the move as Paty had directed. These included such well-known professors as Emmett Carmichael (biochemistry) and Charles M. Goss (anatomy), who updated and rewrote the famous *Gray's Anatomy.*[6] As the move occurred, the previous dean, Stuart Graves, seemed to change his mind about retiring right away. First indicating he would like to move to Birmingham as the new director of admissions, an idea Kracke applauded, Graves ultimately decided to phase into retirement in Tuscaloosa. There, this key figure in the history of UA medical education worked for a short time as a consulting pathologist at Northington General Hospital, a temporary 2,000-bed facility of the U.S. Army, before retiring.[7]

Because of the two additional years of clinical education now in the curriculum, new faculty had to be retained for clinical departments: medicine, surgery, gynecology, obstetrics, ophthalmology, pediatrics, pathology, preventive medicine and public health, radiology, urology, otolaryngology and brochaspy ("ENT"), and the combined unit of neurology, neurosurgery, and psychiatry. Even with limited funds Kracke made some prescient hires. The young internal medicine specialist Howard Holley (native of Marion, Alabama) came from the University of South Carolina to boost Kracke's "house staff." Likewise, the even younger James J. Hicks (native of Enterprise, Alabama), an otorhinolaryngologist, came from Vanderbilt. And from Tulane came the urology resident Samuel K. Cohn (Birmingham native). Kracke also investigated a young Harvard-educated physician raised in Mobile named Champ Lyons whom he wanted for surgery, but found him still committed to the military.[8]

To pursue one of the main reasons for moving the college to Birmingham, Kracke also attained the services of close to one hundred Birmingham physicians for part-time and volunteer roles in the new clinical departments. As he soon would tell the Annual Conference on Medical Education and Licensure in Chicago,

> [An] important consideration in favor of a metropolitan location [for a medical school] is the availability of large numbers of competent physicians to serve on the faculty of the school. . . . [Such physicians] tend to be trained more toward the lines of general practice, rather than toward specialization. There seems to be general agreement that what this country needs in medicine more than anything else today are general practitioners and fewer specialists. It follows, therefore, that an institution whose pattern of training is directed toward the training of practitioners can do so best under the conditions found in a large metropolitan area.[9]

Here were medicine's James S. McLester, James O. Finney, Bert Wiesel, and Arthur Freeman; surgery's James M. Mason, Joseph M. Donald, and Julius Linn; urology's Bruno Barelare and Landon Timberlake; gynecology's Louise Branscomb and Buford Word; neurosurgery's Garber Galbraith; pediatrics' Clifford Lamar, Hughes Kennedy, Beach Chenoweth, and Sam Wainwright; and obstetrics' James R. Garber and Thomas M. Bouleware.[10]

Those hired to chair these departments also served as chiefs of correlating divisions in the hospital. In this case Kracke also went with experienced physicians in the community. He correctly anticipated how difficult it would be to attract senior departmental leaders from other institutions to a medical college yet to start. He also had little money for senior faculty salaries. His state budget permitted him to offer at the most $10,000 to $13,000 per year for a full-time department chair, some 40 percent below the going rate at a national level. Even if Kracke had had enough money, however, the war made experienced academic medical leaders virtually impossible to hire. Just as important, besides believing in the quality of local medical leaders, especially senior physicians above the age for military service but still highly regarded professionals, he needed their involvement to diminish chances for tension that so often developed between academic and private practice physicians in other cities with medical colleges.

On Kracke's enticement, therefore, James Mason accepted the chairmanship of surgery on the condition that Robert Guthrie, a Walker County, Alabama, native who had studied under Kracke at Emory before going on to the Mayo Clinic (and had been exempted from military service because of spondylitis), would leave his current position as a director of research with Johnson and Johnson Company, in New Jersey, to serve as executive officer of the department. Guthrie agreed, with the stipulation that his afternoons would be left free for a private surgery practice to compensate him for the fact that Kracke and Mason only had funds to hire him as a part-time administrator. Two other proven advocates of the four-year school in Birmingham, McLester and Garber, accepted the chairmanships of medicine and obstetrics, respectively. Other chairs included John Sherrill, orthopedics; Walter Nicholas Jones, gynecology; George Denison, public health and preventive medicine; Alston Callahan, ophthalmology; and Melson Barfield-Carter, radiology, one of the few women at such a level.[11]

To advance women in their quest to break into the previously male-dominated profession of medicine was nothing new for Kracke. During his Atlanta days he helped Winton Elizabeth Gambrell become the first woman to earn an M.D. from Emory. Yet each of these quests represented a unique story. Like so many of the initial department chairs, Barfield-Carter had grown up in Alabama, in her case in the Clay County hamlet of Barfield. After a two-year stint at Central Alabama Women's College in Tuscaloosa, she completed a B.S. degree in mathematics at UA, taught at several public schools in the state for a few years, finished medical school at Tulane in 1921, and, after a residency in the breaking field of radiology at Massachusetts General Hospital in Boston, she returned to Alabama in 1929, first establishing private practice out of Hillman Hospital and later with the Baptist hospitals in Birmingham. More to the point, as a highly regarded member of the new field of radiology, Barfield-Carter, on joining Kracke right out of the military, captured the distinction of being the first female department chair in the medical school in a profession in which women, whether in private practice or academia, were few and far between.[12]

Though also recruited out of a private practice background, Callahan was atypical of the first chairs; he was not from Alabama. A native of Vicksburg, Mississippi, and a graduate of Tulane's School of Medicine, Callahan had established a private practice in Atlanta in the early 1930s where he befriended Kracke initially at a Georgia Tech football game, and where he also met Raymond Paty. During World War II Callahan did military service at the Northington hospital in Tuscaloosa, then joined Kracke in Birmingham. Likewise, from Duke University came the founding chair of pathology, Harvard-trained Roger Denio Baker, a native of East Lansing, Michigan, and the son of the famous journalist and social critic of the Progressive Era, Ray Stannard Baker.[13]

Kracke certainly understood Seale Harris's leadership role in bringing the college to Birmingham and had closely followed his progress on two major writing projects: *Banting's Miracle: The Story of the Discoverer of Insulin* published by J. B. Lippincott Company in 1946 and *Woman's Surgeon: The Life Story of J. Marion Sims,* to be published by the MacMillan Company in 1950. Though he worried about Harris's being seventy-five and seeing fewer patients each year, he knew that these publications would make his political connections even stronger, and he needed connections that supported the medical college. Thus Kracke asked Harris to serve as professor emeritus in medicine, holding his breath that the historic competitiveness between McLester and Harris would not erupt into debilitating warfare within the fledgling Department of Medicine, the unit so essential to the overall program. If he discussed the strategies with few, Kracke nevertheless wanted the public to know the role that Birmingham physicians were playing in this development.[14] On June 3, 1945, the *Birmingham News* assisted his cause: "The fact that we are able to open a Medical College of Alabama at this critical time when the country is at war and more than 60,000 physicians are away in military service is due in part to the willingness and spirit of self-sacrifice on the part of our practicing physicians who are willing to devote much of their valuable time to the instruction of young doctors."[15]

In a similar way Kracke drew on the community to build support facilities. Most important was the library. To the 10,000 basic science volumes brought from Tuscaloosa he added a striking gift of 8,000 volumes—the entire library acquired by the physicians of the Jefferson County Medical Society. Birmingham physicians Andrew Glaze and Ralls F. Coston gave their extensive personal collections, and the massive personal library of Luther Leonidas Hill, Montgomery physician and father of U.S. senator Lister Hill, would come shortly. A full-time staff of four, headed by Chief Medical Librarian Mildred R. Crowe, managed and developed this collection, which was spread, ineffectively, wherever space could be found in Hillman. As for laboratories, rudimentary equipment in the basic sciences came with the Tuscaloosa move.[16]

Then there was the matter of student and faculty housing. Here no gift appeared. With Paty arranging a $350,000 loan from the Crimson Tide's football budget, Kracke purchased the old Cullom Apartments, which made up a half block on the west side of the hill going up Twentieth Street. He converted these into 36 faculty apartments and 168 student rooms presided over by "hostesses" to ensure "the best possible environment."[17] The hostesses would have little impact. As one on the scene recalled, "Young doctors need a release for their work stress." Aided mightily by grain alcohol distilled in the basic science laboratories and nighttime social life flowing up and down the fire escapes, the "med-dorms" soon eclipsed the longstanding tradition of George Ward's temples as the prime place for bacchanalian delight on a Birmingham Saturday night. Thirty years later, long after the apartments had been razed for the construction of a hotel, the same contemporaneous observer riding down Twentieth Street chanced a beguiling glance to the left and then quietly recollected, "They called those dorms the red light district." Tradition had the apartments offering prostitution before the UA purchase, yet he of the "beguiling glance" clearly remembered that (unsolicited) late-night knocks on front doors did not immediately end when UA took title of the property.[18]

So with primary as well as support programs increasingly in place, Kracke was ready to open for business. After a registration process presided over by Virginia ("Dean") Baxley, who had moved up from Tuscaloosa with the school, on June 5, 1945, the program began operations on the sixth, fourteenth, sixteenth, and seventeenth floors of Jefferson Hospital. At first there were twenty-two juniors, most from the Tuscaloosa program. Then on October 8, fifty-four freshmen and fifty sophomores—some veterans of World War II and paying their tuition with VA benefits—began their basic science studies. By the spring of 1949 they would make up the first class to complete the new, badly needed four-year program of the Medical College of Alabama. And these degrees would have the essential stamp of approval by the American Medical Association (AMA), for by September 1946 Kracke had placed the entire program through the arduous AMA accreditation process and succeeded. Still, as a sad harbinger for years to come, the AMA's Victor Johnson, who wrote the final report, would indeed note the "minimal acceptable level of [state] funding" for the school.[19]

More than a Medical College

These seminal developments underway, Kracke now tackled the still larger issues of space, certainly knowing that a productive medical center will never have sufficient space but also that his current space was woefully inadequate. The new medical college had begun with the existing Hillman-Jefferson complex. Granted, some of this space was less than ten years old, but all of it was designed for conventional patient care activities, medical education activities Kracke had squeezed into Hillman as best he could. That had to change, plus the dean undoubtedly knew that space had to be provided for research if the reinforcing triad of teaching, research, and service was to function with the appropriate symbiosis. In addition, no sooner had Kracke initiated clinical instruction in 1945 than three other major developments began to occur. One of these increased space needs, while two others eased them—temporarily.

First, in the summer of 1946 on the heels of considerable leadership by Senator Lister Hill, Congress passed what came to be known as the Hill-Burton Act. Designed by Hill and others, including AMA lobbyists, as a way to derail President Truman's health care reform program that included the "socialistic" notion of mandatory health insurance for all citizens, the legislation nevertheless, over time, provided massive federal funds for upgrading and the new construction of hospitals nationwide. Such construction funds, though theoretically targeted chiefly at rural America, quickly became a dramatic source of support for medical school construction in urban areas. Kracke had used his "tight" connections on Capitol Hill to lobby hard for this legislation, and soon there were millions of dollars of Hill-Burton funds headed for Birmingham.[20]

Second, in 1947—following false starts under Governor Chauncey Sparks in 1945—Governor James E. Folsom led the legislature to finally act on pressure from President Paty and a core group of dentists in the state (who anticipated massive veterans benefits) for dental education. The legislature appropriated some $625,000 for the construction of a four-year dental school as another component of UA's Birmingham operations. At the same time the legislature appropriated annual operating funds of $150,000 for the new school. After frustrating efforts by UA's administration as well as Kracke, the hiring of a dental dean would follow in 1948. Still, the leg-islative appropriations of 1947 undoubtedly increased Kracke's excitement about building something more than a medical school.[21]

Finally, in June 1947 Senators Hill and Sparkman advised Kracke that his recent application for a 500-bed, $12 million Veterans Administration Hos-pital now looked good. Formal notification was a few months away, but the medical center expansion plans created the strong possibility for the con-struction of a complex on the block to the west across Nineteenth Street from Jefferson Hospital. Kracke had been anxious about this crucial devel-opment. Through Sparkman he had been named vice chairman of Presi-dent Truman's Special Medical Advisory Group on Veterans Affairs, a key national appointment for access to VA programs; Charles Mayo chaired the group. At first, however, things had not gone well. Since its first submission in 1929 by Birmingham civic leaders Hugh Starnes, Carl Wiegand, and John P. Newsome, Birmingham's VA application had been languishing as a result of the VA's practice of placing hospitals in "scenic areas." This was vexing for the new dean.[22]

Despite Birmingham's nestling among the lush foothills of the Appala-chians, hills prominent enough to host "fresh air" clinics at English Vil-lage and Bluff Park, there was no "scenic area" down where the city lay in Jones Valley. Filthy air accented with red hot "runs" at night may have documented a U.S. Steel payroll for 30,000 or more, but Birmingham re-mained like its namesake in England: an "inferno" of a "valley of fur-naces." Particularly partial to ocean fronts, VA leaders had little interest in Birmingham.[23]

In deliberations of the advisory group, accordingly, Kracke spoke vocif-erously on the need for the VA to develop hospitals with less regard for scen-ery and more emphasis on close proximity to academic medical centers, as had been done recently in Portland, Oregon, where the benefits of "critical mass" were so apparent. To his urging acceptance of the longstanding Bir-mingham proposal, however, Kracke received general discouragement from VA director Brigadier General Frank T. Hines, who adamantly opposed con-necting VA hospitals with medical schools, especially in urban areas.[24]

Turned down, Kracke went back to Mayo and others on the Special Medical Advisory Group. Supported by wide-ranging pressures from the American Legion, the committee reemerged with a frontal assault on the general and his old way as "counterproductive." Indeed, General Hines found himself ousted (and sent off to Panama with the rank of ambassador) and replaced by the august General Omar C. Bradley. The committee's subsequent report, backed up with crucial telephone calls from Hill and Spark-man, a few other senators, and Colonel William Pritchard of the American Legion, soon led to major redirections for planning VA hospitals. By May 1945 the VA placed a priority on hospital development where "proximate location and affiliation" with academic medical centers was a genuine pos-sibility. More to the point, Kracke's application soon appeared on the ap-proval list, and his UA roommate was only too delighted to pass along the encouraging news that the new facility would be a functioning reality by 1953. Kracke's laying the groundwork for a VA hospital to be constructed in Birmingham had to be sized up in only one way: a coup of the first order. And by early 1950 Kracke would celebrate this victory not just for Bir-mingham but for urban health science centers nationwide by writing an ar-ticle for the *Journal of the American Medical Association* titled "The Medical Care of the Veteran," which traced the evolution of the new approach to de-veloping VA hospitals.[25]

The dramatic VA news, plus Kracke's capturing another $1,000,000 building grant from the State Building Commission, filled the new dean with hope about solving at least his most pressing space needs.[26] With the services of the local architectural firm of Warren, Knight, and Davis he set to work. Since the VA would be going up in the next block over from Jefferson—which meant a large pool of patients for "teaching cases"—he knew immediately what the best plan was: a massive expansion and up-grading of Jefferson as an educational facility, not just a "paying" hospital.

Soon he had the basics worked out. On either side of the sixteen-story Jefferson would be new wings, nine stories each though "stressed" for six-teen to permit more expansion as funds permitted. The northern wing would house School of Dentistry administration on the first floor, move upward through dental clinics, and then to floors for educational and re-search endeavors of the Medical College of Alabama: obstetrics and gyne-cology, pathology, surgery, medicine, and finally a top floor with biochem-istry. (The ease of laboratory venting on a top floor was not the only reason he placed biochemistry up there; as a reflection of the crucial perception of the future of medicine shared by both Kracke and McLester, they wanted these particular basic scientists working closely with these particular phy-sicians.) The southern wing would have a first floor for College of Medicine administration, then several floors for the library topped off with floors committed to bacteriology, radiology, and anatomy. Accommodations for nurses and house officers would remain on the top floors of the original Jef-ferson structure, but physiology and pharmacology would be located up there as well, with the resultant loss of bed space for teaching cases being more than accounted for in the VA facility. The closed-in "widow's walk" would be redesigned to house animals used in research. By late 1947, with funds from the Hill-Burton Act to move the old Public Health Department out of Hillman into new facilities on the north side of Eighth Avenue between Nineteenth and Twentieth Streets, plus create additional space for dentistry, and new state funds for basic science and nursing construction, this scheme would be changed some. But thanks to the *Birmingham News,* which printed the plans in a full-page story, Kracke's 1946 vision nevertheless let the public know that out of ground once yielding only iron ore there now was growing a medical center for Alabama.[27]

In these construction plans Kracke and Paty also were determined to address inadequate health care for blacks. Typical of the Southern scene, as Thomas J. Ward shows in *Black Physicians in the Jim Crow South* (2003), black patients long had been admitted to indigent "Negro sections" of otherwise white hospitals, but even in Hillman they could be treated only by white doctors who practiced there. Black patients seeking hospital care at the hands of black physicians generally had admission only to pathetically funded and substandard home-based "Jim Crow clinics." Although a few black doctors had offices in the heart of the city until segregation codes became more rigid around 1900, there is no indication that the more prominent location of these offices paralleled a higher level of care. There was one exception—the Children's Home Hospital for blacks and its descendant institution, the Catholics' Holy Family Hospital. (By 1953 Holy Family would open and soon take the place of Children's Home, closed in 1954 due to lack of sanitation.) More to the point, black physicians of Birmingham had been barred from seeing patients in the modern white hospitals; physician use of these facilities remained restricted to those in the Jefferson County Medical Society, a private organization that had no black members. For professional association and continuing education, black doctors had their own organization, the Mineral District Medical Society, but this had no impact on their access to modern health care facilities.[28]

This general environment of health care for blacks rendered devastating effects in Birmingham. In the mid-1940s, for example, the maternal mortality rate for blacks in the city ran about fifteen per 10,000 live births; for whites it was around five. Infant mortality rates reflected a similar disparity: for blacks about forty per 1,000 live births, for whites twenty-three.[29]

These disparities fit into a larger context with more possibilities for change than some understood. Granted, local customs and UA policy, not to mention state law and city code, had stipulated a segregated society since the early 1900s, and the U.S. Supreme Court had shown no intention of striking down the hypocritical orthodoxy of "separate but equal." By 1943, however, there had been race riots in Mobile, Detroit, and New York City. And in early 1946 President Truman issued executive order 9802 creating the Presidential Commission on Civil Rights; two years later he issued executive order 9981 barring segregation in the armed forces.[30]

The rising national movement for race change was not the only influence on Kracke in terms of how he viewed race relations; something more personal and local was there. In his youth he had spent long hours with his maternal grandfather, William Muller Puryear, a native of Rockspring (Walker County), Georgia, who did what more than a few hill-country Georgians and Alabamians did: opposed to slavery and the Confederacy and white planters' dominance of state politics, in 1861 he enlisted in the Twelfth Tennessee Cavalry Regiment of the Union Army. Ultimately he fought with victorious Union forces at the Battle of Nashville in December 1864. Though some of his relatives and most of his friends refused to speak to him after the war, later as a resident of Town Creek in north Alabama he proudly drew a Union Army pension check until his death in 1941.[31] Puryear led complex family discussions about what was right and what was wrong on the Southern racial scene. Kracke never forgot these discussions, and as these family influences of racial liberalism became reinforced through private conversations with his new friend, Henry Edmonds, and with his boss in Tuscaloosa, Paty, who had vainly sought steps toward UA's partial desegregation as early as 1943, Kracke clearly grasped the hard reality before him: the need for race change, yet also the need for financial and political support to build a medical center in a state that at least for now stood as the most segregated place in America.[32]

In daily life this meant for tricky business. For instance, one of Kracke's closet advisors on Birmingham race relations—and, as his son Robert Kracke recalled, "the first person to invite my father to dinner that summer"— became Charles Zukoski.[33] A St. Louis native and Harvard-trained attorney who arrived in Birmingham in the mid-1920s, Zukoski would be fired from his position as trust officer of the First National Bank of Birmingham (none other than Oscar Wells's bank) in 1962 for his advocacy of worldwide birth control, desegregation, and other "liberal reforms" he urged, among other places, through a local newspaper column signed "Button Gwinnett," the name of a relatively obscure signer of the Declaration of Independence from whom Zukoski occasionally claimed to have descended.[34] Apparently without the knowledge of Wells, however, it was through Zukoski that Kracke made contact with the Camden, Alabama, preacher Renwick C. Kennedy and other 1930s Southern white liberals who were trying to find a nonconfrontational road to racial justice through linkages with the Alabama Council on Human Welfare and through contact with the few racial liberals on Governor Folsom's Committee on Higher Education for Negroes. Established in 1949 to upgrade "Negro education" and thereby make separate but *equal* the continued legal practice despite a growing restlessness with the notion among members of the U.S. Supreme Court, not to mention Folsom himself, the committee included Zukoski and a few other liberals who hoped to move race and education in Alabama beyond separate but equal. Indeed, Kennedy knew of Paty's private position on race change and urged that Kracke move forward "with the belief that he [Paty] would want him to do so."[35]

Encouraged by this small but intense group and with no fanfare, Kracke became the personal escort for African American Charles Richard Drew whenever the noted Howard University medical educator and social reformer moved in and out of Alabama lecturing and recruiting medical students at Tuskegee Institute. In 1948, when Drew was driving to Alabama to give a speech at Tuskegee, his automobile crashed into another and he died shortly afterward in Alamance General Hospital in Burlington, North Carolina. Instead of Drew's lecture on the need for more black physicians, Tuskegee faculty and students received Kracke's moving impromptu remarks on Charles Richard Drew. If the dean was infuriated by the lack of press coverage on Drew's death, it no doubt suited him just fine that the newspapers ignored the eulogy.[36]

Kracke showed the same assertive diplomacy when he quietly admitted three black women to the two-year diploma nurse program in Hillman in 1947, some thirteen years before the civil rights movement made it legally possible for black students to be admitted to UA classes. Apparently, when Birmingham police commissioner Eugene ("Bull") Connor telephoned the dean to ask if blacks actually were in class with whites and thus in violation of state and city laws, Kracke confirmed that this was so. "Mr. Connor, I need nurses. I don't care whether they are white, black, red or green. I need nurses." Then, through a series of telephone discussions over two days, according to his longtime secretary Kay Morgan, Kracke somehow convinced Connor to leave the matter alone with the promise that the dean, if publicly questioned, would say that segregation was well in place in the medical school and its hospital. Kracke stuck with that promise especially in light of the strong prospects for increased state funding to start a full-fledged school of nursing by 1949 located in Tuscaloosa. Still, Kracke's desegregated nursing program ceased within a year when UA board members Hill Ferguson and Gessner McCorvey forced him to remove the black students.[37]

Kracke attempted to use the same nonconfrontational and deal-cutting strategy for race change in planning hospitals open to black patients. When the new dean had arrived in Birmingham in the summer of 1944, Harry Lee Jackson had briefed him on the hard work of the Jefferson County Negro Hospital Association. Led by Bishop B. G. Shaw and members of the Mineral District Medical Society, the association had raised $32,000 toward funding a modern health care facility for blacks. As Kracke soon learned from Bishop Shaw, however, the membership of the association seemed divided on whether the envisioned facility should be built as a segregated component of the new medical school complex or located elsewhere, perhaps four miles east of Hillman in the middle-class black neighborhood of Smithfield. When he was invited to address the association on his vision for the medical school, Kracke jumped at the chance to urge that the hospital be brought into planning for the area around Hillman. In the audience that night sitting right up front with customary legal pad in hand was none other than Zukoski, Kracke's new friend—one of the few white members of the association. The dean argued that a medical school location would help the black hospital defray costs through medical students and interns assisting with patient care.[38]

In response, the leaders of the association concurred, then stipulated that locating it near Hillman could only happen if the new facility maintained its own legal existence separate from UA's as well as its own board of directors. Three days later, after talking with Paty, Kracke assured association leaders that this separate control could be guaranteed. Suspicions still lingered, however, until on Kracke's request Zukoski pledged the credibility of Kracke's promise to the bright young black attorneys representing the group, Arthur Shores and Oscar Adams. In December 1944, the association gave Kracke their written acceptance of his offer, and Kracke, Zukoski, Shores, and others obtained a commitment for a "significant gift" from Birmingham's Donald Comer, president of the international textile firm Avondale Mills, to provide additional funds necessary for construction.[39]

A year later, however, the movement for improved health care for blacks as part of the envisioned UA medical complex seemed stymied. Throughout 1945, VA administrators out of Washington, D.C., kept revising plans on the specific space they would use in building their new hospital just west of

Hillman. In response, Shores and others representing the Jefferson County Negro Hospital Association kept adjusting plans for what particular space they would build on. By January 1946 the VA had decided it would use all the space available in the area at that time. Regardless of the construction funds now available and the powerful support of Comer, no space remained for the development of the black hospital.[40]

Kracke was "distraught," he told Zukoski, but he was not willing to risk losing the VA hospital by fighting the issue. Instead, he figured he would use this setback as a source of an even better approach to black health care. With hopes of attracting funds assembled by the Jefferson County Negro Hospital Association, hopes encouraged by Shores—though with no commitment—the dean announced plans to convert the fourteenth floor of the original Jefferson Hospital into a section for black medicine. Here there would be operating and delivery rooms and sixty beds, some in a private-room setting. Here also would be "Negro physicians, nurses, floor supervisors, interns, and residents." As with white patients, only "pay and part-pay" black patients could be placed on the new floor; indigent black patients would continue to be treated in the segregated indigent section of Jefferson and Hillman as were white indigent patients. In no way denying that this racial formula represented "a hospital within a hospital," Kracke still emphasized that according to 1946 data the plan would provide some thirty-five highly qualified black physicians the opportunity to see black pa-tients with the benefit of a modern medical center—consultancies, nurses, food preparation, laundry, laboratories. To any pragmatic liberal of that time this would have been a breakthrough. To a viewpoint more moderate to conservative, it also was acceptable: as the *Birmingham News* noted, the plan reflected an effort to address a genuine problem and still "be in accor-dance with the social customs of this area."[41]

There is no evidence of Kracke's having checked with the UA president before floating his plan. In view of what close personal friends they were, surely he must have; indeed, there is the possibility that the two concocted it together, for the plan is remarkably similar to Paty's 1943 plan, never unveiled, for gradually desegregating UA first through enrolling blacks on the Tuscaloosa campus in segregated graduate-level courses.[42] At any rate, aware of the boldness of placing black physicians and black patients under the same roof with white physicians and white patients, the dean knew he needed more than pledges of support from some of the press and from a few black and white friends, especially in a state whose powerful, health care–oriented U.S. senator, Lister Hill, had conservative race views. So he decided to look for more substantive support within the faculty and the community.[43]

He got the opposite. When Kracke asked the newly appointed departmental chairs in the medical school to gauge reactions to his plan among their physician friends around the state, he soon received letters from physicians such as Arthur F. Toole, of Talladega, and Gerald G. Woodruff, of Anniston, who said "it was a bad idea" and would "create serious problems." In closed-door conversations Kracke got the same feelings from some of his chairs, particularly James Garber in obstetrics. They could tolerate "the strawberry-blonde . . . hospital house-cat," Minnie, making "a morning tour over the hospital each day," eating lunch in the cafeteria, and indeed giving birth to four kittens—Clavicle, Tibia, Fibula, and Acetabulum—in the social service office. But expanding black people's access to the Jefferson hospital could not find much support.[44]

Simultaneously, the medical dean heard the same message from a few others. As he discovered through conversations with Zukoski and Shores, the plan simply did not go far enough. The plan was not a break from segregation. Yet if he polarized the politics of race and medicine to force the medical lobby in the legislature to exercise its considerable clout, overnight his vulnerable, start-up medical school simply could be eliminated. In Kracke's mind that would take the cause of improved health care for blacks absolutely nowhere. In the midst of this negativism about a "black floor" in Jefferson, however, Kracke was still saying to Bishop Shaw that the developing VA had "created a space problem but this does not mean that we have changed our minds about ultimately having a Negro hospital as part of the medical center."[45]

Still, with the "black floor" concept politically unfeasible, and while he never gave up on mixing the races in the medical center over the long haul, in the fall of 1946 Kracke began to see that the only *immediate* solution was a black hospital located elsewhere. This line of thought seem to gain stronger pragmatic acceptance on all sides throughout the late 1940s, ultimately delivering a black hospital in Ensley, twelve miles west of the medical school. It would emerge as the Sisters of Charity's Holy Family Hospital where black patients and black physicians were welcome, as were whites; it developed out of the combined resources of the Jefferson County Negro Hospital Association, the Catholic Church, the Birmingham Junior Chamber of Commerce, the Interracial Committee (especially with funds raised by Zukoski and Comer), and by Hill-Burton money facilitated by Kracke.[46]

So it was upon a rough sea of social change that Kracke pressed his expanding vision for something more than a medical school—a medical center. It would be 1964 before a black physician would practice medicine in the medical complex Kracke was developing. On the other hand, by 1953 virtually all of his physical plant plans not hinging on race change would be either consummated or on the drawing board. The only exception to this was Five Points South. As early as 1944, with trustee Ferguson's assistance, he had drawn up plans for this once ritzy commercial area (up the Twentieth Street hill just south of the hospital, with its Medical Arts Building [later the Pickwick Hotel] housing private practice physicians) to be revitalized. Then there would be some "unspecified integration" between the resultant medical center properties and adjacent private businesses, restaurants, and shops.[47] That did not happen quite as he envisioned. Still, by the early 1950s the Jefferson project, the new VA Hospital, and the Crippled Children's Clinic (if not a relocated Children's Hospital) all would be realities. Even by the late 1940s, accordingly, Kracke could see his vision beginning to materialize.

Threatening Other Old Ways

Kracke also confronted retarding traditions less directly related to race and real estate. Perhaps these fights would not have been so excruciating if Raymond Paty, his old friend and soulmate in social progressivism, had not left the UA presidency in December 1946 to assume the role of founding chancellor of the University of Georgia system and if Lowe had not gone with Paty as director of the University of Georgia Extension Service. But they did, and a crucial problem emerged: Kracke's two most trusted allies in daily work life were gone.[48]

Amid rumors that Paty favored none other than Kracke to be his successor, rumors apparently fanned by Comer and a few other Birmingham civic leaders, not to mention Governor Sparks's sending a Kracke endorsement to the UA board, Kracke had no plans to be UA's president. As he wrote the board on November 29, 1946, "My entire life's work has been in the field of medicine and medical education . . . and . . . it is my firm conviction that I can be of greater service to the University and to the State in my present position rather than as President of the University." Shortly afterward the board asked Ralph E. Adams, one of its graduates and currently dean of administration, to serve as interim president while a search unfolded. By December 1947 the board concluded its search with a decision surprising to many. It would not go with Adams. Instead, they chose none other than

John M. Gallalee, the man who on Paty's firm encouragement had assisted Kracke on the state building grant.[49]

Gallalee took the reins at a deceptively optimistic time. With educational benefits, veterans now enrolled by the thousands. Between June 1946 and June 1947 total UA enrollment including extension centers rose a staggering 70 percent. In response Gallalee used his connections with the State Building Commission and quickly initiated an expansion of UA's physical plant in Tuscaloosa, the engineer in his element.[50] However, by late 1948 the veterans and their tuition benefits had about run their course; UA now had ongoing construction alongside suddenly unused space and rapidly declining enrollment, coupled with the historic albatross of inadequate state appropriations to offer competitive faculty salaries. On this roller-coaster experienced by so many university presidents in the immediate postwar years, Gallalee tightened control over virtually all financial matters of the institution, including those of the new medical center in Birmingham. As E. Culpepper Clark explains, Gallalee's personality was not well suited for these maneuvers: "Gallalee's attention to detail was exceeded only by his lack of humor. . . . His stiff relationship with students acquired statewide notoriety and prompted a letter from a prominent member of the Birmingham bar who feared that Gallalee would go too far in punishing students involved in a panty raid." On faculty matters, says Clark, things were "no better." "He launched a building program and paid for it in part by diverting a million dollars intended by the legislature for faculty salaries." The campus soon had signs posted that read "G.G.G."—"Gallalee's Gotta Go."[51]

This change of personalities in the president's office had major implications for Kracke. Under Paty, it was well known in UA circles that Kracke could run his own lobbying operation in Montgomery: the dean had been successful in befriending Wallace Gibson, William H. Beck, and other legislators in positions to earmark appropriations for Birmingham activities. If Paty had used Gallalee in his temporary building commission role to assist Kracke's lobby, Gallalee nevertheless was part of a group of UA faculty and administration who never fully supported what Paty and Graves had envisioned for Birmingham. As a leader of what Lowe had called "the conservative element on the campus" developing during the Paty years, Gallalee would become involved in funding disputes that clearly reflected a nervousness about, if not opposition to, growth in Birmingham. As president, Gallalee was not about to stand by while the intense gentleman from Hartselle—and in at least some quarters a favorite to have succeeded Paty—dealt directly with the legislature.[52]

As if he knew what was coming and picked the strategy that the best defense is a strong offense, at the June 1947 meeting of the UA board of trustees Kracke received approval for the creation of a special subcommittee of the board to focus on Birmingham issues. It consisted of Lonnie Noojin, of Gadsden, Paul Salter, of Eufaula, and State Supreme Court justice Thomas S. Lawson, of Greensboro, all of whom had worked hard to create the new medical school. This might buffer Kracke from adverse changes in the president's office and possibly raise the priority of the Birmingham agenda in the board's unfolding deliberations, especially on matters related to indigent care.[53] The subcommittee immediately began periodic visits with Kracke to get a better understanding of Birmingham issues and indeed helped somewhat on Jefferson County allocations for indigent care. By the late fall, however, its activities seemed ineffective to Kracke, and at the November 1947 board meeting, a month before that body named Gallalee president, Kracke raised the stakes by speaking openly of what he first had recommended in his annual report to the president submitted in June 1947, a request that had gone unanswered. Before the board he formally proposed that the best hope for the Birmingham campus was for the special subcommittee to look into ways for Birmingham operations to have more autonomy from Tuscaloosa: "In view of the expanding activities of the University in the medical field . . . and also a constantly increasing University center in Adult Education . . . working as an integrated unit, it is recommended that the type of administration [currently in effect] in this area be changed. . . . It is recommended that a type of centralized authority be developed with one executive officer in charge of the entire Birmingham program."[54]

Kracke gave few details. He had no illusions about how complex the management of such a centralized operation would be. Most medical doctors, the dean soon would tell a group of physicians in Chicago, do not care to "freely participate in general university activities . . . [for] the former receives a higher salary than his [nonmedical] colleagues" and feels "circumscribed" when too integrated into "University activities"; he becomes "just another professor" with not enough "inflating the ego" and loses his role "as a very important person."[55] Even with these irrational appendages of the "authority of the physician," however, Kracke believed that the advantages of the centralized structure in an underfunded place like Alabama, especially considering the various "cultural and financial" leverage factors inherent to the metropolitan scene, far outweighed the disadvantages of management and more than a few egocentric subcultures. Indeed, here was the first openly articulated vision for the expanded profile, structure, and organization of Birmingham affairs, with programs in health affairs as well as in arts and sciences, teacher education, and engineering. Not coincidentally, it was similar to what he had experienced at the University of Chicago and, more recently, at Emory. It is unlikely that Kracke ever convinced Paty of the Extension Center element in this vision; this fits with Paty's implied reluctance to build a new center facility. In remarks to the board, Kracke made no reference to his former boss's embracing this expansive vision for Birmingham. In his comments he also steered clear of calling the vision "a university." However, Kracke now suggested that all Birmingham affairs report to one officer located in Birmingham. At a time when UA administration included no vice presidents, just the standard noncorporate chain of department chairs and deans reporting to the president, Kracke was involved in complicated business. Enmeshed in the final stages of the president's search, the board responded by asking the special subcommittee to look into the possibility of hiring an administrative officer for Birmingham, title unspecified.[56]

Soon after becoming president in December, Gallalee showed at least one sign that he and his medical dean might be able to work together. Alice McNeal, who had come to the medical school in 1946 to manage the anesthesia service within the Department of Surgery, received a lucrative offer elsewhere. A native of Hinsdale, Illinois, with medical training at the University of Chicago (where Kracke had trained), McNeal enjoyed Kracke's strong support. The dean encountered little difficulty in gaining Gallalee's approval to offer McNeal her own operation in Birmingham. The program would emerge out of divisional status in surgery and become the Department of Anesthesiology. McNeal accepted the counteroffer and in 1948 became the second female department chair in UA's medical center.[57]

Such cooperation, however, turned out to be the exception rather than the rule. There soon was little doubt about how Kracke's proposal for expanding Birmingham affairs had gone over. Rather than giving Birmingham more independence, Gallalee spent a year on pressing Tuscaloosa matters, especially construction and faculty salaries. Then he cracked down on Kracke. The first clash involved the longtime issue of deficit spending in the hospital. From the start Kracke and his hospital administrator, John MacQueen, had struggled with shortfalls stemming from inadequate Jefferson County funding for indigent patients. The county would occasionally increase funding but always at a rate well below what was needed to cover costs. In turn, Kracke would have to take funds from his state medical education appropriation to cover real costs in the hospital; the resultant domino effect steadily kept medical center finances teetering on the brink of insolvency. MacQueen's battle with diabetes and regular absences during 1946 added to this problem as Lowe and Kracke tried to save money by not hiring a replacement and seeking, sometimes unsuccessfully, to manage daily affairs of the hospital themselves with Lowe bearing the title of acting director of the hospital. A state audit for 1946–47 revealed that this makeshift fiscal management was sadly lacking.[58]

Shortly before the audit reached the press, as Kracke replaced MacQueen with Arthur Bailey, Kracke wrote his old friend Lowe, now in Georgia, that the indigent care issue continued to plague all Birmingham developments and that his own efforts to deal with the problem by talking one-on-one with legislators had more than irritated some UA officials: "Obviously the administrative officers [in Tuscaloosa] of the University have been rather critical of the fact that the Medical College has not sought counsel, advice, and direction as frequently as they believe we should have."[59] Lowe wrote back with an expansive theory.

In the first place it is obvious that the committee [subcommittee for Birmingham affairs] is confused and frightened. They [individually] seem willing and anxious to appoint an overall director; at the same time, they seem almost severely critical of the fact that we attempted to run our own business. This can only mean that they are now ready to bring the Medical Center under the domination and complete control of the conservative element on the Campus. In the second place, they [the board of trustees] are ready to place the complete financial responsibility on the shoulders of Jefferson County. We all know that the per diem [indigent patient reimbursement] this year has been low, but I do not see how the University [in Tuscaloosa] can escape some feeling of responsibility for the financial success of the enterprise. . . . The University should be willing to bear with Jefferson County a responsibility for success in these unusual times.[60]

With the prediction that UA was in the process of placing Birmingham affairs under the "complete domination of a group of men" on the board "who know little about it and have still less interest in it," Lowe asserted that "the job [in Birmingham] cannot be done successfully that way." Then he offered all that he could—his friendship: "I have felt mighty close to you during these trying times."[61]

Lowe's view had merit but only in the context of a larger picture. If Lowe did not specify who made up the "conservative element" in Tuscaloosa, it is relatively safe to assume that he was referring to Gallalee and others who did not place a high priority on Birmingham expansion. This suggests that although Governors Sparks and Folsom and other Alabama leaders had marshaled the political muscle to create the Birmingham effort, that leadership had never dealt with the perspective of most UA board members in 1947 to which Lowe referred and was likely even Gallalee's, regardless of his personality flaws. The perspective had a reinforcing duality. Notwithstanding their awareness of the strong need for better medical education in Alabama, they were pursuing two strategies: they wanted to avoid increasing mandates for programmatic expansion not accompanied by adequate state funding; then, if that failed, to avoid financing an expanded medical school out of funds desperately needed on the Tuscaloosa campus and in towns statewide where UA had extension centers.

The traditional Alabama view about where public higher education should be, combined with this logical approach to fiscal policy in a poor state, made the perspective unsurprising. Still, in Alabama the perspective assumed historic dimensions that it might not have in other poor states, Southern or not. Alabama's longtime backwardness on funding social services, a backwardness so shrewdly manipulated by the Northeastern-based industry as perhaps in no other state, had produced an especially small state budget for social services. Thus, well-intentioned Alabamians now found themselves pitted against each other: the "conservatives," again to use Lowe's term, seeking to protect money for faculty salaries and library acquisitions, even buildings in Tuscaloosa; and the "liberals" seeking money for health care for the indigent and a new medical school. In actuality, here were two liberal stances in a state with dire need for progressive social policy. Because of U.S. Steel's continuing grip on the polity of Alabama, however, they were increasingly pitted against each other to the point at which they were, collectively, far less effective in helping their state than they otherwise might have been.

The only possible solution to this dilemma was a stronger tax base statewide that could produce funds for better social services and, in turn, catalyze the modern cycle of appropriate economic development—an expanding pool of entrepreneurial profits for more people as well as an expanding tax base. Although this modern cycle could unfold in so many other places in America, it could happen in Alabama only with the appearance of two modern foundation blocks: Alabamians gaining more control over their own economic and social policies; and responsible Alabama leaders stepping forward to assume public leadership roles and using this state autonomy to provide more social services for their fellow citizens. Sadly, at that particular time in 1948 and for some time to come, the reform effort needed to make all this happen remained at most a hazy dream of the future.

Although this conflict flowed out of historic forces of social change larger than any two or, indeed, two thousand people, it nevertheless was personalized for the moment in the developing Gallalee-Kracke feud. If the president seemed unable to stop Kracke's lobby in Montgomery, Gallalee found other ways to rein in his medical dean. He used the legitimate issue of financial crisis in the medical school. Seemingly focused less on the genuine need for more state or county funds to cover indigent care and more on the fact that this problem made it extremely difficult for Kracke to keep his budget balanced, the president told board members, "Never before in its history has the University of Alabama been dunned for its bills," and stated flatly that the dean was "being a bad manager of finances."[62] In October 1948 he informed Kracke that henceforth all requisitions from the hospital and the Medical College of Alabama would be personally countersigned by the UA president, that all hospital personnel matters, including salary decisions, would be managed by the business office in Tuscaloosa, and that he as president would be coming to Birmingham once a week to help oversee all operations—a plan enforced for the remainder of Kracke's deanship. From these developments Kracke, his wife, Virginia, and Kay Morgan suspected that the new president might just possibly want to choose his own medical dean, and Gallalee may have heard rumors that Kracke had had at least some initial feelers about assuming the medical dean's role in Georgia. Kracke, however, had turned down New York City to come home to *his* state and *his* university and was not interested in moving, not even to Georgia where his close friends Paty and Lowe had gone.[63]

What came next left little doubt as to Gallalee's strategy. In conjunction with a striking development in the medical center, the president made one targeted exception to the requisition policy: it did not apply to the person he had hired four months earlier in June as the dean of the new School of Dentistry, Joseph F. Volker. During the late summer and early fall of 1947 Paty, Graves, and Kracke worked closely with three prominent dentists—Centreville's Moran Fuller, Montgomery's Olin Kirkland, and Mobile's John D. Sullivan—to get state money for dental education in Birmingham. By November 1947, Governor Folsom and the legislature delivered a $750,000 appropriation for construction as well as start-up operating costs for a dental school.[64] Acting president Adams started a search for a dental dean, unsuccessfully pursuing George Easton at Iowa and George Teuscher at Northwestern.[65] They saw the effort as too risky. By the spring of 1948 Gallalee, too, had established close contact with prominent Alabama dentists who still recommended that a leader be chosen from the ranks of well-established deans. But he also could find no takers for such an embryonic effort. However, when Kracke presented this predicament to one of his old friends from his Emory days, the Atlanta dentist Thad Morrison, Sr., back came the suggestion that UA go after Joe Volker, the new thirty-four-year-old dean at Tufts University in Boston whom Morrison recently had met when Volker visited Georgia as a public health consultant.[66] Regardless of the growing stress between the medical dean and the president, Kracke was excited and immediately passed the nomination to Gallalee. The president sent two prominent Alabama dentists, Angus M. Sellers and Charles W. Lokey, to visit Volker's operation in Boston. Other Alabama dentists got a look at Volker when he was invited to speak at the June 1948 meeting of the Alabama Dental Association in Birmingham.[67] They found an intriguing Yankee. The grandson of German immigrants and a native of New Jersey, Volker had earned his D.D.S. at Indiana University and a Ph.D. in biochemistry at the University of Rochester where he played a significant role in the evolving use of fluoride to prevent dental caries. Though he found "the rewards of basic science research . . . obvious," he would recall that "the return to clinical dentistry prevailed" and by 1942 he was holding a faculty appointment in dentistry at Tufts. More important, in early 1946 Volker had risen to be dean of dentistry at Tufts, where he was known for innovative management.[68] With a strong informal vote of support from the Alabama dentists, Gallalee rode the bus (being a fiscally concerned executive) from Tuscaloosa to Birmingham and met Volker for lunch at the Tutwiler Hotel. Gallalee immediately saw "developer" written all over Volker and liked his reason for wanting the job: "I want the intellectual challenge of building something from the beginning." A short courtship ensued in which Volker suggested detailed changes to UA's retirement plan, changes that were never made. Still, Volker managed to nail down Gallalee's promise that although the budget would be tight, the dental dean never would be micromanaged and, indeed, would have carte blanche on all staff and faculty hires as well as programmatic development. Sensing these and other advantages of being "Gallalee's hire," unlike Kracke, Volker accepted the offer, rented an apartment on Valley Avenue, arranged to have his wife and two children moved to Birmingham by September 1948, and then headed off to Germany and Austria for several weeks to complete his part of a study of postwar health education sponsored by the Unitarian Church, of which he was an avid member.[69]

Despite Volker's detour through Europe, Gallalee immediately saw that he had his dental dean pegged right. In Volker's first forty-five days on the job in Birmingham, while flying back and forth to Boston to complete "some projects" at Tufts (and, unknown to the Alabama public, actually serving as dean at both institutions with Tufts and UA splitting salary costs), Volker developed a curriculum and recruited a faculty.[70]

He started with two full-time professors in dental techniques, Perry Hitchcock and Dominick Andromaco, the beginnings of the "Tufts Mafia," and seven part-time faculty who had practices in the community, all highly educated: Polly Ayers, Charles Lokey, Jr., Boyd W. Tarpley, Vivian D. Cooper, Leon Farnum, Robert Evans, and Edwin S. Brannon, Jr. Within a year three more full-time faculty would come onboard: Leonard H. Robinson from Tufts, Heyl G. Tebo from Emory, and the esteemed oral surgeon most recently of Tufts, Josef P. Lazansky. In his first forty-five days Volker also arranged with Kracke for the School of Dentistry to have space in Hillman. Kracke had hoped to use some of the $1,000,000 state allocation to build a new nursing dormitory and education building adjacent to Hillman facing Seventh Avenue (though UA's primary nursing programs would continue at Tuscaloosa until 1966, slowing Kracke's project), thus freeing up the old Jefferson-Hillman nursing space for Volker to use in starting dentistry. No sooner had Volker begun planning out of Hillman, however, than he and Kracke developed a strategy for constructing across the street from the envisioned new nursing dormitory a building destined to be a focal point of the medical center. Completed by 1951, it would house dentistry, with construction funded by the $191,000 grant from the Hill-Burton program facilitated by Volker's including beds for oral surgery patients, and it also would house basic sciences with $200,000 for construction out of Kracke's $1,000,000 state allocation. New space for nursing would come later.[71]

The two deans used the term "basic science" in planning this expansion. Before they even knew one another each was awaiting the results of the wartime National Defense Research Committee (NDRC) and its evolution into the Office of Scientific Research and Development (OSRD). Through the lobbying power of these acclaimed U.S. scientists and educators, the federal government's support of scientific research during World War II would be extended into the late 1990s not only to deal more effectively with cold war issues, such as atomic energy, but also to explore broader issues of science and medicine. Although German research and general university life had been the model for U.S. investigators from the 1880s through the 1920s, when this model came under the influence of rigid governmental control by the wartime Nazi regime it had failed to compete with the more decentralized model of independent investigators working in universities emerging in the United States. Hence even before the war was over, in 1944 Congress authorized with appropriation the U.S. Public Health Service to expand funding for medical research underway in universities since 1930 through one of its units called the National Institutes of Health (NIH). No member of Congress played a greater role in creating the NIH than Senator Lister Hill of Alabama. Through his various committee roles, as well as close work with Rhode Island's John Fogarty in the House of Representatives, he guided both the creation of the NIH and the funding of it.[72]

A year later, when one of the NDRC/OSRD group, Vannevar Bush, published *Science—The Endless Frontier: A Report to the President on a Program for Postwar Scientific Research* and urged with even greater force the idea of government funding—not controlling—university-based scientists as the key to future scientific knowledge and therefore power, Congress moved to create the National Science Foundation (NSF). Finally a reality by 1951, the NSF would provide millions of dollars of support for "basic scientists" often working in university laboratories. In short, Volker and Kracke understood the revolution in funding for health science and basic science as it had been touched off by wartime developments, and they carefully planned their nascent medical center bearing in mind these funding sources, not to mention Senator Hill's willingness to discuss with them what sort of construction and research projects these funds should support.[73]

During the first forty-five days of the new School of Dentistry the two deans also refined and implemented a plan first conceived by Kracke, McLester, and Lowe, one that Volker had seen work in Rochester and one strongly encouraged, if implicitly, by Big Science developments in Washington: the pooling of first-year dental students with first-year medical students in the same basic science program. To ensure careful management of this plan, Kracke and Volker named biochemistry chairman Emmett B. Carmichael as assistant dean for both the dental and medical schools. Volker assigned himself some of the biochemistry teaching responsibilities, tightly focused on strong basic science education as a key to the D.M.D. as opposed to D.D.S. Thus, what would be known as the "Joint Basic Sciences," one of the great engines of future interdisciplinary research and extramural funding at UAB, originated out of opposite forces. First, there was current poverty urging "economy of scale" organizational cooperation. Second, there was future wealth in the form of research funding for basic and health sciences beyond the grandest dreams of most scientists and physicians.[74]

As he had promised Gallalee, by the fall of 1948 Volker, aided by Kracke, was ready for fifty-two Alabamians, all veterans, to come to Birmingham as UA's new dental students. Impressed by Volker's beginning and crediting the joint basic science strategy and the Hill-Burton application to Volker alone, Gallalee delivered on the promise to give his dental dean plenty of rein, including exemption from the new requisition policy.

As if by design, this made Kracke "inwardly furious." His shrewdly protective secretary, Kay Morgan, recalled that Kracke confided his anger to only a few, outwardly proceeding in his "quiet" and "always calm" ways though with a red rash of stress plaguing his face more and more. Asked by a close friend if it were not time for him to move on, perhaps joining Paty and Lowe in Georgia, Kracke rejoined, "No. We have much yet to get done; here, have some chocolate." Kindly, the dean did not reference the current (truthful) rumors that his old friend Paty was leaving Georgia because key members of the Georgia Board of Regents, those associated with the Herman Talmadge race-baiting leadership in Georgia and angered by Paty's liberalism on race relations, had Kracke's old friend on the ropes. After a later dismissed drunken driving charge, they would bid him farewell from Georgia higher education, only to see him return to the Julius Rosenwald Foundation as its director, where he had worked before coming to Alabama in the 1940s. Certainly Paty landed well with this eastern liberal Jewish foundation, undoubtedly anathema to the inner conservative circles of Georgia and Alabama.[75]

Tensions between Kracke and Gallalee seemingly had no end. Next there was the Homeric battle over Tom Spies, ten years in the waiting for final eruption. Back in 1937 James McLester, then physician-in-chief at Hillman Hospital, invited the young physician to move his pellagra clinic from the University of Cincinnati to Birmingham for two years, where he could be in the center of a population so devastated by what people called "the Southern poor folks' disease" of "laziness," which led to "insanity" and finally death. A student of the German biochemist Emil Fischer, McLester was an early proponent of the new biochemical approach to understanding disease. Although McLester saw pellagra as chiefly an infectious disease, not necessarily the problem of the poor Southern diet that Spies and others associated with the U.S. Public Health Service thought it to be, McLes-

ter also knew that having the University of Cincinnati operation temporarily based at Hillman could facilitate rapid research and, he hoped, offer
relief to those he saw as the "doomed pellagrins . . . in the South." However, Spies had to work in the pathetic research facilities of Hillman.[76] Un-
daunted, this Harvard-educated physician with a slow Texas drawl and a
quick draw on confrontation with colleagues immediately raised large donations from Alabama business leaders, allowing his project to enjoy a well-
funded staff, equipment, and publicity. However, it soon created a backlash among McLester and others seeking to increase private support not for
a University of Cincinnati project but for Hillman and Jefferson hospital
endeavors in the tough times of the Depression. A few physicians in and
around Hillman and Jefferson nevertheless supported the one they bannered as "the famine fighter," with none more vocal than McLester's arch
competitor and the Alabama physician most eminently experienced in the
political warfare of medicine—Seale Harris. Indeed, Harris helped Spies
develop so much corporate and political support for the Spies Clinic that
McLester was unable to send Spies packing at the end of the planned two
years.[77]

Thus, despite opposition from his original host, Spies was well fortified
on the second, fourth, and fifth floors of the Hillman Outpatient Clinic
when UA and Kracke took charge of Hillman in August 1944. With the construction of medical education wings to Jefferson Hospital still some six
years away, Kracke was scrambling for space to start the new four-year program. On Lowe's advice, however, the new dean took his time in approaching the McLester-Spies-Harris fight, not wanting to run the risk of escalating it into a political crisis that could defeat the initial steps of building the
Medical College of Alabama.[78] Finally, in November 1948, after repeated
friendly conversations with Spies, when the Texan was asked to move on and
Spies responded that he needed *more* space, Kracke felt he had no choice but
to confront him. The dean agreed that Spies was probably right about what
caused pellagra—poor diet—and that injections of vitamin B helped cure
the problem. With congratulations for the medical breakthrough, Kracke
said that he still had to have his space. The Spies Clinic took up space that
the hospital desperately had to recover in an effort to generate more patient
income to compensate for the continued crisis over underfunding for indigent care. (Indeed, short on operating funds, Kracke had to do the unthinkable one year later: close outpatient clinics between December 25 and
January 1.) Kracke ordered Spies and the Cincinnati clinic to move out. And
he had reason to feel confident. If Volker was too involved in other mat-

ters to assist and no doubt happy to stay clear, Kracke still had support from McLester, the chairman of the Department of Medicine, as well as the majority of the faculty of the college.[79]

By this time Seale Harris had helped Spies organize the Spies Committee for Clinical Research, which included some thirty state and national business leaders, as well as a lobbying operation in the legislature with none other than Harris as field marshal. Through Harris's influence, in fact, Governor Folsom, whose own relatives reputedly suffered from pellagra, had visited the Spies Clinic as had Alabama Power president Tom Martin, whose Montgomery lobbyists rarely missed their mark. These and other powerful leaders were convinced that Spies not only was getting at the truth about pellagra but ultimately eliminating one of the primary reasons for underproductivity among Alabama farm laborers and miners. That Spies represented "the paradox of a totally independent kingdom within the confines of the University," as one physician recalled, mattered little to these pragmatists. Shortly thereafter President Gallalee "got the word" from Montgomery that "the budget not only of the Medical School but of the whole University would be in serious jeopardy at the forthcoming legislative session" should Kracke's order prevail.[80] With UA finances so unstable and faculty on the Tuscaloosa campus berating Gallalee for raising buildings instead of faculty salaries, Gallalee feared any interruption in UA funding. Moreover, in view of the old statewide wounds associated with the location of the school in Birmingham, he feared a political crisis becoming something even bigger overnight—all valid points, no doubt, emphasized to him by Harris in a private conversation. So Gallalee told Kracke that Spies would be staying in Hillman. Kracke acquiesced. He might override Brigadier General Hines on VA matters, but Seale Harris was another matter.[81]

The loss to "the squatter," as McLester forces called Spies, had a "seriously depressing effect" on the morale of Kracke's faculty. To Kracke the outcome remained forever "devastating," his perennial stress always mirrored in the red rash on his face. To Spies the victory was sweet. He and his Hillman-based clinic lived on until 1960, deeply engaged in a milk distribution program, even though the Texan had moved to the medical faculty of Northwestern University shortly after Kracke's forced acquiescence. Still, although fatigued and fearful that, unlike Volker, he lacked the necessary support from the top to be an effective dean, Kracke would not quit. He moved forward on new construction projects with his usual intensity.[82]

In 1946 Kracke had worked closely with Senator Hill and UA board member and Birmingham realtor Hill Ferguson to get Hill-Burton Act funds to develop the new Jefferson County Health Department. The first public health facility in the nation built with Hill-Burton aid, it opened in 1953 around the corner from Hillman, facing Eighth Avenue.[83] With a similar plan to treat polio victims he now turned again to Ferguson and other civic leaders and the Birmingham Police Department, which had organized as the "365 Club." Since 1935 the club had been raising money with an annual Thanksgiving Day high school football game. (And by the late 1990s the fund totaled around $700,000.) With these funds as matching and Ferguson working real estate manipulations behind the scenes, Kracke helped the 365 Club get Hill-Burton support and move the Crippled Children's Clinic, devoted to polio victims in this pre–Salk vaccine era, from its old quarters on Eleventh Avenue North to a new modern facility on a square block directly across the street from Jefferson Hospital and next door to the VA site. With its own board and nonstate funds but with physicians from the UA medical school, it opened there in 1951 (later the site of the Spain-Wallace addition to University Hospital).[84]

Kracke sought to do the same with Children's Hospital. Here was a facility dating to 1911, when it was founded by ladies of the Episcopal Diocese in Birmingham in a house near St. Vincent's Hospital in the southern suburbs. Subsequently, the facility got annual stipends from Jefferson County and from the Community Chest. On his death in 1949 local civic leader Robert R. Meyer, one of Kracke's new friends made through Hill Ferguson, left more than $750,000 to assist in the development of Children's Hospital. Kracke's 1946 plan for the medical center could mesh easily with this turn of events. By working closely with the benefactor's son, Jack Meyer, and the hospital's influential building committee chairman, stockbroker Rucker Agee, Kracke convinced the board of Children's Hospital to use the bequest, plus Hill-Burton aid Kracke acquired for the project, to purchase UA property. As he wrote Gallalee in August 1949, "Precisely the same arrangements" of private board control and non-UA funding but UA physicians would exist as between the university and the Crippled Children's Clinic. To Kracke's frustration, financial complications exacerbated by his personal stresses with Gallalee delayed development of the new Children's Hospital for ten more years. It would not become a reality until 1961, on the watch of another medical dean.[85]

Still, again the point was clear. Kracke was not building a medical school but a medical *center*—and one not dependent on state funding in a state that historically underfunded all social services. He also hoped to build something in addition to a medical center, and this is where his striking plan became too bold for President Gallalee.

In the spring of 1949, Kracke and Volker advanced physical plant plans perhaps best described as "entrepreneurial." As they revised plans for the new dentistry/medicine Basic Sciences Building, they knew that in order to get Hill-Burton assistance—funds the U.S. government had targeted for hospital improvements—they would have to plan carefully for "two oral surgery hospital beds" in the dental wing. Likewise, they hoped to use the project as way of achieving something Kracke had been planning for and discussing with the board since May 1946: moving the Birmingham Extension Center into the emergent medical center. I. J. Browder still directed the center in its old house down near Phillips High School, and UA Extension Center dean Tidwell was now seeking to advance his 1944 proposal for construction of a new building at a prime location on Twentieth Street, one block south of Hillman Hospital. Kracke and Volker now joined Tidwell and Browder in their cause, arguing that the new center facility should be planned in concert with the new dentistry/medicine Basic Sciences Building. Indeed, these diverse pro-center forces now urged that an auditorium be added to construction plans so that the center would be merged with the health science facility. This held two important ideas for the future. First, it would meet pressing needs for more center space to serve growing student and community demands in arts and sciences, business, engineering, and teacher education. Second, it could alleviate space needs in the health sciences. Kracke especially wanted the auditorium to get "the public" to the campus—for speeches, public forums, and so forth—ultimately to broaden political support for all Birmingham programs but perhaps particularly those of the College of Medicine.

However, as the lobby for a common auditorium grew, so did the plan. In the same construction project Kracke soon called for "a home economics laboratory" for Extension Center students that also was "quite suitable for dietetics taught to nurses." Volker also had an innovative proposal: construct new Extension Center space for art education that could also be used for the laboratory plaster work required of dental students. In retrospect, some of this proposed "entrepreneurial collaboration" may have been short on common sense. More important, however, both deans saw major possibilities for chemistry, physics, and biology laboratories jointly used for undergraduate science education and the graduate work of dental and medical students—high-powered research laboratories for teaching undergraduate science advocated thirty years before American higher education embraced such an agenda. Both deans also pled the logic of having Extension Center programs and health science programs share a cafeteria, bookstore, and maintenance department. With all this in his mind, in fact with the preliminary architectural plans Kracke had asked Warren, Knight, and Davis to draw up, Tidwell told Gallalee that the time was right to move forward in a major way in Birmingham. Simultaneously, Kracke as well as Volker pushed on Gallalee the "urgency" of the new health science construction.[86]

Never indicating awareness that this was now a shared vision among Kracke, Volker, and Tidwell, President Gallalee categorized the proposal as another one of Kracke's plans for irresponsibly autonomous Birmingham programs. As if Gallalee had never forgotten what Kracke had proposed to the board three weeks before he became president, he quickly delivered a death sentence. Although there remains no indication that he opposed the "two beds" ruse in the dental space, in March 1949 Gallalee said flatly, "We are not ready to start construction on the Birmingham center." He then advised that he had met personally with representatives of Warren, Knight, and Davis and informed them that they were not to "handicap in any way the construction of the joint Medical College–School of Dentistry building by any reference to floor levels in the proposed Birmingham Center building." And to be sure everyone got the point, he then put it this way: "We should not make the joint Medical College–School of Dentistry building cost $1.00 more by any relationship to a proposed Birmingham Center building." The Hill-Burton grant was not to be used for things unrelated to dentistry and medicine.[87]

If Kracke and Volker felt stymied in their bigger vision for Birmingham, they did anything but give up. They still advanced the cause as much as they could by somehow placing a "supstore"—cafeteria and bookstore— on the first floor of the new structure, the second floor housing administrative offices for both deans as well as offices for a registrar and a bursar. Then they waited for another day.[88]

Regardless of the relatively diplomatic resolution to this disagreement over construction plans, the conflict between Kracke and Gallalee continued on matters related to the narrower medical role for Birmingham. Next came the issue of selecting physicians to chair two of the most important departments in the college, medicine and surgery. Back in 1945, of course, Kracke carefully had decided to find chairs for these departments in two nationally recognized Birmingham physicians and key leaders of the old Hillman Hospital—McLester for medicine, Mason for surgery. But both had plans to retire in 1949; McLester was particularly worn out over what he saw as the "fiasco" of the Spies fight. McLester as well as Mason had spoken to Kracke about the possibility of their sons succeeding them; James B. McLester and James M. Mason III enjoyed strong reputations. Careful about such matters not receiving consideration by the faculties of the respective departments, however, Kracke had responded to the outgoing chairs in noncommittal ways. Still, the rumor mill apparently delivered news of "the succession" to Seale Harris, who immediately went to Tuscaloosa to discuss the matter with President Gallalee.[89] Ever the medical politician despite his seventy-nine years, Harris suggested that young Mason was an excellent choice but young McLester lacked some of the personality skills necessary for leadership. Gallalee later recalled that he did not take Harris's visit as an extension of the old McLester-Harris feud; Harris had endorsed one member of the McLester bloc and opposed another. Nevertheless, Gallalee soon advised Kracke that young McLester would not be allowed to succeed his father. In the process, Kracke correctly got the point that an emeritus professor close to the president—Seale Harris—had veto power over many of the dean's major decisions. Kracke never advanced either son for these key positions though he thought highly of both.[90]

Instead, Kracke laid plans for outside recruitment. After a lengthy search in the Department of Surgery he began to focus on one man he had thought about earlier, Champ Lyons. Born in Pennsylvania but through his mother's remarriage raised in Mobile, and through that marriage becoming a cousin of Senator Lister Hill, Lyons had graduated from UA then Harvard Medical School and held a Mosely Traveling Fellowship in London when World War II started. He became an army surgeon and was highly regarded for his investigations into penicillin therapy. After the war, following a brief stint at Massachusetts General Hospital where he wound up being the physician in charge of patients burned in the 1946 Coconut Grove fire, Lyons had assumed the position of associate professor of surgery at Tulane University, where he was in 1949 when Kracke proposed his name to Gallalee. After the president cleared the hire with Seale Harris, Gallalee told Kracke to proceed. Lyons knew of the pathetic conditions in Jefferson-Hillman Hospital, from funding to technology, staff, and space, conditions that had worsened during Gallalee's presidency. Still, like Kracke before him, Lyons ultimately embraced the pull of his home state to achieve something of great significance.[91]

An outside hire also moved into the chairmanship of the Department of Medicine, though tensions with Gallalee kept this from being Kracke's hire. Still, Kracke stayed focused on what he thought he *could do*. As he wrote his friend Lowe in Georgia, on February 13, 1950, "All of our building operations have now begun. The Crippled Children's Hospital is now about four stories in the air. The Veterans Hospital has a deep hole in the ground and [we] are installing foundations. The combined Medical and Dental School [*sic*] are now underway. . . . The *Birmingham News* and *Age-Herald* have become tremendously interested in the problem [of indigent care costs] at last and for the past two months we have had two of their men investigating our operation and that of other medical schools."[92]

Indeed, just as Lowe replied, "[I] hope that your health and resistance hold out" and that "you and I chose the hard way but by far the better way to try to develop professional state-wide services," Walling Keith and Irving Beiman published a long series of articles in the *Birmingham News* based on their investigation of medical school finances nationwide and locally. They openly discussed the stress between the president and medical dean and reminded readers that Kracke never had gotten a formal response on his 1947 proposal for more autonomy for Birmingham affairs. They offered the regrettable conclusion: "Somewhere along the line, the Medical College of Alabama has become a sort of stepchild of the University of Alabama."[93]

If this reinforced Kracke's strategy of brinkmanship, it also heightened tension on all sides. Two months later, in April, he had a mild heart attack in his office. Kay Morgan found him in intense pain at his desk and called in his close friend, William Riser, one of the initial faculty members in the College of Medicine. Kracke extracted the promise from them that they would discuss his heart problem with no one—especially not Gallalee and not even Kracke's wife. On the futile pledge that he "slow down," the two confidants agreed. Kracke then pressed on with wide-ranging matters, naming Riser as acting chair in medicine while the outside search proceeded. However, on June 27, while he was visiting a patient in Sylacauga, forty miles south of Birmingham, a second heart attack killed him. In his obituary, the *Birmingham News* referred to Kracke's accomplishments as including the leadership of "The Birmingham Medical Center": perhaps the *News*'s capitalization of the "C" in center would have meant the most to him; up to this time, the "c" had remained lowercased. There was a memorial service at Independent Presbyterian Church, with Gallalee in the back row and Paty in attendance from Atlanta to present a eulogy. "Bull" Connor did not attend but, perhaps remembering that Kracke had kept his word about black nursing students in Hillman, wrote Mrs. Kracke of his "deep feelings of regret." The family then buried him on the north side of town at old Oak Hill Cemetery, in the Minter plot adjacent to the famous grocer of Twentieth Street. Two months later Kracke's major article on the reorientation of VA hospitals appeared in the *Journal of American Medical Association* alongside an obituary note. Riser and Morgan managed the day-to-day affairs of the school while the search in the Department of Medicine and now for a new dean unfolded. It did not take Gallalee long.[94]

More influenced by Seale Harris than anyone else, the Department of Medicine search committee offered the name of Tinsley Harrison to President Gallalee. A descendant of a line of physicians dating back to the American Revolution and the son of W. Groce Harrison, a noted Talladega, Alabama, doctor whose most recent practice had been in Birmingham, Tinsley Harrison had earned a B.S. degree at the University of Michigan then completed medical education at Johns Hopkins. After a postdoctoral stint in Germany, he became chief resident in medicine at Vanderbilt while authoring *Failure of the Circulation* (1935), in which he explains what happens to the human heart when it "fails." When Gallalee personally interviewed Harrison in 1950, he was the ex-dean of Bowman-Gray Medical College in Winston-Salem, North Carolina, and the ex-chairman of the Department of Medicine at Southwestern Medical College, a bankrupt school about to be acquired by the University of Texas. At age fifty, Harrison had found administration "a wretched experience" and was anxious to return to what he loved—teaching, research, and patient care. Yet like Kracke and, more recently, Lyons, Harrison found going home the right step for family reasons. (His aging father was almost blind.) Unlike Kracke and Lyons, however, Harrison's future where he was, at the reorganized Texas school where he was known as "a cantankerous personality," was at best bleak despite the pending publication of *Principles of Internal Medicine* (1950), a text he helped edit and write and would soon be the foremost such work in the field. Advised of all this by Seale Harris, Gallalee talked Harrison into every-thing *but* faculty life. In July 1950, Tinsley Harrison accepted the position of chairman of the Department of Medicine as well as that of Kracke's temporary successor as dean of the Medical College of Alabama.[95] That same year President Gallalee invited Seale Harris, with seven years left in his life, to come to Tuscaloosa one more time to attend commencement and receive the honorary doctorate of laws for outstanding service to the university and the state. To be sure, the two had found each other useful.[96]

The afternoon before Roy Kracke died he had met in his office with a group of journalists to announce that he had just mailed a copy of the national study of medical education commissioned in the late 1920s by President Hoover to five hundred Alabama political and business leaders. The report urged increased funding for medical education and documented the staggering costs of indigent care that state and county governments pushed off on medical schools. Over the last two decades, the dean explained, the nation had taken virtually no steps to solve the problem. Alabama, he pled, was even worse off than the rest of the nation: "We've had to divert a substantial amount of our Medical College appropriation into operation of the hospital," leaving the entire medical center "in a bad way" for the 1949–50 fiscal year. He called on Alabama's leaders to pressure the legislature to appropriate the funds necessary for Alabama to have a first-rate medical college as well as a hospital complex that could deal with indigent care in a responsible way. Unless Alabamians confronted this issue, he feared, the Birmingham operation would falter and die. Hence it was up to the very end of his life that Kracke relentlessly pursued the plan for a major medical center in Birmingham, a plan undoubtedly set within a comprehensive urban university as he had seen as a medical student at the University of Chicago.[97]

In retrospect, it was against powerful odds that this man from Hartselle would even have had such thoughts. Few would have thought that a four-year medical school—not to mention a medical center or even a university—could have been established during these unpredictable years at the end of the war when so much medical talent remained in the military. Even fewer could have foreseen this happening in one of the poorest states in the union and in a culturally benighted section still known among Northeastern intelligentsia as the "Sahara of the Bozarts." Yet Kracke looked these odds right in the eye and moved forward. For the time being, he knew, he would build a faculty chiefly of part-time physicians. Contrary to the advice of prestigious consultants, he reached out to the medical community of Birmingham where he found numerous modern physicians. Indeed, he found a mature environment of medicine still evolving as a result of urban development connected, ironically, to what helped make the state otherwise so culturally deprived: U.S. Steel. Through the advantage of a Southern sense of place and family, he also recruited a few full-time staff such as Holley and Lyons, an advantage that helped deliver Tinsley Harrison, too. Whether consciously or not, Kracke used broad social forces associated with place and family to confront equally broad social forces—poorly funded social services, fear of Birmingham, medical politics, and postwar talent shortages in medicine. There was a more personal factor, too—his crucial friends: Paty, Graves, Zukoski, Lowe, Hill, Sparkman, Wells, and Sweet. As a result, Alabamians soon had a medical center that may have been "beginning level" by national standards but was still a striking accomplishment in view of the odds, one that included the young star, Volker. Not surprisingly, when Kracke's relationship with the president's office took a 180-degree reversal, he took his shots and kept on doing what he knew his state and his university needed him to do.

In February 1944 when deans at ranking universities were predicting a sacrificial ending for anyone trying to build a medical school in Alabama, the more broadly thinking Dean Stuart Graves of Tuscaloosa wrote his colleague at Cornell, Joseph Hinsey, that the new medical dean for the University of Alabama should be "a younger man [than I am] with strength, training, philosophy and imagination which would enable him to develop a high grade medical school and to live with it for fifteen years." Prescient words. Roy Kracke gave Alabamians everything in the Graves formula— except a long life.[98]

4

Gestation, 1950–62

Reluctant Leadership

From the start, Tinsley Harrison's relationship with President Gallalee was the opposite of that of Roy Kracke. The new (acting) medical dean found that most of the administrative issues of the Medical College of Alabama distracted him from where, as he put it, his "heart was": his other job as chairman of the Department of Medicine together with his own patient care, teaching, and research. Harrison happily conceded to his new boss the micromanagement of many fiscal matters; Gallalee thus often spent as much as two days a week in Birmingham. As a result the two had a workable and generally cordial relationship.[1]

To Gallalee's credit, his sheriff eyes brought about a 23 percent decline in the number of George Barber's milk bottles that were lost or stolen in the hospital during 1950–51, slowing Spies's vitamin D project that Gallalee otherwise, ironically, sought to protect. In the same period, more importantly, the standard state audit complemented the college and the hospital for almost breaking even on indigent care, which was likely a function of Gallalee's making major transfers out of the college's education budget into the hospital's coffers—what Kracke had resisted in the name of the central mission of the college. In response, the legislature increased the college's annual appropriation from $650,430 for 1950 to $1,031,100 for 1951.[2]

Less to Gallalee's credit, neither he nor his acting medical dean pushed ahead on improved health care for blacks. In the fall of 1950 Charles Zukoski wrote Harrison on behalf of the Jefferson County Negro Hospital Association, asking what affiliation might be formed between UA's medical complex and an envisioned black hospital. At about the same time, a black physician associated with the Mineral District Medical Society, L. D. Green, sent Harrison the same inquiry. Zukoski got back what he had undoubtedly anticipated because of his serving on the Governor's Committee on Negro Education, where he served alongside Gallalee, and because he knew about the president's conservatism on race change. To both, replied Harrison, President Gallalee felt that he as an acting dean should take no action on such a proposal; that rules of the Jefferson County Medical Society unfortunately made it impossible for black physicians to practice in Jefferson Hospital; and that even if such rules did not exist severe space shortages prohibited the admission of either black physicians or black patients. Zukoski shot back with a reminder that there was a proposal on the table for new space, a black hospital, but he apparently received no response.[3] The following spring, when a black citizen died after apparently being denied admission to Jefferson Hospital, Harrison received resolutions calling on UA to admit "qualified and licensed Negro physicians" to Jefferson Hospital—one from Jimmie Hess, on behalf of the Birmingham Section of the National Council of Jewish Women, the other from Edward M. Friend, on behalf of the Young Men's Business Club. In each case, Harrison wrote back what Gallalee had given him in response to Zukoski's earlier inquiry.[4] In an April 1951 letter to Friend, he gave an additional—and probably more honest—rationale for the medical center's current stance on black health care.

> We [UA and the medical center] are all most sympathetic to the problem mentioned in your letter. We realize that there is an urgent community need for facilities where negro physicians can furnish high class hospital care to negro patients. Insofar as we at the Medical College can be of aid in such a program by making available certain educational opportunities to negro physicians we shall be most happy to cooperate. You will realize, however, that the basic problem involved in this need is one of community service rather than one of education. It therefore is not the primary responsibility of the Medical Center, which is and necessarily must continue to be education to meet the needs of the entire state.[5]

In short, Harrison reflected the influences of his upbringing, in this case the unarticulated belief that blacks were not full citizens though he did see the issue as a serious one needing a resolution that would improve health care for blacks. This paternalistic view of race, however, did not include high-quality health care for blacks and the related educational enterprise as a "primary [public] responsibility." Instead, it was a well-intended "community service" that one addressed if, and when, other priorities had been met.

As Gallalee remained compulsively involved in the fiscal processes of the medical college, Harrison's aggressive, if diplomatic, colleague over in the School of Dentistry, Joseph Volker—a racial liberal—had a free hand to push through two new organizational developments: the Division of Odontology and the Division of Restorative and Prosthetic Dentistry (evolving toward departments) along with initial continuing education connections with black dentists at Tuskegee Institute.[6]

As much as he tried to be "a caretaker dean only," Harrison was too committed a professional to avoid dealing with some of the unpleasant residuals of the Kracke years, which he tackled from the overly optimistic perspective of reducing the "medical politics" always found in young institutions prior to establishment of clear lines of authority and established personnel policies. No sooner had Harrison moved his wife (his three children were grown) into an apartment in the Plaza, on Highland Avenue, and Kay Morgan had shown her new boss his office in the Basic Sciences Building,[7] than Harrison found himself embroiled in the Spies-McLester fight. Because Harrison's father was an old friend of the great Spies advocate Seale Harris, many physicians in the state assumed that the new dean would soon "oust from key positions members of the McLester group." On reviewing the facts of the case Harrison believed that Gallalee, in fact, had no choice but to protect Spies. However, he invited Spies and Harris to his office where he told them that "first, my father wore no man's collar and second, that not he but I [make] my own decisions." Then to avoid any misunderstandings he took the opportunity of a faculty promotion case to speak to the other side. When McLester called on the dean to advocate promoting a specific individual, Harrison indicated that he promoted people only on the basis of merit as defined by "the opinion of students, interns, and residents concerning who was and who was not an effective teacher." In short, for statewide political reasons the Spies clinic would stay, but this did not mean that Harrison was "pro-Spies."[8]

Harrison likewise sought to depoliticize one of the many crucial medical center issues caused by the underfunding of indigent care—the Great Bed Fight of 1951—involving Champ Lyons, the newly arrived chairman of the Department of Surgery, and Dean Volker. Both desperately needed hospital beds with indigent patients suitable for their programs. However, Harrison as Kracke before him was being forced to reduce the number of indigent patients admitted to the hospital because of inadequate public funds to cover the costs of treating these patients. To make ends meet the hospital needed more paying patients in these beds. This trend plagued Volker in particular, who was in the first stages of implementing a residency program in oral surgery and had no beds designated for it. When Volker requested that Lyons allocate two of the general surgery beds for oral surgery, Lyons said "absolutely no." Both sides appealed to Harrison for help; he met with them individually and repeatedly over the ensuing month, emerging with his typically philosophical reaction: "It has been said that while conflict between right and wrong is melodrama, conflict between right and right is tragedy. Both men were right. They could not agree. Neither would yield." He knew he had to get a solution fast, for Harrison looked upon Lyons and Volker as "the two brightest gems in a crown that, as yet, had only too few jewels." And knowing such frustrations could lead to resignations, which would mean "a major tragedy for the struggling Medical Center," he allocated two beds to the Department of Oral Surgery out of those assigned to the department *he* chaired, medicine. If this permitted the School of Dentistry's new residency program to go forward at no cost to the Department of Oral Surgery (though at definite cost to the Department of Medicine), even more it represented a first concrete step in the binding together of Harrison and Volker, a "warm friendship" among leaders vital to the future of Birmingham affairs.[9]

More immediately satisfying for Harrison was the recruitment of Richard J. Bing. A native of Bavaria who had obtained his medical degree in Germany, by 1938 Bing was in private practice in New York City and had taught at Columbia University's medical school before moving to Johns Hopkins University and establishing an international reputation in cardiac catheterization that enabled the careful "detection of heart anomalies." In early 1951, with the promise that he would "be left alone to work," he accepted Harrison's invitation to bring his teaching and research to the fledgling Birmingham operation. Although Bing moved on in 1955 to a departmental chair at Washington University, St. Louis, his presence along with Harrison's helped make cardiology a major developmental focal point in the medical school and in the hospital.[10]

Harrison also had to take on the issue of a new departmental chair in pediatrics, an effort that revealed the dean's self-admitted "impatience" but was also indicative of the strategy he and Volker saw as the only viable future for their programs—increased funding through research. In 1950, just prior to his death, Kracke had replaced the retiring chair of pediatrics, Alfred Walker, with Beach Chenoweth, who wanted a career in private practice—and who would have a stellar one—but who agreed to run the department until, as later he told Harrison, "the department could find a person of national reputation under whom he would be happy to serve as an unsalaried [and part-time] teacher." More pointedly, Harrison seemed informed about Kracke's plans to have Children's Hospital and the Crippled Children's Clinic functionally part of the medical center (although it would be 1961 before final negotiations permitted the relocation of Children's Hospital from Southside to the medical center); and he wanted the pediatrics head not only to locate the department in Children's Hospital but serve as physician-in-chief in the facility. Hence, Harrison immediately set to work recruiting a chair for the department who would be capable of development.[11] First, Harrison had long meetings with members of the board of control of Children's Hospital to discuss this vision and promise them a role in recruiting the new department head. Here, Harrison encountered serious, talented, and powerful women of Birmingham's civic elite: Margaret Builder Benners, Lucille Hassinger Cabaniss, Rachel London Lamar, Margaret Tutwiler Wimberly, Mary Allen Northington Bradley, and Mary Eva Woods. He emphasized that the pediatrics head must have the ability to attract extramural funds associated with research and patient care, which necessitated a track record for such accomplishment. Alabama's "financial malnutrition" in health and education, he explained, blocked efforts at the hospital's development, particularly the scourge of the times—polio; the only possible immediate solution to this tragedy was extramural funds from the newly created National Institutes of Health, National Science Foundation, and large private endowments.[12]

Understandably, he further explained, few of the initial faculty had research orientations. With war and reconstruction, no such physicians could be hired in 1944–45. Thus between August 1945 and June 1950 only a total of $22,000 in extramural funds had come into the Birmingham campus (excluding construction grants) while, for example, Tulane's established medical programs—begun in the 1880s—had acquired well over $1 million during the same period.[13] Though it was a new idea for them in terms of developing higher education as well as a health care facility, the Children's Hospital board, Harrison would note, immediately saw his point and embraced it as a matter of adjusting to reality, leading him, after futilely trying to get the same point across to male civic leaders, to turn to Virgil's statement still good after two thousand years: "Dux Femina Facta"—loosely translated, "women make leaders."[14] This strategy of development undoubtedly was music to President Gallalee's ears, with whom Harrison continually talked: the less dependent the medical school was on state dollars, the more state dollars allocated to other UA enterprises. Such fire-in-the-gut commitment to increased extramural funding, a strategy that would become one of the hallmarks of UAB, in this particular case led Harrison to what he would call "a serious blunder" in his own judgment regarding, of all people, a woman leader.[15]

At Harrison's strong hand the pediatrics search committee, which included Lucille Hassinger Cabaniss, spent six months trying to attract a young leader "with a strong background in research." Out of a list of six, however, "one after another . . . declined to come and visit us . . . [wanting] no part of Alabama" with its reputation for rigid segregation and paltry state funding for public programs in health and education.[16] Rejected and with Chenoweth applying gentlemanly pressure to hire a chair so he could get on with his private practice, the search committee perked up when Lucy Cabaniss said she had heard excellent reports about a senior pediatrics professor at Vanderbilt, Katherine Dodd. Through informal sources, indeed, Cabaniss had learned that Dodd might be interested in coming to Birmingham. The "pioneering" venture appealed to her. Harrison knew Katy Dodd from his Vanderbilt days; in fact, she was the physician for the Harrison children while they were in Nashville. He knew her "as a superb physician" and "an outstanding teacher" despite her "gruff mannerisms." Even though "she did not always get on well with her academic superiors . . . she was almost worshiped by her juniors, the students, and staff." Yet Harrison blocked Dodd's candidacy. His reasoning: "She had made no significant contributions to research and being already in her late fifties, could not be expected to do so in the future. She could not bring us the grant support."[17]

Twenty years later, with striking intellectual honesty and a more seasoned understanding of academic leadership, premised on the point that not all grant getters make good leaders and some leaders who have not acquired grants themselves can nevertheless lead with a commitment to grants, Harrison held the opposite "conviction": "How wrong I was!" When few, if any, would even look at the UA medical school because of its developmental status and the bad reputation of its city and state, he could have hired one of the best pediatric leaders in the nation and did not. Instead, Harrison moved his strong hand over the search committee and went with an inside appointment.[18]

Impatient about the whole affair, he had the committee select Kendrick

Hare, who held a primary appointment in pharmacology but had extensive training in pediatrics and had begun to develop a track record with extramural funding. But things did not work out. Though a highly regarded researcher and teacher (he taught several future department chairs), Hare was not interested in the diplomatic leadership required for the chairman of pediatrics, who would also serve as medical director of Children's Hospital. Hence this particular joining of public and private facilities envisioned by both Kracke and Harrison had to wait a good while longer.[19]

Harrison perked up for a short while, however, in September 1951 when Gallalee began to move on hiring a regular dean for the College of Medicine. As it turned out, Harvey Searcy, a physician and a prominent member of an old Tuscaloosa family, suggested James J. Durrett to Gallalee. Although Durrett had little experience with either patient care or research, he was from the same old guard Tuscaloosa group as Searcy. His academic record consisted of part-time lecturing in preventive medicine at the University of Tennessee's medical school in Memphis while serving as health officer for surrounding Shelby County. But like Searcy he came from a family with deep roots in Tuscaloosa, was a loyal alumnus of UA, a graduate of the old medical college in Mobile, and had some political connections in Washington as a result of working as an assistant to the surgeon general of the Public Health Service, then as chief medical officer of the Federal Trade Commission working on food and drug matters. His administrative experience in Washington circles might be transferable to a medical school, including what Gallalee liked best: he was known in Washington circles for tight fiscal management.[20]

Although Harrison was excited about his soon-to-be "freedom," the search process bothered him. "My efforts to aid President Gallalee in the matter," Harrison later would write, "[were] totally ineffective." After meeting with the candidate for one hour, Gallalee simply telephoned Harrison and advised that Durrett would "shortly visit us." The visit then occurred— a two-hour tour of the physical plant, then a short meeting with the college's faculty. After the visit when Gallalee asked Harrison what he thought, Harrison reported that the faculty had not been able to get a clear impression. Still, with Kay Morgan braced to train yet another dean, Durrett moved into the office in early October. Harrison later reflected that at last he was "free."[21]

While Dean Volker continued with new initiatives—adding, in 1952, the Department of Dental Hygiene as well as the Division of Dental Medicine and Surgery—Durrett struggled.[22] In 1953, granted, the VA Hospital captured by Kracke and brought through the final stages of completion by Harrison, opened for business and provided badly needed teaching beds, laboratories, and general office space for the medical college. Likewise, over the next year Durrett pushed ahead on Kracke's plan for acquisition of the ten blocks west of the new VA, essentially an area of poor black housing that, despite NAACP opposition, would be razed with urban renewal funds and turned over to medical center expansion.[23] Too, Durrett came across as a genuinely nice person and was rarely one to exercise "the authority of the physician." One Saturday afternoon he cut his face as he fell down some steps at his Altamont home. Instead of "pulling rank," the medical school dean went to the emergency room of Jefferson, quietly registered as "J. J. Durrett" (no "M.D." after his name), then waited for more than two hours to get treatment. Champ Lyons ultimately walked through the waiting room on the way to see another patient and queried, "What are you doing here?" When Durrett replied, "Waiting to be seen by a doctor," Lyons sewed him up.[24]

Because of Durrett's lack of assertiveness no major new programs appeared on his watch. From the start, instead, the new dean did what Gallalee told him to do. He focused on the finances of the medical school and the hospital, which were still unstable, in the president's mind, because of poor management of the indigent care problem. In daily, often hourly, contact with hospital director Arthur Bailey and Gallalee himself, Durrett got hospital bills paid on time and managed to surface from his first year with no additional debts. In the spring of 1952, moreover, with Gallalee's assistance he acquired $150,000 from the State Building Commission matched with $300,000 in Hill-Burton funds to finish the top floors of Jefferson: more bed space and more income to compensate for the state's underfunding of indigent care.[25] Anticipated gains from this investment, however, became offset by a strike among hourly wage earners in the hospital organized by the American Federation of Labor (AFL). Gallalee personally met with individual strikers, agreed to raise wages on the average of 10 percent—the first hospital staff raises he had allowed in four years—then fired the switchboard operator who had helped the AFL open the shop. It suited Durrett fine to sit this one out, though the whole issue revolved around his budget.[26]

Likewise, it apparently suited him to let Gallalee dictate UA's policy on medical center racial matters. In January 1953, with the U.S. Supreme Court's landmark desegregation case, *Brown v. Board of Education* (1954), less than a year away, Birmingham stockbroker and investment banker Mervyn Sterne wrote to Durrett, reiterating the need for UA to admit black physicians and patients. The dean checked with Gallalee and simply responded as he was told: No black physicians could practice in the hospital because of the Jefferson County Medical Society's rule.[27]

It is possible that Harrison agreed with this approach to the push for race change, but he still found himself increasingly dissatisfied with other aspects of Durrett's general strategy to "avoid rocking the boat." This was a problem for the medical school particularly in programmatic matters. When an issue was even too internal for Gallalee to get involved, the dean turned it over to his associate dean, James Foley, professor and chair of anatomy, or to the departmental chairmen. "His training in the Washington bureaucracy," Harrison reflected, "had apparently inculcated a strong conviction that the important thing was not so much to make good moves but rather to avoid bad ones."[28]

Unlike most other chairmen in the Medical College of Alabama, Champ Lyons was a nationally recognized specialist and his department's patient care activities were expanding at a rapid rate. Even in 1950 patients, often with money, came to Birmingham from all over America seeking the aid of Lyons's famous knife. This made bed shortages a "desperate" matter. In a more personal vein, the problem frustrated Lyons in his friendly, if intense, competition with Harrison. Despite the horrors of indigent care funding, Lyons was determined to show that clinical activity—when the physician worked eighty hours a week and communicated "directly" with those reporting to him—could generate at least as much income for the institution as Harrison's extramural funds for research. So Lyons, generally a prima donna, now haughtily confronted Dean Durrett on surgery's "multidimensional space crisis." He urged that the Department of Surgery could generate significantly more income for the college if the department were given more hospital beds. In return, however, he got "endless conversations" on "irrelevant topics," no new space, and the private message from Foley that the dean looked upon him as "public enemy number one."[29]

Just as frustrating for Harrison and Lyons were the rare occasions when Durrett sought to act as a dean. When the founding interim chair of psychiatry, Frank Kay, a part-time faculty member in the Department of Medicine, announced in early 1955 that he would be resigning from his academic post to pursue his private practice full time, the dean appointed a search committee including Lyons and Harrison to find a full-time chair as a successor. Durrett also did the unthinkable for a dean. Months earlier he had privately encouraged the application of one of his Washington, D.C., friends, E. L. Caveny—possibly even offered him the job—and then overlooked this communication when charging the search committee. Chaired by Harrison, who likely got the bad news from Foley, the committee nevertheless advised the dean of its plans to have a national search. Durrett counteradvised that Caveny "looked like just the right man for the job." Although Caveny had little background in academic medicine, he apparently had a strong record with the navy. Durrett persisted with Caveny's candidacy, and the search committee ultimately gave the dean a 3 to 2 vote in favor of the hire. Lyons had opposed the appointment, but it was Harrison, he who had wanted so badly to be "free" to go back to his patients and his Department of Medicine, who led "the fight"; much to Lyons's glee it was Harrison who now unseated him as "public enemy number one."[30]

The fight in psychiatry continued. In late 1955, the recently recruited and nationally recognized hematologist in the Department of Medicine, Walter B. Frommeyer, replaced Foley as Durrett's associate dean. After a private conversation with Harrison, Frommeyer "tactfully but firmly" urged his new boss that the committee was right: "Please, reconsider" on the Caveny hire. The dean proceeded according to his original plan, however, and from then on, at least for Harrison, "every glimpse of Durrett brought to mind the line from Geoffrey Chaucer's *Canterbury Tales:* 'The gretteste clerkes been noght the wysest men.'" Caveny would last for four years; he was replaced with an internal appointment, James N. Sussex.[31]

At the same time, Durrett inexplicably wandered into a mine field of town-and-gown politics. In the late 1940s and early 1950s, as Alabama Power president Tom Martin led the establishment of the Southern Research Institute (SRI), the ranking UA leaders in Birmingham—first Kracke, then Volker and Harrison—intensely sought a harmonious relationship with the scientists two blocks south on Twentieth Street up the hill from the medical center. Even if Martin had been "a problem" in the Spies battle, he remained a man of considerable profile and power. In 1947 *Forbes* magazine counted him among the fifty "foremost business leaders" in the United States, and he had been a significant supporter of the medical center as well as the Extension Center. He also was right on target in urging that SRI could be a vitally needed link between scientific research and the development of Birmingham's economy. Even in the early 1950s, shortly after retirement, Martin was one of the most influential individuals in the state because of the connections between Alabama Power and Alabama's economic future. Significantly, it would turn out, he wanted a diversified economy for Alabama, which meant that he was not at all comfortable with Birmingham's being a one-horse steel town. Nevertheless, Durrett decided he would ask

Martin to withdraw his financial and political support from the executive's special creation, SRI, and bring this assistance to the development of UA's medical college. President Gallalee knew nothing of the approach. The plan of course went nowhere, except to be seen "as an unfriendly act by a sister institution" and one virtually obliterating some five years of "cordial relationship" between UA and SRI—making repairing the "blunder" a priority for a university already in need of fewer backfires left unattended.[32]

Given President Gallalee's less than enthusiastic support for Birmingham affairs, the administrative problem Dean Durrett reflected nevertheless could be traced to the more specific flaw in Gallalee's administrative style, especially as applied to Birmingham. With the notable exception of the hiring of Volker, Gallalee was determined to have his own way on key personnel decisions despite his lack of experience in making such decisions. One weak hire or appointment in an administrative position often resulted in another equally poor personnel decision down the line, which severely damaged the effectiveness of the most committed and visionary faculty and staff and with the ultimate burdens certainly borne by students and patients. So while the School of Dentistry under Volker steadily evolved during the Gallalee presidency (though it was still denied the more ranking nomenclature of "College" of Dentistry), the Medical College of Alabama, despite dramatic start-up with Kracke and the advent of major players such as Harrison and Lyons, still thrashed around awaiting major programmatic development. This soon changed, however, with implications not just for Birmingham but well beyond.

Uneven Development

In the spring of 1953 Gallalee's lack of support among faculty and students in Tuscaloosa finally led him to retire. With College of Commerce dean Lee Bidgood serving as interim president, the board went through the motions of a national search and announced in July that Oliver Cromwell Carmichael would be Gallalee's successor. Here, it appeared, was a coup of the first order.[33]

A native of Clay County, Alabama, and the product of a family known to have turned out more than one devoted physician and educator, Carmichael (close friends called him "Mike") was a UA alumnus and Rhodes Scholar in cultural anthropology. He would come to resemble the University of North Carolina's Frank Porter Graham and other liberal education leaders of the South forged out of the adversities of the 1930s. In the process, he—like Graham but also Raymond A. Paty—emerged at a time when the earned doctorate in a specialized field had not yet eclipsed common sense as the first requirement for administrative mobility in American higher education. After World War I, in which he served with distinction in Europe as an army intelligence officer (he was fluent in Spanish and French), he took an appointment as an instructor of romance languages at Woodlawn High School in Birmingham. Shortly thereafter he became principal of the school, but by 1926 he was a foreign language professor, dean, and executive assistant to the president at Alabama College (now the University of Montevallo, thirty miles south of Birmingham). Two years later, when he asked Alabama College for a sabbatical to go after a Ph.D. in romance languages at Princeton, its board suggested instead that he become president of the institution. He did this for the next nine years, helping enhance the curriculum as well as the state funding for the college. In 1935, following a conversation between none other than W. Groce Harrison—loyal Vanderbilt medical alumnus and father of Tinsley—and Vanderbilt's chancellor, James H. Kirkland, Carmichael decided to roll the dice. He took a salary cut in the middle of the Great Depression and moved to Vanderbilt University where he was held in the wings with the role of dean of the Graduate School and of Senior College—and watched. Then in 1937 he assumed the position for which he had been recruited: he succeeded the great Kirkland as chancellor. After 1943, moreover, he also chaired the board of trustees for the newly created State University of New York (SUNY) system, playing the major leadership role in the creation of that multicampus system.[34]

In the most prestigious American education circles Carmichael was known as "the Alabama legend." Yet he never played college football, never drove a race car, and never sang country music. At Vanderbilt he raised money for academic programs, erected buildings, and increased academic requirements for football players, thus increasing the number of medical students who made the team. He helped align Vanderbilt with the cause of Southern regional change, brainstorming with one of the South's leading intellectual liberals, the Chapel Hill sociologist Howard W. Odum and his noted boss, Graham, on efforts ultimately resulting in the Southern Regional Council. He delivered development through the building of consensus more than through knockout punches from the top, a style well suited for his next move if not the one after that. In 1944 he accepted an invitation to leave Vanderbilt to become president of the Carnegie Foundation for the Advancement of Teaching in New York City.[35]

After nine years of subways, tall buildings, little sunlight, and dirty air, however, the easy dancing of mutual courtship led to Carmichael's acceptance of the offer from UA's board. He wanted to go home. In September he and his wife, Mae Crabtree, and her beloved piano moved into the stateliest place in Tuscaloosa. Carmichael would not stay long. By now in his mid-sixties, like so many other 1930s Southern liberals, he seemed unable to completely turn the corner to the next stage of Southern change: he remained tentative about getting out front on desegregating UA and backing down a board that fought such change in all UA programs, nor was his non-confrontational personality well suited for such a development. As far as developing the Birmingham campus went, however, he picked up right where Bill Paty had left off five years earlier. In view of what lay ahead for the people of Birmingham as the civil rights movement unfolded in the early 1960s, it is both ironic and understandable that the desegregation of UA—a crisis Carmichael soon concluded he was ill-equipped to handle—may well have made him want to focus on affairs of the Birmingham campus which, at least compared to desegregation, seemed to him to be solvable. At any rate, with the board now consumed with race change, Carmichael led decisively on matters ostensibly removed from Tuscaloosa. Quietly, he set out to build a SUNY-style multicampus system for his home state. If his initial steps included gradual expansion of UA extension operations in Mobile, Montgomery, and Huntsville, plus opening a new center at Dothan, where he predicted major "wiregrass development" in the coming years, Carmichael also saw the rapid expansion of UA's Birmingham operations as the most important action he could take toward his multicampus goal.[36]

The new president was well versed on medical center life, having helped guide Vanderbilt's medical school during the difficult days of World War II.[37] Two weeks into the UA job, therefore, he had formed a careful first impression of what was in Birmingham. State auditors had given a good report in 1953: finances at the medical center finally had stabilized. Perhaps this had resulted in part from the "Gallalee reforms," but more important were Hill-Burton assistance, VA developments, a beginning "trickle" of faculty research grants, and greater awareness in the legislature about indigent care costs leading to at least some increase in appropriations. Thus Carmichael felt comfortable in spending his first six months assessing more subtle elements of the scene. He met repeatedly with Volker and Durrett, asking focused questions and listening intently. From these conversations and undoubtedly from his many friends and relatives throughout Alabama he learned that the subtleties were not all that subtle. Their poignancy he found reinforced through talks with his old friend Tinsley Harrison, who had been the Carmichael family physician while they were at Vanderbilt and was now again. The new president, however, assiduously avoided any subjects personal to Harrison's boss, Durrett; and Harrison, knowing "it was not easy for an indiscreet person [such] as myself to remain silent, . . . [still] managed somehow to do so." Restrained for the time being by personal friendship, Carmichael nevertheless got his information and arrived at a firm conclusion.[38]

In five years, he found, despite recruiting difficulties associated with Alabama's reputation for segregation and poorly funded social services, Volker had built a first-class dental school and demonstrated superb administrative skills. The leaders in the Medical College of Alabama also were excellent professionals and visionary planners—indeed they had the advantage of senior status in the national arena, which Volker lacked—and faced the same racial and economic problems specific to Alabama. Unlike Volker, however, they had to drag around the historic deadweight of medical politics, both on and off campus. This usually involved the physician's ego and income alongside underfunded indigent care and presidential oversight once supportive, more recently intrusive, and always problematic for being sixty miles down the road. Given these adversities, some of their own making, in Carmichael's mind the physicians had done amazingly well. But that was not good enough.

From a developmental perspective, he concluded, the Medical College of Alabama as well as some other units had to start growing in the same way the School of Dentistry had. This perspective was confirmed through two sources. First, he read the report on the UA medical college completed in February 1953 by the AMA's Council on Medical Education and Hospitals (the "Manlove Report"), which focused on serious financial and administrative problems in the unit. Second, he went to leaders of the Alabama legislature for more medical school money and received the message that the people of Alabama needed "to be sure that they were going to get their money's worth" before further significant state investments could be made. From that conversation Carmichael captured the promise that the legislature would make a special allocation of $30,000 for Carmichael to get an "outside" evaluation and long-term plan for development of "the medical center."[39]

Carmichael next invited Tinsley Harrison to drive down to Tuscaloosa for "a talk." On the assumption "that he wished to ask my opinion about what was wrong with the Medical College," Harrison "wrestled with how to tell the truth" as he covered the sixty miles. However, the president did not mention the medical school. Instead he said "that the Birmingham branch of the University had a potentially great future" and that he wanted Harrison's thoughts on who would be good for "an external, unbiased and therefore objective" assessment regarding "future plans." Harrison suggested the physician T. Duckett Jones, vice president and medical director of the Helen Hay Whitney Foundation in Boston. No stranger to the East Coast world of medicine, Carmichael heartily concurred and asked Harrison to sit down at his desk, telephone Jones, explain the general plan, and then hand the telephone to him. Jones was reluctant but Harrison asked him to take on the project out of "friendship." Within ten minutes Carmichael officially requested Jones's services, stipulating that he could invite two additional people to the team. Two days later Jones called Carmichael with the word that he along with Maxwell E. Lapham, medical dean at Tulane, and Jack Masur of the U.S. Public Health Service would be at work in Birmingham in one month.[40]

They were. And in August 1954 Carmichael had on his desk in Tuscaloosa "The Report of the Special Survey Committee." Simply known as the "Duckett Jones Report," here was a manifesto for improved health sciences education in Alabama that would speed the state toward the quality urged some thirty years earlier by Abraham Flexner. Though never mentioning the need for official desegregation in the hospital or the academic programs, the great Yankee doctor otherwise clearly used his scalpel. He praised Joe Volker and his entire operation: "The University of Alabama School of Dentistry is at present the best functioning unit of the Medical Center." He gave the opposite evaluation of the hospital, the medical center's greatest problem. After emphasizing that the hospital was "conceived in debt and reared on the ragged edge of poverty," he called for American Hospital Association accounting procedures, with hospital monies kept separate from those of the medical school, as well as more laboratory space, staff, indigent beds, and outpatient facilities. Hospital nursing needed centralized oversight not by the medical school but by the hospital director. Likewise, UA's main School of Nursing needed to be completely removed from Tuscaloosa to Birmingham, merged with nursing education programs long associated with Jefferson and Hillman hospitals, and organized to report to the director of the Jefferson-Hillman hospital complex. These changes would require more money, he urged, but the state needed to pay its fair share rather than ask the medical center to generate the funds through surcharges on paying patients. The report also called for a new, highly trained hospital administrator to implement these enhancements. A sophisticated "public relations" campaign pointing up the statewide implications of indigent care in this particular Birmingham hospital, Jones thought, could help deliver the additional legislative support. As for the medical school, curriculum and faculty were adequate, in some cases strong, but research needed major expansion and general administration was "weak." None of these problems was going to be solved in an effective manner, however, unless something else was done in the way of major organizational enhancement. The report recommended a vice president for Birmingham affairs capable of developing an institutional plan. This plan would, it was hoped, bring to a close nine years of topsy-turvy growth and financial crisis in Birmingham (the Tuscaloosa campus had been having a difficult time, too), help compensate for the instability of four presidents and three medical deans in less than a decade, and provide consistent, innovative development and even the acquisition of more space. Because of its scale, complexity, and potential impact, the position of medical school dean according to Jones might be combined with this new vice presidency.[41]

Jones then turned his attention to what he saw as the heart of the matter: the board. Three years after the founding of the medical school, through Roy Kracke's much publicized report, the board had been advised that Birmingham affairs already had outgrown the existing administrative structure. Kracke had offered sophisticated changes, including the type of offices Jones now urged. Seven years later the board had not responded, much less acted. "Further delay," Jones said, "would offer little hope for the future."[42]

The Duckett Jones Report went down in most quarters as a respected blueprint for progress, although there were whispered dissents. Volker understandably was nervous about changes that had the dental dean report to a new officer who also would be the medical dean, which was especially curious after the School of Dentistry had been praised as the model for development. A few board members wondered if, somehow, not Harrison but Kracke had gotten to Duckett Jones. However, when Jones suddenly died of a stroke (Harrison later discovered that Jones had been reluctant to take on the project because of his severe hypertension), the dissent lost any hearing it might have received.[43] Most board members were taken with the logic of the recommendations, as were the statewide press and key members of the legislature. Birmingham corporate leaders, including Tom Martin, were exuberant. Most of all, though deeply saddened by Jones's death, Carmichael now had what he needed.[44]

The president known for his "innate gentleness" moved like lightning. In a "patient-to-doctor" call to Harrison, who by now must have seen the ironic parallels between his sub rosa connections with Carmichael and the stories he had heard about Seale Harris's connections with Gallalee, Carmichael indicated his plans to replace Arthur Bailey. Who would be "an excellent replacement"? From Walter Frommeyer, Harris got the recommendation of Matthew McNulty.

Here was one of the new breed of professional hospital administrators that took over the field after World War II. With a B.S. in mathematics from St. Peter's College in New Jersey, McNulty had worked for a short while as an actuarial statistician with the Prudential Life Insurance Company before landing at the VA during World War II. With plans for a postwar career in VA hospital administration, he earned a master's degree in public health at the University of North Carolina–Chapel Hill, then rose rapidly through the VA ranks, including a stop at the new Birmingham VA Hospital where he had gotten to know Frommeyer and had met Volker. (McNulty grew up four blocks from Volker in Elizabeth, New Jersey, but the two were several years apart at the local secondary school and never met before their lives intersected in Birmingham.) By the mid-1950s he was a bright young star of an administrator at the major VA facility in Chicago and well experienced in the interface between hospitals, medical schools, and VA facilities. After diplomatic calls to Deans Durrett and Volker, Carmichael called McNulty and within a week had him in Birmingham for tours and meetings. He told McNulty he wanted the changes recommended in the Duckett Jones Report. To help him get the job done Carmichael promised him "dean rank"; the hospital director, the medical dean, and the dental dean would make up a Birmingham executive committee reporting to the president until such time as a chief officer for all Birmingham affairs was designated. McNulty wanted to make it clear that Durrett and Volker would not have oversight of hospital finances. Carmichael agreed (and later would have to enforce the decision on Durrett), stating moreover that all he as president wanted from McNulty on financial reporting were annual figures. "If the figures were bad, he would not move to more oversight," McNulty would recall Carmichael saying; "he would simply get another director." McNulty liked this non-micromanaging approach as well as the fact that Birmingham was a lot closer to Mississippi and the home of his wife, Nell, than Chicago was. Bailey moved on to the directorship of Orange Memorial Hospital. McNulty reported for work on November 1, 1954.[45]

He operated swiftly. With the notable exception of the indigent care issue, which the state tragically would dodge for a long time to come, three years later the facility "conceived in poverty" no longer, in Harrison's eyes, had many of "the barnacles that had multiplied during the several decades." The most noticeable change, perhaps, in the public's eye was that Jefferson-Hillman Hospital became known as the University of Alabama Hospital and Hillman Clinic, or simply University Hospital. Inside, however, McNulty instituted professional fiscal management with the hiring of Kaiser Cox and worked closely with Carmichael and *Birmingham News* publisher Vincent Townsend to raise community funds that "could tide us over" until more funds for indigent care could be obtained through the legislature with the significant aid of Jefferson County legislator Albert Boutwell.[46]

McNulty also did his best to "bring doctors and patients and the physical plant" into some type of efficient operation. For example, the elevators worked "sometimes" and when they did the system was "compromised by human behavior." Champ Lyons had "a special key" permitting him to "board the elevator on the first floor and move immediately to the sixth floor where Surgery was, by-passing all other stops that other physicians, patients, and visitors in the elevator were waiting on." "Getting that key back from Champ was one tough job," McNulty recalled. "He was a surgeon, and, well, you know." The new director subsequently overhauled the elevators, designating one for physicians who needed to move fast for an emergency. "Lyons now had to ride with the other docs," said McNulty.[47]

Ironic Momentum

Carmichael, however, had not waited for the beginning of the hospital reforms to move to the next step. In the fall of 1954, as the U.S. Supreme Court delivered its noted decision in *Brown v. Board of Education* and the UA board dug in to "stand and fight," Carmichael asked for a private meeting with the board where desegregation got full discussion and where the president mentioned that he planned to hire a chief officer for Birmingham, a vice president for health affairs. "It was time," said the distinguished UA alumnus, diplomatically omitting reference to the hard-hitting message to them in the Duckett Jones Report. He had given each board member a "personal copy." Likewise, he added, it was time to modernize the administration of the Tuscaloosa campus with several vice presidents just as Vanderbilt and the University of Virginia had done. Whether the board was too preoccupied with desegregation to focus on the proposed role of vice presidents or it truly concurred with Carmichael is not clear. But he received approval to move forward. The only vice president he ever would hire would be the one for Birmingham.[48]

The path clear, Carmichael immediately called Harrison looking for a recommendation. Back came the name of the forty-two-year-old assistant dean of medicine at Vanderbilt, Robert C. Berson, coauthor of a recently published book on medical education praised in the profession as the first searching study of the topic since Flexner's. Some twenty years earlier he had been Harrison's student at Vanderbilt's medical school, where he shocked everyone—including a new chancellor named Carmichael—with his ability as a star tackle on the varsity football team while excelling as a medical student. Carmichael called old friends at Vanderbilt to confirm what Harrison had found; paid an unhappy visit to Durrett; invited Berson to come try out for a quarterback position; and asked Frommeyer to host a small dinner party for "the gems," Lyons and Harrison, to be sure it was a fit.[49] In late November 1954 he acted. Carmichael accepted Durrett's retirement letter; he was sixty-five. Then he hired Berson as not only vice president for health affairs but dean of medicine. If McNulty was nervous, Volker was livid. Still, in May 1955, as Berson moved into Durrett's office on the first floor of the Basic Sciences Building there were unconfirmed stories of a jubilant "Yes!" echoing down from Oak Hill Cemetery. Roy Kracke now could rest.[50]

But not Carmichael. In Tuscaloosa, stress moved to the breaking point. When a black student named Autherine Lucy sought admission to the university and a few faculty urged that UA needed to abide by the recent ruling of the U.S. Supreme Court, the board—suddenly worried about Carmichael's reputation as a 1930s liberal—increasingly let the president know that it would handle this one. In Birmingham, however, with Carmichael staying close but not too close, the tall, booming-voiced Berson (faculty and students soon called him "Boom-Boom") went to work building the medical center according to other ideas in the Duckett Jones Report and some he concocted with his former professor.[51]

At the outset the medical school's Faculty Council, which had emerged under Kracke's leadership only to become moribund with morale problems resulting from Gallalee's micromanagement, loomed as a matter of crucial concern to Berson. Through it, he hoped, would move major new programmatic developments of the medical school. He revitalized it in a structural sense, to be sure, but to the point that many senior faculty griped about "our endless meetings . . . [leaving] no time [for] real work." Harrison and others also traced the lack of resolution of certain pressing problems, such as costly personnel tensions between Children's Hospital and pediatrics, to the vice president's inclination to "overconsult" with faculty committees, causing him to be diplomatically "termitoid" and ultimately "remote" on tough political issues when informed, decisive judgment was needed. Under these circumstances, the highly regarded faculty removed themselves from formal governance activities; as critical issues arose they worked behind the scenes to keep more seasoned faculty insights in front of key officers. Simultaneously, less experienced faculty gradually assumed governance leadership and accomplished little. With this two-tiered faculty governance system—a formal (junior faculty) system and an informal (senior faculty) system—Berson protected his apparent need for remoteness but at least for a while also stayed in control and appeared to advance several important developments.[52]

Out of earlier programmatic efforts in the medical school he created new departments in dermatology and in obstetrics and gynecology. In 1956 he also blessed the recommendation from Volker, a recommendation produced by the School of Dentistry's more vibrant and integrated Faculty Council, that the Division of Dental Medicine and Surgery become refocused in tune with new practices at Tufts and be called the Division of Oral Medicine and Oral Surgery. To run it, Volker hired the charming Philadelphian Emanuel Cheraskin, whose controversial research on vitamin C fascinated the dean.[53] Just as innovative, Berson and Volker began to recast the basic sciences to be on the forefront of new international breakthroughs in understanding genes and bacteria, research emanating out of Harvard and CalTech. The initial joint efforts in basic sciences developed by Kracke and Volker provided the ideal organizational framework for this new science. In late 1955 Volker and Berson refocused bacteriology and clinical pathology to be in line with major new discoveries in these fields; they called it the Department of Microbiology—the third such department created in the United States.[54]

It also was on Berson's watch that a major UAB figure of the future was recruited, though the acquisition was more Harrison's work than Berson's. Harrison enticed one of his own students from Bowman-Gray, the North Carolinian S. Richardson ("Dick") Hill, Jr., to leave Peter Bent Brigham Hospital in Boston and assume directorship of the new joint program with the VA in metabolism and endocrinology. Hill had been working in the laboratory of one of the leading endocrinologists in the world, George Thorn, chief of medicine at that hospital. Hill not only had published with Thorn and other members of his group, including Marcel Rouche, but had written two chapters in revised editions of *Principles of Internal Medicine*. Then, in the early 1950s, having returned to the Harvard faculty after a brief stint in the air force, he became the physician for the Harvard Crimson's crew team in order to investigate metabolic and psychological factors associated with stress, of which there was plenty when Harvard confronted Yale out on the Charles River.[55] As one carefully attuned to Hill's rare blend of medical expertise and integrative personality, Harrison told Berson that Hill definitely was one to pursue. When it came to Hill's interview in Birmingham, however, Harrison feared that Berson's reclusive personality and his curiously booming voice would work against a successful recruitment. So Harrison marshaled the deal-making technique he had seen Tom Spies employ with such great success. He hosted a small dinner party for Hill beneath the graceful white columns and swaying virgin pines of the Mountain Brook Club with a guest list that omitted "medical center brass" and included several key community leaders. After "a most encouraging evening" with attorney Lucien Gardner, banker Edward ("Red") Terrill, and real estate developers Glenn Cobbs and Bill Jemison, Hill advised his mentor that he was ready to accept a formal offer from Berson and the VA.[56]

Through connections earlier established by Dean Durrett, Alston Callahan, and medical librarian Sarah Cole Brown, Berson also was on hand for the transaction permitting the native Alabamian and famous Detroit radiologist Lawrence Reynolds to donate his entire collection of medical history works to the UA Medical Center. Much to the chagrin of both Yale University and Wayne State University, the Reynolds Historical Collection soon appeared as an intriguing addition to the medical school library, which was at that time still spread throughout Hillman.[57] Assisted by McNulty, Berson began academic programs in allied health sciences as part of hospital programs. Interdisciplinary research programs expanded so much on his watch that grant revenues moved from "a trickle" of $459,000 in 1956 to "a small if steady flow" of $1 million by 1959. This prescient growth owed considerable success to the innovative new Department of Microbiology and behind-the-scenes orchestration by Volker that was yet to surface. On more than one occasion, it also likely resulted from Senator Lister Hill's influence.[58]

As urged in the Duckett Jones Report, Berson had to tackle problems of badly needed space and construction. Like Kracke and Harrison before him, Berson looked to Washington, D.C., where the crisis mentality of the cold war continued to deliver a host of aid programs for both science and non-scientific endeavors. At the National Institutes of Health (NIH) he found funds to construct the Health Sciences Research Building on Nineteenth Street, 100,000 square feet later named the Lyons-Harrison Research Building. Excitement about the new building, which opened in 1960, was mixed with frustration. New research space lead to new research grants, then to more funds to hire more faculty, which always meant renewed space shortages. "Once again," as Tinsley Harrison would recall, "space had become a major limiting factor in further progress." Well before Lyons-Harrison was occupied, it represented more of a shortage-of-space problem than part of the solution.[59]

Berson may have foreseen this crucial issue. After studying Kracke's original plans and talking at length with Carmichael about expansion plans Durrett had advocated under urban-renewal strategies, the Birmingham vice president working with Volker in a less than warm relationship developed a larger "master plan" for physical expansion encompassing some sixty-five city blocks, in a general sense the plan for late twentieth-century UAB. By 1958, with Berson nominally at the helm and Volker deeply involved, this plan saw the medical center incorporate some nine additional city blocks to the west of Jefferson Hospital, an area with a few businesses, restaurants, and churches but mostly consisting of rental homes for the black poor. As the first of two major property additions for Birmingham operations, the other to come a decade later, this effort would expand the Birmingham campus from six to fifteen city blocks. As detailed in Charles E. Connerly's *"The Most Segregated City in America": City Planning and Civil Rights in Birmingham, 1920–1980* (2005), if those associated with the growth of the medical center showed excitement about this development, the projected razing of black housing got anything but approval from those who had lived there and their advocates—Arthur Shores, Oscar Adams, and journalist Emory Jackson—which was consistent with other experiences with urban renewal nationwide. Indeed, a half century later some would wonder if these were the first signs of one type of Leviathan being replaced by another, a questionable notion in that the emergence of a massive medical and university complex in Birmingham would inject millions into the local economy while the old Leviathan, with the exception of a craftily underpaid payroll, sent such funds back to its Northeastern home offices.[60]

To achieve this massive potential for new construction, Volker, Berson, and Carmichael assembled what the historian Blaine Brownell has called an alliance of "commercial civic-elite." The alliance consisted of the medical center leaders working with Hugh Denman, director of the Birmingham Housing Authority; Jimmy Morgan, longtime mayor of Birmingham; Frank E. Spain, senior partner in the Birmingham law firm of Spain, Gillom et al. (and UA's chief legal counsel), and Ehney Camp, executive with Birmingham's Liberty National Life Insurance Company and UA alumni leader a year away from joining the UA board. A sociologist might note this as a classic example of networked "social capital"—for whites only. Expanding on a strategy first developed by Dean Kracke and discussed with his old friend Senator Sparkman, this coalition acquired new properties through an application to the U.S. government's urban renewal program established under the Housing Acts of 1949 and 1954. The federal aid required "matching" monies from the Alabama legislature, which necessitated a statewide referendum for appropriation. In December 1957 the citizens of Alabama approved a $4.5 million bond issue, approximately $2.5 million of which went to the Birmingham urban renewal project. Even with the coalition's orchestration of such strong local and state support, however, the urban renewal expansion of 1958 likely would not have succeeded were it not for an additional Washington, D.C., arm of the coalition, Senators Hill and Sparkman and their colleague in the House, Luther Patrick. Indeed, some have seen the story as reminiscent of Roy Kracke's "arrangement" with Senator Hill to start locating VA hospitals adjacent to urban medical schools: through Hill, Sparkman, and Patrick, a federal program initially designed to support construction of new, low-income housing had its mission expanded to support the acquisition of land for a medical center. Yet the parallel is less apparent when one remembers that the 1954 act saw Congress embracing urban redevelopment efforts of wide-ranging design, not just housing, and that the majority of urban renewal funds actually supported projects nationwide similar to Birmingham's, where redevelopment to produce new types of employment and civic leadership had priority. The stronger parallel between Kracke's development and Berson's is that both cases showed deep South leaders working with representatives on Capitol Hill to bring home "the bacon" on projects that produced long-term and systemic social change. These projects offered marked contrast to military bases and other projects, where most federal aid in the South long had been going.[61]

In June 1958, with official word that Birmingham's urban renewal application would be approved, Berson went after other funding for facilities to occupy the new space west of the hospitals. In 1959, a second-generation Jewish immigrant family, the Smolians, who had found prosperity through a chain of Birmingham-based department stores, Pizitz, gave $100,000 toward construction of what would become the forty-six-bed Smolian Psychiatric Clinic. The next year Frank Spain's own family, which could be traced deep into the region's antebellum aristocracy, provided $500,000 to-

ward the development of the Spain Rehabilitation Hospital.[62] At the same
time, through the good offices of Senator Hill, Berson was permitted to
construct a U.S. Army evacuation hospital. Dedicated in October 1960 as
Fort Mortimer H. Jordan Alabama National Guard 109th Evacuation Hospital Armory, the U.S. Army ostensibly designed this "first of its kind in
America" to provide treatment for soldiers brought back from some distant
cold war conflict, where they might be treated in joint VA/UA medical programs. Word around town also suggested that the facility could be used as
a staging ground for military operations if another conflict, the civil rights
movement, got out of hand. It indeed would be used for National Guard
and Army Reserve activities, some tangentially involved in oversight of
civil rights demonstrations. But by 1968, through some magical fate no
doubt pleasing to two prominent UA alumni, Senators Hill and Sparkman,
the facility found itself becoming Mortimer Jordan Hall—an administration building for an emerging university.[63]

With equal ingenuity, Berson used new state funds to acquire a larger facility for the two-year nursing education program by purchasing and re-
modeling Gus Constantine's Drive-In Restaurant ("Dr. Gus's"), a barbeque
house of more than local fame. He also built multistory dormitories for
nursing and medical students, structures known later as Hixson Hall and
University Hall. Likewise, he facilitated the construction of the long-sought
126-bed structure for Children's Hospital, to open in 1961, amid the new
urban renewal tract, further advancing the plan of a medical *center.* He
also approved plans for a major fund-raising effort to build the 56-bed Eye
Foundation Hospital, which would open in late December 1963. This project reflected the singular leadership of the former chair of ophthalmology,
Alston Callahan. The high-energy eye surgeon not only conceived the idea
for this initially private facility (with an independent board, to which Berson agreed only when pressured by several UA board members) but led the
considerable fund-raising effort and made significant personal contributions toward construction costs. Callahan would serve as the facility's first
director. Additional funds acquired through NIH and Hill-Burton grants
provided the balance in all these projects. And as the additional facilities
began to open in the new space in the early 1960s, Berson could be found
off by himself hard at work planning even more new construction for the
preclinical departments, for a badly needed modern medical library, and
for a second complex of University Hospital with wings for such specialties
as cancer, diabetes, and cardiovascular disease.[64]

Despite these major gains in Birmingham, Carmichael had a problem up at the medical center. It was Joe Volker. The dental dean now was thirty-nine. By any measurement of achievement—even granting that he had had fewer obstacles compared to what the physicians had confronted—he was a dynamic developer. In the early 1950s, students were coming from all over the nation for dental education with Volker's carefully recruited faculty, who, like Volker, were often engaged in extramurally funded research with a strong interdisciplinary basic science orientation. Because he and Senators Hill and Sparkman were becoming trusted friends, it was now even rumored (falsely) that Volker had acquired office space for the School of Dentistry at the NIH. Aided in daily administrative life by associate deans Arthur Wuehrmann, his boyhood friend, and his former student Wallace Mann, the dean himself maintained an active research program on the role of dentifrices in caries prevention, publishing in such top-flight places as the *Journal of Dental Medicine* and the *International Journal of Dentistry.* Yet Volker also was lecturing, consulting, and publishing on issues of institutional development in health science centers. In early 1955, for example, he gave a major presentation at the University of Rochester titled "Integration of Dental Education into the Health Sciences." Though well trained and strikingly active as a health scientist, Volker's focus was increasingly directed toward high-level administration, and Carmichael knew it.[65]

The president also knew from Harrison that Volker had strongly supported every element in the Duckett Jones Report except the assumption that the new Birmingham officer would be a physician also able to serve simultaneously as dean of the medical school. With his track record, so highly praised in the report, Volker believed that he should have been in line for the new vice president's position. Whether because of this, a personality conflict, or professional differences, Volker often treated Berson "in an icy way," though "Berson handled it well." A large portion of the medical faculty had openly stated their belief in the need for a physician at the helm, a point with which Carmichael agreed *at the time,* and initially were excited with the appearance of Berson. Not all, however, felt this way. For example, Carmichael had received a strong recommendation from physician Thomas F. Paine, Jr., who chaired microbiology, that Volker had the "necessary breadth" to "develop the enterprise."[66] In view of all this, therefore, Carmichael was not surprised when Volker finally telephoned on December 14, 1954, to say he would like to come down to Tuscaloosa the next day for a visit. The dental dean took with him in his inside coat pocket a key letter: "I am herewith tendering my resignation as Dean of the University's Dental School. It may be activated at your pleasure. It is my hope that in the immediate future I will be able to find an administrative, teaching, or research position that will be in keeping with my personal philosophy of education."[67]

Whether he ever handed Carmichael that letter is not known. Nor is it clear whether Volker gave his full thoughts on the matter—something he had indeed said forcefully, if quietly, a few years earlier to a young faculty member and former student he had brought down from Tufts, Charles A. ("Scotty") McCallum: "Mobility in academic health centers," Volker advised, "too often is restricted to those with M.D. degrees." What *is* known is that after talking with a man who had led some of the major academic enterprises in America and with no terminal degree of any kind, Volker drove back to Birmingham not only having accepted the suddenly created position of director of research and graduate studies along with continued service as dental dean but strongly encouraged by Carmichael's SUNY-style vision and what the president saw not too far down the road as "UAB."[68]

In anticipation of the problem and having carefully consulted with Berson, the president was not about to let Volker get away just as Birmingham operations were beginning to emerge. Buried in the Duckett Jones Report had been reference to the need for an officer in charge of graduate programs. For the time being the fit was good enough. Even so, as the president no doubt expected, Volker would spend the next decade chomping at the bit. With an office in the Basic Sciences Building just four doors down from Berson's, Volker was frustrated by not being in charge and was occasionally in conflict with Berson. He periodically left on consultancies in dental education—to Jamaica, Colorado, Nevada, Connecticut, indeed for all of 1960 to craft the blueprint for the University of Arizona medical center. With recurring rumors that "Joe is really leaving this time," at least one party was organized to say good-bye. Still, the New Jersey native always came back to his new home. He infused his love of interdisciplinary research into virtually every unit of the campus and spent late nights critiquing drafts of others' grant proposals. In the process, he helped teach the art of raising desperately needed research money to junior colleagues, such as Birmingham native and dental faculty member John B. Dunbar, who, as Volker's assistant director for research, then taught others: nurses, dentists, physicians, basic scientists, and hospital administrators.[69] Volker also paved the way for two young Alabama physicians, Sara and Wayne Finley, to spend a year in Sweden as postdoctoral fellows under the tutelage of the great geneticist Jan Böök. On their return and again with Volker's aid the Finleys would develop, by 1962, the medical center's own NIH-funded cytogenetics program.[70]

Not all of Volker's mentoring in this period, however, involved grants and research. With a different strategy for a different type of development, he urged that Scotty McCallum go to medical school even if this required an overlap with his starting faculty life in the School of Dentistry. Thus, as he pursued an M.D. with plans for a specialization in surgery, McCallum began to be known for his unflagging energy. Even late on Friday afternoons the young dentistry professor/medical student was still going strong. And when there were no more subjects to study, he might be discovered gleefully pouring buckets of water off tall buildings on unsuspecting students. One such target was a psychiatric nursing student from north Alabama named Alice Lasseter, who would become his wife. She never forgot her husband's courtship technique: "A water bomb early on a Friday evening . . . now if that's not a helluva way to ask someone to go to the movies with you!" More to the point, Volker knew precisely what this energy and love of life could accomplish—*if* the individual had an M.D.[71]

Still, the innovative plan for extramural funding Volker and Kracke had conceived for the joint (basic) health sciences to parallel the revolutionary tide of federal funding for science increasingly gained acceptance. Supported by faculty research grants, students now came from points outside the South for doctoral programs as well as postdoctoral clinical residencies in the recently formed Department of Microbiology.

No faculty members better symbolized this high-powered research in the joint health sciences than Samuel B. Barker in physiology and Charles P. Kochakian in biochemistry. First recruited by pharmacologist Kendrick Hare, Barker left the University of Iowa in 1950 and arrived in Birmingham as one of the major basic science researchers in the nation working in the field of endocrinology. He was particularly well known for his work on carbohydrate metabolism. His classic technique for determining lactic acid had appeared in the *American Journal of Physiology* in 1940. Over the next two decades he hit journals such as the *Journal of Biochemistry* and the *Journal of Clinical Investigation* with breakthrough analyses on protein-bound iodine that were considered "the whole basis for clinical thyroid testing . . . for many years to come." Although the University of Vermont lured Barker away from Birmingham for three years in the mid-1950s, Volker won him back. Barker resumed his crucial interdisciplinary force in many of the health science efforts underway in the joint health sciences and throughout the medical center.[72]

Likewise, Kochakian, an Armenian whose self-confidence survived ethnic discrimination in his childhood home of Haverhill, Massachusetts, began his research on male hormones in the mid-1930s as a graduate student at the University of Rochester before there was even a field called "en-docrinology," only to be hired by Volker in 1957 as the scientist most responsible for the identification of testosterone. His subsequent expansion of knowledge on steroids as a crucial component of endocrinology led to great leaps of understanding on how wounds heal and on how "muscle mass" can be expanded in athletes. Years later his colleague Barker would recall that "[Kochakian] did the pioneering work . . . the foundation for all the subsequent work relating to male sex hormones."[73]

Soon flush with congressional funds appropriated to help America's science catch up with Russia's, such agencies as the NIH and the National Science Foundation (NSF) appreciated the innovative investigation coming out of laboratories such as Barker's and Kochakian's and steadily increased their awards to the Birmingham health scientists. As a key indicator of Birmingham's growing reputation, even by 1958 Volker found himself invited to serve on Harvard University's Committee on the Medical School and the Dental School, a premier forum for health science education.[74]

As the research money started to flow to Birmingham projects and Volker's reputation in health science research as well as education program development further expanded, Volker's intensity increasingly left Big Science and Big Medicine. He was becoming enthralled less by the translocal "disciplinary community" of health science in which he had lived since his early twenties and more by what these disciplinary interests had led him to—the local "living community" of Birmingham and Alabama in general. What motivated him most, perhaps, was finding ways to make the health sciences and other international disciplinary communities both reinforce and find reinforcement from the daily life of his new city. In a Newcomen Society pamphlet titled *The University and the City* (1971), he laid out his belief that cities and universities could catapult each other as mutually reinforcing agents of social change.[75]

Still, though Volker read widely on the history of higher education, it is questionable that he understood the precise historical connections he was reactivating in Birmingham. He had a general understanding of how the earliest of urban universities, such as those of Leiden and Salamanca, had evolved out of a rush of social change as the medieval era gave way to the Renaissance; certainly he understood the role of social change in the late 1950s and 1960s as it prompted the creation of urban universities in such cities as New Orleans, Charlotte, Richmond, and Atlanta.[76] He left no evidence, however, of understanding connections behind the growth of the great nineteenth-century civic universities of Britain—those of Manchester, Leeds, Birmingham, and Liverpool—that had emerged out of the industrial revolution. Nor did he demonstrate awareness that what he was seeking in Birmingham was also being sought in the form of "concrete universities" of the mid- to late 1950s in Britain—in Warwick, Essex, East Anglia, Sussex, Kent, and York.[77]

His possible lack of knowledge about English civic universities reflects a fascinating irony with respect to Unitarianism. It was the Unitarians who played such a disproportionate role in building the nineteenth-century institutions across the Atlantic. Unitarians embraced the religious fervor that improvement of the mind and advancement of social progress through civic engagement were moral imperatives. And Joe Volker, though born a Catholic, became a Unitarian in his twenties while he lived in the American center of Unitarianism, Boston, and he helped lead the establishment of the Unitarian Church in Birmingham in the early 1960s. If he revealed no understanding of his own beliefs in the context of English higher education, however, his own vision for city and university becomes even more fascinating. He seemingly rediscovered *on his own* at least some of these earlier connections between learning and social change rather than emulating something he had assimilated through external means. More to the point, out of what possibly was a Unitarian-style epiphany, he seemed to be increasingly convinced that both types of communities—the local living community and the translocal disciplinary or professional ones— "could come to be more than if they were operating without the help of the other."[78] Or, as Samuel Barker recalled, "Big Science and Big Medicine truly were not big enough for Joe. He may never have realized this about himself, but this is what was going on."[79]

As an American Unitarian, Volker offered a special twist on the notion of civic engagement, education, and social progress. One way or the other, in Dutchman seminars, Great Books discussions, or "sermons" at the Unitarian Church, he managed to bring into this vision the only human force he knew for sure to be his superior, his self-proclaimed "daily companion": Thomas Jefferson. The Sage of Monticello would have been more than agitated if he had overheard Volker use his name in advocacy of public higher education in any place other than out in the woods and in circumstances not carefully reserved for white males. Still, Volker accurately viewed Jefferson as a proto-Unitarian and used Jeffersonian logic to argue that effective democracy in Alabama, that is, sophisticated voting, could not develop through advanced health care alone. "Physicians only seek to keep people alive and well," he told Barker, "and well people can be dumb voters unable to choose good leaders for changing times, as we know well from the history of Alabama."[80] More pointedly, a large number of Birmingham citizens, whites and—with the civil rights movement—blacks, were too place-bound to get the public higher education they had a legal right to attempt and which they needed to have to vote in an informed way. And the logical path to solving this problem was expanding UA's Birmingham programs into a full university.[81]

In short, this Unitarian missionary and East Coast urbanite had it all figured out. More than an "administrative style" or a philosophy of education, his was an ideology for social change. Though key national and international currents of the immediate post–World War II period dictated that Kracke advance a similar plan with considerable camouflage, by the mid- to late 1950s America was headed in a different direction on matters of race and urban life. As one who understood these changes to be as irreversible as Sherman's assault on Atlanta, Volker crafted an idea for a university that would simultaneously advance, and be advanced by, this powerful wave of social change. Hence in the spirit of the Dutchman UAB found final gestation. Out of the beer and the talk, incessant reading, and undoubtedly much private reflection, a vision for a new institutional life took form.

Carmichael knew much of what Volker was thinking. Indeed, in Volker's nonresignation discussion with the president, the dental dean may have mentioned briefly his early discussions with Kracke and, in the context of the ongoing racial crisis in Tuscaloosa, said that things in Birmingham could be different. More than his acumen as a scientist and administrator, Volker's brief comments about the coming social change, despite "the strong ego that he usually showed," may have been what most impressed Carmichael that day.[82]

If doubts remained, they did not exist just two weeks after the nonresignation discussion. Late on the afternoon of December 31, 1954, not being one to get an early start on New Year's Eve, the dean had written Carmichael that he wanted the School of Dentistry to offer continuing education courses to black dentists in Birmingham organized as the Jefferson County Dental Study Club. Similar programs, Volker explained, had been underway in the UA medical school since 1949 and now were taking fuller form at the Medical College of Georgia and the medical campus of the University of Tennessee–Memphis. Carmichael gave him vague directions to proceed: "Because the situation is rather sensitive in the area of race relations, I have a little fear of what may happen if you respond to the request of the Study Club. However, if you are willing to run the risk, I will back you in it. . . . I am willing to follow your judgement in the matter." Immediately Volker proceeded in this initial step of desegregating the School of Dentistry. Granted, even by mid-1950s standards Carmichael's moderate position on race, like ideas of all reformers, ultimately had not kept pace with changes in society. But his views had been shaped by the era of the 1930s, one as rich with progress as the times now shaping Volker's. It was in this context that the president likely saw the Yankee as right and having the will to act.[83]

Other developments shed significant light on how Carmichael came to view Volker's progressivism as part of something larger. On the most personal of levels, Tinsley Harrison—a social conservative—remained the president's confidant and undoubtedly sought to guide Carmichael away from some of Volker's "nonscientific enterprises."[84] Even more, there was the matter of the UA board. Often dominated by Birmingham real estate developer Hill Ferguson, a man of deep conservatism on race, the board remained virtually paralyzed with defending UA operations from another Yankee invasion. This put Carmichael in a tough position, particularly because Tuscaloosa was increasingly singled out by civil rights leaders as an important symbol of segregation that had to fall. Even if Carmichael had developed decisive plans to force integration on the campus, which he could not bring himself to do, the board would have fired him and put a solid segregationist at the helm. Nevertheless, the board's focus on this issue permitted Carmichael a relatively free hand with the more subtle forces of change up in Birmingham.[85]

Carmichael had already made a few moves on behalf of a Volker-style vision in the Magic City, reversing more than the Alabama public knew. To put these moves in proper perspective, however, one needs to return for a moment to Carmichael's predecessor, Gallalee, and his aversion to the type of Birmingham development that Volker—and, it turned out, Carmichael—advocated.

Since the late 1940s UA's longtime dean of continuing education, Robert E. Tidwell, had wondered about the strength of the "local market" in Birmingham. His on-site administrators, I. J. Browder, then Richard Eastwood, joined by Kracke and Volker, urged movement out of the old home near Phillips High School and construction of a modern facility facing Twentieth Street that would be physically and programmatically connected with the medical center. However, Tidwell's caution about the market continuing after the rush of veterans, reinforced by costly overexpansion problems in Tuscaloosa, made him reticent to try to reverse Gallalee's general dislike of the idea. Thus, much like the medical center, continuing education was on its own stand-alone budget. If center expansion in Birmingham failed financially, Gallalee would take it out of Tidwell's hide statewide, at Huntsville, Montgomery, Dothan, and Mobile. For Tidwell, expanding Birmingham operations was not worth the risk of losing a high statewide profile in extension service and the accomplishments of a major thirty-year career.[86]

Thus Tidwell was both excited and nervous when, in December 1952, pressures orchestrated by Tom Martin—a longtime advocate of economic diversification, including more higher education in Birmingham—finally forced Gallalee to inch forward on an altered version of the Warren, Knight, and Davis plans developed in 1948 at the request of Kracke and Volker. Budgeted at $500,000, construction began in the winter of 1953. Meanwhile, Eastwood remained unable to find space for badly needed general education courses for students in the extension nursing program; said Gallalee, "I cannot at this time . . . set aside permanently space for courses for Nurses [in Birmingham]." Likewise, despite encouragement from Volker, Martin found it "not feasible" to get Gallalee's office to locate the space for master's-level graduate work in physics, biology, and chemistry needed by SRI employees.[87]

More revealing, Martin got the same answer on his proposal to reestablish the full engineering program in Birmingham to serve those working in heavy industry, even with letters from U.S. Steel, Stockham Valve, and other major employers in the area. Undoubtedly, Martin had U.S. Steel's letter of support in perspective. He knew what other Birmingham leaders knew: Arthur Wiebel "didn't give a hoot about education or [the idea of] community in Birmingham, nor did his bosses in Pittsburgh and the chief stockholders of U.S. Steel; and he did absolutely nothing—not even give a small-audience speech in Birmingham—without advance approval of every word and every action by [superiors in] Pittsburgh." If U.S. Steel and Wiebel could not afford *not* to write at least a letter of lukewarm support for an engineering program in Birmingham, Martin and a few others also suspected that Wiebel was on the telephone to Gallalee making it clear that this was not to happen.[88] As longtime UA administrator Jefferson J. Bennett recalled, "U.S. Steel still owned Birmingham at that time. If Wiebel had wanted engineering in Birmingham, it would have happened overnight. He did not want it, however." John Patterson, at that time on the verge of a political career that would include his election as attorney general and then governor of Alabama, likewise recalled that "Wiebel was the top guy in town [and] a cold person. You had to go to him to get anything done, and anything new in the state [he] opposed." The advantage of training engineers in Birmingham, Bennett reflected, would be "quickly offset by new people, new white-collar forces, which threatened the hell out of U.S. Steel." Similarly, as the Birmingham attorney Jerome ("Buddy") Cooper recollected, "If Birmingham developed in any way different, new businesses might compete with U.S. Steel for labor, and the whole reason U.S. Steel was in Birmingham, besides the ore and coal, was the cheap labor—cheap white labor and even cheaper black labor." U.S. Steel would lose not only its huge profit margin but its control.[89]

So, as Gallalee prepared to step down from the presidency in the spring of 1953, he undoubtedly had these issues on his mind. Despite Tidwell's recommendation that the sign on the new facility—one that did not include engineering—say "Birmingham Center," reflecting the vocabulary increasingly used by continuing education programs in cities across the nation as land grant institutions spun off universities in neighboring cities, Gallalee made sure that it would carry the more restrictive title, "Birmingham *Extension* Center."[90]

Then in the summer of 1953 the new leader, Carmichael, came to town with SUNY on his mind. Quiet and gentlemanly, he simply told Tidwell and center director Richard Eastwood to move full steam ahead. Carmichael decided against altering the sign plans; the press already had announced the revised signage. But he increased the construction budget so that two additional classrooms would be available, and in June 1954 the new Birmingham Extension Center opened for classes, well ahead of schedule, with Carmichael and Martin standing out front.[91]

Within a year, reversing another Gallalee action, Carmichael added a second building to Extension Center operations, Clark Memorial Theater, and in the process permitted the emergence of new people, programs, and ideas in the life of Birmingham. For the previous five years the C. Powell Noland family, a family with extensive steel fabricating interests in the city, had been seeking to give this community theater, located at South Twenty-Sixth Street, off Highland Avenue, to UA for its extension activities in Birmingham. Gallalee had stalled on the gift as he had on other Birmingham expansion projects. Essentially he was worried that even if received as a gift, the theater's operating costs would eat into funds targeted for the Tuscaloosa campus.[92]

By January 31, 1956, the UA board under Ferguson's leadership happily had resolved that its Birmingham operations included what now would be called Clark Memorial Theater. Ostensibly reporting to Eastwood, James

Hatcher, an Extension Center teacher, immediately started raising money among relatively wealthy Birmingham families, some of whom wanted their children to "see what it was like to play a role in *Oklahoma* or *The King and I*."[93]

Volker rarely missed one of those mid- to late 1950s performances. Here he saw another key piece falling into place for the university he knew could exist. Here also he came to know Hatcher's foremost community supporter, Cecil Roberts, the "strange-talking" iconoclast from Surrey, England, and war bride of David Roberts III, Princeton graduate and head of one of Alabama's premier coal and steel families.[94] Although well regarded as an advocate of the arts in Birmingham, Roberts had ideas about politics and city life that were not particularly popular in the city, though they were similar to Volker's. She was vocal about the lack of a cultural life in the city. She helped found the Alabama State Council on the Arts, the Alabama School of the Fine Arts, and the Birmingham Festival of Arts. Yet the desegregation of Birmingham seemed her passion. Roberts found that though she had not completed a university education she appreciated Volker's understanding of the University of London and shared his vision for higher education as an agent of social development in Birmingham, development not limited to musical theater. Even before 1960, when she walked down the aisle of Boutwell Auditorium alongside the black dentist and civil rights activist John Nixon to help desegregate audiences of the Birmingham Symphony Orchestra, beginning in 1958 there were racially mixed audiences at the Town and Gown Theater and racially mixed "après theater" social gatherings at the Roberts' home in Mountain Brook. She also hosted visiting journalists covering race relations, such as Harrison Salisbury of the *New York Times*, author of the noted 1960 exposé of Birmingham segregation, "Fear and Hatred Grip Birmingham."[95]

Volker kept Carmichael posted on the high drama ("It's not exactly *Oklahoma* up here") resulting from UA's recent acquisition of Clark Memorial Theater.[96] And Carmichael had at least one reason to be pleased as he dealt with Ferguson on UA's racial policies. As the single most potent force in the UA board's attempt to reject desegregation on the Tuscaloosa campus, Ferguson had inadvertently advanced the cause of race change in his own city through an expanding program of the Birmingham Extension Center.

Of even greater historical significance, the new president supported science and engineering education in Birmingham. Carmichael had full appreciation of the fact that in 1955 half of UA's total enrollment came from extension centers and 25 percent of this was in "pre-engineering." In that context, and in the course of their discussions about the Tidwell Hall expansion, Tom Martin and Carmichael had come to share the same ideas for engineering education in Birmingham. Martin had told Carmichael how he resented the way UA had initiated a full engineering program in the city during World War II then within two years pared it back to a two-year program, requiring students to complete the last two years of the program at Tuscaloosa. Though he had no proof—it may reside in the "off-limits" files of U.S. Steel—he had a circumstantial argument for U.S. Steel's using key UA alumni practicing law in Birmingham to achieve this discontinuation once the dynamics of wartime had passed. A complete engineering program in Birmingham could have a ripple effect in terms of expansive public higher education in Birmingham—the subtext being socioeconomic diversification that ultimately would challenge U.S. Steel's control. In support of this critique, Jefferson Bennett, admittedly a strong advocate of engineering education in Birmingham, recalled years later that "powerful alumni, some connected through legal practice with U.S. Steel, likely played a role in helping shut it down." At any rate, frustrated by his inability to correct this problem under Gallalee, Martin was determined that whoever succeeded Gallalee would see the matter differently.[97]

Carmichael needed little encouragement. With Eastwood as the key operative, the Martin-Carmichael-Bennett team quietly began approaching Richard J. Stockham, Harry Brock, and a few other Birmingham business leaders about making sizable corporate gifts. With the UA president's office on his side, Martin's plea for an investment in the city's future would not be turned down by at least some local corporate leaders regardless of where U.S. Steel stood on the matter. Birmingham now moved closer to controlling its own destiny. In what was probably a battle of epic proportions, but one kept out of the press no doubt because of U.S. Steel's long arm into the office of the *Birmingham News*, Carmichael and Martin took on Wiebel and won. As Buddy Cooper recalled, Wiebel was known privately to be "one mean man," and the fight was kept quiet because even those supportive of Martin were scared to criticize U.S. Steel openly.[98]

By early 1956, the Carmichael-Martin money drive for engineering education in Birmingham was prevailing. Perhaps they were aided by the fact that U.S. Steel was preoccupied with the pending revolution in race relations. As Judith Stein shows in *Running Steel, Running America* (1998), the civil rights movement ultimately meant that black union members would gain the same clout in union matters as white union members because the U.S. Supreme Court would rule that "separate seniority" no longer would be

permitted within the United Steel Workers Union.[99] So, if U.S. Steel virtually departed from Birmingham in the years following the apex of the civil
rights movement for reasons more associated with global changes in the
steel industry, and less for reasons associated directly with the civil rights
movement, Wiebel and some others of Northeastern origin who in the mid-
1950s represented the hierarchy of U.S. Steel management in Birmingham
and in Pittsburgh still had racial attitudes aligning them with the conservative elite of Birmingham and of the Black Belt. On entering his political
career in the mid-1950s, John Patterson recalled receiving a telephone call
from Senator Bruce Henderson of Wilcox County, a "Big Mule" strategist.
Henderson advised Patterson that if he wanted to win any statewide election, he would "need Art Wiebel's money and private endorsement." Subsequently, Henderson drove Patterson to Birmingham for a meeting with
Wiebel at the Fairfield office. Wiebel to Patterson: "We'll give you all the
money you'll need. Just do what we say."[100] More pointed, as Wiebel advised Cooper in a discussion about black union members beginning to
hold the seniority that would enable them to have an equal position at the
collective bargaining table with white union members, "I'll tell you one
thing: no bunch of burr-headed niggers is going to tell me how to run U.S.
Steel." Nevertheless, as winter gave way to spring in 1956, and U.S. Steel
officers above Wiebel under White House pressure ordered him to appear
more progressive, it was increasingly clear that private monies raised out
of downtown Birmingham (and U.S. Steel's becoming less of an obstruc-
tion) would be sufficient for the construction of a new building near the
medical school. This would be the start of a full-scale engineering school.
New lights in the valley.[101]

Still, the very desegregation crisis in Tuscaloosa that resulted in limited
board objection to Carmichael's role in the Birmingham engineering effort also kept the president from seeing it consummated. In February 1956,
polarized by the board's acceptance then expulsion of Autherine Lucy, the
Tuscaloosa scene and the world's view of it contained too much conflict for
Carmichael to survive. A "Personal and Confidential" letter from Mobile
board member and attorney Gessner T. McCorvey to Hill Ferguson, dated
September 1, 1955, encapsulates the predominant board sentiment: "I cannot possibly imagine any defense [of segregation] that would be too dras-
tic to have my hearty concurrence. . . . I feel that practically every right-
thinking man and woman in Alabama not only expects us 'to go to the
limit' in keeping negroes out of the University, but that the people of our

State will be very much disappointed in our Board if we leave a single stone unturned to prevent negroes entering the university."[102]

In this environment Carmichael's heretofore brilliant diplomacy no longer could work. Only full and open confrontation would work, and like many Southern leaders of his generation he was not good at confrontation. All sides nailed him. Ferguson continued to depict Carmichael's 1930s liberalism as too prone to accepting desegregation. Bypassing the president, board members managed critical developments of the Tuscaloosa campus even more tightly with telephone calls from their own offices around the state. Moreover, as if to personalize board sentiment, Tuscaloosa's social elite refused to join Carmichael on the country club golf course. From the other side, too, he lost. Liberal faculty and students in Tuscaloosa saw Carmichael as "an old style conservative." The *New York Times'* Arthur H. Sulzberger and others of the Eastern liberal elite of which Carmichael had once been a part cut him off socially and professionally no doubt because he would not confront his board. Often seen strolling the campus "bowed lower and lower," Carmichael undoubtedly knew that the board could sense his weakness, in Culpepper Clark's words, "like a dog smells fear." So, acting on a decision he made in the fall of 1956, he departed UA's presidency on December 31 of that year, becoming a consultant for the Ford Foundation while living in retirement in Asheville, North Carolina.[103]

Of course, the engineering education program and other nonmedical as well as medical developments Carmichael sought in Birmingham continued to unfold with the opening up of the city, more than once aided by the *New York Times*. Curiously, it would again be the board that inadvertently helped make this happen. The coming years delivered the greatest heights of the civil rights movement: Martin Luther King leading demonstrations, the U.S. Congress finally responding with troops, and new legislation implementing desegregation. It is understandable that so visceral an upheaval would set off big changes in the UA family, including its life in Birmingham and with its rising leader, Volker.

A Team of Leaders

After a year with the interim presidency of James H. ("Foots") Newman, who had been dean of administration, UA's board brought a thirty-seven-year-old Mississippian, Frank A. Rose, most recently president of Transylvania University in Lexington, Kentucky, to become the twentieth president of the University of Alabama. An ordained minister in the Christian Church, a man with no faculty experience much less an earned doctorate but with fulsome ego, here nevertheless was a Southerner who would "understand how to deal with the racial problem." This preacher, however, would surprise them all. He turned out to be a charming young star of an educational modernizer. Indeed, if he were so charming that on occasion he would lose sight of the truth, he still would exhibit no counterproductive lost-cause bonds to Alabama's old order. Once again in Ferguson's efforts to halt change he advanced it.[104]

In Rose's first year two crucial changes in the UA board had significant implications for Birmingham. Confident he had put a man at the helm who would steer the ship in the right direction, Ferguson retired after forty years of service. Shortly thereafter, his equally conservative colleague from Montgomery, Robert Steiner, died. Winton M. ("Red") Blount replaced Steiner, and the Birmingham businessman who had played such a significant role in the urban renewal proposal, Ehney Camp, replaced Ferguson. Both were leaders in UA alumni and football circles. After World War II Camp prospered as an executive with Liberty National Life Insurance and Blount returned home to Union Springs, near Montgomery, to join his younger brother, Houston, in the family pipe and construction materials business. If the transition on the board brought younger, more racially moderate blood to UA leadership, depending on the issue it also brought less opposition and at times genuine support for the development of Birmingham operations.[105]

That same year, 1958, Rose asked Richard Eastwood to leave his role as director of the Birmingham Extension Center and become the special assistant to the president for Birmingham affairs. Rose needed Eastwood for the thorough, objective advice he could offer on Birmingham matters: Eastwood had no personal stake in medical center politics, but his sharp mind was a repository of all Birmingham affairs dating back to the very beginning—the clapboard house on Sixth Avenue North. He now moved his office from Tidwell Hall over to the first floor of the Basic Sciences Building, down the hall from Berson, not to Berson's pleasure. On Eastwood's recommendation, Rose then moved George Campbell—the Dadeville, Alabama, native who had taught mathematics at the Extension Center during the late 1930s, then earned a doctorate in education at UA—to leave his position as director of the UA Extension Center at Mobile and take over the Extension Center in Birmingham. To replace Campbell, again on Eastwood's suggestion, Rose hired a young philosopher trained at Emory University, Fred Whiddon. This native of Dothan, Alabama, and graduate of Birmingham-Southern College had been making a name for himself as a fund-raiser for private Athens College in north Alabama. As Eastwood explained to Rose, hiring Whiddon not only placed another innovative UA leader in the Port Town, but effectively shut down Athens College fund-raising in Birmingham. In his first and only year with Athens, it was reputed, Whiddon had gotten more money out of the Birmingham banks than the whole UA Medical Center ever had. Within a few short years Rose would discover just how innovative Whiddon could be.[106] In 1958, however, when his mind was not on Tuscaloosa, Rose was thinking chiefly about Birmingham, and he was delighted with the advent of his new Extension Center director sixty miles up the road. Campbell knew the politics of the legislature and its higher education priorities as well as "the inside plans" many powerful Alabamians had in the works.

Indeed, Campbell knew that Auburn University had serious thoughts about bringing both undergraduate and graduate engineering programs to Birmingham. Alabama Power's Tom Martin played hardball: either the UA family got behind engineering education in Birmingham in a serious way or Martin would encourage Auburn to do it. Immediately, Campbell saw to it that the new president understood this threat through conversations with Eastwood and with his old Tuscaloosa friends, dean of continuing education John Morton and dean of engineering James R. Cudworth. As the UA historian Robert J. Norrell explains, Cudworth always had reservations about expanding engineering programs in the Birmingham Center. The dean, his Tuscaloosa colleagues, and others questioned whether "the state could . . . justify or afford that much technological education, which, when done correctly, was as expensive as medical education."[107] Subsequent history would bear out some of the wisdom in Cudworth's preoccupation: as one of the poorest states in the nation and with one of the lowest per capita state allocations for students in higher education, Alabama would find itself as overly developed and inefficient in numbers of separate engineering schools as it would in two-year colleges.[108]

As real as this fiscal issue was, however, in the early 1960s Rose quickly sized it up as offset by long-term educational, political, and economic developments in Birmingham. He then told Cudworth and Morton to cooperate in every way possible with Eastwood and Campbell to meet with Martin to seal the financial deal. Shortly thereafter, the non–U.S. Steel part of the Birmingham business community, spurred on by "the final straw [of] a large business plan expansion" from outside investors that had been lost because "the city had no degree granting program for engineers," had Martin raising $650,000 to build a new engineering facility in Birmingham on Eighth Avenue a half block west of Twentieth Street and looking directly out on the other extension center's main building.[109]

With Cudworth continuing to warn against the main campus being "penalized in any way," but with Martin and now Steve Moxley, president of Birmingham-based American Cast Iron and Pipe Company (ACIPCO) pressing harder and harder on the need for engineering education in Birmingham, Rose assigned Cudworth to work with Campbell and the Birmingham donors to make sure the Birmingham program succeeded. The president then went off to a UA board meeting with the message that "they [the Birmingham folks] have their money and they have Tom Martin, and as long they understand that no funds targeted for the [Tuscaloosa] campus can be used for the effort, we need to proceed." Even before formal board approval, Campbell had called one of his Birmingham friends, corporate engineer Joe Appleton, and suggested that he talk with Dean Cudworth about working full time in Birmingham as professor in engineering. Appleton did, beginning a career with the Birmingham campus that ran some thirty years.

Thus in January 1963, after having been shut down in 1948, the four-year program started up again under Appleton's direction, and two years later a master's program was instituted. To open for business, Appleton used laboratory space and conference rooms all over the city; certain local industries were more than willing to help. But by September 1964 the new Engineering Building opened for Birmingham's 25 full-time and 375 part-time engineering students. In June 1963 a Birmingham native transferred from Tuscaloosa, John Duncan, had the distinction of receiving the first engineering degree under this new program. By 1967 another Birmingham native, Jerry Abbott, would become the first master's graduate, and a year later yet another Birmingham resident, Imogene Baswell, would be the first woman to earn a baccalaureate degree in the program. For the time being the diplomas bore the institutional title "University of Alabama."[110]

From expanding the engineering effort in Birmingham, Rose gained prescient insights into how a modern University of Alabama might work. For the time being, however, he stored these thoughts. Even before the deal with Martin had been consummated, as Rose had come to know more about the general Birmingham scene he had encountered developments in another area that required his immediate attention. In 1962, against the backdrop of not just engineering negotiations but the larger scene of mounting civil rights tensions in Birmingham and Tuscaloosa and inaction on the part of the U.S. government, Rose felt that he had a solid enough understanding of the medical center's complicated existence to bring bigger changes to Birmingham, which meant leadership changes.

For insiders, this was not unexpected. Despite his superior skills as a physical plant planner and his large physical presence and booming voice, Vice President Berson had a remote personality when it came to many management matters. Throughout Berson's Birmingham tenure it was Harrison, Volker, and others who had been getting most of the crucial work done.[111] Most recently, instead of Berson it was the newly appointed chair of medicine, Frommeyer, who had seen the need to create a separate Division of Gastroenterology and had pulled off the major coup in 1959 of recruiting the internationally recognized South African Basil I. Hirschowitz to develop the division in the still bright afterglow of his recently invented fiberoptic instrument for observing hollow organs of the human body.[112] The medical school was growing, as was the dental school, but more through the forcefulness of others, not Berson.[113]

For Rose this problem showed most clearly in the crisis over the selection of a chairman in pediatrics—getting a chair who could be more than a superior teacher and researcher, as Kendrick Hare undoubtedly was. There was a need for someone who could work diplomatically in crucial joint activities with Children's Hospital. The new president got full details on the pediatrics problem from Eastwood, who had personal contacts throughout the medical center, and from Tinsley Harrison. Indeed, with Eastwood steering Rose to Harrison, the smooth president and the crusty physician quickly developed a close friendship during weekends at Lake Martin, ninety miles south of Birmingham, where they both had cottages. Harrison seemed fixated on leadership in pediatrics and its implications for Berson. During his interim deanship it was Harrison who placed Hare over pediatrics, and it was now Harrison who urged that Hare lacked the necessary diplomatic skills for the nonteaching, nonresearch elements of the job, regardless of Vice President Berson's refusal to deal with the matter.

To Rose, Harrison also criticized Berson for his waffling support of Alston Callahan. As the founding chair of the Department of Ophthalmology and by now the author of the acclaimed two-volume *Surgery of the Eye-Injuries* (1950–56), Callahan recently had become professionally vulnerable because he had been openly critical of some of Alabama's private practice ophthalmologists for allegedly receiving kickbacks from optometrists over recommendations for eyeglasses. Here was physician-to-physician criticism in public; in the words of one Birmingham physician, the "doctor code" allowed physicians to "criticize each other through physician organizations or under the cover of darkness," but Callahan had crossed the line: he had been critical in the open—in communication with legislators, journalists, and other "non-physicians," "something you just did not do if you wanted to stay in the fraternity." More important, when many members of the Jefferson County Medical Society who were angered by these allegations as well as upset about Callahan's known photographic interests of an "eclectic nature" (nudes) and sought to remove Callahan's license, Berson—in Harrison's mind—had not stood up for his beleaguered colleague in conversations with Carmichael and with prominent physicians throughout the state. Berson had not asserted in public that Callahan had a superb track record as a teacher, a surgeon (he had treated Harrison's father), and a fund-raiser, besides being "right" and "courageous" on "ethics and eyeglasses."[114]

One cannot conclude that Harrison dictated to Rose on these matters. On his own, Rose had formed reservations about the organizational chain of command in Birmingham: the dean of medicine also serving as vice president and therefore boss to the hospital director and the dental dean. But Harrison reinforced the president's opinion. Though Harrison had been Berson's professor at Vanderbilt and a major advocate of his coming to Birmingham, not to mention a supporter of the chain of command that Berson assumed, within just three years of the new vice presidency Harrison saw major gaps and administrative entanglements resulting from this organizational structure. Out of its complexities, this structure inherently led the vice president to appear indecisive on personnel as well as other internal matters. To Rose, the operation "just wasn't working." Professionally hurt by the structure, Berson nevertheless remained unwilling to be a part of changing it. Yet he was smart and mobile and undoubtedly knew that Harrison wanted a change. After Rose called him to Tuscaloosa to discuss this and other problems, Berson read the tea leaves and headed for the South Texas Medical School in San Antonio, part of the University of Texas system, where he was named dean of medicine (and not vice president) in 1962.[115]

With Berson's departure set for July 1962, in March Rose quietly eliminated his role as vice president and asked special assistant Eastwood to assume the suddenly created position of executive director of university affairs on an interim basis. Already in an office on the first floor of the Basic Sciences Building, Eastwood now assumed command over all deans, including Berson, as well as Extension Center director George Campbell. Apparently unnoticed by the board, but undoubtedly perceived by Eastwood and Volker, the administrative framework for a new university had evolved yet another step, and in this vital stage it reflected medical center leaders reporting to Eastwood, an experienced administrator with a doctorate in business administration. Yet Rose, Eastwood, and Harrison all understood that this was only a transition step.[116]

The president now moved to complete the transition. He wanted not just a new leader but a new leadership *team* in Birmingham. In late March 1962 Rose and his trusted confidants, Harrison and Eastwood, hatched the plan in a marathon conversation at Harrison's Lake Martin cottage. Trustee Camp joined them toward the end of the talk. The discussion of course focused on Joe Volker. Harrison urged that he had been "wrong—Volker should have been placed in the job [the vice presidency] to begin with, and someone else taking over in Dentistry." Camp, who had gotten to know Volker from the urban renewal project, strongly concurred. Eastwood apparently expressed less enthusiasm. Rose telephoned Volker before the four parted to see if he would take the job. He defined the position as vice president for health affairs, reporting to the president. All deanships would be separate positions and report to the vice president for health affairs. Campbell, however, as director of the Birmingham Extension Center and associate dean of continuing education, would report jointly to Eastwood, whose title changed to assistant to the president, and to UA continuing education dean John Morton. One can only speculate that Rose wanted to see how Volker functioned at this level before broadening his charge to include the Extension Center. Still, with restrained excitement Volker replied, "Yes, under the right circumstances." He then added two stipulations. First, no doubt recalling the plan that had worked so well some fourteen years earlier when he was negotiating with President Gallalee over building a dental school, he would need "a totally free hand in lining up the rest of the team, and there will be some new people rather swiftly." Second, he wanted to begin to eliminate the "vaguely defined" position of director of graduate and research programs; operationally these matters would be administered by the respective academic unit deans, although Volker continued to carry the graduate studies title for three more years and remained strongly involved in guiding all graduate programs. Rose agreed and then, with Harrison no doubt whispering in his left ear, added a stipulation of his own: "And fix pediatrics!" On March 26, 1962, after formal board approval, Rose announced that Volker would be succeeding Berson as vice president for health affairs. The same day Eastwood, a person of long-term administrative effectiveness and an admirer of Volker, yet one of ambition, quietly resigned to take a high-level administrative position at the Texas Medical Center in Houston. He left Birmingham in July.[117]

Volker did not wait to assume his new responsibilities before lining up his team. In early April he and Rose had charged search committees to help select new deans for medicine and dentistry. But the focus was "inside," and it was clear that Volker would "lead" both efforts. In a quiet office conversation he asked one of his "Dental Mafia" from Tufts, Scotty McCallum, to succeed him as dean of the dental school. It was a logical choice. Thirty-seven-year-old McCallum had completed his M.D. some five years earlier and now had several years of experience as chair of the Department of Oral Surgery as well as service as one of Volker's assistant deans. To Volker's utter shock, McCallum said, "No, Joe, I just can't do it." The oral surgeon had a commitment as a senior consultant to Project HOPE with its health care vessel then cruising the shorelines of South America. He also was developing new techniques in maxillofacial surgery and did not want to be taken away from this contact with patients.[118]

Two days later Volker had the same experience across the street in the Department of Medicine. There, he asked Dick Hill to become dean in medicine. On Harrison's urging, Volker long had been watching Hill as a diplomatic organizer—skills vital to the development of Hill's joint VA/UA programs in metabolic and endocrine medicine and, as Harrison himself often noted, skills not that apparent in Hill's mentor at Bowman-Gray, namely, Tinsley Harrison. Though working long hours in the medical center (he had taught McCallum in medical school), Hill still had "the personality of the developer" perhaps in part because he, like Volker, had been profoundly affected by the chaos of Europe after World War II. During 1946–47, just graduated from Bowman-Gray's medical school, Hill received funding from the Rockefeller Foundation "to evaluate the effectiveness of medical education in postwar Europe." Despite some pleasant distractions—"We were mistakenly treated as visiting dignitaries" who "could actually give away Rockefeller money"—these travels placed him in contact with major health scientists and other leaders of Europe and gave him a perspective on what "large sums of money" invested in education might do for the reassertion of "social and economic progress." These ideas clearly had application to the historic backwardness of social services in Birmingham and across Alabama, which were prostrate more because of a social system than a cataclysmic event such as war or depression, but nevertheless prostrate. Volker saw Hill's perspective on education and social change as well as his likeability as crucial to the transition he had in mind for the medical center and more. Yet Hill, too, gave a firm but polite "No." Indeed, at this stage thirty-nine-year-old Hill had plans to move back into the more conventional medical center life of research, teaching, and patient care, the life he had known at Harvard, letting someone else assume his joint VA/UA administrative role. As Volker approached him, Hill was finalizing plans to take a leave of absence to study chromatographic separation under the direction of Ian Bush at the University of Birmingham in England.[119]

Frustrated but far from defeated, Volker telephoned Rose to report these developments. The president indicated his strong desire to help. A week later, accordingly, with Rose scheduled to take a late afternoon flight from Birmingham to Washington, D.C., Volker managed to corral McCallum and Hill and deliver them to a first-floor room of the Airport Motel. In that room Frank Rose waited, accompanied by four glasses, a bucket filled with ice, and a quart of Cutty Sark scotch. Two and half hours later, ten minutes before Rose had to board and with one light-amber inch left at the bottom of that bottle, Volker had his team.[120]

As if conversations at the Dutchman were but dress rehearsals for the meeting at the Airport Motel, Volker had talked eloquently about the *university*, not just the medical center, that he knew could be developed in Birmingham. Rose then promised that "Volker's vision" was a real possibility, that he as president would support it, and that changes in the board could eliminate old obstacles to this and other changes in Birmingham affairs. The scale and force and responsibility of this "exciting possibility of a new endeavor" turned out to be too powerful and too challenging to decline. Hill agreed to take the medical deanship, though it represented a 180-degree reversal in career plans. McCallum agreed to take the dental deanship so long as he also could stay involved in maxillofacial surgery and coach Little League baseball in Vestavia.

By September 1, 1962, Volker had set up his vice president's shop on the first floor of the Basic Sciences Building. In the new administrator suite, he had Hill on one side of him and McCallum on the other. John Dunbar, with the assignment of managing extramural funds, moved in two doors down from McCallum. The team was in place except for one.[121] The new vice president's first order of business that first day was to call George Campbell over in the extension center building to see if just the two of them might get together for "a private talk about the future."[122]

5

Stage One Delivery, 1962–65

The Team Takes Charge

Only in retrospect do the years leading up to the 1960s appear as a time of preparation for UAB: a time for the formation of complicated relationships, a time for the conception of an idea, a time for gestation to transform the idea and its proponents into a new institution. To all but the most exceptional observers, despite the Great Depression, Birmingham had not moved from its hypocritical "New South" stance assumed back in the 1920s.

Indeed, when *Holiday* magazine commissioned Carl Carmer, author of the 1934 classic *Stars Fell on Alabama,* to leave his home in Cooperstown, New York, and return to Alabama for several weeks to see what had happened in the state since *Stars* first appeared, the sixty-five-year-old writer published an essay in the March 1960 issue titled "Back to Alabama," which depicted Birmingham as a place still led by "a *nouveau riche.*" Not only did these city leaders continue to extol such Shades Mountain "curiosities" as "the recreated temple of Vesta . . . [all of which] hardly improves the general opinion of the city's taste," but they had erected another "curiosity" on Red Mountain, "The Club." In this glassed building of "neo-Miami-character . . . patrons [could] dine listening to the music of violins and a mother-of-pearl piano [while] looking down into the valley where the steel furnaces flare in the night exuding the same feeling that Nero got—the fiddles play while the city burns." Still, while Carmer saw that "the grime of the steel city persists in downtown Birmingham," he noticed "the beginnings" of change: "a new art gallery happily situated among the buildings of the city government, a little theater [Clark Memorial/Town and Gown Theater] that has existed long enough to establish a tradition, a few clean-cut towers of business . . . and air-conditioning." One Birmingham busi-

ness executive who was thrilled about air-conditioning typified for Carmer just how much and how little change had occurred—again, no more
than "the beginnings." *Holiday* had "explicitly instructed" Carmer to stay
away from all "sensitive issues" such as desegregation. Yet the aging iconoclast could not resist asking the executive if he had ever seen an air con-
ditioner in a "Negro shack." "I guess so," came the reply, "though Negroes
can stand heat better than anybody else."[1] Hence "Back to Alabama," despite Carmer's general soft-pedaling of social criticism, got the same reception *Stars* had. Progressives such as C. J. Coley of Alexander City found it
"essentially accurate." The editorial page of the *Birmingham News,* however, railed against "outsiders" critiquing Birmingham. Under the less than
imaginative headline, "Carmer Falls on Alabama," followed the pronounce-
ment that "this always happens when people from elsewhere start trying to
explain what Alabama and Alabamians are like."[2]

No record remains of what Joseph Volker, at the time an engaged resident of Vestavia (he was the founding chair of the Vestavia Library Board)
thought of Carmer's criticism of the temples of Vestavia.[3] In retrospect,
however, Carmer's undisguised message about Birmingham came close to
the mark. In the early 1960s Birmingham appeared to be approaching a
juncture. One road led to a burning; the other led to the gradual embracing of modernity. From a still later perspective it would appear that Birmingham may have pursued both routes for at least a while. More to the
point, however, although Carmer's article vaguely referred to Clark Memorial Theater, "Back to Alabama," as a piece of journalism based on local interviews conducted in 1959 and written by the most noted writer about
Alabama, included not a single mention of University of Alabama activities
in Birmingham. In the public eye of Birmingham, not to mention that of
a savvy social commentator, such activity remained nowhere near "significant" in the high-profile life of Birmingham. It remained unnoticed for it
still remained essentially unborn.

As with the delivery of any new life, timing was crucial for UAB to finally
spring forth from the influences of the past and out into the forefront of
Birmingham's civic reality. An effective leadership team had to take control
of the enterprise precisely at a time when momentous societal changes provided the advantages they needed to achieve their goal. Neither major social
developments nor effective leadership alone could have delivered the new
university: it took both—at the same time—where they could nurture each
other. And that is what happened. Overwhelming movements in race rela-

tions, economics, and city growth along with revolutions in microbiology, organ transplantation, computer science, and federal health care policies permitted the leadership team the leverage it needed for "the final push."

In this context, Volker set to work building a public urban research university with a major medical center. Indeed, just one year after Carl Carmer assessed Birmingham with no mention of any UA endeavors in the city, the noted televised CBS update on Birmingham narrated by Howard K. Smith, "Who Speaks for Birmingham?" profiled only two positive "developments" in the otherwise backward city: Cecil Roberts and the UA Medical Center. The following year the *Washington Post* featured the UA Medical Center as "Birmingham's second biggest industry ranking behind only . . . the giant U.S. Steel," and as "providing a dynamic new force in the city."[4]

Aided by two executive assistants, Blanche Alexander and Jane Williams, and soon by financial aide Paul Brann, a Mississippian with a Ph.D. in economics whom Volker had discovered while consulting in Arizona, the new vice president for health affairs moved forward on all fronts.[5] Volker's first meeting with George Campbell was only partially concerned with programs over which Volker had official chain-of-command responsibility. They talked about wide-ranging mutual interests, including how the Extension Center might offer even more graduate-level courses in certain fields of science and how some of the medical center faculty might also assist with undergraduate offerings. Campbell brought Volker up-to-date on engineering developments. They talked briefly about what connections might be found between engineering and medicine, a new field Volker called "biomedical engineering," as well as medical center faculty who had recently enlisted the aid of Extension Center faculty to form a new chapter of the American Association of University Professors (AAUP). In short, Volker already thought of himself as head of all Birmingham affairs, not just those of the medical center. Moreover, he was finding that he and Campbell had similar visions for the place, Campbell's having evolved since 1936—a full decade longer than Volker's. So Volker saw Campbell as someone with whom he easily could work.[6]

Their growing association would be remarkably free of the standard turfdom, ego, and self-defeating pettiness of university life. Indeed, when some medical center people potshotted Campbell for his having an Ed.D. rather than an M.D. or a Ph.D., Volker flipped aside "the stupid degree matter" as "vexing and narcissistic and irrelevant to high-level leadership," remembering the sting of the physician's condescension toward the dentist. So, not just in need of each other but liking each other, the Yankee and the Southerner joined forces. At first to the public eye it looked simply ceremonial. They stood together that first year at openings of the Spain Rehabilitation Hospital, the Smolian Clinic, and the Engineering Building. They also appeared as a team when the medical center received the small white structure known as the Life of Georgia (Insurance) Building at 1909 Eighth Avenue to be remodeled as the Computer Research Laboratory and when it received the Smolians' new gift, their personal estate up on Red Mountain to be used as a club for faculty of *both* the medical center and the Extension Center. Shortly, however, there followed something that was much more than symbolic.

Renewed Efforts in the Medical Center

In health affairs new programmatic developments came fast. At the dental school, Volker eventually practiced his often-stated administrative philosophy of "hire good people and get out of their way," though behind the scenes it was a little different.[7] "That first year I stuck real close to Joe," the new dean McCallum would recall. "He considered it his baby, and was always walking around . . . sitting down in faculty offices and checking on things in my area," a practice facilitated by Volker's having located McCallum's operation in offices in the same hall as his own. Still, out of a process best described as "publicly smooth" and "ultimately, Joe letting me do what I thought was right," McCallum reorganized the School of Dentistry during 1962–63. Aided by executive assistant Trudi Sinette and well-established faculty committees,[8] he replaced Volker's organization of divisions with something better suited for growth. Volker had seen this need for a couple of years, but his interests increasingly were elsewhere. McCallum ushered in the era of more focused departments that could advance the new specializations in dental practice. By 1963, there were ten: crown and bridge chaired by William D. Powell; odontology chaired by Harold Askew; operative dentistry chaired by Adeeb E. Thomas; oral diagnosis chaired by Stanley E. Kellar; oral roentgenology chaired by Lincoln Roy Manson-Hing; prosthetics chaired by John M. Sharry; oral surgery chaired by McCallum himself; orthodontics cochaired by Perry Hitchcock and Boyd Tarpley; pedodontics chaired by Sidney B. Finn; periodontics chaired by Gilbert Parfitt; and oral medicine chaired by Emanuel Cheraskin.[9] The following year he introduced one more, the Department of Oral Biology, chaired by Robert C.

Caldwell, which integrated new basic science knowledge into dental education while also establishing a beachhead for preventive dentistry, over time evolving into the public health field of community dentistry.[10]

Long-needed action also appeared in the medical school. This unit had the "jewels in the crown," Harrison and Lyons, and in the year 1962–63 UA medical students would be in the top one-third nationally on board examinations. Even so, as Hill moved into Robert Berson's old office complex on the first floor of the Basic Sciences Building and received Kay Morgan's now well-honed welcome, the medical school still lacked momentum.[11] The lag stemmed from the systemic problem of underfunded indigent care as well questionable appointments at the top. As Volker and Harrison had anticipated, however, Hill had both the inner toughness and political skills to make the locomotive not just move forward but pull quite a load.

In public, Hill simply preached optimism backed up by selected facts. "We are on the threshold of a golden era," he repeatedly stated to the press and community groups, and he meant it.[12] Internally and privately, however, he also confronted the basic issues head-on. To upgrade clinical instruction Hill wanted a significant change in the hospital hierarchy. Much like the separation of the medical school deanship from the office of vice president for health affairs, this involved fine-tuning one of the major changes brought on by the Duckett Jones Report. On the authority of that document the position of hospital director, in 1955, had been taken out from under the dean of the medical school and made to report to the new position of vice president for health affairs. Although this was a modernizing change in the eyes of American hospital administrators because physicians were trained to heal patients, not manage complex organizations, the change still had little immediate consequence in Birmingham because the report also provided for combining the dean's position with the new vice presidency, to whom the hospital director reported. However, with the separation of the dean's position from the vice presidency in 1962, Matthew McNulty, director of University Hospital, began to report directly to Vice President Volker. If at first Hill acquiesced to this plan, he soon developed reservations over the medical school's lack of influence as to which physicians served as chiefs of staff in the hospitals; these chiefs were pivotal positions in the medical school's clinical education programs. In a power struggle typical of all developmental organizations and reminiscent of the Great Bed Fight of 1951, Hill and McNulty "debated" for some three months.[13]

Hill wanted chiefs strongly grounded in the research and educational enterprise and with a primary chain of command leading to the medical dean. This fit into the traditional model of administration "where deans as line officers almost outrank the president and where vice presidents, assistant and associate vice presidents, and directors, even of hospitals, clearly are viewed as 'staff officers,' not line officers." By contrast, McNulty emphasized the need for "the modern model" where chiefs were well attuned to hospital management and, after appropriate consultation with the dean and appropriate department chairs, "often were chosen by the director out of private practice or clinical faculty ranks." This is what McNulty consciously had implemented as part of the hospital reforms called for in the Duckett Jones Report. Still, in November 1962, after Tinsley Harrison had "quietly talked with Joe on several occasions," Volker saw continued "debate" as unacceptable. He settled the Great Chief Fight with the announcement that henceforth, while reporting jointly to McNulty and Hill, the chiefs would be appointed by the medical dean. As if he already had known what was coming, Hill immediately announced that Champ Lyons, chairman of the Department of Surgery, and Walter Frommeyer, chairman of the Department of Medicine, would be assuming the additional titles of chief of surgery and chief of medicine, respectively. The diplomatic Hill would recall this episode as a source of "some stress within Matt" but "certainly not defeating our cooperation on many different projects." Likewise, even though McNulty would be gone within four years (he ultimately spent fifteen years at Georgetown University), he would remember that "regardless of this big issue, Dick and I could work side by side on issues facing the medical center overall." Indeed, to the public of Birmingham and Alabama in general, the major hospital happening was simply a change in what the joint facilities were called. In 1963, by action of the board, "University Hospital and Hillman Clinic" became "University of Alabama Hospitals and Clinics," a subtle reminder that the growth unfolding in Birmingham operations still occurred under the auspices of UA.[14]

While working behind the scenes on the hospital hierarchy, Hill also developed a badly needed committee structure to help develop the medical school. "The administration needs advice from the faculty with regard to existing programs and proposed new ones," announced the new dean, "and faculty members should know what is going on in other areas which might be helpful in their own." With help of an ad hoc planning committee that included John Bruhn, John McKibbin, and four other faculty, Hill thus delivered a structure of a Committee of the Whole made up of all medical school faculty—full-time as well as part-time or clinical appointments, physicians as well as basic scientists. Through elections, this committee sent representatives to join administrative officers in forming three subgroups: the Committee for Academic Affairs, the Committee for Faculty Policy, and the Faculty Council, the latter of which was made up of the dean and seven faculty and served as an executive committee advisory to the dean. Implemented in March 1963, this reorganization gave virtually every endeavor of the school, from teaching and patient care to research, the benefit of broader as well as more focused discussion.[15]

Hill hoped this new breadth in governance would ensure that the educational program would stay well infused with a "real life, an after-medical-school" perspective while simultaneously infusing the program with new scientific ideas and teaching techniques. In the spring of 1963 he held a retreat at UA's Ann Jordan Lodge in southeast Alabama to overhaul the entire curriculum. This process produced joint instructional endeavors in the medical center, including combining the teaching programs of the Department of Pediatrics and Children's Hospital, as well as "A Revised Curriculum for the Medical College of Alabama," implemented in the fall of 1964 and 1965, respectively. On Emmett Carmichael's advice, he launched through the medical center the *Alabama Journal of Medical Sciences,* then promptly convinced Carmichael that he should serve as founding editor. At the same time, again turning to Carmichael for leadership, he inaugurated the medical center's Distinguished Faculty Lecture Series, leading off with the dean's mentor, Tinsley Harrison, lecturing in March 1964 on the eclectic topic of "witches and doctors."[16]

Hill also had hoped that the new committee structure would ease town-and-gown stresses. As he had seen in the Great Chief Fight, such relations had the potential to do considerable damage to both the city and the medical center. Thus he hoped that the inclusion of private practice physicians who had clinical appointments in the medical school might head off some of this tension. In coming years, however, even with the presence of such well-intended community physicians as the surgeon Thomas Patton and the psychiatrist Charles Herlihy, the peace-making abilities of the system would be pushed to the maximum. There even would be times when part-time faculty from the community out-flanked full-time faculty in deliberations of the executive committee. In these cases, after reminding everyone that the structure was only advisory to the dean, Hill would have to intervene with his increasingly noted diplomacy.[17]

To his general plan of reinvigorating the curriculum with the latest science, Hill connected another strategy for change, one necessitated by financial planning but one that could increase tensions between clinical faculty and full-time faculty. He expanded the research orientation of the unit. Granted, research dollars were going up as Hill took over. In 1959 the medical center faculty and hospital staff had captured in excess of $1 million in research and training grants, chiefly from the National Institutes of Health (NIH) and the National Science Foundation (NSF). By 1962 that number had grown to $3,888,514, and by 1965 it would be $4,445,900. The possibilities for research support in the world of science and medicine had never been greater.[18]

Indeed, in his first year as dean, Hill himself had captured NIH funding for the establishment of one of the six initial General Clinical Research Centers (GCRC) in the nation. Designed to translate basic research breakthroughs into new clinical practices, the accompanying inpatient renovation in the hospital provided free space to patients participating in clinical research projects. Out of this program sprang new knowledge, new clinical care, and new medical leaders.[19]

For example, Buris R. Boshell, who had begun his medical training in Birmingham then completed it at Harvard and the Brigham Hospital, studied "treatment of diabetes mellitus with the new oral hypoglycemic agents." He then went on to initiate the Diabetes Trust Fund and the development in the medical center of the nation's first public hospital devoted to research, teaching, and clinical care related to diabetes.[20] Tinsley Harrison and E. E. Eddleman worked on "hemodynamics and chest wall changes in angina pectoris," and Champ Lyons and Holt McDowell studied "renovascular hypertension." Along with colleagues Charles Baugh, Carlos Krundieck, and Jerome Hershman, the Floridian and Harvard-trained James A. Pittman made great strides in the discovery of TRH, the "thyrotropin-releasing hormone secreted at the base of the brain" crucial to the functioning of the endocrine glands. Unknown to Pittman and his colleagues, other scientists had made the discovery one week earlier and by 1968 would have a Nobel Prize. Still, if Hill's GCRC produced excellent science and health care, it also gave the new dean a chance to nurture leadership. In the coming years, virtually every young faculty participant in the GCRC ultimately would have institutional and societal impact well beyond their own specialties.[21]

Moreover, Hill long had supported Volker's contention that the backwardness of Alabama's economy would likely mean limited state funding for the foreseeable future, which meant the medical school's growth in part depended on the ability of its faculty to attract large amounts of research support just as the dental faculty had done from the start. So, with careful use of the new committee structure, Hill went after new faculty who were attuned to the type of research that the NIH and NSF wanted to fund. Most of these hires occurred after his first year in the dean's office. But he started off strong in 1962–63; he hired Claude Bennett.

A native son of Birmingham—his family long had been associated with Yellow Label syrup company—and 1954 graduate of the city's Baptist-affiliated Howard College, Bennett had set his sights on scientific research even before he had finished West End High School. There, as a participant in an honors curriculum and a member of a science club called the Junior Electrons, he became fascinated by the fact that fresh pineapple kept gelatin from gelling. Hence, as one of his old friends suggests, "the enzyme bromelin" and "the persisting memory of a child's wonder at failed gelatin [likely] catalyzed his life's work, . . . [his] consuming interest in science and in the structure and function of proteins." At Harvard Medical School, where he earned his M.D. in 1958, these interests evolved into "a desire to explore, at a molecular level, the specifics of protein function in health and disease."[22]

Thanks to fortunate timing and his intense intellectual curiosity, Bennett became one of the key players in the scientific revolution springing out of James Dewey Watson's 1953 determination of the molecular structure of deoxyribonucleic acid—DNA. Quickly setting off heated debates between evolutionary biologists and new molecular (and cell) biologists, the research on proteins, molecules, and genes fostered by the "test-tube jockeys," as Harvard's Edward O. Wilson called them, would prevail in superseding the germ theory as the new orthodoxy in biomedical research targeted at cancer and other diseases. Yet, as Wilson would muse, "the sheer force of this new wave of scientific insight would produce a generation of physician-scientists with massive egos, people who would thrive on building empires within medical centers and many of whom would lose all ability to think that they could do wrong, in science or in anything else. If they understood DNA, they of course understood everything else."[23]

Despite the hubris of the movement, *Science* and *Nature* as well as the *Proceedings of the National Academy of Sciences* reverberated with the new knowledge. Hill knew that while Bennett had not studied with Watson—the Nobel laureate was across the river at Harvard College, not at the medical school—Bennett had been trained in an environment profoundly influenced by this cutting-edge science. Ironically, years later Bennett opposed the creation of a department of genetics, preferring to keep such investigations in the Department of Medicine; he held to this position even after having a conversation with Watson himself at a dinner at Birmingham's Relay House, where Watson urged UAB to develop a department of genetics. More to the point, Bennett became one of the "young test-tube jockeys" Hill wanted to hire. In fact, Bennett already had completed a residency in immunology at the UA Medical Center under the direction of Howard Holley and was in the first of a four-year postdoctoral fellowship plan in molecular biology at CalTech and the NIH when Dick Hill recruited him during 1962–63. However, the new dean made the offer with the stipulation that Bennett had to complete all his postdoctoral work before returning home. Bennett arrived in Birmingham in July 1965 at the age of thirty-two. And he and others of "the test tube" genre would begin to make grant support leap forward at a pace probably unmatched in the nation.[24]

Challenge from Mobile

By the time Bennett came back, however, more than science had changed; America had changed as well. And President Rose seemed less focused on the concrete steps the new leadership team was taking in Birmingham and more on these "larger" social and organizational matters. The cold war of the late 1950s and early 1960s led to a rapid expansion of Marshall Space Flight Center and adjacent engineering enterprises in Huntsville. Rose in turn began to envision significant growth for the UA Extension Center in the north Alabama town. At the same time, however, given the tenuous assumption that he had ever embraced Carmichael's SUNY model of a multicampus UA system, Rose began to retreat from that notion and embrace the idea of UA's Tuscaloosa operation being a "main campus" with perhaps two specialized campuses—in Birmingham (health sciences) and in Huntsville (space and engineering)—as well as two remaining extension centers at Gadsden and Mobile. His reasoning likely sprang from a nearly accurate reading of higher education politics of the time. On the specific matter of Montgomery, UA had no significant future there; out of proximity reasons alone, Rose thought, Auburn had distinct advantages over UA in the Montgomery market. Hence Rose began to phase out the UA center in Montgomery as well as its satellites at Dothan and Selma—a process completed in the late 1960s—and began to have similar thoughts about the Mobile center. Not everything, however, went according to plan. If Gadsden folks seemed pleased with their center remaining a center and ultimately coordinated it with a state two-year college, Mobilians were not about to go along with Rose's statewide vision of a slowly suffocating UA center in the major urban center at the southern end of the state.[25]

As early as 1961 Port Town civic leaders catalyzed by the new director at the center, Fred Whiddon, had approached Rose on how important it was for their UA operations to offer a full four-year degree and perhaps even medical education. Rose flatly refused. Something, however, had to give. The Mobile center had been operating out of the old customshouse structure at the foot of Royal Street, and that building was now slated for demolition to allow construction of the new First National Bank of Mobile. So, joined by Mobile civic and business leaders Ernest Cleverdon, Finley McRae, George Denniston, and Alfred Delchamps, Whiddon decided to act "more like John the Baptist" than an educator and proceeded to get legislative approval to create the Mobile County Foundation for Public Higher Education. This foundation not only garnered local private monies to be used for "development," that is, lobbying in Montgomery, but retained the legal talents of Alfred Rose (no relation to Frank Rose) of the Bradley, Arant, White, and Rose firm in Birmingham to develop a public bond issue for the construction of a new building on the acreage. Rose was a Phi Beta Kappa graduate of UA and a significant donor to UA's law school as well as its Town and Gown facility in Birmingham; he was also the leading public bonds attorney in the state with close ties to the new administration of Governor George Wallace, who had been installed in January 1963.[26]

They had flexed some muscle. Still, Mobile civic leaders gave UA one more chance. In April 1963, as the legislative session in Montgomery was cranking up, they sent Frank Rose a registered letter urging the creation of the University of Alabama at Mobile. A week later, in a meeting with these leaders at Mobile's historic Battle House Hotel, Rose personally delivered his reply to the letter: "No." In addition to a community college appearing at nearby Bay Minnette, he replied, the Baptists' Mobile College was on the rise and the historic Jesuit institution, Spring Hill College, was doing well. There was no need for a city the size of Mobile to have more of a UA presence than an extension center.[27]

Privately, he told Jeff Bennett that there was no way the Alabama legislature would appropriate sufficient funds for expanded public higher education in Mobile, even if it was connected to UA, and "he could not afford probable reallocation of Tuscaloosa-bound appropriations to make the endeavor even partially successful." More to the point, by taking this position, Rose demonstrated that he likely did not appreciate the symbiotic relationship between *public, urban* universities, the development of cities, and the future of America—what Joe Volker had been advocating. This, in turn, suggests that it was more the momentum of operations in Birmingham, rather than agreement with Volker's vision, that had prompted President Rose to inch forward on Volker's autonomy. For if Rose had believed in such a vision for Birmingham, he likely would have done the same for Mobile. At any rate, against Jeff Bennett's quiet advice, and, as it turned out, in apparent ignorance of several key social and political changes in Alabama, Rose "drew a line in the dust" by remaining adamantly opposed to further development in Mobile.[28]

Still bitter about the movement of the medical college away from the Port Town, Mobile leaders at this stage were only too happy for the line to be drawn. Yet "the stealing of the medical college" and the denial of a University of Alabama at Mobile were only lightning rods. Deep in the ethos of Mobile's civic elite there abided an enduring feeling of offense: the end of antebellum Mobile's "Golden Era" and its continued loss of vibrancy in the New South era paralleled steel mills replacing cotton fields (and cotton exports from Mobile) and "that dirty city north of Montgomery" replacing Mobile as the economic center of the state.[29]

Understandably, a significant gap existed in Port City perceptions as to how this upstate shift of cultural clout related to the politics of medical education. When UA had moved the public medical college from Mobile to Tuscaloosa, UA simultaneously had assisted in shutting down the private medical college in Birmingham and moving its remnants to Tuscaloosa; after only the most intense of struggles had Birmingham, in 1944, recaptured its momentum of over fifty years as a developing center for medical education. Hence, for Mobilians the historic enemy remained a broad based Birmingham-Tuscaloosa axis (which had a partial reality in the political alliance known as the Big Mules): in this axis, they erroneously believed, was the heart of a longstanding assault on the past, present, and future of public medical education in the state's oldest, and for a long time only, urban area.[30]

Whiddon clearly understood how the proud oaks of Government Street long had awaited this chance for rectification. So, just as Volker drew on Birmingham's emerging desperation to show the world that it indeed could have a socially progressive post–steel era, Whiddon spent day after day talking with Mobile civic leaders about their sense of grievance and urging that their renaissance, the transition to what others have called the "post-port era of Mobile," could be assisted through "an urban university . . . with a medical center." Here was a rational plan for the future bolstered by emotional attachments to the past. It also had good political timing.[31]

Armed with "gallons upon gallons of gumbo" brought up from Mobile to Montgomery and handed out free to any legislator so inclined, by the late spring of 1963 Whiddon and the Mobile legislative delegation stormed over Goat Hill. They had more than gumbo behind them. Federal court orders springing out of the civil rights movement had led to significant reapportionment statewide. As a result, Mobile County's seats in the state House increased from three in 1960 to eight by 1963. At Whiddon's encouragement, the shrewdly gentle Mylan Engle, a Summerdale farmer who had become a lawyer and legislator, led the expanded Mobile delegation forward with unprecedented cohesiveness, vastly increasing Mobile's clout when county delegations from the north, such as Jefferson's, warred within. Engle also knew that the close Wallace ally and powerful chair of the Alabama House Ways and Means Committee, Rankin Fite (who hailed from rural Hamilton in the northwest section of the state), had a general antipathy for Birmingham as an urban area of growing influence. It was well known to Engle and to others of the Mobile delegation, such as the young attorney Bill McDermott, that Fite "especially disliked the haughty Birmingham doctors at the medical school, in part because he was unable to inject political favors into their medical school admission decisions." For "these reasons," Fite normally was "in the mood to really gig Birmingham." Just as important, Engle knew that Fite liked him personally. Even though Engle was a Mobile lawyer, "in Rankin's eyes [Engle] came from the country—not the city—just like he did." Likewise, Engle understood how much Fite needed Mobile's "eight cohesive votes" to create the legislation and appropriation for the new state two-year college system, an education plan far more Fite's than Governor Wallace's. "So," Engle recalled, "we [from Mobile] just did the deal. We traded with Rankin. We gave him our votes on the two-year schools . . . he got his gig into Birmingham . . . and he got us the University of South Alabama." With the crucial aid of state senators John Tyson and Sage Lyons, of Mobile, Fite worked with the governor simply to hold up the entire state education budget until Mobile had what it wanted. With little difficulty "Whiddon's team" beat down a last-minute lobby by UA and Auburn.[32]

Later that summer this team returned to the Port Town with a charter for a new university separate from both UA and Auburn and an appropriation to get it started. Within two years, the Whiddon group had a ninety-nine-year lease on a massive block of land in west Mobile off Gaillard Drive and a contract with a local builder for the construction of a first, all-purpose building. Shortly thereafter, Alabama had a new university president: Fred Whiddon, and his institution would be named the University of South Alabama (USA). Mobilians took the whole episode as further evidence that although most of Alabama really did not care what happened at the bottom of their state, Mobile *would* resurge. "South," as they soon called the new institution, would be one of the keys to this future.[33]

If during the first year of his vice presidency Volker had quietly opposed the creation of USA through several private conversations with Governor Wallace and key state legislators, it was not because Volker failed to see some good and exciting things in the development. Privately, he described Whiddon's victory of 1963 as "a beautiful piece of political development—a brilliant coup." He considered Mobile an urban area perfectly suited for an urban university. Still, he quietly had opposed USA because he knew that as a non-UA institution it would seek to reestablish medical education in Mobile, costly duplication with Birmingham efforts Volker considered wrong for the entire state.[34] Yet no one in Birmingham at that time, not even the cagey Volker, foresaw that Whiddon's secession movement also would pressure Rose to give Volker's own vision a genuine chance to succeed. Perhaps this is understandable when one reflects on higher-profile developments then enveloping Birmingham.

Race Change

The civil rights demonstrations climaxed as Reverend Martin Luther King, Jr., joined forces with the White House and took a bead on Birmingham. President John F. Kennedy told King that passage of new civil rights acts enforcing blacks' right to vote, eat in restaurants, and sleep in hotels could become reality only if powerful Yankee and Midwestern liberals in Congress ceased kowtowing to their wealthy white conservative constituencies. In Kennedy's view and even more in the opinion of the man who succeeded him the following November, Lyndon Johnson, those on Capitol Hill who represented these elites held the crucial key to changing race relations in America. If these leaders got behind civil rights legislation, and they needed to as part of Kennedy's cold war strategy, the legislation would pass despite opposition from the South.[35]

Moreover, King believed that U.S. Steel needed segregated, cheap labor to make its Birmingham plants profitable. Growing competition from Japanese metals, plus nascent movements in new materials and environmental protection, were making things hard enough for U.S. Steel. Loss of profits out of Birmingham before the corporation could reposition itself for the post-steel era could be disastrous. Hence Birmingham's police commissioner, Eugene "Bull" Connor, with a lack of sophistication matched only by that of national television audiences, would be told through a couple of local attorneys to whip up "the people" in a "true Christian crusade" to block desegregation the same way it had been defeated ten years earlier. In King's mind Birmingham was made to order, though he never gave up hope of avoiding violence—he planned to use marches and economic boycotts to change Birmingham. He undoubtedly anticipated that while many Birmingham retailers and some manufacturers would desegregate on confronting civil rights boycotts, U.S. Steel would drag its feet in doing so.[36]

King knew he had to act fast—U.S. Steel's foot-dragging would not last forever. AFL-CIO leaders in Birmingham were moving rapidly toward a strong stance on behalf of eliminating discrimination at U.S. Steel; whenever the union made that move, as it indeed would in May 1963, U.S. Steel likely would begin to make plans to phase down its Birmingham operations. In short, the great corporate force reputedly responsible for much of segregated Birmingham would no longer be there to instruct members of the Birmingham white establishment, or their small-time operatives such as Connor, to stand and fight. Moreover, after segregationists beat up Freedom Riders at Birmingham's Trailways Bus Station in May 1961, and Connor and his fellow city commissioners, Art Hanes and James T. Waggoner, closed city parks rather than desegregating them in January 1962 according to recent federal court order, a group of moderate and liberal whites had coalesced in the Young Men's Business Club of Birmingham, which had been originally established in 1946. Here were several Jewish civic leaders from the suburb of Mountain Brook—Ferdinand Weil, Emil Hesse, Fred Sington, and Edward Friend, Jr., leaders long interested in race change and recently outraged over cross-burnings in front of synagogues—actions attributed to the Ku Klux Klan. Other members included the attorney (and former Hugo Black law clerk) David Vann and business leader James Head. The club openly agreed with Harrison Salisbury's characterization of Birmingham and increasingly urged both "racial justice" and change in the city's government. By November 1962 their pleas delivered a city vote to throw out the old commissioner government and move to a mayor-council system.[37]

Although the new moderate leaders failed to achieve their primary goal of Birmingham annexation of wealthy suburbs, they had at least some success. By early 1963 they won elections to fill the new positions of mayor and

councilmen, ultimately eliminating "Bull" Connor and leaving steel interests in a quandary. So to reiterate, King had to act fast, before Connor was
out of office, to get the major confrontation he needed.[38]

In April 1963, King moved his demonstrations and boycotts out of Georgia and over to Birmingham. Ultimately, the strategy worked. On Good
Friday, April 12, in violation of an injunction against marching, King led a
group forward. As they kneeled and prayed in front of the federal building,
around the corner from city hall, a paddy wagon moved in swiftly to whisk
King to jail. National television cameras whirred. King's subsequent "Letter from a Birmingham Jail" heightened the drama but nothing matched
the fire hoses and police dogs turned on black demonstrators on May 3.
The cameras whirred yet again during King's riveting "I Have a Dream" address on the Washington, D.C., mall on August 28, 1963. Then in the following September, back in Birmingham, something occurred far beyond
King's orchestration: the horrible death of four black children in the Ku
Klux Klan bombing of the Sixteenth Street Baptist Church. Finally, after all
this, the Yankees got off the fence. Congress began to work on serious civil
rights legislation while U.S. Steel—according to the *Wall Street Journal*—
continued to practice de facto segregation regardless of public statements
out of Pittsburgh that U.S. Steel favored race change.[39]

In bold relief to the UA board, not to mention the majority of Birmingham's white citizens, the new UA team in Birmingham—Volker, Hill, and
McCallum, plus Campbell and McNulty—did not *react* to these developments in Southern race relations as much as they *engaged* them in a measured way. Pragmatically following Rose's direction to stay out of the demonstrations and worried about retaliation from Governor Wallace and the
legislature, they knew the wave of change was coming, and so far as high-
profile public actions went they waited for the wave to pick them up and
carry them along on different aspects of desegregation. Still, from the pul-
pit of his Unitarian Church and in private discussions with friends, Volker
preached the need for desegregation, at times using Harrison Salisbury's
own phrase—"Fear and hatred grip Birmingham."[40] Then, as the wave slowly
got stronger, he and his colleagues made incremental changes on the Birmingham campus.

During October and November 1962, with local civil rights leaders dem-
onstrating at several lunch counters in downtown Birmingham and King's
appearance still some five months away, Volker received anonymous letters
and telephone calls about his "communist views." Dissenters seemed especially concerned about a recent racially mixed meeting of the Alabama

chapter of the American Psychiatric Association (APA) hosted by the Psychiatry Department in medical center facilities. With Volker's approval, nine black members of the APA who had joint appointments at Tuskegee Institute and the neighboring VA had been invited to attend. Callers advised "Pink Joe" to cease such activities. If he did not, urged one anonymous writer, UA alumni would demand that "Dr. Rose . . . be called in for an accounting" and that the legislature would retaliate with reduced appropriations for the medical center.[41]

The following spring and summer, of course, had its seemingly inevitable experience with Reverend King, social change, and concomitant tragedy. The medical center physicians Joe Donald and Alan Dimick had the "very sad experience" of pronouncing the four children caught in the church bombing dead on arrival at the hospital emergency room. Meanwhile, in Tuscaloosa in June, Governor Wallace unveiled his contrived "schoolhouse door showdown" involving U.S. attorney general Nicholas Katzenbach and the young U.S. marshal from Birmingham, Peyton Norville. While President Rose maneuvered the Tuscaloosa campus through this mine field, ultimately implementing token integration in Tuscaloosa, sixty miles up Highway 11 Volker and his team worked on the same "social engineering project," though with a much lower profile.[42]

Also in June, through contacts of Charles Zukoski—who a year earlier had been quietly dismissed from the First National Bank and now could work full time on "community projects"—Volker and George Campbell made arrangements to admit a black English teacher from Ullman High School, Luther Lawler, into a master's program in education offered in the Extension Center. As the first (token) black student enrolled at what would become UAB, he began his course of study in September 1963. Several black nurses had been admitted unofficially to Dean Kracke's nursing education program in Hillman Hospital in the late 1940s, but Lawler became the first black student officially admitted to regular academic programs in any of the units destined to be part of UAB.[43]

That same month, September 1963, the new Faculty Council in the medical school passed a resolution calling for desegregation of the cafeteria in the Basic Sciences Building. Volker gave no immediate response. On October 9, 1963, the "Negro Employees" in the basic sciences sent a memorandum to Volker urging desegregation of the cafeteria.[44] Shortly thereafter, with Volker's private encouragement, dental and medical school faculty and staff began to pull down "White Only" and "Colored Only" signs above water fountains and restrooms in the building. By October 17 Volker had approved the complete desegregation of the building and black employees began using the facility—the cafeteria, the bathrooms, the water fountains—just as whites did.[45]

At the same time the historic barricade in the medical profession began to come down. Volker wanted black physicians to practice in University Hospital. However, as more than one UA official had explained over the years, practice was limited to physicians who had membership in the private Jefferson County Medical Society. With Volker's knowledge, James T. Montgomery, a black cardiologist, quietly set out to penetrate the barricade; having grown up in Alabama and recently completed his medical training at Howard and Harvard, he was not about to limit his practice to Holy Family Hospital in Ensley. In 1958, he connected with Abraham H. Russakoff and a few other white liberal private practice physicians to integrate the Jefferson County Medical Society.[46]

At first the cause seemed to go nowhere. Despite instruction on persistence from his close friend Zukoski, Russakoff got back "the message": "Now is not the right time." By early October 1963, however, things had changed. Aware of Montgomery's medical treatment of civil rights leaders beaten in recent demonstrations, and concerned about Birmingham's increasingly bad image, Volker, Zukoski, Russakoff, McNulty, and Walter Frommeyer initiated a full-court press on the society's discriminatory practices: telephone calls, "serious conversation" over lunches, letters, and McNulty's pleading remarks before the society. Montgomery finally acquired the requisite five letters of endorsement from current members, and with a unanimous vote of the membership committee, in late October the wall of segregation in Birmingham's medical profession began to crack. It would be two years before another black physician, T. J. Barfield-Pendleton, gained admittance and the wall finally came tumbling down.[47]

Just as important, within several weeks after Montgomery's admission to the society the other wall was cracked. In a conversation with Frommeyer about the substandard "segregated hotel rooms" at the upcoming New Orleans meeting of the American College of Physicians, Montgomery inquired, "By the way, Wally, when am I going to start practicing medicine in [University] hospital?" To which Frommeyer replied, "Jim, when are you going to apply?" With that invitation Montgomery recalled, "I took my application blank from [Frommeyer's] office . . . and sent it back in a matter of approximately one month." Immediately, "I received an appointment to the active staff of the University of Alabama Hospital, and an appointment [effective November 1963] as Clinical Assistant Professor of Medicine" at the University of Alabama Medical School. Though his was a part-time, non–tenure track appointment, he was the first black faculty member in UA's Birmingham operations.[48]

These were significant changes, and Volker wanted more. But he also became increasingly nervous. Regardless of Rose's effectiveness as a leader and the growing critical mass of desegregationists among Birmingham's white professionals, the vice president feared getting too far ahead of the wave. Retaliation against him, the "Pink One," could easily be played out through cuts in state funding and elimination of Jefferson County support for the hospital. When he learned from emergency room physicians that they were treating lacerations on the arms and faces of blacks—wounds inflicted upon them by Birmingham police officers—he did not go to the press. Instead he quietly telephoned "Bull" Connor and said he *would* go to the press if Connor did not intervene, which he apparently did for a while. As one of his close medical center colleagues in these years, biochemist Roger Hanson, recalled,

> Joe and I had different approaches to social activism. He was incremental in most cases because as the administrator he had to watch out for political backlash that could hurt our budget. But I was a faculty member, truly with more freedom to act. . . . A good example would be his reaction to my work with Robert Hughes, the white Methodist minister-turned-desegregation activist. Joe did not object to my working with Abe Siegal and Frederick Kraus [two other medical center scientists] in talking Chuck Morgan [the white attorney of emerging race change leadership] into providing legal defense for Bob. We did this in a virtually all-night session in Kraus's other office, in the Veterans Hospital, technically U.S. government property, not university or state property. But when I orchestrated a "call for change" speech by Chuck before medical center faculty in the University Hospital auditorium . . . and Joe shortly found out that I was responsible for all this occurring on state property, he called me to his office and verbally took me apart for risking the institution's political and financial support. When I presented him with an AAUP letter supporting my use of freedom of speech on a campus, he backed off . . . never really said another word about it. So I would say he definitely wanted racial change, and in some cases played a leading role, but he still was careful.[49]

Volker's cooperation with Hanson on fighting the Nettles and Hawkins bills bears out this characterization of Volker. State House Representative Hugh Lock of Birmingham saw Volker, Hanson, Kraus, and other medical center liberals as a serious threat to the "old racial order" and constantly referred to them in the state House, making it clear to his conservative constituency that he was ever vigilant against their integrationist proclivities. Representative Sam Nettles of Wilcox County and John Hawkins of Jefferson County joined Lock in what Albert Brewer recalls as "constant pontification" about these liberals at the university in Birmingham and across the state in other institutions.[50] Hence, in the spring of 1963, Volker was in a bind when Representative Nettles pushed a bill to force State of Alabama employees to sign a loyalty pledge to historic racial laws of Alabama by placing that pledge on the back of their paychecks: one could not endorse the check without agreeing to the pledge. Although state senator (and attorney) Larry Dumas of Birmingham counseled Hanson and Kraus that such a law, if ever passed, certainly would be struck down as unconstitutional for its violation of the First Amendment, Hanson still went to Volker and asked him to use his relatively well-known, if quixotic, influences with Governor Wallace to make sure that the draft of the bill never got to the floor. Hanson feared that if it even came up for a vote or were introduced as a bill, it would create so much negative national attention that faculty recruitment for the Birmingham campus would be made even more difficult than it already was. Ever so quietly, but swiftly, Volker delivered and so did Wallace. The so-called Nettles Bill disappeared. It was never even introduced.[51]

However, in the same session, the Hawkins Bill establishing a "Peace Commission"—providing for a secret police force to report to Wallace on race reform activism by university faculty—did indeed make its way into law despite the hard lobby against it by Hanson and his AAUP colleagues statewide. Volker "likely tried to go to Wallace again," recalled Hanson, "but did not take an open stand." Indeed, despite regular protestations by AAUP chapters statewide but with leadership coming out of Birmingham, the commission continued to function though with less and less activity until 1968, when Acting Governor Brewer "ended it by terminating its funding."[52]

Volker's role in desegregation became even more complex with the intensification of racial issues within UA board politics. In the midst of the "schoolhouse door" crisis, Rose had told Volker the only way he could let Birmingham affairs expand would be to have two clearly distinct state budgets for Tuscaloosa and Birmingham operations. If Birmingham affairs, whether extension center or medical center, could be self-sustaining or, better, self-expanding, then in Rose's mind Birmingham operations could continue to move toward the vision discussed that historic evening in the Airport Motel. With the climax of desegregation almost over, however, Rose expected the board soon to regain its focus on Birmingham growth; even though the board had a few new members, in Rose's mind the best way to keep nervousness about Birmingham from blocking the vision was for the president to be able to show that Birmingham was in no way consuming funds that Tuscaloosa might have had.[53] In this context, the pragmatist as much as the visionary, Volker saw the possible pincer movement headed his way and in the winter of 1964 decided to slow down on race change. Before he moved further, he would wait until the spring or summer when he expected Congress to pass the Civil Rights Act of 1964 and cause the wave to reach its full force according to the plans of President Johnson and Reverend King.[54]

Unsurprising to Volker, this strategic delay did not sit well with Oscar Adams, the chief NAACP attorney in Birmingham, nor with other black citizens in the city. In April 1964, Adams telephoned then wrote to Volker about segregation in the hospitals of the medical center. Though James Montgomery was practicing medicine there, hospital regulations still isolated most black patients on a floor known as "2 West"—long visited by white physicians but now known behind closed doors as "Montgomery's floor." Further, black patients and any visitors who were black had to enter the building through an alley door then move up to "2 West" via the freight elevator, where they often rode alongside garbage.[55] Volker subsequently met with Adams, pledging his plan to correct these "obvious wrongs of local custom." Adams urged immediate action. According to the U.S. Department of Health, Education, and Welfare, Adams reported, any medical center facilities benefiting from any federal funds, whether from Medicaid, Hill-Burton, NSF, or NIH, "certainly had to be free of racial discrimination under the Civil Rights Act working its way through Congress." Strategically, Adams kept the focus on the historic symbol of segregated health care in Birmingham, University Hospital (including Hillman Clinic). Even so, trying to buy time for the law to find passage and give him leverage with conservative Alabamians who could destroy his state appropriations and thus tacit support from his board about the future of a university in Birmingham, Volker urged upon Adams and Louis J. Willie, the black civic leader and vice president of the Booker T. Washington Life Insurance Company, that (1) with slashed state and Jefferson County funding he could not provide adequate service to anyone, black or white; and, (2) counting on passage of the new civil rights act, he planned to have no signs of segregation anywhere within UA operations in Birmingham by the coming fall. To protect the budget he had to have some type of "legal rationale."[56]

In July 1964 Congress finally passed the Civil Rights Act with its specific stipulations regarding public accommodations and federally funded facilities. Worried and frustrated about the continued force of segregationist thought despite the new law, Volker proceeded on desegregation—though hesitantly, watching for conservative reactions after each step. In the first of many "summit" meetings in his office, Volker evolved his plan to move forward with low-profile, gradual steps. Though technically reporting to the Tuscaloosa campus, Campbell had Rose's instruction to function as part of Volker's strategy. Volker understood that federal compliance officers likely would be visiting the medical center "relatively soon." He hoped that as word of this spread among Birmingham's governmental officials and corporate leaders, combined with the low-profile approach, the segregationists' negative political, that is, state budget, influence would be minimized.[57]

Even with this approach, "Pink Joe" became a hot topic in racially conservative, politically influential circles "over the mountain" where many referred to him as "the Communist educator" who preached in the Unitarian Church on Cahaba Road alongside "Mr. Zukoski." Still, Volker, Zukoski, and other liberals never lost "cocktail contact" with educated conservatives, including the attorneys James Simpson and Ormand Somerville and John ("Parking-Lot King of the South") Hendon, not to mention moderates like the attorney and state senator Larry Dumas. Here was continued reflection of a pattern rooted deeply in the antebellum agrarian background of many of Birmingham's socially prominent families. In social life, if not in business, the formal expression of personalism called "good manners" found extension even to "Yankee-Communist dentists" so long as they were educated and sophisticated. In fact, though ultimately forced out of the Birmingham banking business, Zukoski not only had served several terms as unpaid *mayor* of the conservative enclave of Mountain Brook, but for over ten years played tennis two mornings a week at the Mountain Brook Club with a partner who represented his utter opposite on race and politics—Hendon.[58]

Volker understood the complexity before him. His private counsel on such matters came not just from Zukoski, Russakoff, and Miles College president Lucius Pitts. His counsel also came from Birmingham-Southern

College (BSC) president Henry King Stanford through meetings often facilitated by Roger Hanson.[59] A Georgian trained in political science at New York University, and one who had served as vice chancellor of the University of Georgia system as well as president of Georgia Southwestern College—Bill Paty had been his boss—Stanford had become president of BSC in 1957.[60] Here on the Hilltop dramatic racial events quietly unfolded each day, creating "a mood" among the elites of Birmingham that was deeply troubling to Stanford—and to Volker. Despite a BSC board that felt differently, Stanford urged desegregation of BSC. He also met with city commissioners Hanes and Connor in futile efforts to talk them out of shutting down public golf courses and swimming pools as part of their efforts to avoid desegregation. "Doctor," Connor told Stanford, "I don't give a good Goddamn what you want for Birmingham. I'm just gonna tell everybody I know not to send their children to Birmingham-Southern."[61]

Stanford, in Volker's view, wanted what was right but was not making much progress. Indeed, by the spring of 1962 Volker was witnessing a community leadership once strongly behind BSC beginning "to flee it like rats from a sinking ship." As an open racial liberal, Stanford was reinforcing the image of BSC as the college "filled with liberals." In fact, BSC had a moderate faculty (there were several notable exceptions who were "liberal"); a generally conservative student body (again, notable exceptions—e.g., Martha Turnipseed and Tommy Reeves—could be found associated with the Methodist Student Movement); and an even more conservative board, alumni, and community constituency. Out front on social change with few following, Stanford would give up by June 1962 and take the presidency of the University of Miami. Around town the move was chalked up more to the specific incident of "Bull Connor and the Klan" burning a cross in his yard at the corner of Arkadelphia Road and Eighth Avenue North.[62]

Stanford told close friends—Joe and Bertha Smolian, Mervyn Sterne, and others who also were close to Volker—that there was another reason he left. Granted, the Miami job was first class: "The president even gets his own yacht," urged the ever-witty Stanford, "and yachts are better than flaming crosses!" More important, most Birmingham leaders were capitulating to Connor's crowd. Indeed, Stanford was awestruck to find that for several nights after the cross-burning a black maintenance man at BSC, Willie Sweeney, armed himself with a shotgun and secretly stood guard behind some large bushes in the president's front yard to protect Stanford against further harassment—at serious risk to his own life—while most members of the BSC board refused to lift a hand to assist the institution through these devastating developments. For several months Stanford had had the pledge of W. Cooper Green, then one of Tom Martin's vice presidents at Alabama Power, to head up a fund drive to build a new fine arts facility. The night before the campaign drive was to be kicked off at a dinner at the Mountain Brook Club, however, Green advised Stanford that he was unable to participate and that an anticipated $1.5 million from the Henry J. Stockham family would not be forthcoming. Shortly thereafter, the Stockham family became significant supporters at Samford University. This changeover of support for the shrewdly orchestrated "conservative alternative" to BSC became so infuriating for a few BSC racial liberals, Stanford would recall, that they later referred to the neocolonial campus at Samford as "the Bastard Williamsburg of Lakeshore Drive." Although the BSC art building ultimately appeared chiefly through funds raised by two BSC alumni, with few exceptions Henry King Stanford could not get the Birmingham community leaders on his board to help him fight back against predominant reactionaries on racial change. So he left.[63]

With declining enrollment as well as endowment, BSC entered hard financial times. Hemmed in and needing to replace Stanford, its board opted for an acting president, the college's treasurer, Neuman ("Red") Yielding, son of an old Birmingham mercantile and banking family. Under his leadership and after a year of that of his successor, Howard Phillips—who came from Emory University via Montevallo College—BSC quietly admitted three black students. Simultaneously, however, the college's administration cooperated with Bull Connor's bugging telephones in student dormitories and placing undercover police officers in classrooms to monitor what was being taught. Through this turn to the right, some board members sought to throw off the unjustified label of "liberal BSC" as a strategy for financial recovery. Some thirty years later and under new leadership, however, Samford University, now with a robust endowment, would join a revitalized BSC in helping create the new progressive leadership of the city.[64]

Through conversations with Stanford often facilitated by Roger Hanson and Mervyn Sterne, Volker developed a keen understanding of how the "BSC story" of 1960–62 had polarized the daily environment in which he worked at both city and state levels. Granted, Volker's operations at that time were not as dependent on local endowment as were those of BSC and Samford. Still, the medical center's budget sorely could afford to lose any of its increased state appropriation slated for 1963–64 and 1964–65, not to mention Jefferson County funding for the hospital. On the other hand, he also could not afford to lose federal funds—some $5 million—that clearly would be cut off if the hospital continued segregation. Still, he determined to wait for "the right timing" to do anything more than the low-profile admittance of Luther Lawler in September 1963, an action *following* by some five months the desegregation of UA's Tuscaloosa campus. Hence the Birmingham campus was among the last in the deep South to implement token integration of its student body; the final ones were Vanderbilt and Auburn in 1964 and Mississippi State, Jacksonville State, and Furman in 1965. Zukoski disagreed with Volker's strategy. He urged his fellow Unitarian to push ahead aggressively on genuine desegregation of the campus as well as the hospital. Still, with the "BSC story much on his mind," Volker stood his ground. It was not until a year later, with "the awaited congressional cover" of the passage of the Civil Rights Act in July 1964, that Volker worked with Campbell to enroll forty-four black students in various programs of the Extension Center, many of whom lived within three miles of the campus and some of whom had spent their youth in ramshackle housing now replaced by urban renewal programs and by the medical center. Likewise, in September 1964 McNulty enrolled a black student, Wilma Barnes, in the hospital's School of Medical Technology. Such steps were taken quietly and with no backlash in either Birmingham or the state legislature.[65]

Racial integration in other health-related programs, however, proved more difficult. Faculty committees in the medical and dental schools had developed strategies for desegregating their professional graduate education programs, too. Indeed, as McNulty would recall, "Some of the medical faculty who were most committed to this cause were physicians whose lives went way back into the traditional family life of Alabama and the South, people like the gynecologist Nick [W. Nicholson] Jones." Because strong black college graduates increasingly were in the position of simply naming whatever excellent medical or dental school in the nation they cared to attend, and Birmingham's racial image was knocking the bottom out of the "best place to live in America" scale, it would be 1966 before the medical school team could entice two black medical students, Richard C. Dale and Samuel W. Sullivan (both graduates of Birmingham's Parker High School and of Howard University), to attend the UA medical school in Birmingham.[66] With the prominent NAACP leader and black dentist John W. Nixon of Birmingham advising the dental profession that the UA dental school in Birmingham was not good enough for black students to even want to attend—an opinion that led to a direct verbal confrontation between Nixon and McCallum and one likely motivated by black dental schools fearing a loss of enrollment due to desegregation (Nixon later apologized)—the Birmingham dental school team would not be able to recruit a single black student until Wilson Wright, in 1969, and Jimmie Walker, Jr., in 1970.[67]

Progress on the black faculty recruitment front proved just as difficult. In October 1966, McCallum hired the second black faculty member for any of the UA Birmingham programs, Clifton O. Dummett, the dentist of international reputation working under VA auspices in Tuskegee. Still, McCallum could convince Dummett to take no more than a clinical (part-time and nontenure) appointment, what James Montgomery had received three years earlier in the Department of Medicine, and Dummett would travel from Tuskegee to Birmingham once a week for the next five years.[68] At about the same time, in November 1966, McCallum also hired Bronetta L. Scott, a black woman from North Carolina who had a Ph.D. in anatomy from UCLA. Scott, whose research included electron microscope analysis of salivary glands, also had a non tenure track appointment, though full time, and would eventually leave Birmingham for Howard University after nine years.[69]

Likewise, it was July 1968 before Hill hired the local Meharry-educated black physician Herschell Lee Hamilton as a general surgeon. Formerly practicing only at Holy Family Hospital, Hamilton was known as the "dog-bite doctor" for his taking care of black protestors in the early 1960s. Hamilton's recollections help document why the medical center experienced such difficulty hiring black faculty. The outside image of Birmingham had a lot of truth behind it: though board certified, he "was scrutinized by everybody" and nurses, elevator operators, and parking guards just could not fathom that he was a doctor. At the time, he found that he was more accepted by physicians in University Hospital, where he had the title of clinical assistant professor—his background being far more that of a practicing clinician than an academic-clinician. Notwithstanding Hamilton's major significance, it would be 1969 before a tenure-track black faculty member appeared in the medical center. In short, throughout the late 1960s and 1970s the persisting racist reputation of Birmingham and Alabama frustrated efforts to recruit black professors and students.[70]

To be sure, however, the hospital represented the highest profile of the desegregation projects. In September 1963, after the church bombing, Abe Siegal—head of clinical laboratories—privately expressed his "fury" over hospital segregation; McNulty essentially said to wait for change. By the fall of 1964, however, faculty openly removed more "white" and "colored" signs from bathroom doors and water fountains. In early December the "white" signs came down from the regular elevators. Still, there is no doubt that Volker and McNulty were using a gradual approach and with the new year, despite promising key black leaders that "we're getting there," they in fact were not "there" yet. Finally, on March 15, 1965, eight months after passage of the Voting Rights Act, a week before the Selma-Montgomery protest march delivered a dying Reverend James Reeb to Alan Dimick's emergency room, and three months before the rumored date for the compliance inspection from the Department of Health, Education, and Welfare (HEW), Volker got a telephone call from Oscar Adams. He was filing suit in federal court for desegregation of "the Medical Center complex," and he did just that. The hospital, he restated to Volker, was his central target.[71]

Volker was not surprised. And judging from his supportive reaction to his faculty participating in activities of Concerned White Citizens and the Selma-Montgomery protest walk in late March—Frederick W. Kraus (dentistry), Abraham Siegel (physiology), Roger Hanson (biochemistry), and Harold Wershow (sociology)—he likely welcomed the resolution that certainly had to follow. Throughout April he stayed in close contact with Adams, continually reassuring him that there would be no problem: "We can do what we all know is right." Meanwhile, he worked the telephone trying to solidify support from key physicians in the community and the medical center, as well as powerful alumni of the medical school who were active in the Medical Association of the State of Alabama (MASA). The majority were good-willed but lacked firm conviction to support the change even with the backing of a federal law. Perplexed by these circumstances and possibly trying to buy some time to ward off rumored demonstrations in front of the hospital, on Thursday, April 15, he invited Adams, Willie, and Reverend John Porter to his office to ask them to serve as "a type of ad hoc community advisory committee or Kitchen Cabinet on totally desegregating the hospital." Willie carried the conversation. He first pledged his understanding of how complicated a situation his friend faced. Then he made the crucial point: "Joe, on behalf of your newly formed 'Kitchen Cabinet' I want to advise you of something. Joe, you've got to open the hospital—right now." Volker replied, "I'll have it done in four days." Years later, Willie recalled leaving that conference "feeling good." "I long had known that Joe was a man of his word. If he said he was going to do it, he *was* going to do it."[72]

Volker now ceased being gradual in his actions, no doubt in part because he knew that HEW inspectors were due in Birmingham by the second week of May to determine whether the hospital was in compliance with all civil rights laws. On Thursday, April 22—one week after the Kitchen Cabinet meeting—Volker notified the medical center faculty that he would like to meet with it, en masse, in the Engineering Building auditorium on the following afternoon. There, sitting on the edge of the stage in a seersucker blazer, his noted bow tie casually dipping to the right, he announced that he and McNulty had developed a plan for desegregating the hospital and that by Monday morning, April 26, that plan would be implemented. McNulty made a similar announcement in a special assemblage of leaders of the Jefferson County Medical Society.[73]

True to his promise, by late afternoon on Sunday, April 25, Volker had done all he could do to remove all indications of segregation from the hospital. Specifically, as confirmed in McNulty's summary report to Volker, written Sunday night, "each patient is assigned a bed accommodation without regard to race, creed, or color." On April 26, physicians who had not followed the relocation of patients over the weekend arrived to fine-tune the process: appropriate physicians and nurses were connected with appropriate patients. The medical center was ready for federal inspection—at least Volker thought so.

On either April 27 or 28, Paul Brann telephoned an old friend associated with a hospital in Jackson, Mississippi, where federal inspectors had just completed the same type of evaluation destined for the UA hospital. The message Brann took back to Volker was that *all* floors and sections of the hospital had to reflect thorough racial integration regardless of how a patient's illness might otherwise locate him or her in the hospital. In response, Volker and McNulty spent the next two days looking for medically sound ways to meet this additional standard. In the end they did not. Beginning Friday afternoon, April 30, and working through Sunday night, May 2, they saw to it that a full blend of races existed on every floor and in every section of the hospital, at times locating patients at a significant distance from sections and nurses' stations specifically designed to treat particular illnesses. On Monday morning, May 3, physicians had a far more extreme version of "hunt your patient" than a week earlier. The formerly "black" floor, "2 West," took on a different complexion. Despite this last-minute "adjustment," Volker again thought he had a plan to pass the inspection, the only plan possible in view of Birmingham's racial reputation.[74]

The hospital did indeed settle down under these "medically odd" conditions. At first patients and visitors of different colors would not look at each other; some even turned their backs on each other. However, by Sunday afternoon, Willie recalled hearing from black friends in the hospital, patients as well as visitors, who were "struck by the point that they had something pretty powerful in common—sickness—which made their different colors seem less significant." They not only started looking at each other but "smiling and talking, trying to have good manners." McNulty personally spent the night of May 2 roaming the hospital and occasionally sitting in the emergency room and recalled the same "efforts to be polite to one another" as black and white "sat side by side in the waiting room." Concerned that it would not be the patients but their visitors who would disrupt this harmony, McNulty had Birmingham police officers check on waiting rooms (in retrospect, a questionable step considering the racial views of some of them). McNulty also located "an oversupply" of visitors' chairs in all rooms holding "two or more patients": "We could not risk a situation where visitors of one race were the first ones to enter and took all the chairs, leaving a stand-up-only circumstance for visitors of the other race."[75]

Thus on the morning of May 3, McNulty again notified Volker that the hospital was desegregated, privately adding that physicians were "wandering all around the hospital looking for their patients." All tiptoed through this racially blended, medically confused situation for "close to a week." Volker the pragmatist held his breath, assuming that the situation was doable at least until the inspectors had completed their work, now confirmed for Sunday, May 9. This assumption proved more lucky than right. Given that the passing of each hour, each day increased the chances for this medically unsound scheme to deliver significant tragedies, it was sheer luck that the HEW team decided to pop in on Birmingham two days early, on Friday May 7. The team stayed one day, seemed pleased, and headed on to its offices in Atlanta and filed its report with HEW officials in Washington, D.C. Relieved, and not counting on any further luck, McNulty then spent May 8 and 9 reassigning patients to the sections of the hospital most appropriate for their illness. Looking back on this complex development years later, the physician Durwood Bradley mused, "You know, it's amazing: the desegregation of this hospital did not cost us one life."[76]

With relief evolving into cautious celebration, on Tuesday, May 11, Volker and his Kitchen Cabinet quietly walked through the hospital, ate lunch in the cafeteria, and jointly pronounced the reforms a "real success." Volker explained to them precisely what he had done, perhaps compromising sound medicine briefly to illustrate compliance. Willie later stated that he "understood exactly what Joe was up to and I would have done the same thing; the most important thing was that he *had* opened the hospital."[77] Indeed, a few days later Willie wrote McNulty from an even broader perspective: "All of us enjoyed the luncheon, the tour of your facilities, and especially the witness of human dignity which you have made by your actions. May God bless you, and let each of us pray for His special grace as we seek to advance the ministry of reconciliation."[78]

On Tuesday, May 18, James Quigley, assistant secretary of HEW, notified Volker that the hospital needed a few walls torn down in the cafeteria to make sure there was no return to the old ways. That was done over the next two months, and on July 20, 1965, Federal District Judge Hobart H. Grooms dismissed the suit Oscar Adams had filed some fifteen months earlier. In subsequent years Birmingham operations, of course, would reflect far more racial mixing, no doubt in part because Volker continued to meet periodically with his Kitchen Cabinet, including Adams, at least through October 1967. By the summer of 1965, however, the cause of racial equality in these academic and clinical activities at last reflected major advances in the situation first confronted by Roy Kracke, Oscar Adams, Charles Zukoski, and the other Birmingham reformers of 1947.[79]

6
Stage Two Delivery, 1965–69

Urban Change

Even as he worked day and night on desegregating the hospital, Joseph Volker was beginning to implement his social change strategy in other areas of the medical center, too. He subtly used the desegregation issue to bring about the greatest development project in UA's Birmingham operations as well as a new era, though not without overcoming more than a few obstacles.

In October 1964, extending a strategy he, Roy Kracke, James Durrett, and Robert Berson had followed for over a decade, Volker laid plans to acquire forty-five blocks west of the medical center through another application for urban renewal funds. This space—similar to the first urban-renewal plan—included large stretches of low-rent housing where many black laborers and their families lived. It also included several revered churches and, in the northwest sector, a cultural icon of the black community: Ullman High School. Founded in 1901 as an elementary school for whites (and named for Samuel Ullman, a lay rabbi and the single most important person behind the creation of the Birmingham Public School system), since the early 1940s the school had been a secondary school for black students living near the medical center and in the adjacent neighborhood of Titusville. Though poorly funded, Ullman High School benefited from the leadership of George Crenshaw Bell, a strict disciplinarian known for sending graduates on to college and out into wide-ranging professional careers. Volker was fully attuned to the iconic nature of "Mr. Bell's school." Still, he saw its location as too suitable not to be included in the forty-five-block plan. Over time, however, what Volker saw as suitable would prove to be a far less than popular move.[1]

At the time Volker had reason to be optimistic about this second urban renewal application. Despite Birmingham's racial reputation—indeed, in Volker's mind, *because of* this reputation—its funding connections with Washington, D.C., recently had delivered in major ways. Because of the radical alteration in Birmingham's form of government brought on by Martin Luther King, Jr.'s demonstrations, "Bull" Connor was out of power. A more moderate segregationist, Albert Boutwell, was in power. And despite Connor's continuing role as police commissioner, Boutwell's lieutenants along with moderate business leaders associated with Operation New Birmingham were planning to apply for federal aid to build a new post office and a new sewer system. President Johnson's recent creation, the U.S. Department of Housing and Urban Development (HUD), and his "War on Poverty" still viewed Birmingham as a relatively good place for federal aid. It was a place of poverty within the general population, a place notoriously in need of social change, a place where U.S. senators Lister Hill and John Sparkman wanted more investments, and a place that Mayor Boutwell's executive secretary, William C. ("Billy") Hamilton, and the director of the Birmingham Housing Authority (BHA), Hugh Denman, had begun to "sell" to War on Poverty leaders in Washington, as would the succeeding mayor, George Seibels. Yet there would be opposition. It would come from a few well-to-do white realtors who owned the dilapidated rental houses and the realtors' strange bedfellows, the black people who lived there, and a few black leaders who strategized for revitalizing other areas such as Ensley.[2]

To deal with this problem, Volker and Ehney Camp worked with Denman and Hamilton to create the 136-member Mayor's Advisory Committee on Medical Center Expansion. On December 24, 1964, Mayor Boutwell announced the formation of the committee. It included business people who were well known for civic leadership: Harold Blach, president of Blach and Sons department store; Robert Jemison, Jr., president of Jemison Realty; Mortimer H. Jordan, vice president of Southern Natural Gas Company; Lillian G. Meade, executive director of the American Cancer Society; and Camp, UA board member from Birmingham. It also included individuals with business interests in the immediate vicinity of the medical center, people like Cecil G. Etros, of the Phoenix Cafe, and Roy H. Adwell, of Adwell Tire and Marine Supplies. On Camp's advice, Volker got Mayor Boutwell to ask Jack McSpadden to chair the committee. McSpadden and Camp long had been friends, having risen together through the ranks of Liberty National Life Insurance Company; in the mid-1960s both were executive vice presidents with the company and, though far more moderate in social and political views than Zukoski, McSpadden still had much in common with business leaders who helped build the civic universities of late nineteenth-century England. Indeed, McSpadden had married a local artist, Louise Lathrop, whose family roots went deep into the early steel and railroad origins of Birmingham. These powerful civic-elite connections, both to old Birmingham and to what lay ahead, permitted McSpadden to work through the 136-member committee and ultimately deliver what Volker, Boutwell, Denman, and Hamilton needed.[3]

On February 23, 1965, McSpadden's group hosted a public (press invited) meeting on the proposal. A product of Volker's orchestration, it began at 2 p.m. in the auditorium of the new Engineering Building. Volker led with a presentation titled "The Growth of the Medical Center." President Frank Rose supported "the message" as long as "no Tuscaloosa money" was used. Then, Volker delivered what soon would be known as his "litany." Birmingham was going through difficult but important social changes, he said. However, just as Tom Martin had advised ten years earlier, Volker urged (using Martin's exact words) that the city should not "dream too small"—"to do so would be to do our community a great injustice." He cited urban renewal projects then underway in San Antonio, Houston, and Hartford, Connecticut, and explained that through a similar project UA's medical center could acquire some forty-five blocks. This space would create possibilities for other new federally funded enterprises: a cancer center, a stroke and heart attack center, a regional health science library, a mental retardation center, the movement of UA's main School of Nursing from Tuscaloosa to the medical center, an expansion of the current Extension Center and School of Engineering into a College of General Studies that could offer full baccalaureate and graduate programs, and even the possible relocation of Carraway Methodist Hospital and St. Vincent's Hospital into the area. The new vision delivered, Volker now turned to "old Birmingham" for "legitimacy."

The next person slated to speak was the revered former mayor, James B. Morgan, president of the powerful Molton, Allen, and Williams mortgage and real estate company. He presented a talk titled "The Value of the Medical Center to the Community." With remarks drafted by Volker and then refined by media aide Gloria Goldstein (a graceful if wily thirty-eight-year-old Fayette, Alabama, native who, since 1961, had worked for Volker, Hill, and McCallum in various public relations positions), Morgan emphasized that Birmingham's current image did not encourage private investment and the badly needed economic vitality to accompany the medical center—a state appropriation of $6.5 million, an operating budget that had escalated from $1.5 million in 1944–45 to $20 million in 1964–65, and a workforce and payroll that matched that of U.S. Steel. He predicted that the expansion proposed by Volker would increase "Medical Center jobs" from the current 5,000 to 10,670 and raise the current payroll of $18 million to $38.4 million. No wonder the Birmingham Real Estate Board had given the plan a unanimous endorsement after Morgan gave the group a sneak preview of it on February 10, 1965. (Morgan omitted the arm-twisting he had had to go through to get that vote. Some rental property owners had a hard time "seeing the future.") Then up to the podium came Frank Spain, UA's attorney and already a major donor to the medical center. His job was to explain the Urban Renewal Act. With a fund deriving 75 percent from urban renewal and 25 percent from a City of Birmingham bond issue, over a two-year period the BHA would purchase parcels of land in the targeted area. Then the land could be granted to UA for the expansion projects. BHA's Relocation Office, already open at 1426 Tenth Avenue South, would work closely with all individuals living in the area to move them into public as well as private housing, some being constructed with Urban Renewal Act funds, with moving costs for all covered by BHA.

Finally, to emphasize the true international significance of what could happen in Birmingham with an expansion of the medical center, to the front of the auditorium strode William R. ("Billy") Lathrop, the charming French consul in Birmingham, adorned with signature ascot, and the president of Southern Life and Health Insurance Company. As a person "simply concerned about the future of the city"—he also happened to be McSpadden's brother-in-law—Lathrop felt it was his responsibility to introduce a resolution. It read: "The City of Birmingham should proceed with an application for the necessary Urban Renewal funds and thus acquire the area bounded on the east by 20th Street, South, on the North by 5th Avenue, South, on the West by [proposed] Highway I-65 (the same as 10th Street, South), on the South by 12th Avenue, South, including the projection of 12th Avenue, South from its Western terminus to [projected] Highway I-65." With a second to the motion offered by another concerned citizen, Wilbur H. Hollins, vice president of Acamar Realty and Insurance Company (and who ultimately would direct the BHA Relocation Office), McSpadden presided over an hour of open discussion. He then called for a vote of the 136-member committee. The voice vote delivered unanimous approval. McSpadden adjourned the meeting with the announcement that the committee's recommendation would be considered at the next meeting of the city council.[4] Zukoski, who had been uncharacteristically quiet in the back row of the auditorium, walked out with the smiling vice president. Volker: "Charles, this is the first meeting in Birmingham where you haven't lectured." Zukoski: "I feared that if you and I both talked they'd think this project was communist." Volker: "Good thinking." Here was a chapter out of the history of higher education presaged less than a century earlier, though with different names and different social forces, in such transatlantic places as Liverpool and indeed Birmingham, England.[5]

On March 3, 1965—just days before Reverend King's Selma march began—the Birmingham City Council convened to take up Lathrop's resolution. It passed unanimously with the urging that the BHA speed up the schedule, to which Denman replied that the envisioned schedule was necessary to ensure careful relocation of people living in the area.[6] Aided by a $241,000 Urban Renewal Planning Grant, Volker, George Campbell, and Denman, plus E. Todd Wheeler and Art Garikes, began immediately to prepare the necessary "Expansion and Land Utilization Study," which was in final form by February 1966.[7] Meanwhile, on April 18, Birmingham voters "solidly approved" eleven bond issue proposals including funds for a new civic center, a new public library, two new schools, expansion of the art museum, sewer and street improvements, and $400,000 as Birmingham's "match" in the urban renewal venture. The vote on the urban renewal bond was closest: 10,968 in favor, 6,896 against. Because the Voting Rights Act of 1965 did not pass until August, this was a virtually all-white vote. Opposition to "medical center expansion" likely came from some small-scale white property owners in the target area; from the few white renters in the area; from a few black renters in the area who had fought through the maze of bureaucratic blockades to vote and who feared replacement housing would even be worse; and from homeowners in Southside neighborhoods west of Twentieth Street and south of the target area who feared further expansion right up to "the shadow of Vulcan." Still, by late May 1965 the team had a $5.7 million grant application in the mail, destined for success. It would be 1969, however, before the complicated negotiations on property in the area would be completed and all titles changed hands.[8]

Prescience

Not coincidentally, at about the same time that Volker's urban renewal application reached its climax, something even more dramatic occurred. After attending the June 1965 commencement exercises in Tuscaloosa, Volker and Campbell accepted Jeff Bennett's invitation to drop by his home, on the east side of Tuscaloosa, and have a drink before they returned to Birmingham. The three talked for two hours about the likelihood of Birmingham operations "seceding from UA" the way Mobile operations had. Especially in view of all of the growth, Volker affirmed what Bennett suspected. "Either Tuscaloosa would have to get out of the way," Bennett would recall Volker saying, "and let Birmingham have more autonomy, or Tuscaloosa almost certainly would see the development of something totally outside the UA influence, such as a University of Birmingham, on *our* side of the Atlantic." None of this surprised Bennett. He had tried (and failed) to get Rose to understand these dynamics in the case of Mobile. He now tried again regarding Birmingham.[9]

Armed with the accuracy of his Mobile prediction, not to mention recent news of Auburn University's plan to develop a branch campus in Montgomery to fill the void left by UA's phasing out its center there, plus "several good quotes" from the conversation with Volker and Campbell, Bennett went to visit Rose the following Monday morning. And that afternoon in early June, Bennett telephoned Volker with the crucial message: "Develop 'a new plan' for the Birmingham campus." Rose had said to "proceed with a plan."[10]

Out of numerous conversations between Volker, Campbell, Paul Brann, and Bennett the plan evolved through the summer and fall of 1965. By late summer these discussions turned into a written document. Shortly thereafter, Volker called Rose to summarize this report, and he concluded with a "strong suggestion" that the University of Alabama in Birmingham (UAB) become one of three semi-autonomous campuses within an envisioned three-campus UA system—Huntsville and Tuscaloosa being the other campuses. Rose replied: proceed with "planning" related to the Birmingham campus and deliberation regarding other proposals would come in time. With this invitation, on December 13, 1965,[11] Volker sent Campbell and Brann to Tuscaloosa to give Rose a simply stated two-page outline for the Birmingham campus. "I will never forget it," Campbell told a UAB history student years later. "It rained all the way on us, a very dismal day, and as I recall, Dr. Rose's attitude was about as dismal as the weather. I didn't feel very good about his reaction at the time; he seemed to be preoccupied about other matters. [And then] he sat on the report until he just about wore all of us out."[12]

However, under Bennett's savvy influence, Rose only appeared to be sitting on the report. Throughout the fall of 1965, a good three months before "the plan" even made its official entry into Rose's office, Rose had begun to have brief, informal, and confidential talks with board members whom he thought might feel comfortable about his use of the term "University of Alabama in Birmingham" to describe what was about to happen sixty miles northeast of Tuscaloosa. Indeed, during September, October, and November, Rose occasionally used the acronym "UAB" in talks to civic groups and with board members. He probably first heard the acronym coming from the lips of Volker, but Volker likely got it from former president O. C. Carmichael, who had helped establish the SUNY system in New York and had been fascinated by the recent growth of the University of California–Los Angeles (UCLA).[13] At any rate, on September 20, 1965, H. Brandt ("Brandy") Ayers, the young editor of the *Anniston Star* and who had become increasingly well known for his new New South message, "You Can't Eat Magnolias," ran an editorial under the lead, "The Rolling Tide Campus": "Plans of the University of Alabama to make its Birmingham operations an expanded, semi-independent entity, reflect the rapidly growing status of the entire school. . . . Dr. Frank Rose . . . says the new 'University of Alabama in Birmingham' will take in the medical and dental schools and the extension center, which will become a college of general studies offering bachelor and master's degrees. . . . [This] is something to be proud of even if it means more responsibilities, but Alabamians can happily bear such fruitful burdens."[14]

If Ayers was ahead of board action by a good eight months, it suited Rose, Bennett, and Volker just fine. The waters could be tested. Political influences on the board could now be orchestrated more openly. Moreover, the higher-profile element of UA, Paul "Bear" Bryant's "Crimson Tide," which was now poised to win another NCAA football title, nurtured UA's self-esteem that was otherwise left yearning from desegregation crises and made alumni and board members less nervous about growth sixty miles up the road. The timing could not have been better.[15] Within two months, Volker had news that added to this already positive environment. He had formal approval on the urban renewal grant from HUD: "We've got it," he advised Rose, "and we also have won the award for the best Urban Renewal project in the Southeast for 1965."[16]

And that was not all Volker had to keep fuel on the fire. During the spring of 1964, while immersed in desegregation, Volker had watched with keen interest congressional debates on the proposed Appalachia Bill, a centerpiece of the War on Poverty. Originally targeted at poverty in the Appalachian Mountains, especially in West Virginia, as the 1960s unfolded the program increasingly focused on urban blight; and, as a reflection of the influence of

Senators Hill and Sparkman, this included hills much further south—into Birmingham's Jones Valley. In May 1964, some three months before the bill passed Congress, Volker urged President Rose to help him seal the deal that he apparently had been working on through "informal channels." "[The] Appalachia [Bill], as I understand it, is to be a concerted attack on the economic problems of several depressed states. These problems have employment, educational, and health components. All are interrelated, and all are represented in the Medical Center. . . . [These] circumstances make the University and its Medical Center a natural focus for Appalachia's endeavors."[17] Volker concluded the letter suggesting that "we" work through Alabama's congressional delegation so that President Johnson himself could see how "compatible" the medical center was with Johnson's developing program. "Your early action would be appreciated," Volker wrote.[18]

What Volker had in mind was federal money to construct new buildings not just in the existing medical center space but in the envisioned urban renewal acquisition. Rose began lobbying not just Senators Sparkman and Hill but President Johnson himself.[19] Then, in September, after Johnson had had a few months to establish the new Appalachian Regional Commission (ARC), Volker wrote to ARC cochairman John L. Sweeney asking if he could come to Washington and make a presentation on what the UA Medical Center could do to help eliminate poverty in Jefferson County, Alabama, a county—as the national press was reporting—desperately needing racial change that only could occur through economic change. He copied Senators Hill and Sparkman. His letter arrived even before criteria for the award of grants had been established. But Senator Hill apparently telephoned Sweeney on the matter as well as the special assistant to the president and one of the key architects of the Great Society programs, Senator Hill's good friend and fellow Montgomery native, Douglass Cater. Within three days Sweeney wrote Volker inviting him to serve on the ARC's Advisory Committee on Health. The committee would develop criteria to be used in awarding construction grants under section 202 of the law, which had an initial fund of $41 million to distribute. Volker "just had to accept" the invitation—so long as his institution was not barred from applying for funds, which it was not. Within the following year, serious heart problems would take Cater to "Volker's hospital" and then to extended recuperation at Rose's Lake Martin retreat. Personal bonds cemented those of politics and social vision.[20]

Remembering his early dental dean days, where he worked both in Birmingham and Boston, Volker shuttled between Birmingham and Washington for a year. Just as important, throughout 1965 and 1966 Rose relayed this unfolding news to board members, reinforcing the point that Birmingham leaders were attracting their own major funds.[21] Not unexpectedly, by late December 1966, Volker and John Dunbar had managed to submit a $952,000 proposal for Birmingham ARC. When matched with state funds, this ARC grant would deliver a new building for a Regional Technical Institute (RTI) for Health Occupations. Originally conceived as a component of University Hospitals—a school of "Paramedical Studies"—that would educate poor Southern "Appalachian people" of Jones Valley and its surrounding area, because that education would help them get jobs and climb out of poverty, RTI soon would find approval plus set the stage for six additional ARC grants.[22]

Some eighteen months before final approval of the first ARC grant, however, still bigger news arrived. Confident that space for expansion and money for new construction looked like genuine possibilities in Birmingham, Rose and Ehney Camp spent the early spring of 1966 extolling the phenomenal growth in Birmingham to UA board members. They also gave board members copies of the report Rose had received in December 1965. Prepared by Volker, Campbell, and Bennett, it had been kept under cover until "the time was right." Such timing ultimately was the result of both luck and hard work. It derived from "Joe's having even more expansion projects up his sleeve," Bennett recalled, "and with nonstate money to pay for them." And it derived from the fact that "Bear" Bryant's Crimson Tide further bolstered the self-esteem of powerful Alabama alumni by claiming a set of postseason bowl victories as well as national championships in 1964 and 1965.[23] The psyche of many white Alabamians and particularly of numerous UA alumni now began to reflect a renewed sense of security, and with that came more comfort with change. They had lost the Civil War as well as the deciding confrontations in civil rights. But by God they had won the Orange Bowl and, as the sardonic Jeff Bennett recalled, "the future now looked damn good." Accordingly, the man who later would oppose visions of UAB athletics, especially football, "the man himself, The Bear" in winning that Orange Bowl helped create a new environment in Alabama without which UAB (and UAB varsity athletics) perhaps never could have arisen.[24]

At any rate, aided by the curious confluence of forces of 1965–66, in early May 1966 Rose and Bennett began planning Rose's comments to the board on the future of Birmingham operations. His discussion would include ideas for an administrative structure that would permit medical programs to reach full potential, the status of the availability of land and funds, and some thoughts on the possible competition from Auburn, which was considering the development of a full program branch in Birmingham the way it recently had done in Montgomery.[25]

Rose decided that the May 28, 1966, board meeting in Tuscaloosa was the right time to move forward on "the University of Alabama in Birmingham." When the time came for the meeting, however, Rose found himself stuck in a Washington, D.C., hospital recovering from an emergency appendectomy. Still, he proceeded using a combination of previously written remarks, long-distance telephone calls, and Jeff Bennett, who was present at the meeting. After the board passed a resolution wishing Rose a speedy recovery (not planned), it adjourned into executive session (as planned). Rose said simply that he had told Volker repeatedly, with board approval, that Birmingham operations could grow as long as the expansion did not cut into state allocations for the "mother campus." Volker, he emphasized, had complied completely. He now had federal funds for capital development totaling $7 million with more on the way. Likewise, he had increased research grants and contracts from $3,888,514 in 1963 to $4,445,900 in 1965, continuing the trend of constant growth since 1945. Birmingham enrollments also were burgeoning. In 1964–65 there were 299 medical students, 221 dental students, 177 in the hospital's nursing program and 22 in its medical technology program, 191 in medical and dental residency programs, and around 3,500 (1,000 full-time equivalents) students in the Extension Center. Clark Memorial Theater, moreover, had offered five major productions in Birmingham over the previous year and had delivered twenty additional performances throughout the state, with total attendance approaching 40,000. Extension Center enrollment, Rose emphasized, had grown 24 percent between the fall terms of 1964 and 1965.[26]

Rose neglected to mention that Volker, working through Campbell and his friend at the state ARC office in Montgomery, J. Rudolph Davidson, had Governor Wallace's promise to call a special session of the legislature to provide new state funding for Birmingham operations. Most of these funds were to be earmarked for something to be called either "Birmingham College" or "the College of General Studies," a term Volker first had used in the 1964 ARC application.[27] Though this was to be new state money, Rose correctly believed that some members of the board looked on any state money for UA as targeted for Tuscaloosa affairs. Withholding clear definition of "self-generated," Rose next stated that because of the Birmingham operation's striking "self-generated funds" as well as the scale of current instructional and cultural activity, "progressive management" in Alabama called for "the College of General Studies" to replace the Birmingham Extension Center and for this new unit to join the medical center in reporting to Dr. Volker, who would have the title of vice president for Birmingham affairs. Camp moved that the change occur as President Rose had suggested. Winton Blount seconded the motion. A unanimous vote, carefully checked out before the meeting, made it official. Three days later Rose telephoned Volker with the bottom line, a reiteration of the budget reality: "Joe, I've done all I can do for you. You are now on your own."[28]

Rose's assent to the progressive change Volker and others had developed in Birmingham contained some interesting twists. U.S. Steel's Arthur Wiebel may have been so preoccupied about desegregation that he failed to defeat other forces in Birmingham aligned with a full Birmingham engineering school, forces wanting Birmingham to be something other than a company town with a low wage scale. Some members of the UA board seemed so overwhelmed by UA's desegregation crisis in Tuscaloosa that they inadvertently left the door ajar for O. C. Carmichael to gear up Extension Center programs in Birmingham. Granted, there were notable exceptions, especially Blount and Camp, who increasingly advocated Volker's vision irrespective of race change in Tuscaloosa. Then there was the palliative of football. The board and scores of powerful UA alumni, including Birmingham faculty who were helping build the Birmingham campus, became so excited about the way Coach Bryant and his rolling Crimson Tide commanded national media attention, so recently focused on failure and embarrassment associated with desegregation, that an uplifting aura of relief, pride, and harmony settled over relations between Birmingham and Tuscaloosa. And in that era of good feelings Joe Volker—who rarely missed a UA home game whether at Denny Stadium in Tuscaloosa or Legion Field in Birmingham—moved his plan to the next stage.

On September 15, 1966, as the fall term began in Birmingham, Rose took this "old news" to the Birmingham faculty. Most knew what they would hear, but the faculty were not about to miss the show. In the Cudworth Auditorium Rose began his address to "the joint faculties of the University's Birmingham campus" with a slip of the tongue tantalizing even to those who knew nothing of Sigmund Freud: "I have come here today to discuss significant advances in the work of the University of Birmingham." Seemingly unconscious of the slip, he continued.

As of this afternoon, the various operations of the University of Alabama in this city will be known as the University of Alabama in

Birmingham . . . [to] include: the School of Medicine, the School
of Dentistry, the School of Health Services Administration, University Hospitals and Clinics, and the College of General Studies. . . .
Nearly one-fourth of all the people in Alabama live within twenty-
five miles of this campus. These three-quarters of a million people deserve the best use of the University's resources. . . . More college-age
young people live [in this area] than in Mobile, Huntsville, and Tuscaloosa combined. . . . The people *must* be served. . . . The baby bird has
grown and is ready to fly. We are pleased to see you spread your wings
and soar to new heights above Birmingham.

This did not mean that UAB had become an autonomous or even semi-
autonomous institution. After all, Volker as vice president would report to
Rose and not to the board, and Rose always would think of Tuscaloosa operations as "the main campus." It did, however, permit the movement toward the semi-autonomy Volker and others long had wanted. Final delivery lay just ahead.[29]

The College of General Studies

Volker wasted no time in heralding the new enterprise as "UAB." The December issue of the medical center's *Bulletin,* a community outreach and
medical alumni publication, urged participation in "the UAB blood donation campaign."[30] The *Birmingham News* and *Birmingham Post Herald* were
slower to embrace the acronym, for years still using "medical center" rather
than "UAB." However, longing for something good about Birmingham, these
newspapers saw Rose's announcement alongside Birmingham-Southern College (BSC), Samford University, Miles College, Daniel Payne College, and
the two new state community colleges developed under Governor Wallace's
expansion program, Jefferson State Community College and Lawson State
Community College, to be firm evidence of Birmingham's bright future as
"a growing center for higher education."[31]

The most striking new component of UAB immediately appeared: the
College of General Studies (CGS). On Volker's direction "Birmingham Extension Center" came off the front of the building on Twentieth Street, and
the vaguely descriptive "College of General Studies" went up in its place.
With the new title of dean of CGS, George Campbell spent the Christmas
break preparing for expanded, degree-offering programs of study that would
start in January 1967.[32]

Since August 1966 Campbell had been meeting with faculty to plan "the future." Out of the forty full-time faculty of the Extension Center, he had chosen "a core group," an advisory committee, to accomplish three main tasks: develop a curriculum, hire new faculty, and lobby members of the legislature. Indeed, during 1966–67, Rose kept his word: CGS did not receive one dime out of the Tuscaloosa appropriation (even though many medical units by now had their own line-item funding from the state), which meant that CGS had no state funds that year—just CGS tuition and fees running about $280,000. Hence lobbying for a state appropriation for 1967–68 was very much on Campbell's mind as he drew his faculty leaders around him.[33]

They were a resourceful bunch. There was Joseph Appleton, a former Birmingham corporate engineer who had become a professor and since 1959 had been a crucial builder of the engineering program. There was John S. Coley, from an old Alexander City, Alabama, family, who at age forty-five had ended his first career as a pharmacist, gone to Vanderbilt to earn a Ph.D. in English, then joined the center's faculty in 1965. Soft-spoken while intellectually intense, Coley often arrived in the classroom early for the first meeting of a freshman composition course in order to take a seat in the back row of chairs; only after all the new students had assembled would he slowly rise and, from the rear of the class, introduce himself as "not just the teacher but one of the learners in this class." There was Hubert H. Harper, a Birmingham native and BSC graduate who had postponed use of his noted talents as an actor to obtain a Ph.D. in English at Chapel Hill. He arrived at the center in 1964 to teach both literature and—where he shined—Latin. There was mathematician Adrienne Rayl who, with Campbell, held the longest tenure of anyone in any of UA's Birmingham operations; he had started teaching mathematics in 1936 in the old clapboard house on Sixth Avenue North. There was Percy B. ("Corky") Reed, a behavioral scientist trained in Tuscaloosa's own excellent program in experimental psychology, who spent weekends on his boat docked at Dauphin Island, below Mobile, where he dragged for shrimp to use in his laboratory but occasionally boiled, chilled, and ate most of them before they could reach Birmingham. There was Charles Wilson, a teacher education specialist also trained in Tuscaloosa whom Campbell soon would name to serve as associate dean. And then there were the historians. There was Jack D. L. Holmes—New Jersey native, star student of the great Hubert Herring at the University of Texas. There was Virginia Van der Veer Hamilton, already a seasoned professional from AP reporting in Washington, D.C., and from her public relations work at BSC during the tough if exciting era of Henry King Stanford. The gutsy Hamilton had left BSC in the mid-1960s to be the second woman to complete a Ph.D. in history at UA. Still taking a few courses and with her dissertation ahead of her, she arrived at the Birmingham Center in September 1965 and became one of the leading faculty of the emergent university; she was also a rising star among history faculty nationwide because of her exceptional abilities as a writer. Finally there was Gardner McCullom with a brand-new doctorate in teacher education from UA, who would corner state representative Frank House on the Bessemer golf course and not let him finish his round before he had promised to support a special CGS appropriation.[34]

By December 1, the faculty leadership committee had developed a diversified program to be offered through seven primary units. There would be four professional education units: the Division of Business Administration chaired by John E. Lewis; the Division of Engineering chaired by Joseph Appleton; the Division of (Teacher) Education chaired by Fain A. Guthrie; and the Division of Allied Health Sciences, formed out of University Hospital programs in occupational and physical therapy, dietetics, and radiology, chaired by Charles H. Winkler, an Austin, Texas, native and long-time medical center neurobiologist.

In anticipation of at least twenty years of burgeoning undergraduate enrollment, the planning group elected not to have a conventional arts and sciences college but instead three additional primary units: the Division of Natural Sciences and Mathematics, to be chaired by Roger W. Hanson, the Minnesota native and a faculty member in the Department of Pharmacology in the medical center since 1953 who had worked hard to change race relations in the state; the Division of Social Sciences, to be chaired by George E. Passey, a Massachusetts native who had helped build the experimental psychology program at UA before going to Georgia Tech, only to return to Alabama for the new division post in Birmingham; and the Division of Humanities, chaired by John Coley.[35]

Through these seven divisions CGS would offer a full array of undergraduate majors and minors and select graduate programs as well as wide-ranging noncredit courses for the surrounding urban constituency. The adoption of UA's baccalaureate degree requirements, not to mention tuition and fee structure, would facilitate what Campbell and Volker correctly anticipated as the major influx of Birmingham students who had initially enrolled on the Tuscaloosa campus but who now could transfer to their hometown campus and pursue a degree while developing a career or meeting family responsibilities. They chose a different route, however, on the matter of the academic calendar. To better serve an urban population in need of as many "start-up" times as possible—people working while going to college—they adopted a quarter calendar. Yet to facilitate transfer students from UA and from the developing state two-year college system, they implemented semester credit hours, with each course incorporating sufficient "contact hours" to justify semester credits. As logical as this planning seemed, over time the hybrid system would defy classification as either a semester or a quarter system. Students and faculty alike simply would refer to "fall *term*."[36]

Campbell's planning group also laid plans for faculty recruitment. The college would enter the upcoming 1967 winter term with 35 full-time faculty and 50 adjuncts. By the fall of 1969, 120 full-time faculty would be needed, and to get moving on this massive hiring they planned to fill at least 20 new slots over the next six to nine months.[37] Moreover, under the careful eye of Clay Sheffield, Campbell's recent appointee as director of student affairs, they also developed a catalog. To reinforce the idea that CGS was opening to serve an urban population, the catalog published a class schedule from 8 a.m. to 10:00 p.m., Monday through Friday; the offices for student records and advising would be open from 9:00 a.m. to 8:00 p.m. Monday through Friday and 9:00 a.m. to 12:00 p.m. on Saturday. Campbell briefly considered a separate "evening division," but immediately dismissed it as "sending the wrong signal"—"night students were just as important as day students and in many cases they were the same people, modern working citizens." The start-up library located on the second floor of the CGS building, developed under the part-time direction of Virginia Hamilton, kept the same hours as student advising offices, plus Saturday and Sunday afternoons.[38]

When classes began on January 4, 1967, Campbell was already at work on the vital next step. He was on the telephone lining up a state appropriation to cover faculty salary commitments and operating needs for the fall of 1967–68. The golf course promise Frank House had given Gardner McCullom had to be followed by much more.

Under the plan by which UAB would receive its own state appropriation, and counting on "the understanding" Campbell had with "folks close to" Wallace that a special session of the legislature would increase funding for education, Campbell and Volker set their sights on the CGS budget moving from $280,000 for 1966–67 to $900,000 for 1967–68. Then they drove the ninety miles down to Montgomery for a personal visit with Governor Wallace. They took Jim Simpson with them: he was the single most powerful supporter of recently deposed Eugene ("Bull") Connor, the senior and scholarly partner in the Lang, Simpson law firm, and the man some identify most with brokering U.S. Steel's crucial support for Connor's racist grip on Birmingham. Indeed, while Simpson represented so much of what Volker and Campbell opposed, they badly needed this indefatigable former state senator and leader in the Jefferson County delegation. Simpson had given a young George Wallace his first job as a clerk on Goat Hill, and if Wallace ever valued anything other than his own power it was loyalty to those who had helped him. Campbell recalled that the three sat down in front of Wallace. With all four parties knowing the business at hand, Simpson got right to the point.

> Simpson: Governor, I just want to ask you one question.
> Wallace: What's that Mr. Jim?
> Simpson: Governor, are you going to give us the money?[39]

Although the Birmingham contingency departed without a firm commitment, they were encouraged by the governor's parting words spoken loudly but directly at "the Doctor" (Volker): "Mr. Jim got me started. It's hard to say no to him." Here is one of the most personally revealing, if murky, statements Wallace ever uttered. No doubt it was the exciting priority of personal politics, rather than any large view of society, that most motivated the governor.[40]

As he had done before, Volker had proven to be the careful pragmatist. He had employed one of the scions of Alabama's Old Guard, not just a noted segregationist but a leader of the historic Big Mules alliance between Birmingham industrialists and Black Belt landowners, to garner political influence and, he hoped, money to build an urban educational institution that would soon have the highest percentage of black students in any major research university in America. And Simpson was only too flattered to be asked for help.[41]

That done, three days later Volker and Campbell returned to Montgomery to visit a more likely ally, the moderate Democratic lieutenant governor out of north Alabama, Albert Brewer, who presided over the state Senate. They pled the case of social progress for Alabama's urban areas and the need for place-bound citizens, many of whom were black, to get a college education. Brewer would recollect, "I listened carefully but I don't recall giving them a concrete answer." Seven months later, however, in July when the special session for education funding got down to the last day, and the rural delegations were still trying to do what they usually did—block any "liberal project" headed for Jefferson County—Brewer, noticing that the powerful Crenshaw County senator, Alton Turner, had left the chamber, came down from his chair, made a brief talk on behalf of the new College of General Studies in Birmingham, then quickly returned to his chair and hammered through a call for a vote before Turner returned. Brewer could "not recall" if he and Wallace and Turner had this all planned in advance. But the CGS had its money—not $900,000 but $1.1 million. From the gallery overlooking the Senate floor, Campbell caught Brewer's eye with a solemn and heartfelt stare of gratitude. Then he and Volker drove on back up to Birmingham. Campbell would remember "this [as] one of the best days of my life at the University."[42]

In the broadest sense there was more at work here than the constant political maneuvers and personal contacts of Volker and Campbell, which were essential for high-level university leaders. These and other massive increases in state funding for UAB also could be attributed to the fact that the shrewd "quarterback-of-a-lobbyist" named J. Rudolph Davidson (soon to be Campbell's son-in-law) had signed on as full-time director of state governmental affairs at UAB. These increases could be traced even more so to Davidson's old employer and friend, George Wallace, who had decided that "investments in education" represented the best investment a state could make. This made Volker a "true believer" when it came to advice from Davidson regarding Wallace's "strange brand of conservatism and liberalism."[43] Yet it also foretold that alongside these desperately needed gains for the education of everyday and poor Alabamians would be the creation of a two-year college system.

Initially the idea of Wallace's House floor leader, the shrewd Rankin Fite, this system found Wallace's strong support as a way for him to deliver political favors and, ostensibly, as a means of creating educational opportunities and economic activity—jobs—at a time when out-of-state investors stayed clear of "Wallace's racist Alabama." In the process, however, Wallace let the two-year system become not only dominated by political appointees, precisely the way Fite had envisioned it, but overbuilt to the extent that (despite its inclusion of some excellent campuses) it came to represent one of the most tragically inefficient uses of tax dollars anywhere in America. The victims of this tragedy were thousands upon thousands of poor people of Alabama, black and white. Wallace consistently said he stood for "the working man" and "the little man." Yet he never sought to use his virtually dictatorial power to rid Alabama of a regressive tax structure, in which most tax dollars came not from wealthy owners of large tracts of land (some of whom lived out of state) or from corporations but from poor people— through sales taxes they paid on food and drugs and taxes they paid on their paltry incomes. To the contrary, with the major assistance of Fite, through the two-year college system (initially duplicated, like four-year public institutions, to avoid racial integration) Wallace launched the state onto a grossly inefficient use of the "little man's" hard-earned tax dollars.[44]

Although the CGS became a long overdue step toward meeting some of the needs of urban Alabamians—needs met a century earlier outside the South—this happened in an overall context of weak public policy. And here lie the central ironies behind the expanding state support for CGS and, indeed, much of the growth of UAB during the late 1960s and 1970s. Given the political reality of the times, only one person, George Wallace, could have filtered the process to achieve a larger net gain for a benighted state. Wallace was not about to apply such a filter, however, for along with inefficiency the filter would have diminished his expanding power. Yet if it had not been for Davidson's earlier career with Wallace, the "new money" delivered to UAB via political connections likely would not have been available. These core issues produced much of the serendipitous, yet excitingly complex, daily life of Volker and his team.

Medical Center Expansion

While Campbell was launching CGS, Volker, Charles McCallum, and Dick Hill had been bringing more developments to the medical center. Here would be the greatest single surge in medical center programs since Kracke's start-up in 1945.

In 1963 Hill had replaced Kendrick Hare with Herschell Paul Bentley, a Mississippian with medical training at UA and the University of Minnesota, as head of the Department of Pediatrics.[45] By late summer 1964 the new chair working with Hill not only had reunited but expanded the joint programs of Children's Hospital and the Department of Pediatrics, a cooperation expanded even more after 1968 when Bentley left and was succeeded by John W. Benton, an Enterprise, Alabama, native with an M.D. from UA. By the summer of 1964, moreover, Hill's interdisciplinary hire, Claude Bennett, was at work in his new molecular biology laboratory. And in July 1965 the old Hillman Hospital nursing residence hall reached completion as the Roy R. Kracke Clinical Services Building. It stood as the only physical marker commemorating the individual who had first led the medical center and who had planted the seeds for something far larger.[46]

There were setbacks, too. On October 24, 1965, Champ Lyons suddenly died of a brain tumor. After a funeral service in Birmingham, he was buried in Magnolia Cemetery in Mobile. Granted, the Department of Surgery still had a first-class senior surgeon in Sterling Edwards. A Birmingham native and a graduate of the University of Pennsylvania's medical school, Edwards had joined the department in 1952 and had become well known for developing a prefabricated artificial artery that became important in artificial heart research. Still, even with Edwards in the wings, by any measurement Lyons's death was a huge loss not just in terms of skill but national profile and leadership. By the mid-1960s Lyons had become experienced in open heart surgery, not to mention well connected nationally through his cousin, Senator Lister Hill. Indeed, Lyons chaired the board of regents of the National Library of Medicine, which he had helped create with his famous relative. In short, one of the "two gems" was gone. No sooner had Lyons's funeral taken place than Hill was at work searching for a replacement.[47]

With yet another one of "Tinsley's boys," T. Joseph Reeves, chairing the search committee, Dick Hill moved into the search aided by the external consultancy services of Francis D. Moore, Mosley Professor of Surgery at Harvard University and chief of surgery at Brigham Hospital in Boston. Even with Moore's assistance, however, Hill and Reeves struggled through a year of frustration as few major figures seemed interested in coming to "Bull Connor's Birmingham." Then, in June 1966, an abrupt turnaround occurred. Moore called Hill to say that John W. Kirklin at the Mayo Clinic in Rochester, Minnesota, was more than interested. Here was one of the pioneers in open heart surgery and one of the foremost surgeons in the world.[48]

Elated, Hill notified Volker that Kirklin might well leave Rochester to take Lyons's place as the Charles and Fay Fletcher Kerner Professor of Surgery, chair of the Department of Surgery, and chief surgeon at the hospital. The Harvard-trained physician was at a stage in his career when he placed a premium on freedom to work, freedom to develop a transplant program, and freedom to develop a department. "It was merely a question of whether I wanted to keep on doing, the last fifteen years of my life, what I had done the first fifteen, or whether I wanted to do something different . . . make a contribution to surgery in general . . . bring into being some of my ideas about a department of surgery and the training of surgeons." When Hill explained Volker's philosophy of "hire good people and get out of their way" to Kirklin, he became even more enthusiastic. At the time Kirklin also had an offer to be chief of surgery at Children's Hospital in Boston, no doubt the premier children's hospital in the nation. Still, despite the lack of comparable hospital facilities whether one looked at the Mayo or to Boston, Kirklin would recall that "the opportunity [in Birmingham] was better, freer." And the cause was not hurt, as Kirklin emphasized during his recruitment, that Birmingham offered several opportunities for him and his wife, Peggy, to stable their beloved horses close to their home—this was not possible in Rochester or Boston.[49]

A longtime admirer of Kirklin put a different spin on the rationale for his move to UAB and the recruitment of others close to his league.

When we told folks like Kirklin they could come here and build something with no interference, what we really were saying is that we understood the great-doctor ego: we were saying "You can build an empire in Birmingham—no barriers. In fact, if you haven't built an empire within a year, you're either sick or no good." And, of course, as the place matured we would pay the price for letting this be the founding ethic. Still, it was either do it that way or, realistically, not at all in view of how poor our funding and general state support were and how few people were willing to come to the South of George Wallace in those years.[50]

But there was an additional "Southern factor," a positive one. Unlike other physicians who had spent their careers in the North, Kirklin—born in Muncie, Indiana—believed that Birmingham's racial problems were similar to those "everywhere else in the country, and that given just a little bit of luck [the South] might have an opportunity to work these problems out better than some other parts of the country." Although to confirm that at least some change seemed in the offing, he telephoned the biochemist Roger Hanson—the two had crossed paths in Minnesota—for more details on social activism in Birmingham; Kirklin did not see "the down side to Birmingham" as a developing medical city that many national-level professionals did. (Some nationally known health scientists did not even realize that the UA Medical Center was in Birmingham. In 1960, Birmingham native Donald Kahn, as a recent UA medical graduate interviewing for a surgical residency at Harvard, encountered the question: "Now where is that medical school you went to, Tuscaloosa?") At any rate, on September 1, 1966, Kirklin moved his seventy-hour work weeks to Birmingham, accompanied by his former student and junior colleague from the Mayo, Albert D. Pacifico, a native of Brooklyn, New York. Within three years Edwards moved to the University of New Mexico medical center to become chairman of the Department of Surgery.[51]

The ultimate significance of Kirklin's move would be more than developing a major surgery program with his son, James, and with young Arnold Diethelm and others whom he gradually moved to Birmingham—a program with internationally acclaimed specialties in heart and kidney transplants. It would be more than coauthoring the definitive textbook *Cardiac Surgery* (to be published some twenty years later) and over time more than helping create a new outpatient clinic named in his honor.[52] These and other medical and institutional accomplishments likely were eclipsed simply by the statement made by Kirklin's leaving the Mayo to come to Birmingham. At a time when many progressive citizens of Birmingham were beginning to believe what they heard about their city, that "Bombingham" was a dirty, racist place certainly beyond reconstruction, Kirklin's arrival in the fall of 1966 began the slow revitalization of an *entire city's* heart. At that time, the visceral changes underway in the city's leadership, government, and economy were too far under the radar for most people in the city to know what was about to happen. However, Birmingham citizens could indeed focus on Tuscaloosa perhaps having the No. 1 football team in the nation but Birmingham the No. 1 heart surgeon in the world. Although these statements perhaps added to a counterproductive competition between UAB and UA, they did provide "psychic relief from Bull and the police dogs." The Kirklin story helped desperately needed civic leaders—black and white leaders organizing through such groups as Operation New Birmingham—begin to believe that a new Birmingham could be built and that a public university with a major medical center could be a key to this reconstruction. In the words of an intense young Miles College biology professor then in transition to city politics, Richard Arrington, "All of us who were then trying to find a way to a new city took Kirklin's arrival as a strong indication of the future. Dick [Hill] really did something when he did that one."[53]

Other less heralded but vital developments justified this feeling. In June 1965, Hill and Volker opened an additional two floors on the psychiatric hospital with more philanthropy from the Smolian family. By March 1966, Volker announced the establishment of a third primary unit in the medical center, the School of Health Services Administration. With Matthew McNulty continuing to serve a short while longer as director of University Hospitals plus dean of the new school, the unit offered graduate work in hospital administration as well as training for hospital workers. This had been evolving as part of the hospital and was funded out of urban renewal allocations.[54]

Moreover, in late August 1966, with Kirklin in town for social visits and a lecture, Volker dedicated the new 100-bed north wing of the hospital, which had been designed for short-term care of the mentally ill and for mental health educational programs; one floor was for children and the other for geriatric patients. Surgery and radiology also picked up new space in the addition as did emergency room services, ending the historic, though badly outdated, emergency clinic at Hillman. The $4.2 million addition had been financed by a grant from the Hill-Harris program of the Department of Health, Education, and Welfare (HEW) and from a state bond issue passed in 1960 after a crucial endorsement by Birmingham commissioner "Bull" Connor.[55] In November 1966 Hill and Volker renamed the Health Sciences Research Building, including its new 45,000-square-foot addition, the Lyons-Harrison Research Building. They took the occasion to host the tenth anniversary celebration of the U.S. government's Health Research Facilities Act, which had made the building possible. Senator Lister Hill along with noted officials of HEW and the Public Health Service came to Birmingham for the event. The combination of the two names on the building captured considerable attention, even making the front page of the national newsletter *NIH Trends*.[56]

Next came a major development in terms of public perception of the hospital. In part because of Kirklin's appearance, the hospital made *Ladies Home Journal*'s February 1967 list of "America's Ten Best Hospitals," a coup that reverberated throughout Alabama as John L. Wright, of Selma, took over public relations for the hospital. Likewise, in the October 1967 issue of the *Journal of the American Medical Association* (*JAMA*) the UA medical school captured a major accolade. Two dozen medical deans in the South were polled on two questions: (1) "In terms of research, what medical school is on top?"; and (2) "What school is progressing most rapidly?" The answer to question number one was Duke, to question number two was UAB. Everywhere they went, Hill and Volker took copies of these articles—from private parties to Rotary Club talks to lobbying visits to Montgomery. As a result, the historic "indigent reputation" of the UAB Medical Center and hospital began to dissipate. Even "over the mountain" residents started to go there for treatment. Shortly thereafter, the local press bannered the AMA's appraisal, repeating what Hill had stated in the article. If Volker and Hill had decided to go with a senior individual like Kirklin to reinvigorate clinical services and instruction, they had not excluded risks with less experienced minds in the new frontiers of research on diseases. With clear reference to Associate Professor of Microbiology Bennett and UAB's now being among the top twenty-five medical centers funded by the National Institutes of Health (NIH), the *Birmingham News* praised the Birmingham strategy "to gamble on several bright young men . . . reasoning that without good, young investigators, the distinguished senior man would only stagnate."[57]

Other developments in the medical center reinforced this point. As if to reassert a Birmingham influence first established by Kracke, the VA had decided it should construct a "research bridge" across Nineteenth Street connecting the VA Hospital with the Lyons-Harrison Research Building and the whole University Hospital complex. Here, dedicated in September 1967, was the first physical connection between a VA hospital and a university hospital in the nation. At the same time, to no one's great surprise, Dick Hill was rising from vice chairman to chairman of the Special Medical Advisory Group of the VA.[58] The same year Wayne and Sara Finley used NIH funds to expand their operations into the Laboratory for Medical Genetics and began to host international seminars in this rapidly developing field of science.[59] Other key personalities arrived at about the same time: Richard D. Morin, a chemist in the Psychiatry Department with a specialty in hallucinogenic amphetamines; the Australian Hazel Gore in pathology and in gynecology; Anthony C. L. Barnard, a physicist who launched computer science studies first in the medical center and then across the university; Jiri F. Mestecky and Raymond H. Hiramoto, founding forces in microbiology; and Thomas W. Weatherford III, a relative of the noted Native American chief William (Red Eagle) Weatherford and one of the foundation blocks in periodontology.[60]

As of 1968, however, certainly one of the most exciting new hires had to be the biochemist Charles E. Bugg. At twenty-seven and already having completed a postdoctoral stint at CalTech, Bugg was known as a potential leader in the new molecular revolution because of his intense pursuit of "X-ray crystallographic studies of nucleic acid components." His marketability also was not hurt by the fact that his mentor at CalTech was Linus Pauling, the only individual to win two unshared Nobel Prizes. To follow through on early plans for the joint health sciences, though Bugg's primary appointment was in biochemistry and his secondary in medicine, McCallum covered Bugg's salary out of the School of Dentistry with funds Volker had acquired through a basic research grant from the National Institute of Dental

Research. Bugg soon would be recognized as an international expert on using crystallography for drug design and far more.[61] Years later, reared back in his desk chair, he reflected on the significance of his own inter-disciplinary hire.

> I wasn't a dentist. By the same token, I must say that's the way the place was built—people working together, not worrying about dis-ciplinary boundaries. The place was just too young to have an en-trenched outlook, and then along came the molecular revolution and that characteristic of youth made us prime for the new way of doing science—interdisciplinary. It was that wide open intellectual envi-ronment, plus the people. . . . The search committee wanted to go to a colleague's birthday party that night. I got to go along. Was that a party! And Joe [Volker] set the pace! I knew this was the place for me. Not stuffy. Plenty alive.[62]

The growth continued. In 1968, while Hill was helping recruit Bugg, the medical dean also captured an NIH National Heart Institute grant to es-tablish the Cardiovascular Research and Training Center (CVRTC). Shortly thereafter he turned over the center to Thomas N. James, a recently recruited professor of cardiology, and by the early 1970s the unit would bring to the Birmingham medical center more NIH funding for cardiovascular research than went to any other medical center in the nation. Also in 1968, with the leadership of Kirklin, Hill opened the Alabama Transplant Center; Arnold Diethelm performed the first kidney transplant in the medical center not long afterward.[63] At the same time Kirklin did something he had wanted to do since his Mayo days: he launched a surgeon's assistant training program in the Department of Surgery, one of the first such programs in the nation following the founding of the discipline at Duke in 1964. The UAB program was soon broadened, renamed the physician's assistant program, and relo-cated in the School of Community and Allied Health.[64] Moreover, under Peter B. Peacock, the Department of Preventive Medicine and Public Health became the Department of Public Health and Epidemiology. The second en-dowed chair appeared: Ruth Lawson Hanson donated funds for a chair in diabetes, and with Volker's strong approval Hill named Buris Ray Boshell to the chair. Hill captured more NIH funding to begin the development of the Myocardial Infarction Research Unit (MIRU) in University Hospital. Com-mitted to the study of "hemodynamic and anatomic abnormalities occur-ring during and after heart attacks," two cardiologists, Charles E. Rackley and Richard O. Russell, Jr., would sustain this key element of research with continuing support from the National Heart, Lung, and Blood Institute of the NIH while also saving lives, including that of the new mayor of Birmingham, George Seibels.[65]

Hill also brought onboard three new chairs—Guenter Corssen in anesthesiology, Patrick H. Linton in psychiatry, and Charles E. Flowers, Jr., in obstetrics and gynecology. An early advocate of "family-centered" medical practice, Flowers's arrival from Baylor University represented the first full-time chair for obstetrics and gynecology; private practice physician Nick Jones had run it on an acting basis since its inception in 1955. Flowers would become nationally known for his progressive, if controversial, stances on the reproductive rights of women and the humanization of women's medical treatment.[66]

Other medical center units also developed during this period. In 1968 the new chair in pediatrics, John W. Benton, with the aid of NIH funding, established the Center for Developmental and Learning Disorders (CDLD), which was committed to training pediatricians in the diagnosis and treatment of children with such disorders. One year later the name "Sparks" was added to the name of the center in honor of the governor who, back in 1944–45, showed the political fortitude to bring the start-up four-year medical school to Birmingham.[67] More new developments occurred almost daily. McCallum captured an NIH grant to found the Institute of Dental Research and named Wallace Mann as the new chair in periodontics. To complement Bennett's interdisciplinary research, Volker split the responsibilities of graduate programs administration and grants administration, which he personally had managed through much of the 1950s and which his chief aide, John Dunbar, had run since Volker had become vice president in 1962. In July 1965 Dunbar assumed the single role of coordinator of research grants. Soon, when he moved to the NIH, Dunbar was succeeded by an assistant professor of biochemistry, Birmingham native Robert P. Glaze, whose physician-father, Andrew, had made the first donation of books to the fledgling medical school library in 1946. Longtime member of the joint basic sciences faculty, Samuel B. Barker, then took the position of director of graduate programs. To further advance the interdisciplinary research agenda, in 1965 Hill and McCallum changed the name of the Department of Physiology to the Department of Physiology and Biophysics. Warren S. Rehm, who had joined the faculty the year before as a specialist on the neutral carrier exchange mechanism for the secretion of gastric acid, continued as chair. The same year they created the Department of Biostatistics under the chairmanship of David C. Hurst, then in 1966 formed the Department of Biomathematics, which focused on nonstatistical applications of mathematics to biological sciences, with Edward A. Sallin as chair.[68]

Also in 1966, McCallum and Hill created the Department of Biomedical Engineering. Although the new chair, Seymour S. West, retitled the department the Department of Engineering Biophysics, biomedical engineering began to grow as an interdisciplinary field consistently nurtured by another new hire, Jack E. Lemons. At the same time they recruited Josiah C. Macy, the New York mathematician currently director of the Physiology Computer Center at Albert Einstein College of Medicine (in Bronx, New York) to become director of the newly formed Division of Biophysical Sciences. On Macy's request, they then created within this division the Department of Information Sciences, which Macy also would manage while he established a computer center. Although this center emerged in the anachronistic setting (Doric columns, small but still white) of the Life of Georgia Building, it still represented a gigantic step of moving the medical center into the still pubescent revolution in high technology.[69] Still more interdisciplinary development occurred in 1968 when McCallum created the School of Dentistry's Department of Biomaterials, chaired by Theodore E. Fisher, and acquired funding to build the Regional Maxillofacial Prosthetics Treatment and Training Center.[70]

Then in March 1968, alongside the announcement that UAB extramural funding for research had reached $18 million, Volker broke ground on what would become the Rust Computer Center (the local Rust Foundation contributed $150,000 toward the project), a modern building prominently facing Eighth Avenue in the medical center (leaving the old Life of Georgia Building, at least for a few years, for other start-up endeavors). The Rust Center would expand the university's capability in this exciting new technology so vital to virtually every interdisciplinary endeavor as well as the general management of the institution. It would be guided by a variety of individuals including Gerald A. Hutchison, James Murdock, Janet Wixson, Jeanne B. Alexander, and Sheila Sanders.[71] By July other ground-breakings had occurred. Aided by an $8.9 million NIH grant, there soon would be a new medical center library—the Lister Hill Library for the Health Sciences, including a specially designed complex for the Reynolds Historical Collection. By 1971 the longtime librarian, Sarah Cole Brown, would be able to offer a modern facility to physicians and medical students. As state funds came through, a massive new basic sciences building would be joined to the new library—both facing the increasingly busy Eighth Avenue South.[72]

More glacial organizational developments also occurred. In October 1967 personnel matters on the Birmingham campus finally ceased being a hodgepodge of uncoordinated departmental mandates and occasional memoranda from Tuscaloosa: Rose let Volker establish his own Office of Personnel Services and hire Leonard D. Harper, who had worked at both the University of Oklahoma and the University of Illinois Medical Center, to be the founding director. Moreover, in May 1968 Rose obtained board approval to get Volker some help in managing medical center affairs. He named Volker executive vice president for Birmingham affairs, then Volker named Paul Brann his vice president for fiscal affairs and convened a search committee to advise him on filling the health affairs vice presidency. The new executive vice president soon announced that Dick Hill would be leaving the position of medical dean to assume the role of vice president for health affairs. Few were surprised.[73]

Then it was Hill's turn to form a search committee. By September 1968 Clifton Meador, a Selma native and product of the Vanderbilt Medical School, had agreed to leave his faculty position in the Department of Medicine to be the medical dean. (This made the Meadors a two-dean family in Alabama: Clifton's brother, Daniel, had been UA Law School dean since 1966.) Hill and Meador immediately went to work on the overhaul of the basic medical curriculum. Over a two-year period their faculty committees took long, hard looks at the four-year curriculum, the "modern curriculum" urged in the 1920s by the Flexner Report and implemented with the move of the medical school from Tuscaloosa to Birmingham in 1945. For reasons associated with physician shortages nationwide as well as new emphases on specialization acquired through post-M.D. internships, the faculty committee ultimately came forward with a more modern three-year curriculum (basic medical science, core clinical experience, individualized experience), which would be implemented with the freshman class of 1970. Moreover, during the mid-1960s Meador had established an enviable record researching the regulation of adrenal function in Cushing's disease under the auspices of Hill's (NIH-funded) General Clinical Research Center. In subsequent years, Dean Meador demonstrated that he also knew how to make this type of fast-breaking medical knowledge reach immediately into the lives of patients and physicians located far beyond Birmingham.[74]

As these administrative and curriculum changes were taking place other developments were unfolding. To pursue a quiet promise he had made Volker in the early 1960s, in December 1966 President Rose announced that UA's School of Nursing, established in 1950 on the Tuscaloosa campus as a strange salve for the movement of the medical school to Birmingham, no longer would admit students and that all nursing programs soon would be offered through UAB; that is, the School of Nursing was being moved to Birmingham and combined with nursing education programs begun in Hillman even before there was a medical school. In August 1967, as planned, Dean Florence Hixson moved her entire unit to Birmingham and began reporting first to Volker and shortly thereafter to Vice President Hill, now giving the medical center four primary units.[75]

Still, Rose let the Tuscaloosa campus keep its state-allocated budget for nursing education to use on other endeavors, including—oddly—a replacement nursing school for the Tuscaloosa campus. Even though "the legislature had been appropriating these funds for nursing for some twenty years," Jeff Bennett recalled, "several crucial board members would not let Frank deliver on his promise to Birmingham unless we kept the money in Tuscaloosa. . . . The promise did not overtly stipulate that the budget was included, so it did not travel with the school to Birmingham." More to the point, already faced with the perennial problem of little funding for indigent care in the hospital, Hill now had the additional burden of an indigent nursing school. It would take almost a decade of reallocating already committed funds and working with the legislature for Hill to develop the replacement funds.[76] From other perspectives, however, the move was good, and Hixson seemed happy. "Most university schools of nursing are in the medical centers of the respective schools," she would tell the Metropolitan Business and Women's Club at the Relay House in November 1967, the new private eating club in downtown Birmingham. In the progressive setting of Birmingham with its medical center she foresaw great expansion of the program. Out of temporary facilities in the CGS building, she started classes in September 1967 with 276 baccalaureate students and 32 master's students, plus another 60 still in Tuscaloosa with plans to be in Birmingham soon. Hixson anticipated "500 students in our program in the next three to four years . . . and . . . a graduate track . . . leading to the doctorate." In March 1969 she hired a specialist in psychiatric nursing, Delois Skipwith. A Tuscaloosa native educated at UA and Indiana University, she was the first tenure-track black faculty member not just in the School of Nursing but in the entire Birmingham operation. Then Hixson retired. In July 1970, Marie O'Koren, Hixson's associate dean and the individual who had managed the daily details of the move to Birmingham, succeeded her and immediately wrote a grant providing $2 million in federal and state funds for a new nursing education building, to open by 1971 on Eighth Avenue, directly across the street from the Hill Library.[77]

At the same time, a fifth primary academic unit was developing in the medical center: a school of optometry. In the late 1940s Alston Callahan and Dean Kracke had opened a small optical dispensary in Hillman Hospital so that patients would not have to obtain glasses through certain private practice ophthalmologists who, they felt, were receiving kickbacks from opticians. Even so, Callahan long had urged Volker to stay clear of a separate *school* of optometry, a point he urged even more fervently on both Volker and Hill as the Alabama Optometric Association (ALOA) began to lobby for such an initiative in the early 1960s.[78]

Forces of history and politics would not see the ophthalmologists prevail. The Kennedy-Johnson Medicaid/Medicare programs included a Bureau of Health Manpower report that showed the Southeast's ratio of optometrists to population as the worst in the nation and the Alabama ratio of 4.8 to 100,000 as next to the bottom in its region, with Mississippi at the bottom. U.S. congressman Kenneth Roberts, of Piedmont, Alabama, was the chair of the Health Manpower Committee and in 1963 saw to it that an Anniston optometrist and chairman of the Health Manpower Development Committee of the Southern Council of Optometrists, Donald Springer, testified in Washington on the need for federal funds to help solve Alabama's optometric manpower problem. Unlike optometrists in other states, however, Springer and others of the ALOA wanted such an initiative to occur within the context of public higher education—Springer had completed his O.D. at Ohio State University—where it could have the qualitative development associated with university life.[79]

By the mid-1960s three developments significantly increased the momentum for this project. First, Springer met with Volker to discuss locating an optometry school within what would become UAB, vaguely mentioning that Auburn would want the program if UA did not. Volker responded, as Springer recalled, with his "characteristically cagey words." He told Springer that ophthalmologists, that is, those with an M.D., in his medical center would strongly oppose such a plan and hence he could not show "any type of open support for it." Yet he also advised Springer that he needed to have a locally produced proposal for the legislature which, while incorporating national and regional data, focused on Alabama's needs and why Alabama higher education should embrace this cause. Springer replied that he had anticipated this and was in fact "prepared to approach Harold Wershow," a Penn-trained sociologist and social worker who had joined the early Extension Center faculty in 1963, about developing the proposal. Always the pragmatic liberal, Volker nixed this plan: "Wershow is capable," Springer recalled Volker saying, "but he [had just] protested for racial change by walking in the Selma march and that will work against you in the legislature." Instead, Volker recommended a scientist at Southern Research Institute, Sheldon Shaffer, for the work, and shortly thereafter the Shaffer Report was part of Springer's arsenal. Second, the ALOA in league with state senator Alton Turner of Luverne, Alabama, who chaired Alabama's Joint Legislative Committee on Finance and Taxation, pushed through the Alabama legislature an increase in the annual license renewal fee for optometrists from $12 to $112. Most of the new funds would be earmarked for helping start an optometric education program in one of Alabama's universities. Third, and most important, by January 1967 the optometry lobby delivered passage of a resolution in the legislature for a joint committee to study the need for an optometry school in the state.[80]

Callahan now found himself publicly aligned with his former opponents, Joseph Dixon and other ophthalmologists who viewed optometrists as lacking in sufficient medical training, although Callahan could support an optometry *program* with restricted curriculum—still anathema to the optometry lobby. If there were more federal or state funds for eye-care education, Callahan and other ophthalmologists, not to mention Hill, wanted the funds to enhance the Eye Foundation Hospital or the Department of Ophthalmology in the medical school rather than be used to start a new venture for which they held great skepticism. Callahan's board of the Eye Foundation Hospital, led by Frank Spain, took on the fight by orchestrating a flood of letters to legislators. The Medical Association of the State of Alabama (MASA) and the Jefferson County Medical Society also supported Callahan's position. In only three places, it seemed, had optometry been accepted into university settings: at Ohio State University, Indiana University, and the University of California–Berkeley. Otherwise, universities, especially university medical centers, had steered clear of optometry. Such programs had remained at the proprietary (privately owned) stage. This was the message that most Alabama physicians, including Hill, sent to Governor Lurleen Wallace and, after her death in May 1968, to her successor, Governor Albert Brewer.[81]

Still, with a well-organized response in the legislature orchestrated by Springer and voiced in the House by Roy Coshatt, a Pell City optometrist, and in the Senate by Turner, the ALOA countered that although they were not medical doctors, optometrists could diagnose and treat numerous eye problems at a lower cost than ophthalmologists could and thus increase public access to certain types of eye care. Shrewdly, Turner also convinced many others in Montgomery that physicians simply did not want the competition and the resultant loss of income. A few physicians agreed with the ALOA critique, including Tinsley Harrison, but they did not speak out. Rarely would physicians critique physicians in public. Ultimately, the ALOA succeeded in having the legislature's study, managed by Representative Hugh Merrill of Anniston, conclude that there was considerable need for an optometry school in an Alabama university.[82]

Next, the legislature and Governor Lurleen Wallace approved the establishment of a school of optometry and appropriated $50,000 a year for two years to fund the planning for such a program. At the same time, the legislature also asked Volker to submit a "needs assessment" for an optometry school's curriculum, faculty, space, and equipment, which he did.[83]

Then in the spring of 1969, when the Alabama legislature held hearings on proposed legislation to fund an optometry school and Hill received an invitation to testify, Volker instructed Hill to "follow [his] conscience, take the position on this issue that you think is best for Alabama." Hill continued to lobby against the project. At the same time, however, Volker was in close contact with Birmingham optometrist and city council member E. C. Overton; Volker wanted the ALOA to endorse the UAB Medical Center as the best location for the school *if* the program ever became a reality. In June, Hill went to Montgomery to testify against the plan. Despite his eloquent presentation of the ophthalmologists' arguments, Turner, Merrill, and others in the legislature had the vote wrapped up. The legislature not only embraced the report to create such a school *at UAB* but appropriated $200,000 for its establishment during fiscal year 1969–70 with additional funding of $300,000 for fiscal year 1970–71.[84]

Always pragmatic and reading the tea leaves on Goat Hill almost as well as anyone, as far back as December 1968 Volker had told Hill, Meador, and McCallum, "If it's going to be anywhere in the state it needs to be here. And if we are going to do it, let's do it right." Accordingly, Volker had assigned John Dunbar the task of writing a UAB proposal for $750,000 of federal construction monies to be folded in with initial state appropriations for optometry and ALOA-raised private funds to start the new unit. Likewise, in 1968 ALOA had launched a national fund drive that by 1969 yielded $350,000 in cash and pledges. Even before the legislature's initial appropriation, Volker and Dunbar would have a telephone commitment for NIH funds contingent upon the actual state appropriations, all of which soon became reality. Complicated business.[85]

Likewise, Volker and Hill moved swiftly to land a dean to run the operation. In some ways resembling Volker himself in 1948—someone young, who wanted to take a risk, and was curious about the South, though more "in your face" than Volker when confrontation arose—Henry B. Peters had just become an associate dean of optometry at Berkeley when he accepted Volker's offer. Later recalling that he "must have been insane, for when [he] arrived for work in August 1969 state funds had not yet been appropriated and even after that decent funds were a long time in coming," the Porsche-driving Californian proceeded to deliver just as Kracke and Volker had done some twenty years earlier. By September 1970, Peters not only had hired an initial faculty but was instructing a "pilot class" of eight students and writing grant applications to obtain badly needed funds for the unit's programmatic and physical growth.[86]

With the outcome of war clear, Volker, Hill, and Peters went to work building what shortly would be one of the premier optometry schools in the nation and certainly the most innovative. What few optometry programs there were with university connections, that is, those at Berkeley, Indiana, and Ohio State, had been located in applied optics programs in physics departments or had not been stand-alone departments within a university. UAB's School of Optometry was fully contained in a public university academic health center and with the inherent advantages of this setting. Peters employed the already established medical center philosophy of expanding critical mass by developing within the Birmingham VA Hospital the nation's first clinical teaching program in optometry. Into the UAB School of Optometry would be infused other influences of interdisciplinary health science, including the Vision Science Research Center and the Center for Biophysical Sciences and Engineering. Such innovative relationships were available only in a university setting.[87] To maximize this approach, after beginning the program in the Life of Georgia Building on Eighth Avenue (which also housed the start-up university computer center) Volker, by the 1970s, placed the new School of Optometry building squarely in the middle of the medical center, next door to the epicenter of Alabama ophthalmology, the Eye Foundation Hospital. Doing it "right" also meant doing it with all hatchets dulled if not exactly buried. Still, Volker never ceased working both sides of the fence on this issue: for years to come, when physicians asked him how UAB could have sponsored an optometry program, out came the pat response: "I asked for a school of public health [which would appear in 1981], and in its wisdom the legislature gave me an optometry program."[88]

Further Challenge from Mobile

Meanwhile, Volker and Hill had been deeply involved in another development of even greater statewide political ramifications: the move to create a second medical school in Mobile. By 1966, with USA buildings rising among majestic pine trees and vibrant azaleas on a massive block of land in west Mobile, Volker had begun to work through members of the Jefferson and Tuscaloosa delegations in the legislature—people who rarely did anything together—to block President Whiddon's openly advocated plan to build a USA medical school. After severely underestimating the Mobile-autonomy movement a few years earlier, Rose was not about to let Volker and Dick Hill go this one alone. All three began to publicize a fair question: If the state could not provide adequate funding for the medical school in Birmingham, what business did it have creating another one in Mobile? Far from threatened, Whiddon and other Mobilians rejoined that the tragic state of health care in Alabama as documented in the recent report of the Bureau of Health Manpower demonstrated the urgent need for more physicians. Another medical school, they said, was a critical step toward meeting this goal. And the message had the clout of realpolitik. By this time Whiddon had assembled a USA board of trustees capable of getting something done. Several board members were from powerful pro-Wallace ranks in the Alabama legislature, with crucial committee appointments capable of blocking the entire state education appropriation if they did not get what Whiddon wanted for "South."[89]

Volker and Hill, if not Rose, had a strong working relationship with Wallace and his wife, Lurleen, who had succeeded her husband in 1966. (The Alabama legislature, by narrow vote, had refused to amend the Alabama Constitution of 1901 to let George Wallace succeed himself, so he just ran his wife in his place.) They had become even more comfortable, however, with the New South liberal out of north Alabama, Lieutenant Governor Brewer. Not only had Brewer recently assisted the CGS funding for 1967–68, but he had been working with Volker and Hill to bring "rational planning" to Alabama higher education through sponsorship of the Alabama Commission on Higher Education.[90] The UAB team, joined by Rose, formed a strategy. If Mobile influences for the time being likely could control the Wallace team's position on the issue of a second medical school, Mrs. Wallace (though sick with cancer) seemed fully capable of finishing out her term and there was a strong sense that Brewer would then run for governor and win. Thus Volker and Hill decided to buy time on the Mobile issue and stick close to the one whom they thought would be Alabama's first New South governor, Brewer, ultimately counting on him to steer developments away from Whiddon's plan.[91]

Meanwhile, Whiddon kept the pressure on. In August 1966, Representative Mylan Engle introduced a resolution in the state House urging the USA board to move toward admitting medical students by the fall of 1972.[92] In response, Volker told the lieutenant governor that Hill would resign if the legislature created a new medical school while leaving the one in Birmingham in such an underfunded situation. Hill "may" have meant this at the time, but the threat also was "carefully orchestrated" by Volker, Hill, and Brewer to give Brewer "something to work with" in defending against Whiddon's opening charge. Brewer "politicked around" to the point at which Engle's resolution was not passed, mightily aided with the argument, quietly designed by Hill, Brewer, and the Alabama Medical Association lobbyist Bob Ingram, that the state should retain the Chicago consulting firm of Booz, Allen, and Hamilton (BAH) to assess Alabama's future needs in medical education. Given Hill's close connections with the AMA and in turn its close connection with this firm, it is an understatement to say that the consultants soon had the opportunity to study a carefully written paper, "The Development of a Second Medical School in the State of Alabama," in which Hill set forth all the reasons why the state should not establish a second medical school at USA. Seven months later, in November 1967, BAH delivered its findings. After stating the obvious fact that Alabama needed more physicians, they recommended the following: (1) the legislature should provide the funding for the UAB medical school to increase annual entrance enrollment from 80 to 100 by 1969 and to 125 by 1971; (2) with Birmingham expansion, the state should design a long-range plan for *possibly* reestablishing the two-year basic science medical program in Tuscaloosa and opening a similar program in Huntsville; and (3) with Birmingham expansion, the state should design a long-range plan for *possibly* developing an additional "four-year medical program" at Mobile. Volker, Hill, Rose, and Brewer always viewed the report as "balanced, even-handed," and "in a rational world an effective document." It urged more funding for the Birmingham operation while not denying that Mobile, as another major urban area, represented a logical place for the *possible* expansion of medical education. They just hoped such expansion, if it occurred, ultimately would happen under the joint auspices of Mobile General Hospital and the UA medical school.[93]

In March 1967 Tinsley Harrison had resurfaced after completing (with colleague Joe Reeves) another major book, *Principles and Problems of Ischemic Heart Disease* (1968), wrote to Dick Hill applauding this "Birmingham perspective" and offering prescient advice: "I am in complete agreement with everything you say about the unwisdom of development of a second medical school under the aegis of the University of South Alabama." Still, in his sixty-seven years Harrison had witnessed too much medical warfare to believe that whatever the impending BAH report would say could come close to settling the matter, regardless of who was governor. He recalled that when he had moved back to Alabama in 1950 "the smoke had still not cleared between Birmingham, Tuscaloosa, and Mobile, from the battle fought some 7 years before about the location of our present medical school." Well attuned to the "considerable feeling [still remaining] on the part of a group in Tuscaloosa and another group in Mobile, that their cities had been slighted," Harrison urged Hill and Volker to move fast in implementing a UA medical program in Mobile dedicated to clinical training even before such programs might be started in Tuscaloosa or Huntsville. Otherwise, there likely would be "a major battle in the Legislature and throughout the state" from which UA easily could emerge the loser.[94]

Subsequently encouraged by the door left ajar by the BAH report and aided significantly by USA board members also in the Alabama legislature, men such as Mylan Engle, L. W. Brannan, Ray Lolley, John M. Tyson, and Roland Cooper, the USA president undoubtedly had the same insight and began swift action toward the opposite goal.[95] Then came political developments of pivotal importance. Governor Lurleen Wallace died in May 1968; Albert Brewer automatically ascended to the governorship; then Alabamians denied Brewer a full term of his own when they yet again elected George Wallace as their governor. In short, these developments, as opposed to medicine or fiscal resources, would prove to be the deciding factors as to whether Alabama would have a second medical school.[96]

The Complexity of Social Change

In the spring of 1969, one year into Albert Brewer's two-year term as governor and with the movement for a USA medical school temporarily in check, the UA family implemented a change as progressive as Brewer himself. In January 1969 Frank Rose had announced his plans to leave Tuscaloosa and, indeed, all of higher education to spend the rest of his career chairing the board of General Computing Corporation in Washington, D.C. It was time to go, and he knew it. As winter gave way to spring, rumors spread through UA operations that Rose was leaving with the recommendation to the board and to Governor Brewer for a new administrative structure to succeed him. There is no evidence that in reaching this decision Rose gave any special consideration to his failed Mobile strategy as represented most poignantly in the ongoing political battle over a second medical school. Quizzed on this matter, one of Rose's closest advisors, Jeff Bennett, replied, "Frank was not really focused on these connections at this time. It was more of a general feeling of frustration with Alabama higher education under Wallace and with the board's unwillingness to give him more room to operate."[97]

Still, Volker left nothing to chance. If overwhelming programmatic momentum and pragmatic politics had produced the watershed organizational developments of 1962–63, 1966, and 1968, this was no time to change the strategy. Developments in Mobile, as problematical as they were in Volker's mind—and, again, there is no indication that Volker understood how they might in fact be helping him achieve his own ultimate goal—must not divert him from the most important issue of all: more steps toward autonomy.

Hence, despite his various maneuverings on the second medical school, Volker began to meet regularly with twenty-seven Birmingham citizens, whom he called the UAB Urban Council. The urban renewal application, not to mention desegregation of the hospital, had shown him how vital it was for UAB to have a structured approach to its community relations as well as its urban educational outreach. He turned to the Urban Council for advice on how this structure should be formed. John Monro was a key member of this group. In the early 1960s Monro had resigned as dean of students at Harvard College to move to Birmingham's Miles College, where he not only sought to improve higher education for black students but where—aided by Charles Zukoski and Cecil Roberts—he developed a series of quietly unfolding civil rights endeavors in the city. On Monro's advice the Urban Council recommended that Volker create a Center for Urban Affairs. The center could assist with wide-ranging community affairs but also help the City of Birmingham obtain grants that would benefit both the city and the university, smaller versions of the urban renewal and ARC projects. Volker wasted no time. By March 1968 he had assigned his trusted grant-writing colleague, John Dunbar, to begin planning the Center for Urban Affairs. Volker also hired as Dunbar's assistant director an energetic young urbanist, Edward S. LaMonte. A New Yorker and student of Monro's at Harvard, LaMonte had completed coursework for a Ph.D. in urban history at the University of Chicago under the direction of Richard C. Wade when he arrived in Birmingham in 1968 to do dissertation research on social welfare in modern Birmingham. His joining the Volker team would turn out to be a development of striking significance not just for UAB—Dunbar turned over the center to LaMonte in 1970—but for all of Birmingham.[98]

Still, the public focused more on the way Volker continued to grow the campus physically. In April and May 1968, he announced the final approval of the urban renewal plan for the forty-five-block expansion. This would include the five-building CGS complex as well as medical center additions such as a cancer center and a genetics institute, although it would be January 1976 before the city negotiated the urban renewal takeover of all the parcels of land and a state bond sale of $8.5 million fully committed this massive deal. At the same time he sent forth a press release on the acquisition of an additional $2.2 million in ARC funds to at least begin CGS construction.[99] On into summer the news of physical growth kept coming. In July, as earlier noted, Volker had ground-breakings on three medical center buildings: the new Basic Health Sciences Building, the Lister Hill Library, and a new high-rise School of Nursing building—a "main event" for public consumption including all three "turns of the shovel" on one day.[100] Finally, in December 1968 the anticipated but still striking news appeared—the funds for the urban renewal grant were available for use, which meant that large-scale CGS development could now start in earnest. This included the Regional Technical Institute (RTI), conceptually crucial to all ARC and urban renewal applications, where citizens of the Birmingham/Appalachia area could train at sub-baccalaureate levels for careers as health technicians— Johnson's War on Poverty at work in Jones Valley.[101]

This vigorous development was not without problems, however. The Birmingham Planning Commission, the Birmingham Housing Authority, and the Birmingham Board of Education were assisting Volker's vision by making the old Ullman High School—at the corner of Seventh Avenue and Fourteenth Street and originally slated for demolition along with neighborhood housing to its southeast—available to become a UAB facility. These groups saw less need for Ullman as a high school since a substantial portion of the 970 families who long had the opportunity to send their children there were now moving to new public housing developments provided through the Urban Renewal Act.

Still, critics of the closing of Ullman were not timid. The Titusville community, which began just two blocks northwest of Ullman and was one of the most historically significant all-black middle-class communities in the South, had sent its children first to Washington Elementary School and then, after 1940 when Ullman changed from a white to a black school, to Principal George Crenshaw Bell's Ullman High School. Indeed, out of this neighborhood educational network presided over by Bell there emerged a wide array of leaders: UAB mathematician Louis Dale; UAB nurse Charlie Jones Dickson; Reverend John Porter; civil rights activist Arnetta Streeter; University of Maryland educator Freeman Hrabowski; and Yale University public health specialist Curtis Patton. Where would such Titusville talent go to high school if Ullman became part of the UAB complex?[102]

Indeed, in 1968, the Birmingham public schools were on the verge of embracing bussing as part of desegregation, where "the Negro high school students" would scatter to became an explosive issue not just for Titusville families but for hundreds of families *not* of Titusville. From Woodlawn to Bessemer, black children had been going to Ullman because of its high quality and longstanding reputation with an esteemed middle-class community. Hence the loss of Ullman High School would have citywide implications. Faced with this stress, called "the Ullman issue," the Birmingham city schools proposed the creation of a new school three miles southwest of Titusville, near the all-black Goldwire neighborhood. Reverend Porter labeled the proposed site "horrible," among other reasons because it was "too far from Titusville."[103] In the *Birmingham World,* the noted editor Emory Jackson not only queried which black leaders involved in the decision had actually gone along with the relinquishment of Ullman to UAB, but urged that the new school be located "in the . . . Medical Center development area." With the threat that "we are not afraid to help bring to the front the kind of leadership needed at this hour," Jackson called on the whole matter to be "properly and effectively challenged."[104]

It was, but only to a degree. The new school, Porter recollected, "somehow was never built." Mary Cargle, an Ullman graduate and civic activist, recalled, "Actually funds were allocated by the Birmingham [School] Board for construction of the new school, but no neighborhood wanted it squarely in its area, and after several years of debate the money—like money will do in any bureaucracy—just disappeared . . . went on to other projects." On

Volker's urging, and with Porter's cautious endorsement, the Birmingham city schools made plans for some of the Ullman students to be admitted gradually to Ramsay High School, which was located three blocks north of the emerging university campus. This certainly had the advantage of being closer to Titusville than a Goldwire location. Volker had in fact seriously thought of including Ramsay in his early expansion plans. In view of the tensions over Ullman High School, however, he was only too happy for Ramsay to be an accommodating factor for Ullman students.[105]

For over a decade the change gradually occurred, though at first it lacked the spirit of accommodation for which Volker had hoped. The first Ullman student to transfer to Ramsay for 1963–64, before UAB took over Ullman, the "unflappable" senior Richard Walker, ultimately became an accomplished ENT physician in Birmingham as well as a civic leader. Yet none of this success eradicated clear recollections of social snubbing and other forms of discrimination Walker endured before heading on to college and then medical school at the UAB medical school.[106]

As Walker moved on, so did the times. By early 1969–70 far more Ullman students were at Ramsay. Indeed, against that background, in 1971–72 UAB took over what was now known as the Ullman-Bell facility on a rental agreement, and a year later—after renovations—purchased it as the new site for programs in social and behavioral sciences.[107]

It is unclear whether Volker, who was always fascinated by the subtleties of history, caught the irony of this story of race change occurring in what once was such a stronghold of the Confederacy's lost cause: Ramsay rested atop a neighborhood long known as "Confederate Hill" because so many ex-Confederate officers built stately homes there in the 1880s and 1890s.[108] What is clear is that the "solution" to the problem was never fully satisfactory. The Birmingham city schools designated Ramsay to be a magnet school for the arts—for reasons unconnected with its having had such well-known white alumni as Fannie Flagg (born Patricia Neal), Wayne Rogers, and Sheldon Hackney—and would be carefully planned to ensure a racial makeup of around 50 percent black and 50 percent white, not typical of most Birmingham city schools in the era of "white flight" that followed desegregation. Hence, as it turned out, many students from Titusville who were not oriented to the heavy arts curriculum at Ramsay never went there. Instead, along with many other black students in Birmingham, they found themselves bussed to schools far from their neighborhood: to Jones Valley, Hayes, Carver, Ensley, Wenonah, Parker, and Phillips high schools. Likewise, by the mid-1980s when the Alabama legislature determined that no state appropriations could be used for capital (physical plant) expenditures in four-year institutions of higher education, UAB would begin its move from the twentieth to the twenty-first century with the four-story Ullman Building, which was overwhelmed with "increasingly deferred maintenance problems" and did not have elevators. Still, the building remained an icon of black culture in Birmingham, having its own *national* as well as local alumni societies, in part out of tribute to the rigorous education it hosted under the leadership of Principal Bell. And Volker understood this. In May 1970, for UAB's first commencement, Volker asked Virginia Horns and other faculty planning the program to decorate the stage at downtown Boutwell Auditorium with the Ullman football colors, brown and black. A month later, Volker placed Mr. Bell's name on the auditorium wing of the Ullman building complex—there now was a Bell Building.[109]

Odessa Woolfolk had about as many connections to the Ullman Building as anyone could have. She was a Titusville student at Ullman and then taught at the school during the 1963 civil rights demonstrations. Years later, after graduate school, she directed UAB's Center for Urban Affairs located in Ullman. The "community leader" personified, Woolfolk softly reflected on Ullman's complicated evolution into a university facility and how the building's story mirrored that of the city and of the university: "Social progress is so, so complicated and Joe [Volker] understood this."[110]

Final Push: The Birth of UAB

Philosophical though he was about social change, Volker still stayed focused on the pragmatic issues before him. In the winter and spring of 1969, he and his team, especially George Campbell, tackled the legislature. Their mission included much more than coming home with enough money to expand the medical center as BAH had suggested. They wanted to return with enough state money to complete the CGS package, where student enrollment (graduate and undergraduate) had increased annually from 25 to 45 percent during the late 1960s. It was an awesome task in view of the general poverty of the state, and it took two years to complete. But they focused on the office of the new governor, Albert Brewer, and on developing at least temporary cohesiveness in the Jefferson County delegation. By June 1969 the word had reached Frank Rose. Though not official until the vote in July, there would be a state bond issue benefiting all universities, not just medical education associated with the BAH report. The Birmingham campus would receive $7.5 million for CGS construction as well as for matching funds to complete construction of the new Lister Hill Library and Basic Health Sciences Building. Moreover, the state appropriation for CGS general operations in 1969–70 would be $2,430,000, a 15 percent increase from the previous year. If different from Wallace on many issues, Brewer obviously shared his passion for funding education.[111] In early June 1969 Volker iced the cake with word that by July—in the midst of the legislature's special session—there would be official announcement of an $800,000 ARC grant for more CGS construction. There seemed to be an unstoppable momentum toward an urban research university in Birmingham—exactly the perception Volker wanted.[112]

On the heels of the early summer meeting of the UA board, on June 16, 1969, Governor Brewer announced that effective September 1970 the various operations of the University of Alabama would be organized as a three-campus system; each campus would be autonomous within the context of a system and each would have its own president reporting to the UA board. UA attorney Rufus Bealle would serve as executive secretary to the board on system matters. This change was at the discretion of the governor and the UA board only—no action of the legislature and, for once, no amendment to the state constitution were involved in the decision. Volker would be president of UAB, David Mathews—Rose's executive vice president—would succeed Rose, and a search would begin for a leader of the Huntsville campus.[113] Over the succeeding four years the eight board members would find themselves overwhelmed with paperwork and general administrative duties and not entirely clear as to how much autonomy should rest with campus presidents and how much board oversight should be involved. Changes would be needed. Still, "the history of development of the three campuses made this a wise move," Brewer recalled. "Through such independence each campus could become even more. Yet it was UAB's development that made it necessary. The old way was just too confining. To give UAB more room to operate we had to give it to the others, too." Accordingly, out of well-planned momentum, momentum springing out of innovation, risk, and social change, and accompanied by fiscal success in a state unaccustomed to public institutions being anything but poor, UAB had become a university. The Special Medical Education Subcommittee of the board, however, continued to watchdog medical center money, the only difference being that it was now a UA system board committee, not a UA board committee.[114]

In announcing the advent of the UA system, Governor Brewer suggested that the multicampus system model had been borrowed from Arizona higher education; Volker had indeed mentioned Arizona developments at least once to Rose in August 1965. But to attribute UAB's final delivery solely to "the Arizona model" risks possible extension of a significant historical inaccuracy. Such attribution implicitly denies the crucial role of O. C. Carmichael and the SUNY model in the birth of UAB: Carmichael likely planted the idea that Volker later found affirmed in his Arizona trips. Volker had not forgotten how some members of the UA board had rejected Carmichael for what they perceived to be his liberalism. So with his finely honed sense of pragmatism, Volker probably lobbied the idea of a system, which meant a vaguely defined autonomy for UAB, with no reference to Carmichael yet with ample mention of his visits to Arizona. Perhaps he and Volker even planned it this way back in 1954 when Carmichael encouraged the Yankee dentist to stick around just to see what might be possible.[115]

7

Volker's Vigorous Youth, 1969–76

The Woodward House and the New Era

In the summer of 1969 Joseph and Juanita ("Neet") Volker left their home on Mountain Laurel Circle in the recently established southerly suburb of Vestavia Hills, where they had raised their children, Joe Jr., Anne, and John. They moved to the top of Red Mountain to a thirty-six-acre estate that the descendants of Pennsylvania-born iron baron Allen Harvey ("Rick") Woodward and his wife, Annie Jemison Woodward, had sold the year before to "the University of Alabama medical center" at the cost of $325,000, which included furnishings and works of art valued at $63,000. Conservatively appraised at $500,000, the estate represented anything but a bad deal. Indeed, the land was so valuable that Volker's original plan, on the advice of Paul Brann, was to develop the home "into a conference center at the main house and a real estate development of town houses and condominiums . . . on the adjoining land." Volker and his family would live instead in a modern home nearby valued at around $800,000 and projected to be given to the university. These plans changed swiftly, however, when a major gift failed to materialize and the Woodward House, with board approval, became the official residence of the university's president.[1]

For many universities, placing the president in pleasant surroundings created an unending series of problems in terms of both campus and community politics. In 1952, for example, when the new chancellor of Vanderbilt, Harvey Branscomb, moved out of the relatively humble house on the campus where O. C. Carmichael had lived and into a restored home out in stately Belle Meade, it reinforced the already growing image of Vanderbilt, to use the words of that institution's biographer, Paul Conkin, as a place where the "upper classes" sent their "snobbish rich kids." In 1969, however, if UAB, like any organization, had its share of unappealing characters, the institution was in no danger of encountering the pitfall Vanderbilt had. Indeed, two decades would pass before most socially prominent citizens of Alabama, their perceptions of higher education still overwhelmed by the traditionalism of the 1950s, could accept the reality that UAB's academic programs as well as health care were for anyone other than "the indigent." It would be close to three decades before much of America's intelligentsia, their perceptions of "college" frozen in the early 1960s, would think it possible that an innovative public research university could be emerging in a place called Birmingham. With those thoughts at home and beyond there was little chance that UAB or its new president were going to be tagged as "arrogant," regardless of where the president lived.[2]

To the contrary, the Woodward House with Volker in it immediately became "a positive thing for UAB." On a personal level, of course, it was a special place for Volker to make the most of his limited family time, lick his wounds, toast his victories, and, most of all, cut new deals.[3] For sensitive and analytical citizens, however, certainly including Volker himself, it also became far more. It became a powerful metaphor for the past, present, and future of Birmingham.

Since its completion in 1926 as the largest residence in Alabama, the Woodward House had been a stage of poetic complexity. Styled as a villa of the Spanish Revival, it reverberated with historic universals of culture and learning. Yet the home also offered the secret sliding bookshelves and even more secret passages of escape so essential to the well-lubricated corporate and political entertainment of the Roaring Twenties (especially among the film moguls who had popularized Spanish Revival in Hollywood) and into the following decade when the experiment with Prohibition finally met its inevitable end. Physically, this curious stage would remain essentially unaltered through the latter half of the twentieth century. The succession of those who spoke from it, however, had striking differences. In the late 1920s the majestic fireplace in the front parlor, equipped with what Alice McCallum would call "those alluring no see 'em brandy warmers," provided crucial props for quiet after-dinner steel deals negotiated by Rick Woodward and other industrialists who sought to modernize the South by colonizing it.[4] By 1969 that fireplace framed still other low-toned talks but the participants were different. Volker and numerous city and state leaders and faculty and students were helping heal the hurt left by the Leviathan's pernicious grip and delivering in its place a new era for the people of the valley below. Hence by 1969 the Woodward House represented something far more complex than, say, Vanderbilt's Belle Meade mansion. The Woodward House symbolized evolving definitions of Southern life, major shifts of power, and ultimately the changing of a city's culture. In 1969, at the dawning of an age in which power derived more from knowledge and other elements of human capital—and less from steel, coal, shovels, and other forms of material capital—the people of Alabama and especially those of Birmingham were beginning to gain control of their own lives, with a public urban research university helping them do it. New lights in the valley and some on the hill above, too.

Indeed, after the crack *New York Times* writer Jack Rosenthal visited Birmingham in the spring of 1970 just to see what had happened since Harrison Salisbury's noted investigation, this veteran of the Selma march concluded that UAB's influence on the city represented quite "a face-lift." The "infant" institution already was "reshaping social attitudes and patterns of life" in what was once "a stronghold" of steel and segregation. He reported concrete signs of change the university seemed to be bringing to the daily life of the city. "A middle aged grocer," he recounted, "lies ashen in the intensive care unit [with] a red rope of a scar [showing] the open heart surgery he has just undergone. Next to the bed stands a computer complex . . . that both observes and treats. The patient is white. Fred Wallace, the electronic technician at the computer console, is black." Rosenthal went on: "In the [hospital] cafeteria, white and black nurses lunch together at the same tables. In the College of General Studies, black enrollment is already 13 percent. . . . Of the 5,500 employees of the university and medical center one-third are black."[5]

These changes were but part of the larger evolution in Birmingham's social and political life after the tortuous 1960s. The early 1970s saw recently reenfranchised black voters—who made up a greater and greater majority of the city's 275,000 voters—become a growing political force in the City of Birmingham and help elect not just the black Miles College professor Richard Arrington to the city council but the progressive white Republican and former city councilman George Seibels to the position of mayor. Although not an open civil rights activist and one who would not embrace affirmative action hiring, Seibels won the mayoral race with 98 percent of the black vote and represented a major upgrade in both image and substance for the city. As Arrington would recall, here was the first Birmingham leader to "reach out to the black community." A descendant of one of Montgomery's most storied families and a graduate of the University of Virginia, Seibels was a political moderate and an impeccably honest insurance executive. As mayor, he would be criticized for "unilateral hardheaded leadership" resulting in the destruction of the Birmingham Terminal Station instead of turning the magnificent Beaux Arts structure into usable historical space; he was also identified with initiation of a controversial occupational tax. Perhaps more significant, however, he would be recognized nationally for his advocacy of neighborhood associations designed to bring grassroots sentiment ("sentiment from people of all colors," he would recall) to the fore of city government; for increasing the number of black police officers from two to forty-eight; and for initiating major urban revitalization construction projects such as the Birmingham-Jefferson Civic Center (BJCC) and Birmingham Green, which changed the inner city's major thoroughfare of Twentieth Street into a boulevard lined with trees and flowers. Some called him a "compassionate conservative."[6]

In 1975, another white professional, the attorney David Vann, culminated three decades of seeking racial progress by succeeding Seibels as mayor; Vann would be aided significantly by black support orchestrated by Vann's close friend, Councilman Arrington. And then in 1979, accompanied by a temporary if visceral split between Arrington and Vann over Vann's handling of a police shooting, the complex spirit of the new Birmingham reached epic proportions when Arrington himself—a sharecropper's son with a doctorate in zoology—won election as mayor, receiving 10 percent of the white vote. In part owing to the shrewd political use of the very neighborhood associations first established by Seibels, this election signaled the beginning of the twenty-year "Arrington era" in Birmingham—an era when even the most casual observer had to notice not just a racially oriented "Arrington political machine," the Jefferson County Voters Coalition, trying to cope with the fact that no more than 10 percent of the white vote in the city would ever go for Arrington, but more jobs, a diversified economy, dramatic new buildings in the inner city, and equally striking city annexations adjacent to the rapidly growing and overwhelmingly white municipalities to the south of the city.[7] Still, at the dawning of the "Arrington era," Howell Raines, then Atlanta bureau chief for the *New York Times,* reported that the newly emergent aspect of Birmingham—in contrast with the old and in many cases lingering elements of the city—had at its core a *lack* of uniqueness within the context of the national scene: "Thousands of white-collar workers and professionals flocked to new corporate headquarters here and to the university and its medical center that, with a payroll of 8,500, now rivals United States Steel as the major employer. These new-comers were, as often as not, Easterners or Middle Westerners with no ties to the world of Sunday chicken dinners and Wednesday night prayer meetings."[8] Indeed, Raines raised the question of whether the rapid changes in Birmingham, though clearly a step forward, were not leaving the city at least temporarily in a condition described by Alvin Toffler as "future shock," a characterization of many American cities recovering from the "tumultuous Sixties."[9] In the 1970s what once was the Leviathan's Birmingham at last seemed on the threshold of relative autonomy and joining the American mainstream.

Although some would argue that *New York Times* writers unduly represented the viewpoint of their subterranean hostess, the thoughts of "that amazing woman named Cecil Roberts," as Jack Rosenthal described her, and that they overstated UAB's progressive impact,[10] key statistics document UAB growth during Volker's presidency that certainly made the university capable of the type of impact Rosenthal, Raines, and others attributed to the university in the story of rapidly changing Birmingham.

Out of new central administration offices created in Mortimer Jordan Hall, when the fledgling CGS library moved to yet another home, total revenues jumped from $63 million in 1970–71 to over $200 million in 1977–78. Income from grants and contracts played a big role in this increase—from $18,750,000 in 1970–71 to $40,337,000 in 1977–78. Yet, in direct opposition to what lay ahead for the young university, significant jumps in state appropriations under the leadership of governors Brewer and, after 1971, Wallace also were major factors behind this increase. The state allocation for 1970–71 was $8,958,000; by 1977–78 it was $47,707,789. To be sure, it had been Volker's juggernaut grantsmanship that had proved so crucial to UAB's final birth; and years later striking growth in extramural funds would be the key to institutional survival, not just growth, as legislative allocations per university student in Alabama descended to the bottom of the national scale. Still, during the 1970s the State of Alabama's investments in UAB were significant by any standard, not the least of which was the $8.5 million bond issue, in January 1976, needed to finalize negotiations for the forty-five-block campus expansion deriving from the second urban renewal project initiated in 1968. More to the point, with this increase in revenue, it is not surprising that other growth signs appeared.[11] The institution's full-time workforce, including faculty, increased from 4,800 in 1970 to 7,000 in 1977; the total payroll increased during the same period from $35,300,000 to $89,970,000.[12] Even by 1971, such growth prompted Vice President for Administration Paul Brann to get Volker's approval to create a university police force (developed first by Chief Thomas C. Seals) as well as centralize virtually all personnel management under Director of Personnel Services Lionel C. Skaggs, formerly of the University of Missouri–Kansas City.[13]

The growth and emergent complexity of the institution led to other new administrative positions. With silent engineering on the part of Charles Zukoski, James H. White III, a Birmingham native and son of Zukoski's regular tennis partner, James H. White II, left the law firm of Bradley, Arant, Rose, and White after three years of practice to assume the role of chief counsel and head of governmental affairs (lobbying) for Volker. Technically J. Rudolph ("Rudy") Davidson reported to the young Yale-educated attorney, a curious but highly effective mix of Ivy League and Avondale carefully orchestrated by Volker. White: "We definitely were a team: Rudy knew Montgomery folks I did not know and I knew some he did not know . . . no doubt about it, Rudy was extremely smart and one of the greatest lobbyists ever to operate in the state."[14] When White left UAB in 1973 to form his own investment firm in Birmingham, Volker replaced him with another bright young attorney, R. Lee Walthall, a native of New Bern, Alabama, deep in the old plantation county of Hale and a recent graduate of both the UA and NYU law schools. At the same time, Volker let Vice President Brann hire a director of program planning and analysis. The job went to the Chicago native with a doctorate in psychology, John M. Lyons, who had been performing similar duties for the Illinois Board of Higher Education. At first Lyons's role included monitoring and reporting on all credit-hour production and other indexes of productivity related to state funding, but his duties and title expanded repeatedly over the next three decades as UAB's connections with the legislature, higher education oversight committees, and the UA board became a job not just for him, later a vice president, but for a growing office of analysts.[15] Throughout Volker's presidency, from 1969 through 1976, about 60 percent of the students were full time and 40 percent were part time. During the same period, about 75 percent were undergraduates and 25 percent were graduate students. Total enrollment, however, more than doubled: 6,142 in 1970 to 12,540 in 1977.[16] Not surprisingly, the increased tuition revenues alongside great jumps in state appropriations permitted the same thing to happen with the number of full-time faculty. In 1970 there were 600; in 1977 there were 1,163. There were, on average, ten new positions a year in the College of General Studies (CGS), for a 1977 total of 250; and an average of sixty-seven new positions a year in the medical center for a 1977 total of 913.[17]

The only growth component lacking during these years, with the special exception being certain medical center units that ran their own fund-raising efforts based on "grateful patients," was philanthropy targeted at the university as whole. To start up the Office of Development, which initially reported to Volker and then to Brann, the new president hired Nettie E. Edwards as development director in 1971. She was a longtime leader with the Jefferson County Community Chest, a former journalist, and a friend of Zukoski. After 1977 she reported not to Brann but to the new vice president, Walthall. "Papa Joe," as the student newspaper, *The Kaleidoscope*, increasingly called him, clearly had on his hands not just an agent of progressive change but a vigorous youth.[18]

University College

Beneath all of this progress and good news lay both careful planning and frustrating misunderstandings. Through a "direct" conversation with Rose's handpicked successor, the young and dynamic David Mathews, Volker finally reversed a longtime stance by UA graduate dean Eric Rogers and changed the title of the chief graduate program officer in Birmingham from "director" to "dean." By the fall of 1970 it was *Dean* Samuel B. Barker. "This was no line position," as Barker recalled, for he "was not a 'real dean,' an officer responsible for the primary appointments of faculty." Still, the title and office allowed Volker and Barker to give more focus and management to graduate programs in Birmingham.[19]

By the same token, Volker trod lightly on competitive issues even closer to the heart of Tuscaloosa. In Volker's first general faculty meeting in the fall of 1969, Warren Rehm, chair of the Department of Physiology and Biophysics, asked *the* question: "Joe, can you tell us when we'll get a football team?" Without cracking a smile the new president replied, "Not currently part of the plan," then moved swiftly to other queries.[20] He applied the same charming savvy to faculty recruitment, working closely with George Campbell in hiring more nonmedical faculty. The place was still small enough for the new president to interview virtually every prospective faculty member. If they were hired, he made a habit of remembering crucial details on their vita and calling them by their first name. The first nonmedical faculty member he helped recruit in this way was Thomas L. Alexander. A native of Mississippi educated at Atlanta University and the University of Alabama, Alexander joined the Mathematics Department in September 1969 as the first tenure-track, full-time black faculty member in CGS.[21]

Just as important, Volker worked with Campbell to change the standards of CGS programs from those of an extension center to those of a university. He and Campbell immediately applied for provisional accreditation with the Southern Association of Colleges and Schools (SACS). A site-visit team came to the campus for three days in April 1970. By November the crucial stamp of approval for a new university was in place, and within three years they had captured full (nonprovisional) accreditation. As far as signs of development went, however, the public and the faculty and staff seemed less interested in SACS accreditation than they did in the sheer burgeoning population of the place, which Volker's public relations experts Janis Hawk and Gloria Goldstein made sure UAB folks had on the tip of their tongue when talking with anyone of political influence in Alabama.[22]

In the fall of 1969 and for a decade thereafter CGS undergraduate enrollment ("head count" or majors) in regular credit courses skyrocketed. In the fall of 1969 there were 3,800 undergraduates. By the fall of 1971 this number had grown to 5,300, by 1974 to 6,500, by 1978 to 9,000—in nine years a 237 percent increase. While this happened, moreover, master's and doctoral students in the sciences and education (not including those pursuing the M.D., D.M.D., and other professional-school degrees), moved from 520 in 1968, to 2,500 in 1975, and to 4,000 in 1978, a 769 percent increase over the decade. Graduation rates showed the same trend. Total degrees awarded, graduate and undergraduate, went from 570 in 1970, to 1,800 in 1974, to 2,800 in 1978, a 449 percent increase over an eight-year period.[23]

Beneath these CGS statistics were fascinating human stories. Because so many of those enrolled had family responsibilities, or confronted the obstacles of being "first-generation" college students, or got transferred by their employers, student retention remained at under 40 percent—the way it was at Wayne State University, Temple University, and other urban institutions. Unsurprisingly, therefore, the striking jumps in numbers graduating were accompanied by stories of persistence and boldness. At UAB's first commencement in 1970, downtown at Boutwell Auditorium, Elzira Pearson Finley, a seventy-year-old African American native of Birmingham, completed a forty-seven-year effort at overcoming life's obstacles and earned a B.S. in education. With her family shouting congratulations, a grand applause swelled from the entire assembly. Nonplussed, Ms. Finley headed off to graduate school at the University of Tennessee.[24]

In most respects this growth permitted Volker to breathe easier. It further demonstrated to the UA board and to the public of Alabama the pent-up need for UAB's new status *with* nonmedical programs, while producing rapidly expanding tuition revenues to develop even more programs and hire more faculty. Still, even with funding on the increase, enrollment growth stayed so fierce during 1969–71 before the new CGS buildings opened—when the only instructional space George Campbell had was the extension center (CGS) building and the Engineering Building, when social science and humanities faculty worked out of offices rented in the recently constructed Central Bank Building (later UAB's administration building) across Twentieth Street from the CGS building—Campbell capped new full-time undergraduate admissions at 500 annually.[25] This made for an undergraduate profile of around 60 percent full-time and 40 percent part-time students. Neither Volker nor Campbell, however, appeared bothered by this pattern. They saw quality part-time education at both the graduate and undergraduate levels as a crucial component of urban life and of changing Birmingham so that it would have an educated population that would be even more supportive of UAB.[26]

What did preoccupy Volker on a regular basis, however, and Campbell, too, was hiring faculty with scholarly credentials suitable for the big vision. Just a sampling of these individuals illustrates how CGS leaders went after faculty who, collectively, represented richly varied backgrounds as well as demonstrated commitments for being more than extension center–style teachers, that is, for being active scholar-teachers. In mathematics Tennessean Roger Lewis began that department's surge toward an international reputation in differential equations. In history Floridian David E. Harrell III became an international figure in American religious history and James F. Tent an equally noted scholar of modern Europe and World War II. In foreign languages Georgian William C. Carter was already engaged in what would be a thirty-year study of Marcel Proust, resulting in his receiving the highest cultural award offered by the French government, the Palmes Académiques. In teacher education Nebraska-born Gary and Maryann Manning were nationally recognized experts on why some children learn to read well and others do not. In chemistry Birmingham native Lee Summerlin offered national-level summer institutes for high school science teachers. In engineering Birmingham native Barry Andrews developed new materials used in the construction of spacecraft. Then there were the philosophers: Birmingham native (and son of Cecil) David Roberts IV, who specialized in iconoclastic views on virtually anything; and the New Yorker George Graham, who was rarely without his signature New York Yankees baseball cap as he pushed on the interdisciplinary frontier that would become cognitive science. In biology Missourian Ken Marion held high the head of evolutionary and environmental biology in the face of the molecular revolution and was a destined protector of Alabama's free-flowing rivers. Moreover, in sociology, Rhode Island native Michele Wilson would become the driving force behind UAB's women's studies program. In art North Carolinian John Schnorrenburg shared his expertise in eccle-siastical architecture. Finally, in business, Michigan native Dalton McFar-land continued his work on management and was joined by his young pro-tégé from Birmingham, Jack Duncan, who applied many of McFarland's theories and some of his own to the rapidly emerging field of health care management.[27]

Arriving at the best organizational structure for this dynamic young faculty proved a perplexing problem for Volker and Campbell. Since 1966, connections with the medical center and Southern Research Institute had been leading to the development of departments in Roger Hanson's Division of Natural Sciences and Mathematics: Blaine H. Levedahl over chemistry, Charles P. Dagg over biology, Robert Bauman over physics, and Adrienne Rayl over mathematics. Indeed, under the watchful eye of the new graduate dean Samuel Barker, chemistry, physics, and biology would have doctoral programs in place by the early 1970s. This growth now led Volker and Campbell to similar departmental structures elsewhere, though with the exception of teacher education, doctoral programs were a good distance down the pike.

In 1969 John E. Lewis's Division of Business Administration evolved into two departments, accounting and business administration chaired by Keith Bryant and Norman Ringstrom, respectively; shortly thereafter, economics was chaired by David P. Lewis. In 1969, George E. Passey's Division of Social Sciences (renamed that year Social and Behavioral Sciences) also evolved into departments: the Department of History led by Virginia Van der Veer Hamilton; the Department of Psychology chaired by David L. Sparks; the Department of Political Science under Grady Nunn; and the Department of Anthropology-Sociology led by Charles S. McGlammery. In Fain A. Guth-rie's Division of Education, the retired U.S. Navy captain Eddie P. Ort as-sumed the role of chair in elementary education as did Charles E. Wilson in secondary education. Overwhelmed by the numbers of students need-ing the required English composition course, Campbell had asked John S. Coley to establish the Department of English back in 1967, with Coley himself as chair, and by 1969 that department was part of the Division of Humanities with Coley in charge. Otherwise, however, this division con-tinued under such heavy financial pressures to offer composition that it would not be able to assume departmental organization until the early 1970s.[28] Likewise, while limited not so much by resources as by political agreement with the Tuscaloosa campus to offer one general engineering degree program at the undergraduate level and another at the graduate level, a full decade would pass before Joseph H. Appleton's Division of Engineering assumed departmental organization. Still, his programs reached a crucial milestone in the fall of 1971 with accreditation by the Engineers Council for Professional Development.[29]

Enrollment increases and expanded departments also caused more university-wide development. In the fall of 1971, Volker and Campbell changed the name of the College of General Studies (CGS) to University College (UC).[30] In Volker's mind, if one of the oldest and most revered urban universities in the world, the University of London, had used the term "University College" at least by the eighteenth century and continued to use it, so could UAB. Still, much like other U.S. educators he employed the term however it suited his needs. The University of London originally applied the term to the unit to which all non–degree seeking students were assigned for academic advising. By contrast, Tulane University in the 1940s used it to connote a newly formed night school. The University of Florida and Michigan State University installed a university college in the 1930s as the unit responsible for a required, liberal arts–oriented undergraduate core curriculum; no undergraduate was allowed to focus on studies in the major until the third year of study or when all "University College [core curriculum] requirements" were satisfied. By the late 1960s and early 1970s, however, Florida and Michigan State agonized over the elimination of their university colleges because they had devolved into a "general buffet" approach to undergraduate education and thus posed a dishonest oxymoron, as Gerald Grant and David Riesman show in *Perpetual Dream* (1978), that is, an extreme relaxation of curriculum requirements occurred as a 1960s supra-individualism descended upon much of U.S. higher education. Hence, at a time when many established universities were dropping the name and the structure of *university college,* Volker looked upon the term as one with "a good ring" that denoted all programs (degree and nondegree) in arts and sciences, engineering, business, and teacher education, that is, all "nonmedical programs." Again, although Volker likely did not understand the specific *nineteenth-century* transatlantic connection, the way he used *university college* bore remarkable similarity to the way in which most of the civic universities of England, for example, Liverpool, ultimately employed the term: the college was a section of the university primarily for commuter students interested in the fields Volker had aligned with it and had committed to improving educational levels of the local citizenry; it was a unit reflecting strong civic engagement.[31]

Volker also changed Campbell's title from dean to vice president. As vice president of University College, Campbell would find vital staff aid in three assistant vice presidents—initially, teacher education specialist Gardner McCullom (1968–71), then mathematician-engineer John Anderson (1971–73), and again a mathematician-engineer, James H. Woodward (1973–78).[32] With these three monitoring and advising behind the scenes and with Campbell always having direct contact with faculty leaders on crucial issues, the new vice president soon allowed two divisions to become schools with chief titles changing from director to dean: Guthrie, dean of the School of Education, and Appleton, dean of Engineering. A bright young professor of management with a doctorate from Washington University who then became dean of the School of Business at Rochester Institute of Technology, Jerry W. Young came aboard as dean of the School of Business. The national search producing Young, however, also turned up others whom Campbell wanted to hire, including M. Gene Newport of the University of Nebraska–Omaha, who came to Birmingham as chair of the Department of Business Administration.[33]

Still, as a former professor of mathematics and physics, Campbell was sensitive to, if not totally sold on, a cohesive approach to arts and sciences education. Moreover, Volker had a personal preference for (though, like Campbell, no steadfast opinion on) keeping arts and sciences together. So the new UC structure reflected earlier arts and sciences divisions continuing, if tenuously, under the single School of Arts and Sciences, and Campbell wound up with an old friend, Frederick W. Conner, running it— for a while.

A well-known literary historian and author of *Cosmic Optimism* (1949), Conner had served as dean of arts and sciences at UA where he befriended Campbell before moving on to the University of Florida as vice president of academic affairs. It was Conner who, as a faculty member in the 1930s, had strongly supported the required core curriculum concept of the "university college" in Gainesville. As Florida's academic vice president in the late 1960s, Conner sought to abolish Florida's University College after it had changed into a structure where students could virtually design their own core curriculum. Later, Conner would recall that "George and I discussed the term ["university college"] and its application in Birmingham, I believe, a good two years before I came to Birmingham. Maybe Joe got the idea through those conversations." Conner continued, "Joe identified it with the University of London. And he never did use it—the concept—as he should have."[34]

By 1970, when Campbell wrote to Conner asking who would make a good division director in humanities to succeed John Coley, who was resigning from administrative life, Conner said that he had wanted "to go gradually back to faculty life" and would be happy to move to Birmingham and, at least for a while, take the position himself. Campbell immediately signed him. By the time Conner arrived in the spring of 1971, however, Campbell and Volker had pressed him into taking the humanities division director job, as well as the position of interim dean of arts and sciences.[35] Still, by August 1972 Conner wrote Volker in no uncertain terms that (a) as a person with long experience in arts and sciences education, he viewed the UAB unit as too cumbersome and administratively unnecessary; and (b) he would be resigning from the arts and sciences dean post.[36]

Meanwhile, Volker formed a planning group to assess the organizational structure for the arts and sciences. It consisted of George Campbell, Vice President for Finance Paul Brann, plus the newly appointed executive assistant to the president, Robert W. French (formerly business dean at Tulane), and the Miles College dean, John Munro—none of whom ever had had high-level experience with arts and sciences education. They urged Volker to stick with the "revered" organizational structure, "all under one roof."[37]

In the end, however, Volker went with Conner's recommendation and ultimately Campbell's that the split offered "better management opportunities for the academic disciplines experiencing rapid and, to a degree, unpredictable change." Two other, more pragmatic factors likely entered into Volker's final decision, too. First, in October 1973 University College programs were scheduled for final review and, as it turned out, full accreditation by SACS. Volker wanted no visceral debates on organizational structure going on as the institution prepared for this crucial legitimation.[38] Second, throughout the early 1970s Volker had a "bigger issue on his hands, the increased taxation of Professional Service Funds" of medical center physicians; at a time when he was worried about having "too many hot potatoes on his plate at once," he did not need to be fighting a battle on reorganizing arts and sciences when there was no compelling reason to do so.[39]

On June 7, 1973, accordingly, George Passey became dean of the School of Social and Behavioral Sciences; Hanson took over as dean of the School of Natural Sciences and Mathematics; and Conner "not quite reluctantly" became dean of the School of Humanities. For the foreseeable future, UAB now consisted of twelve primary academic units (thirteen if the joint health sciences is included) distributed between the medical center and University College.[40]

Meanwhile, new programs supported by both new and old faculty brought further development to the infrastructure. In 1972 Jerry Young's School of Business initiated the Center for Labor Education and Research with Higdon Roberts coming from Ohio State to run it. The same year the Department of Criminal Justice emerged with George Felkenes as chair, and the Division of Special Studies (continuing education) arose under the initial leadership of Rudy Davidson. In 1973 the School of Business won accreditation by the American Assembly of Collegiate Schools of Business (AACSB), one of only 150 of the over 900 schools of business so accredited in the nation and the youngest ever accredited. Campbell's stretching his budget to bring in several experienced professors in business had paid off.[41] Moreover, the Department of Foreign Languages appeared in 1973, as did the Department of Art, chaired on an interim basis by Martha Johnson, then by the nationally acclaimed art historian Virginia Rembert. The Department of Performing Arts (later split into two departments, theater and dance, and music) likewise took off under the leadership of D. Ward Haarbauer, who returned to his hometown after earning a doctorate in theater at the University of Wisconsin.[42]

In 1974, Guthrie and his new associate dean, Milly Cowles, led the School of Education to full accreditation by the National Council of Accreditation of Teacher Education (NCATE). In addition, that year M. Gene Newport assumed the dean's position in business, as Jerry Young moved up to vice president of finance—a domino effect touched off by Paul Brann's moving to Tuscaloosa to become chief operating officer of the UA system, as Rufus Bealle moved on to become secretary to the board. Changes kept unfolding that year. The Department of Urban Studies (later merged with political science) took shape under Birmingham native Blaine A. Brownell, who most recently had taught American studies and urban history at Purdue University. Moreover, a native of Opp, Alabama, Thomas K. Hearn, who had attended Birmingham-Southern before earning a doctorate at Vanderbilt, left the faculty of the College of William and Mary in 1974 to start the UAB Philosophy Department. By 1976 Hearn would have succeeded Conner as dean of humanities; Conner retired permanently in Gainesville, Florida.[43]

Even more new programs appeared. In 1977, Campbell and Hill agreed that the unfolding technology revolution dictated that the medical center's program in information sciences in the Division of Biophysical Sciences be expanded and refocused as the Department of Computer and Information Sciences and be relocated in the School of Natural Sciences and Mathematics. Warren T. Jones, trained at Georgia Tech, came onboard to chair it. The same year the nation's continuing preoccupation with oil and other sources of energy prompted Campbell to move ahead with another development, the creation of the Department of Earth Sciences (after 1982 called the Department of Geology) with former Birmingham-Southern professor Denny Bearce as chair.[44] On the strong encouragement of Volker himself, Campbell also worked with Passey to launch the Department of Social Work, what Volker saw as "crucial to any urban university." They hired a University of Chicago PhD, Norman E. Eggleston, previously at Catholic University of America, not only to establish the B.S.W. curriculum and faculty but to lay plans for an M.S.W. program. Although the B.S.W. program immediately became strong, the M.S.W. program proved more than elusive probably because Volker never obtained political clearance for it via the UA system office with regard to the existing M.S.W. program at UA.[45]

Broadly speaking, Volker and Campbell initiated University College the same way Kracke, Harrison, Volker, and others began the medical center. Some of the leading faculty had educational and professional backgrounds in Alabama. Others either were Alabamians who had gone to major graduate schools out of state and had begun careers, or were part of a national, even international mix, with graduate training in places as diverse as the University of Berlin, the University of London, the University of Alabama, Vanderbilt University, the University of Texas, Columbia University, and Georgia Tech. As Samuel Barker recalled, all seemed excited about "Volker's experiment" of "building something ultraprogressive right in the middle of a city known in some ways to be quite the opposite."[46]

Many academics who were from Alabama who either had not left or had returned also felt as Kracke had. Virginia Hamilton counseled an aspiring historian who had spent his early years in Birmingham but who wanted little to do with "Bombingham": "You really need to consider coming back here. This is where the action is. With Volker out front we will change this place." Some four years later, by then a young assistant professor at UAB, the historian chanced to get the same message from Volker himself, if circuitously. It was around 10:00 p.m. in early May, a clear sky and still warm. The historian departed the Ullman Building and headed out front to the dirt parking lot and to his ancient oxidized-blue Volkswagen minivan. He found Volker dressed as always in blazer and bow tie leaning up against the spare tire mounted on the front of the young man's vehicle. The president greeted him with a question: "Well, what do you see out here tonight?" Excited that the president was addressing him but nevertheless relatively fresh out of graduate school—long on cocky knowledge and short on subtlety— the historian shot back: "I see a city." Volker replied, "I . . . I see a city, and a university, and their lights, and where there are no lights right now I know there will be . . . new lights in the valley." All but oblivious to the metaphor just offered up by the scientist turned sophisticated generalist, the young historian headed home wondering when lights would be added to the Ullman parking lot. Yet the conversation—word for word—stuck, and with the passage of just a few days the power of the metaphor did, too. As light is a form of energy, so too in the metaphorical sense can light in the human mind and spirit be a force of creativity and, if channeled properly, one of social energy delivering positive societal change. An emergent university. New lights in the valley. He got it.[47]

For others, however, it was not so much the profoundness of the possible social change by itself but a 1960s reform sentiment blended inextricably with a sense of loyalty and mission about a Southern home-place. "Drawn to home," they wanted "to do something for [their] people" at a time when these people had been going through "a lot of changes," Samuel Barker would recall.[48]

No faculty exemplified this Southern sentiment more than two black scholars. Descendants of slaves, both could have used the new federal pressures to hire black faculty and virtually named their jobs at many more established institutions in the nation and at higher salaries. A native of Greenville, Alabama, but a graduate of Birmingham's Parker High School, Ernest Porterfield completed his B.A. at Tuskegee, an M.S. at Atlanta University, and a Ph.D. in sociology at the University of Illinois–Urbana then returned to Birmingham in September 1971 as a tenure-track faculty member in UAB's Sociology Department. Ultimately he chaired the department as well as authored a path-breaking book, *Black and White Mixed Marriages* (1978), a work that led to his being the first UAB faculty member from any field to be interviewed as a feature story on national network television (*The Donahue Show*, April 1983).[49]

Louis Dale attended Washington Elementary School in Titusville and Ullman High School, then completed his B.S. at Miles College, an M.S. at Atlanta University, and a Ph.D. in mathematics at the University of Alabama. He had started his doctoral program at Wayne State University in Detroit, where he found that he "and, to be fair, perhaps graduate students from all other colors" were not given any "personal attention—there was no human warmth to the place," which made him feel that he was "the main character in Ralph Ellison's book *The Invisible Man.*" In 1968, after talking with several members of the UA mathematics faculty at a professional meeting, he moved his doctoral training to Tuscaloosa. There "people showed real interest in each other, ate together, stood by each other. . . . I was *never* discriminated against, and I felt like I could be part of the inner circle just like a few other Ph.D. students of different colors were." Dale subsequently began a teaching career at Miles College where he was a colleague of Richard Arrington. In September 1973, however, he joined the UAB Mathematics Department, ultimately earned the rank of professor of mathematics, and then became a senior administrator at the institution as well as a nationally recognized National Science Foundation specialist on expanding black participation in mathematics and science careers. Years later, when asked why he had spent his career in Birmingham when he had numerous opportunities to move, he reflected a strong Southern identity— as James Cobb has shown—so emergent among some black scholars in the years following the apex of the civil rights movement.

> This is my home. I can be at my farm in an hour. I do grow beautiful tomatoes. But more than that I have liked it here because here I have been able to help build something from the beginning; and also here, in the deep South, to be honest, it's just that race relations are less hypocritical. . . . Southerners, ultimately, are the ones who will solve their racial problems, just like Northerners will solve theirs. In that sense George Wallace *was* right. I wanted to be a part of solving the problems of my people—*all* my people, black and white. So I'll return the question: Why would I want to be anywhere else?[50]

Much as Dick Hill had moved swiftly to develop effective faculty governance when he became dean of the Department of Medicine, Campbell now did the same. Unlike Hill, however, Campbell had a positive starting point. Since 1966 he had worked closely with standing faculty committees on virtually every aspect of university life, from physical plant to finances and academic programs and personnel decisions. Thus, on Campbell's request a scholarly gentleman trained at New York University and serving as chair of the Department of Political Science, Grady Nunn, assumed the task of chairing a committee to draft a blueprint for the CGS Senate. What came out of the process was less an extension of his formal and traditional exterior and more a reflection of Nunn's values: his 1930s/1960s commitment to shared power and collective decision making reinforced by his experience in the more mature urban setting of New York City. Following intermittent discussions with Volker as well as Charles Zukoski, his friends at the new Unitarian Church, Nunn proposed representatives from the faculty—deans and department chairs considered part of the faculty—as well as from students, staff, and the community. Altogether there would be thirty-nine members, serving on committees ranging from finance to student affairs, academic affairs, and external relations.[51] Nunn had produced something in keeping with the spirit of the Dutchman. It just as easily could have come out of a 1960s Berkeley, California, or Madison, Wisconsin.

By October 1969 faculty, students, and staff gave strong votes of support. The following January elections determined the actual membership, and, curiously, "administrators" carried the day. Fain Guthrie, dean of education, won the position of general chairperson, though he was succeeded the next year by psychology faculty member William Farrar. Robert Bauman, head of physics, found himself elected to chair the constitution and by-laws committee, which organized the first senate. The dean of engineering, Joseph Appleton, received a mandate to chair the all-important Academic Programs Committee, which immediately took up consideration of four new graduate programs, doctorates in physics, chemistry, and biology and a master's degree in mathematics. In ways yet to be unraveled (Nunn: "It just seemed to happen that way"), Zukoski "discovered that [he] had been chosen to be the community representative."[52]

Campbell also moved quickly to establish vital vehicles for faculty governance at the school and department levels, and his key advisor on "governance and academic life" was the new dean of social and behavioral sciences, George Passey. In the process, Campbell got from Passey much more than advice on faculty governance. He got help on how such faculty governance, if done right, relates to everything else of priority in the university, and in this new university research was a priority.[53]

Passey had an intense interest in and understanding of the relationship between faculty governance, reward structures, and the instruction-research role of faculty. As he told Campbell on numerous occasions, for there to be a strong *university* faculty, as opposed to that of a liberal arts college faculty or a faculty just involved in instruction of commuter students, research and instruction, including graduate-level instruction, must be "joined at the hip, one in the same." Hence, if Passey understood the revered land grant triad of teaching, research, and service, in his own mind he saw it all as one seamless enterprise motivated by research. Likewise, he knew that University College, much like the medical center, could not evolve into "a high-quality educational operation which has money to function" unless graduate programs were available, and this would not happen unless faculty governance and reward structures embraced research and scholarship. Though this shift in emphasis went unnoticed at first by all except those involved in University College daily affairs, here was a striking addition to Volker's original plan for University College to function essentially as a civic university: the faculty and in time the students grafted the values of a research university—expressed through graduate education and research—to those of a civic institution. And in the process, according to the recollections of then assistant vice president for University College, James Woodward, "the quality of undergraduate education steadily surged forward, too, as researching faculty also taught first- and second-year undergraduates."

From these premises, and working with Virginia Hamilton, David Sparks, and a few other intense researchers, during the summer and fall of 1973 Passey developed a draft document that set forth a collection of faculty committees for the School of Social and Behavioral Sciences, by then located in the Ullman Building. The following spring a faculty vote approved the plan. The school had a faculty affairs committee, an academic affairs committee, and a faculty-student relations committee, membership chosen chiefly with faculty elections though each committee had a few dean-appointed positions. Campbell had considerable experience with committees focused on new academic programs and student issues; however, Passey's plan was a structured step forward in the way its faculty affairs committee handled matters pertaining to tenure, promotion, and salaries. Immediately, members of the Social and Behavioral Sciences faculty affairs committee called on all departments in their school to develop their own specific *written* departmental guidelines, guidelines that would not permit a proposal to the dean that an individual be promoted or tenured without "substantial peer-reviewed scholarly, creative or research activity" and guidelines that emphasized the necessity of *only* merit raises "counting" *only* research and creative activities judged "of significant quality" by national peers. Indeed, by the spring of 1974 most departments in the school, notably psychology and history, had formally adopted general guidelines for decisions on merit raises.[54]

Meanwhile, Volker and Campbell with the major aid of Assistant Vice President Woodward had been working hard to solve another of the continual growth problems of University College: library resources. Much as medical center programmatic successes virtually always resulted in the need for greater laboratory space, the new faculty hires and curriculum developments in University College had brought library needs to the breaking point. And just like medical center leaders, during the early 1970s Campbell and Volker, aided powerfully by the political contacts and fiscal strategy of Rudy Davidson, had been carefully developing a war chest of federal funds—Appalachian Fund monies, urban renewal funds, and revenue-sharing funds—to build the badly needed library for arts and sciences, teacher education, business, and engineering.[55]

The collection had started in two rooms of the CGS building, then had been moved to Mortimer Jordan Hall, and then in 1971 to the recently constructed Building No. 1 (later known as the Education Building), which also housed the Departments of Teacher Education, Business, and Humanities. To prepare for the expansion, in 1971 Campbell contracted for the consulting services of a Ph.D.–level librarian out of the University of Illinois library science school, Paul Spence. The next year Campbell hired Spence to replace acting director Perry Cannon, and Spence subsequently hired as his chief accountant and administrative aide a young Birmingham native and recent graduate of UAB's accounting program, Jerry W. Stephens. Thus by early 1973, under the joint supervision of Spence, Stephens, and Woodward, the $3 million project moved forward.[56]

As it did, however, the project encountered two problems. First, there was the matter of what to call the new library. For at least three years planning documents had referred to it as University College "Building No. 4." Even the most uncreative of bureaucrats knew that this would not do for long. Ultimately, as word got out that Campbell and Volker were searching for a name for the new library much as "Lister Hill" appropriately graced the front of the new medical center library, two names emerged as frontrunners: George C. Wallace, who unquestionably had poured millions into the new campus; and Martin Luther King, Jr., without whose leadership the new Birmingham surely would not have been taking shape the way it was. Behind the scenes the constituencies of the two leaders began to square off. "Whichever way he moved Volker was in trouble," recalled Spence. Then, once again, Zukoski eased out of the shadows. After church one Sunday he suggested to Volker that the noted Birmingham stockbroker-philanthropist, advocate of desegregating the hospital, close friend of Zukoski, and long-time supporter of UAB and the medical center, Mervyn H. Sterne, might be willing to have his name on the building out of "general recognition for his longtime support for UAB." On Volker's approval—he knew Sterne through their service on the Birmingham Public Library board—Zukoski made the contact. Sterne quickly agreed and also offered some vague indication about a gift toward the cause "to keep the old [racial] fights from coming back on us." He died before such a gift was consummated, although his widow, Dorah Sterne, would become a significant benefactor of the library. Still, a good nine months before the building opened it had a name: the Mervyn H. Sterne Library.[57]

As a result of expanding library facilities, however, the university encountered a second problem. Now, as never before, there was the issue of prioritizing collection funds. Would the library need to become a "college [teaching] library"? Or should it be developed into a "university [research] library"? Spence understood the vital nature of the questions. At the core was the central question facing University College: Would it be part of a research university with vibrant graduate programs? Unable to get clarification on this complicated point from either Campbell or Volker, Spence turned to Woodward, "who always was easy to talk with. Not that he was always easy-going, but you always knew where you stood when you left his office. Trust me, behind closed doors Southerners can be just as direct as folks from other sections." These two direct-talking Southerners simply made the decision that the type of faculty being hired—a faculty rapidly embracing research emphases on promotions and salaries—would have to have a library supportive of research. They recognized that "short of a gift of many millions of dollars to close the gap, we never will make this library catch up with research capabilities of more established universities." Still, "praying that such a gift would someday, somehow come in," they decided that Sterne funds would be used for acquisitions "supportive of a faculty and student body interested in research." For Woodward, here was one of the essential cores of University College: "If you have any sophistication about higher education, when you walk into a library quickly you can get a feel for what faculty and students are doing: we needed this to be a research library not just for the sake of [then] current students and faculty but in the name of the future—the recruiting of both faculty and students." In January 1973, this new facility for research and teaching opened for business with a collection of 300,000 volumes with experienced reference librarians such as Bonnie Ledbetter and, in addition to Spence, well-honed managers like Jerry Stephens.[58]

Careful programmatic development certainly had its place; politics did, too. To ensure that state funds were available for faculty raises and library acquisitions that year, on May 20, 1973, Volker had Governor Wallace on campus for an official dedication of the library (not yet named for Sterne) and the three other buildings in University College, which Volker saw as directly connected to Wallace's support.[59]

Starting Student Life

Just as Volker, Campbell, and other leaders knew that faculty life in University College had to develop for UAB to emerge as a high-quality university, they also understood that student life needed major development. In a few areas their vision for student affairs was in fact prescient. They understood the great potential for the hub known as Five Points South four blocks southeast of the campus. Beginning in the late 1960s, with the decline of the Dutchman east of the campus near St. Vincent's Hospital, students and faculty began gathering at the Five Points watering hole known as Joe Bar (no connection to Volker) at the corner of Twentieth Street and Eleventh Avenue; across the street at Gene Crutcher's bookstore (in space later occupied by the Five Points Grill); or in Charlemagne Records located next door to Joe Bar. Aided by early discussions with Kracke, Volker fully comprehended that the once posh 1920s shopping and entertainment center of Five Points South was slowly becoming a "type of Southside Soho" for faculty and student life elements of an academic community, in a smaller and younger way, "something comparable to Greenwich Village's interaction with NYU or Georgetown's connection with the university behind it on the hill." Yet Five Points South also represented to Volker the potential revitalization of an urban business district and the creation of part-time jobs for students. Many already were in the area working, and many more would follow. Among the most unforgettable was Jack Bergstresser. A soft-spoken, intense UAB student on his way to becoming an industrial archaeologist, as well as a superb campfire cook (he had grown up fishing along the Cahaba River thirty miles south of Birmingham), Bergstresser's early reputation on campus was as part-time maker of slow-cooked chili at Joe Bar. On a cold and rainy February evening it was an utterance of warmth and place: "I'd like a mug of Bud and a bowl of that stuff Jack makes back there." *Playboy Magazine* found Joe Bar sufficiently charming to describe it in a case study on owning such a neighborhood place. Volker held to the more focused view: the weaving together of the city with the university.[60]

Although Volker and Campbell placed appropriate value on this "campus-without-walls" social and intellectual scene of Southside, they also wanted more conventional student life programs directly on campus. This was no easy task. Similar to the vast majority of American higher education leaders, they and virtually all of their key officers erroneously saw the development of systems in student records and programs in student life as "an easy add-on . . . anybody with common sense can make it happen," which initially reflected the myth that student life is really not a "profession" within higher education. And, again, much as other university leaders nationwide they apparently did not understand that common sense and political savvy are not always found among faculty and administrators eminently successful in research and instruction. They erroneously asked people successful in these more "prestigious" elements of academia to call the initial shots on the formation of student life programs instead of staying true to their own scientific method of consulting those who know the most about the subject.[61]

In 1969, when Volker named his chief aide, John Dunbar, to be the director of the new Center for Urban Affairs, he also gave him the title of director of community and student affairs. A superb grant writer, Dunbar nevertheless had no experience or training in the field of student life, and he allowed student government associations (SGAs) to pop up all over the campus. By 1974 there were seven SGAs on campus: five in the medical center, one for graduate students, and one for University College. With scant oversight, these organizations could produce significant problems when student leadership lacked quality. One early president of the University College SGA decided that he and his vice president should have university cars like other "university officers" did. He promptly went to Edwards Chevrolet in downtown Birmingham and charged two new Chevrolets to "Dr. Joseph F. Volker and UAB." Some other early SGA officers followed suit on a lesser scale, running up large bills in the community for "everything from food and drink to printing services" with no budget "but the most ad hoc" to pay their "usually unauthorized debts." When Volker got the bills he would send Dunbar and Joe Volker, Jr., who worked for Dunbar on student life matters, to "either return the charged item or pay the bill." Word spread fast. Local merchants began "police-like inquiries" of UAB students when they sought to write a check using a UAB student identification card. Despite the reputation of Bergstresser and other excellent student employees in businesses near the campus, for several years local merchants did their best to stay clear of hiring UAB students and began to weigh the pros and cons of the general economic influence of the burgeoning UAB.[62]

Compared to life in Berkeley, Madison, and Athens, Georgia, and indeed in Tuscaloosa, early student life at UAB showed relatively few signs of social reformism. Many UAB students had full-time jobs and family responsibilities. As explained in a January 1969 article in *The Kaleidoscope,* UAB political scientist Charles Bulmer asserted that this left little energy or time for structured campus activities or even expression of opinion on campus issues beyond the need for a new commuter-student lounge with soft drink machines that returned proper change.[63]

There were, however, exceptions. During the late 1960s and early 1970s, medical center faculty and students agitated for press coverage and litigation to clean up Birmingham's filthy air. The pulmonary specialist Ben V. Branscomb and pulmonary residents Randy Cope, Marshall Brewer, and Dan Prince joined biochemistry doctoral student Cameron Spain McDonald (granddaughter of attorney Frank Spain, who helped Volker create UAB) to form GASP—the Greater Birmingham Alliance to Stop Pollution. Through GASP they kept newspaper attention on the way heavy metals production was polluting Birmingham's air. In turn this activism assisted Jefferson County health officer George Hardy and Alabama attorney general William J. Baxley in ultimately forcing U.S. Steel into compliance with the federal Clean Air Act of 1970. On reflection about cleaner air subsequently coming to Birmingham, McDonald mused, "In the context of the times, we were radicals—hopefully, I was a radical; we needed to be radical."[64]

In 1968, moreover, UAB microbiologist and dental professor Frederick Kraus, a noted racial liberal who had participated in the Selma march, worked with Zukoski and Dean Roger Hanson and the Alabama Council on Human Relations to hold a student rally on the UAB campus to protest the U.S. bombing of North Vietnam. This fit into a national pattern. Throughout the late 1960s and early 1970s local reform groups initially motivated by the need for greater racial tolerance also branched out to advocate change in other areas, such as the environment, discrimination regarding gender and sexual preference, and foreign policy. (And in Kraus's case the connections ran even deeper: as a young dentist in Prague in the 1930s, he had opposed and then fled Nazism.) Two UAB faculty, the sociologist Harold Wershow and the biochemist Abraham Siegel, attended the meeting in the engineering auditorium along with such community liberals as Eileen Walbert and the television news broadcaster Bette Lee Hanson (wife of Dean Hanson), as well as some younger people who said they represented Students for a Democratic Society (SDS), though they were not enrolled as students at that time. "A few" UAB students attended. A year later, however, a group of students and young faculty reported by *The Kaleidoscope* as totaling 200 gathered in front of the CGS building, on Twentieth Street, to show support for brethren recently involved in the Kent State University tragedy and protest U.S. involvement in Vietnam. And, unconvinced that serious student radicalism so apparent in recent riots at Columbia University could not happen in Birmingham, by July 1969 Volker had a fifteen-page strategic plan—"Procedures for Dealing with Major Campus Disturbances or Major Demonstrations"—distributed to all vice presidents. Above all, it emphasized the importance of university authorities using minimal force in dealing with a student outburst, which never came to pass.[65]

During the 1960s a few UAB white students had joined black students from neighboring Ullman High School to participate in civil rights demonstrations in Birmingham and beyond. Vocal beyond their numbers because most students left campus after class for home or work, they bonded with their faculty and the high school students through strong feelings about social reform, which was often reflected in heated classroom discussions. Ironically, a black specialist on teacher education and urban outreach, King Chandler, was so preoccupied with outspokenness in UAB's classrooms that he declined George Campbell's offer to take a faculty position on the campus, professing deep concern about "a rebelliously tempered society." Still, as early as 1971, just two years after the founding of the university and at a time when black students made up no more than 10 percent of the undergraduate student body, a black student named Bracie Watson easily won election as president of the UC SGA. Both as a candidate and as an elected student official, he urged "greater progress on the race-relations front." Although there were few episodes of open racial hostility on campus, despite (or because of?) intense classroom discussions, he was concerned about undercurrents of racial tension and about the few outbursts that did indeed mar campus life.[66]

Two other elements of student life remained pubescent: dining and bookstore facilities—standard, crucial parts of higher education. Well into the early 1970s dining options were limited to the following: the hospital cafeteria; small sandwich shops in the basements of the Engineering Building and the Basic Sciences Building (later Volker Hall); Ziggi's, a beer and pizza joint on the eastern side of Twentieth Street across from the university; and, unquestionably the place of choice among students, Pete Graphos's *original* Sneaky Pete's Hotdogs, managed with flowing efficiency by Pete himself. In 1973, Volker managed an incremental move in the right direction by opening in Building No. 3 (later called the Humanities Building) a grill called the Hideaway Cafe, which over time assumed a small, but venerable, role in the social and intellectual life of the campus. Likewise, in the mid-1960s Volker and Campbell had come up with a makeshift bookstore in the CGS building, but by 1973 they developed a new (temporarily) effective building for books and supplies just off the main thoroughfare of Eighth Avenue at Fifteenth Street.[67]

Student registration, records, and other elements of student life also appeared slowly and erratically. Under the general direction of teacher education professor Clay Sheffield, part-time history instructor Richard Wallace served as the registrar for University College and Rozelle Reynolds as the bursar. They operated out of the CGS building until 1972. Then they moved to the second floor of Mortimer Jordan Hall. As an appendage, to the west in the Ullman-Bell Gymnasium, faculty performed advising duties at student registration. Much like faculty all over America, here were professors with little knowledge about the finer points of general degree requirements. Yet they were excellent advisors in their own areas of expertise, and given the slightest opportunity they could hold forth on the questionable merits of a colleague's specialty. For all its vigor, the advising "system" was "developmental."[68]

By 1969 Campbell and Sheffield had made a stab at computerizing student records, from transcripts to financial accounts. The new technology "never could be made to work right," however, and frustrated students usually wound up at Wallace's desk seeking correction of errors made by the "faculty advising system" or the "always down" computer. They then moved over to Reynolds's desk, where their tuition bills were corrected to reflect "what they really were taking." Although underdeveloped and misunderstood by senior management, this nascent student records effort could also produce good results. Both Reynolds and Wallace had an intuitive understanding of the types of students coming to the new university: students who were often paying their own way while working one, if not two, jobs, students desperate to get in classes at 8:00 a.m. and 10:00 a.m. so they could get four hours of sleep in the afternoon before awakening to study and then returning to the night shift at U.S. Steel or University Hospital. And Reynolds and Wallace were overtly humanistic, as opposed to technocratic. They often knew students on a first-name basis and worked out payment plans when somebody came up short, undoubtedly circumventing state auditing practices in an effort to help people be the first in their families to earn a college degree.[69]

Then, in 1973, came a crucial hire for student life. In an effort to increase black faculty and administrators and "to get some of the chaos out of student affairs," Volker, Campbell, and Dunbar recruited Aaron Lamar as a faculty member in counselor education and as director of student affairs.[70] The son of one of Alabama's leading AME ministers, Lamar had grown up in segregated Birmingham and Montgomery. He had attended Thomas Elementary School and Rosedale High School in Birmingham, then graduated from Booker T. Washington High School in Montgomery. After a stint as a seaman first class aboard a U.S. Navy destroyer, in 1948 he returned to Montgomery to earn a bachelor's degree in English at Alabama State University. Throughout the 1950s and 1960s most members of Lamar's family marched, protested, and in other ways took public stands on behalf of desegregation. However, following a strategy embraced by many black families in the South of this era, Lamar's parents decided that Aaron would keep a low public profile on race change *and keep a job*—in his case, a job teaching English at Carver High School in Birmingham. They assumed that other family members who protested would lose their jobs, which often happened, so young Aaron would "maintain diplomatic relations" with "the white management folks who ran the city" and bring home the money necessary to help feed the family so they could stay engaged in the movement. "Behind the scenes my parents permitted me to make sandwiches for the early marches," he recalled, "but otherwise I was supposed to keep my head down. That was so hard for me. Everybody else in the family got to go to the front line, where the action was. Over time, however, I came to understand [my parents'] wisdom."[71]

Indeed, by the mid-1960s, on the heels of finishing a master's degree in counseling at Atlanta University, the strategy of being diplomatic catapulted Lamar into a doctoral fellowship program in administration at the recently desegregated Auburn University. While there he served as part of a statewide team of educators charged with developing desegregation plans for county K–12 systems. Diplomacy and education had brought him to one of the most significant front lines. Fain Guthrie, at that time still a faculty member in UA's College of Education, served on the same team. After completing his doctorate, Lamar returned to Birmingham to teach writing and literature and counsel at Lawson State Community College, a state two-year school recently reorganized as part of Governor Wallace's two-year college expansion program. But in the summer of 1973, several years after Guthrie had left Tuscaloosa to become education dean in Birmingham, Volker and Campbell asked Lamar to come to work at UAB. Guthrie had recommended him, and his initial title would be assistant professor of counselor education and director of student development. He would be in charge of student life programs. "It was a major opportunity for me," Lamar would recall, "but I always would miss the teaching of literature and writing."[72]

By 1979 Lamar's title had changed to dean of student affairs and associate vice president. Later the scholarly gentleman would receive the UAB President's Medal for Distinguished Service. On wide-ranging issues of city and university—on issues, as one Lamar observer remembers, "where a problem suddenly was solved but there was no one shouting, 'I'm the one who fixed it!'"—he would prove to be a quietly powerful influence on behalf of "social progress without people killing each other." Confronted years later about how some black people labeled him an "Uncle Tom," Lamar shot back, "How simplistic. How ignorant. Show me an army developed with only one type of soldier, and I'll show you an army that has never won a war."[73]

Lamar moved into his office on the second floor of Mortimer Jordan Hall in the fall of 1973. He had a secretary but no professional staff. He *was* the student life program, and he reported to no one but Dunbar, an executive assistant to the president. As Lamar recalled in one of his rare undiplomatic moments, "The hierarchy of the university simply had no concept of how older, more sophisticated universities staffed and managed their student life endeavors. It just wasn't in their background and they were hard to teach because they were research scientists and as you well know most research scientists and physicians only listen—truly listen—to other research scientists and physicians: this keeps their knowledge from getting too complicated and contradictory."[74]

For the time being, however, Lamar kept such angst to himself. He just went to work. Much to Dunbar's delight, the first thing Lamar did was tackle the chaos of student government. He soon had the "seven centers of anarchy" reorganized into an undergraduate SGA for University College (UC/SGA), a graduate SGA for University College (GSA), and school-based student organizations in the professional schools of the medical center. "Not ideal—still so diffuse," Lamar would lament, "but necessary considering the essentially professional, rather than university or academic, orientation of faculty and students in a medical center." Still, the more conventional elements of undergraduate student government now began to take shape. Larry Langford, an African American who had grown up in a local public housing project only to become mayor of Fairfield and later a Jefferson County commissioner, cut his political teeth as an early UC/SGA leader.[75]

Also under Lamar's general oversight—"You have to know when to step back and simply encourage the right academic folks to get involved outside the classroom"—other student life programs developed out of the drive and maturity of certain students and faculty. *The Kaleidoscope,* the student newspaper first established in 1967 with faculty oversight and later brought under Lamar's supervision, had an array of well-qualified editors. By 1974 the paper won a "first class" rating by the Columbia Scholastic Press Association, the first of many such awards it would capture.[76] Under Hubert Harper and John Coley's leadership, *Aura,* a student literary magazine, first appeared in 1969 with Kay Haslam as founding editor, and by the early 1970s other student editors such as Carolyn Massey had evolved the magazine into a well-developed outlet for student poetry and essays, many of which addressed issues of the surrounding urban scene.[77] James Hatcher's Town and Gown, now a unit of the School of Humanities, occasionally cast UAB students alongside community and guest actors in such performances as *Member of the Wedding* and *Sweet Charity.* In 1971 the noted choreographer and performer Stevan Grebel and his wife, Melanie, joined the faculty and began the University Ballet, a reconfigured version of the earlier successful Alabama Ballet. The next year Ward Haarbauer's student theater program opened in newly acquired Bell Auditorium and premiered that summer with Martin Duberman's plea for progress in American race relations, *In White America.* Dependent on an interracial cast, Haarbauer offered the play in response to "black students urging [him] to do a play with blacks in it." When it came time for casting and filling other positions associated with the production, however, Haarbauer "could not find any black students willing to participate." So he had to fill black roles "with community people and high school students."[78]

At about the same time the UAB Concert Choir gave its first performance in Bell Auditorium. Moreover, the UC/SGA Entertainment Committee brought to Boutwell Auditorium such national billings as Little Anthony and the Imperials and the Preservation Hall Jazz Band; to the engineering auditorium the consumer advocate of growing reputation, Ralph Nader; and to Clark Theater the recent poetry consultant to the Library of Congress, James Dickey, who had just published his major novel, *Deliverance* (1970). In 1972 the GSA hosted "the youngest and most irreverent member of the British Parliament," Bernadette Devlin, for a lecture in Bell Auditorium as well as a campaign debate between incumbent U.S. senator John Sparkman and challenger Winton M. ("Red") Blount. In 1975, engineering professor John Anderson led the establishment of a chapter of the national honorary society extolling outstanding scholarship, Phi Kappa Phi, with Volker, Hill, Campbell, and Barker as well as management professor Joe Van Matre and engineering professor Martin Crawford serving as charter leaders who then, within a year, initiated fifteen UAB student members. The same year Omicron Delta Kappa opened a chapter at UAB, and by May 1976 this new chapter hosted the first annual Student Honors Convocation begun with an address by the renowned economic historian and national security advisor for President John F. Kennedy, Walt Rostow.[79]

In the spring of 1971, UAB commencement sported the ultimately "permanent" colors of the institution, vibrant gold and deep green. Despite the growing "systems" approach to student life, the decision on these colors showed that some of the old ways persisted. In the spring of 1970, when UAB hosted its first commencement, Volker had leaned on teacher education professor Virginia Horns to manage the occasion. And as the 1971 commencement approached, he again telephoned Horns, late in the afternoon, to see how the details were lining up. Horns recalled the end of the conversation: Volker: "Virginia, those brown and black colors we used last time seem sort of dull. Don't you think we need something brighter?" Horns: "Dr. Volker, what colors would you like?" Volker (after a bad day?): "I don't give a goddamn what colors we have just as long as there is some brightness in the flowers on the stage!" Horns: "Yes sir, I'll get some bright colors." As Horns related twenty years later, "Back [in August] 1970 we had tried to work through a committee," which gave Volker a statistically detailed report on campus opinion related to different colors, concluding that there was a consensus about green and gold. But Volker never acted on the report. "So in the end [in the spring of 1971] I just went to a florist near the campus and ordered some goddamn green and gold flowers for [Boutwell] stage, and that's where we got our goddamn colors. People seem to like them, don't you think?"[80]

Certainly with a less abrasive approach, in 1976 Volker, Dunbar, Hill, Dudley Pewitt, and two community leaders devoted to classical music, the attorney Jerome Cooper and the journalist Oliver Roosevelt, brought a public radio station to the campus and community, with facilities at 1028 Seventh Avenue South. Certainly one key to the emergence of WBHM was the grant-writing ability of Dunbar: start-up hinged on funds from the Department of Health, Education, and Welfare, and they got them. Yet the influence of longtime Birmingham civic leader Thad Holt, so crucial in the beginning of UA's Birmingham Extension Center in the early 1930s, and of his son Sam Holt, who served in the mid-1970s as a vice president with National Public Radio, certainly provided "the ace card at the crucial time," mused Cooper.[81]

In addition, with gifts from two prominent and intermarried families of longtime Birmingham prominence, the Shooks and Ingalls, and from the enigmatic local attorney James A. Simpson, Campbell initiated the Ellen Gregg Ingalls Award for Excellence in Classroom Teaching, whereby students voted on outstanding professors. In 1969, students chose Hubert Harper as the first recipient of the Ingalls Award. A specialist on early English literature as well as the language and literature of ancient Greece and Rome, Harper also had become a noted Town and Gown actor. In fact, in 1968 he had made his Hollywood debut in the film based on Carson McCullers's classic novel, *The Heart Is a Lonely Hunter* (1940). Subsequent early Ingalls award winners were Charlotte Gafford (English), James S. Dupuy (mathematics), Robert Penny (English), and Glenda Elliott (teacher education).[82]

Medical Center Takeoff

Just as medical center grants and state funding began to flow, the Birmingham Medical Center encountered two setbacks. First, in January 1969 Lister Hill retired after forty-six years as a senator in Washington; he had provided crucial political aid in the development of medical education in Birmingham. Senator Sparkman stayed in office until 1978. Even so, Hill's leaving Washington, preceded some five years by Congressman Carl Elliott's reelection defeat at the hands of Governor Wallace's strategists, continued the gradual dissipation of an Alabama congressional delegation that had been forged out of Depression-era politics and for some twenty years had added dramatically to national leadership on congressional legislation related to health and education. The UAB Medical Center, and many other constituencies in Alabama and beyond, would have to work much harder to compensate for the demise of this forward-looking delegation out of the Heart of Dixie.[83]

Second, as the Alabama legislature worked through the summer of 1969, Governor Brewer began to make vague public statements foretelling the development of some type of second medical school, a shift from his earlier lack of enthusiasm about such a school dictated by the upcoming Democratic Party primary and Brewer's need for crucial south Alabama votes in the election. Still, he also advised reporters that increased funding for the UAB Medical Center would indeed allow it to expand medical and dental student admissions to reach the level recommended by the Booz, Allen, and Hamilton (BAH) report. Under these circumstances, he believed that the UA medical college certainly would work with Mobile General Hospital to start third- and fourth-year training programs for medical students in the Port Town as well as establish two-year basic science programs for beginning medical students on UA campuses in Tuscaloosa and Huntsville.[84]

By July, Governor Brewer's intentions became clearer: $2.5 million in bond money would go toward the construction of two additional floors on the new Basic Health Science Building then under construction in Birmingham, and by September 1970 the Birmingham medical college—now with its new three-year curriculum—could then begin to admit classes of 125, instead of 80. As this happened, "the two-year program at Mobile would remain under the control of the Birmingham medical school and possibly expand to a full program running fifty to a class." Moreover, when Dean Clifton Meador privately visited with Fred Whiddon in Mobile to seek clarification of what the Mobile leader actually sought, Whiddon assured him that a full-curriculum medical school reporting up through USA certainly was not part of his plans. Meador remained skeptical of this assertion. However, as long as Brewer was governor and the former AMA lobbyist Robert Ingram served as the state finance director, Volker and his Birmingham colleagues believed they held the balance of power in the always tricky game of politics, money, and medicine. Still, each new dollar flowing to Birmingham undermined their leverage. Increasingly, a change in politics could tip the scales toward Whiddon.[85]

And that is what happened. Throughout 1969 and early 1970 Whiddon's "gumbo lobby" pressed harder and harder for the return of George Wallace to the governorship. Then in 1970, ignoring his pledge not to run, Wallace beat Brewer in the Democratic primary and easily carried the general election. More to the point, during the campaign Wallace had promised Mylan Engle (who had supported Brewer in the primary) and other Mobile leaders that, if elected, he would deliver an enabling act for their medical school as well as a start-up budget. By the summer of 1971, with Wallace back in power and Mobile legislators once again working with the governor to hold up the state's education appropriation until there was "at least an additional $600,000" to get USA's medical school underway, the die was cast. As a last-ditch effort, Hill asked Alston Callahan, who had had George Wallace as a patient, to approach the governor about blocking Whiddon's strategy—to no avail. "It was as simple as this," Brewer recalled, "Fred had the votes."[86]

Hence, on August 3, 1971, regardless of his earlier statements to the contrary, Whiddon told the Mobile Builder's Association, "The medical school is a reality . . . the first class is scheduled in thirteen months and the new dean [Robert M. Bucher] is on the job." In late September 1971 it was official. By January 1973, only a half year behind Whiddon's breakneck schedule, twenty-four medical students enrolled for classes on the USA campus—pretty much the way Tinsley Harrison thought it could happen and with much the same strategy of "overwhelming momentum" that Volker had been pursuing in Birmingham.[87]

Although the civic elite of the Port Town now believed that the convoluted offense their city had endured for close to a century finally had found vindication, as Whiddon recalled, they "never [would] forget the way Tuscaloosa, then Birmingham stole the medical college from Mobile." Volker, Hill, and Mathews also would "never forget" Frank Rose's "flawed judgment" about an expanded UA presence in Mobile and what this "error" produced. Still, striking new successes at the UAB Medical Center made at least some wonder whether excessive implementation of the BAH report, that is, placing Mobile medical education under USA rather than Birmingham, had resulted in the slowing of any Birmingham developments.[88]

Despite intense, time-consuming work regarding the Mobile effort, Dick Hill in his new role as vice president of health affairs and director of the medical center made Birmingham take off. Although behind the scenes such growth involved tense moments between leading figures, such as Hill and John Kirklin, to the Alabama public this takeoff appeared foremost in the form of even more rapid physical growth. Foreshadowed with its much heralded ground breaking back in 1968, the new Basic Health Sciences Building (by 1977 renamed Volker Hall) kept growing up and out. Finally completed in 1971, it represented an additional 400,000 square feet for basic science research and instruction, some of which over time would pose a major problem in terms of asbestos removal.[89] At the same time Callahan's Eye Foundation Hospital, still technically separate from UAB, expanded and beside it Henry Peters's 71,000-square-foot School of Optometry building came out of the ground. To the southwest on Eighth Avenue the new School of Nursing building became a reality. A new wing to University Hospital, also planned since in 1968, opened in April 1970.[90] Full steam ahead, Hill and his colleagues also acquired the Crippled Children's Clinic (at Sixth Avenue South and Nineteenth Street) to be part of the medical center. With Jonas Salk's breakthrough research, however, the early 1970s witnessed rapidly diminishing focus on polio and the facility was converted to other uses, including temporary quarters for the School of Optometry while its new building went up as well as a makeshift ambulatory (outpatient) unit of University Hospital. The Regional Technical Institute (RTI) for Health Occupations opened in 1970, as did the Lister Hill Library for the Health Sciences in 1971, under the direction of long-time medical center librarian Sarah Cole Brown. Through a gift from Birmingham civic leader Sam Nakos, the new library immediately hosted on its front plaza an oversized statue of the ancient Greek ethicist and "father of medicine," Hippocrates. On Eighth Avenue, next to the Engineering Building, the first of many high-rise parking decks opened by mid-1970. In addition, an occupational rehabilitation center, first opened in 1964, received in 1969 a large two-story addition and continued to be known as the Spain Rehabilitation Center, honoring the family whose leader, Frank, had played such a crucial role in the birth of UAB.[91]

Moreover, as University Hospital increasingly became a facility specializing in extreme medical problems, as opposed to general health care, and as Medicare and Medicaid appeared to be a solution to funding for indigent care, the Jefferson County commissioners decided to build a special county facility for indigent patients. Though county managed, Mercy Hospital opened in 1972 right in the heart of the medical center to facilitate a continued "critical mass" approach. By 1975 it bore the name of W. Cooper Green, whose leadership on the commission had been so instrumental in this and other developments in the area.[92]

Likewise, in 1970 the William P. Engel Psychiatric Day Treatment Center opened, followed the next year by the Ziegler Research Building, endowed by Rebel and Sophie Ziegler, of Selma, who owned a hotdog manufacturing company. In 1973 the Diabetes Research and Education Building opened; a decade later it would bear the name of the complex personality so identified with its construction, the physician Buris R. Boshell. In 1975, a high-rise apartment tower shot up to house medical and nursing students, receiving the name Denman Hall in honor of the civic leader so instrumental in urban renewal developments. In 1976 the Ambulatory Dialysis Center opened as well as another parking deck.[93]

It kept coming. A seemingly endless stream of buildings emerged out of ground once prospected just for coal or iron ore: a massive new five-story, 71,000-square-foot addition to the dental school, plus a comprehensive University Hospital expansion labeled "UH2." This included the Alabama Heart Hospital (Monday Morning Quarterback Tower), aided by substantial gifts from the Kresge Foundation, the Rich Foundation, and local philanthropist Hall Thompson, and dedicated with a major address by the UAB cardiologist Harriet P. Dustan while she served as president of the American Heart Association.[94] In essence, according to the *Birmingham Post-Herald*'s Chris Conway, medical center expansion during the early to mid-1970s was of "mammoth proportions," involving close to $80 million. This not only represented the striking growth of a medical center but a significant increase in jobs for Birmingham citizens as well as significant projects for such Birmingham companies as Brice Construction, Brasfield and Gorrie, Inc., Dunn Construction Company, and Robins Engineering, Inc. The bumper year remained 1974, with expenditures of some $24 million. The biggest ticket was the new Basic Health Science Building at $17,178,800 ($2 million over budget). The smallest was $191,600 for the heartfelt pavilion at the Spain Rehabilitation Center given in memory of Edward M. Holmes, a place where patients in wheelchairs could see the sky and feel the sun, one of whom was Governor Wallace as he sought recovery from a thwarted assassination attempt during the presidential primary of 1972.[95]

Much of this money clearly represented funds the city and state otherwise would not have ever seen. Fifteen percent came from crucial private gifts—notwithstanding hotdogs and Montgomery connections, most from Birmingham. A whopping 65 percent came from competitively awarded federal grants and contracts, notably from the National Institutes of Health (NIH) and the National Science Foundation and strongly supported by Alabama congressman John Buchanan. In view of the major increases in education funding launched by Governor Wallace, it is ironic that only 20 percent of this construction derived from State of Alabama funds. Despite Wallace's general support, therefore, grants and contracts proved crucial to the development of the physical plant of the medical center. Moreover, this federal funding record underscored one of the central UAB lessons for the New South: a willingness on the part of at least some to embrace social change *could* get the generally poor Alabamians a badly needed return on their federal tax dollars for something other than military bases and, occasionally, highways. (As the historian Christopher Scribner has emphasized, however, this does not mean that the majority of Birmingham or Alabama citizens embraced such modern thoughts.) It also provided an important lesson to Volker, Hill, Charles McCallum, and other UAB leaders: indeed there *was* life after Lister Hill and Carl Elliott—and, from another perspective, after Fred Whiddon. It would be many years, in fact, before one could fully fathom the significance of Jack Rosenthal's metaphor of "a face-lift" for Birmingham.[96] Of course, what drove this physical takeoff were equally striking faculty and programmatic developments. Between 1969 and 1976,

Volker and Hill increased the full-time faculty in the medical center from 464 to 1,163, involving a rich array of scholars and clinicians.[97]

Just as Volker and Campbell had had to make adjustments in organizational structures to accommodate developing needs, Volker, Hill, and the medical center deans had to do the same. True to the spirit of the Appalachian Regional Commission grants, medical center expansion created a seemingly insatiable demand for well-trained professionals in the wide array of allied health fields, even more than Volker had expected—a point he continually urged to U.S. representative Bob Jones, from Huntsville, who chaired the commission. To deliver even more people for these jobs and to do so with a modern approach to their education, therefore, Hill and Campbell agreed to a programmatic merger and the creation of a new school in the medical center. Supported with Rudy Davidson's delivery of a line-item state appropriation, they merged the School of Health Services Administration that Matthew McNulty had established in 1966 in the medical center with the Division of Allied Health Sciences that Campbell and Charles Winkler had established in 1966 in the Extension Center. Hence, by the fall of 1969 the new School of Community and Allied Health Resources (SCAHR) opened in a new facility and reported up through Vice President Hill.[98] When McNulty, who had been director of the hospital, moved to an administrative position with the Association of American Medical Colleges then on to another high-level administrative position at Georgetown University, Hill named Keith Blayney, who had a Ph.D. in hospital administration from the University of Iowa and was McNulty's "right-hand man" in the old school, to serve as dean of the new school and James Moon, McNulty's "right-hand man" in the hospital, to the role of director of University Hospital.[99]

Beneath the surface of these developments were complications well beyond personalities and organizational charts. As one deeply steeped in the field of hospital administration and attuned to its organic nature, Moon was charged with working with hospital chief of staff Durwood Bradley to further redirect the hospital away from being a place for indigent patients and toward one focused on private-paying patients who needed secondary and tertiary care, particularly on health problems where UAB medical faculty and staff were engaged in research such as cancer, organ transplantation, and cardiology.[100] By the same token, with the massive increase in new medical technologies as well as jobs associated with them, employment and education in allied health fields caused reverberations throughout both universities and two-year colleges. As the new dean, Blayney continued to chair the long-range planning committee of the Alabama Regional Medical Program, providing crucial "articulation" linkages between Governor Wallace's new two-year colleges and the two-year (associate degree) allied health programs at UAB. In this endeavor Blayney received the assistance of Charles L. Joiner, who had joined the faculty in 1968 and now served as director of the school's Bureau of Research and Community Service. Within five years the Blayney-Joiner team would have cleared a crucial hurdle. One of their flagship programs, occupational therapy, won accreditation by the American Occupational Therapy Association. The association praised the unique connection the UAB team had formed between junior and technical colleges and SCAHR's RTI, a program led by James Truelove, whereby the great need for more occupational therapy assistants—those who aid registered therapists in treating the physically and psychologically disabled—could be met by students completing one year of study at a two-year college and a second year of "intense and practical" training at UAB.[101]

Hill, however, also moved forward on programmatic developments external to the Birmingham campus. One such effort evolved alongside something about as internal to the medical school as anything could be: its name. No sooner had Clifton Meador taken over as medical dean than he and Hill huddled and then recommended that the "College" of Medicine become known as the "School" of Medicine to make the unit conform to the organizational vocabulary most commonly used in the new university. Volker approved—it could have been his idea to begin with—as did the board, and Meador put in an order for new stationery.[102]

Shortly thereafter, the naming of medical education units received more attention as Meador and Hill moved forward on establishing a second "college" of medicine. In the summer of 1971, when pressures associated with the BAH report delivered state funding for the Birmingham Medical Center to open additional third- and fourth-year medical education programs at Tuscaloosa, Huntsville, and Mobile, Meador most willingly pursued the BAH report's recommendation as a way of increasing the number of primary care physicians trained in family practice, internal medicine, and pediatrics—physicians who might help serve the nonurban areas of the state where doctors were so badly needed. In a sense, beyond the BAH report, here was a positive response to the AMA's *Meeting the Challenge of Family Practice* (1966), which called for renewed attention to training more specialists in family practice medicine to balance what some, including Meador, saw as too much specialization in other fields, such as cardiology and oncology. (In 1965, Meador spoofed his profession's overindulgence in certain traditional specialties with a *New England Journal of Medicine* article titled "The Art and Science of Non-Disease.") Working through vaguely defined relationships with the other campuses, Hill and Meador discovered at a board meeting that UA was already establishing a College of Community Health, reporting up jointly through the Birmingham Medical Center and Tuscaloosa administration, and the Huntsville campus was starting a School of Primary Health Care with the same organizational plan. At UA, the preferred vocabulary for an academic unit was "college"; at Huntsville it was "school." To complement these "off-campus" efforts, Meador sought to build a family medicine program in Birmingham, but his faculty rejected the idea out of what they viewed as the lack of specialized depth in such a program. Still, by the fall of 1972 Hill and Meador had hired administrative staff and clinical (private practice) faculty, which enabled advanced medical students interested in such careers to find appropriate off-campus placements. Here, ostensibly, were three intertwined missions: more broadly reaching health care for Alabamians, more health education opportunities for medical students, and an implicit system for referrals of "very sick" patients to University Hospital.[103]

These efforts did not meet with universal success. Some physicians who specialized in family practice, for example, could be considered "simply undertrained internists" by prominent physicians (academic as well as private practice), since they were discouraged from such fields as surgery and gynecology.[104] For Dean Meador, however, though an endocrinologist, the new primary care fields may have lacked effective organizational structure in Alabama, but they were needed. They correlated with something vital in his past. His early medical career as a physician in Selma, where he saw numerous health problems stemming from the disconnectedness of Black Belt life, motivated him to take this project as far as he could go. He seemed pleased when, in 1972, David Mathews, UA president, hired the "Father of Family Medicine," William R. Willard, to serve as dean of the Tuscaloosa operation as a way of expanding rural health care, which Mathews viewed as lacking at UAB's medical school. As a professor at the University of Kentucky, Willard had led the AMA committee responsible for *Meeting the Challenge of Family Practice*. Likewise, Meador supported President Benjamin Graves's hiring of G. Gayle Stephens, the recent president of the Society of Teachers of Family Medicine, to assume the dean's role on the Huntsville campus, though this hire appeared, as the UA hire did, with no consultation with him or anyone else at the medical center in Birmingham.[105]

Meador also delivered direct Birmingham involvement in this outreach.

Even before the legislature appropriated "BAH funds" for outreach, he had sought to increase connections between the Birmingham medical faculty and patients and physicians in Alabama's small towns and rural areas. Journals and continuing education, he knew from his clinical experience in Selma, had obvious limitations as quick access to new lifesaving information on specialties such as surgery, internal medicine, pediatrics, and obstetrics and gynecology. Indeed, if Dick Hill's GCRC had permitted Meador a chance to translate research knowledge into clinical information, it also had convinced Meador of the need for "extending the system further." So, with assistance from physicians Thomas W. Sheehy (recently a medical advisor for the U.S. armed forces in Vietnam) and Margaret Klapper, he initiated Medical Information Service Via Telephone (MIST). One of the relatively rare commonsense approaches to the distribution of knowledge, here was a toll-free telephone line open twenty-four hours a day, seven days a week, permitting physicians practicing in remote areas of Alabama to get information on special problems, such as rare defects in blood clotting, new research, treatments, and cures unfolding in the urban medical center in central Alabama, as well as help with referrals. Soon featured in *Time* magazine ("the concept [is] simple, the effects far reaching"), MIST ultimately "enrolled" all faculty in the School of Medicine and some in dentistry. Over time the program assisted patients and physicians throughout the United States, facilitating upward of 100,000 incoming and outgoing calls in a single year—"distance learning" well before modern technology.[106]

This outreach from Birmingham was criticized for its "duplication and inefficiency," especially at a time when USA's new medical school was rising rapidly on the horizon and threatening to make Alabama's medical appropriations spread thinner and thinner. To counter these criticisms, Volker and Hill borrowed a concept from the University of Texas system and worked with the board to create an arm of efficiency and oversight; they proposed that the longstanding Special Committee of the Board for Medical Education Programs, now extending to the UA system, would provide overt oversight for their endeavors. Through this committee, high-profile UA board members then could assure the governor and legislature that there were no plans for UA to have three separate, costly medical schools, nor to blanket Alabama with health care "another institution" to the south might provide—hardly a phenomenon about to occur especially in large areas of poverty. On a more pragmatic level, through the committee's oversight and efficiency, Hill could argue that proposals for increasing medical education appropriations for Birmingham programs, now in competition with the Mobile programs, should be perceived as worthy of funding. Likewise, in the wake of the board's decision to move the nursing school from Tuscaloosa to Birmingham, the board had then looked the other way while the Tuscaloosa campus simply built a "replacement" nursing program at UA; the new oversight committee, Dick Hill hoped, could be used to defeat rumored efforts out of Tuscaloosa to accomplish similar "development" by turning its two-year medical program into yet another medical school for Alabama. Indeed, out of all these reasons, Hill repeatedly asserted that UA medical programs could accommodate an increase in class size from 125 to 200 "conditioned on . . . annual increases as funds become available." Hill remained nervous about the growing strength of a special board committee focused on medical education and its finances; physicians like their autonomy. Still, any realistic appraisal of the situation in 1972 told Hill that this strategy, if risky, was right for UAB and right for Alabama.

On November 18, 1972, the board passed a resolution strongly endorsing this expansive medical education outreach plan along with the increased role of the oversight committee. Known as "The McCall Report [No. 1],"—trustee Daniel T. McCall, Jr., offered the plan to the board and assisted in the drafting of it—the plan resulted out of careful deliberation by Volker, Hill, Wayne Finley, and their political sage so familiar with similar developments in the University of Texas system, the aging but sly Tinsley Harrison. In that the politics and money of medical education often are better understood within the context of international relations than university development, the plan was remindful of the key tactic employed by every nation to assume world power since the Renaissance: "defensive expansion." Even more, the Hill-Meador strategy had ideals and self-interest in full harmony, another crucial characteristic of effective "foreign policy."[107]

The medical center takeoff also included more developments in the School of Dentistry. On a daily, indeed hourly, basis, perhaps no individual proved more essential to McCallum in getting through his fifteen-hour days than his executive assistant, Kitty Robinson. Through night classes ("preferably nothing before 8:00 p.m.") and using vacation to get in an occasional mini-term day course, she completed her B.A. as well as considerable graduate work in medical history all while managing the kinetic dental dean. She often found herself forced to be frank with those needing to meet with the dean as well as with the dean himself. McCallum: "Hey, Robinson, I've got fifteen minutes to get to the airport—in which briefcase did I put those airline tickets?" Robinson: "Hey, McCallum, try looking in your right hand." McCallum: "Oh."[108]

More recently arrived on the scene but of more programmatic assistance was Juan Navia. A native of Havana, Cuba, and one of several high-level professionals whose flee from the regime of Fidel Castro ultimately brought them to Birmingham (oral pathologist Mario G. Martinez had arrived at the dental school in the late 1950s), Navia earned B.S., M.S., and Ph.D. degrees at the Massachusetts Institute of Technology (MIT). After several positions in Latin America, this public health–oriented biochemist served as assistant director of MIT's Department of Nutrition and Food Science before Volker and McCallum hired him in 1968 to become the senior scientist in the School of Dentistry's new Institute of Dental Research (IDR). More to the point, if the Birmingham dental faculty already had attracted considerable attention by creating "four-handed dentistry," an early 1960s innovation in which dentists using chair-side assistants revolutionized the efficiency of clinical care in dentistry, McCallum wanted the charming but hard-driving Navia to develop more basic research in the school's faculty; to do this he gave him the additional title of director of research training in dentistry. McCallum offered a clear charge: between 1974 and 1977 the School of Dentistry recorded total grants and contracts of only $3.2 million; regardless of the coup of "four-handed dentistry," extramural funding in dentistry had to increase.[109]

In response, Navia began offering courses such as Research Approaches and counseling young faculty and postdoctoral fellows on how to develop better research designs that would be attractive to funding agencies. He showed an array of young scientists, including future UAB faculty member Luis Aponte-Merced, how to capture grants funded not just from conventional sources, such as the National Institute of Dental Research, but from "more innovative places," such as the M&M Mars candy company. To follow through with the proven plan of knitting together crucial units, however, Navia also held appointments in comparative medicine and in biochemistry and served on the Biochemistry Executive Committee. And he set an example as an interdisciplinary researcher. With the use of "Siamese twin rats" (pairs of rats surgically connected at infancy—parabiotic rats), he quickly expanded his already nationally recognized research on how "TMP," sodium trimetaphosphate, inhibited tooth decay more through surface activity than through ingestion.[110]

This new emphasis on fundable research began to pay off. By 1983–84, dentistry's grants and contracts totaled $4.7 million, $1 million of which flowed through the now decade-old IDR, which conducted wide-ranging studies of oral vaccines against dental caries and of mouthwashes to combat periodontal disease. Here was Milton Schaefer's public health breakthrough creation of a small plastic cup located between the cheek and the teeth for catching saliva secreted by the parotid gland; collected in this uncontaminated way, as Schaeffer explained in the *Journal of Dental Research,* the saliva could then be used for immunological research on metabolic disturbances, mineral levels, and enzyme abnormalities.[111]

In concert with Volker's plan of using the university to enhance targeted segments of local employment, much as the Blayney-Joiner team had been doing, McCallum also worked with the VA Hospital across the street to initiate the Dental Laboratory Technology Training Program. Housed in the VA, the certification (nondegree) program began in 1976 "to fill an acute need in the state [of Alabama] for trained dental laboratory technicians," especially for employment removed from the major urban areas of Alabama.[112]

McCallum also pushed harder on affirmative action. The dental school had experienced a 40 percent enrollment increase between fall 1966 and fall 1978, by which time there were 288 D.M.D. students, more than 70 postdoctoral students, and 75 auxiliary (or dental hygiene) students. Twelve percent of the D.M.D. class in the fall of 1976 were women; the national average was 11 percent. Because of its location in a city known for civil rights tragedies, the UAB dental school had more difficulty than most of the other fifty-nine dental schools in the nation in attracting black students. For 1976–77, the school received six applications from blacks; three were accepted. To help solve this problem, McCallum turned to a new faculty member, Wilson Wright, Jr., whose own experiences documented the virtues of McCallum's goal.[113]

In 1970, Wright—a Prattville, Alabama, native with a B.S. from Alabama State—had been admitted to the dental schools of both Meharry University and UAB; he was one of the first three black students admitted to the UAB dental school. However, his UAB acceptance had been conditional upon his satisfactory completion of organic and inorganic chemistry at Birmingham-Southern College (BSC) during the summer of 1970, that is, "Double O" in one summer, no easy task and frankly one of questionable pedagogy. When Wright replied to McCallum that he wanted to go to UAB but that he had no tuition to attend BSC, McCallum called the black corporate leader A. G. Gaston. Shortly thereafter, Gaston notified BSC that he would cover Wright's costs for the summer.[114] Still, just as Wright conquered "Double O" and proceeded to his first year of dental school at UAB, he encountered an obstacle of another sort—social discrimination.

Along with the other two black students admitted that year, Jimmy Walker and Richard Rudolph, Wright failed to receive invitations to social gatherings other first-year students received, engagements that could lead to the joining of a dental fraternity. As Wright would recall years later, "This hurt us and embarrassed us." However, in the early winter of 1971, when McCallum discovered what was happening, he called into his office the student presidents of all the dental fraternities. They received a flat statement: "This next year, 1971–72, our black students will be included in the fraternity system or there will be no dental fraternities at UAB. Mark my word." And the following year there was a smooth transition in the interracial social life of the dental school.[115]

By the fall of 1974 Wright had completed his D.M.D., turned down a private practice offer in Montgomery, and joined McCallum's faculty as a tenure-track specialist in restorative dentistry. It now became McCallum's turn to get some assistance. The dean asked Wright to help get the same opportunity for other black students that he had had: he asked Wright to join him in increasing the number of black students who applied to the UAB dental school by sending over Wright's own signature letters to black dentists all over the Southeast, advising that Birmingham was a good place for a black student to pursue dental education. One such letter went to the prominent resident of Huntsville, Alabama, John L. Cashin, respected equally for his dental practice and his civil rights activism. Wright urged that Cashin, "as a local minority practicing dentist, help in encouraging minority students to apply to the UAB School of Dentistry." "There should be one dentist for every 1,200 people," he stated. "However, in black communities the average ratio is one dentist for every 12,100 people . . . [and] in many counties in Alabama, there are no black dentists to treat black patients." Then Wright's central point: "You can see that there is a great need [for black dentists]. Being a black graduate of Alabama State University and the UAB School of Dentistry, I am convinced that we can change this applicant pool. . . . In most instances, if a student is accepted, the University can provide some financial aid. . . . If you are interested in receiving additional material about the [UAB] School of Dentistry for distribution in your office or have any questions, please let me know."[116]

Such efforts brought limited results. In 1973–74, only 4 percent of the total D.M.D. enrollment were blacks, all of whom were from the deep South. By 1977–78, the D.M.D. program, made up of 273 students, included 12 (4.4 percent) blacks, all of whom were from either Alabama or Mississippi. This frustrated Wilson Wright. He received no reply from Cashin nor from the twenty-five other people to whom he sent letters. Recalling a similar frustration, McCallum later would put it plainly: "The Birmingham image was still defeating us and it's always possible that some of the traditional black dental colleges were working against us. . . . Understandably, we wanted the same students."[117]

Other aspects of the School of Dentistry's outreach and student recruitment moved more quickly. From Volker's deanship, indeed from the very grassroots dental forces that enabled the creation of the dental school in 1947–48 and from Volker's own connections with Thailand, dentistry had a strong record of balancing service to the taxpayers of Alabama with service to the world beyond Alabama. McCallum followed through with this complex outreach, often with the assistance of Margaret Klapper, a physician working for Hill on public outreach matters. Between 1948 and 1977 more than two hundred students from over fifty nations received some of their dental training at UAB, often postdoctoral training. Likewise, faculty and graduate students from dentistry traveled throughout the world, especially to Latin America, to assist local efforts at public health and sponsored international dentistry conferences in Birmingham.[118]

Still, Alabama remained dentistry's chief service target. In the words of McCallum's longtime associate dean of administrative affairs, yet another of the dental school faculty trained at Tufts, Lewis Menaker, "One obviously did not have to go out of Alabama to find people living in third-world health conditions." In the fall of 1978, despite opposition from some dentists around the state who feared loss of revenues, McCallum initiated a B.S. program in dental hygiene. Graduates could work as key components of public health teams, especially in rural counties where access to dental care remained limited. He also continued to keep the D.M.D. program focused on turning out dentists who would practice in Alabama. For example, out of sixty-six in the graduating class of 1977, only one headed for private practice outside the state. Not surprisingly, the School of Dentistry's alumni provided key leadership for the Alabama Dental Association and through its structure (just like the School of Medicine's alumni organization and the Alabama Medical Association, pragmatically organized along lines of state legislative districts) served as a potent lobbying force in the legislature, delivering, among other things, state scholarships for Alabama students attending the UAB dental school.[119]

The School of Nursing showed the same pattern of applying high-level programs to improve the welfare of the state and local citizenry. By the late 1970s, Dean Marie O'Koren had built a program consisting of 800 undergraduates and 200 graduate students that reflected steady increases in the types of people the profession lacked: men and people of color. In its rural areas and particularly in the old cotton plantation sections of the state where there were high concentrations of poor black citizens, Alabama needed all the nurse practitioners it could get. Moreover, as part of a national trend toward more prevention education in all aspects of medical education, O'Koren and her colleagues established a master's program (one student in the program was future UAB president Carol Garrison) and a doctoral program for training nurses with the research skills so badly needed in the development of prevention programs. This was the first doctoral program in nursing in the Southeast. O'Koren, likewise, led an overhaul of the B.S.N curriculum and refocused it on prevention. By their third year, students studied prevention in target populations such as adults, mothers and children, and the mentally ill. In their fourth (final) year students engaged in practical training for serving one of these target populations, with opportunities to specialize in low-income urban or rural areas as well as in tertiary care facilities such as UAB's University Hospital. No faculty member proved more ingenious in this effort than Charlene McKaig, who found extramural support for school-based clinics in Birmingham's inner city through which she both trained nurse practitioners and provided free health care screening and education for adolescent minority females.[120]

Henry B. ("Hank") Peters had developed the School of Optometry similarly and focused on solutions to local problems, something Volker and Hill increasingly called "research service." From the year it opened its doors, 1969, through 1977, the School of Optometry produced ninety doctoral-level optometrists on its own as well as over fifty optometric technicians in conjunction with RTI programs in SCAHR. A rotating fourth-year internship program for O.D. students connected the program to the university's service mission. Free eye health screening went to patients in the VA Hospital as well as to developmentally disabled patients at the Center for Developmental and Learning Disorders (CDLD), to diabetes patients in the diabetes research and education program, and to retired Birmingham citizens associated with local Eldergarden activities.

Like nursing, optometry extended this free service to K–12 students. By 1977, 12,000 students per year across the state received free eye health screenings.[121] To keep this service one of modern health care, however, optometry added master's and Ph.D. programs in physiological optics in 1975. The faculty recruited for this interdisciplinary program held doctorates in psychology but primary faculty appointments in optometry. With the blended insights of physics, psychology, and optometry, and in time behavioral neuroscience and cellular biology, they plowed new ground on how the eye interacts with the brain. Soon they advanced their research even further through the creation of the Vision Science Research Center, which anticipated many of the scientific connections at the heart of a new field to be known as cognitive science. Simultaneously, through instruction based on their research they produced researching faculty for optometry schools across the nation, including UAB's. Unknown to the Alabama citizens receiving this futuristic health care, at times in conjunction with the VA Hospital, this was the only physiological optics program in the Southeast.[122]

On Dean Meador's watch in medicine, John W. Benton cemented a long-developing (and much needed) relationship by chairing the school's Department of Pediatrics and serving as medical director and physician-in-chief of the Children's Hospital, which had been since 1961 a well-established (though privately owned and managed) component of the medical center. This innovative medical *center* arrangement soon facilitated Hugh Dillon's expanded understanding of streptococcal diseases; Charles Alford, Sergio Stagno, and Robert Pass's new discoveries pertaining to rubella, toxoplasma, and, most important, cytomegaloviruses, especially among newborns; Richard J. Whitley's work on herpes simplex and varicella-zoster virus infections; and Max D. Cooper's study of human immunodeficiency diseases. For this work Cooper ultimately won a coveted fellowship of the Howard Hughes Medical Institute as well as the honor of being the first faculty member from the State of Alabama invited for membership in the National Academy of Sciences, although Volker was an original member of the academy's Institute of Medicine.[123]

No doubt equally striking became the work of Meador's new star of a hire, Dan W. Urry. In 1970, Meador and his Department of Medicine chair, Joe Reeves, enticed Urry, a biochemist, to leave the AMA's Biomedical Research Institute in Chicago for a joint appointment in biochemistry and medicine in Birmingham, the Kracke and Volker plan still at work. A physical organic chemist on the cutting edge of the ongoing molecular revolution, Urry identified the "beta helix" factor in the structure of peptide molecules, the corollary to Linus Pauling's 1948 identification of the "alpha helix," within a year of his arrival at the medical center. Two years later, in 1973, he nailed down "beta spirals" as yet another crucial component of peptides and proteins. From these discoveries and others he then jumped to the still younger field of biomaterials where new discoveries about molecules were helping create new materials that were simply nonexistent before the molecular revolution of the mid-twentieth century. To the intense interest of the Office of Naval Research as well as the National Heart, Lung, and Blood Institute, and with their financial support, Urry invented biodegradable, nonadhesive membranes that could protect burns and wounds while preventing fluid loss and infection. With the same intriguing mixture of basic and applied science (indeed, intriguing to the point at which "basic" and "applied" appeared to lose differentiating relevance), he also helped make synthetic arteries that were *not* biodegradable and in modern academic fashion started a private company, Bioelastics.[124]

The flexible center approach to programmatic development also continued to reap benefits during Meador's deanship. With the combined forces of the Spain Rehabilitation Center and the Medical Rehabilitation Research and Training Center focused on spinal cord dysfunction, the Department of Rehabilitation Medicine—especially through the efforts of John Miller, Samuel L. Stover, and Phillip R. ("Russ") Fine—launched the Regional Spinal Cord Injury Care System and the Urological Rehabilitation and Research Center.[125] The oldest of the UAB centers, the Cardiovascular Research and Training Center (CVRTC), first established by Reeves in 1967, also continued expanding. Thomas N. James, who had left Henry Ford Hospital in Detroit in 1968 to join the Birmingham faculty in medicine, assumed command of the CVRTC in 1970 and propelled the unit to worldwide reputation. Despite his additional responsibilities after 1973 of chairing the Department of Medicine, James made CVRTC research funding skyrocket. These funds came primarily from the American Heart Association but also from the NIH. In fact, more NIH cardiovascular research funds went to UAB during the 1970s than to any other academic medical center in the United States. For these and other accomplishments James would be chosen president of the American Heart Association, president of the International Society and Federation of Cardiology, president of the Association of University Cardiologists, and ultimately chair of the Tenth World Congress of Cardiology, in Moscow, especially for his leadership in the USA-USSR Symposia on Sudden Cardiac Death, which convened in Birmingham at a time when the cold war remained anything but over.[126]

In 1971, in the midst of President Richard M. Nixon's proposed "War on Cancer," Congress provided massive funds for the NIH to establish eleven regional and comprehensive centers for cancer research as well as treatment. There was the standard call for proposals.[127] An oncologist from Philadelphia named John Durant, educated at Swarthmore College and Temple

University Medical School and who had joined the faculty of the UAB Department of Medicine in 1968 as director of the Division of Hematology/ Oncology, took the lead in submitting UAB's proposal.[128] The NIH cancer grant required substantial local- or state-level matching funds. State-level tragedies facilitated this support. Cancer finally had killed Governor Lurleen Wallace in May 1968. Her enduring popularity among rank-and-file Alabamians, combined with Governor Brewer's generally strong support of UAB "as a place truly of the future" and the possibility that George Wallace would reverse his promise not to run and would beat Governor Brewer in the 1970 gubernatorial election, made it a strong bet that Montgomery somehow would promise matching funds for UAB's application to the NIH. Indeed, unrelated to the UAB-NIH connection, no sooner had Lurleen Wallace died than several of her close friends began to create a foundation for the construction of a cancer hospital in Montgomery. On hearing of their plans, Dick Hill immediately visited with these Wallace family friends— and brought them onboard with the idea that such a hospital in Birmingham, tied in with the existent medical center, could have a far larger impact on the fight against cancer than a smaller operation in Montgomery. Ultimately, more than 44,000 Alabamians contributed to this foundation, a significant portion of whom were UAB employees. During 1969 and early 1970, the now full-time UAB lobbyist Rudy Davidson had Volker, Hill, Meador, and Durant—not to mention ENT specialist James J. Hicks, who had "serious Wallace-country connections"—visiting with these friends and Wallace himself, bereaved but more and more acting like a candidate for 1970.[129]

They also visited extensively with Governor Brewer. Not hedging their bets but simply caught in an oddly flexible situation, Volker and Hill saw themselves as getting cancer center support if Brewer remained a permanent fixture: Brewer as governor likely would block USA from taking over medical education in Mobile, then easily would have the funds for state support of the Birmingham cancer center. However, Volker and Hill had reason to be optimistic about the cancer center even if Wallace unseated Brewer the following year: if reelected, Wallace, while undoubtedly going forward with USA's medical school, had promised to deliver major state funding in memory of his wife to aid the UAB cancer center. As it turned out, of course, Wallace returned to the governorship in 1971. Accordingly, the UAB team adjusted "relatively quickly" to Wallace's new administration, especially his supporting USA medical education, and, with Davidson's strategy, began to collect on the promised assistance to the Birmingham cancer center. By late summer 1975, Davidson telephoned Volker with the news that "the cancer center support from Montgomery and other places was a sure thing": $5 million from citizen contributions to the foundation (with a significant portion from the Henderson Foundation of Troy, Alabama), $3.1 million allocated by Governor Wallace out of Federal Revenue Sharing funds, and $6.5 million from the sale of UAB bonds.[130]

Meanwhile, with the crucial aid of John Dunbar, Durant submitted his application to the NIH. Optimistic, by late 1970 the hippie-looking if brilliant Durant—long hair, beard, and acerbic wit—had relinquished his role as division director in medicine to Marc Conrad and was working full time as director of the planned facility. The NIH grant delivered $2.3 million. With total funding, then, of some $16.9 million, the Cancer Research and Training Center, including the Lurleen B. Wallace Radiation Therapy and Tumor Institute, opened officially in January 1977, and two years later its eighty-bed tower also became a reality. Under the leadership of Durant and after 1983 that of Albert LoBuglio, who came from the University of Michigan's Simpson Cancer Center to direct the facility, here emerged one of the top cancer centers in the world.[131]

Through the establishment of the Cancer Research and Training Center the irony of the Wallace legacy spoke with unique poignancy. The Wallace political machine, which not only smashed Brewer but other progressives, too (e.g., Carl Elliott in 1964 and George McMillan in 1982), in many ways rendered Alabama's public policy nonfunctional some three decades after the end of Wallace's career. Yet Wallace also helped deliver crucial money and support for UAB to go forth on many fronts and in this case to attack one of the most devastating diseases of our time. Guided by Durant and later LoBuglio, the facility still stood strong at the advent of the new millennium, helping people from all over the world.[132]

The Great Money Fight

No doubt because of its rapid growth, the School of Medicine in the 1970s still encountered problems. The most acute of these revolved around the Great Money Fight of 1972. In May that year "all hell broke loose," to use Clifton Meador's recollection, over the role of patient care revenues in the general fiscal development of UAB. In a sense this was but a Birmingham chapter in a nationwide story unfolding wherever there were medical centers with physicians generating the large revenues available through billings passed on to the new Medicaid and Medicare programs created in the

1960s. UAB's experience, however, was particularly intense. The institution was in a state with historic underfunding for indigent care. Alongside this poverty were much sought-after specialties, such as coronary bypass surgery, involving physicians who commanded relativity high salaries, much of which was generated by the specialists themselves. For example, if a physician was salaried at $250,000 annually, only about $40,000 of this sum derived from state funds—the remaining $210,000 was paid out of the physicians' departmental Professional Service Fund, a fund that received patient payments for care rendered by physicians in a given department—"the doctor's money." Out of this departmental fund might also come contributions toward physical plant renovations within the medical school and the hospital. Here was a surreal blend of poverty and wealth and the attendant complications of management.[133]

Since 1969 President Volker had been "taxing" these physician-generated revenues at around 4 percent per year to assist hospital funding (in addition to voluntary physician donations to the hospital) and to develop the general university budget, including that of central administration, the new SCAHR in the medical center, and University College.[134] But in April 1972, word broke inside the institution that the following developments were forthcoming: (a) University Hospital and its clinics likely would complete the fiscal year between $600,000 and $1 million in deficit due to staggering indigent care costs (the state reimbursed only 10 percent of the hospital's costs); (b) Volker likely would increase the "tax" on Professional Service Funds to make up for this shortfall; (c) Volker had considered significant raises for medical school faculty and hospital staff after a three-year dry spell but was backing away from the idea in view of the deficit; and (d) some "close to Volker" had preliminary plans for renovating the Woodward House. Amid these rumors, some more substantive than others (e.g., Woodward House redecoration had been mentioned and dropped), key faculty in the School of Medicine screamed foul. What exacerbated these tensions was the legal, but at times counterproductive, practice that Volker and Paul Brann had been following with regard to where such transfers ultimately landed: into one "general pot" out of which certain expenditures for non–medical center operations were covered; that is, it was virtually impossible for physicians to trace where their taxed funds were going. To further escalate matters, Volker had been using projected University College revenues from the state and from tuition and fees to guarantee the sale of bonds used in various medical center construction projects. Whether one views this as innovative financial practice behind futuristic growth in a state often considered backward, or nontransparent financial processes engendering a lack of trust, the fact is that the Great Money Fight began to heat up.[135]

By late April, doggedly pressed by two powerful department chairs, Reeves in medicine and Kirklin in surgery, Dean Meador and hospital chief of staff Durwood Bradley urged Hill and Brann to reconsider: it was unfair that physicians were unable to use the revenues they were generating to build their own programs. When the two vice presidents looked to Volker for help, the president told Hill to "come up with a plan."[136] Hill had to act fast. In communicating with Brann, Kirklin held little back: "Kind words, bland reassurances . . . will not be useful any longer," and he would resign and take one of several offers including "one at Harvard" if the problem were not solved to the satisfaction of the School of Medicine faculty. But Hill's situation was more complicated than this threat from the School of Medicine and from the new "jewel in the crown" he had recruited from the Mayo. Hill had instructions from Volker that there had to be at least some medical center–generated funds behind the development of the university in general.[137]

By early May, despite Hill's already noted skills as both a negotiator and a diplomat, there had been further communications from Kirklin to Brann, followed by Brann's resignation. Through these communications even more of the genuine complexity of the crisis became clarified. To avoid unionization of certain hospital employees, which the board wanted him to avoid, Volker recently had approved an increase in the wages of hospital employees well beyond what they were budgeted for in the state appropriation. While this was happening not only did the state's payments to the hospital fall far short of what was needed to cover the costs of indigent cases, but Jefferson County's did, too, as it had for years. Indeed, in this context, UAB had determined it could not provide medical staff for the emerging county-managed Mercy (Cooper Green) Hospital, which was to focus on indigent care. UAB also emphasized that where patient costs were being covered by Blue Cross/Blue Shield health insurance, reimbursements to the hospital "are paying off at a rate far less than University costs." Managing University Hospital, they also urged, remained far more expensive than managing other hospitals in the state because of the teaching role and the high technology costs accompanying new specialties, such as organ transplantation, which citizens urged UAB to offer.[138] Here were enduring reverberations of Roy Kracke's dilemma in the late 1940s, just more complicated because of the intervening development of the institution and the complexities of federal funding, especially regarding new specializations within the medical faculty and the hospital.

On May 5, as Volker publicly professed "optimism . . . that differences of opinion . . . can be resolved," the president again told Hill to "fix the problem." Shrewdly, Hill hoped the crisis, though real in every sense, would deliver additional state funds. He was buoyed by a message from Volker that representative Tom Gloor and state senator Pat Vacca, of Jefferson County, wanted to have a summit of the Jefferson County delegation in Birmingham to determine what increase out of an anticipated special session of the legislature might be necessary to bring an end to the crisis. Not counting on new money, however, Hill continued to draw a hard line on his colleagues in medicine and refused to promise that further patient revenue monies would not be necessary to "get us out of the bind." Instead, he appointed a broadly based ad hoc committee, drawing from leadership in medicine as well as the hospital, to make proposals for a way to "fix the problem."[139]

While the committee worked day and night, the problem intensified. On May 6, Meador and Bradley resigned their administrative posts. Kirklin followed two days later. On May 10, through the *Birmingham News* (whose crack reporter, Anita Smith, had been covering the story with fresh information daily), Hill politely confirmed the Meador and Bradley resignations only and announced that the chairman in pediatrics, John Benton, would take over as interim dean of medicine and surgeon Holt McDowell would serve as interim chief of staff in the hospital. Hill hoped that Meador and Bradley "would reconsider." Aside from these personnel changes, however, neither side budged either publicly or in the private committee meetings. Volker kept quiet the resignations of Brann and Kirklin, who was on the verge of being named the 1972 recipient of the Lister Medal by the Royal College of Surgeons of London, and Hill also stuck with a public vagueness on these two: "Some others, yes, have submitted their resignations." Joined by Hill, Volker went to work trying to get them to reverse their decisions.[140]

Finally, on the morning of Friday, May 12, a breakthrough came. Through the committee Hill had been able to work out a "back to work" solution. Outlined as phase 1 (the remainder of fiscal year 1971–72), phase 2 (implementation on October 1, 1972), and phase 3 (during fiscal year 1972–73), the settlement in effect reduced Professional Fund transfers to the university by the amount of the hospital's deficit, while transfers from the Professional Funds to central administration operations remained essentially the same. How bonded indebtedness for School of Medicine buildings would be paid, especially regarding use of funds generated by University College, would be left "to further study." By the same token, state funds appropriated for the hospital and the School of Medicine would come to those units "intact," then would be "taxed" at negotiated percentages for support of central administration and the university. A new senior-level fiscal officer representing the hospital as well as the School of Medicine would be appointed to help handle these negotiations as well as many other fiscal affairs of the two units.[141] Finally, representing implementation of an idea first suggested almost a year earlier, in July 1971, in a communication from Kirklin to Brann, patient-income funds generated by the School of Medicine and the hospital would be placed in separate accounts with "management and investment by these units" and earnings from the investments coming back to the units. The most immediate impact of this agreement was the retraction of the resignations by Kirklin and Brann, Meador and Bradley, all of whom were back in their administrative jobs by the afternoon. Of perhaps greater long-term influence, phase 3 of the agreement, originating out of a conversation with Kirklin—he had experienced similar operations at the Mayo and for some time had been interested in an approximate replication in Birmingham—led to the creation of the Health Services Foundation (HSF). Shortly to be a striking source of entrepreneurial capital (desperately needed in a state that by the mid-1980s would actually ban appropriations for capital improvements in research universities), the foundation also intensified the power of clinical chairs and added to general UAB affairs the new power-broker position of president of the foundation with leaders chosen from a variety of fields in the coming years: 1973–75, radiologist David M. Whitten; 1975–88, surgeon John W. Kirklin; 1988–92, pulmonary specialist Dick Briggs; 1992–2001, neurologist John N. Whitaker.[142]

If the board had strongly encouraged Volker to get a solution before the adjournment of the board meeting, scheduled for May 12 and 13, the board also seemed to grasp the difficulty of what he and Hill had accomplished. In the wake of approving the creation of HSF in 1973 (with one dissenting vote), it adopted a "statement" recognizing the "special sensitivities necessary to guide successfully an institution of higher learning through both its triumphs and its tribulations" and extended its "deep appreciation" and "continued confidence and support of" Volker, Hill, and Brann. Publicly, thereafter, Volker reflected confidence in the process and the outcome spawned by the crisis. Privately, however, he saw to it that a few medical center leaders knew that he stuck by his guns on the matter of University College: while clearly benefiting from taxation of physicians' Professional Service Funds, UC also played a role in helping expand the medical center. As he wrote Dean Meador, "It is evident that a substantial portion of the recent building program of University Hospital and the School of Medicine was made possible by revenue bonds guaranteed by the pledge of University College and other non–University Hospital revenues. Hopefully, the administrative leadership of University Hospital and the School of Medicine will attempt to correct these misconceptions."[143]

In short, even during the Great Money Fight of 1972 Volker had the leadership skills to keep the momentum of his urban research university moving full steam ahead. This could not have happened, however, had it not been for Dick Hill's not only having the diplomatic toughness to bring the crisis to an end, at least as far as anyone could predict at the time, but his sharing Volker's vision for the future of the whole university.

More Medical Center Takeoff

The "bizarreness of Alabama's developing a second medical school—not just the objective but the way it was achieved"—combined with stresses of the Great Money Fight in Birmingham convinced Dean Meador that high-level administration in a medical center was not for him. "I wanted no part of it ever again," he would recall. Hence in late October 1972 he wrote Hill that he wanted to do something else, either at UAB or elsewhere, though he would stay on as dean until the end of the 1972–73 academic year if necessary to facilitate the selection of a suitable replacement. No lingering acrimony led to his decision. Pressed on this point by Anita Smith, Gloria Goldstein—the consummate diplomat—assured folks that "no one's mad . . . everything's amicable."[144]

Hill appointed a search committee, and in March 1973 it made a recommendation he and Volker endorsed. They offered the deanship of the School of Medicine to James A. Pittman, a Floridian who had graduated from Davidson College then Harvard Medical School. Pittman had been one of "Tinsley's boys"—one of his last residents in Birmingham—and had worked at UAB from 1956 to 1971 as instructor through professor in the Department of Medicine and as director of the Division of Endocrinology and Metabolism. In 1971 he moved to Washington, D.C., to become professor of medicine at Georgetown University and assistant chief medical director for research and education in medicine at the central office of the VA. In

July 1973, however, this nationally acclaimed endocrinologist with intense interests in everything from World War II airplanes (which he collected) to Renaissance art (which he read about) returned to Birmingham to run the school his mentor, Harrison, helped create. His old friend, Meador, assumed a faculty position in the School of Medicine at Vanderbilt University.[145]

Arriving on the very same day as the official creation of HSF and with the "medical politics" of that development still unfolding, Pittman found no regular slot on the HSF board allotted for the medical dean; he "vowed to Volker either to get [him] on that board or [Volker] would find that the whole thing would not work." Six months and Volker's personal action finally saw Pittman take a seat at this table, which was all-important to the medical school. Shortly, two developments long in the works reached fruition. From a significant array of existing programs, and after considerable planning with Vice President Hill, he created the Department of Neurology chaired by James H. Halsey, Jr. Likewise, Pittman let the Sports Medicine Institute take off under the direction of Kurt W. Niemann.[146] Pittman also encouraged new projects to surface and take form, including the Center for Aging, which spun out of the Division of Gerontology and Geriatric Medicine, in the Department of Medicine. Directed by the physician most responsible for the division, Harold Schnaper, the center advanced research service and community outreach on multiple issues of aging, burgeoning tasks as American society got older and as the NIH and other agencies saw the need for increased grant support in such areas. By 1979 Schnaper's center moved out of the Department of Medicine into the Community Health Services Building (formerly the Blue Cross/Blue Shield Building). At the same time, Schnaper developed the Gerontology Education Program (including a baccalaureate-level certificate) through joint efforts with the School of Social and Behavioral Sciences, initiated by the new chair in social work, Norman Eggleston.[147]

Pittman also picked up where Meador left off on medical education outreach and referrals—the ideals and the self-interest. To the chagrin of Tuscaloosa leaders, especially President Mathews and Dean William R. Willard, Pittman immediately reorganized the reporting chain for branch campus health education programs: on paper at least, because of his strong regard for Gayle Stephens, in Huntsville, he had the Tuscaloosa primary care program reporting up through Stephens, and from there to the Birmingham dean, though an uneasy murkiness continued to characterize the management of these operations. Then, in 1975, Pittman entered into lengthy discussions with Hill about the pros and cons of national trends in primary care training, and ultimately created a new unit at the UAB medical school campus—the Department of Family Practice. At first Pittman turned to Robert Sherrill, director at Cooper Green Hospital, to take on the additional role of chair of this new department. When Cooper Green physicians prevailed in their point that this left Sherrill overextended and conflicted regarding management of their Professional Service Funds, Pittman brought Gayle Stephens down from Huntsville to run the new Birmingham department, replacing him in Huntsville with the internist J. Ellis Sparks. From this new position, despite continued and time-consuming behind-the-scenes tensions over who really managed Tuscaloosa's program, Stephens wrote *The Intellectual Basis of Family Practice* (1982). Likewise echoing national trends, Pittman worked with Thomas N. James in the Department of Medicine to create a separate Division of General Medicine. As Pittman distilled the plan, this would be "internal medicine without a sub-specialty such as hematology or cardiology but with an emphasis on ambulatory [mobile patients] care"—an old idea, but one being advanced across the nation and in Alabama. Pittman often pointed to renowned Jack Kirschenfeld, of Montgomery, as a model of such training in a general medicine practice; he was board certified both in internal medicine and, by the mid-1970s, in family practice medicine and would soon be the head of a UAB satellite clinic in Montgomery.[148]

Although he followed these national trends in medical education, Pittman also continued to worry about how such new programs were managed and evaluated within the UA system and how they could influence the national accreditation of Birmingham operations, despite the Special Committee of the Board that had been charged with clarifying such problems. Rumors of development about to happen out of Tuscaloosa turned Pittman's concern into "more than agitation." President Mathews, some said, sought the development *not* of an expanded family health/rural health program (an area in which, he asserted, UAB was lacking), but a full-program medical school in Tuscaloosa. Such rumors, Mathews later recalled, had no foundation, and no substantiated fact remains to back them up. Still, the maelstrom of politicking inside the UA system created by this rumor resulted in the board's special committee accepting Pittman's recommendation that, after years of disputed authority among the three campuses, the chief reporting lines of the Huntsville and Tuscaloosa programs *would be* up through the medical dean in Birmingham, with secondary reporting up through the presidents of the Tuscaloosa and Huntsville campuses. Otherwise, accreditation issues watched closely by the Liaison Committee on

Medical Education (LCME)—that is, quality of faculty, funding, and student admission standards—in the branch medical programs could not be managed effectively by the UAB medical school. Advocates of more autonomy for the Tuscaloosa and Huntsville programs were furious. As for Pittman, while he had a multicampus program whose utility he worried over, he at least thought he had taken a step toward bringing the program under his control. As for Tuscaloosa reactions, Willard soon retired. An extended search for a replacement ultimately produced another nationally recognized leader in family medicine, the Floridian Wilmer J. Coggins, who saw the Tuscaloosa program into a new era—renamed Capstone Medical Center in 1982—and programmatic fine-tuning Pittman generally endorsed.[149]

Pittman's contentiousness over the Tuscaloosa program should not be taken as opposition to broadened medical care. Quite the contrary. In 1978, UAB opened the Russell Ambulatory Center on land once occupied by the Crippled Children's Clinic. The center facilitated referrals from across the state for diagnosis and treatment, skipping over the referral by a subspecialist. To underscore the significance of the step, Pittman and Thomas N. James, chair of the Department of Medicine, enticed a former governor of the American College of Physicians for the State of Alabama, the internist Alwyn Shugerman, to leave his lucrative private practice in Birmingham to head up the new division. At the same time, to further develop the outreach strategy laid out by Meador, the School of Medicine increased the numbers of physicians and programs that attended to rural patients across the state. UAB's gynecological oncologists established nine clinics throughout Alabama where new technologies, such as the colposcope (a binocular-type instrument for detecting cervical cancer), could be employed, while local physicians simultaneously could get continuing education training on use of the new technology. In a similar fashion, clinical immunologists and rheumatologists such as Howard Holley and the young William J. Koopman, newly arrived from Harvard Medical School via the NIH, opened arthritis centers in Huntsville, Tuscaloosa, Sylacauga, and Mobile; ENT specialists such as James and Julius Hicks provided services at the Talladega Institute for the Deaf and Blind; and nephrologists such as Thomas Andreoli created kidney dialysis centers statewide, which not only treated patients and taught them home dialysis techniques but offered continuing education programs for local physicians.[150]

These joint efforts at generalist education as well as having specialists meeting more needs of the medically underserved reflected the extreme

disparities in the quality of life in different areas of Alabama. It also reflected the convoluted nature of higher education politics in Alabama woven together with exciting, yet vexing, cross-currents of modern medical
education and practice. For years to come, in Birmingham and across the
nation, the jury would stay out on family practice medical education: Was
it essentially nostalgic remembrances of doctors seeing patients in their
homes (something that would later be revived for those able to pay)? Was
it effective reform in medical education? What individual social values
were reflected in the advancement as well as the reservations about family
practice medicine? Hence, even more than complicated streams of medical
education knowledge, here was the ultimate intellectual challenge: understanding the connections between social and scientific institutions and individual values. Pittman, the eclectic intellectual as much as the physician
and medical dean, could not have come back to Birmingham at a more intriguing time.[151]

8

Reach for Maturity

The Hill Years, 1977–86

The UA System and the "New" UAB Team

On June 16, 1976, the UA board moved Joseph Volker out of the presidency of UAB and into the newly created position of chancellor of the UA system. He would be the chief operating officer through whom the board worked in managing the three campuses—Huntsville (UAH), Birmingham, and Tuscaloosa—resulting out of the reorganization of 1969. At Volker's behest and with board approval, the vice president for University College, George Campbell, took over as acting president of UAB. At age sixty, Campbell was nearing retirement. When the *Birmingham News* queried him regarding his succeeding Volker, he responded in his usual straightforward way: "I think it would be appropriate to get a younger person. . . . All I'm looking forward to is being acting president for three to six months." He also would retain responsibility for daily operations in University College, but by this time such operations also enjoyed the assertive leadership of Campbell's assistant vice president, James H. Woodward.[1]

In the press, in the power halls of Montgomery, and on the streets of Birmingham this transition generated much ado. Some of the talk revolved around who would succeed Volker. A lengthy search seemed not to be in the works. Most fingers pointed to Dick Hill, noticeably not the acting president, and to Campbell's repeated statements that he was comfortable taking the interim job because he definitely would not be a candidate.[2] Likewise, for six months before Volker's transition, Hill had been courted by the University of California–San Francisco to assume the position of chancellor of that chiefly medical facility. Much as Volker had not hidden his opportunities to go elsewhere back in the 1950s, Volker made sure board members and corporate leaders knew that losing Hill would be a huge loss for the state. Not known perhaps even to Volker, however, was the unlikelihood of Hill's ultimately making this move. Hill remembered:

> When we got down to the final stages [of the recruitment] and they invited me back out there to talk about salary and a house, I of course took my wife, Janet, with me; and when our hosts met us at the plane, and I was to go on to the campus for some meetings and the itinerary included Janet going with some of the women to participate in a protest march down in the Haight-Ashbury district, we knew we wouldn't be moving. Being from Birmingham, we knew something about social turmoil. But we viewed it as a means to an end, and those folks just thrived on it . . . an end unto itself. It may sound odd, but we were ready to get back as fast as we could to the relative order of Birmingham.[3]

While the San Francisco leverage worked its way through the search for a new UAB president, the public focused even more on what Volker's move to the chancellorship indicated about the larger picture of higher education in Alabama. There were two lines of thought.

A conspiracy theory held that Volker's leadership at UAB had been so successful that the only way for the board to keep him from dominating higher education in the state—and grossly overshadowing the "mother" campus in Tuscaloosa—was to take him out of the presidency. The tried and true corporate strategy of moving him "up and out," according to this theory, seemed to be the smoothest way of handling "the Volker problem." Circumstantial evidence lends a modicum of credence to this theory.[4] Several years prior to Volker's transition the local press had been printing story after story about UAB's success. Under such headlines as "City and UAB Are Growing Great Together" and "UAB Construction Is at Mammoth Level," the *Birmingham News*, though long supportive of the campus in Tuscaloosa and filled with writers who had UA degrees, nevertheless heralded Volker's victories. Insiders also credited the cordial relations the UAB press manager, Gloria Goldstein, had developed with journalists.[5]

Praise also derived from well beyond the South. In an overly optimistic profile of Alabama, "Dixie with a Different Tune," *National Geographic* urged that a genuine "New" South finally was emerging in the state, and the clearest example of this was the UAB Medical Center. The *Chronicle of Higher Education* issued an even more pointed story. With the lead, "Suddenly It's

Birmingham," there was the direct statement: "[The] Tuscaloosa campus used to be 'the' University of Alabama—but now the power is shifting."[6]

There was another "circumstance," too. In the midst of all the press coverage and bold planning, in 1974 the Alabama Commission on Higher Education (ACHE) under John Porter's direction had sought to curtail the development of graduate programs at UAB, even some with a health science orientation. Although the effort eventually failed, Samuel Barker and others believed that "the threat of UAB eclipsing Tuscaloosa" had led UA to push this "reform" up through ACHE, what Garland Reeves of the *Birmingham News* called the "amputation of the graduate school of UAB." In short, one also could make a case for threat and counterattack in the Volker transition.[7]

Though not denying the circumstances supporting it, however, this "up and out" conspiracy could be refuted by nonconspiratorial explanations—rational thought. According to the *Tuscaloosa News* writer Jack Wheat, the UA board needed a chief operating officer who not only could provide regular checks against the unwise actions of presidents and bring order to a wild, wild West approach to individual institutional lobbying, none more effective in this environment than UAB's J. Rudolph ("Rudy") Davidson, but also as a check against a board that "[can] atrophy into the kind of rubber-stamp board that in the 1960s was helpless to prevent the chief executive officer [i.e., Frank Rose] from making major policy decisions by fiat, such as pulling UA out of Mobile and Montgomery." Further, ACHE easily argued that duplication of certain graduate programs needed to be avoided. Finally, there is little to deny the board's open statements as to why it needed a chancellor, and why it ultimately named Volker to this position. As reported first in December 1975 by the Associated Press, whose writers talked with "some members of the Board," "since 1969" worries about in-fighting among the three campuses along with the need to have one key leader for the board to interact with (i.e., other than the three presidents) gradually had been guiding the board toward such a change in administrative structure.[8] Board member Thomas E. Rast, a Birmingham real estate executive and strong UAB supporter, later confirmed this "rational explanation."

> From a management standpoint there was too much activity among the three campuses for it to be reporting just to a board. Whoever was serving as head of the board at a given time—mind you, someone with a full-time professional career in addition to board service—just couldn't do it all, even with a highly active board helping him and

with some significant support staff. [In February 1974, the board had moved Volker's chief financial aid, Paul Brann, to Tuscaloosa to assume the position of administrative officer of the board; at the same time, J. Rufus Bealle joined the UA system staff as vice president, secretary, and general counsel.] We had to have help. And so we ultimately turned to the most proven academic leader in the state for that help. We turned to Joe. Paul [Brann] . . . assured us that he was as good as we thought. He was.[9]

Of course, Rast related, it did not happen quite that easily. Some board members were in contact with David Mathews, on leave from the UA presidency to serve as secretary of the U.S. Department of Health, Education, and Welfare (HEW). As the search for the chancellor, under the direction of trustee Samuel Earle Hobbs, unfolded in the winter of 1976 alongside press reports of over 120 nominees, some on the board and many in Montgomery and Tuscaloosa hoped that Mathews would return to Tuscaloosa as chancellor. For example, state senator Richard Shelby of Tuscaloosa and his colleague, state senator Bert Bank of Northport, wanted Mathews to have time to be a candidate, but Mathews said he would not be willing to leave Washington before January 1977. Hence, Shelby urged that the process slow down. Moreover, he emphasized that the state education budget was, at that particular time, not strong enough to handle an additional office such as the new chancellor's.[10]

Reminded of this debate, Rudy Davidson mused that "some of the old rural versus urban stuff" probably influenced the "inner conversations." A UA graduate, Mathews was a favorite son of south Alabama. He grew up in Grove Hill in Jackson County, which also had produced another politician who urged going slow on the chancellor search, House Speaker Joe McCorquodale. By contrast, Volker clearly was a city person: as Davidson put it, "You couldn't find a person in Alabama with fewer rural Alabama credentials than Joe Volker." And for a "noted city man" to head up the UA system "likely was hard on a few board members."[11] Still, Mathews had not been a major success as the UA president—certainly nothing comparable to Volker at UAB. After Rose departed and Mathews took command, he had changed from being an open, engaging individual to someone known for negativity and almost reclusiveness. Mathews especially alienated the engineering faculty with criticism of their utilitarian role in higher education. So, as winter gave way to spring, Mathews—who never really liked the idea of a system—probably knew it was Volker's job and said he could not be a formal candidate without compromising his current position in Washington, a compelling argument since the HEW awarded grants to all three UA campuses.[12]

In mid-June 1976, trustees John Caddell, Samuel Earle Hobbs, and especially Ehney Camp carried the day both within Montgomery and the board. Volker immediately moved to Tuscaloosa with an annual salary of $55,000, an expense account of $9,000 a year, plus housing in the refurbished Pinehurst home adjacent to the system office building, a sprawling structure bequeathed to the university by the late Mr. and Mrs. Herbert Warner and their son, Jack Warner, of Gulf States Paper Corporation. Some board members, including Winton Blount, hoped Volker's ascendancy would reduce system staff duplication and bring a net savings to the public. However, they were mistaken. With little board opposition, the chancellor's budget, reflecting steady staff expansion, moved from $64,000 in 1976 to over $700,000 in 1978—with $312,904 taxed off of UAB's budget, $312,904 taxed off of UA's budget, and $69,537 taxed off of UAH's budget.[13]

On all fronts, not just that of his own budget, the new chancellor moved forward in public with typical aplomb. Behind the scenes, however, he reflected limited action, what Jack Wheat described in the *Tuscaloosa News* as "a *laissez faire* approach to system governance . . . often describ[ing] his role as 'advocate for the presidents and agent for the board.'" If, as Wheat suggested, "Many of the authorities the Board gave the Chancellor when it amended its bylaws were never activated by Dr. Volker," those close to Volker recall his feeling restrained by the board—sometimes unable to act according to the bylaws. Still, against a backdrop of House Speaker McCorquodale, joined by Lieutenant Governor Jere Beasley, of Dothan, trying to outflank the UA chancellor development by now urging a single "regents system" for the whole state, Volker proceeded to name George Campbell interim president at UAB, sent Paul Brann back to Birmingham as vice president of administration to assist Campbell, and charged a search committee to find a new president for UAB.[14]

By December 1976 the "known" became "better known": S. Richardson Hill, Jr., became UAB's second president. On February 1, 1977, shortly after the opening of the cancer center, Hill took over officially; he and Janet and their four children moved from their longtime home in Mountain Brook into the Woodward House. The august setting had its disadvantages. While they made plans for the addition of a swimming pool just off the east wing, they also found that they had to dodge copperheads and other venomous snakes while walking on the grounds of the estate or even in the basement.

When a large copperhead shot its venom into Hill's right foot, the president headed for the UAB emergency room where top surgeons, Janet would recall, struggled frantically to find a manual on dealing with snakebites. Copperheads aside, however, Hill's noted dynamism only increased.[15]

As the second president assembled his team Campbell returned to full-time work in University College. After a quiet conversation with the new chancellor, Hill immediately named Charles McCallum acting vice president of health affairs and director of the medical center; a national search turned up no better-qualified candidates and McCallum was officially installed in September 1977. Others completed the team. Now sixty-six, Samuel Barker left the Graduate School for faculty life and also to pursue his passion (using his personal funds) to bestow the emergent campus with modern outdoor sculpture, ultimately requiring the establishment of the Committee on Works of Art to "regulate" such aesthetic additions to increasingly valued green spaces. Subsequently, six months of debate over whether there should be two graduate schools, one for University College and one for the medical center, was finally settled. Hill decided that, as it always had been, one such school best represented the growth directions of the university. To ease worries about "too much blending of Medical Center and University College endeavors," however, Hill went with "co-deans" for the unit: Blaine Brownell out of University College (his urban studies program was phasing out as part of a temporary but dramatic, national-level lessening of interest in city life); and Kenneth J. Roozen, a Wisconsin native who had been serving as vice chair in the medical center's Biochemistry Department. When the vice president of administration, Paul Brann, retired in April 1977, Hill replaced him with the former assistant vice president of administration, Dudley Pewitt. Jerry Young, whom Volker had moved out of the deanship in business in 1974 to become vice president of finance—triggering M. Gene Newport's moving up to the dean's position in business—stayed on under Hill in the finance position. Robert Glaze, a Birmingham native and biochemist, had moved into the position of vice president of research under Volker; he continued, too. In similar fashion, long-time dental faculty member Leonard Robinson took McCallum's place as dean of the School of Dentistry.[16]

In addition, Lee Walthall, who had served as chief legal counsel under Volker, continued in that role but also in the elevated position of vice president of institutional advancement and legal affairs, which encompassed not just legal but governmental affairs (lobbying), public relations, private fund-raising, and a fledgling alumni operation—a job too big to hang together for long in such a dynamic setting. Indeed, by 1980 Walthall had resigned to join his friend James H. White III—Volker's first in-house legal counsel—in an investment firm. Hill then divided Walthall's responsibilities among the new chief counsel, Ina Leonard; a new director of alumni affairs and development, M. Sanders Murell, who had broken into development work at Georgia State University; and Gloria Goldstein, who was responsible for marketing, media relations, and university publications. So, if the "new" team seemed augmented and evolving, much of the original core of leaders remained at the top of the organization and, more important, they stayed tightly focused on Volker's original vision—an urban research university with a major medical center. Despite the setbacks inevitably accompanying an institution's movement from youth to maturity, with this continuity—so rare in higher education—institutional momentum continued to grow.[17]

Student Life and Athletic Life

Hill had more the personality of a socially gregarious developer than of the less-than-gregarious and elitist medical scientist—what Edward O. Wilson called "the personality aberrations" of the microbiology revolution. Indeed, from his first days on the campus as a young physician in the 1950s he had been known as someone "reluctant to decline an invitation to a party . . . not one to avoid having a good time." Though equally gregarious, Volker after a few drinks at a cocktail party guided you into a corner and drilled you on the relevance of Thomas Jefferson. By contrast President Hill constantly beamed (in public at least) and gracefully brought out all elements of an occasion, including the frivolous and the fun. By virtue of his own socially integrative personality, therefore, not to mention crafty strategy, he seemed utterly at ease with all aspects of university life—from poetry magazines to microbiology laboratories. Granted, he always believed that the driving force behind the university was the School of Medicine and within that framework, more precisely, the Department of Medicine. Still, unlike some of his medical center colleagues, Hill felt certain that this epicenter could remain secure and indeed be enhanced if the university stopped being "two ends of a campus—the medical center and University College." Others would advance this notion even further. In Hill's mind, still, the meshing had to occur "at least up to a point" for UAB to have both the substance and the public identity of a mature university.

In that context, among other initiatives, he led the institution through significant leaps in student life.[18]

Student life was ripe for this takeoff. Despite the overwhelming difficulties of developing extracurricular programs for students where the majority of undergraduates are commuters, Aaron Lamar had used the "interregnum" of Campbell's acting presidency to implement a host of new student programs. He formed his own leadership team. At the core was the Philadelphia native Michael Raczynski, right out of graduate school at Southern Illinois University who had come to UAB the same year Lamar had. At that time ("with plans only to stay one year") and for years to come, Raczynski would serve as chief financial officer for the ever-evolving and complicated programs of student life. Kathleen Faircloth, a young psychologist originally from Georgia who signed on with Lamar to run research and evaluation in student life, would, in time, be the first in a significant line of UAB leaders to be hired away to high-level jobs in the better-funded university life of North Carolina. There was James A. Clark, a Mississippian, who had come to UAB in 1968 to share registrar duties with Richard Wallace but who now moved into the newly created position of director of special student programs—chiefly scholarships and financial aid. There was Anthony G. ("Tony") Dew, a native of Illinois who had worked in student career counseling and job placement at the University of Illinois before accepting Lamar's offer to develop similar programs at UAB. There was the other Mississippian and battle-proven Vietnam veteran, Joseph A. ("Buzz") Sawyer. Besides taking on an incipient Greek fraternity and sorority system, personal counseling, and nonacademic disciplinary issues, Sawyer was charged with developing reentry counseling for Vietnam veterans who initially had come to Birmingham because of the VA Hospital but who then wanted to use their "VA package" to enroll in courses.[19]

Each Vietnam veteran student was an individual with unique "adjustment issues" owing in great part to the uniqueness of the war. Several former medics bore the emotional scars of "America's longest war" so severely that although they quickly gained admission to the physician's assistant program because of their extraordinary battlefield background, they struggled and some dropped out. The horrific experiences that made them such strong candidates in the program gave them residual emotional difficulties that defeated some of them as students.[20]

Still, many Vietnam veterans were hard-driving and sensitive students, and none was more interesting, and tragic, than the Pennsylvania native

Charles Hartz, who during 1966 and 1967 served as a member of the U.S. Army's Tiger Force, elite (at times called "rogue") fighters who spent up to forty days at a time in the jungles of North Vietnam. Hartz had survived shrapnel, jeep explosions, imprisonment, and torture—a broken knee, a broken arm, a crushed right foot, and lingering jungle rot in the left foot—when the stoic veteran, having been diagnosed with brain tumors, moved to Birmingham to be near relatives, the VA Hospital, and a university where he planned to get his college degree no matter what. As a student he stood out not because of his size but because this large, hardened man also could contribute soft-spoken, keen analysis to class discussions. In social science classes in the Ullman Building, he politely decimated fellow students often in ROTC uniforms who urged naive rationales for war. Thrilled with the learning of a university life, he nevertheless found himself being torn down by recurring tumors on the brain—tumors generated by the defoliating chemical known as Agent Orange secretly used by U.S. commanders in Vietnam. Hartz was one of the first Vietnam veterans to join an eventual group of 15,000 in the successful class-action suit against the U.S. government known as the Agent Orange Case. Unflinchingly using crutches to make the long climb up the stairs to the fourth floor of Ullman to meet regularly with his history professors, Hartz died in February 1983 at his home in the Glen Iris neighborhood near campus, five months short of being awarded a baccalaureate degree with a double major in history and sociology—subjects he had experienced in the most surrealistic of ways through commando military life and what followed. "If any of those chemical company executives [with Dow, Monsanto, and others] believe this chemical [Agent Orange] doesn't hurt," he often said, "just let me spray some of it on them and their kids." And as his legal counsel, Hy Mayerson, recalled, "Nobody took him up on that."[21]

Lamar also worked through physical education professors James E. Sharman and Benjamin Bingham (known for his work with the U.S. Special Olympics) to expand extramural sports. Lamar created an intramural athletic league through which teams from all over the campus—both "ends" of the campus—played basketball, tag football, and volleyball at George Ward Park, the Southside YMCA, and Bell Gymnasium (adjacent to the Ullman Building). Laced with former intercollegiate varsity stars moving onto medical school or graduate work in the other health sciences, medical center teams usually dominated. Intramural baseball reflected so much talent that students organized their own UAB club team. Overconfident and with only one "rough" practice they lost their opener to Miles College.[22]

Even so, impressed with the student athletic talent all around him and with a grant from the NCAA, Sharman began the University College Summer Sports Program for disadvantaged youths on the Southside, using UAB students as teachers, coaches, and counselors. Here was one more small but carefully placed step for an urban university using its resources to assist those living directly adjacent to the campus, some of whose families Lamar knew well from his own family's life in Birmingham.[23]

Yet Lamar and even more so Hill saw the need for a far larger step involving athletics—something to help bind together "the two ends of the campus" while simultaneously binding the campus with the city and expanding the national identity of the institution. It was a maturing step that virtually all other major universities had taken, universities with far smaller budgets than that of UAB, and a step that most of the new urban universities of the 1960s, notably the University of North Carolina–Charlotte, had implemented successfully. It was intercollegiate athletics. In 1969, when Volker had held his first faculty meeting as the new president of UAB, he had fielded the lighthearted question, "What about starting a football team?" with the reply, "Not currently part of the plan." And it still was not in 1977. But other things were: basketball.[24]

Jerry Young, the new vice president of finance, gladly accepted the role of Hill's chief aid in this endeavor. Young's gleeful enthusiasm about dunks and layups was so intense that some could attribute it only to "Indiana genetics" (he held B.S. and M.S. degrees from Indiana State University). Aided by budget officer Don B. Young (no relation), Jerry Young took the operational lead in building an NCAA-level basketball program. They had Volker employing his role as chancellor to block (certainly not silence) opposition out of Tuscaloosa led by Coach Bryant, who claimed that there were not sufficient high school basketball talents in Alabama to justify another team, and that basketball could never really succeed at UAB without a football program as well—and that was "out of the question." Volker, however, quietly reminded the board that starting up intercollegiate teams was a presidential prerogative that did not require board approval. Moreover, Young had Rudy Davidson, not just a lobbyist but also a former Birmingham-area high school football and basketball coach, shore up any possible political cracks in the movement by securing a joint resolution out of the legislature in Montgomery calling on UAB "to give serious consideration to establishing a major college basketball team forthwith." Coach Bryant shortly withdrew his reservations, assuming—like President Mathews did—that UAB efforts would result in a relatively low-profile program.[25]

Such a basketball team could, at best, practice in the old Bell Gymnasium. This facility, however, hardly had the seats to handle the crowd of a Department of Psychology/Department of Medicine intramural basketball game much less a crowd coming to see an intercollegiate game involving "big name" teams—the only kind Hill and Young wanted to play. The Birmingham City Council, with its rising star Richard Arrington, however, seemed only too happy to have the business in his new civic center coliseum downtown. The Birmingham Chamber of Commerce enthusiastically concurred. Hill and Volker purred over the implications of "city and university moving forward together."

And what about a leader, a coach? Fully aware of the risk he ran in taking the university down this path, Hill decided that he had no choice but to "use a medical center approach . . . when starting up something risky like we did with heart transplants: hire the best you can get." In that context, Young brought him the "sports intelligence," gleaned from continuing news from one of Don Young's friends at Memphis State, that Gene Bartow of Missouri, who had recently enjoyed major coaching success at Illinois and Memphis State, was anything but happy in his new position with the preeminent basketball program in the nation at that time, UCLA's.[26] Indeed, Jerry Young and Bartow had first met each other during their graduate school days at Washington University, St. Louis, and during George Campbell's interim presidency, Campbell and Young had received quiet encouragement from some board members, especially Winton Blount and Ehney Camp, to have a conversation with Bartow about being a consultant should UAB decide to develop a basketball program. Moreover, on May 14, 1977, Hill went to Tuscaloosa to meet with all members of the UA board and, separately, with UA president David Mathews to give all a heads-up on UAB plans. (Coach Bryant was invited to the meeting with Mathews but could not attend, though within a few days he told Blount he had no objections to UAB's plans.) Hence Hill got no red lights, only green. What he found, however, was that Bartow might be interested in something beyond consulting. Although Bartow could praise famed UCLA coach John Wooden for "winning ten out of twelve national championships" in his last years as UCLA's head coach, Bartow also could recall Wooden as "determined to keep an office right down the hall from mine, . . . and alumni—not to mention UCLA administrators—continued to go to him as if he were still the coach. He even had the summer basketball camp for pre-college kids all wrapped up." Bartow's recollections continued. "Those fans expected no losses. And when we'd lose one, they'd be in there the next day talking with

Wooden about what coaching flaws produced the defeat." The whole thing was intolerable. "So," Bartow recalled, "when Jerry contacted me, he honestly said that UAB had nothing, that they wanted to build something from the start, and I was in the frame of mind where that sounded mighty good." "Plus," he went on, "with Birmingham so close I thought I could recruit effectively out of 'the Memphis connection' where high school ball had been so good [for] so long." Indeed, after several visits to Birmingham, Bartow seemed ready to sign. When, however, in mid-May 1977 the momentum slowed with Bartow writing Jerry Young, "I would like . . . to think . . . I'll be in touch" and as late as June 9 Bartow told AP reporters, "I know [UAB] is interested in setting up a basketball program, but that is all I know," Hill thought he might possibly be losing the chance to "get another jewel in the crown." So Young flew back to Los Angeles. On the night of June 13 Bartow telephoned J. D. Morgan, director of athletics at UCLA, to request a release from his contract, which he was granted immediately. On June 14 Bartow signed with UAB.[27]

With several members of the UA board more than nervous about an individual of Bartow's stature actually coming to UAB, Bartow officially started in Birmingham on September 1, 1977, and promised to field a team, league to be determined, for the 1978–79 season. His budget was $300,000 a year and, as he urged at a Birmingham press conference, there "should be no problem in making the program balance the books at the end of the year." Although Hill, accompanied by Camp, opened the press conference with his usual wit—"I would like to put to rest all rumors that UAB has hired Ara Parseghian [then head football coach at the University of Notre Dame]"—in introducing Bartow he pointedly presented him as "head basketball coach and director of intercollegiate athletics" at UAB. More than men's basketball seemed in the works.[28]

The tone at UAB changed as a result. Since the late 1960s it was commonly heard on the UAB campus that "UA might have the number one quarterback in the nation but UAB has the number one heart surgeon in the world—and which would you *really* rather have?" After the Bartow press conference on Tuesday, June 14, however, automobiles all over campus and out in the community brazenly sported green and gold bumper stickers proclaiming, "UAB 1–UCLA 0."[29] Shortly thereafter the press raised the stakes. As if he had just reread the 1974 article in the *Chronicle on Higher Education*, Philip Rawls, state editor of the *Montgomery Advertiser*, came forward with the Sunday headline, "Will Junior [UAB] Campus Eclipse Tuscaloosa?" More pointedly from an athletic standpoint, Rawls's colleague at

the *Advertiser*, Roy Thomas, mused, "While basketball may well be the answer to UAB's identity crisis, the school probably will never field a football
team due to the money and the years it would take. . . . Basketball will have
to whet the athletic appetite of Birmingham because anything but the best
is not the UAB way."[30]

With private thoughts quite different on what this whetted "appetite"
might deliver, Bartow went to work. By July he hired one of his former
Memphis State stars, Larry Finch, as an assistant coach and a recruiter, and
Lee Hunt as associate coach; Hunt had worked with Bartow at Memphis and
UCLA. The new head coach was serious about going after the "Memphis
connection." In August he hired Fran S. Merrell, a coach at Birmingham's
Jackson-Olin High School, to build a women's intercollegiate basketball
program. In October he obtained the standard initial "associate member"
status in the NCAA (full status was to follow), and a month later he had
UAB teams entered into the two-year-old Sun Belt Conference, which consisted of such urban universities as Jacksonville University (Florida), the
University of North Carolina–Charlotte, the University of New Orleans, the
University of South Florida (Tampa), and—Fred Whiddon had had the same
thoughts Hill and Volker had about building a university—the University
of South Alabama.[31]

By February 1978 Bartow had a 1978–79 Division I schedule to announce:
it would begin in November with a nonconference matchup against the University of Nebraska, at the Birmingham Civic Center, then move to home
and away games with members of the Sun Belt Conference, and wrap up in
February in Chicago with the traditional powerhouse, DePaul. With local
recruits like Oliver Robinson (Birmingham's Woodlawn High School) and
Donnie Speer (Sylacauga's B. B. Comer High School), and "Memphis connection" recruits such as Raymond Gause and Larry Spicer, Bartow began
to galvanize the group into an initial team. Simultaneously, Fran Merrill
began to announce recruits for the women's program—leading off in March
1978 with the Atlanta High School Metro Player of the Year in Class 3A,
Kathi Cunningham of Tucker High School.[32] Then a committee of students,
faculty, and administrators got down to the serious business of naming the
team. Any person—student, faculty, staff, or community member—could
submit a suggestion on a printed form; "The Blazers," submitted by students Eddie Smith of Birmingham and Ted Greer of Quinton, just north of
Birmingham, got the big nod in May. By the end of May the season ticket
sale for the men's program had netted $8,000, a good start but insufficient
over the long haul. The 16,000-seat civic center "did not exactly encourage

folks to buy a ticket in advance," Bartow noted not so subtly, as an opening suggestion that other "accommodations" might be necessary.[33]

As it turned out, President Hill had the same expansive idea. For the time being the basketball program, not even into its first season, would need to stick with the plan of playing games downtown in the civic center; Mayor Arrington was counting on it. However, as Hill, Young, and Bartow almost immediately laid plans for other sports programs, intercollegiate athletics portended a massive new component to student life in need of additional administrative expertise, namely, a full vice presidential officer in student life. Lamar had done a superb job building many extracurricular endeavors, but by his own admission he had no experience in intercollegiate athletics. On Bartow's suggestion, accordingly, Hill called the vice president of student affairs at Memphis State (later the University of Memphis), John D. Jones, to come to Birmingham to be a consultant on student life programs at UAB.[34]

A former football player at the University of Arkansas–Monticello and subsequently a leader in the Arkansas Boys State program (where he futilely sought to "keep a young William Jefferson Clinton focused on public policy issues rather than social activities"), Jones had earned his doctorate in higher education at the University of Mississippi and, by the early 1970s, was considered "one of the senior deans" of student life in American higher education. A talented public speaker with a resonant voice, he had given keynote addresses before all the national student life organizations in the country during the early 1970s. More important, he had played a key support role in developing intercollegiate athletics at Memphis State, where he and Bartow had become close friends and where Jones became an expert on NCAA regulations pertaining to student athletes. As a white man from the state of Orville Faubus, he also had managed the desegregation of the Memphis State student body with an effectiveness that garnered national attention. Further, he had built dormitories and student activity centers, managed fraternities and sororities, and developed programs for urban and commuter students. In February 1978 Jones visited with Hill, Young, McCallum, Campbell, and Lamar; he promised to deliver a report on how to expand student life endeavors at UAB. The "consultancy," however, soon "turned into a hire." Jones became UAB's first vice president of student affairs on May 5, 1978. Promoted to associate vice president of student affairs and dean of students, Lamar would recall that he "wanted the vice president's position, badly." Still, "John had far more professional experience than I had in areas where we needed to go, especially athletics, and we became close friends . . . almost like brothers learning from each other. And to set the record straight," he emphasized, "the decision had nothing to do with race—just credentials."[35]

Later that May the brotherly combination of Jones and Lamar moved the student life offices, including student registration and accounting, out of "broom closets" in Mortimer Jordan Hall into the first floor of new Campbell Hall at 1300 Eighth Avenue, where the Department of Computer Science also was housed. (Campbell Hall's upper floors became the new homes for the Department of Biology, which was removed from Building No. 3, and the Department of Psychology was removed from the fourth floor of the Ullman Building.) Though he had new quarters, Jones also had a private promise from Hill that even this would be a temporary home for student life.[36] However, at the top of Jones's agenda was getting intercollegiate athletics up and running as "something for the students, and not just those on the court." Virtually overnight a student dance team appeared, along with a student cheerleading team and a student pep band; often practicing in the muddy parking lot in front of the Ullman Building, all went off to regional clinics to prepare for their debut in the fall. Shortly thereafter Jones also established a university ambassadors program, based on an earlier one he had created in Memphis, which gave the twenty-five students who "could make the cut" the opportunity to polish their social and professional skills while serving as "assistant hosts and guides" at official UAB functions, such as basketball games and large formal dinners at the Woodward House. Civic leader Emil Hesse, CEO of Parisian, donated the first set of dark green blazers—official uniforms for the ambassadors.[37]

The opener against the University of Nebraska was on November 24 at the Birmingham Civic Center. "An almost sell-out crowd" of 14,800, heightened considerably by a booster party with free beer, urged the Blazers onto the court. Cheerleaders cheered. Dancers danced. Vice President Jerry Young's daughter, Jennifer, sang the national anthem. A wheelchaired, plaid-suited George C. Wallace made a special on-court appearance accompanied by President Hill. As if the governor had learned something from the way "Bear" Bryant's boys had responded to the Nebraska players in the 1966 Orange Bowl, Wallace frantically shook hands with black players on both benches. However, the Blazers had their debut spoiled by the Cornhuskers, who were ranked in the top twenty, with a final score of 64–55. Not a bad first showing. Ten days later, again at the civic center but minus the beer and the governor, the Blazers claimed their first victory against San Francisco State, 67–51.[38]

January 1979 was a big month for the Blazers. Halfway through the season the men's Blazers claimed a record of 9 wins and 5 losses. Then the even bigger news: because of an NCAA rule change, UAB athletics gained "full membership" status in Division I, a year in advance of what was expected.[39] Here was intense motivation indeed for the celebration of January 25–27: the first UAB Homecoming with dances, bonfires, pep rallies, and a tip-off party in the city center at a new watering hole on Morris Avenue named for the city's first hotel, the Morris House. A revered ritual for more mature institutions, this was a watershed start-up for the maturing student life of UAB. W. Sanders Murell wrote to all students, staff, faculty, and alumni, and to "hundreds of folks in the city": "Please accept this personal invitation to be a part of UAB's inaugural Homecoming celebration this weekend." Although the 8,000 in attendance at the basketball game saw the Blazers go down to the Jacksonville (Florida) Dolphins, 84–76, from here emerged Murell's latest creation, the UAB Alumni Association.[40]

Earlier "excited by all this," however, the emotionally charged Bartow had nothing but "disgust" on his mind as his team soon fell again, this time to the University of South Florida. Ultimately the men's team finished 15-11 for the 1978–79 season, dropping its final game against powerhouse DePaul in Chicago on February 29. Yet here was an exceptionally strong start by anyone's standards, even Bartow's. Indeed, at the end of the season, when the head coach position opened at Memphis State and Bartow received an invitation to apply, he declined: "We have come too far too fast for me to leave," Bartow publicly pronounced. "We are going places." And they were. The 1979–80 season delivered an 18-12 record and a bid to the National Invitational Tournament (NIT). The 1980–81 season showed a dramatic 23-9 record, a Sun Belt Conference championship, and a bid to the NCAA postseason tournament where they went all the way to the "Sweet 16."[41]

The momentum of basketball reverberated through other elements of student life. In 1981, during halftime at the Homecoming basketball game, the UAB community applauded the first winners of the "Mr. and Ms. UAB Competition," David Bolus and Kondra Ellis (both chemistry majors), as the team rolled toward a 25-6 record, a Sun Belt championship, and an NCAA "Final 8" finish. The Sun Belt championships and NCAA tournament appearances would continue through the late 1980s accompanied by national television coverage.[42] Meanwhile, if tension mounted over the prospect of UAB playing UA, UAB—still sporting "Memphis connection" stars such as Steve Mitchell—began playing Auburn University, usually on the same weekend as the iconic Auburn-Alabama football game. After losing the first such encounter in 1982, in 1983, after the Blazers beat an Auburn team including future NBA star Charles Barkley, UAB proceeded to dominate the friendly in-state competition. Even though the Blazers soon moved into seasons with fewer national-level victories, UA leaders remained unwilling to schedule the upstart team in Birmingham. It took the NIT a decade later to force such a matchup in Tuscaloosa. In short, as the "grandiloquent commentator" for ESPN, Dick Vitale, pronounced, the emergence of Bartow's program was "one of the two greatest basketball stories of the 80s" in the East.[43]

Though not as striking as men's basketball, other programs inaugurated in 1979–80 made more than respectable showings as start-up endeavors. Women's basketball, like the men's program, went 15-11 its first year, including a dramatic victory in Birmingham over UA with the stately Wanda Hightower, out of Memphis, bringing home 25 percent of the Blazer points. After a spate of winning seasons, the Lady Blazers took a dive for a few years then resurged by the late 1980s with a Sun Belt championship and still later made it to the NCAA's "Sweet 16" before being defeated by no. 2 seed Rutgers.[44]

Initially coached by former Major League manager Harry ("The Hat") Walker (St. Louis Cardinals, Pittsburgh Pirates, Houston Astros) and then for some thirteen years by Pete Rancont, men's baseball started in 1978–79 with a losing season (21-29) that included a March 7, 1979, victory over UA. By 1981 UAB baseball claimed a Sun Belt Conference division championship before moving into the mid-1980s with generally even seasons, when it received a bittersweet boost.[45] In May 1983 Jerry Young suddenly succumbed to a heart attack in Tampa, Florida, while serving as president of the Sun Belt Conference; in honor of Young, Hill, Bartow, and Dudley Pewitt garnered major civic donations to construct a modern baseball park on the southeastern edge of the campus appropriately named Jerry D. Young Memorial Field and had Brooks Robinson, former star with the Baltimore Orioles, on hand to throw out the first pitch in the park in April 1985. Though with weaker facilities, after slow starts in the late 1970s and early 1980s, men's soccer and women's volleyball ultimately rose to national stature; soccer finally got "a serious field" in part due to the "serious lobbying" of UA trustee Cleophus Thomas, Jr.[46]

Other new elements of student life appeared before more athletics did. In late April 1982, Hill hosted a news conference to unfold a new "master plan" for the UAB campus. Designed by Helmuth, Obata and Kassabuan, out of St. Louis, and orchestrated by the new director of UAB architecture and campus planning, James A. Garland—who would be the single most important influence on the development of the growing campus for the next twenty-five years—the plan sought to halt private sector architects' "free hand" approach to each new building; instead, the Hill team had requested that they develop something that would let the seventy-three square blocks assume "more of a campus feel," something John Jones had helped develop at Memphis State. It hinged on three centers designed to be "friendly to students and patients and also staff and faculty": a Medical Center Plaza, a University Square, and a Fine Arts Plaza.[47] With considerable controversy, streets also would be slated for closing to assist with the "mall effects" that were springing out of plazas. The greatest "street closing of all," however, would never occur—and not even appear in the final published version of the plan. It involved running a tunnel underneath the length of Eighth Avenue South (much as a tunnel ran underneath Mobile Bay connecting the main city with the eastern shore) from approximately the beginning of the medical center at Twentieth Street to the entrance to I-65, and the creation of park-like green spaces in place of the ribbon of asphalt. "Too costly, too involved, too many potential objections, and perhaps even bumping into an old U.S. Steel mine shaft, but still fascinating as a possibility," Garland would recall. Still, the unfeasibility of this idea led circuitously to the renaming of Eighth Avenue South. In 1983 it became "University Boulevard" in keeping with mature college traditions nationwide.[48]

Full implementation of the "master plan" remained years in the offing, and it would be "amended" more than once as Hill, beginning in July 1983, initiated UAB's first capital campaign with a goal of $25 million to pay for the expansion. Well before Hill had announced the campaign, however, in 1982 John Jones had his eye on something in addition to intercollegiate athletics: the planned University Square, more precisely the corner of it located at Fourteenth Street and soon-to-be University Boulevard. Here he would create what Hill had discussed with him in vague terms during his "consultancy/recruitment talks." Opening in the spring of 1984 with funding from student fees as well as the ongoing capital campaign, it consisted of a four-story center committed to student organizations, the *Kaleidoscope* newspaper, the Student Government Association (SGA), a bookstore, a cafeteria (shortly serving the "Bartow Burger," ingredients changing with chefs), accounting and registration offices, financial aid, a game room, the Center for International Programs, a large auditorium for lectures and student recruitment, student life administrative facilities, and offices for the Graduate School staff. If Jones now saw a dream actualized, he and Hill nevertheless took some heat for the gamble; critics (some perhaps overly sentimental about the Hideaway Cafe in the Humanities Building) urged that commuter students, who made up 60 percent of UAB undergraduates, never would use it or anything else north of University Boulevard. "Above all," Jones retorted, "it is an undergraduate student population of commuters that so badly needs these centralized facilities and a place to hang their hats when they are not in class." The *Birmingham News* concurred. UAB was fifteen years old and had over 15,000 students: "It was about time." Initially called the University Center, the facility ultimately bore the name of the gregarious developer, S. Richardson Hill, Jr.—named buildings being better than generic descriptives, not to mention Orwellian numbers, in profiling a sense of history so essential to the maturation of an institution.[49]

University College Takeoff

While Hill and Bartow had been pushing ahead with new players on the court, University College added more than a few people and places, too. Many of the personnel changes were a result of retirements. As he had implied when he became acting president, Campbell was about ready to hang it up. In early spring 1978, when Hill named the new classroom building not "Building No. 5," as anticipated, but "Campbell Hall" and had an "all-hands-on-deck" dedication honoring the namesake, folks began to wonder not what but when. After all, Campbell had devoted thirty-eight years to various operations within the UA family.[50]

Campbell retired September 30, 1978. Hill appointed Thomas K. Hearn, dean in the School of Humanities, to replace Campbell as vice president of University College. At the same time, when Joseph Appleton, founding dean of the School of Engineering, returned to the faculty, Hearn confronted two strong inside candidates for the engineering post: there was James H. Woodward, Campbell's most recent assistant vice president, and Woodward's close friend since graduate school days at Georgia Tech, John Anderson, who also had experience as a Campbell assistant vice president and by then was a senior professor in electrical engineering. Another key opening also appeared. Long wanting Davidson full time in governmental affairs and reporting to the president, Hill had asked Davidson to give up his University College role as director of continuing education (special studies). This fit with Campbell's urging that the vast untapped market in continuing education of the surrounding area be tapped. So Hill and Hearn named Woodward to the engineering deanship and the entrepreneurial Anderson to the directorship of special studies. (For several more years, however, the two would pursue their love of engineering instruction by team teaching the infamous, interdisciplinary EGR 495, "a bear of a course" exploring connections between civil and electrical engineering and necessitating that the two old friends hold special "before class tutoring sessions" at 7:00 a.m. two days a week.)[51] Hearn's departure from humanities, however, left that deanship open; it went to the individual Hearn had hired as his own replacement as chair of philosophy, James Rachels, who had grown up with Woodward in Columbus, Georgia, before earning his doctorate at the University of North Carolina, teaching at New York University, and becoming a renowned ethicist, especially on death and dying.[52]

Although national searches were conducted for each vacancy, inside talent prevailed in the filling of these University College administrative positions much as the medical center administrative teams had been built. The downside for such personnel development was the euphemistic "no new blood," a vital consideration but nevertheless one which, if mismanaged in the slightest way, can ignore the hard reality that "new blood" can turn out to be "bad blood" as often as "good blood." The upside appeared not just in proven, known people moving into positions of greater influence. It facilitated continued internal agreement on already proven institutional strategies. It permitted the formation of a team bonded by a common base of experience and long-term friendships and trust. It advanced an institutional mission experienced on a daily basis as a deeply felt personal commitment. Here were crucial, common sense elements of "organizational effectiveness" accomplished some two decades before these traits were advanced in the name of "strategic planning" and "restructuring" of the 1990s.[53] In later years at least one experienced observer, Philip E. Austin (UA system chancellor and later president of the University of Connecticut), pronounced this continuity of leadership as "one of the chief reasons" for the rapid emergence of UAB: "continuity not just among presidents, with no president staying 'too long,' but continuity within the general leadership team." Under these influences UAB continued to broaden and deepen, mature and grow.[54]

The Medical Center: Maturation through Innovation

Clinical and academic programs in the health sciences also matured despite an increasingly difficult environment. In early 1980, the UA board, the legislature, ACHE, and key officers of the three UA campuses once again engaged in contentious "discussion" over the autonomy and budget development for medical education programs in Huntsville and Tuscaloosa. In short, despite McCall Report No. 1, of 1972, through which Hill had sought to manage the medical education branches at UA and UAH, on a daily basis Dean James A. Pittman had not been getting much cooperation. So now the new team—President Hill, Vice President McCallum, and Dean Pittman—again went to work with the board's Special Committee on Medical Education. Ultimately, this effort produced McCall Report No. 2, of 1980, which reinforced the key tenets of the first McCall Report and established that the UAB vice president of health affairs also would serve as assistant to the chancellor of medical affairs. UA's College of Community Health Sciences and UAH's School of Primary Medical Care clearly would report *not* to their own higher campus officers but to the new assistant to the chancellor of medical affairs, in Birmingham.[55] This meant that the Tuscaloosa and Huntsville programs reported to Dean Pittman in actuality, although Vice President McCallum had a "hands-on" administrative style and worked more closely with Pittman, not to mention board members, than some vice presidents might have.[56] More to the point, just as in the 1970s, the change had been recommended by the nationwide Liaison Committee on Medical Education (LCME), which was focused on significant accrediting problems in the Tuscaloosa operation. Indeed, if this change had not occurred, LCME accreditation for the UAB School of Medicine would have been seriously jeopardized as well because of its administrative connection, if heretofore loose connection, with the Tuscaloosa operation. Still, from Mobile to Tuscaloosa to Huntsville came murmurs of "UAB imperialism"; Governor Fob James (who succeeded Wallace in 1979) heightened the tension by using the case to illustrate inefficient "duplication" that would not even be practiced "in a Waffle House." The *Birmingham News* still blessed the "medical consolidation" with the hope that the Birmingham administration, especially Dean Pittman, could sort out the difficulties with the "branch" operation in Tuscaloosa.[57]

Less contentious developments occurred in other places. Through the expansion of research funded by the National Institutes of Health (NIH) and the National Science Foundation (NSF), medical center faculty continued to increase during the Hill presidency: from 857 in 1977 to 1,188 in 1986, averaging over thirty-three newly funded faculty positions per year. These increases, combined with resignations, adverse tenure decisions, and retirements, permitted major hires and eclectic additions to an already diverse group.

Organizational changes also continued to unfold with the maturing of the medical center. The new dean in the School of Dentistry, Leonard Robinson, reorganized the Department of Prosthodontics into the Department of Fixed Prosthodontics chaired by William D. Powell, then established the Department of Removable Prosthodontics chaired by Dwight Castleberry. He also reorganized the Department of Oral Surgery into the Department of Oral and Maxillofacial Surgery, chaired by Charles Alling.[58] In the School of Medicine, under Pittman's leadership, the national trend in public health found its way to Birmingham. Although in 1976 William Bridgers became chair of the Department of Public Health in the School of Medicine, by 1981 Pittman followed a long-term plan and spun the department out of his school to form the School of Public Health, with Bridgers as dean. Blending fields earlier developed in the School of Medicine, the School of Dentistry, and in the joint health sciences, Bridgers soon had rapidly increasing enrollment in the Department of Environmental Health Sciences chaired by Walter Mason; the Department of Health Care Organization and Policy chaired by Edgar D. Charles; the Department of Epidemiology and Biometry chaired by Philip C. Cole; the Department of International Public Health chaired by Juan Navia; and the Department of Health Behavior chaired by Richard Windsor, not to mention the John J. Sparkman Center for International Public Health Education funded by the NIH, which was first directed by Bridgers and later by Navia.[59]

Numerous other centers soon appeared across the health science units. The Gregory Fleming James Cystic Fibrosis Research Center—the first of its kind in the nation, named in memory of the deceased son of Governor Fob James—emerged under the leadership of Roy Curtiss, then reached international prominence when directed by the precocious Eric Sorscher. Charles Bugg created the Center for Macromolecular Crystallography, then passed it on to his colleague, Lawrence DeLucas.[60] To the outsider these units seemed to keep popping up overnight: Virgil Wooten's Sleep/Wake Disorder Center, William Bridgers's Lister Hill Center for Health Policy, William C. Bailey's Lung Health Center, James Halsey's Parkinson's Disease Association Information and Referral Center, Claude Bennett's Center for Interdisciplinary Research on Immunological Diseases, Michael Friedlander's Neurobiology Research Center, Sara Finley and Hugh Shingleton's Center for Reproductive Health and Genetics, and Russell Fine's Injury Control Research Center.[61]

Indeed, when one looked collectively at these units alongside centers that had begun earlier—for example, Joseph Reeves and Thomas N. James's

Cardiovascular Research and Training Center and Alan Demick's Burn Center—it was possible to see a mind-boggling array of nondepartmental structures, which the UA board, not to mention more than one governor, perhaps understandably had a hard time following. And ultimately for this reason the board severely limited further such developments.[62] Despite outward appearances, however, these were innovative academic and clinical research enterprises that provided the flexibility to capture extramural monies so necessary for improved health care at a time when the U.S. government and private agencies seemed to change their funding priorities every other year. This flexibility was particularly crucial for a university in Alabama, where state funding for health, education, and general human welfare remained so low. From the perspective of a maturing university, faculty from wide-ranging departments engaged in the interdisciplinary research and clinical care that eventually facilitated UAB's reaching a national research status alongside far older, more "prestigious" institutions such as the University of Chicago and the University of Pennsylvania. Much like the earlier story behind the joint health sciences, accordingly, these and many other centers sprang from the severe financial disadvantages of Alabama as much as from the new interdisciplinary focus and expanding monies out of Washington, D.C. Once again, ironically, out of the obstacle came the innovative success.

Centers aside, especially between 1982 and 1984, departmental chair changes also sparked this growth in the School of Medicine. Managing such rapid change was one of Dean Pittman's main priorities. When medicine's chair, Thomas N. James, departed for the University of Texas Medical Center in Houston, Claude Bennett, who long had chaired one of the joint departments, microbiology, ascended to one of the most crucial department chair positions in the university, the leadership of the Department of Medicine. In turn, after two interim chairs in microbiology, Kenneth J. Roozen and David H. L. Bishop, one of Bennett's former doctoral students, the native Alabamian Gail Cassell, took over microbiology. Likewise, in 1982 John Kirklin stepped down from the chairmanship of surgery, though he continued as director of that department's Division of Cardiothoracic Surgery through 1984 and as president of the Health Services Foundation through 1988.[63] To fill this major department chair position, Pittman named Arnold G. Diethelm, who had joined the department in 1967 after earning his M.D. at Cornell University and doing specialty training at New York Hospital, Harvard Medical School, and the Peter Bent Brigham Hospital in Boston. At the same time, Albert D. Pacifico ascended to the newly created endowed rank of Kirklin Professor of Cardiovascular Surgery and by 1985 also assumed Kirklin's role as director of the Division of Cardiothoracic Surgery.

Over the following two decades, under the leadership of Diethelm and Pacifico, the international reputation of UAB surgery grew, especially in heart, liver, and kidney transplantation. A man committed to time efficiency in surgery as well as shorter hospital stays for patients, Pacifico by the end of the century would have completed over 25,000 surgeries on patients from around the globe. As for Diethelm, despite chronic leg pain (from playing football for Cornell), he also mastered the use of long hours in surgery. A study of kidney transplants between 1982 and 1985 ranked UAB's renal transplant program fifth in the United States. And in 1986 alone, with the recent development of the Alabama Kidney Center (a thirty-bed operation in the Spain-Wallace Hospital) and new surgery connections with Children's Hospital, UAB surgery completed 223 kidney transplant procedures: patients with "cadaveric renal transplants" had one-year survival rates of 80 percent and five-year survival rates at around 70 percent; those who received "living related donor kidneys" had an 88 percent one-year survival rate and an 80 percent five-year rate.[64]

University College Maturing

In University College, the intermittent cuts in state funding that accompanied Fob James's first term as governor (1979–83) had a far greater impact on new faculty lines because so many of these faculty fields, with several notable exceptions, had little or no access to the NIH and NSF funds that had aided the growth of medical center faculty. Moreover, UAB enrollment from the mid-1970s to the mid-1980s ceased its striking jumps of the Volker presidency. With enrollment leveling off at around 14,000, tuition and fees also ceased the rapid growth of the earlier years, which again meant relatively less money for faculty expansion outside the health sciences. On Hill's watch, therefore, University College faculty moved from 306 to 397, averaging slightly over nine new lines per year compared to the average of thirty new lines per year during the same period for the medical center.[65] Nevertheless, these new slots and numerous replacement positions—many from retirements, a few from mid-career resignations, and some from adverse tenure decisions—were filled with individuals from diverse backgrounds who had a wide variety of high-level graduate training, all of whom enriched the campus and the community. For example, the historian E. Culpepper Clark (Ph.D., University of North Carolina), while chairing the Department of Communication Studies, commenced a twelve-year project and later as a UA administrator published it as *The Schoolhouse Door: Segregation's Last Stand at the University of Alabama* (1993).[66]

Although by the time of Hill and Hearn's leadership most programs in University College that could be justified had been implemented, facilitating a full range of undergraduate opportunities offered by a nationally recruited faculty, a few necessities remained. The new dean in engineering, Woodward, reorganized programs developed by Appleton into full-fledged departments more along the lines of what he had experienced at Georgia Tech: a Department of Electrical Engineering chaired by David A. Connor, a Department of Civil Engineering chaired by Natarajan Krishnamurthy, a Department of Biomedical Engineering (combining existing personnel in the School of Medicine and in the School of Engineering) chaired by Louis C. Sheppard, and a Department of Materials Engineering chaired by Raymond A. Buchanan.[67] Similar reorganizations followed Milley Cowles's succeeding Dean Fain Guthrie in the School of Education: the creation of the Department of Counseling, Human Services, and Foundations chaired by Clay Sheffield for one year and thereafter by James S. Davidson, as well as the Department of Curriculum and Instruction chaired by Bernice J. Wolfson.[68]

In much the same way the new dean in the School of Humanities, James Rachels, broke out the early Department of Performing Arts into two new units—the Department of Music chaired by Ronald Clemmons and the Department of Theater and Dance chaired by Ward Haarbauer, who also served as associate dean in the school.[69] And the same growth leading to re-structure happened in the School of Business. Dean Newport added finance to the Department of Accounting (and within four years finance would have its own department under chair Keith Bryant), and the old Department of Business Administration, with finance split off, became the modernized Department of Marketing, chaired by Warren Martin.[70] Finally, when Edward Lewis, who had succeeded Brownell as urban studies chair, left the university at a time when there was a national as well as local decline of preoccupation with problems of the city, Dean Passey in the School of Social and Behavioral Sciences merged urban studies into the Department of Political Science, with David Sink succeeding the retiring Grady Nunn as chair. Passey also backed up Virginia Hamilton's efforts in history to create a new interdisciplinary undergraduate minor in African American studies and to hire Horace Huntley (Ph.D., Pittsburgh) to run it.[71]

Perhaps most striking from the standpoint of graduate education and interdisciplinary research, however, was what happened in psychology. During the late 1960s and early 1970s the psychology chair and University Scholar David L. Sparks had initiated discussions with Dean Passey about the possibility of a doctoral program in medical psychology. Over time, Passey and Spark's ideas evolved into something far greater: a major UAB role in the behavioral medicine revolution. Even if one does not view behavioral medicine as former UAB medical dean and later Vanderbilt medical professor, Clifton K. Meador, would assert—"after the revolutions in knowledge related to genetics and biomedical engineering, the prevailing frontier will be the psychosocial approach to health care"—the emergent field of behavioral medicine loomed as dramatic as the microbiology investigations Claude Bennett had underway in the medical center. To fully understand where Passey and Sparks were headed in an almost serendipitous way, one first has to look well beyond Birmingham, Alabama.[72]

Since the early 1970s the psychologist Neal E. Miller, of Rockefeller University in New York City, had been leading his field toward a new symbiosis to be known as "behavioral medicine" through which biomedically trained psychologists could assist in solving problems about the human brain and nervous system ranging from depression to stroke. There was nothing particularly new about this general approach: over a century after narrowing and specializing in response to revolutionary discoveries about germs, then genes and computers, some health scientists once again sought to understand and treat the "whole person," not just body parts or microscopically perceived chemical complexes.[73] Viewed within the time frame of one century, many physicians saw this "new" approach as a "less than productive deviation from the biochemical tradition" that made up the foundation of their education and professional lives. On the other hand, some physicians understood that certain human health problems could be understood better and treated more effectively by a team made up of, say, a surgeon, a psychologist, and a sociologist trained in behavioral medicine.[74] Ironically, it was Bennett plugging away in his specialized microbiology laboratory who began urging physician colleagues in the 1970s, unbeknownst to Passey and Sparks, that this broadened approach to medicine was an essential element of future research, teaching, and clinical care in medicine. Other physicians of the 1970s, including Bennett, also extended the approach to their own professional culture. The social-behavioralist medical approach could provide new insights even into doctor-patient relationships. This easily led to analysis of health care management issues and ultimately to matters of effectiveness and efficiency—"assessment." Still, at this particular time—the 1970s and even into the early 1980s—Bennett was not confident that UAB's non–medical center faculty could be effective cross-campus partners in such interdisciplinary endeavors. Indeed, in communications with President Hill, Bennett characterized UAB's faculty in the arts and sciences as at best "mediocre" and with little chance for improvement.[75]

Still, in no contact with Bennett, Sparks began to feel his way along toward this emergent field of behavioral medicine, with at least as much luck, at first, as strategy. Recalls Sparks, "Of course we knew the importance of [Neal Miller's] work—I had heard him speak and read his publications—and what it likely would do to funding patterns in the NIH and NSF, and I and a few others actually were working in the field, especially with primates. But it was other more practical things that had the greatest impact."[76]

Indeed, as with so many successful developments at UAB, the most pronounced being the development of the joint health sciences in the late 1940s and the urban renewal grants of the 1960s and 1970s, it was a strategic *disadvantage* that first moved Sparks and his colleagues down the road to innovation. Sparks continued,

> [Graduate dean] Sam Barker, also aware of NSF and NIH funding possibilities in psychology, proposed that we look at building a doctoral program. But we knew that the psychology faculty in Tuscaloosa would scream foul—and then the board and ACHE would—if we tried to build a general Ph.D. in psychology. So we designed the program in a way that we thought politics would let it pass—we tied it to the more accepted medical research role for UAB and to something we knew the Tuscaloosa psychologists were not doing. Actually, only after we had approval for the Ph.D. program in psychology did it really dawn on us what a few of us had been doing, behavioral medicine psychology, and what the new program set us up to do even more: it could become *so* connected to the revolution that Miller had been fostering and what the NIH wanted to fund at such high levels.[77]

Changes in people and places—good and bad—also influenced this overtly practical development. By 1977 Passey had convinced outgoing Vice President Campbell that the Department of Psychology should be moved from the top floor of the Ullman Building to the new Campbell Hall where, alongside biology and computer science, it could have the requisite "wet lab" and computer facilities—what Sparks and others said they had to have.[78] Leadership also changed. Though he had been the chief influence in the establishment of the department, Sparks had little desire to be an administrator: "Just working on the doctoral proposal, I found, took time away from what I loved, research." And the chair who had succeeded Sparks in 1974, John Ost, was both ill and close to retirement. Hence, in 1977, on the advice of Sparks and his new colleague, the behavioral neuroscientist Joan Lorden, Passey hired a new psychology chair out of Southern Illinois University, Robert E. Levitt, with the specific assignment of completing the doctoral proposal. Passey also convinced the new vice president, Hearn, that any new state monies invested in new psychology hires would deliver not just an innovative and needed program, but grant revenues including salary release savings that could be used for the general fiscal development of the whole school, assisting departments whose disciplines did not have access to the large funds associated with health-related research. (To this end, Passey also reallocated existing monies of the school, moving salary out of the history department into the psychology department when David E. Harrell, a senior, highly paid historian, left UAB to take a similar position at the University of Arkansas.) With the program proposal implemented in 1981, accordingly, Levitt began to use resignations as well as new slots to hire medical psychologists.[79]

As so often happens with such futuristic developments, however, the initiative temporarily spun out of control. Although Levitt worked with Sparks and others to develop a first-class proposal for the doctoral program, Levitt was more a researcher and program designer—and a clinician, it turned out—than a personnel manager. The increasingly health science–oriented faculty in psychology was not moving forward cohesively. In that environment, and increasingly finding he could not compete for grants against medical center–based neuroscientists if he were teaching anything close to a standard arts and sciences teaching load, Sparks left the Psychology Department to take an appointment up the street in the medical center's Physiology and Biophysics Department, where he had a far lighter teaching load and more time for research and grant development. Despite the fact that he was from "down the street," Sparks's huge extramural funding made him attractive to a few medical center leaders. Soon Sparks left that department, too, however, as he found an endowed chair at the University of Pennsylvania, solid testimony indeed of an Ivy League medical center's embrace of behavioralism.[80] One of the great faculty losses in the history of UAB, Sparks's leaving pointed up the difficulty of going beyond the conceptual nature of interdisciplinary science and into the human resource management issues springing from the various academic subcultures undergirding the interdisciplinary effort.[81]

Meanwhile, Passey and Levitt agreed that Levitt's talents lay in practicing medical psychology, which he proceeded to pursue in a strikingly successful practice in south Florida. At the same time, in 1982, Passey turned to Carl E. McFarland, whom Ost had hired fresh out of the doctoral program of the University of Kansas, to "bring the plane back under control and make it fly straight." McFarland did just this. While completing his own research and moving through the ranks to full professor, McFarland showed a subtle understanding of the constantly changing nature of psychology and psychologists, and he had the management skills to guide such a health science enterprise, which was emerging as a crucial part of the arts and sciences.[82] Hence, as the 1980s unfolded the UAB Department of Psychology, increasingly under the influence of behavioral medicine, assumed the life—the productivity, intensity, and in some ways the self-image—of a medical center department.[83] While educating some 600 undergraduate students a year, UAB psychology ultimately offered three different doctoral tracks—medical psychology, behavioral neuroscience, and developmental (life cycle) psychology. In 1985, the department delivered its first two doctorates in medical psychology, and by 1991 broke the $2 million mark in total grants and contracts awarded—a smattering of what lay ahead.[84]

Meanwhile, beginning in 1977–78, Vice President Hearn had charged a group to develop an equally unique program in undergraduate studies: the honors program. Initially designed to attract more highly talented students to counteract the inaccurate image that UAB was a place where you pursued college if no other institution would take you—much as the medical center took bold steps to counteract its image as "a place for the indigent"—the group planning the program included Theodore M. Benditt (philosophy), Daniel Lesnick (history), Richard Crittenden (mathematics), John Swann (business), Patrick Linton (medicine/psychiatry), Beverly Head (community representative), Nancy Johnson (teacher education), and Ada Long (English). They debated throughout 1977–81. Although the committee concluded that a university-wide undergraduate honors program should be built around an interdisciplinary curriculum, drawing on the wide faculty resources of the institution, including health science faculty, it debated endlessly over the issue of "exclusivity."[85]

For many faculty involved in the planning this was a reassertion of the social and intellectual issues dominating their own education in the 1960s:

"anti-elitism," "shared decision making," the sanctity of traditional disciplines pitted against interdisciplinary inquiry. After a series of reports, counterreports, dissenting reports, and meetings where the level of discussion moved to "fairly high decibels," as well as the termination and reconstitution of the committee, the process finally produced a report written by Benditt. The proposal called for a program that would not only include students with high SAT or ACT scores but allot approximately 25 percent of the thirty slots to students who might have relatively low standardized test scores but who, when interviewed by a faculty committee member, revealed something uniquely strong: a desire to do something for society, a curiously creative bent, a personality from whom other students could benefit. Likewise, the curriculum, guided by an honors council of faculty, students, and community leaders, would emphasize the "complex whole of knowledge," not traditional disciplines, and would consist of thematic courses reflecting some of the most pressing issues of the day. Finally, the program emphasized close relationships between faculty and students in the context of "an egalitarian academic community" and sought to bind the students together into a social network where they could learn from each other's diverse backgrounds as well as intellectual interests. Hence, in the early 1980s, a time when American society in many ways seemed shifting to the right and reacting against the social and intellectual openness of the 1960s, the UAB Honors Program seemed to jump right out of 1968.[86]

But there was more than the 1960s social and intellectual values of certain faculty behind the plan; it was craftily designed for UAB to turn a disadvantage into an advantage, much like other UAB innovations. As part of the resurgence of conservatism of the early 1980s, elite honors programs appeared all over American academe. Rather than try in vain to compete with those of Yale University or the University of Georgia, whose longtime institutional reputations permitted major advantages, UAB's start-up program in a relatively unknown university offered an alternative. In 1981, with the aid of funds from a National Defense Education Act (Title III) grant, Vice President Hearn asked literature professor Ada Long, whose views clearly had prevailed in the debates and the report, to direct the program. With Hill's help, Hearn and Long then acquired an ancient wooden house at 1527 Ninth Avenue South on the north-central fringe of the campus as a location for the new program. One side of the house became a large seminar room, the other a director's office and space for study and social activities.[87]

The honors program opened for business in the fall of 1983. An intriguing faculty mix—Louis Dow (economics), Carter Hudgins (history), Lee

Mohler (biology), and Long herself team taught the core course, Witchcraft to Space Craft: Man, Society, Science, and the Modern World. Reflective of the rich social composition of the urban university, students ranged from eighteen-year-old Cassandra Warner, a recent graduate of Jess Lanier High School in Bessemer, Alabama, to Helene Robertson, a seventy-four-year-old New Yorker who returned to college after first enrolling at Elmira College in 1928. Robertson's enthusiasm reflected the spirit of the program. Asked by Melanie Jones of the *Birmingham News* why she was pursuing the honors program, Robertson replied, "For the same reason I do everything—to see if I can do it." Robertson earned a baccalaureate degree "with honors" and then headed off for the Peace Corps.[88]

In 1985 the honors program received larger and better physical facilities in the "Old Church" at 1153 Tenth Avenue South. Established in 1901 as the all-white Second Presbyterian Church, by 1963 the facility had become the all-black New Hope Church. UAB had acquired the facility in the mid-1970s with urban renewal funds for use first as a student government meeting place, then by the late 1970s as a studio for Stevan and Melanie Grebel's dance program. In this ironic setting—Victorian-gothic architecture for a 1960s-style program premised on "question the orthodox"—Long's program, increasingly co-managed by scientist Dail Mullins, soon gained national recognition; in 1995 Long was elected president of the National Collegiate Honors Program Council.[89]

Urban and State Affairs

Meanwhile, Hill continued to shape the university's identity and increase its influence with regard to issues well beyond the campus. Volker had been a founding member of the Committee of Urban Universities within the National Association of State Universities and Land Grant Colleges (NASULGC). During 1977 and 1978, Hill and William G. Croker, UAB's chief lobbyist, worked through the liberal Republican U.S. congressman from Birmingham, John Buchanan, and Senator John Sparkman to influence national legislation. Much like a few other urban institutions, for example, Wayne State University, UAB already had created a Center for Urban Affairs, which linked UAB with the surrounding community, though UAB never put significant state dollars into the center the way other urban universities did. Now Hill sought to bring his institution into the national movement for federal funding lobbied by the Committee on Urban Universities, which consisted of thirty-one urban universities nationwide and was led by an Ohio consortium. Indeed, through UAB's Capitol Hill connections the

U.S. House of Representatives Subcommittee on Postsecondary Education, chaired by William D. Ford of Michigan, chose Birmingham as one of five cities for field hearings on the need for the Urban Grant Act. With this act, urban universities as a *national group* might receive federal funding to help solve problems of urban poverty, urban housing, urban race relations, and urban education the same way Congress a century earlier had funded land grant institutions for rural development. With the Birmingham testimony occurring on March 25, 1978, in the UAB Nursing School Building Auditorium, the congressional tape recorders whirring away for replication in the *Congressional Record,* Hill told much of the story of the vibrant interconnectedness between UAB and Birmingham, offering "documentation" of the need for Congress to make massive grants to universities across the nation. Others giving testimony included Odessa Woolfolk, director of public services with the UAB Center for Urban Affairs; David Vann, mayor of the City of Birmingham; Richard Arrington, a member of the Birmingham City Council; Ben Erdreich, one of the three members of the Jefferson County Commission; and Louis J. Willie, executive vice president and director of the Booker T. Washington Insurance Company, plus a key member of Volker's "Kitchen Cabinet" of the 1960s.[90]

Because the general public was not concerned about urban issues in the 1970s, the act never received decent funding. But more than national trends were at work. The act placed many powerful committee chairs in both the U.S House and Senate in the politically awkward situation of defining an "urban university": Could an "urban university" also be a land grant university located far from the city yet with a few outreach or extension programs in the city?[91] Or was an "urban university" what Hill and other presidents of the Committee on Urban Universities said it was, namely, one located in a city and with a large portion of its students coming from that city and in other ways deeply involved in the daily life of that city? Some congressmen worried about alienating longtime constituencies associated with the old extension services of the land grant institutions if they defined it the latter way. For example, Congressman Ford might commit a major offense against the University of Michigan if he permitted a definition that would allow Wayne State University, which was located *in* Detroit, to be Michigan's "urban university." And such inclinations often were increased as some key urban university presidents, such as Wayne State's (and UAB's?), never directly articulated "the urban university" as their *top* priority in lobbying Capitol Hill. Hence leaders on the Hill never pushed the act to the point of significant appropriation.[92]

Then, too, perhaps the inaction of Congress could be traced to timing on issues beyond its control as much to its conviction about city life. Advanced a decade *after* the unrest of the 1960s and during declining attention to urban issues, yet *before* the end of the cold war in the late 1980s returned the American public interest to domestic issues, the Urban Grant Act could not compete. Instead, Congress stayed clear of defining an "urban university" and remained focused on what was politically "safe," if also exciting, such as NSF and NIH research projects and science education as the best use of education money in finishing off the Soviets. The act would have to wait until 1989 and the end of the cold war to receive even scant funding. Even then, caught up in the Reagan revolution of increasing the federal debt at a staggering rate but lessening federal spending on "domestic social programs," the act received only $8 million—a small sum compared to public monies associated with the Morrill Act or post-1945 health science funding.[93]

President Hill, however, maintained strong identification with the Urban Grant Act. In 1981 he published a major article on the topic in *Phi Kappa Phi Journal*. To emphasize UAB's urban focus and to further differentiate it from UA, Hill and Hearn, in November 1984, received board approval to change UAB's name from the University of Alabama *in* Birmingham to the University of Alabama *at* Birmingham—a step of questionable significance. More significant, Hill sought to raise the national profile of UAB as an urban university *as well as a research university*, in no way seeing the two as mutually exclusive, by helping Vice President Hearn with his leadership in developing the Urban 13, a group of urban universities including such old and revered research institutions as the University of Pittsburgh and the University of Cincinnati. The Urban 13 advanced the "urban cause" before every possible source of funding and, down the line, even prompted NASULGC, a direct product of the Morrill Act, to create a section on urban education. In view of the origins of NASULGC, that organization ultimately hedged on the crucial matter of definition, just the way Congress had, by creating a "Commission on the Urban *Agenda*" (emphasis mine), thereby sidestepping any tight and effective focus on the urban university. From another perspective, Hill also could find more than solace in what happened to the Urban Grant Act. One of the reasons the act did not obtain funding at the outset was the intense lobbies from the NIH and NSF, agencies whose monies increasingly placed UAB health scientists among the most well funded in the nation.[94]

Though with similar mixed results, Hill also increased UAB's profile within its own state. In his most recent campaign, Governor Wallace had not admitted that many of his previous economic and political policies left something to be desired: in late 1982 Alabama had a staggering 15 percent unemployment rate while most of the nation had fully recovered from the economic stagnation of the 1970s and early 1980s. Yet Wallace indeed had called for a "blueprint" to deal with some of the economic "chaos" in the state. And it is not surprising that Wallace asked Hill to chair the Governor's Task Force on Economic Recovery. Hill managed the largest single budget outside Montgomery; Hill had worked closely with the governor to create the Cancer Research and Training Center; and Hill accurately depicted UAB to Wallace as the most successful public thing in "your [Wallace's] state," although Wallace always would refer to the facility as the "Medical Center" rather than "UAB." Hence, at the start of Wallace's final tenure as governor, beginning in 1983, the UAB president found himself chairing a committee of some of the major civic leaders of the state. The thirty-eight included John Woods, president of AmSouth Bank; A. G. Gaston, president of Booker T. Washington Insurance Company; Joseph M. Farley, president of Alabama Power; Richard Arrington, mayor of Birmingham; Donald Comer, president of Avondale Mills; Wyatt Shorter, president of McMillan Bloedel Timber Corporation; Joab Thomas, president of the University of Alabama; and Johnny Ford, mayor of Tuskegee. It also included two people long associated with promoting Wallace's political career: Ralph Adams, president of Troy State University, and Elton B. Stephens, president of EBSCO Industries in Birmingham.[95]

Although Hill remained politically close to Wallace, this hardly tempered Hill's thoughts on what Alabama needed. Submitted to the governor in January 1983, with a follow-up report on taxation policy dated February 2, 1984, Hill's "blue ribbon report" urged the following: (1) increased efficiencies among the trade schools and junior colleges started in 1960s (which only could occur through merger and closure); (2) reorganizing the State Development Office so that career professionals (as opposed to gubernatorial friends) could apply their expertise to attracting outside industry (thus increasing the tax base that could provide more funds for social services); (3) developing alternatives to prison for "less-serious offenders" (to save funds on a costly prison system that could then be reallocated to other social services and education); (4) establishing health insurance for catastrophic illness for the newly unemployed (which also would help lessen the unfunded indigent care expenditures of UAB and USA hospitals); (5) making the state's general approach to medical education more efficient by reducing the total number of physicians the state's programs sought to produce; (6) reviewing (and if necessary increasing) taxes with special attention to property taxes; and (7) a decade before Georgia embraced such an idea, a state lottery as a source of educational funding. Although one member of the task force, Joe Adams of the Ozark, Alabama, newspaper the *Southern Star,* filed a dissenting opinion on tax increase provisions, Hill spoke with the apparent force of the committee behind him—including Wallace's longtime compatriots, Adams and Stephens—when he wrote Wallace in January 1983 that "overcoming the problems . . . which impede this state's economic progress will require . . . extraordinary actions" by both the governor and legislature. To Hill, such action even included reducing the number of physicians he would train, despite recent moves to increase this number, with the trade-off in the committee of getting strong support for a more progressive approach to property taxes. "To seize this opportunity," concluded Hill, "is the challenge of leadership which is now before you and the other elected members of state government."[96]

From the standpoint of the state's immediate future, all this was mostly for naught. As usual, despite his self-proclaimed "populism," Wallace was unwilling to confront corporate lobbies, both in state and out of state, that had contributed to his campaign and that stood to lose in the short run by tax reform: with few exceptions, it was a long-time Alabama custom—rail against "special interests," get in power, and then do what "special interests" tell you to do. In fact, some of these lobbies likely were well represented on the "blue ribbon" committee, continuing their strategies of assuming high-profile public stands for "improving Alabama" only to work behind the scenes to block the necessary steps if they ran counter to their short-term profits. Overtly sensitive to these interest groups as the key to his political power, Wallace sent Hill a "Dear Dick" thank-you note, expressed "disagreement" on "the lottery proposal," and urged all to work for "a better life for all Alabamians." The product of a few hardworking and high-minded Alabamians alongside more than a smattering of corporate hypocrisy, this "blueprint" for taking Alabama into the genuine New South soon found its way into the Alabama State Department of Archives and History. There it came to rest alongside many other worthy ships of change wrecked on the lighthouse atop Goat Hill, at times emitting a faint glow but to all intents and purposes unlit and immovable.[97]

Years later, however, Hill recalled, "I'd do it again if there were just a chance that we could get [such a reform] to help this state."[98] He pointedly said on another occasion, "[T]here was a limit to how far UAB—and all other things in the state—could mature" as long as state public policy remained in the nineteenth century. Still, just as his advocacy of the Urban Grant Act expanded UAB's national image as something more than a medical center, Hill's chairing the highly publicized committee of corporate and civic leaders likely helped solidify and mature the public image of the Birmingham institution as a significant social force in the state.[99]

Refining a Vision for Maturity

In the early summer of 1984, on the heels of helping Hearn and Long start the honors program, Hill received an inquiry from his baccalaureate alma mater, Wake Forest University, regarding its opening in the president's office. Hill nominated Hearn, and by September Hearn was on the job in North Carolina, taking with him John Anderson to fill the newly created position of executive vice president. The two expatriates from UAB turned out to be an eminently successful team at Wake Forest—Anderson shaving his beard, donning pinstripes, and managing the "inside," while Hearn focused on fund-raising and other external matters. Both were significant losses for UAB, however: Hearn had built Birmingham community support for the arts at UAB (which included hiring the dynamic pianists Sam and Delores Howard away from Birmingham-Southern), and Anderson had expanded special studies into one of the most financially successful ventures in continuing education in the nation, providing year-end profits that were plowed back into basic undergraduate programs.[100]

Hill moved carefully in replacing them. First, on Hearn's advice, Hill named the dean of humanities, James Rachels, to the position of acting vice president of University College; Rachels then moved Benditt out of the philosophy chair into the dean's office and George Graham became chair in philosophy. Hill also named Sara Ruiz de Molina, the daughter of one of the founding members of the medical faculty, Robert Guthrie, and Anderson's director of credit programs, to serve as interim director in special studies. Then Hill started a search. After six months the search committee had three candidates to interview: M. Gene Newport, dean in business; Anthony C. L. Barnard, the founder of computer science programs in the medical center and most recently Hearn's assistant vice president of academic affairs; and James H. Woodward, dean of engineering, formerly Campbell's assistant vice president and an executive periodically courted by major corporations. Chiefly on the grounds that Woodward not only had helped develop many of the policies and procedures undergirding University College but had been a dean with a considerable track record in raising money, the committee ranked Woodward as the first choice. Hill, who had had conversations with several members of the search committee, seemed unsurprised by the outcome and warmly concurred. Woodward became vice president of University College in July 1984 and his old friend from boyhood days in Columbus, Georgia, James Rachels, assumed a university professor position based on his acclaimed writings on death and dying and his ongoing investigations into the philosophical significance of Charles Darwin. Then, after an interim deanship of Edmond T. Miller, Woodward filled the engineering post through a national search with Jay Goldman, a Duke Ph.D. who had been at Washington University, St. Louis. At the same time, the founding dean in the School of Social and Behavioral Sciences, George E. Passey, decided to retire; Blaine Brownell left the position of UAB Graduate School dean and took what he called "a real dean job" in the School of Social and Behavioral Sciences. Anthony C. L. Barnard prevailed in an internal search to succeed Brownell in the Graduate School; through this new role Barnard also became one of the major national figures charged with the development and administration of the Graduate Record Examination (GRE). Again, here was a plethora of "inside" appointments, evoking standard reactions on campus: good, for it kept the institution focused on its mission of being an urban research university with a major medical center; bad, because of "no new blood."[101]

Money matters also changed dramatically under Hill. The massive programmatic growth of the 1970s and early 1980s had left many infrastructure needs unmet. To meet these needs took money, and there were a number of budgetary obstacles. First, in May 1981 at the annual meeting of the UA board Volker surprised many board members in announcing that he would be leaving the chancellor's post as soon as a replacement could be found. The transition took longer than expected, however, partly because it was not clear what authority a new chancellor would have. Thomas A. Bartlett, formerly president of Colgate University and also of American University in Cairo, finally replaced Volker in the summer of 1982. Although Volker had managed some important UA system developments—among them the appointment of Hill as UAB president, the replacement of Mathews with Joab Thomas as UA president, and Benjamin Graves with John Wright as UAH president—he was approaching seventy and wanted out of high-level administration. If he was glad that O. C. Carmichael had talked him into sticking around back in the early 1960s just to see what might happen, at this particular stage of his life a distinguished professorship and an active civic life back in Birmingham would do just fine. Still, not to have Volker presiding over the key budget issues of the system was not exactly encouraging news for Hill.[102]

There also was the more concrete problem of enrollment. During 1979–86 the profound enrollment growth of previous years slowed, a standard problem all institutions sooner or later have to confront as they move from youth to maturity. Total fall enrollment in 1979 was 14,214; by the fall of 1986 it was 14,248. By the mid-1980s the national as well as Birmingham economies finally had recovered from the recession touched off by the international oil crisis, and the increased availability of full-time jobs in the Birmingham area meant fewer folks wanted to enroll at UAB. In contrast to nonurban universities, here is a standard pattern in most urban universities: the hotter the economy, the colder the enrollment; the colder the economy, the hotter the enrollment—making the budgets of urban universities one of the best safety nets for city economies. The ubiquitous "credit hour production" (CHP) upon which ACHE recommended a state allocation for UAB paralleled this enrollment: fall term 1979 CHP ran 96,489; fall term 1986 CHP was 95,681. Beneath these statistics were fascinating trends. Undergraduate CHP increased slightly during this period as growth in the metropolitan population of Birmingham engendered by new economic diversification helped offset the hot economy effect on enrollment. Graduate enrollment, where the formula "weight" (based on the Texas formula) in CHP is higher, however, declined slightly, especially in programs strongly oriented to the local job market—business, teacher education, and engineering.[103]

Although in retrospect the leveling off of enrollment is understandable, it still engendered more than nervousness in an academic community accustomed to skyrocketing numbers of students. And it fell more to Vice President Woodward than to any other key officer to deal with this problem. He was an intense leader. A good decade before cellular phones made humans talking into technology commonplace among rapidly moving automobiles, Woodward often was sighted on metropolitan freeways lecturing into his dictaphone as he sought to confirm virtually all business discussions with written summaries. In his office in the Education Building on certain afternoons the dictaphone occasionally got a rest as he turned to his cigar. As smoked wafted out from under his office door, deans and others knew to ask his assistant, Faye Holtzclaw, "What sort of day has he had?" The cigar signaled both victories and defeats. He relaxed only when his office staff—Holtzclaw, Joan Davis, Mary Perry, and Patricia Jeffery—

surprised him with birthday parties filled with devilish pranks. (Davis: "A plastic foam birthday cake, disguised with homemade icing that cannot be cut with even a sharp knife . . . now that just doesn't sit too well with someone trained in engineering.")[104]

More to the point, after extensive discussions with deans Newport, Goldman, Clint Bruess, Peter O'Neil, Brownell, Barnard, and Benditt, Vice President Woodward rapidly evolved a three-point plan for increased enrollment. Certainly such hands-on leadership came from his working with Vice President Campbell. No doubt it also emanated from Woodward's previous experience in the private sector where successful visioning and marketing tied to detailed data are crucial determinants of success.

First, Woodward reinvigorated UAB's commitment to part-time and working students. To him, the maturing of UAB did not mean a loss of focus on "the local living community," the city encircling the university. He personally spot-checked the course offerings of different UAB schools to ensure there were sufficient classes at night, especially for undergraduates.[105]

Second, he initiated a revision of the undergraduate general education or "core" curriculum. This curriculum had remained essentially the same since the mid-1960s, when George Campbell had implemented the relatively "loose," or unstructured, "distribution requirement" curriculum in vogue at UA and many other institutions. Still, Woodward was a believer in the current "back to basics" movement in American higher education, for example, reestablishing as *requirements* certain courses in mathematics, history, science, literature, and philosophy, as well as ensuring a UAB graduate was computer literate. However, he also was determined to have a curriculum carefully attuned to "transferability" out of Alabama's two-year colleges, private and public. Indeed, at the time approximately 55 percent of UAB juniors and seniors came to the institution after completing one or two years of work elsewhere, often at junior colleges. Through curriculum reform he sought to maximize this flow of incoming students.[106]

Accordingly, he established a faculty committee on "goals and philosophy" and another on "specific requirements"—committees including representatives from neighboring feeder institutions, public Jefferson State Community College and private Walker [Junior] College. For a year and half their debates reflected the standard disciplinary and departmental turfdom over what was "important," as well as the struggle between a curriculum "with unique UAB strengths" as opposed to one facilitating transfer students. On several occasions the vice president used his authority as "chief academic officer" to keep the committees focused on "transferability" but not without tension between himself and certain faculty regarding the role of "faculty governance." Perhaps the climactic moment came when he explained the realpolitik undergirding their endeavor to the "specific requirements" committee. He pulled no punches. Because of their placing numerous employees in the legislature and also out of their alignment with the Alabama Education Association (AEA), state two-year colleges could have the legislature dictate much of the curricula of four-year institutions if universities such as UAB did not show sensitivity to students' need to transfer credits to senior institutions. Whether the committee liked it or not, this was going to happen, sooner rather than later. So, it would seem that the committee would prefer to have at least *some* influence over what UAB faculty taught by building a curriculum that engaged transferability from the two-year institutions. The committee ultimately acquiesced, listening carefully to specifics offered up by Henry ("Hank") West and Joe Morris, committee members with leadership positions at Walker College and Jefferson State, respectively.[107] Woodward's assessment of these politics was prescient. Over the succeeding decade, as some four-year institutions in the state embraced transferability and others—including Auburn University and UA—did not, the precise legislation Woodward predicted was enacted: a standardized state core curriculum was put in place for all public institutions.[108]

Third, he concluded that overt undergraduate recruitment efforts, not to mention retention efforts, should be far more focused. Benefiting from Urban 13 reports, he increased formal retention efforts where most students would drop out or "stop out" if they were so inclined: during the freshman and sophomore years. He created the Division of General Studies, essentially five full-time professional advisors who were to stay in constant contact with these students until they had declared majors, at which point school-level advisors were programmed to pick them up. Then, from the opposite perspective, he pursued recruitment and retention of students well focused on a major as they entered the institution, increasingly "traditional" students in their late teens and early twenties who attended college full time who often came from high schools south of Birmingham. Within the Birmingham Metropolitan Study Area (MSA), southern Jefferson County and northern Shelby County by the early 1980s already were showing on all state studies as the hottest areas for population and economic growth in Alabama. New freeway connections in the area, especially the intersection of Highway 280 and I-459, plus U.S. Steel's continuing withdrawal from the Birmingham area by selling off thousands of acres in southern Jefferson County for retail and residential development, began a booming traffic-snarled brand of growth so recently responsible for the metroplex of Atlanta. To Woodward, however, here were burgeoning numbers of college-educated families, earning a good living thanks to Birmingham's increasingly diversified economy, with children who would go to college. He wanted them at UAB—not just enrolled but staying enrolled through graduation.[109]

To make this happen, while continuing to advise deans that they should never let up on scheduling classes in time slots popular among working and part-time students, he initiated a multilayered strategy to overtly "market" UAB as a traditional college. He welcomed faculty proposals for new interdisciplinary programs that appealed to traditional college students. At the undergraduate level he implemented a new B.A. major in international studies, developed by the French professor William C. Carter, the historians Eul-Soo Pang and Canfield Smith, and Dean Blaine A. Brownell. He also implemented two new academic minors to go along with the recently instituted minor in African American Studies: one in American studies and one in women's studies. Likewise, at the graduate level he implemented new interdisciplinary programs not just to grow the institution internally but in direct response to the new chancellor of the UA system, Thomas A. Bartlett, who called for multicampus doctoral programs that exhibited to ACHE and the legislature that the UA system could use its resources efficiently. In this context, multicampus doctoral programs rapidly emerged in applied mathematics, materials science, health education, and educational leadership. Here were some of the new high-demand graduate programs found at such premier traditional institutions as Duke or the University of Virginia, and Woodward saw the chancellor's strategy as well serving his own.[110]

Woodward initiated more direct "marketing," too: a redesign of the undergraduate catalog, especially the cover, which showed students on a *campus* and had the UAB seal on the cover. So as to make the new image real, he also developed more campus "green space," an idea strongly reinforced by architect Garland, who was interested in the ideas of urban landscape first propounded by the nineteenth-century landscape architect Frederick Law Olmsted, who created Central Park in New York City. It was more and more the Olmstedian "green space" that Woodward, Garland, and Hill urged as opposed to blacktopped parking lots; and at every chance, buildings both new and refurbished were wrapped in a consistent dark-red brick veneer. Red brick silhouetted against trees and grass: here was a "college campus," and, unknown to UAB leaders, the reassertion of a look first developed by civic (or "red brick") universities in mid-nineteenth-century Britain.[111]

Strategic planning seemed to work. Enrollment is always the result of complex forces, and UAB's undoubtedly would never repeat the striking increases of the early 1970s. Yet Woodward's strategic maturing of UAB recruitment likely was one of the main reasons why the institution overall again reflected robust enrollment gains by the late 1980s and early 1990s. University College, which housed the programs under Woodward's supervision, grew from approximately 10,500 students in the fall of 1984 to almost 11,500 in the fall of 1988, a trend that continued well into the next decade and encompassed both qualitative and quantitative development.[112]

Nevertheless, the developing shift in the UAB "vision" evolved by Hill, Woodward, and others—more of a traditional campus with significant intercollegiate activities—certainly did not go unnoticed beyond Birmingham, as revealed in the traumatic fight over board appointments that culminated in the summer of 1983. Several years earlier, in response to the burgeoning scale of the three UA campuses as well as President Hill's urging that there be more board members attuned to UAB's growth, the board advocated a state constitutional amendment that would enable the board to have fifteen members instead of eight. In turn, state senators Earl Hilliard and U. W. Clemmon, both African Americans, urged that they could support the proposal as long as a certain number of the new slots went to black leaders; at the time there were no black members on the board. Opposed to quotas, the board managed to get the amendment passed on the ballot of April 1982 with promises to black leaders of the state that an expanded board would reflect racial diversity.[113]

Then things got dicey. In 1981, anticipating the board expansion issue, Lieutenant Governor William J. ("Bill") Baxley, a UA graduate and a fulsome Crimson Tide fan (on occasions he flew on the team plane with Coach Bryant), quietly—but legally—had the state senate rules amended such that if the Senate failed to confirm a particular board nominee, the Senate, not the board, would make the nomination to fill the open slot. (During the 1990s the role of lieutenant governor in Alabama became far less powerful.) How might this rule change affect the board's slate? A hint: Baxley openly said that he opposed confirmation of any new board members who had not done "something of significance" for UA and who might acquiesce to or support other board members who supported building a traditional campus at UAB. Indeed, years later he recalled,

I long had played a role in getting budget increases for the UA medical school. This was a jewel in the crown for all of Alabama. However, the state did not have the money for the development of a traditional campus in Birmingham. Such developments were appropriate in Auburn and Tuscaloosa and, because of distance, probably Mobile [USA]. But undergraduate education in Birmingham needed to be held to a commuter program with a student life that included, at most, low-profile intercollegiate sports. I long had thought this, and I wrote at least one board member about it and was told it was none of my business. When Hill hired Bartow at a salary slightly higher than C. M. Newton's [the UA basketball coach] and I discussed this with Coach Bryant, I saw clearly where UAB leaders were headed—a traditional campus with big-time athletics. This was wrong for the state, and that's the reason I eased through the rules change. The board as of the early 1980s was not going to block what UAB was trying to do. So I had to try by changing the makeup of the board at the first opportunity.

Confronted with the point that most vibrant cities have vibrant, fully developed universities, Baxley replied, "As a generalization that may be true, but Alabama's horrible record with a retrogressive tax system and lack of funds for general social services makes us unique. There was not enough state money to develop a traditional UAB without limiting the continued growth of AU, UA, *and* the medical center in Birmingham." At any rate, in 1983 the relatively unrecognized rule change and Baxley's firm beliefs about where Alabama higher education needed to go were the dominant political factors the UA board faced as it submitted its slate of nominees to the Senate.[114]

The seven nominated for the new slots included William Mitchell, Louis J. Willie, Robin Swift, Juliette St. John, Margaret P. Stabler, Margaret E. M. Tolbert, and Sandral Hullett. On receipt of the list, Baxley telephoned his friend on the opposing side, the UAB lobbyist Rudy Davidson, with the direct message that two of the nominees looked appropriate—the white business executive and UA graduate, Mitchell, and the black physician and graduate of UA's community health program, Hullett. The other five, he indicated, would not be confirmed, the most prominent of whom was the black business executive from Birmingham, Willie. A Texas native with an M.B.A. from Michigan State University, Willie long had used his leadership positions with Booker T. Washington Life Insurance Company and his friendships with Volker and Hill to advance developing growth agendas at UAB, not the least of which was fully embracing civil rights. Willie was not an easy turn-down for Baxley. The lieutenant governor previously had served as attorney general for Alabama, and in that role he had fought the Ku Klux Klan at every opportunity, most notably in seeking to prove its guilt in the Birmingham church bombing. But in the end Baxley did not bend: he thought Willie, if confirmed, would have been exactly what President Hill wanted—an effective advocate for a traditional-campus UAB.

Through Davidson, then, back went Baxley's reactions to Hill, the chancellor, and the board. Unflinching, and undoubtedly believing that the long-established precedent of no political intrusions into UA board matters would prevail, Chancellor Bartlett (remembered as "clueless" by one lobbyist) and the board held to its nominees. In formal Senate hearings, therefore, Baxley first commented on Willie's lack of connection with UA and then asked Willie if he had ever attended a Crimson Tide football game. Willie said no. Subsequently, at the end of some forty-eight hours of intense politicking and similar questions being asked of other nominees, Willie and the four others were rejected (two withdrew before the end of the proceedings). Shortly thereafter, Baxley and cooperative colleagues in the Senate forwarded new names to fill the now open five slots. Their first-cut list included at least one current state senator, Michael Figures of Mobile, a black man well identified with the civil rights movement. But Baxley soon saw that this would lead to other senators wanting to serve on either the UA or the AU board and stopped further consideration of Figures. Baxley's final slate included no members of the legislature but men known for their advocacy of UA: Mobile grocery retailer Oliver Delchamps, Jr.; Jasper (and Birmingham) coal executive Garry Neil Drummond; statewide jewelry store owner (of Birmingham) Frank Bromberg; Montgomery real estate developer Aaron Aronov; and attorney Cleophus Thomas. Much like Hullett, Thomas in Baxley's view represented significant progress toward diversity on the board. The first black SGA president at UA, Thomas had graduated from Harvard Law School and recently joined a practice in his hometown of Anniston. The lieutenant governor quickly prevailed with these "Senate-proposed" confirmations.[115]

Backwash from this storm held strong and conflicting currents. President Hill and many others in Birmingham saw the board fight, with an implied litmus test of always placing a priority on UA needs, as a type of "reverse referendum" on the future of UAB. To them, UAB confronted an amorphous sentiment, on the board and in the Senate, that a thriving Crimson Tide and a vibrant UA campus could not exist alongside UAB's vision for maturity. And, though supportive up to a point of Hill's fear, Baxley's position on board appointments was shared by substantial Alabamians, though there is no scientific public opinion poll to document such sentiment. Within the general population many UA fans looked at all these developments through the prism of athletics: UAB's hiring a person of Bartow's stature was heresy. Further, inside the Birmingham medical school—where Baxley was known among older faculty as the cousin of the esteemed medical school registrar Virginia Baxley—support for Baxley's position likely emanated from concern over financing an ever-expanding medical school and continuing sensitivities over "internal transfers" for "the University." Despite substantial support for Baxley's stand, however, the episode also reflects the UA board as anything *but* monolithically opposed to the continuing evolution of UAB—a mythologized version of board dynamics advocated by many proponents of a traditional-campus UAB. Baxley recalls that in the days following the showdown some board members, such as Ernest G. Williams of Tuscaloosa, seemed relatively satisfied with the outcome, while others, such as Winton M. Blount of Montgomery, were angry—and one or two others normally very supportive of "pro-UA" actions resented Baxley's intrusion. Indeed, Baxley recalls that during the most intense hours of the storm the board placed significant pressure on him to cease his political intrusion into board affairs, which Baxley recalls he did not accede to and with "appropriate justification." From a distance another, broader insight emerges. Though a public entity, the board did not go public on how it viewed the fight, even if there were differences of opinion as there obviously were. In the process, the board and the chancellor's office lost a badly needed opportunity to mitigate longtime and still escalating tensions inside the UA system. Such tensions occupied increasing time and energy of campus officers and system staff as well as board members, which undoubtedly kept all of them from doing as much as they might toward the advancement of teaching, learning, research, and service in Alabama.[116]

Money: Proration, Capital Campaign, and Physical Growth

Even with these complex issues of campus life and the resulting distractions of politics within the UA system and Montgomery, President Hill still managed to expand the institution's overall budget to meet the pent-up needs of infrastructure and physical plant—at least some of them. Indeed, total UAB revenues for 1979 ran $235,300,000; by 1986 they were $409,884,784—a 43 percent increase. A breakdown of some of the sources of this money reflects a trend that makes the expansion and maturing of

UAB during the Hill presidency all the more interesting. Despite little enrollment growth in the early to mid-1980s, tuition and fee revenues increased from $12,685,000 in 1979 to $20,148,000 in 1986, a 37 percent increase owing to a general statewide pattern of tuition rate increases touched off by an ancillary problem—decreased state funding. Granted, state appropriations for UAB ran $78,780,000 in 1979 just as Fob James was about to temporarily displace Wallace as governor; and by 1986 at the end of Wallace's final term as governor they had moved up to $131,000,900. These gains, however, are deceptive.[117]

During much of the Hill presidency, state funding for public education began to be influenced by the Budget and Financial Management Act (Fletcher Act). As detailed in Ira Harvey's landmark study, *A History of Educational Finance in Alabama, 1819–1986* (1989), this act, which was originally enacted in 1932 with the onslaught of the Great Depression and enforced last in the late 1950s and early 1960s, provided that original appropriations (biennial until 1975 and annual after that year) to education would be lowered retroactively if sales tax revenues, the major source of income for the Alabama Special Education Trust Fund (created in 1927), failed to come into the state coffers in sufficient amounts to match the appropriations. At the same time, State of Alabama appropriations were adversely affected by the longstanding practice of "earmarking," that is, in many cases a particular administration could not move funds from one part of the state budget to another to help avert a crisis in funding in a special area, such as education. In this context, should sales tax revenues not come into the state treasury as anticipated, K–12 as well as higher education budgets would be "prorated," that is, educational entities would be required to return a certain percentage of their annual allocation to the state so as to avoid state education indebtedness, regardless of what time of year—what stage in education's fiscal year—the economic downturn occurred.[118]

Though on the surface proration spoke to statewide fiscal accountability as well as Alabamians' historic distrust of politicians and government in general, it often became a tool of sinister manipulation. As David Bronner, the noted director of the Teachers' Retirement System of Alabama, put it, Alabamians "may have some common sense but [they] don't have much financial sense." In election years legislators and governors made appropriations well beyond what economic trends could justify in order to have the monetary levers to help them get reelected, then they called back some of the education allocation because sales tax receipts "somehow" did not come in as expected. In turn, proration placed all of public education in Alabama on a constant roller-coaster of unpredictability, as the state's economy and hence its sales tax receipts rose and fell with national trends.[119]

Paul Hubbert, the shrewd leader of the K–12 teachers union, the AEA, further complicated this problem. His dilatory effect emanated not so much from his ability to get K–12 a greater and greater share of the annual education appropriations, for K–12 did indeed need greater allocations because county-level funding in some areas was so weak. Instead, he used his money-bought influence over legislators and governors to manipulate the all-too-regular instances of proration to pit K–12 against higher education as a way of building his own organization, which consisted of 65,000 teachers in 128 school systems for the 67 counties of Alabama. One ponders what would have happened if this native of Hubbertville, in Fayette County, and a former Troy, Alabama, school superintendent, instead had used this power (and his striking intelligence) to help solve the systemic education funding problem his state faced during the 1980s.[120]

Where Hubbert's power needed to be directed was at Alabama's regressive use of sales taxes as the foundation for education funding: not only did this make for unpredictable education funding but it placed the heaviest education tax weight on the vast majority of Alabamians, who were in the lower-middle and lower-class income brackets. Throughout the 1970s, 1980s, and 1990s, however, both he and Governors Wallace and James essentially stayed clear of confronting this situation. In the late 1990s, only the most optimistic held to an enduring hope for systemic change.[121]

More to the point of these convoluted education politics, during the Hill presidency UAB's original appropriations showed a healthy upward trend; in actuality in many years these appropriations were prorated: in 1978–79 (under Wallace), 2.98 percent; in 1979–80 (under James), 6.14 percent; in 1980–81 (under James), 3.57 percent; and in 1985–86 (under Wallace), 4.12 percent. To add to this deceptiveness was the issue of "line-item funding" whereby historically a university president and lobbyist could pressure the Alabama legislature to earmark in some cases a million dollars or more for a special project. This permitted a lobbyist such as Davidson, who represented a university with a medical center, to work magic on a particular legislator who might have a personal or family interest in a special health issue—the strategy of working the "grateful patient." Yet it also created utter chaos because Davidson and Hill often did not know until it was too late which assertive UAB physicians, for example, a diabetes specialist, also might be working his own independent agenda on the same legislator, acquiring earmarked money that effectively reduced the expected *institu-*

tional UAB budget. To add to this complexity, the press and the people (including many UAB faculty and staff) only focused on the total *original* UAB appropriation, generally unaware that large portions of the money in certain years had been both prorated and earmarked for "innovative faculty" and their programs.[122]

In a far clearer context, however, during the Hill years grants and contracts underwent genuine growth. These revenues moved from $48,784,000 in 1979 to $78,132,000 in 1986—a 38 percent increase. Overwhelming blocks of this money came from medical research institutions. For example, in 1979 the NIH alone provided $26,009,980 and by 1986 this figure had moved up to $42,500,890, as interdisciplinary research in the biomedical sciences continued to be funded at higher and higher levels by the federal government.[123]

Likewise, Hill launched UAB into its first capital campaign. Formally announced in July 1983 (though in the planning since 1980), Hill and his team raised nearly $30 million over the next three years ($6.6 million from the faculty alone) and then raised the goal to $55 million which, joined with state bond money, UAB bond funds, patient fees, and grants and contracts, produced a $160 million physical plant expansion. With notable exceptions, virtually all of these funds were earmarked for construction or faculty endowment in the medical center. More to the point, by the mid-1980s the medical center enjoyed special attention from wealthy Alabamians. Particularly as a result of Kirklin's heart transplant program and the new cancer center, the hospital complex and its physicians were perceived less and less by prominent citizens as something "suitable for indigents but not for my family." Savvy marketing by medical center leaders helped close this gap between myth and reality, not coincidentally assisting Hill's fund-raising.[124]

With these chiefly nonstate funds, Hill began to make a dent in the shortages of space, support personnel, and operating issues. The full-time workforce including faculty moved from 7,900 in 1979 (with a payroll of $121,800,300) to 9,097 in 1986 (with a payroll of $227,027,800). During the same time medical center faculty increased from 945 to 1,159 and University College faculty from 368 to 403. If this reflected modest faculty gains in an effort to fill in gaps left by the massive programmatic development of the Volker presidency, clearly the chief impact was on infrastructure staff often associated with NIH and NSF research grants rather than with the hiring of additional state-funded faculty or staff.[125]

A similar infrastructure and funding problem had existed, however, beyond the medical laboratories and hospitals. If they did little about operating funds in general education programs, Hill, McCallum, Hearn, and Woodward did indeed tackle several other matters in University College. With major gifts from Harold Abroms and Emil Hess, owners of Parisian, the Hill team provided scholarships for students in the new undergraduate honors program—a key component in the strategy to mature the institution by attracting more talented and "traditional" college students.[126]

Then there was the issue of the libraries. Although Lister Hill Library for the Health Sciences, including the Reynolds Historical Collection, continued to keep pace with the expanding medical center, in Mervyn H. Sterne Library—the facility focused chiefly on nonmedical programs—books and journals had not kept pace with the new programs, students, and faculty added during the Volker presidency. A major infusion of onetime funds, accordingly, some from the capital campaign, allowed holdings in Lister Hill Library, under the direction of Richard B. Fredericksen, to move from 152,359 volumes in 1979 to 176,400 in 1986. In the same period, with the aid of a $1 million line-item (and one-time) increase from the legislature facilitated by Rudy Davidson, the Mervyn H. Sterne Collection, under the direction of Paul Spence, moved from 467,500 volumes to 707,400. Somewhere entangled in the allocation was the understanding, too, that Sterne would receive a vast collection of fishing caps, fan letters, and assorted press clippings from the recently retired George Wallace, all of which ultimately would find their way to the place where the main body of Wallace's papers went, the Alabama State Department of Archives and History in Montgomery. These new books and journals in Sterne Library represented a major improvement. Yet the Sterne collection still remained strikingly limited by the standards of the high-level research faculty hired over the previous decade, faculty trained in research libraries such as those of the University of North Carolina, Columbia University, the University of Texas, and Vanderbilt University. Frustrations mounted, especially among "nonlaboratory" arts and sciences faculty. Their "laboratory" may have been well managed as Paul Spence passed the directorship to Jerry Stephens in 1985, but this facility remained clearly underfunded while their science, engineering, and health science colleagues often worked in state-of-the-art laboratories.[127]

Hence, through the Faculty-President Liaison Committee and other faculty forums, Hill and Vice President Woodward repeatedly explained the complexity of the problem. In other states, public universities had been receiving state dollars for library development in some cases for well over 150 years. In UAB's case, not only was the institution less than twenty-five years old, but the state generally remained strapped with retrogressive public policy including an antiquated taxation policy resulting in small budgets for everything from indigent health care to library operating funds. When pressed on why a capital campaign could not do even more for book and journal acquisitions, especially in view of the overt decision to build Sterne collections for a researching faculty, Hill delivered the unvarnished truth. In a straightforward admission that Sterne Library's budget then and for the foreseeable future was at about 50 percent of the average of libraries in research universities in the Southeast, short of unrestricted gifts that could be directed to library development, it was virtually impossible to find donors for library books on the same level that "grateful patient" donors stood eager to endow medical research laboratories. Plus, he noted, federal policy widened the gap even further as Congress appropriated millions each year to the NSF and NIH that could be used for conventionally defined laboratories, while Congress provided the National Endowment for the Humanities a less than paltry sum for "core grants" for libraries: it was a problem of "national and state priorities."[128]

Woodward was even more direct. Unless "long-shot luck" delivered a multimillion-dollar gift, UAB's Sterne Library "will never come close to catching up with libraries of the older institutions." Indeed, he went on, what collection there was always would have even less of an impact on faculty and student scholarship because it was politically unfeasible for Sterne's collections not to be open to virtually all Birmingham citizens, including high school students. Struggling for a way through this daunting dilemma of the declared policy of building Sterne into a genuine research facility yet not having the funds to do so, a historian essentially uninitiated on UAB's current political economy, or Alabama's, suggested that each time UAB hired a "nonlab" arts and sciences faculty member, the institution would provide the individual with "library start-up funds" the same way new health scientists, for example, received special monies to start up their "wet" laboratories. Hill kindly responded that the idea had "possibilities" but would require "major participation by deans and vice presidents." The problem persisted.[129]

Physical plant development of the mid-1980s was altogether another matter, once again targeted as much at catching up with programmatic and faculty development of the previous decade as with new initiatives. As Claude Bennett, among other chairs in the medical center, had been emphasizing, "Wouldn't it be a shame if we lost chances for some scientific breakthrough . . . by failure to act decisively in terms . . . of space for imaginative, frontier-type endeavors?" Indeed, if one uses the UAB physical plant of 1977 as a baseline, during the Hill presidency physical facilities (i.e., gross square feet for teaching, research, and service, including clinical) increased by 40 percent. This massive growth, however, was not without considerable controversy, as some citizens protested about "the University that ate Birmingham," especially regarding the street closings that were necessary for new construction.[130]

During 1979–80 Dean Pittman, with the major assistance of the local corporate leader Hall Thompson, built the Center for Advanced Medical Studies (CAMS), by lore (if not fact) a structure as odd in origin as in appearance. Pittman's many medical center friends enjoyed telling the story that Pittman, an avid pilot of antique planes, took Thompson aloft in a World War I biplane, turned the rig upside down at 6,000 feet over downtown Birmingham, and secure in the knowledge that "We both had on seat belts" refused to right the plane until his good friend committed on the gift facilitating construction. Pressed hard on this account, Pittman tweaked the story into truth: "I did take Hall up, and we did wear seat belts, and he did make the gift; but I never turned us upside down." Still, with plane returned to hangar and gift virtually in hand, Pittman proceeded with plans for a neo-antebellum home replete with white columns smack-dab in the middle of the futuristic medical center where the original Reynolds Library once stood. On the luxurious sofas of CAMS, select students soon to receive their M.D.s met as the Harrison Society (named for Tinsley Harrison, who fostered similar discussions) to explore connections between medicine and the larger issues of modern society—a breadth of inquiry typical of Pittman's own broadly expansive interests—while lunching with the likes of Sir George Pickering, Regius Professor of Medicine at Oxford University.[131]

Other construction projects seemed more conventional. The Twin Towers dormitory went up, housing nurses and "a few others"—a prescient sign of an emergent full-time residential student population at UAB. The following year, 1980, the Hill team added new primate facilities, an addition to the nursing building, and a flammable storage facility. Then came the Kidney Transplant Unit, another addition to the nursing facility, and the Webb Nutrition Sciences Building, facilitated with major gifts from two local foundations, the Susan Mott Webb Charitable Trust and the Pepsi Cola Corporation. By 1984–85, there also was an addition to the Spain-Wallace Hospital as well as the new Tinsley Harrison Tower; an expansion of the diabetes hospital (renamed Boshell Diabetes Hospital); the addition of a

Nuclear Magnetic Resonance Imaging system to the cancer center; and a massive 111,974 gross square foot basic science education and research facility aided by a large donation from the Callaway Foundation of Georgia, which much later would bear the name of Charles A. McCallum.[132]

Not all construction, however, related to the medical center. Hill and Vice President for Administration Dudley Pewitt, who simultaneously chaired the Birmingham Chamber of Commerce, worked with city and county officials and the Birmingham Convention and Visitors Bureau to erect an information center on the far western end of University Boulevard. The growth of the previous two decades, not to mention current construction, made the seventy-two-square-block campus "more than difficult" to navigate for guests; the new facility could assist the city as well as prospective students and patients.[133]

In addition to the University Center and the Jerry D. Young Memorial Baseball Field, Hill with Hearn's assistance upgraded the facilities of WBHM and added a performing arts wing to the Humanities Building— the Hulsey Center, named for one of the chief donors, William F. Hulsey of Birmingham—although for acoustical reasons the facility was better suited for classes and guest lectures than music and theater. (The Yale historian C. Vann Woodward, one of the preeminent intellectuals of twentieth-century America, helped christen the hall shortly after it opened in 1981.) Moreover, while still dean in engineering, Woodward called on corporate friends at Rust Engineering, BE&K Engineering, and American Cast Iron and Pipe Company and found support to build the 133,000-square-foot Business-Engineering Complex (BEC), which envisioned more interdisciplinary instruction between business and engineering. Heretofore, engineering had been housed where it had begun in the 1950s—in Tidwell Hall and later in Cudworth Hall just off Twentieth Street—and business had been in Building No. 1 alongside education. The new BEC went up in 1983 at the far west end of the campus.[134]

In the normal domino effect of any campus growth, John Anderson, just before he left for Wake Forest, arranged for the relocation of engineering to open up Cudworth Hall as a modern conference center. Implemented by his successor as dean of special studies, Sara Ruiz de Molina, the project permitted special studies, heretofore limited to space in a series of apartments at the west end of the campus, to benefit from funding by the Birmingham Hilton Hotel (later the Radisson). From the Hilton at the southwestern corner of University Boulevard and Twentieth Street a skywalk bridge was constructed to the new conference and continuing education facility, with minimal financial risk permitting UAB food service and hotel accommodations for the already nationally acclaimed continuing education program. As this project reached completion in the mid-1980s Hill and Woodward, working closely with the new Sterne Library director, Jerry Stephens, were well underway with an $8.5 million addition (105,000 square feet) to Sterne Library wrapped, of course, in dark red brick, conveying "traditional college."[135]

Simultaneously, just north of Sterne Library, Hill and Woodward also started construction of anything but a traditional new business incubator facility, to be known as OADI, the Office for the Advancement of Developing Industries, designed to encourage UAB scientists and also those of the Southern Research Institute to remain in research while still benefiting themselves, not to mention the community, by taking a major new discovery out of the laboratory and into a venture-capital enterprise based in Birmingham. Over the next decade, the UAB facility relocated south of the city center in Shades Valley (land strategically annexed to the city of Birmingham by Mayor Arrington, some of which he "gifted" to UAB for the project) and became, in the city-booster words of the *Birmingham News*, "a five mile fuse that will ignite Birmingham's next growth explosion." "Explosion" overstated the impact of OADI in the late 1980s and 1990s, but the success stories included Zortec, TRACS Software, CMS Research Corporation, and Upgrade Technologies. These and related entrepreneurial endeavors advocated by subsequent UAB presidents and their faculty would be prime examples of a national pattern of research universities advancing high-tech developments.[136]

In the summer of 1986, with much of the $160 million expansion completed, the presidency of S. Richardson Hill, Jr., effectively came to an end. In addition to the capital campaign and wide-ranging growth in programs, faculty, students, and staff, the Hill era saw UAB's total annual budget move from $168 million in 1977 to $455 million in 1986, which included a hospital budget growing from $69 million to $195 million, and total grants and contracts go from $38 million to $79 million. The era also witnessed UAB's economic impact on the Birmingham area reach $640 million, which included the direct and indirect creation of 32,645 jobs—about 7,000 shy of what U.S. Steel had produced some fifteen years earlier but with cleaner air and a more diversified social and economic life. Proud but understandably tired, through a July letter to all faculty and staff and many in the community, Hill at age sixty-three advised that he soon would be leaving "the adrenalin-pumping atmosphere of UAB" for his first sabbatical in twenty-four years. The medical metaphor spoke to Hill's remaining an endocrinologist even during his presidential years. He and his wife, Janet, would be gone for about a year, much of the time in London, and on their return Hill would not go back in the president's office. He would be a faculty member, a Distinguished Professor of Medicine, which actually developed more into a dynamic fund-raising life than a teaching life. With Hill working hard through the summer, especially on some discretionary fund projects with the Wallace administration, Chancellor Bartlett and the board respected Hill's wish that Charles A. McCallum, vice president of health affairs, assume the interim presidency on September 1, 1986.[137]

9
Reach for Maturity
The McCallum Years, 1987–93

"Smooth Change of the Guard"?

For the time being, the administrative heart of the institution barely skipped a beat. Charles A. McCallum named the Birmingham native and chief of staff of the hospital, Durwood Bradley, to serve as interim vice president of health affairs. The board slowly began a national search for the selection of UAB's third president. Interviewed on the transition, Hill received what would become a standard question of the future as, oddly, memories of non-physician Volker already were fading though he was back in Birmingham and quite a campus presence. Asked if a nonphysician could govern UAB, Hill replied, "Yes, I can envision a non-M.D. president. What's important is that the person has been through the process of faculty life and experienced various levels of administration and understands research."[1]

By April 2, 1987, the third president was the dentist *and* physician Charles A. McCallum. He was chosen out of a field of 127 candidates; the seven top contenders were medical doctors. According to Trustee Yetta G. Samford, who chaired the search committee, McCallum's age of sixty-one did not work against him in the search because he would "not need a learning period." Likewise, while the UA system had a standard retirement age of sixty-five for administrators, the board could waive this annually. Chancellor Thomas A. Bartlett publicly blessed the arrangement: "Under Dr. McCallum, UAB can move ahead without missing a stride." Indeed, questioned by the *Birmingham Post Herald* about his age, McCallum replied, "I've just got too many things to do. . . . Some people are happy to hang up their shoes at a certain time. I'm not. I've worked long hours . . . and I don't see why that would change." In fact, throughout his interim role and straight through the search, McCallum continued his longtime practice of jogging three to five miles at least four days out of seven even when traveling. Hence, UAB press releases deemphasized McCallum's age and instead bannered this as "a smooth change of the guard." And in some ways it was. It was an extension of a successful team of leaders all focused on essentially the same mission and strategies.[2]

Still, what the public did not know, and what all but a few inside UAB did not know, was that this "smooth change of the guard" almost did not occur. As the search unfolded "several high-profile UAB docs" associated with the Health Services Foundation (HSF) established their own lines of communication with "several board members and the chancellor" urging "informally" that an increasingly integrated UAB as developed under Roy Kracke, Joseph Volker, and Dick Hill be reversed and that a new administrative structure be implemented allowing the hospital and certain other medical center units to have greater control over their administrative and fiscal affairs. It remains unclear what specific formula for reorganization these Birmingham folks sent to Tuscaloosa.[3] What is clear, however, is that Chancellor Bartlett with approval of "at least some of the board" entered into an intense planning mode, producing a typed document titled "Review of Administrative Structure of the University of Alabama at Birmingham." There remains no indication that the press or the general community of Birmingham knew about this document. It laid out three options.

1. *Continue the 1969–86 Structure/Single President* . . . the single presidency and a base of common support services have generated a public image of a single institution [and also] . . . some economies of scale.
2. *Two Presidents* . . . There is . . . a very desirable dual mission for UAB and promotion of both without undue conflict may require more separation of the University College from the Medical Center. Some separation may also ease some existing tension between the Medical Center and University College regarding fund transfers and lifestyle differentials [i.e., salaries and operating funds]. . . . The time has come . . . for the broader university to be more on its own and for the Medical Center to reconcentrate its efforts on its ever-present needs to grow, expand, and take the final steps to certain national and international prominence. . . . In this model the University and the Medical Center would become two distinct universities, each with its own president. . . . But [this] would dismantle the very successful efforts that have been made to generate local and state support for

an entity known as UAB to the community and the state. The community outside UAB would feel damaged and threatened—a needless price to pay.

3. *Dual Structure/Single Image* . . . This structure would feature an Executive Vice Chancellor and Provost for medical affairs who would serve as a peer to the Presidents of other University of Alabama campuses and report directly to the Chancellor. There [also] would be a President of the University of Alabama at Birmingham who would be responsible for the operation and development of University College. . . . The UAB president would continue to be the public spokesman for UAB while the Executive Vice Chancellor/Provost would be the chief medical spokesman for the University System. . . . In the new process, the President of UAB and the Executive Vice Chancellor/Provost or their representatives not only would negotiate the division of costs but also would have more direct input into the nature and level of services provided. In case of inability to agree, the Chancellor could play a mediating role.

The report continued, reflecting Chancellor Bartlett's recommendation and "some sentiment" of the board that the third option of "Dual Structure/Single Image" was clearly the preferred model. The report concluded with a detailed map of how to implement the new structure, including a new organizational chart.[4]

One sticking point remained, however. As the search narrowed and the inevitability of McCallum as president became clear to Bartlett, he presented the "new plan" to McCallum as something that he would need to implement at least as his own presidency wound down. And McCallum would not agree.[5]

To McCallum the plan fit into Bartlett's gradual increase of UA system office authority in ways running counter to his—and Hill's—perception of UAB's self-interest. Much as Hill did, McCallum saw the 1983 board fight in this context. McCallum also saw this threat associated with how, and where, lobbyist J. Rudolph ("Rudy") Davidson would work. Despite Davidson's successes on behalf of the entire state on matters such as limiting malpractice suits, Bartlett perceived Davidson as tightly focused on UAB's development *not* within the context of system growth. Indeed, Bartlett knew that Davidson personally wanted the legislature to move UAB out of the UA system, and had him reassigned to the system office where he futilely tried to control him.[6] Simultaneously, Bartlett had been seeking legislation that would deliver to the UA system a "unified budget," that is, state appropriations would go directly to the chancellor's office and then be allocated to the three campuses instead of each campus getting its own budget from Montgomery, each of which was then "taxed" to provide operating funds for the system office. Owing to strong campus lobbies (the Davidson factor?), such fiscal realignment never made it out of the legislature. In short, while Bartlett viewed the plan as necessary centralization in the name of efficiency, to McCallum and others within UAB here was one more in a string of actions to rein in UAB's political force and growth. (UA president Joab L. Thomas also bridled under such centralization, moving to the presidency of Pennsylvania State University in 1990.) Bartlett's reorganization plan, in McCallum's mind, was yet another action in this behind-the-scenes assertion of system control. It undoubtedly could frustrate campus leadership in Tuscaloosa and Huntsville and usher in an era of generally weaker presidents; as far as Birmingham went it also could block the vision for institutional maturity that Hill clearly had passed on to McCallum.[7]

The reorganization plan also struck McCallum from another perspective. The plan "seemed hypocritical." Bartlett continued to tell the public that he was "trying to operate in a very restrained manner" with regard to UAB and other campuses. At the same time, however, while he was trying to convince the public that there was still a UAB and endorsed plans for continuing the capital campaign, asking for money in the name of one cohesive institution, he quietly was advancing a plan that would eliminate UAB. McCallum recalled, "The plan would have brought structural division to a campus which had risen to prominence on being 'a university without walls.'" It would have done this at a time when many national leaders, including some at the NIH and NSF, were beginning to appreciate the advantages of places like UAB. Said McCallum, "At UAB we had the reassertion of the whole. Interdisciplinary knowledge, certainly including medical knowledge, had to be the top priority of teaching, research, service, and most particularly clinical health care. But he [Bartlett] wanted to cut this up."[8]

McCallum steadfastly refused to go along with Bartlett's reorganization. He refused when Bartlett initially presented him with the plan, and he refused even more emphatically several weeks later, in April 1987, when the chancellor drove him from Birmingham to Huntsville for the board meeting where the final decision on the new president was to be made. "Driving up I-65 he asked me again to go along with it," McCallum mused. "He twisted my arm, implying that my getting the job depended on it. But I said if that was the condition, I would not accept. He could have it." Then an afterthought. "While we were driving to Huntsville, I knew that the chancellor had woven John Kirklin's vague endorsement of the reorganization plan into his conversations with some board members; but I had talked with John myself that morning, and I knew that he did not want the place cut up even though he had strong feelings about internal transfers. I'll have to say that that meant a lot to me, and I told that privately to several board members at the start of the meeting . . . that John's views had been misrepresented. That helped a lot in backing down the chancellor's request." In the end, despite a powerful riptide just below the surface of what the public knew, through an executive session at the board meeting McCallum assumed the presidency with no "conditions." One can hardly overlook McCallum's prevailing, however, as an indication that the board clearly included more than a few strong supporters of not just McCallum but UAB.[9]

Money Problems, New Thought

Immediately, McCallum moved Alice and the boys as well as the family hot tub out of their Vestavia home up to Woodward House, the hot tub—next to the swimming pool—melding relatively well with the spirit if not the actual design of Spanish Revival. Tub left chiefly for family, McCallum rapidly immersed himself into fast-breaking developments of UAB.[10]

At the top of the list—despite other high-profile projects such as Vice President James H. Woodward's chairing a statewide committee to bring a supercomputer to Alabama—were enrollment and revenue issues in University College, where budgets suitably remained more dependent on state appropriations than other sources and where the slashing effects of Governor Fob James's anti–higher education policies seemingly were being extended by the new governor, the Republican and evangelical minister and former Amway salesman Guy Hunt, who had been elected in 1987. Granted, the original state appropriation for UAB in 1986–87 (under Wallace) moved from $97,162,640 to an original appropriation in 1992–93 (under Hunt) of $136,230,017. Yet Hunt seemingly had little understanding of the matrix of complicated issues related to education finance. He made a high-profile appearance at the UAB-Auburn basketball game in November 1985 as prelude to appointing a statewide task force to recommend massive changes for education funding, a committee heavily weighted toward Birmingham. But after the operational arm of the task force dutifully wrote an intelligent report, ultimate action on the report was limited to filing in the state archives.[11]

With such leadership at the state level, UAB's annual state appropriation during the McCallum presidency was at best strange. Fiscal years 1986–87 through 1988–90 reflected steady increases, but at times because certain other functions of the state (such as mental health care) were attached to the UAB budget and were not to be spent by UAB. Then in fiscal year 1990–91 the appropriation of $128,399,290 (under Hunt) was prorated 6.5 percent and the fiscal year 1991–92 appropriation of $140,081,381 (under Hunt) was prorated 3 percent. Again, here was only the most recent set of cuts in a litany of historic transgressions against education funding, where state leaders refused to confront the need to fund the Special Education Trust Fund, not to mention the general fund, out of predictable revenues such as property taxes and, instead, used unpredictable and unfair strategies such as sales taxes.[12]

McCallum and Woodward comprehended this problem in terms of their continued need to recruit and retain more students, and hence increase tuition dollars, in order to compensate for inadequate or reduced state allocations. Yet they also understood that increased enrollment by itself would not solve the problem. Even with economies of scale, more students often meant more costs. In short, they understood that they, like their predecessors, were being forced by the state to raise tuition and fees in many cases beyond a standard increase associated with the consumer price index. They were being forced by the state to implement the insidious "policy" of placing more and more *public* higher education costs on the backs of many Alabama families and making baccalaureate-level education increasingly unreachable. In turn, this only compounded the problem, whereby only 16 percent of Alabama's citizens had baccalaureate degrees—third from the bottom in the nation.[13]

In this context, much as Woodward had established curriculum and advising changes several years earlier, the vice president set to work with student affairs vice president John Jones to create in place of a relatively passive admissions office an overtly activist Office of Enrollment Management, which reported to both Jones and Woodward. The new enterprise not only provided more focused recruitment but far more demographic data to support "segmented marketing." Woodward and Jones agreed that the best person to run this new operation was Virginia D. Gauld, a native of Gadsden, Alabama.[14]

Originally brought to UAB in 1977 as part of John Anderson's team of continuing education directors in special studies—she specialized in "reentry education" for women in their thirties and forties—Gauld held a B.S.

in mathematics from Emory University and a doctorate in higher education from UA. She had shown administrative acumen in a special assignment: designing and implementing the UAB Benevolent Fund, which provided aid to employees in financial trouble. She knew the UAB market. She was comfortable with the newly dominant tool of the high-technology revolution: statistics. And beneath her warm, outgoing personality (she was known to all students, faculty, and staff as just "Jenny") there surged an intensely competitive spirit and the drive to work the sixty-hour weeks most of Woodward's lieutenants found necessary. Hence in February 1986, much like others of the emergent wave of "enrollment managers" at universities nationwide, she went to work crunching numbers with the benefit of a new (but quickly outmoded) computer data system known as STARS (Student Administration and Records System) and in other ways seeking to increase all sectors of enrollment but with special emphasis on the sector where Woodward remained convinced that UAB could capture the greatest net growth, the "traditional" college student—eighteen years old, attending college full time, and living on or near campus.[15]

Yet Gauld's job included far more than statistical analysis and market strategy. It also involved building new relationships inside UAB. For example, as Gauld assumed her new role, aided by her unflappable staff assistant Cynthia Holmes, the university was in the midst of planning a new component of both its undergraduate programs and its medical education, the Early Medical School Admission Program (EMSAP). In December 1987 Woodward first had encountered such a program via Urban 13 connections, especially through a presentation by the University of Missouri–Kansas City (UMKC) whereby that institution recruited high school seniors with exceptionally high SAT scores who wanted to become physicians by admitting them into medical school at the same time they admitted them into college to work for the baccalaureate degree and by offering them extensive summer research internships on issues of health care.[16] In a telephone conversation Woodward tried out the idea on medical dean James Pittman. While intensely interested, and aware of some twenty similar programs at such highly regarded traditional institutions as the University of Pennsylvania and Case Western Reserve, Pittman pointed out that the UMKC program was not ideal (indeed, the whole medical school there had gone on a temporary probation) and he favored UAB's developing its own unique approach. Indeed, Pittman initially favored UAB's developing "programs, plural," as opposed to a single program for all of UAB. One program might be of a liberal arts orientation based in University College, as Woodward urged; but others would "be programs in conjunction with other schools within the Medical Center, particularly the School of Nursing and the School of Health-Related Professions." Woodward rejoined that "we actively pursue discussions" on the matter, but that such discussions stay focused on one program for UAB: "I think it would basically be wrong to have a University College program, a School of Nursing program, and a School of Health-Related Professions program.... There must be a common core of undergraduate experience.... I think it is not helpful ... to continuously emphasize the dichotomy of the institution, especially at the undergraduate level."[17]

Certainly attuned to McCallum's approach of "one university," Woodward's strategy was gaining acceptance within private practice medicine as well as academic medicine owing in part to the growing emphasis on psychosocial factors in medical education and research. And right in the middle of UAB's medical center, Claude Bennett, who in 1982 left the chairmanship of microbiology to assume the chair's role in the Department of Medicine, was one of the most assertive advocates in the nation for broadened medical education. Pittman was amenable to Woodward's approach. Indeed, he eventually would teach courses in the program. And throughout January, February, March, and April, the two had the project being planned in detail by others, including the deputy dean in medicine, Charles W. Scott, the pre-health advisor in University College, Kathy Angus, and of course the new director of enrollment management, Virginia Gauld.[18]

By July, Gauld urged official approval of the new program, and McCallum, who viewed the proposal as "an excellent initiative" especially because it included "money for scholarships to help attract more black students," prepared to take it to the board in September as an "information item." Further, "[the program] cut anxiety about getting accepted [into medical school] and prompted students to delve into broader academic studies.... [The board] will be most pleased to learn about this initiative," predicted McCallum.[19]

And he was right. Throughout the academic year of 1988–89 Gauld's recruiters pushed EMSAP in conversations with students who had excellent high school records and who wanted to be physicians. Twelve were enrolled in the fall of 1989, all from Alabama. First-year students included Lacey Langston (Hoover), Lyn Dykes (Trussville), Jennifer Reed (Albertville), Scott Crumpton (Opelika), Jason Gamble (McCalla), Dawn Davis (Bessemer), John Mauer (Jacksonville), V. K. Gadi (Decatur), and David Lin (Birmingham). Edward Yeh (Mobile) was "grandfathered" in as a sophomore.[20] Some eventually changed their minds about becoming physicians. On the other hand, some admitted to the program decided to decline. In this case, none was more fascinating—and uplifting—than Edward Shackleford, who was from the tiny, poor, coal-mining town of Sulligent in Walker County, Alabama. Shackleford declined "free rides" both to UAB and to Harvard in order to stay in Sulligent for a year to work to help his family. Yet Shackleford eventually earned a baccalaureate degree from Harvard and over time a medical degree from UAB.[21] Even though some students did not complete the program and others went elsewhere, from the perspective of Woodward and Gauld the program was a striking success—"high-end" students living in dormitories, excelling in broad liberal arts studies, not just science, and involved in campus life: a traditional college producing broadly educated physicians. And over time, as the program deepened and expanded under the leadership of the philosophy professor Gregory Pence, the impact would be even greater as a significant portion of the EMSAP students also participated in Ada Long's honors program and used summers to tackle research projects in the medical center.[22]

To complement this continued effort at growing enrollment in terms of both numbers and quality, Woodward and Gauld worked with special studies dean Sara Ruiz de Molina to begin offering both credit and noncredit courses in the late afternoons and evenings at wide-ranging locations south of Birmingham off Highway 31: from the Hoover Public Library and Berry High School in south Jefferson County to Valley Elementary School near Pelham in north Shelby County. The object: introduce adult and working populations to the quality of UAB programs and through them market the idea of having their children, as well as themselves, attend UAB full time. Ultimately, in October 1987, this strategy led to the establishment of a small UAB satellite campus called "UAB South" in south Jefferson County off Highway 280 at International Park, a corporate village near the mind-bogglingly busy intersection of Highway 280 and I-459. In short, faced with the complex issues of "Fob cuts" and "Guy cuts" simultaneously with the "maturing university" problem of at times stagnant enrollment and hence stagnant levels of tuition and fees, Woodward steered the non-medical component of UAB toward the equally maturing status of campus life and far more full-time students while sustaining outreach to varied types of part-time students. Subsequent UAB leaders would push this strategy even more.[23]

This plan coincided with Gene Bartow's growing intercollegiate athletic programs, the new UAB Arena, and Jones's new student life center as well as Jones's establishing an organized effort to advance a student to the august national rank of Rhodes Scholar.[24] Still, the Woodward strategy would not be able to deliver immediate results. Other institutions in Alabama, also facing chronic underfunding from the state, intensely recruited the same sector of students—and at least two of these institutions had advantages of family football allegiances that bordered on xenophobia. Likewise, a split within the UA system board over developing new dormitories at UAB, which were necessary for the full-time residential students, slowed Woodward's plan. Trustee Aaron Aronov of Montgomery viewed such construction as a break with the established notion that as far as undergraduates went, UAB should be a commuter institution. For him, echoing the strong words of Lieutenant Governor William J. Baxley, who was most responsible for Aronov's appointment to the board, undergraduates wanting a full-time residential experience could attend the Tuscaloosa campus. Yet each time UAB sought to expand its capability to serve nonresidential students by creating more parking lots—space that had to be purchased on currently developed urban space prices, not given to UAB—Aronov balked at how much UAB was having to spend on new parking areas. Frustrations mounted not just within UAB administration, faculty, and the increasingly vocal student body, but among some board members. Not denying the new UAB strategy to be a "significant change," Thomas E. Rast and, later, Garry Neil Drummond, of Birmingham, ultimately led the board toward acquiescence. Indeed, after listening to another UAB plea before the board for taking the step into residential campus life, and hearing Aronov's standard response, Rast erupted, "I'll be damned if I don't have enough confidence in [UAB officials] to back them up. . . . We've been beating this dead horse a long time [and] it stopped moving a long time ago." In the summer of 1990, a major new dormitory complex appeared on the southern perimeter of the campus, appropriately named Rast Hall, and the Highrise Apartments (at 1512 Ninth Avenue) building was renamed Blazer Hall. Shortly thereafter, the earlier constructed Twin Towers dormitory received the new name of Camp Hall, honoring another longtime supporter of developing the Birmingham campus, Ehney Camp.[25]

With the same plan of expanding the traditional campus look and atmosphere to attract and retain more talented traditional college students, as well as nontraditional students, President McCallum and architects James Garland and Jim James, using $1.3 million of City of Birmingham bond issue funds made available by Mayor Richard Arrington, upgraded University Boulevard into four lanes surrounded by trees and blooming shrubs, with crosswalks suitable for wheelchairs, bicycles, and skateboards. In a similar vein, with UAB funds they added new "green space" in the heart of the medical center, complete with a fountain, to be known as Unity Park. They also developed (red) bricked and flowered pylons at the western approach to University Boulevard (from the I-65 down ramp and from Green Springs Highway); and at the northern approach from "mid-town" on Eighteenth Street South. As simple as they seemed at first, the pylons were destined for recurring photography as UAB "branded" itself into the surrounding cityscape. Likewise, on the southern perimeter of the campus, where dormitories existent and envisioned met private residential and commercial real estate, they added a park filled with benches, trees, and children's playground equipment, as well as an outdoor basketball court. No doubt the most striking addition to the "traditional campus look," however, was a life-size statue of Joseph Volker, erected in the mini-park shortly after his death in May 1989.[26]

Woodward's plan resulted in a return to enrollment growth: during the McCallum presidency total enrollment moved from 14,245 in the fall of 1987 to 16,788 in the fall of 1993, an 18 percent increase with attendant financial implications. Some of this growth for the next decade occurred among graduate and professional students as well as commuter undergraduate students. The latter were a result of the revolutionary growth in the Birmingham economy, that is, from more jobs no longer reliant on steel and from the social fabric that went with this change. On the other hand, although efforts to capture a Phi Beta Kappa chapter failed, owing at least in part to "disproportionate" numbers of professional education students compared to arts and sciences undergraduates, the succeeding decade of the 1990s would show the refined vision premised on traditional college students bearing major fruit.[27] The 1980s redefinition led by Woodward, Garland, Hill, and McCallum stands alongside the creation of the Birmingham Extension Center in 1934, the movement of the medical school to Birmingham in 1944, the fiscal and programmatic independence of Birmingham operations in 1966, UAB's becoming an independent campus in 1969, and the creation of HSF in 1973 as one of the seminal developments in the history of the institution. Indeed, over time, this refocus would appear as a crucial step in the gradual social and economic modernization of Birmingham.

"Personnel Development"

Wide-ranging personnel matters also emerged on McCallum's watch, some of which resulted from retirements, some from well-funded universities in other states continuing to steal Alabama's highly skilled personnel, some owing to McCallum's wanting new people, and some owing to the return to significant increases in student enrollment. Indeed, personnel developments represented a human drama all unto itself in the McCallum presidency, keeping the president's office life a whirligig of appointments from 6:30 a.m. to 7:00 p.m., all somehow juggled into harmony by McCallum's aide, Kitty Robinson.[28]

The growth of computer-based data and its impact on institutional planning led McCallum to move John M. Lyons, who had served as director of the Office of Institutional Advancement, to the vice presidential level and to charge him with responsibility for the Office of Planning and Information Management, reporting to the president. Immediately, Lyons completed development of "one of the most cohesive administrative units ever to function on the campus," recalled McCallum, including Glenna Brown, John Byrd, Ann Day Hunt, and Mary Beth Bridges. Also, with Katherine Howard's retirement, McCallum hired Torrey Smitherman to handle operational communications between UAB and the board; a Mobilian, UA graduate, and former member of the UA system staff, Smitherman brought a smiling face and a savvy understanding of the importance of confidentiality on developing relations between UAB and the board. McCallum also approved Woodward's plan to replace longtime School of Education dean Milley Cowles with the nationally recognized health education specialist Clint Bruess, who had directed that program at UAB since 1981.[29]

He also stuck with Woodward on further expansion of the faculty in University College. Under McCallum and Woodward, University College faculty grew in numbers from 397 to 443, a total of 46 new lines, averaging six per year. While this remained insufficient to keep pace with enrollment growth, it was all that was possible in view of the state's continued addiction to prorating education budgets and McCallum's determination, despite proration, to keep merit raises averaging 5 percent per year. Still, these new positions, and even more so replacement slots, permitted the hiring of many new faculty. During this time, Christopher Taylor (Ph.D., University of Virginia) came from the University of Chicago to the UAB Anthropology Department and began his ultimately excruciating research in Africa that would lead to *Sacrifice as Terror: The Rwandan Genocide of 1994* (1999). Likewise, James D. McClintock (Ph.D., University of South Florida) joined the Biology Department, from which he launched (via very long trips) studies of organisms underneath the polar ice caps that could have dramatic implications for medicine and pharmaceuticals. In 1998, the U.S. Geological Survey honored McClintock's contributions by spearheading the designation of "McClintock Point" in Anarctica.[30]

Two additional hires during this time are particularly noteworthy. One was Henry Panion, an African American native of Birmingham and graduate of Birmingham's Parker High School, who attended Alabama State University before earning a doctorate in musicology at Ohio State University. He joined the music faculty of UAB as a specialist in musical compositions using the computer, but soon gained international recognition for being selected by Stevie Wonder to direct orchestras all over the world when the acclaimed pop singer performed in formal concerts. So effective was Panion's role as guest director of orchestras that in 1990, when the Alabama State Orchestra, based in Birmingham, moved to the brink of insolvency and had no funds to pay a conductor, Panion served for over a year as director—an oft-repeated development in many cities in the 1980s and early 1990s as orchestras nationwide hit upon hard times and invariably turned to their local urban universities for help.[31]

Then there was Edward Taub. A Neal Miller–trained psychologist working out of several different institutions, including the University of Maryland, Taub long had been examining why certain stroke victims lost the use of an arm or leg and, more to the point, how such paralysis could be eradicated. His research using primates received such negative (and inaccurate) depiction by leaders of People for the Ethical Treatment of Animals (PETA), however, that virtually all of his funding from the NIH and NSF had vanished by the early 1980s—and ultimately his employment, too. Still, Taub's name turned up in a faculty search in UAB's Psychology Department, and the departmental chair, Carl McFarland, instantly understood what possibilities there were for UAB if Taub were to come to Birmingham to complete his revolutionary research. Still, when McCallum received uncomplimentary comments from physician friends regarding Taub's work—comments, in retrospect, which likely emanated less from Taub's recent downturn in extramural funding and more from the laborious M.D./Ph.D. tension— McCallum initially discouraged Woodward from endorsing McFarland's plan to hire Taub. McCallum, however, altered his position after a lengthy exchange with Woodward revolving around the point that universities, above all else, are for exploring frontiers of knowledge and that the PETA-type attacks should be given little credence in a university with a medical center constantly engaged in primate research.[32]

So Taub and his wife, Mildred, who was an opera singer (the Metropolitan Opera in New York City had hosted her on many occasions), moved to Birmingham in the fall of 1986. With his wife quickly joining the Music Department at Birmingham-Southern College, Taub began to regain his momentum. Since he had completed the primate phase of his research, he began writing article after article explaining how lessons about paralysis learned from primate brains were applicable to human brains. Over the next decade, indeed, Taub's work found publication in journals such as *Nature* and *Science* and ultimately garnered wide acceptance by psychology colleagues and many physicians as well. Award after award came his way, including the Henry James Prize of the American Psychological Society. After a series of successful human trials, Taub's treatment for "rewiring the human brain" with nonintrusive therapy (e.g., strapping the "good" arm behind the back of the patient for a certain period of time in order to teach the brain to reactivate its sending of movement signals to the "bad" arm) came to be known worldwide as "Taub Treatment" or "CI" (Constraint Induced) Therapy. In a story broken by the *New York Times,* Taub's work began to be heralded as the major health science breakthrough that would eradicate paralysis in certain types of stroke patients and perhaps even in paralysis among some cerebral palsy–stricken children, too.[33]

Personnel developments in the medical center began to take place from the very start of McCallum's administration. Barely in the president's office, McCallum launched a national search to replace the retiring dean of nursing, Marie O'Koren; by November 1987 Rachel Z. Booth, dean of nursing and vice president at Duke University, had moved to Birmingham and was hard at work grappling with the complicated supply and demand issues that faced nursing nationwide. McCallum also geared up a national search for a vice president of health affairs—his own replacement (Durwood Bradley had been holding the position on an interim basis while McCallum served as interim president). By April 1988 the job went to John Durant, who had led the building of the UAB cancer center in the early 1970s but who more recently had served as president of Fox-Chase Cancer Center in Philadelphia, his hometown.[34]

In turn, with McCallum's approval, Durant moved Terry Hickey (vision science) and Marlon Priest (emergency medicine) into his office as assistant vice presidents in October 1989 and replaced the hospital director, James E.

Moon, with Clark Taylor. Moon went to the faculty of the School of Health-Related Professions, where his vast experience in the field and his upbeat, unpresumptuous personality and wry humor made him a vibrant professor and consultant until his retirement in 1991.[35]

By contrast, as one who also had come up through the ranks in hospital administration in several different states, serving most recently as Moon's associate administrator for operations, Taylor still seemed less the nuts-and-bolts guru of modern health care and more the futuristic soothsayer about hospitals as evolving institutions in a rapidly changing high-technology society—a different style from Moon's and one Durant initially found engaging. Indeed, at heart an intellectual, Taylor followed closely the writings of the famed economic theorist Peter Drucker and often sought to apply Druker's tenets about modernization in the microcosmic context of UAB health care. A Swarthmore graduate, Durant also enjoyed such intellectualizing about health care. Yet Taylor exuded a self-confidence not always well suited to the diplomacy so useful to life in an institution with as many health science subcultures as UAB's. He also sought more hospital autonomy within the general UAB organization, including on matters related to human resource management. Hence Taylor's tenure under Durant and McCallum wound up rocky. Such tensions increased as the UAB hospital, like virtually all others across the nation, encountered caps on Medicare and Medicaid reimbursement (declining revenues) along with the application of new medical technologies (increasing costs), plus a pay incentive plan Taylor had introduced for hospital executives. By the fall of 1992, when Taylor raised the possibilities of "privatizing"—selling—the UAB hospital as an initial step toward dealing with these huge money matters, McCallum and Durant replaced Taylor with James Lee on an interim basis, who had held major fiscal positions under both Moon and Taylor; and Taylor headed to Chattanooga to manage another hospital.[36]

Although of far smaller scale than the hospital, the Center for Aging experienced an equally complicated transition in leadership begun in 1990 when Harold Schnaper announced his retirement. In tackling the problems of aging (for example, Alzheimer's disease, arthritis, atherosclerosis, and immobility), the center drew from wide-ranging fields: from medicine to sociology, from public health to social work and psychology—campus-wide implications to say the least. Carefully attuned to these "one university" implications, McCallum initiated a study to determine exactly what a future Center for Aging should look like before starting a formal search for replacing Schnaper. The six-month analysis urged keeping gerontology and geriatric education spread throughout the interdisciplinary campus and not creating a new department or doctoral program, as a few institutions were attempting. That study accepted, then reconsidered, then accepted again—a process reflecting medical center interests competing for state funds Schnaper had garnered for the program. McCallum and Durant named two institution-wide committees: one to choose a new director, the other to provide temporary management of the center with Schnaper's longtime assistant director, Glenn Hughes, guiding daily operations. Finally, in 1992, following an exhaustive national search, a young geriatric physician in UAB's own Department of Medicine, a person with the diplomatic skills to manage such an interdisciplinary enterprise, Richard Allman, assumed the Center for Aging directorship. To be sure he personalized what McCallum called an "axiom for higher education": "the greater the interdisciplinary inquiry through a university without walls, the greater the difficulty of management and personnel issues; yet the greater the interdisciplinary inquiry through a university without walls, the greater the results of the inquiry—for certain, it's worth the trouble."[37]

The early 1990s brought other key personnel developments in the medical center, though with less stress over organizational implications. Several of the most established departments in the medical center received new leadership.

In 1990, Michael Harrington assumed the chair's role in family and community medicine; the same year Jay McDonald left Washington University, St. Louis, to become chair of pathology, and Stephen C. Harvey (unknowingly on the eve of Faculty Senate leadership) ascended to chair of biochemistry. One of the younger departments, health behavior (established in 1984), in the School of Public Health, also experienced a change in leadership when the psychologist James Raczynski—first appointed in psychology, then in medicine—assumed the chair's role, succeeding Richard Windsor.[38]

In addition, McCallum soon found he needed to hire a vice president to preside over University College, that is, over programs in arts and sciences, business, teacher education, engineering, and continuing education. For in late June 1989, James Woodward, after being pursued by several universities as well as one multinational corporation, left his position as vice president of University College to become president of the University of North Carolina–Charlotte. McCallum and Woodward asked Tennant S. McWilliams (not a candidate to replace Woodward) to serve as interim vice president until a regular successor could be chosen.[39]

Before the search began, McCallum changed the title of the position from vice president of University College to the more traditional title of vice president of academic affairs. "This was one of the few developments [initiated by Volker] that I ever tweaked," McCallum recalled, and as a result "shrieks of protest came from the medical center over even the suggestion that medical center life did not involve 'academic affairs,'" as it surely did. So McCallum changed "the Medical Center" to "the Academic Health Center," certainly a term of more current usage for similar programs nationwide. Still, McCallum felt strongly about moving away from "University College" as a "maturing step" for the institution. Much like Volker years before, at that time neither McCallum nor McWilliams had a clear understanding of the way the originators of "University College," the civic universities of England, had used the term. Even more, neither was familiar with rapidly breaking "new" usages of the term as a generic description (less so a formal title for an academic unit) of a higher-education environment increasingly found in elite colleges, as explained by Harvard's Henry Rosovsky in *The University: An Owner's Manual* (1990), where researching faculty taught both graduates and undergraduates—precisely what UAB offered. Equally, they were unaware that Indiana University-Purdue (IUPUI) would be using "University College" to sponsor freshman learning communities. Still, McCallum accurately perceived "University College" as not in synchrony with contemporary mainstream public American higher education, a mainstream that included faculty and students who worked and lived in an *academic* enterprise—some of the keys to the formula for the maturing UAB and obviously crucial steps that the west end of the campus had in process at the time. In retrospect, to most on hand at the time of the change, it was just a name change that sounded more traditional.[40]

Simultaneous with this name change and Woodward's departure were other personnel changes. Lydia Alexander, who had directed the advisors in general studies since its 1985 inception, assumed the position of assistant dean of the School of Education (while she held this position, in 1996, she coauthored the courageously tender book about African American women and friendship, *Wearing Purple*); and Nancy Walburn, an Anniston, Alabama, native and a historian who had been an advisor working with Alexander, moved up to the directorship of general studies, which shortly migrated from its original location in the Education Building to new space more accessible by students in the University Center. Blaine Brownell resigned his deanship in social and behavioral sciences to assume the position of provost at the University of North Texas, near Dallas, leaving his associate dean, the criminologist Belinda McCarthy, in charge. So McCallum had that deanship to nail down, too, with McWilliams indicating a desire to enter the search to be dean in the school where he had spent over a decade of his career. By August 1990 the search committees recommended a Kansas State physicist, William A. Sibley, recently on leave to the NSF, to be vice president of academic affairs, and McWilliams to be dean in social and behavioral sciences, with McCarthy moving to a deanship at the University of Central Florida.[41]

Sibley immediately assembled his team. Louis Dale, a senior mathematician, came onboard as associate vice president of academic affairs; and Shirley Salloway Kahn, long connected with the office and with Birmingham civic life, continued as associate vice president of administrative and fiscal affairs. Meanwhile, in 1990 one of the cornerstones of student affairs, John D. Jones, decided to leave the vice presidential grind to become director of the Center for International Programs—which Brownell also had been handling—for a few years before he fully retired. Again there was a national search. The net result was that Virginia D. Gauld, director of enrollment management, moved up into the position of vice president of student affairs where she—as the first female vice president at UAB—rapidly assumed Jones's role as a major national figure in the field. Gauld named Stella Cocoris to the position of director of enrollment management. A Birmingham native who had been an academic advisor, an English composition teacher at UAB, and most recently a member of Gauld's staff, Cocoris long had been known for her encyclopedic knowledge of student advising issues and transferability policies, crucial components of enrollment management.[42]

More major personnel changes followed. Three months before McCallum had taken over as acting president, he honored Leonard Robinson's request to retire as dean of the dental school and went with the recommendation of the search committee to replace him with Richard Ranney, a sitting dean from Virginia Commonwealth University (VCU). Ranney's efforts to reorganize the dental school, however, and some clashes with McCallum resulted in his returning to VCU by 1989. McCallum and Durant replaced him with longtime UAB oral surgeon, Victor J. Matukas.[43]

Likewise, at the time of the Hill-McCallum transition, the founding dean in optometry, Henry Peters, retired and on his outgoing recommendation McCallum elevated to the dean's role the Massachusetts native Bradford Wild, who had served since 1974 as Peter's associate dean. Soon other changes occurred. Biochemist Robert Glaze, who had served under Hill as vice president of research, retired. McCallum elected not to fill the position but instead to merge it with Kenneth Roozen's expanding role from assistant to the president to vice president of university affairs and research. Dudley Pewitt, who had served Hill, too, as vice president of administration and finance, retired and joined Rudy Davidson's private lobbying firm; McCallum split the jobs, naming longtime personnel manager John Walker to the position of interim vice president of administration and human resources, and an M.B.A. graduate of UAB and current UAB budget director, Linda Flaherty-Goldsmith, as director of finance. After William Bridgers retired from his post as dean of public health in 1989, McCallum and Durant asked the senior UAB public health professor Juan Navia to serve as dean. Navia returned to faculty life in 1991, however, and a national search brought to the public health deanship O. Dale Williams, a biostatistician from the University of North Carolina–Chapel Hill. It took a scorecard to track all this—and there still was more.[44]

In 1990, pulmonary specialist Dick Briggs, who had succeeded John Kirklin as president of HSF in 1988, announced that Samuel W. Jackson, a Clio, Alabama, native, attorney, and certified public accountant (most recently with Ernst and Young), had been moved up from general counsel to HSF to vice president and chief financial officer—one of the most demanding jobs in the state. Then in 1991 Keith Blayney retired from the dean's position in the School of Health-Related Professions (which had been the School of Community and Allied Health until 1987), and Durant replaced him with Blayney's longtime associate dean, Mississippian Charles L. Joiner, Jr. Next, in the School of Medicine several key steps occurred. In 1991, Durant and Pittman brought in William B. Deal as associate dean of graduate education and community relations; the intense competition between the six hospitals in the metropolitan area, touched off by lessening Medicare and Medicaid reimbursements, helped make such a position necessary. A North Carolinian with extensive administrative experience in Florida and Maine, Deal had the diplomatic personality for the task.[45]

Perhaps most striking for the School of Medicine, the next year Jim Pittman decided that nineteen years of deaning was "enough for any person." Shortly thereafter, he left for a sabbatical leave at Harvard, thrilled to have time to pursue his medical history interests, renew old acquaintances, and make new friendships with noted scientists such as Alabamian Edward O. Wilson. After a short stint with Pittman's experienced deputy dean, Charles W. Scott, serving as interim dean, Durant's national search brought in Harvard-trained Harold J. ("Hal") Fallon, a sitting dean at VCU, to manage the UAB

School of Medicine—the oldest, certainly best developed school on the campus with Fallon as its ninth leader.[46]

McCallum and other medical center leaders also continued to grow the faculty. Between 1987 and 1993—the years of the McCallum presidency—the size of the medical center faculty increased from 1,118 to 1,438 for a total of 320 new positions. The new faculty included entry-level faculty as well as senior specialists.[47]

More Capital Campaign

In the midst of this constant swirl of personnel developments McCallum reinitiated the capital campaign, first begun under Hill, closing it out on March 30, 1990, at just shy of $70 million—some $30 million more than the original goal. New scholarships and endowed chairs ran $5.2 million, which, when combined with a futilely planned state matching ("Eminent Scholars") program, would have produced fourteen new endowed chairs. One of these involved the single largest family gift so far in the history of the institution, the Drummond Chair in Psychiatry, filled by the new department chair in psychiatry, the New Yorker and Duke-trained Robert Friedel, who succeeded interim chair David Folks in January 1992. All in all, the campaign managed to produce seven faculty-endowed chairs.[48]

Not all of the capital campaign funds under McCallum, however, went to endowed chairs identified chiefly with medical research and clinical care. A significant gift from Mrs. Caroline P. Ireland, widow of Charles W. Ireland (one of the principals in Vulcan Materials, Inc.) permitted McCallum to begin to showcase UAB arts and sciences, where major scholars rarely enjoyed much public recognition in state and local perceptions of UAB—even though they did nationally and internationally—owing to the longer-standing and far larger collection of health science faculty. Hence, as a parallel to the Distinguished Faculty Lecture Series in the medical center, the Caroline P. and Charles W. Ireland Award for Scholarly Distinction began to go annually to a UAB arts and sciences faculty member considered "eminently outstanding" by a committee of peers. The first such award, in 1991, went to Joan Lorden, a psychologist on her way to full-time administrative life as dean of the Graduate School. Subsequent awardees included the philosopher James Rachels, the historian James F. Tent, the biologist James McClintock, the mathematician Roger Lewis, the psychologist Edward Taub, the philosopher Harold Kinkaid, creative writing professor Dennis Covington, and the psychologist Craig Ramey. Out of the same gift McCallum also created the Ireland Distinguished Visiting Scholar Award chiefly, again, to heighten public awareness of UAB arts and sciences by annually bringing acclaimed scholars from other institutions to lecture on the UAB campus. Martha Nussbaum, an ethics and law professor at the University of Chicago, began the program in 1992. Others included the historian Stephen Ambrose of the University of New Orleans, the biologist Edward Wilson of Harvard University, the historian Charles Rosenberg of the University of Pennsylvania, and the psychologist Amos Tversky of Stanford University.[49]

In the same vein, on McCallum's invitation, the President's Leadership Council—high-profile community leaders who both advised the president and disseminated information about UAB developments to the community at large—joined forces to create an endowment to fund Presidential Teaching Awards: annually, one faculty member from each of the academic units campus wide would be chosen by his or her colleagues for recognition with a Steuben Apple and a $2,500 check, part of a nationwide trend among research universities to focus more attention on teaching.[50]

Close to $30 million (41 percent of the total of McCallum's phase of the capital Campaign), however, became joined with bond issue money to create new physical facilities, some carefully orchestrated to continue the strategy of building a traditional university campus that would be appealing to "traditional students." In the middle of the west end of the campus emerged the $11.9 million UAB Arena. Located at the corner of Thirteenth Street and Seventh Avenue South (a street soon to be eliminated, though not without considerable city tension), the arena had a seating capacity of around 8,500. With a special curtain system, this could be telescoped down to 2,000 for volleyball games or a small lecture series. As it turned out, one of the largest types of crowds it would accommodate were those attending student commencements—student commencements *on the campus*, not downtown in the civic center. In June 1988, just three weeks after the dedication of the building, some 3,200 graduating students and three times as many faculty and guests descended on the complex.[51]

Coach Bartow saw the facility as a strong advantage in recruiting varsity basketball players. His teams no longer practiced in "dilapidated" Bell Gymnasium, Bartow explained, plus there was the new weight-training center built into the arena, which gave expert trainer, James Hilyer, a greater opportunity to do what he was hired to do. Just as important, there was the "Green and Gold Room," where McCallum and other presidents might use halftime to entertain Blazer boosters, including such community leaders as

Alice and Tom Williams—Alice embracing the torch of civic engagement passed to her by her father, the early UAB supporter Jack McSpadden.[52]

In his dedicatory remarks at the opening of the arena in May 1988 McCallum stated, "Thanks to Dick Hill and the trustees [but] it's because of Gene Bartow that we are here today." Here was a physical symbol of UAB's moving into intercollegiate athletics as a step toward making it a more mature, nationally recognized institution. Yet it also showed the relatively narrow view with which most Americans, not just Alabamians, perceived big-time higher education—intercollegiate sports had to be part of it all. To continue the strategy, McCallum went to work carefully orchestrating efforts to have Bartow inducted into the Alabama Sports Hall of Fame, which he was in January 1989, and to have the arena dedicated to Bartow—which took almost a decade longer to achieve. Shortly after the arena opened, however, banners appeared on the ceiling, banners naming all-stars whose numbers had been "retired": the number 10 of Wanda Hightower, the number 20 of Oliver Robinson, the number 14 of Steve Mitchell, and the number 40 of Jerome Mincy.[53]

In a similar effort to use the capital campaign to help move the university beyond "a scientific institute and medical center and a constantly flowing river of commuter students," and following through on one of Volker's special themes, McCallum gave international programs a greater physical presence on the campus. Ever since its opening in October 1983, the University Center had provided spacious offices for the Center for International Programs under the successive leadership of codirectors Blaine Brownell and J. Stephen Smith (who also served as McCallum's associate vice president of health affairs) and then, after 1990, under the directorship of John D. Jones. With the continual expertise of Carol Argo, these offices managed the operations of many international programs, for example, visa and immigration assistance for faculty and students as well as linkages between UAB and foreign universities. What was lacking was an on-campus facility to actually host international students. The evolution of such a facility touched on one of the first examples of philanthropy ever to influence the fledgling institution.[54]

Back in 1963, Joseph and Bertha Pizitz Smolian, a family who had amassed considerable wealth from their retail businesses, left their expansive, maze-like estate up on Red Mountain just north of Key Circle to the UA Medical Center. By the early 1970s, after a complete renovation, the facility to be known as the Smolian-Friendship House offered a faculty club with buffet lunches (hosted by "generalissimo" Billie Fliegel and the engaging Caribbean gentleman, Sam Gibbs), as well as formal gardens filled with sculpture and plants from around the world. While the Smolians on their own strongly advocated greater world tolerance through more people traveling, and thus appreciating and understanding different cultures, the gardens and the many international artifacts inside the home soon became in Joe Volker's Unitarian mind crucial symbols of the institution's global programmatic connections, especially through public health and medicine, as well as symbols to remind people in weighty garden conversations that "there really is a big world out there beyond Birmingham." During the Volker and Hill presidencies these gardens also hosted receptions for epidemiologists, cancer experts, and others from medical centers around the world. Too, the founding faculty such as the political scientists Grady Nunn, John Carmichael, and Charles Bulmer, and the psychologist Jesse Milby made a regular habit of driving the four miles from the campus to the Friendship House for lunch and talk. By the mid-1980s, however, the development of other eating facilities adjacent to the campus slowed the midday business of the house—its key source of revenue—to the point of its not breaking even.[55]

Accordingly, when in 1987 Bertha Smolian, at age ninety-four, died at the family's Hollywood, Florida, home, McCallum decided to sell the Smolian estate and combine the proceeds with certain unrestricted capital campaign funds to give John Jones an opportunity to build another Smolian International House where it would have more campus impact. Located on the northern perimeter of the campus on Tenth Avenue South close to an emerging collection of dormitories, the two-story center completed in 1989 did more than host international receptions. Under Jones's leadership, it became a "landing point" for international students ("far more appealing than Ellis Island," Jones would muse), a place for them to live until they could make more permanent arrangements. With its expansive kitchen the facility also permitted people from around the globe to have a place for preparing foods of their native cultures—eclectic smells emanating year-round as holidays from all over the world found celebration.[56]

In a similar vein of enriching the international tone of the campus, McCallum raised interest in Samuel Ullman, the early Birmingham civic leader and author of the poem "Youth." Published posthumously in *Reader's Digest* in 1946, the poem extolled the enduring spiritual and psychological traits of feeling young as opposed to the more ephemeral physical traits of youth. Through an odd series of coincidences, a large printing of the poem came to decorate the office of General Douglas MacArthur while his forces occupied Japan at the end of World War II, and from that point until well into the 1990s "Youth" clubs—bordering on positive cultism—emerged all over Japan as Japanese citizens associated their postwar resurgence on the world scene as tangible evidence of the wisdom in Ullman's poetic advice.[57]

Indeed, since the late 1970s once or twice a year small groups of high-ranking Japanese corporate officers had been paying low-profile visits to Birmingham in hopes of discovering an Ullman shrine, which normally led them into the Ullman Building on the campus and to the Ullman portrait hanging just inside the main entrance. Simultaneously, the Birmingham attorney Wyatt Haskell had been telling anyone who would listen that Ullman represented a positive part of Birmingham's past that deserved serious celebration: if Japanese corporate leaders could fund an Ullman scholarship at UAB, at least Birmingham should know who the man was. Then, in 1993 an unveiling of an Ullman statue in front of the Ullman Building accompanied by a Woodward House reception for Japanese "Youth" club leaders as well as for descendants of Ullman—most particularly his grandson Mayer Newfield, a Birmingham attorney—led to the proposal that the Tuscaloosa plant of JVC, a multinational Japanese electronics firm, would purchase Samuel Ullman's home south of UAB, just off Highland Avenue, and give it to UAB for the creation of an Ullman shrine and museum. McCallum accepted the gift and helped fund restoration of the structure. The museum opened on March 21, 1994, after McCallum had completed his presidency, with UAB historian and Ullman's biographer, Margaret Armbrester, serving as curator.[58]

If the single drawback to the Samuel Ullman Museum was its relative remoteness from the UAB campus at a time when growing the core campus was an institutional priority, developments in the performing arts under McCallum had a different outcome. Specifically, the idea of using the capital campaign to bring into the campus otherwise far-flung programs helped motivate the creation of a new performing arts center. When McCallum became president UAB's musical performances normally occurred in Hulsey Hall adjacent to the Humanities Building, though its acoustics were better suited for lectures than for high Cs. Likewise, academic theater unfolded in the former high school auditorium called Bell Theater (which got a $75,000 "facelift" in 1989), next to the Ullman Building; and university-sponsored community theater, of course, unfolded some three miles to the southeast of the campus off Highland Avenue at the historic Town and Gown (Clark Memorial) Theater. Granted, all of these settings could host quality performances and certainly, in the case of Town and Gown, had the profile of a community icon—and was identified with the long, hard work for racially mixed cultural life by its key civic supporter, Cecil Roberts, who died in 1990. Indeed, in the mid-1980s Jimmy Hatcher's Town and Gown production offered the well-reviewed portrait of African American artistry, *Speak to Me As I Am* starring the Alabama civil rights leader John Nixon, which even traveled to the nation's capital. Still, Hill and Hearn had focused on the severe physical limitations of all these facilities, and a high-level performing arts center at the west end of the UAB campus was on the agenda as McCallum and Woodward took over.[59]

To position the university for this move, in 1988 Dean Theodore M. Benditt changed the name of his unit from the School of Humanities to the School of *Arts* and Humanities.[60] Things really started to happen, however, when numerous civic leaders pleaded with McCallum to develop a facility that could meet not only UAB's needs but those of the struggling Alabama State Orchestra (ASO). In this context, McCallum approached Alys R. Stephens—wife of businessman-philanthropist Elton B. Stephens—about a core gift. With an initial pledge from her, McCallum and Woodward, plus UAB development director M. Sanders Murell, Dean Benditt, architect James Garland, and Shirley Salloway Kahn (a close friend of a Stephens' in-law), laid plans for a facility located adjacent to the arts and humanities complex and joined to the Hulsey Center that would be budgeted at around $5 million and designed to house both music and drama as well as community and academic productions, including performances by the ASO.[61]

As Woodward left for UNC–Charlotte, however, closer study, especially by performing arts faculty Ward Haarbauer, Ron Clemmons, and Karma Ibsen, indicated that the plan to build a multiple service hall under one roof had the same serious flaw that the Hulsey Center had, namely, insufficient differentiation of acoustical needs of music and drama. Garland's studies of similar facilities nationally confirmed this insight. Hence, in the year of McWilliams's interim vice presidency, and following a lengthy visit with him by music faculty Sam and Delores Howard and Dean Benditt (Benditt: "We will build one of these things only once in the foreseeable future, so it needs to be right the first time"), it was decided that multiple facilities with specialized acoustics should be built but housed under one roof. Persistent community voices calling for a large facility that the ASO might use certainly reinforced this approach. The proposed budget moved to $10 million. Accustomed to visionary construction projects from his years in medical center life—and, at the time, he was embracing far larger projects than this—McCallum moved forward.[62]

He started to work on "doubling the giving" with a visit to longtime Birmingham attorney and patron of the arts, Morris Sirote. Ultimately, out of the same logic that "You will only build one of these things once," over the next few years—and another capital campaign—other campus leaders joined McCallum in expanding what would be known as the Stephens Center into a majestic $30 million facility incorporating the 1,350-seat Jemison Concert Hall, the 350-seat Sirote Theater, the 150-seat ("black box") Otis Theater, and the 168-seat Reynolds-Kirshbaum Recital Hall. With Hatcher's death in 1993 and Clark Theater ultimately returning to its original status as an independent community theater supported by such philanthropists as Virginia Samford Donovan, the Stephens Center under the general direction of Caron Thornton opened in incremental stages during the 1990s, initiated by a performance of Leonard Slatkin's National Symphony Orchestra. It would rapidly become known as one of the most "perfectly toned," as Slatkin put it, facilities of its kind in the nation, not to mention an uplifting core of UAB campus life. Tragically, only a portrait of Alys Stephens, painted by Birmingham's Arthur Stewart, would be on hand for most of these openings. Cancer took the vivacious pianist and opera fan in February 1996.[63]

Not all capital campaign construction under McCallum, however, had "traditional college campus" stamped on it. Indeed, medical research and clinical care facilities lunged forward yet again during the six years of his leadership. As a reflection of how massive the medical center had become both in terms of programs and people, McCallum opened a second bookstore—the Health Sciences Bookstore—facing Twentieth Street as part of the ground level of Parking Deck 4.[64] In terms of origin, however, one of the most curious medical center projects was the Civitan International Research Center.

Unlike funding for the arena and the Stephens Center, which came from hundreds of corporate and individual donors, here was a one-source project: a gift of $20 million. In the early 1980s, the service organization known as Civitan International, with board members from all over the world but founded and headquartered in Birmingham, decided to cease its fifty-year-old small grants program attacking various aspects of "mental retardation" and to start up, instead, one complex and highly funded program committed to the reduction of "developmental disorders." The Civitans looked nationwide for proposals for use of the $20 million gift, virtually all of which was money accumulated from sale of peppermint candy at restaurant cash registers worldwide. When Kenneth Roozen found the Request for Proposal (RFP) on the Civitan project and took it to his boss, and McCallum said, "Let's go for it," Roozen personally assumed the monumental task of pulling together UAB's manifold talents in this area of health care research and treatment and of submitting the application. When Roozen's application nailed it, UAB needed to find someone to run the project.[65]

After some of the standard M.D. versus Ph.D. rivalry, Durant asked Craig Ramey and Sharon Landsmon, two Ph.D.s from the University of North Carolina–Chapel Hill, to serve as consultants in finding a leader. In late December 1989 they completed a site visit to Birmingham, then flew back to Chapel Hill to work on their analysis of what, beyond Roozen's proposal, should be done with the center and who should do it. Although they had finished drafting their report for Durant by the afternoon of New Year's Eve, on January 2 they called Durant and asked if they could return immediately to Birmingham to talk about *their* moving to Birmingham—as a married couple—to manage the project. Durant concurred. And by May 1990 the Chapel Hill psychology team had jobs as codirectors of the Civitan International Research Center in Birmingham.[66]

To underscore the interdisciplinary, university-wide nature of their vision, Craig Ramey's primary faculty appointment was in the Department of Psychology and Sharon Landsmon's was in psychiatry (one in academic affairs, the other in the medical center), though for all intents and purposes the center would report up through medical center ranks. On returning to Chapel Hill, the two notified UNC officers of their plans to leave, married, and in July 1990 Craig and Sharon Ramey arrived in Birmingham to oversee the construction and programmatic development of the Civitan center. Soon the center, with its explosive record on extramural funds and its codirectors working daily at matched desks facing each other, joined forces with the Department of Psychology to create a new doctoral program in developmental psychology.[67]

Simultaneously, the McCallum presidency brought other exciting capital campaign projects out of the ground. In November 1991, the West Pavilion addition to University Hospital opened its doors. With fleshed-out plans in the last days of Hill's presidency, the project was the single most expensive medical center addition at $48 million. The nine-story tower arose over a three-year period between the Spain-Wallace Hospital and Eighteenth Street; ultimately it replaced outdated patient care facilities in "ancient" (by medical center standards) Jefferson Tower on Nineteenth Street. Led by John N. Whitaker, recently arrived from Memphis to chair the Department of Neurology, and by Richard B. Morawetz, the new division director for neurosurgery, most programs in the new tower involved neurosurgery and neuroservice intensive care. Orthopedic surgery, the General Service

Clinical Research Center, and some 160 beds also were included. Among these West Pavilion beds were those on the ninth floor called the Camellia Pavilion. A "VIP-style" collection of patient rooms, modeled on a similar facility of the University of South Carolina Medical Center, the Camellia Pavilion was for "patients who want more exclusive surroundings than a traditional hospital room." As with most projects of such magnitude, the Civitan center being the exception, the capital campaign only funded a portion of overall costs for the West Pavilion. A $1.5 million gift by the Bruno family was the largest single gift in the project. Other donors provided funds for the Camellia Pavilion. The remainder, however, came from a UAB hospital bond issue and monies generated by the institution through grants and patient care income. Although the state of Alabama continued to fund construction for the two-year colleges, it provided no funds toward this additional 300,000 square feet of public space in Birmingham, just as it had done in other recent UAB construction endeavors.[68]

In March 1992, McCallum opened the Center for Psychiatric Medicine (psychiatric hospital). The $15 million project allowed psychiatric care to move from University Hospital's old north wing next to Jefferson Tower to a modern seven-story, seventy-five-bed site on Sixth Avenue South. Gifts, monies from the State Mental Health Department, and UAB bond issue funds made it happen.[69] Three months later McCallum opened the $125 million Kirklin Clinic. What prompted this "super-clinic" was not so much a specific strategy within the capital campaign but John Kirklin and a few other medical center leaders staying in close touch with galactic trends in academic health centers.

The grand expansion of such centers in the years following the Flexner Report and even more so following World War II, with UAB's academic health center being a prime example, had been undergirded not just by direct federal aid from such agencies as the NSF and the NIH but by President Lyndon Johnson's "Great Society" legislation, which provided massive increases in patient-derived revenues via Medicare and Medicaid programs. While the NSF and NIH budgets could dip and then resurge, by the early to mid-1980s a host of new forces arrived on the scene. Paul F. Griner summarized these forces in his 1997 "President's Address" before the American Clinical and Climatological Association: everything from the "capping" of funds available for paying physicians (resulting from cutbacks in Medicaid and Medicare) to "deregulation" of the health care industry, encouraging more for-profit health care providers, to "the growth of medical knowledge," most profoundly seen in new and expensive medical technologies, and on to the increasing awareness that people in the United States had an "overall health status. . . . well below that of many other industrialized nations." Out of these and other forces a stark reality began to dawn on leaders of academic health centers. The practice of medicine was undergoing a revolution often experienced as costs increased and overall revenues decreased, which was driving managers to place a premium on efficiency while causing them to rethink job descriptions and reward structures for medical school faculty. The matter of faculty research in this era of systemic flux was of particular concern to Dwight E. Monson, not to mention medical school deans nationwide: "[T]he ability to grow the research mission is jeopardized when cross-subsidies from clinical surpluses [as a result] shrink."[70]

Fully attuned to these complicated forces, Kirklin as a man of brilliantly eclectic thought (his 1975 Distinguished Faculty Lecture was "Training Horses, Quarterbacks, Pilots, and Surgeons") and others in Birmingham sought to cut such fixed costs by reducing the amount of time and the number of patients involved in overnight hospital stays, and to implement this they focused on a massive outpatient clinic. Moreover, as a response to striking growth in private practices and hospitals in Birmingham, notably from the HealthSouth System and the St. Vincent's Hospital System, and hence stiffer competition for the "needed" market share of patients for UAB, such a clinic would eliminate what John Durant called the "patient-unfriendly" and "mind-boggling chaos" of each UAB medical department having its own outpatient operation: the new "super" outpatient clinic would centralize virtually all such services in an "easy access" situation for patients. Finally, the clinic also would permit "economy of scale" centralization—and elimination of redundancy—of the costly medical technologies, further reducing costs.

What likely made these thoughts move rapidly from "plan" to "action" was a "rumble in the profession," subsequently documented, that the Mayo Clinic in Minnesota and the Ochsner Clinic in New Orleans, facing similar dynamics, had completed patient market surveys targeted at the construction of satellite outpatient facilities in other cities; and that both hospitals had decided that in the Southeast, Birmingham and Jacksonville, Florida, were strong prospects. In response to the news, Kirklin felt that if the Mayo could "do it" in Birmingham, so could UAB. And "do it" he did. In May 1988, Sam Jackson and others administering the HSF began using foundation resources and borrowing power to develop the new clinic.

Still, despite its logic, what Kirklin in a rare moment of noneclectic thought wanted to call the "Ambulatory Patient Care Center" was not easily achieved. To make it happen, medical center leaders, notably department chairs, the key powers in most academic medical centers, had to accept what they called among themselves the "Kirklin Tax." At the deepest level, perhaps, this violated the autonomy of their departmental clinics, the century-old maxim of scientific medicine known as the "authority of the physician." Although this sense of authority could pit physicians against nonphysicians, it also made daily life in a medical school an unending stream of conflicts between physicians. If understandable, *encouraging* such physician and departmental autonomy had been one of the key strategies Volker and Hill had used to recruit stars such as Kirklin. However, it was now time to move beyond this founding ethic of the medical center; and, as a comment on his sheer analytical power, something that could slice through ego, money, and revered tradition, it was Kirklin who led the charge. In broadest perspective, just as UAB's academic affairs sought maturity by embracing more research and traditional campus life, medical center units had before them the crucial maturation step of more cohesiveness and fewer silos of money and power.[71]

On a more concrete level the "Kirklin Tax" required all medical school departments to provide a portion of their HSF-managed fees to amortize bonds for this massive construction project. The tax never reached the level that Kirklin thought appropriate, however, and perhaps it was more than coincidence that he resigned from the role of president of the foundation when his idea of how far the tax should go was rejected by his colleagues. Years later, reflecting on the tax, Kirklin recalled that the medical center "has a lot of selfishness in it." The famous surgeon even failed to show up for the unveiling of the model of the new facility. Still, through a modified tax the 430,000-square-foot project arose in the 500 block of Twentieth Street South, designed by the international architect I. M. Pei, with Kirklin omnipresent for the ribbon-cutting ceremony followed by an elaborate party. The facility could be criticized for large open spaces and wasted space, "Taj Mahal building materials," and at the outset insufficient physicians to avert long waits by patients. But the strengths were there, too. It brought easier doctor access to UAB outpatients. It reflected centralized technologies and laboratories, paralleled by a drop in the average number of nights patients spent in a hospital bed. It forcefully demonstrated that the 650 physicians of HSF indeed were capable of adjusting "at least to a degree" to "the old autonomous ways of doing things" and in the process creating something easily competitive with other super-clinics in the nation.[72]

There was another prism, however, through which one might look at the rise of Kirklin Clinic—the "external fallout." Some private practice physicians in the city saw "HSF docs" as having unfair, publicly funded advantages in the increasingly competitive marketplace of patient care brought on by downward turns in Medicaid and Medicare reimbursements. The *Birmingham Post Herald* sought to capture this reservation with an old UAB metaphor: "[The] Kirklin gem may shine too brightly." Still, as UAB media relations director Mike Ellis continually emphasized, either with "UAB Clinic" (Ellis's preference) or "Kirklin Clinic" (McCallum's preference) placed on the facility in time for McCallum's presiding at the grand opening in June 1992, there was a ring contributing significantly to what national media pointed to as the "New Birmingham," not coincidentally the same impact Kirklin had had when he first arrived in Birmingham in 1966. In addition, some of the local private practice physicians who were unhappy about the Kirklin Clinic in fact had served, early on, as crucial faculty of the medical school, which had ultimately made all this growth in health care and general city life possible.[73]

By April 1993, some six months before stepping down as president, McCallum completed his final major capital campaign construction project. Much like the Kirklin Clinic, the Bevill Biomedical Sciences Building was inspired less by capital campaign strategy and more by innovative thought on how UAB might continue to advance new approaches to science and medicine, in this case the now long-held but constantly evolving faith in interdisciplinary inquiry. Over the previous decade the molecular revolution had advanced understanding in all areas of health science, but in UAB laboratories especially as related to vascular diseases under the direction of Gerald Pohost; AIDS under the leadership of Eric Hunter, Michael Saag, Victoria Johnson, and Beatrice Hahn; and vaccines led by Max Cooper and Christopher Ackley. In fact, by the early 1990s each of these areas of inquiry, bonded by overlapping examinations of the structure of molecules, were being pursued at UAB by emergent research centers well funded by the NIH and NSF. Owing to this powerful interdisciplinary bond, accordingly, Vice President Durant, Department of Medicine chair Claude Bennett, and others conceived of a building that would maximize contact among these investigators whose departmental appointments ranged across the board in the School of Medicine. The net result: a $40 million research facility wedged into Nineteenth Street South, funded in part by some $20 million from the U.S. Department of Energy guided through to UAB by Alabama congressman Tom Bevill, of Jasper, and the remainder covered out of UAB bond funds. In just a few short years, work in this building not only delivered new molecular-based knowledge, especially regarding the AIDS virus profiled by *Newsweek* magazine in an article titled "How the Plague Began," and connected to the new 1917 Clinic, but called for yet another facility targeted at exploration into genetics.[74]

From Extraterrestrial to Very Terrestrial

If scientific investigation at the molecular level caused the movement of a good deal of earth during the McCallum presidency and afterward, such inquiry also had its extraterrestrial features under McCallum's leadership. In 1985 the biochemist Charles E. Bugg had led the establishment of the UAB Center for Macromolecular Crystallography, which was committed to innovative drug design to attack viruses such as AIDS by using crystals. Because the examination and manipulation of molecules in crystals functions best in a nongravity environment, Bugg quickly built a close relationship with the National Aeronautics and Space Administration (NASA) through his plan of executing molecular experiments out in space, well beyond the gravitational pull of Earth. Before the end of the center's first year of operation Bugg's experiments were up in space. But not Bugg. For him, remaining in his UAB laboratory or peering into space from his home perched on the northerly edge of Red Mountain was just fine. He offered the "Buck Rogers bit" of going with the spacecraft and personally executing more refined experiments, instead of having machines do them, to Lawrence J. DeLucas.[75]

By 1990, DeLucas was the forty-year-old outwardly calm, inwardly daring assistant director of Bugg's center. Originally a New Yorker, he had earned a B.S. in chemistry from UAB plus two doctorates from UAB—one in biochemistry, the other in optometry. As an amateur astronomer who "had wanted to [fly] since high school," he jumped at the chance to take the molecular investigations out where there was no gravity. In August 1990 NASA notified him that he had been accepted for the astronaut training program in Houston, and in June 1992 he was one of two scientists who proceeded to Cape Canaveral for the launch. He would be one of six crewmen to take up *Columbia* on June 26 for another Space Lab mission. Interviewed live from space by Connie Chung on *CBS This Morning,* DeLucas participated in the longest flight up to that time: 14 days, 221 times around the Earth, 5.76 million miles. More important for him and his scientific colleagues, DeLucas returned with large, clearly formed crystals crucial to understanding how the AIDS virus infects immune cells and hence how drugs can be designed to block the virus.[76]

Meanwhile, back on Earth, no sooner had DeLucas returned to Birmingham and to a hero's welcome on the campus than McCallum, Durant, and Bennett were in Washington, D.C., to cement the deal that would bring the Gorgas Memorial Institute of Tropical and Preventive Medicine from Bethesda, Maryland, where it had been since its establishment in 1921, to its new home at UAB as part of the Gorgas Center for Geographic Medicine. With new scientific and medical priorities such as molecular research, plus political instability in Panama where much of the institute's work had been focused, Congress no longer could afford to foot the whole bill for this agency. But in engineering the transfer to UAB, Bennett's senior executive officer in the Department of Medicine, James L. Lewis, a geographer by doctoral training, was attuned to more than the poetry of an agency bearing the name of William Crawford Gorgas, of mosquitoes and Panama Canal fame, being moved to the home state of the famous physician. He thought the transfer would boost the international profile and the grant-getting abilities of UAB's recently created Center for Geographic Medicine, which seemed the perfect complement to the mission of the older institute— training researchers, physicians, and public health workers in the developing world—while simultaneously expanding the international network of patient referrals to UAB hospitals.

Lewis and Bennett anticipated not being totally dependent on research grants for funding. U.S. congressman Ben Erdreich, of Birmingham, had joined with Congressman Bevill to produce legislation that would enable the Centers for Disease Control, in Atlanta, to review the status of tropical disease research on an annual basis; from that review federal monies could become available to assist the expanded center. Though the expected congressional line item for the center never materialized, McCallum saw this as "[adding] even more to the international activities of the University, a priority for the institution since the early days of Joe Volker's leadership."[77]

McCallum sought a similar "takeover" or "annexation" regarding undergraduate programs. In the summer and early fall of 1990 he had begun to consider UAB's inclusion of a junior college (which would offer associate of arts and associate of science degrees) program by joining to UAB the private Walker College, which was located forty miles north of Birmingham in

Jasper—an idea first explored by Volker in the mid-1970s. The current president of Walker College, Jack Mott, and chancellor of the college (and its president from 1956 to 1988), David Rowland, had approached McCallum about such a merger chiefly as a way of maintaining the vital presence of the programs of the fifty-two-year-old campus in the civic life of Jasper. Before talking with McCallum about such a radical step during these times in which Alabama higher education "need[ed] to do more with less," Rowland had contacted Garry Neil Drummond, the Jasper native and president pro tem of the UA board, and had received a tentative "green light" to pursue the matter.[78]

Drummond understood not only the vitality that Jasper long had received from having Walker College in its midst, but that the relatively recent appearance of Bevill State Community College in Jasper, with its competitive edge of massive state funding, made it nearly impossible for Walker College, which had a higher private school tuition, to compete with Bevill for students. If Walker joined with UAB, however, as Rowland soon explained to McCallum, there would be the commensurate state funding for the credit hour production (CHP) it produced, resulting in a lowering of tuition to the point at which a "UAB Walker College" easily could compete with Bevill State for students. In follow-up discussions with McCallum, Rowland urged several additional points of pragmatism: (1) the closeness of Birmingham and Jasper; (2) the longstanding pattern of Walker College graduates continuing their higher education at UAB; (3) with the influence of Congressman Bevill, the plan for a federally funded "Corridor X" freeway from Memphis to Birmingham that would make the Jasper area even more of an "economic encatchment area" as well as, over time, a northerly suburb of Birmingham in the same way that Shelby County communities had developed to the south of Birmingham; and (4) if UAB were not interested in such a merger, he felt sure that either UA or the University of North Alabama, at Florence, indeed would be interested.

An Ohio native always fascinated with the longtime growth of Ohio State University and a retired major in the U.S. Army, Rowland had been a strong-willed and effective leader of Walker College. He once had a heavy metal ashtray crammed into his left eye by the massive hand of a disgruntled faculty member who outweighed him by a good hundred pounds. Though the blow came close to eliminating the eye, the next day—with the faculty member out of jail on bond—Rowland dressed himself in appropriate academic regalia (accented with bandaged eye) and presided at his institution's commencement exercises. That strength of personality was evident in his talks with McCallum, whose forcefulness was just as great. If the two had been on opposite sides there undoubtedly could have been sparks. In fact, however, the two bonded out of mutually reinforcing needs and respect.[79]

After digesting the oral proposal, McCallum called several deans and vice presidents to a meeting in his office to discuss its pros and cons. In the meeting it was clear that McCallum had great interest in such a project, but for reasons in addition to those Rowland had given. Over the previous thirty years McCallum had seen "the public two-year college system" rapidly grow into something that cut an already small pie for state education funds into smaller and smaller pieces: at the time such colleges numbered forty, the greatest number per capita in the United States: "gross inefficiency." But, he also propounded, if, by taking on this private junior college, UAB could show the state that some of the "high quality State two-year schools" could be merged with neighboring four-year institutions in "a fashion that permitted the continuation of the two-year programs," and then other state two-year schools—"the weaker ones"—could simply be shut down, the resultant economies of scale could begin to "reverse the inefficient distribution of state funds that so long had plagued Alabama." Indeed, for starters, Shelton State Community College could merge with UA, Faulkner State Community College with the University of South Alabama, and, most exciting—for it would involve UAB possibly acquiring one of the strongest educational leaders in the state, President Judy Merritt—UAB would acquire Jefferson State Community College.

It was a "large plan filled with numerous political pitfalls," including not just the extreme power of the two-year college system in the legislature but the extreme sensitivities in "the UA family" about signs of radical new development at UAB. But most of McCallum's deans and vice presidents agreed that if done correctly, starting with UAB including Walker College as a model for a university sponsoring such a two-year program, it could represent major gains for the state.

McCallum handed out assignments. One vice president headed to Pennsylvania State University to study its highly regarded integration of two- and four-year programs. Another went to work on how the Southern Association of Colleges and Schools (SACS) would view such an initial step. Still another worked closely with Walker College budget director David Abrams and developed a careful analysis of every financial implication of a Walker College merger. Still others began an examination of what types of Walker students and programs could prosper, or lose ground, in the arrangement. While these studies were taking place, McCallum initiated confidential talks with various members of the board, including Drummond, another Jasper-based trustee, John Oliver, and with UA chancellor Philip Austin. McCallum got "no red lights," though all agreed that the step was "risky" at a time when Governor Fob James was cutting education appropriations based on "too much duplication." "The problem," McCallum later recalled, "was that the initial step regarding Walker College might create so much backlash that we would never be able to get the far larger, cost-savings plan before the proper forum."[80]

Still, on September 28, 1990, with particular assistance from trustees Drummond and Blount, McCallum managed to get the passage of a board resolution that authorized him "to pursue discussions with officials at Walker College . . . concerning the possibility of closer ties between Walker College and UAB." So far so good. Then, on December 7, 1990, McCallum sought to return to the board with the completed proposal. Chancellor Austin asked that the proposal follow standard procedures, however, and be reviewed first by appropriate board committees, in this case a joint meeting of the Committee on Finance and the Committee on Academic Affairs. As reported that evening in the *Birmingham News* with an article closely resembling a press release crafted by James Bosarge and Mike Ellis, and also as reflected in the board minutes, in his remarks before the joint committee McCallum decided to risk revealing the whole plan, minus a few specifics, and thus try to head off criticism that the action represented inefficient expansion of UAB: "[The merger of Walker College into UAB] will serve as an experiment in combining two-year and four-year institutions in a state where merging educational institutions is a perennial topic."[81]

In response to McCallum's presentation, however, Chancellor Austin told trustees that he was opposed to the merger on the grounds that Walker College was a *private* institution, that is, the proposed merger represented a net increase in fiscal responsibilities for Alabama higher education. In addition, the Alabama Commission on Higher Education (ACHE) had no guidelines for assessing or approving such an action. Hence, because of Austin's action, McCallum's plan received a "no action" response and did not move forward to the general board meeting the following day, although Drummond, while not seeking to override Austin's position, urged McCallum to "seek all ways of cooperation with Walker College short of formal merger" while Austin and ACHE gave the matter further consideration. In retrospect, Austin's fiscal reservation, if considered short term and with reference only to Walker College, had merit. Still, the larger plan of which Walker was only a starting point, if ever implemented (and granted this would have involved nothing short of warfare in the legislature) could have saved Alabama millions of desperately needed education dollars.[82]

The succeeding two years proved stressful. Robert Potts, president of the University of North Alabama, entered into serious negotiations that would have brought Walker College into his institution. Linda Flaherty-Goldsmith, who as McCallum's treasurer, then vice president of finance, had played such a crucial role in McCallum's planning for Walker College, departed UAB to become vice chancellor of financial affairs at the UA system office, reporting to Austin. Still, with longtime director of risk management John Walker replacing Flaherty-Goldsmith on an interim basis, McCallum continued to marshal financial data showing that Walker College would be a fiscal advantage, not a fiscal liability, for the UA system. Ultimately, after McCallum had taken the proposal yet again to the board in a special "called meeting" on the UAB campus—where the "usually persuasive" Drummond backed the merger and Austin advised that the "environment" now looked more positive for such action—and after the board of Walker College decided to withdraw from negotiations with the University of North Alabama, the plan found board approval on October 29, 1993, soon after McCallum's presidency had ended. Still, the development of the Walker College merger between 1990 and 1993 produced high tension among all the key players—the chancellor, McCallum, and most trustees, not to mention numerous leading citizens of Jasper. The merger also lacked clarity on certain financial issues, especially regarding how CHP generated out of UAB Walker College would be factored into UAB's annual budget allocation from the state, as if such allocations had ever truly functioned via a rational formula. For certain, any legislator with close ties to the two-year college system, of which there were some twenty in 1993, would have opposed a positive budget outcome for UAB in view of the overall plan McCallum had so honestly articulated. Hence, despite the progressive boldness of McCallum's vision, the marriage of Walker College and UAB began with what therapists call "unresolved issues" and had the rough future normally attendant to such beginnings.[83]

Indeed, it is virtually impossible to tease out of the Walker College tensions other strains McCallum experienced during the same general time period with the chancellor and some board members over yet another project for UAB expansion: football, with its attendant implications for state pride and UA institutional self-image.[84] Remember that Volker, in 1966, showed deference to UA when he answered a faculty member's query about the emergent autonomy of UAB. Though he did not rule out football at some point down the line, Volker treaded lightly because, as former UA administrator Jeff Bennett recalled, "Joe understood that football was the ultimate source of security for UA after the embarrassments associated with desegregation, despite many *non*-football accomplishments at [the University of] Alabama." Writing for the *Wall Street Journal,* former UAB vice president Thomas K. Hearn, from his perspective as the new president of Wake Forest University, sharpened the point: UA football elicited "a kind of mythic quality that has to do with people's [need for] confidence in themselves." In fact, in Bennett's view, it was chiefly this relatively recent iconic experience with football that had prompted "Bear" Bryant and his followers on the UA board, especially Tuscaloosa businessman Ernest Williams, to be less than supportive about UAB's entering the world of big-time college basketball. Soon, many identified with UA athletics feared that UAB basketball would only be the beginning. And they were right.

The same motivations leading to President Hill's hiring of Gene Bartow to start up intercollegiate basketball and other sports programs at UAB moved McCallum in the spring and summer of 1989 to agree with Gene Bartow's urging that UAB begin to think about football. "Dick and I talked about it a long time," Bartow remembered, and although McCallum made several neutral statements on the matter while he was interim president, as his full presidency unfolded "Scotty picked right up." The idea was to build a full, mature university with growing enrollment; and in the deep South, from where the overwhelming number of UAB undergraduates would be coming, it was football more than anything else that the general population identified with "college." The *Wall Street Journal* distilled McCallum's strategy: "While UAB is one of the state's biggest employers, many Alabamians think of it as nothing more than an urban night school." Through athletics, especially football, the plan was "to change all that."[85]

It was no coincidence that McCallum made his move on football as Vice President Woodward and others sought to remold and market UAB's undergraduate programs with a greater sense of collegiate traditionalism—dormitories, campus "green space," and so forth.[86] Further, it was no coincidence that, upon the retirement of longtime media specialist Gloria Goldstein Howton, McCallum hired away from UA one of the most experienced higher education experts on marketing and media relations in the nation, Birmingham native Mike Ellis, perhaps most noted for his "Bama Bound" marketing strategy for UA. Although McCallum did not mention football to Ellis in the hiring process, at the time McCallum seemed fully aware of the lightning rod football represented, not just from the perspective of relations with UA but from the standpoint of fiscal austerity recent governors had brought to Alabama higher education. He also understood the risk successful football represented in ultimately skewing the priorities of his university. Still, to grow UAB further, McCallum decided he had no choice.[87]

In August 1989 McCallum gave Bartow the go-ahead to initiate a "student-organized" football program as a "club team" (no league affiliation, no scholarships) under the coaching of James Hilyer. A man with several graduate degrees and one well experienced in the world of sports—he had been an assistant football coach at Mississippi State University and at Auburn University as well as with the Washington Redskins and the Birmingham Stallions—most recently Hilyer had been attached to Bartow's athletic department working on strength and conditioning, as well as counseling. That first season the interesting assortment of players who turned out for Hilyer, some with exceptional high school football experience, struggled through six losing games against virtually any team they could schedule, such as the junior college team at Marion Institute. McCallum attended most of the games, which were normally played on the intramural athletic field just west of the Ullman Building, and the team's losing record suited him fine: low profile. The next year, however, the talented Hilyer fielded a more competitive club team. Completing 1990 with a 3-4 record, the Blazers beat Marion Institute, Albany Turner College, and Lambuth College. Still low profile: fine.[88]

At the next board meeting, in March 1991, McCallum reported that UAB planned to field a NCAA Division III team the following year. A strong majority of the board felt such a step was unnecessary because of where it might be headed, and Chancellor Austin concurred. Still, according to UA board policy, the initiation of intercollegiate athletics remained a matter *technically* under the control of the president, if *politically* on this matter the line of authority between the board and president lacked such clarity. Exercising his technical prerogative to move ahead, McCallum—carefully primed by Mike Ellis—held a press conference on March 13, 1991, and delivered the message. It was all the fault of the NCAA.

At the recent NCAA meeting in Nashville several propositions were approved which will require changes in the athletic program at UAB. The recently approved Proposition 45 specifically requires all Division I members to sponsor seven sports each for men and women. Our preference is to add men's football at the Division III level since it is the only non-Division I sport that will be accepted to meet the minimum of seven sports without adding additional scholarships. We also will add soccer for women. . . . Although I have objected to and continue to object to a move to Division I football because of the potential financial burden on the university [with scholarships], I think Division III football has the best chance of being self-supporting with the least amount of investment. . . . I believe this is a program our students want and deserve. . . . Since this will be a non-scholarship program, the players will truly come from the student body.[89]

With Hilyer still at the helm, football and higher education now became intertwined as they had during the years of UAB's infancy—this time, however, the centerpiece was a strident UAB, not an exuberant Crimson Tide. UAB opened the 1991 season with a thrashing by Millsaps College. Two weeks later the Blazers bounced back with a 34–21 victory over Washington and Lee University. Even though convincing ESPN and CNN score reporters to refer to the Blazer team not as "Alabama-Birmingham" but as "UAB," emphasizing UCLA as an appropriate parallel, proved frustrating, the die seemed cast. McCallum clearly was working with Mike Ellis to ensure a distinctive UAB identity wherever possible, certainly among national television sports audiences. There was a reassertion of school colors: vibrant green and gold with occasional splashes of white. Appearing on football uniforms and those of virtually all other UAB athletic teams, the colors sought maximum television appeal and what Ellis called "institutional branding." Yet the notion of maturing institutional identity through athletics could be affected, too, by matters decidedly *non*athletic. In September 1991, in the midst of Ellis's athletic branding, UAB failed in a year-long effort to gain the state senate's confirmation of Michael Goodrich as a UA trustee. A UA law graduate (as well as a Tulane engineering graduate), Goodrich seemingly was shot down because his corporation, BE&K Engineering, generally did not hire union laborers. Something did not fit: When had advocating rights of organized labor become a litmus test for service on the UA board? To McCallum and his followers, the Goodrich defeat not only saw one of the most talented civic leaders in the state denied a role in higher-education leadership but it smacked of the "politics" of the mid-1980s when Baxley, a UA graduate, stifled UAB (and some members of the UA board) when it futilely advocated another Birmingham leader, Louis

Willie, for trusteeship. In short, as in any university's life, beneath the sublime (choosing school colors better suited for television) often could be found the serious (intense politics). More to the point, this perceived blow to UAB's stronger identity in 1991 only fueled the fire for *far* more UAB football.[90]

After a year of careful planning, on November 12, 1992, McCallum again raised the stakes. Through a letter to Chancellor Austin, McCallum told the board what he planned to do next and why he had to do it. Again the NCAA left UAB little choice.

> It seems appropriate to reiterate some of the issues covered in the recent discussions I have had with you and the Board of Trustees concerning football at the University of Alabama at Birmingham. . . . It has always been my hope that that we could remain a Division III football team and maintain our other sports in Division I. As you know[, however,] action by the NCAA precludes an institution's participating in sports in more than one division. Therefore, unless things change at the forthcoming meeting of the NCAA in January of 1993, we are forced to reevaluate the future of football at UAB. . . . [On the other hand], . . . use of State funds to supplement athletics at a time of proration, the need to improve salaries for the faculty, buy equipment, etc., would in my opinion be inappropriate and an action that I do not support. Therefore, unless things change at the NCAA meeting, it is my intent that we will move to a I-AA non-scholarship program. [And] if the Athletic Department can raise the money, I would have no objection to a limited number of scholarships . . . from outside sources. . . . I recognize the concerns of the Board of Trustees who have been so very candid with me relative to football at UAB. I respect and appreciate their opinions, but I hope they understand that I must make the decisions that I believe are best for this institution.[91]

By early 1993 the NCAA had acted as McCallum had anticipated. On January 22, he met with Bartow and Hilyer to give them the news and followed the conversation with a letter of confirmation: "I have made the decision that UAB will move to I-AA football beginning in the fall of 1993. . . . If you wish to raise money from the private sector to assist in the support of the football team, including scholarships for the football players, I would have no objection providing you do not solicit gifts from individuals, corporations or organizations that we are already approaching." He followed this with his key honestly spoken belief, separate from connections with NCAA rules: "Having a football team at UAB is important to the activities of the university, and I trust that my decision will prove to be the right one for UAB." The same day, January 22, 1993—in the midst of tensions over Walker College—he wrote the chancellor of his decision.

> It is [now] my feeling that it is in the best interest of [UAB] to move to a I-AA football program. . . . In my opinion football is an important part of the student activities here at the University; and as long as it does not detract from our continuing quest to maintain and enhance the academic excellence that this institution has achieved, I will be supportive of a football program. . . . I had a meeting with Coach Bartow and Coach Hilyer at which time I made it absolutely clear that . . . I will not provide monies from state resources to provide scholarships for the athletes in the football program. If they are capable of identifying funds from private sources to provide scholarships, this would have my approval.

And then the crucial point:

> I appreciate your candidness, as well as that of the Board of Trustees, on this very sensitive issue, and it is my hope that you understand that I realize the majority of the Board feel that this is not the best decision for this institution. [Trustees Drummond, Loftin, and Mitchell apparently led a minority opinion unopposed to McCallum's plan.] I . . . respect the fact that they have indicated quite clearly that the decision relative to football is a presidential one and not one to be made by the Board of Trustees. I am making the decision which I think is in the best interest of this institution. It is my fervent hope that this shall prove to be the appropriate and best decision for the University of Alabama at Birmingham.[92]

With the aid of Mayor Arrington, corporate leader John Harbert, and others, including McCallum himself, Bartow raised the football scholarship money, and by March 1993 UAB could announce plans to enter the next season as a Division I-AA team.[93]

Through a coincidence no one could have foreseen, tensions associated with the football announcement were heightened further that March by a basketball game. Under basketball coach Winfrey ("Wimp") Sanderson—and under the supraguidance of Athletic Director "Bear" Bryant—UA long had refused to schedule Bartow's team, a stance interpreted at least in Birmingham as evidence that UA feared either losing to UAB or the further "legitimation" of athletics at UAB that playing UA would provide, which if so, was an absurd idea since Bartow's team already had had appearances in NCAA basketball tournaments, plus had taken on and beaten Auburn several times. In 1989 UA even had refused participation in a basketball tournament involving only UA, UAB, USA, and AU, an exciting prospect advanced by the businessman and civic leader Larry Striplin. However, in March 1993, with Bryant dead some eight years and UA basketball under the coaching leadership of David Hobbs, UA found itself in a box with only one way out: it was compelled to play UAB in the first round of the National Invitational Tournament (NIT), and indeed required to play the game in Tuscaloosa because of the NIT policy on location tied to average attendance over the previous season. The result: with about 14,000 in the packed house—some 30 percent from Birmingham—UAB beat UA by the score of 58–56. With increased internecine tensions over this victory, and UA standing firm on not permitting UAB a regular place in its basketball schedule, supporters of UAB football only became more intense. Ultimately, however, such growth persisted without McCallum at the helm.[94]

More Urban Engagement

Although McCallum had spent a good deal of time and energy on the football project and Walker College, he also had been pushing on a totally different institutional frontier. This effort brought him little tension from the board, and on several occasions brought him praise. He continued the drive to make UAB part of mainstream urban university life in America.

As a dental dean mentored by Volker, McCallum had experience working outside conventionally defined health care; much of his "thinking outside the box" is reflected in his own Distinguished Faculty Lecture, "The Challenge of Service," which he had given in April 1972. He also had helped desegregate the Birmingham Medical Center and sought to expand the number of black Alabamians who went to the UAB dental school. Moreover, as vice president he had worked alongside President Hill in UAB's advocacy of the Urban Grant University Act; and then in the earliest years of his presidency McCallum had worked behind the scenes to assist Mayor Arrington and Odessa Woolfolk, director of the UAB Center for Urban Affairs

(CUA), in leading the ten-year effort that culminated in the creation of the Birmingham Civil Rights Institute. But these were not the focal points of his professional life. In terms of both faculty and administrative life, he had grown up deeply immersed in the world of health care and was not known publicly for articulating the role of the assertive, reform-minded urban university.[95]

All this changed. Two years into his presidency—at a time when it was increasingly apparent that the American civil rights movement lacked anything approaching consensus on what the "next step" should be—one of McCallum's key focal points became unmet goals of the civil rights movement in Birmingham, particularly UAB's obligation as an *urban* university to do something about increasing African American access to the higher socioeconomic levels of life in Birmingham and elsewhere.

Cynics could argue that McCallum's tight focus on UAB and African Americans resulted out of contemporaneous litigation. The Perry Woods case, a class-action lawsuit brought against UAB for alleged discrimination against black maintenance workers with regard to salary and promotions, began in the mid-1980s and was dismissed a decade later with UAB not found guilty of breaking federal civil rights laws but nevertheless agreeing to provide back pay to certain employees and making promotions in the facilities management area purely on the basis of seniority, not merit.[96] Then there was the higher-profile *Knight v. Alabama* litigation, a latent result of the U.S. Department of Justice's implementing the "compliance review" component of the Civil Rights Act of 1964 as it pertained to desegregation of Alabama's public institutions of higher education. Certainly the convoluted case, initiated in 1978 but reaching its crescendo between the mid-1980s and the mid-1990s in a federal courtroom in Birmingham presided over first by federal judge U. W. Clemon and later by federal judge Harold L. Murphy, quickly documented what all with common sense knew to be true. Going back a century or more, there had been a clear pattern of segregation and other forms of racial discrimination in many of Alabama's public four-year institutions. Again to the surprise of few, Judge Murphy's initial 366-page opinion provided remedies involving over $50 million of "back allocations" from the state government of Alabama to Alabama State University (ASU) and Alabama A&M University, the two historically black public four-year institutions in the state. Yet to the surprise of many, he accompanied this remedy with the order that ASU and A&M also were not to be segregated (i.e., all black).[97]

Still, the Birmingham campus postdated the pronounced era of segregation. Indeed, UAB not only owed much of its complicated origins to the success of the civil rights movement, but even in recent years many of its faculty and staff (e.g., geographer Charles R. Clark in the CUA) had been providing statistical data to the state legislature and local governments to assist them in eliminating the persisting pockets of Jim Crow politics. Hence, by 1989 Judge Murphy was beginning to make it clear that UAB, while part of the UA system, was not an individual campus to be considered part of the historic pattern of Alabama segregation. In fact, he pointed to the significant numbers of blacks who were students, faculty, and administrators at UAB. Nevertheless, during much of the 1990s, he allowed Alabama A&M to employ some of its proceeds from the suit to launch outreach programs that duplicated UAB's inside Jefferson County.

More to the point, by the late 1980s and early 1990s the backdrop of the Woods and Knight cases clearly occupied some of McCallum's mind, not to mention long hours of work by Ina Leonard, Robert Potts, and Glenn Powell. (Since 1984, Leonard and other chief campus attorneys had been reporting to the chief system attorney, Potts, then Powell, as part of the effort to centralize management of the system.)[98] However, two lower-profile developments well beyond Birmingham were perhaps most responsible for heightening President McCallum's positive action on race and his city.

In the summer of 1989, he received an invitation to attend an Urban 13 meeting at the University of Cincinnati; the meeting would probe new strategies for the recruitment and retention of more African American faculty. McCallum had a schedule conflict, but he sent three UAB representatives: Louis Dale, senior mathematician and an African American; the executive assistant to the president, biochemist Kenneth J. Roozen; and the historian and interim vice president for academic affairs, Tennant McWilliams. On their return to Birmingham, the three were wary of the financial implications of "solutions" to the problems they had been discussing. UAB had more African American students (27 percent of total undergraduate enrollment) than virtually any other predominantly white state research university in the nation, but UAB's faculty was 2.5 percent African American— barely above average. The three filed a report telling McCallum of these findings. McCallum, however, wanted more. Granted, he knew there were high-profile examples of UAB helping launch the health science careers of certain African Americans. With pride he could point to certain individuals in academia and more outside academia. There were academicians such as the UAB dentistry professor Wilson Wright. There were private practice physicians such as Richard Walker. And there were public health physicians such as Sandral Hullett and, most recently, Regina M. Benjamin, a 1984 M.D. graduate destined to be an Alabama-based rural health specialist of international reputation. But he recognized that UAB's high African American enrollment, plus its location in a city with high African American population, permitted UAB to do much more, influencing broad fields of education and professional life. He believed that UAB had a preeminent opportunity to help "fix the national pipeline problem" with regard to African American faculty. And so he fired back, "Tell me how we are going to do this better and do it right away."[99]

With little notion of where the president would find funds to support such a project in light of unpredictable state appropriations, plus the anticipated reallocations out of the Special Education Trust Fund to pay "the remedy" in the Knight case, the three nevertheless assembled a plan revolving around summer institutes for African American high school students, increased partnerships between various units of UAB and high schools in the city with high African American populations, and UAB scholarships for African American students, graduates and undergraduates. It was a classic pipeline approach, as it turned out, much like proposals being developed by other Urban 13 institutions (e.g., the University of Pittsburgh and the University of Illinois–Chicago). The only difference was that these were public institutions in states with relatively strong tax bases, sophisticated state-level policymaking (no dependency on sales tax for education funding), strong funding-per-student at the higher-education level, and no anticipated reallocation of state dollars as compensation for a history of segregation—the exact opposite of what Alabama had. Accordingly, it came as a shock when Roozen advised Dale and McWilliams, "He's going to do it. He's going to take about $1 million off the top of the State allocation next year no matter what it is; and he wants a detailed budget showing how the money will be allocated within the program . . . immediately."

McCallum got his budget. There would be $170,000 for African American undergraduate merit scholarships; $500,000 for African American graduate fellowships; $20,000 for retention (research and travel support) for current African American faculty; $90,000 for visiting African American faculty; $120,000 to assist departments with recruitment of new African American faculty; and $50,000 to create an infrastructure in student affairs—led by the African American UAB graduate Cynthia Scott—to establish mentoring and advising for African American undergraduates.[100]

While campus announcements of the program brought mixed reactions, especially from women who emphasized that they were minorities, too,

McCallum held firm. "We're going to do it," he told Faculty Senate leaders. "In Birmingham, with a city school system that is over 90% African American, we have the chance to make a difference, and we're going to do it." Despite a 1990–91 state budget prorated by 6.5 percent (partially offset at UAB by a 5.3 percent increase in tuition and fees), he implemented the program that year.[101]

Spin-offs then occurred. By using the President's Minority and Recruitment Fund as matching money, Terry L. Hickey, associate vice president of health affairs, and Roozen obtained from the Coca Cola Foundation an additional $300,000 per year for five years for a summer scholars program focused on African American high school students, chiefly of the Birmingham area, who were interested in careers in science and medicine. Similar funds soon were acquired from Time Warner, Amoco, and 3-M. Likewise, the mathematics professor Louis Dale, working with the new vice president of academic affairs, Sibley, also used the President's Minority and Recruitment Fund as matching funds to obtain an Alliance for Minority Participation in Science (AMPS) grant from the NSF that funded undergraduate and graduate students interested in careers in science and mathematics. Ultimately expanded into an NSF commitment to UAB of $1 million a year for ten years, Dale's program became a model for the nation. Applauded at a White House meeting, Dale found himself escalated among NSF ranks as one of the national leaders in bringing more African Americans into scientific careers in both academia and private industry.[102]

These funding programs, considered collectively as the Comprehensive Minority Faculty Development Program (CMFDP), produced significant results. By its sixth year, of the 121 undergraduate students who had been funded by the program (not all of whom had first held summer internships but virtually all of whom focused on study in the sciences, mathematics, or engineering), 93 percent had completed their degrees. This was a significant accomplishment in view of the fact that UAB, much like other urban universities, had a general six-year graduation rate of about 35 percent. Of these 93 percent who had graduated with CMFDP support there also were some inspiring success stories. For example, ten went on to medical school, one to dental school, and three to Ph.D. work in the sciences and engineering. At least five others skipped graduate school and headed into well-paying industry jobs, especially in computer engineering. The original pipeline-to-academia approach was not a total success, however, for a disproportionate number of the graduates pursued careers in nonacademic life where salaries were so much higher.[103]

From the more general standpoint of increasing the numbers of African American faculty at UAB, however, regardless of where they completed baccalaureate or graduate training, the program delivered more consistent results. With the use of a one-time award of $30,000 to any department that hired an African American to a tenure-track position—an award originally made to the department but earmarked shortly thereafter for use by the new African American faculty member in the department—the program sought to add four new African American scholars to the faculty each year. It did this with difficulty: the percentage of African American tenure-track faculty moved from 2.5 percent in 1987–88, to 3.4 percent in 1992–93, to 4.3 percent by 1999, and in the process gelled to create a chapter of the National Congress of Black Faculty. Undoubtedly cuts in state funding and an inability to increase the *number* of faculty lines in most schools kept the program from being even more successful.[104]

Such overt efforts at increasing the presence of African American faculty at UAB and beyond likely had an additional, if difficult to pinpoint, effect: the growth of the general African American enrollment at the university. With an already strong base of African American students dating back to the 1970s, by the early 1990s the number of African Americans attending UAB began to grow steadily to the point at which, well after McCallum's presidency, a freshman class could be over 35 percent African American. The vast majority of these students were from Birmingham, and a significant number were top scholars who just ten years earlier would have looked only at the Ivy League or prestigious historically black institutions such as Morehouse or Tuskegee.[105]

At the same time, owing in part to some African American businessmen and African American UAB faculty, such as the management professor George Munchus, publicly criticizing UAB for local African American entrepreneurs not getting more UAB construction contracts, a point strongly urged also by Vice President Robert Glaze in September 1987, McCallum asked an eight-person committee to study who in fact was benefiting most from a business standpoint as a result of UAB's burgeoning economic impact in Birmingham. Although the study concluded that African American entrepreneurs were pathetically underrepresented in this business, it did not recommend moving to a "quota system" to solve the problem. Instead, it looked for a vehicle to disseminate information on UAB construction and other business opportunities to African American business people to facilitate their submission of bids. Ultimately, McCallum asked George Perdue, an African American accountant from Birmingham who had served as a senior internal auditor at UAB as well as a member of the Alabama legislature, to help him create and then manage an office specifically designed to make all business opportunities with UAB known to the African American business community of Birmingham, and to begin to track annually the number of UAB jobs and their dollar values that went to such businesses in Birmingham.[106]

Under Perdue's leadership, with the significant assistance of Beatrice Newton, this effort facilitated a steady growth of the percentage of UAB business going to African Americans. Such business grew from .21 percent ($295,000) in 1987–88 to 1.50 percent ($2,000,000) in 1992–93 and up to 7 percent ($9,500,000) by the late 1990s. No doubt some of this success was a result of Perdue's soft-spoken but persistent salesmanship. He connected the UAB effort with national meetings on African American business development by awarding trips to conferences for staff of different UAB units that did the most business with African American enterprises in Birmingham. Often the winners were white female fiscal agents who returned to the campus after a trip to, say, Miami Beach, excited about new friendships and filled with information about race and economics in America—continuing education for current professionals in its most compelling form.[107]

Meanwhile, another conference invitation arrived at McCallum's office. This time the president of the University of Pennsylvania, Sheldon Hackney—a historian and Birmingham native—invited McCallum to bring a small team of urbanists with him to a meeting in Philadelphia. Joined by seven other teams from universities in cities nationwide, they engaged in far-ranging discourse on the role of the urban university, past, present, and future. Each team discussed its experience with university-community partnerships: UAB focused on its experience with the Titusville partnership. Hackney also had a pragmatic goal. Increasingly, the University of Pennsylvania, as an elite private Ivy League institution with little programmatic connection to its surrounding city, had been the scene of considerable conflict between university personnel and students and Philadelphia citizens living and working a stone's throw from the campus. Flash points covered everything from race and religion to business opportunities, campus expansion, homelessness, and Penn's lack of interest in the Philadelphia public schools. In response, and at the urging of Penn historians Ira Harkavy and Lee Benson, Hackney had authorized the creation of the Penn Center for Community Partnerships. Under Harkavy's direction here was a research-service center designed to encourage Penn students and faculty to be a part of programs that would permit them to learn from their surrounding community and also to help solve its problems. Hence, Hackney wanted to bring in fellow urbanists to interact with the Penn Center, learn what other urban universities were doing, and lay the foundation for multi-institutional grant applications.[108]

If McCallum and other UAB participants shared with Harkavy and his Philadelphia colleagues the lessons they had learned, especially regarding ethnic diversity and university development, they also returned to Birmingham with new ideas about what could be done at UAB on matters of community partnerships. With his usual fast-action approach, McCallum telephoned directives. First, he was convinced that the university-community partnership he recently had initiated in Titusville, the African American neighborhood adjacent to the UAB campus whose residents knew McCallum personally from their mutual 6:00 a.m. jogging jaunts on the UAB track, should be expanded to include more than endeavors involving essentially UAB faculty in social science and teacher education. To Odessa Woolfolk, a Titusville native who had managed the Titusville Project since stepping down from directing UAB's CUA to become special assistant to the president for community affairs, he pledged his support to get more health science faculty into the project. He was convinced—in part from the Philadelphia trip and also from reports about health screenings in local schools by nursing faculty member Charlene McKaig—that "systemic health issues" had a "disproportionate influence" on children's ability to succeed in school.[109]

Shortly thereafter, Woolfolk and her Titusville friend Roger White had UAB faculty from public health, nursing, dentistry, and optometry working in Washington Elementary School, in Titusville, offering a wide range of health screenings for children. One of the results: the conclusion, one acted upon, that students with poor eyesight would have more success in reading and mathematics if they had proper eyeglasses, that is, if they could see. In a similar vein, Robert Corley, Betty Bock, and others of the CUA acquired city and private foundation funds to redevelop housing in and revitalize the economy of the once prosperous neighborhoods of West End and Woodlawn.[110]

The Birmingham Compact was more expansive and therefore difficult, but McCallum pushed on. Begun in 1991 with a small grant from the Pew Charitable Trusts, the program provided a structure for UAB, neighboring Jefferson State Community College, and the Birmingham city schools to develop careful strategies for more Birmingham K–12 students to graduate and move into successful college careers. Focused on "algebra and reading as the [disciplinary] gatekeepers" and massive numbers of dropouts among sixteen-year-olds (when state truancy laws no longer kept them in school), the compact captured additional Pew funding—$500,000 over three years—and hired UAB teacher education specialist Barbara Lewis as its executive director. Under her leadership the Birmingham Compact worked well for over three years on *planning* strategies to solve severe student dropout problems. The *implementation* of strategies, however, proved far more difficult. Infighting within the Birmingham Public School system, touched off by Cleveland Hammonds's desire for major new efficiencies in the system (many of which hinged on ending tenure for principals and assistant superintendents who long had been protected by the statewide K–12 union, the Alabama Education Association), and other stresses brought the city's K–12 system to a near grinding standstill and ultimately led not just to Pew's withdrawing its money from the compact but to Hammonds's resignation. For all of the positives associated with Birmingham joining America's social mainstream in the years following 1963, here in the 1990s' crack-up of the inner-city public school system—a devastating trend nationwide—was one of the tragic negatives. From another perspective, however, this effort along with more successful and tightly focused ones in Titusville and West End, and a new program for teacher education students committed to inner-city teaching *in* Birmingham, clearly reflected McCallum as an institutional leader capable of development not just within his "translocal disciplinary community" of health science, to recall Tom Bender's words, but in research-service endeavors central to his "local living community."[111]

Accolades and History

Although the Birmingham Compact clearly deconstructed in the eyes of the Pew Charitable Trust and others, McCallum's personal and institutional role as an urban activist persisted. Behind the scenes, he orchestrated a letter from Dick Hill to Hill's close friend, Birmingham corporate leader Houston Blount, whereby Blount—a leading Republican of Alabama—in turn wrote to President George Bush pleading the (futile) case for increased funding for the Urban Grant Act of 1978. Repeatedly, moreover, McCallum spoke before national urban reform groups assembled in Washington, D.C., and Philadelphia by Nevin Brown, Ira Harkavy, and others. Sparked by these appearances and what lay behind them, in August 1991 the *New York*

Times sent yet another reporter to check up on Birmingham, this time an African American reporter named Karen DeWitt. The result was a front-page story in the paper titled "Universities Become Full Partners to Cities in the South."

Accompanied by a photograph of President McCallum and Mayor Arrington standing in front of the Kirklin Clinic in deep conversation about their city, DeWitt underscored UAB's role in "actively nurtur[ing] its city's blacks." She profiled Woolfolk and the CUA's role with the Birmingham Civil Rights Institute, and she described McCallum's Minority Recruitment and Retention Fund as flying "right in the face of [national] political efforts to end affirmative action." DeWitt presented these and other developments as examples of what urban universities across the South, not just UAB but the University of New Orleans, the University of North Carolina–Charlotte, and others, were doing to assist the growth of the region's cities. A former college professor, DeWitt quickly grasped a central point of history related to higher education and a changing American South. Just as land grant institutions had provided a major engine for the socioeconomic growth of the nineteenth century when the nation was essentially rural, the urban universities, especially those of the South, were providing the same type of "special function" in the increasingly urban life of the late twentieth century. Why this type of higher-education impact might possibly be greater in cities such as McCallum's, she posited, "is that the painful passage through the civil rights struggles of the '60's gave some [Southern] communities [such as Birmingham] a more open attitude toward diagnosing and treating other community problems." Although undoubtedly some in Birmingham thought DeWitt had gone too far, hers remained heavy affirmation for UAB regarding urban reform. In October 1991, Congress selected UAB as one of a handful of campuses nationwide to hold public hearings on the need for greater federal funding in order for urban universities to assist their surrounding cities. The proceedings included DeWitt's article being entered into the public record.[112]

There were other types of accolades, too. In September 1992, a *Reader's Digest* survey of health care specialists announced that cancer, arthritis, and heart disease treatments at UAB were ranked alongside those of the Mayo Clinic and Johns Hopkins University as "the best in the nation." The same month, *U.S. News & World Report,* in its annual survey of American higher education targeted at those about to select a place to go to college, named UAB the "No. 1 Up and Coming University in the Nation." Then in November 1992 the *Atlanta Business Chronicle* published a feature story on UAB's leading Birmingham into an era of serving as the "health hub" of the South. Early the following year the tiny *Eastern Shore Courier*, of Fairhope, Alabama, an enclave of reformers on the eastern shore of Mobile Bay, zeroed in on UAB for its economic impact. In 1992, the *Courier* reported, UAB-related "local business volume was $1,222,000,000, which had increased from $409,000,000 in just ten years." From at least one perspective, these and other stories were more significant than detailed reports of a particular faculty member's research in a specialized journal or a student's receiving an award before some international disciplinary organization. Such coverage in popular journalism, from national circulation magazines to a careful chronicler of small-town life in south Alabama, echoed from the all-important outside world what those on UAB's inside gradually had been experiencing, day by day, over the previous two decades: the maturing of a university in tandem with the modernization of a city.[113]

As no small footnote to this process, but as a comment on McCallum's comprehension of the historical significance of what had been happening around him for some forty years, he sought to protect his institution's history. Over the years archivists from the University of North Carolina and the Alabama State Department of Archives and History, notably Edwin Bridges, had urged UAB to establish a records management system. In 1983 the UA board had passed a resolution (Rule 160, later renumbered Rule 105) encouraging all UA system campuses to develop records management programs. In response, McCallum asked James Lowery in institutional studies and services to move forward gradually on this high-cost endeavor.[114] Of greater practicality, no doubt because it involved less funding, not to mention a decade of inside lobbying by the physician Wayne Finley, in November 1992 McCallum followed a route pursued by virtually all of the young, Urban 13 universities and established a university archives. With Virginia Fisher, a UAB history graduate, named the founding director, the UAB Archives emerged with a sound budget and space in Mervyn H. Sterne Library—space that had stored such items as Governor Wallace's fishing caps. Joe Volker's massive papers (171 cubic feet) immediately became the first project for curatorial process under the careful eyes of Jane Williams and later Timothy Pennycuff, who succeeded Fisher as director of the facility.[115]

In the midst of this continued internal growth and national acclaim, as well as serious tensions over UAB Walker College and UAB football, in November 1992 McCallum announced his plans to step down. He was sixty-seven; for two years the board had been waiving its age sixty-five retirement rule for those holding administrative positions so that McCallum could continue as president. For McCallum, however, six years was long enough at the helm, indeed it was double the national average for a presidential stint. And he had accomplished a lot. In addition to the more important qualitative developments, from a quantitative standpoint on his watch total enrollment had moved from 14,200 to 16,600; grants and contracts from $82 million to $130 million; physical plant from 6 million gross square feet to 7.5 million gross square feet, including the 1993 acquisition of the Central Bank Building across from Tidwell Hall on Twentieth Street to be a new administration building; total revenues from $498 million to $872 million; institutional endowment from $40 million to $90 million; annual economic impact on Birmingham from $634 million to $1,579 billion; and, despite state government, which cut higher education in Alabama to one of the lowest levels of funding per pupil in the nation, pay raises for faculty and staff averaging over 5 percent a year.[116]

On September 30, 1993, McCallum vacated the presidency to assume the role of Distinguished Professor of Dentistry. Shortly thereafter he had coronary bypass surgery. But soon he returned to patient care and teaching as well as fund-raising and urban activism in areas both old and new for him. He also chaired the Birmingham Metropolitan Development Board, headed up a record-setting fund drive for the United Way, led revitalization of the local symphony, and then—at age seventy-four—won election as a drafted "reform candidate" to be mayor of Vestavia Hills, the municipality south of Birmingham where his family had lived off and on for thirty years. In short, the maturing of McCallum bore an uncanny resemblance to that of his university. In both cases, the process of maturing did anything *but* preclude an enduring vigor—at least that is the way it seemed in the early 1990s.[117]

10

Reach for Maturity

The Bennett Years, 1993–96

Old Momentum with New People

In November 1992, shortly after Charles McCallum announced he would be leaving the presidency, Chancellor Philip Austin and the UA board initiated plans for a national search to select the fourth president of UAB. Some board sentiment favored an individual with no previous connection to UAB. Such a selection might assist the chancellor in bringing a more cohesive approach to UA system development and by definition, therefore, lessening the "sometimes strident sense of autonomy" of UAB. Whispers of this possible strategy energized old beliefs on the Birmingham campus regarding the board's "discontent," to use Wayne Flynt's word, about UAB's maturing as a full university.

Perhaps the most extreme response in this vein came from John Rogers, a UAB employee and member of the Alabama House of Representatives, who talked openly of the need for Alabama to consider making UAB a fully independent public institution, that is, making it the University of Birmingham just as Earl Hilliard and Rudy Davidson had advocated in the early 1980s.[1] Others inside UAB, such as Dick Hill and several of his corporate friends, began quiet inquiry about an inside candidate who, in their minds, "could protect UAB." One possibility was the current UAB vice president of health affairs, John Durant, a man of extensive administrative experience and of international reputation as a cancer physician. Yet these "insiders for an insider" found this option untenable because in recent years Durant had had to assume a conflict role with the board, and its new vice chancellor of financial affairs, Linda Flaherty-Goldsmith, who represented the board's desire for more influence over medical center finances. For this reason,

Durant—though an honest and brilliant man—likely would not be acceptable to the board.[2]

"Insiders for an insider" soon settled on Claude Bennett. All who knew Bennett recognized that he found administration distasteful and, indeed, at age fifty-eight had had no administrative role above the level of department chair in medicine—where he had used a senior executive officer, James Lewis, to manage most administrative affairs. Yet they also knew Bennett had a major reputation in medical education and research. Also, at least in Dick Hill's mind, Bennett came from the unit of the university "which always had formed the intellectual, leadership, power, and financial heart of the institution," the Department of Medicine, as this department often did in many universities with academic medical centers and especially those in which medical education, by design, had outdistanced arts and sciences in spurts of rapid growth. Bennett also had a reputation for being smart, for having eclectic intellectual interests, and for public speaking abilities "as smooth as Ronald Reagan's." Moreover, his 1980s memoranda to then president Dick Hill, reflecting an outmoded approach to undergraduate education and little knowledge of west-end campus developments, rested deeply in a file of the S. Richardson Hill Papers in the UAB Archives, undoubtedly long forgotten by both sender and receiver.[3]

In fact, virtually all nonmedical faculty who had had professional contact with Bennett, such as sociology chair Kenneth Wilson, viewed him as an intense advocate of interdisciplinary research and graduate programs between medicine, social science, and the humanities at UAB. For example, as a strong supporter of a social medicine program sponsored jointly by the Departments of Medicine and Sociology, in 1991 Bennett helped provide salary funds to bring William C. Cockerham, a noted medical sociologist, from the University of Illinois–Champaign to UAB.[4]

Bennett remained publicly coy about leaving the Department of Medicine for the presidency. As he told one UAB dean in a conversation at the Birmingham airport, he just was "not sure" if he ever could leave "real academia" for high-level administration, and he was enjoying his deep engagement in coediting the twentieth edition of *Cecil Textbook of Medicine*. Still, during the winter and spring of 1993 the momentum for his candidacy grew steadily among Birmingham leaders, on and off the campus, as well as within the mind of Chancellor Austin, who increasingly found Bennett's personality and credentials "so impressive."[5]

As the chancellor and several board members made clear, however, the national search during this time was turning up a relatively strong pool of candidates. Ultimately 150 individuals joined the search, including several with extensive administrative experience. In the end, besides Bennett, two of these made the "short list": Rita Colwell, a biologist and president of the Maryland Biotechnology Institute, well known not just as a leader in American science but for her marshaling the dramatic urban renewal of the harbor section of the city of Baltimore; and the physician Charles Putman, executive vice president of Duke University. By mid-July 1993, however, both of these external candidates had withdrawn. On July 20, with the UA board meeting in Birmingham's Hill University Center, Bennett emerged as the fourth president of the University of Alabama at Birmingham.[6]

Overall, reactions to the Bennett announcement seemed positive. The *Birmingham News* bannered Bennett as a "consensus builder." The *Birmingham Post Herald* emphasized that Bennett's appointment forecast the "steady" continuation of UAB folks leading UAB to an ever-expanding reputation in American higher education, though the paper also saw an ancillary issue.

> Most universities would have turned to an outsider [for] at least one in four presidents. Most university trustees would have felt compelled to, not necessarily because of a lack of qualified inside candidates, but because outside candidates clearly out-shined the home-grown ones. Some universities would deliberately have sought out a leader from outside the institution because they need the renewing vigor of new blood and new ideas. . . . Fortunately, UAB did not have the latter need. Although the rapid physical growth of its childhood and adolescence is behind it, the University remains a vibrant, forward-looking institution as it continues to adjust to its maturity.[7]

In short, the *Post Herald* assumed, as did many of the UAB family and a significant number of board members, that inside UAB there just had to be a continued strong pool of high-level talent to lead the institution—and that individual was Bennett. After all, because of the continuity of inside leadership, to recall Philip Austin's assertion, UAB had been on a trajectory of development virtually "unparalleled" in American higher education.[8]

A few dissented. Some, including UAB management professor George Munchus, could not document it but nevertheless viewed the outcome of the search—a search with no African Americans on the short list—as controlled by insiders and best described, in his words, as "plantation politics." Others, including some UAB female faculty and perhaps a female board member, believed that UAB and the UA system had missed an opportunity to bring "diversity" to high-profile leadership in Alabama. A strong female candidate, Colwell, had done well in the search up until she withdrew. Although her stated reasons for doing so related to how strong, ultimately, she felt about staying where she was, some questioned this explanation.[9]

Primed for such issues via the speechwriting abilities of Mike Ellis, Bennett set out to bring people together in his initial press conference directly following the announcement on July 20. With calm delivery, he pledged to be a president committed to "diversity." Sensitive to the point that some UAB faculty felt that the president need not necessarily be a physician—a point McCallum had emphasized in a well-publicized interview in December 1992—he also offered himself as a "consensus builder" and an advocate of "one campus," not an advocate for a "medical end and a nonmedical end." Moreover, though UAB's secession from the system and its formation as a University of Birmingham had little, if any, grounding in realpolitik, Bennett flatly declared, "Those who seek to distract us from that concept [of being in the UA system] I do not believe serve the university well." And on possibly the most pressing issue of all in the minds of some board members, he went on record with the not overwhelmingly precise statement about moving Blazer football up to the next level of Division I-A: he would not use state money to "build scholarship football."[10]

All present, with the exception of a few intense UAB football advocates among the student body, apparently felt the press conference went well. Interviewed immediately following the press conference, Kenneth J. Roozen, the vice president of research and university affairs, predicted, "I don't expect us to skip a beat." Retired board member and longtime supporter of UAB Tom Rast concurred: "He'll do fine."[11] So on these notes of continuity, diplomacy, and optimism, this internationally known medical scientist, this soft-spoken scholar considered by his friend from Episcopalian circles, UAB sociologist Mark LaGory, to be "smart but very complex," this first Alabama native to become president of UAB set out to continue the dynamism that so characterized the preceding twenty-four years of the institution's history.[12]

From the new president's suite on the tenth floor of the new Administration Building on Twentieth Street, Bennett set to work on wide-ranging issues. He moved quickly on a redecoration of the Woodward House, something that had not happened since the Hill family had moved in back in 1977—a project undoubtedly justified in that the home had been used regularly for professional entertainment of large crowds. Moreover, recalled Bennett, his wife, Nancy—a person with longtime allergy problems—was "not particularly keen on leaving their Mountain Brook home for the Wood-ward House" because of "dust and other things in the air" in the 1920s structure. Bennett hoped that "more than a full cleaning . . . new paint throughout, [and] new lighting" would make the place more suitable for his wife. With the project completed over the next nine months, Bennett and his wife moved into the home by April 1994, marking the event with an Episcopalian "blessing of the house" ceremony presided over by Nancy Bennett's close friend, John Claypool's associate priest at St. Luke's Episco-pal Church, Joy Phipps. Some twenty guests attended, most members of Claypool's congregation.[13]

Other first-year developments seemed to unfold under their own mo-mentum. With an unsolicited gift of $2 million from Jarvis Ryals—a Ft. Deposit, Alabama, native, a 1965 graduate of the UAB medical school, and a successful private practice neurologist and entrepreneur in Pueblo, Colorado—the new president presided over groundbreaking ceremonies for the new School of Public Health facility located in the middle of the cam-pus on University Boulevard.[14] He also managed ribbon-cutting ceremonies for the vastly enlarged Lister Hill Library for the Health Sciences. Thanks to hard lobbying, plus private fund-raising by Dick Hill and Wayne Finley, the library also included spacious new digs for the Reynolds Historical Li-brary. More indicative of how far the institution had matured since its early days, however, was unfolding news from the Carnegie Endowment for the Advancement of Education. In 1994, resulting out of a process several years in the works, Bennett found his institution classified as a Carnegie I Re-search University, the only institution of this type in Alabama. Its research peers now were the University of Pennsylvania, Duke University, and other older, more prestigious universities, an accomplishment in which Bennett the physician-scientist clearly had played a pivotal role over the previous quarter century.[15]

Finally, in January 1994, earlier momentum also consummated the UAB "annexation" of Walker College. By December 1996, UAB announced that Foster Watkins, an Alabama native well regarded for his presidency of Shorter College, in Georgia, would be taking leadership of Walker Col-lege. Nothing suggests that in dealings with the board and others Bennett advanced the larger political plan hatched by McCallum, that is, UAB's ac-quisition of Walker College as initiating a plan to reduce the number of two-year colleges in the state—a reduction plan that by the mid-1990s the two-year colleges were implementing on their own. Still, in Bennett's completion of the Walker College acquisition, he indeed offered the rationale of increased credit hour production and hence funding, initially advanced by McCallum. He also joined trustees Garry Neil Drummond and John Oliver of Jasper, not to mention Walker's chancellor, David Rowland, in explaining that Congress soon would be awarding significant freeway expansion funds for the Memphis to Atlanta connection, expansion destined to enhance the value of Walker College properties as well as the population in the area. This point garnered less than overwhelming acceptance by a majority of the board members and the chancellor. In coming years, however, predictions about freeway construction near Jasper showed every sign of being true.[16]

Decorations, ceremonies, major accolades, and carry-over momentum aside, early on of course Bennett also found himself involved in key personnel decisions. To the surprise of few, he named his longtime colleague Roozen to be executive vice president.[17] He also appointed Samuel W. Jackson, who had been serving as executive director of the Health Services Foundation (HSF), to the role of vice president of finance and administration, replacing John Walker—who had been holding the administration position—and Thomas C. Thrasher, who had done likewise with the finance slot. Jackson was an attorney, a CPA, and a former executive with Ernst and Young, with a specialization in health care finances. Still, his appointment elicited the same expressions of dissatisfaction among medical center leaders that Flaherty-Goldsmith's move to Tuscaloosa had created, with a slightly different twist. As if Bennett himself did not have basic knowledge of HSF money, one physician recalled, "This appointment placed a substantial knowledge of HSF financial matters, not in the hands of the board (as was the case with Flaherty-Goldsmith) but directly with the senior UAB administration." Others were just stunned; was Bennett making a 180-degree turn in his general university vision, planning infusions of more HSF funds into general university life?[18]

Despite this rumble in the background, Jackson swiftly established a corporate-style office, retaining some who had been with finance and administration for years as well as adding new blood. He hired a UAB student affairs officer and decorated Vietnam veteran, John Wesley Ault, to serve as associate vice president of business services. He hired a UAB health affairs finance officer, Mary Lee Rice, to serve as associate vice president of financial affairs. He hired the Harvard M.B.A. (and former press secretary to U.S. senator Edward M. Kennedy) Richard A. Berliner for the position of senior real estate officer—a key position for the ever-growing institution. He also hired the attorney Susan Barber, most recently at Birmingham's Children's Hospital, as associate vice president of human resource management.[19]

Likewise, Bennett moved swiftly to conclude a search for a new hospital director. In October 1993 he hired Kevin Lofton to be executive director of the hospital and associate vice president of health affairs. At thirty-eight years old, this African American native of Texas held an M.S. in hospital administration from Georgia State University and already was well experienced in the field; most recently he had been the executive director of Howard University Hospital in Washington, D.C. At the time of his hiring, he was the highest-paid executive (in terms of state money, not including HSF funds) on the campus.[20]

Within a year of his hiring, Lofton found himself immersed in the perennial debate over reporting lines for the chief of staff in the hospital: in early December 1994, Bennett issued a memorandum indicating a "medical center re-organization" in which Durwood Bradley, M.D., chief of staff, no longer would report up through the vice president of health affairs but, instead, directly to Lofton. Moreover, by altering such lines of responsibility associated with John Durant, Bennett essentially sent a signal to Durant that he might want to look around. Durant did, toward the National Cancer Institute in Washington, D.C., to which he moved in March 1995 as the executive director.[21] After prevailing upon his longtime colleague, Sergio Stagno, chair of pediatrics, to fill Durant's slot on an interim basis, Bennett entered into a national search and emerged with Michael Geheb, a physician/manager from SUNY–Buffalo, to replace Durant as UAB's key health affairs officer. Geheb had the augmented title of executive vice president, which Bennett spelled out as part of his medical center reorganization to include all clinical endeavors. Hence, in hiring Geheb, Bennett melded into one position the responsibility for what he now called the "UAB Health System," including oversight of University Hospital as well as the HSF, plus the Kirklin Clinic and any health insurance program UAB might develop. More than grumbling emanated from medical center faculty as they saw further diminishing of their semi-autonomy over clinical activity and the revenues it delivered.[22]

Other developments of 1995 caused less strain between Bennett and medical school faculty. In October, T. Scott Plutchak, a Wisconsin native with degrees in both philosophy and library informatics (plus significant credentials as a country music singer) and most recently of St. Louis University, took over as director of the rapidly expanded Lister Hill Library for the Health Sciences. Then there were crucial matters inside the School of Medicine. William Dismukes assumed the position of chair of the Department of Medicine, replacing Bennett on an acting basis while a national search unfolded. By 1995, the search delivered the name of William J. Koopman, the Harvard-trained rheumatologist whom Bennett had been mentoring at UAB since the late 1970s. Bennett warmly endorsed Dean Fallon's naming Koopman as the seventh chair of the Department of Medicine. By April 1997, however, Fallon himself retired, and Associate Dean William B. Deal took that position on an interim basis while another search unfolded.[23]

Strategic Planning Initiated

On to broader matters, through a set of formal strategic planning discussions beginning in January 1995 and orchestrated by the Kaludis Consulting Group, out of Nashville, Bennett met with vice presidents, deans, center directors, and ultimately many others to reach deep into UAB's institutional life. He looked for ways to move the institution, in his words, "to the next level . . . a university recognized across the board as a national level university . . . one university (not two ends of a campus) with national reputation." Clearly, Bennett had on his mind an institutional identity not of "youthful vigor" but of "maturity" and "one with Nobel laureates." In comments before the downtown Kiwanis Club of Birmingham, Bennett distilled more of his vision behind the meetings. He hoped a strategic plan could deal with the problem of too many resources being committed to the instruction of underprepared undergraduate students and not enough funds to making UAB an institution of choice for more outstanding undergraduates. He wanted to deal with deferred maintenance problems in the physical plant, exacerbated by the state's reluctance to develop public policy to assist with capital needs. He believed UAB needed to convert funds committed to research into marketable biotech products that could produce new revenues for the institution. He saw a "very stormy" health care industry, characterized at least on the surface by an oversupply of hospital beds, not enough general doctors, and too many specialists. He also saw an academic culture in which faculty are slow to change even though "the world they're living in is going to change rapidly."[24]

As memoranda of blueprints for strategic planning sessions began to emanate from the tenth floor of the Administration Building, both negative and positive reactions arose and from opposite poles. Some quietly wondered why the goal of "one university" when there had been just this, one university, for a long time.[25] Others of nonmedical programs, however, seemed excited about Bennett's concept as they—often ignoring crucial state funding problems—had watched development of health science programs far outstrip those in such areas as arts and sciences, business, and engineering.[26] On the other hand, many health science faculty grew even more nervous about the "one university" notion, remaining perplexed as it came from one of their own: What sources of money would be used to increase development of nonmedical programs, transfers from health affairs? If so, how could internal transfers be increased at a time when UAB's medical center, much like all others in the nation, was struggling with lower Medicaid/Medicare reimbursements while the costs of new medical technologies were shooting up, the health insurance industry was in chaos, and physicians wanted their salaries going up, not down?[27] Then there were medical center faculty who wondered about something broader—Bennett's general view of UAB. Had the recent ranking of UAB as a Carnegie I Research University, combined with his elevation to far larger administrative responsibilities than he had ever known, radically altered Bennett's view of UAB? If so, the transformation was as striking as Hugo Black's reversal on race (Black had once been in the KKK) upon arrival at the high post of U.S. Supreme Court Justice. As he reflected on all this and on his friend in the president's office, sociologist LaGory mused, "It's all very complex."[28]

Strategic planning did indeed unfold, however. On increased student standards, Bennett took a noteworthy approach. With Roozen, he expanded the number of students in the undergraduate honors program (from thirty-three to forty-four per class), long a magnet for high-end students from around the region. Roozen also worked through Ada Long, director of the honors program, to encourage departments engaged in undergraduate education to develop departmental honors tracks, hoping for the same effect on a broader scale.[29]

If the expansion of opportunities for more outstanding students seemed uncontroversial, the stated mission of UAB as an interdisciplinary *urban* research university became a topic of intense university-wide debate. Few on campus rejected the notion that a university could be engaged in urban outreach regardless of how *urban* found expression in the institution's mission statement. Questions arose, however, over whether *urban* should be emphasized sufficiently to appear in UAB's mission statement. History complicated matters. Since the publication of the first UAB catalog in 1967–68, under Volker's leadership, "urban university" had figured prominently into UAB's statement of mission. And for some faculty who felt strongly about keeping *urban* in the statement, chiefly faculty in academic affairs but also in public health, nursing, and optometry, overt inclusion of *urban* (or a proposed substitute, *metropolitan*) represented a crucial component of UAB's identity and what it badly needed to do for Birmingham and for all of Alabama, a state sadly lacking in numbers of college-educated citizens.[30] To others, however, primarily scientists and others in health affairs, *urban* had the ring of "substandard": the goal should be Harvard, Penn, Berkeley, and other institutions known for high-level doctoral education and exceptionally strong undergraduate students, certainly the "counterpoint to 'urban university,' which identifies us with weak students and a faculty with only teaching and service duties." This was an odd perspective when put in broad context. At the time of this debate in Birmingham in the mid-1990s, and in continuing response to two high-impact books—*Universities and the Future of America* (1990), by Harvard's Derek Bok, and *Scholarship Reconsidered* (1990), by Ernest L. Boyer of the Carnegie Foundation—none other than Harvard, Penn, and Berkeley were feverishly advancing more urban research service in Boston, Philadelphia, and the Bay area of California, respectively. Even more feverish about including *urban* in their institutional outreach were revered old land grants such as the universities of Michigan, Texas, and Missouri, as well as Auburn University. They saw urban affairs as their key new frontier of outreach. It should be noted, however, that none of these traditional institutions, whether private or public, began to call itself an "urban university."[31] Still, for others in UAB health affairs, *urban* raised the specter of all-too-familiar internal monetary issues. As J. Russell Lindsey in comparative medicine wrote Bennett,

> On the issue of UAB's role in solving problems of the urban community, I am fully supportive. . . . [However,] we cannot afford to bleed the Medical Center of funds to build up the west campus as a major center of urban problem solving, as laudatory as that may be (this is also the view of the majority of Medical Center faculty). . . . Thus, my greatest fear (and the fear of most Medical Center faculty) all along, that the Medical Center would foot the bill for "The Great Urban University" concept, now seems to be coming true. I believe that the UAB should definitely be very involved in solving the problems of the urban community, but *not* at the expense of [the] Medical Center.[32]

With this complicated dialogue still underway Bennett took his first step into applied urban activism. He helped lead the creation of the

Birmingham Area Committee on Higher Education (BACHE), a consortium of five baccalaureate-level institutions in the Birmingham area—UAB,
Birmingham-Southern College, Samford University, Miles College, and the
University of Montevallo—dedicated to "cross-serving" students of all the
institutions, plus increased exchange of information, to whatever purpose
it might result, among area faculty and administration. Ultimately modeled on Five Colleges, Inc., in the Holyoke-Amherst, Massachusetts, area,
UAB and a grant from the Greater Birmingham Foundation provided initial funds for BACHE with annual dues from member institutions soon providing the budget. Longtime UAB history professor and Birmingham native
Margaret E. Armbrester, most recently named curator of the Samuel Ullman
Museum, assumed duties as BACHE's first executive director.[33]

Soon, however, James Lewis (somewhere along the line his title changed
to executive assistant to the president) engaged in a flurry of faxes with several deans, assessing the ways other urban universities in the nation with
medical centers presented their mission statements. With that information, Bennett authorized a slightly altered statement for the next (1997)
UAB catalog: "UAB is an urban research university with an academic health
center complex." *Urban* stayed. Likewise, Bennett announced in the *UAB
Report* in February 1995 the following: "We have expended much institutional energy considering the question of whether UAB is an 'urban university' or a university in an urban setting, and trying to understand the implication of each possibility. The fact is, UAB is—and must be—both; we have
a blended mission. We must be both 'in' and 'of' Birmingham."[34] Leaders
in the Urban 13, at such institutions as Wayne State University and the University of Pittsburgh, who had been viewing the inner UAB debate about
"being urban" as something "incredulous," breathed easier over not losing
one of their strongest peer institutions. Closer to home, after temporary
sputtering, the momentum and complex vision for education, research,
and service evolved first by Roy Kracke, Joseph Volker, George Campbell,
and Dick Hill, and most recently by Charles McCallum and James Woodward, moved forward again.[35]

Academic administrative organization also came under the scrutiny
of strategic planning. In the name of "one university" as well as foster-
ing a more change-oriented faculty, Bennett eliminated the basic roles
of vice president of academic affairs and vice president of health affairs
(offices first created by Volker and continued—with tweaks—up through
McCallum) and created in their place the new position of provost, that is,
chief academic officer, to which all twelve academic schools (medical and

nonmedical) plus the two libraries would report. In the summer of 1995, he placed in this new position his executive vice president, Kenneth J. Roozen.[36]

In the new organization, Roozen then not only had the augmented title of provost and executive vice president, but continued his longtime role as director of the Research Foundation *and* as vice president for research. In effect, with Geheb presiding over all things clinical (and his title revamped to "director") Roozen managed the daily administrative affairs of the university, including the academic component of the medical center. In a university as complex as UAB with its medical center, even with the strong administrative talents of Roxie Speed, Roozen's assistant in this new role, Roozen's job description represented one heavy workload. Indeed, as Roozen told the *Birmingham News* after being quizzed on why his salary was so high, "There probably isn't a job comparable to it in the United States."[37]

Such organizational overhaul had domino effects in the university. William A. Sibley, who had been serving since 1991 as academic vice president, went on leave to the National Science Foundation (NSF). Bennett advised two proven vice presidents, Virginia Gauld in student affairs and John Lyons in institutional planning and services, that they now would be reporting to Roozen, not to the president as they had before.[38] Roozen asked Joan Lorden to remain as dean of the Graduate School and assume the additional role of associate provost of research. Terry L. Hickey assumed the role of associate provost of undergraduate programs, which included management of UAB special studies (continuing education).[39] Shortly reorganized as UAB Options, Hickey's changes included decentralization of "for credit" overload faculty teaching into primary academic units. And so the Bennett-Roozen changes rapidly unfolded. And there was more.[40]

Louis Dale, the African American mathematician now with a national reputation for NSF grants encouraging more minorities to enter careers in mathematics and science, became associate provost of minority affairs. Fred Brooke Lee departed the University of Maryland to take the newly created position of vice president of development at UAB, with promises of significant increase in the development budget to hire at least four new development officers. Dorothy Mueller, who first entered faculty ranks in 1965 associated with what would become the Lister Hill Library for the Health Sciences, and who had spent the previous twenty years working in a variety of administrative positions in research and faculty administration as well as being the mainstay behind the *UAB Faculty Handbook*, became assistant provost of faculty affairs. Melanie Markle and Margaret Coshat, respectively, took on fiscal and personnel matters for Roozen.[41] There was still more.

On Dale Williams's leaving the public health dean position to return to faculty life, Eli Capiluoto—who had departed UAB's School of Dentistry Faculty to earn a doctorate in public health at Harvard, then returned to UAB with an appointment in his new field—moved up from chair of the Department of Health Care Organization and Management to be acting dean of the School of Public Health. An extended national search ultimately delivered Capiluoto as the dean, just in time for him to preside over the construction of a new public health building on University Boulevard.[42] In addition, Arol Augsburger came from Ohio State University to succeed retiring Bradford W. Wild as dean of optometry, and shortly thereafter the new dean changed the name of his building from the none too prosaic School of Optometry Building to the Henry B. Peters Building, signifying a new leadership fully apprised of his school's dynamic (and politically active) past reinforced by the continued work of John Amos, as associate dean, who had worked closely with Peters and Wild since the mid-1970s. Harry Marzette, a Birmingham native with over thirty years on the New York City Police Department and recently appointed as UAB's deputy chief under retiring Patrick Murphy, moved up to the chief of police position. After trading police uniform for corporate pinstripes and emphasizing college education for all of his officers, Marzette upgraded UAB's force to be one of only twelve departments among U.S. universities accredited by the Commission on Accreditation of Law Enforcement Agencies (CALEA).[43]

Considerable discussion in strategic planning meetings revolved around finances related to greater development of west end (nonmedical) programs. In 1987 President McCallum and Vice President Woodward had worked hard to assist Sterne Library director Jerry W. Stephens in his statewide leadership regarding the Network of Alabama Academic Libraries (NAAL), a consortium approach to increasing state funds for library development. In 1992, McCallum also made a one-time allocation of $2.2 million for sophisticated computerization of Sterne Library. More focused on the library's acquisition budget per se, Provost Roozen raised the recurring allocation for Sterne Library by $150,000 annually, the first base increase the library had received in ten years. Even after the Roozen increase, however, Sterne Library's budget remained at the bottom (thirty out of thirty-four) among budgets of the Association of Southeastern Research Libraries—a ranking it would continue to have for years to come.[44] Likewise, the higher education–friendly governor, James E. Folsom, Jr., aided west end programs with three years of significant increases, virtually all of which went to salaries. But these were followed by the devastating 1995–96 proration cut of 7.5 percent levied by returning governor Fob James, increasingly known for his higher education philosophy of "just run it like a Waffle House."[45]

In this context, the strategic planning process concluded that some version of Responsibility Centered Management (RCM), recently offered as the gospel for higher education in Edward D. Whalen's *Responsibility Centered Management* (1991), was the key for nonmedical programs. Such decentralization had made the medical center succeed, went the mantra of the planning meetings, and it could do the same in other areas of the university. The Economic Rules Committee of the strategic planning effort began a protracted, and complex, discourse on implementing some form of RCM, but never reached a clear conclusion.[46]

Faculty Developments

In 1996, upon Jay Goldman's stepping down as engineering dean, Bennett and Roozen hired Stephen Szygenda from Texas A&M; on Gene Newport's retirement as business dean the same year, they hired Albert Neimi from the University of Georgia. The new deans had outstanding credentials as scholars and administrators. But they required not just high salaries but significant new programmatic money.[47] Corporate leaders of Birmingham, noted Bennett, strongly recommended that such development through reallocation represented the appropriate future for nonmedical education at UAB. This elicited months of grumbling among arts and sciences faculty, who wondered if *nonprofessional* (arts and sciences) education at UAB ever would be considered a genuine priority among Birmingham's civic elite, not to mention UAB leadership, the way it was at other major universities.[48] Grumbling also emanated from medical faculty who assumed that at least some of the new funds had to have been derived from health affairs revenues, which was no doubt true.[49] Roozen showed every awareness that such actions were of concern for a significant spectrum of faculty (Roozen: "I'm probably a short-timer here"). In a reflective moment with one dean, he explained that the president had charged him with modernizing "the institution and some people did not understand that this required consistently swift and often unpopular actions." Still, such honest responses on his part evoked a third wave of dissent. From both ends of the campus came the question: From a structural standpoint, did Bennett's creation of the provost position centralize too much power, responsibility, and workload in one office, that is, was UAB too complex to have one provost? Although a decade later Bennett would recall, "I tried to move too much too fast," at the time the president and the provost remained resolute that the structure was right for the major changes needed.[50]

Indeed, Bennett stayed focused on melding even more of the university into a cohesive whole, including faculty governance. Since the early 1970s the Faculty Senate had consisted of representatives from the six nonmedical units and had reported in an advisory capacity to the vice president for those programs. With that vice president no longer existing, however, and, more important, with many nonmedical faculty viewing some of their concerns as university wide, not academic affairs wide, Bennett responded positively to a report of the ad hoc Committee on Faculty Governance that urged that the senate's representation derive from all faculty units, including those of the health sciences.

No faculty member played a greater role in this transition than senate president LaGory, who first pitched the idea to Bennett in a conversation in the parking lot of St. Luke's Episcopal Church. Throughout 1994–95 LaGory and the committee worked with minority opposition to the change emanating from both "ends of the campus." Some nonmedical faculty feared they would be subordinated in such a transition because of the far larger number of health science faculty; on the other hand, some health science faculty viewed their school-level governance system more than ample and were not interested in anything that would pull the campus closer together. In the end, however, the change occurred. The key was giving all academic units appropriate representation—generally based on numbers of faculty—and having the senate executive committee meeting regularly with the president as well as the provost and the deans' council, where discussions on crucial issues ranged from salaries and state politics to health insurance and plans for campus expansion.[51]

Other aspects of faculty life, however, seemed stymied as a result of what repeatedly were called "Fob Cuts." With UAB salaries, much like those of university faculty statewide, slipping further and further behind the going rate at peer institutions, some faculty just left. For example, as a senior-level professor in public administration, chair of the Department of Government and Public Service, and president of the National Association for Schools of Public Administration, Mary E. Guy easily accepted Florida State's offer of an endowed eminent-scholar position rather than remain in a state where the governor used "the Waffle House" as the best model for managing higher education.[52]

There were other frustrating developments. Bennett approved Roozen's plan to expand the Comprehensive Minority Faculty Development Program (CMFDP) with a new component—several *new* faculty lines a year—but the badly needed change only stayed in effect for one year, after which it fell victim to "Fob Cuts."[53] Fair-minded faculty could not blame the institution's leadership for this failure. Another effort to enhance the role of minority faculty at the institution fared even less well. In his opening remarks as president, Bennett had emphasized how strongly he felt about increasing "diversity" on the campus; during the first two years of his presidency he urged to various faculty groups that "if you will identify highly regarded, senior-level African American faculty who will help you get a national reputation, I'll find you the money to make the hire." Chairs and deans jumped at the chance to do so. They identified several such candidates and in at least one case brought the distinguished scholar to the campus and the community for extensive interviews. Thereafter, however, chairs and deans confronted continual obfuscation about commitments of new money, placing the university in embarrassing positions with several internationally acclaimed African American scholars.[54]

New faculty did arrive, however, and diversity slowly increased. Some appeared in the health sciences where federal monies and clinical revenues facilitated new positions. Others, beyond health affairs, mainly were replacements of retired or resigned faculty, slots that managed to survive "Fob Cuts." During the Bennett presidency, some 160 faculty hires occurred in the medical center and about 45 in what many continued to call "academic affairs." Several of the new hires were African American, which increased the number of African American faculty during the Bennett presidency from 3.4 percent to 4.0 percent.[55]

Still, if these new faculty happened to be in programs significantly influenced by state policies and funding (as opposed to clinical and research endeavors associated with NIH and NSF funding), they arrived at a time ranging in perception from "acute flux" to "ineffectiveness." For example, in February 1994, the Alabama state legislature, under the strong influence of two-year colleges, passed legislation signed by Governor Folsom that forced standardization of essentially the first two years of college at all public institutions in Alabama, with an Articulation and General Studies Committee (AGSC) stacked to ensure that two-year colleges controlled what this curriculum would be.[56] From one perspective, here was the realization of something Vice President Woodward had warned about throughout his leadership at UAB: for reasons related to efficient use of public funds as well as sensitivity to student needs, four-year institutions needed to take a positive approach to transferability issues as they developed their undergraduate curricula. UAB had a long track record for such positive action (even including two-year college faculty on its own core curriculum committees), while other institutions that received few two-year college transfers, such as AU and UA, basically did not. This gave two-year college leaders significant ammunition in lobbying curriculum standardization through the Alabama legislature. From another perspective, however, this reform eliminated much of the uniqueness of many undergraduate programs in the state, reducing the choices for types of education that Alabama citizens might pursue.[57]

Then there was the relatively undebatable realpolitik regarding the AGSC changes and faculty salaries. Curriculum standardization brought more students into two-year colleges and thus more money for faculty salaries to those colleges. Increasing enrollment at two-year colleges also was a function of funding formulae: two-year college tuition and fees were lower than those of four-year colleges because such colleges, due in part to their severe clout in the legislature, were funded by the state at a higher level per pupil than were four-year colleges. Once again, more money for two-year faculty salaries. Finally, by the mid-1990s the two-year college system, as *Birmingham News* writer Thomas Spencer has shown, was eliminating administrative positions, combining programs, and eliminating some of its colleges. Still, if the freed-up funds could be reallocated to increase faculty salaries, in some cases the money also found its way into funding curricula well beyond standard two-year college offerings—courses normally associated with junior and senior years at public universities: "unnecessary duplication." In short, a virtually omnipotent two-year college lobby in the legislature, connected to the influence of the Alabama Education Association (AEA), hardly could escape notice behind most of these developments. In September 1996 Samuel Webb, a UAB historian and one intimately familiar with the political machinations in Montgomery (he had served as an assistant attorney general in the 1970s under Attorney General William Baxley), explained the consequences: "I have two doctorates, a J.D. and a Ph.D., plus seven years of college teaching experience and ten years of legal experience, plus I am a published scholar in political and legal history. But one of my M.A. students upon graduation, and with no teaching experience, can go to an Alabama two-year college and start at a higher salary than I am making right now. I teach here [at UAB] because I love it, certainly not for the money—though the salary situation Montgomery has given us is grossly unfair, an embarrassment for the state."[58]

Such relatively weak funding of four-year institutions manifested itself in other ways. Out of fiscal shortages, the School of Health Related Professions discontinued all certificate programs. Likewise, the School of Arts and Humanities discontinued the B.A.-level major in dance and the B.A.-level major in German.[59] Although the Alabama Commission on Higher Education (ACHE) deemed these changes suitable, other citizens saw such changes as cause for even more worry about *high-quality* university opportunities for Alabamians. Most striking, however, were related developments in UAB's Schools of Nursing and Dentistry.

Between 1993 and 1996 School of Nursing faculty at UAB declined from eighty-one to sixty-three.[60] Beneath these statistics one could see the Waffle House strategy for managing Alabama higher education exacerbated by complicated national-level supply-demand dynamics. During the final decades of the twentieth century, demands for nurses of virtually all types increased across America and, for that matter, all over the world as people lived longer as a result of wide-ranging new medical technologies and drugs, as well as preventive medicine. More people, especially of the World War II "baby boomer" generation, began to move into "old age," which dramatically increased the demand for nurses. At the same time, with more professions now open to women (for example, in science, architecture, law, and high-level corporate management, as a result of the persisting reform sentiment of the 1960s), percentage-wise far fewer women entered the profession of nursing—a profession, along with K–12 teaching, once the bittersweet domain of women. Such relative drops in women entering the field of nursing were not accompanied by commensurate increases in male nurses to fill in the gap. As might be expected, with supply and demand so out of balance, at the national level salaries for nurses, particularly nursing educators, increased significantly. On top of this, during the same period the U.S. government phased out massive federal assistance to major university nursing programs, such as UAB's, which for some twenty-five years had bolstered nursing faculty salaries so that at least some nurses would stay in higher education instead of heading off into the even more lucrative private hospital practice.[61]

For nursing dean Rachel Booth, local factors brought these broad dynamics to a virtual breaking point. Gross fluctuations in state funding further reduced the resources she had to offer competitive faculty salaries. Simultaneously, two-year colleges in Alabama, which had long been involved in nursing education, expanded such programs as their clout in the legislature associated with the AEA union gave them steady budget increases not only to hire nursing faculty but to expand undergraduate programs in nursing. In short, with fewer Alabama-based nursing students wanting to attend UAB, where tuition and fees were not defrayed at the level they were in two-year colleges, Booth's enrollment and therefore income declined. At the same time, however, her costs skyrocketed as a result of the national escalation of nursing faculty salaries. Her "only option," therefore, "was to use significant monies derived from resignations and retirements and, instead of hiring more faculty, plow the freed-up funds into existing salaries." "Under these circumstances," she recalled, "not only did [her] faculty size shrink but, accordingly, [her] ability to offer programs did, too," which of course further exacerbated enrollment, tuition, and fee problems. Here was "an utterly dysfunctional fiscal situation." Although at UAB Alabamians had "a nursing program ranked among the top fifteen [out of five hundred] in the U.S." by the prestigious *Nursing Educator* magazine, certainly here was a ranking that could not be maintained for long unless systemic policy changes occurred at the state level.[62]

The School of Dentistry had similar difficulties. Between 1993 and 1996, the number of full-time UAB faculty plummeted from ninety to sixty-three.[63] Dean Victor J. Matukas confronted national dynamics similar to what Booth was encountering. Beginning in the early 1980s, U.S. population expansion accompanied by new standards for preventive health care in dentistry, breakthroughs in new materials for reconstructive oral surgery, and a strong new emphasis on extending appropriate dental care to large pockets of poverty-stricken areas in both rural and urban America all combined to significantly increase the demand as well as salaries for dentists in private practice. This created a problem for the recruitment of dental faculty because state funds for salaries in Alabama stayed well below the national rate and were not competitive with private practice salaries. Not only did Matukas find it hard to hire, but he had faculty leaving to enter private practice.[64]

Ultimately, Matukas felt forced to follow the same strategy as Booth's but in a more extreme fashion. As department chairs in dentistry left UAB, he appointed interims from existing faculty and plowed whatever monies that could be saved into salary increases for existing faculty with hopes that they would not leave, too. Moreover, the additional burden of proration of UAB's state appropriations in the mid-1990s forced Matukas to eliminate two programs of significant need in the national efforts to improve dental elements of public health—the Dental Assisting Program and the Dental Hygiene Program. Matukas also eliminated several faculty positions through an early retirement program. By 1997, when Matukas himself retired, several of the research faculty in dentistry had left the school for other positions. Altogether, by 1997, the School of Dentistry, which long had held the reputation as one of the most internationally acclaimed academic units of UAB, found itself in a compromised condition because of reduced state funding and loss of faculty.[65]

Despite continued external problems associated with state funding, programmatic development in the mid-1990s at times reflected victories at UAB. The academic minor in African American studies received increased funding and programmatic development under the leadership of the literature professor Virginia Whatley Smith.[66] Out of local private donations, the Stephens Center for the Performing Arts officially opened. In virtually all other cases of expansion, however, the continued flow of federal health science dollars for the competitive investigator provided the key to growth. With such funding new endeavors found ACHE and board approval: the Department of Neurobiology, the master's degree in basic medical science, the baccalaureate-level major in respiratory therapy, the doctorate in environmental health engineering, and the doctoral program in medical sociology—a joint offering of the departments of Sociology and Medicine (housed in sociology) in which Bennett first as department chair in medicine and later as president played a crucial leadership role.[67]

Likewise, new interdisciplinary centers, normally funded with federal research dollars, came on line: the Center for Health Promotion and Disease Prevention; the Center for Industrial and Applied Research/Genesis Center; the Specialized Caries Research Center; the Cell Adhesion and Matrix Research Center; the Center for Educational Accountability; the Comprehensive Sickle Cell Center; and the Center for Social Medicine and Sexually Transmitted Diseases. And there was more: the Osteoporosis and Treatment Center; the Center for Metabolic Bone Disease; the Comprehensive Stroke Research Center; and the Center for Radical Free Cell Biology—title to the contrary, a science endeavor not connected to any brand of politics. At the department level appeared new names for existing programs reflecting new advances in knowledge: the Department of Maternal and Child Health in the School of Public Health, and the Department of Leadership, Special

Education, and Foundations in the School of Education. The Department of Biochemistry and Molecular Genetics appeared in the joint health sciences, and the Department of Emergency Medicine emerged in the School of Medicine. Also, there was preliminary development of a massive center for human genetics (to bear the name of philanthropist Hugh Kaul), which, on completion, ushered in UAB's expanded move into the revolutionary era of the human genome.[68]

Not surprisingly, with such programmatic growth involving both research and clinical care, extramural funding continued to grow throughout the Bennett presidency: $150 million in 1993 to $200 million in 1996. Usually originating out of NIH and NSF grants, projects contributing to this growth certainly included awards such as Albert LoBuglio's $4.1 million for cancer research, Robert E. Pitt's $566,000 for civil engineering research, Joyce N. Giger's $750,000 for nursing research, William Koopman's $20 million (over nine years) for rheumatoid arthritis therapies, and Craig and Sharon Ramey's $5 million for developmental psychology research. To the *Birmingham News* writer Betsy Butgereit, Provost Roozen held forth: "In 1954, [our] fledgling university had about $240,000 in research grants. . . . In 1985 . . . we were at $60 million . . . [and] in 1990 . . . at $100 million. Now, we're over $200 million. We continue to double every five to six years."[69]

Perhaps more useful, if only because it derived from an "outside" source, just as Roozen was touting the continued growth of UAB as a research institution, two analysts in no way associated with UAB—Hugh Davis Graham (a historian at Vanderbilt) and Nancy Diamond (a Goucher College specialist on public policy)—completed *The Rise of American Research Universities* (1997), in which they offered these sweeping yet documented conclusions about UAB:

> The final entrant in the Research 1 group not to have been included in the 1987 Carnegie Research 1 category [but included in 1994], Alabama-Birmingham [UAB], represents . . . a postwar urban strategy designed to compensate for a nineteenth century bias against establishing major state universities in cities. In this familiar scenario, a state's historical flagship campus [UA], secluded in a university town to shield students from the sins of the city, is too distant from the state's major urban center(s) to satisfy metropolitan leaders. . . . In no other American state has a new urban campus of the state university so surpassed the traditional flagship as a research university.[70]

If this was heady stuff, as in any university, UAB research also could experience its share of unfortunate controversies. For example, there was the
case of physician Jian-Yun Dong, who left UAB in 1994 after two of his
female employees said he forced them to have sex with him. There also
was the high-profile accusation by Pamela A. Berge, an epidemiologist with
Pfizer, who urged that UAB pediatricians Sergio Stagno, Robert Pass, Charles
Alford, and Karen Fowler unethically used data on transmission of a virus
from a mother to a child that Berge had employed in her Cornell University
dissertation. After a lower court decision held the UAB investigators guilty
and ordered the payment of $1.9 million in damages, the U.S. Supreme
Court ruled in favor of the UAB defendants. They were innocent on the
grounds that *they* had provided Berge tapes of *their* data to assist her with
her dissertation and hence had every right to use the data themselves.[71]

More Student Life, More Sporting Life

With the exception of the expansion of the undergraduate honors program,
a gift of $2 million to reconstruct the Honors House made by William and
Virginia Spencer, and the establishment of the Academic Programs Council to increase communication among vice presidents, deans, and student
life staff, UAB's undergraduate academics had a relatively low profile in the
mid-1990s. Enrollment remained steady at about 10,500.[72] On the other
hand, under Vice President Gauld's leadership, the number of "traditional"
students for the first time began to make up an increasingly greater percentage of the student body: from 60 percent full-time students in 1992 (about
the same percentage since the early 1970s), to 61 percent in 1994, to 65 percent in 1994, to 66 percent in 1995, and to 67 percent in 1996. Still, many
of UAB's undergraduates, much like their counterparts at Pittsburgh, Virginia Commonwealth University, or the University of New Orleans, continued to be employed either full or part time *despite* their attending college
increasingly on a full-time basis. In 1995, for example, 68 percent of undergraduates were enrolled full time; 60 percent of them were also working.
For financial reasons, many of these students from time to time reached a
breaking point and either dropped out or at least "stopped out," a crucial
factor in comparing retention rates under 40 percent with higher retention
rates among nonurban universities, not to mention small liberal arts colleges. Yet here was a powerful comment on the seriousness of urban university students as well as the compelling societal need met by urban univer-

sities in general—and a reason why commencement each year at UAB was such a genuine, heartfelt celebration.[73]

With this maturing of the institution also came complexity and greater diversity, as well as more moments of stress. In tune with national patterns, the percentage of women enrolled in UAB increased from 54 percent in 1992 to 55 percent in 1996. Much like virtually any university of the late twentieth century, moreover, poignant moments emerged out of a society still not certain about the revolution in sexual identification and values spawned, most recently, out of the 1960s. For example, a male teaching fellow departed UAB following multiple accusations of sexual harassment by female students. The UAB Gay-Lesbian Bisexual Pride Alliance, a continuation of the Gay-Lesbian Student Union begun in 1990, held a fulsome rally in nearby Rushton Park, protesting discrimination. UAB police removed a female undergraduate from the campus for repeatedly stalking a male professor, ignoring serious warnings, then attempting a right cross to the face of a vice president.[74]

None of these student life issues involving sexual identity caught the eye of the press, however, as much as the showing of one particular film. When student affairs leader Andrew Marsh signed off on students showing on campus the recently released film *Showgirls* as part of a film series designed by students for students, though the film had been deemed inappropriate for showing in theaters around the city, a few state politicians led by Senator Bill Armistead, formerly Governor Hunt's chief economic advisor, clamored about the moral decline of university life. Yet these attacks left unaddressed Marsh's positions that (a) universities within reason are places for freedom of thought and expression; (b) "no students were required to see the film"; (c) a small portion of UAB students attended the showing; and (d) a group of university personnel and community leaders, including a minister, had approved the showing of the film. When the *Birmingham Post Herald* columnist Elaine Witt discovered that Armistead, too, was among those who had never seen the film, she could not hold back: Armistead's critique represented "drive-by shootings into ivory towers . . . good political sport."[75]

Student life under Bennett also reflected trends and issues unique to UAB. As for ethnicity, the African American portion of total enrollment grew from 17 percent in 1992 to 21 percent in 1996, certainly unique among Carnegie I Research Universities and indicative of a UAB trend bound for growth in coming years. Although this trend was overwhelmingly positive from the perspective of campus diversity, occasionally it could reflect ethnic block-voting in undergraduate student government elections. The percentage of Hispanics increased from just under .5 percent in 1992 to slightly over .9 percent in 1996, small numbers by national standards and virtually infinitesimal by Southwestern standards. Nevertheless, this upward trend forecast general increases in Hispanic students just over the horizon as Hispanics flooded into Southeastern states at the turn of the century, creating, in Raymond Mohl's words, a "Nuevo New South." Likewise, measured against national standards, Asian students made up a small, if growing, percentage of UAB enrollment: from 1.4 percent in 1992 to 2.7 percent in 1996.[76]

UAB athletics also continued to be unique or developmental compared to standard higher education profiles, which often was partly a result of lack of space—something with which old land grant institutions had fewer problems. Here one could find both excitement and tension. In tune with the still subterranean vigor of serving more traditional students, for example, UAB looked for ways to expand intramural softball facilities. In reaction to its efforts to develop a facility in Betty Estelle Park, near the Glen Iris neighborhood southwest of the campus, strong neighborhood responses echoed the old objection: Would UAB "eat the city" it sought to serve? With the careful diplomacy of Mayor Richard Arrington, UAB ultimately turned to another city park, George Ward Park (located a mile west of the campus), for both intramural softball and, over time, an excellent NCAA women's softball team.[77] On more minds within the UAB community and indeed among the citizenry beyond the campus, however, were the two men's intercollegiate sports programs of football and basketball. Although both, it was anticipated, could bring the institution more traditional students because of Alabama's intensely legitimating sports culture, each had its own points of stress.

In August 1994, still with much of the momentum of the previous administration behind him, Bennett held a press conference in the UAB Arena to announce that UAB football would be moving up to Division I-A for the 1996 season. "We live in an environment where college athletics is . . . very important," and regarding the "one university" theme, "[athletics] is one of the things that provides the glue that holds the educational institution together." There also was the urban theme: "I believe in the spirit and personal commitment to Birmingham . . . [and] I am willing to take this risk because we are the University of Alabama *at Birmingham,* and we're in this city to stay."[78]

Considerable machination preceded this announcement, and considerable machination followed it. The team under Jim Hilyer's coaching had had some success despite serious obstacles (e.g., intramural football at times having first priority over the practice field and players buying their own pregame meals). Perhaps more important, with the aid of Hilyer and assistant coach Larry Crowe, Bartow had convinced Bennett and Roozen that significant home crowds and television opportunities, the keys to football finances (besides winning), would follow such an escalation because of the quality of teams the Blazers would be playing. Bartow admitted that so far UAB football was not breaking even, but it would if it were playing fewer teams of the caliber of, for example, Butler University and Morehead State University, and more teams like Nebraska, Tennessee, Missouri, and Florida.[79]

Just as important, Legion Field, the historic setting of many UA football games and perhaps the chief reason Birmingham's business community hailed its city as the "Football Capital of the South," was losing more and more UA games. From the perspectives of campus development as well as business profits, UA and AU had plans, eventually, to play the annual Iron Bowl in Auburn and Tuscaloosa. By itself this yearly conflagration had been delivering a $10 million economic impact on Birmingham. Therefore, as the teams announced that 1999 would be the last year of the Iron Bowl in Birmingham, the *Birmingham News* saw the symbolism of "the flaking paint on Legion Field's girders" and UAB's plan to start a Division II-A "football homecoming" in October 1994 as not exactly the solution needed.[80]

Then a singularly powerful football fan, Richard Arrington, stepped into the breach. The mayor had just made several frustrating efforts to capture some type of professional football program for the city when his old friend Gene Bartow came calling. Over time and with proper funding for scholarships and a "name" coach, the two agreed, UAB as a Division I-A team could begin to fill the gap at Legion Field created by the departing Tide and Tigers. Shortly thereafter, Bennett and Roozen joined Bartow in another meeting with Arrington where the mayor indicated his hope that the City of Birmingham would underwrite UAB football to the tune of around $2.2 million (paid out between 1994 and 1997), money invested heavily in ticket purchases (to be donated to children of the city) and in improvements to Legion Field.[81]

When the plan hit the press and city council, however, it did not meet with unanimous approval. Some believed it was wrong for the city to aid UAB because the institution had pending several suits alleging racial and gender discrimination and the city had significant needs in K–12 education. In response, Arrington did not deny that such litigation and needs existed, but urged that UAB's growth was good for the city, including its black citizens. For example, he said, "I personally negotiated [the Kirklin Clinic] deal with [UAB] and guaranteed a 20 percent minority [business] participation in that [project] . . . and we got it." In the end, although many in the city correctly anticipated that Arrington would not run for reelection in 1999 and wondered if his clout remained sufficient to prevail in the UAB football endeavor, the mayor emerged victorious, climaxing almost twenty years of advocating the symbiosis between city and university.[82]

With his significant subvention in hand and corporate promises engineered chiefly by Bartow and McCallum to support athletic scholarships, that is, no state money in football scholarships, on August 17, 1994, Bennett sent the obligatory "information item" to Chancellor Austin. Accompanied by a specific budget for the project, he wrote, "[I]t is my belief [that] UAB is well positioned financially to take this step and that the opportunities and advantages of Division I-A football outweigh the potential risks and disadvantages." Some on the board continued to view the whole idea of UAB football as "not necessary," a point accentuated by the *Wall Street Journal* with quotes from two well-known professors from the state of Alabama—AU historian Wayne Flynt and UA law professor Wythe Holt.[83] Other board members—Mitchell, Drummond, and Lofton (a former UA football player)—seemed supportive. UAB's plan for I-A competition moved inexorably forward according to the plan Bartow, Hill, and McCallum had quietly launched at least a decade earlier. Indeed, by January 1995, with a new Blazer marching band rehearsing on the football field adjacent to the Ullman Building, Bennett announced that the former star quarterback at Vanderbilt University, and most recently an offensive coordinator at the University of Oklahoma, Watson Brown, would be coaching the team in its last year of II-A play in the Great Midwest Conference and preparing for the big transition to I-A in Conference USA beginning with the 1996 season.[84]

In the first few years of the higher-profile competition, the Blazers perhaps understandably did not capture a winning season, although they made more than respectable showings against such traditional powerhouses as Nebraska, Auburn, and Tennessee.[85] Detractors had various arguments. Some who lived in the vicinity of Legion Field, such as Henry C. Randall, a retired Birmingham-Southern history professor, found UAB's gunshot-like sounds—indeed, "battlefield sounds"—following touchdowns to be "a disturbance of the peace," as he urged in a letter to Bennett. In fact, they likely encouraged real gunshots to be fired off, "more gunshots than [Randall] had heard in any one evening during [his] thirty-two-year residence" in the area—an area once known for its relatively high crime rate. Others undoubtedly agreed with George Graham, a UAB philosophy professor, who despite being a UAB athletics fan looked upon recent lackluster attendance at UAB football games alongside the institution's growing deficits related to football and pronounced: Alabama "needs another football team the way we need more kudzu." Behind the scenes, Vice President Samuel Jackson kept giving Bennett reports on how football was needing more and more money from other parts of the UAB budget: "Claude, note the subsidy!" Roozen, too, stayed focused on budget problems related to lack of attendance, constantly encouraging Bartow and Sports Information Director Robert Staub to rustle up more fans.[86] Yet out in the public, deeply committed fans—some hard-core students such as Terry C. ("TC") Cannon and some equally fierce alumni such as Keith Hutchison and civic leaders such as Alice Williams—and certainly Arrington and McCallum—held steadfastly to the notion of big-time UAB football. As McCallum privately reflected in September 2002, "It was all a matter of time, something Tuscaloosa interests always were willing to give the Crimson Tide . . . so why not UAB?"[87]

Over in men's basketball, a different type of clock ticked away during much of the Bennett presidency. Bartow's teams lacked the meteoric success they had had in earlier times: no NCAA tournament appearances, one losing season—granted, some strong showings by standards of virtually all but a few coaches in the nation but frustrating for Bartow, who was generally considered to represent what Birmingham journalist Paul Finebaum called "one of the most distinguished and remarkable careers in college basketball." To make this more difficult for Bartow, in private he did not have a warm relationship with Bennett and Roozen.[88] When Wayne Martin of the *Birmingham News* covered one of the Blazer's lackluster preseason appearances, noting that the insult to injury was the fact that tournament directors in San Juan, Puerto Rico, identified Bartow's team as "the University of Alabama," Roozen reminded Bartow, "If we're going to have a first-class athletic program we need first-class PR. . . . You've got to have pros doing that job. . . . We've never gotten a strategic plan."[89] Finally, in March 1996, Bartow began to let the word out that he was ready to stop coaching. Not so privately, he laid plans to step down as head coach while remaining as athletic director, with the stipulation that his son Murry, a UAB graduate, a former assistant coach at Indiana as well as William and Mary, and most recently one of Gene Bartow's assistant coaches, would succeed him as head coach.[90]

Things then got more unpleasant. As discussed openly in the local press, Bennett and Roozen would go along with Bartow's staying on as athletic director but—appropriately—had intended to conduct a national search for the selection of his successor as head coach. Over an intense two-week period, Bartow dug in his heels on the point that his son would succeed him and marshaled his significant corporate and political support to that end. Resolution finally arrived after Bennett heard from several of these leaders, including Hall Thompson. On March 26, 1996, Bennett held a press conference to announce that son would succeed father.[91]

Responses were mixed. The local press quoted several noted coaches on Murry Bartow's abilities; William and Mary's Chuck Swenson: ""Murry worked hard and he worked smart." Moreover, Bennett described his new coach as "energetic," "enthusiastic," and well trained. With little reference to the son's abilities as a coach, however, faculty simply asked the question among themselves: "Why is it that we in faculty searches are required to go through a laborious process of national searches in conformity with federal guidelines," as philosophy chair George Graham queried, "while in athletics such standards are just waived?" Jessie Lewis of the *Birmingham Times*, known for relatively conservative views on social policy, weighed in even heavier: "This has nothing to do with affirmative action; this is about fairness. . . . No one can convince me that there is no black qualified to be head basketball coach . . . at UAB." When John Archibald of the *Birmingham News* asked UAB leaders about Murry Bartow's appointment representing a violation of nepotism rules, they were passed over to Mike Ellis's "crisis-command post" in media relations: "The nepotism rule was set up 'to raise flags so that we could examine these situations on a case by case basis,' Ellis explained, and not to eliminate them."[92]

At the same time, however, major sports journalists of the city provided retrospective analyses of Gene Bartow's coaching career: "striking," "one of the greats," "no coach has ever built a major program so rapidly." And Arrington underscored yet again his theme of symbiosis: "Coach [Gene] Bartow has been very good for the university and the city." Then there was the "let's move on" editorial by Clyde Bolton. A year earlier the *Birmingham Post Herald* writer Chet Fuseman had asked UA athletic director, Cecil ("Hootie") Ingram, what he felt about a regular season basketball game with UAB. According to Fuseman, the bottom line of Ingram's reply:

"I don't have to answer that question with a 'yes' or 'no.'" With reference to such historic tensions between UA and UAB, Bolton emphasized that now "Wimp" Sanderson as well as Gene Bartow no longer were coaching, which offered a perfect opportunity for new basketball coaches to begin regular play between the two institutions. Aware that UA still would not want such a development, he bore down: "Colleges are supposed to teach young folks how to interact in a civilized society. . . . Given the events of March 18, 1993 [when UAB beat UA in the NIT tournament] a haughty attitude hardly becomes Alabama." Still, as Murry Bartow ascended to the job of head basketball coach, much of UAB basketball life picked up where it had left off the year before.[93]

Projects: "Blazer," "Capital," "Managing Board"

Other elements of UAB life headed toward anything but normalcy. As part of his public salvo, in January 1995, about the need for UAB to undergo rapid change and the initiation of a formal strategic planning program, Bennett with every justification emphasized the complex transformations coming to "all academic health centers, including UAB's." Soon the board, the campus, and anyone in Alabama who read the newspapers knew that Bennett had far more on his mind than smoothly delivered words.[94]

Out of quiet but intense planning (which bypassed the formal strategic planning process), by July 1995 Bennett and Jackson brought Geheb on-board. Escalating health care costs, caps on Medicaid and Medicare reimbursements, the projected hospital loss of some $10 million in Medicaid Disproportionate Share Payments (indigent care reimbursements) beginning October 1995, combined with an "oversupply" of hospitals in the Birmingham area—all these factors called for "a strategic course correction," which the three identified with the code name "Project Blazer." They kept the endeavor out of the public eye, and indeed out of the eyes of all but a few at UAB, for a brief time. Still, key medical faculty already were nervous about Jackson, the former HSF leader, being part of Bennett's inner circle, plus Jackson's receiving a portion of his salary from the HSF (an action officially approved by the UA board). With rumors related to Project Blazer, they began to be "more than nervous."

Jackson hoped that some of this nervousness among influential people, such as cancer center director Albert LoBuglio and HSF president (and neurology chair) John Whitaker, would "ease up" as Bennett's small planning group moved to the next level of including key members of the UA board and the system office. Hence, by September there was a low-profile Project Blazer task force consisting of Bennett, Jackson, Geheb, Chancellor Austin, Vice Chancellor Flaherty-Goldsmith, attorneys Ina Leonard and Glenn Powell, and two trustees, Jack Edwards and Garry Neil Drummond. Before this group, Jackson "put all the numbers on the table" pointing to the need for "strategic course change," including the sale or lease of the hospital. UAB's Academic Health Center (AHC) was headed toward insolvency five to ten years out. And what made the UAB situation far worse than that of many other AHCs nationwide was the state's historic refusal to deliver anything approaching adequate reimbursement for indigent care at a time when several Birmingham-area hospitals were sending more and more indigent patients to UAB. Bennett summed up with a statement he soon used with numerous civic leaders: "There is no way we can carry out any part of our teaching, research, and service missions if we are broke." Finally, he posed the possibility that in dealing with this crisis UAB might derive funds sufficient not only to make the health system vibrant but to invest in the west end of campus. (Jackson later recalled that west-end investment was never a possibility: "Claude never intended to do this—just misguided public relations.") With the concurrence of the task force, Bennett assigned Geheb the job of presenting "the strategic course correction" to the UA board in an October 1995 meeting held in Huntsville.[95]

In that meeting, Geheb explained that to increase revenues and offset debt there had to be "a regional or at least statewide integrated health care delivery system." Ever since the mid-1980s UAB had been moving toward a small constellation of remote clinics across Alabama in part as a place for training family practice physicians but also as a way of building referrals to the UAB hospital within the context of the intensely competitive health care scene in Birmingham, which included HealthSouth, Brookwood Hospital, St. Vincent's Hospital, and others. But what Geheb now presented clearly represented the boldest approach to a "health system" ever proposed by UAB. The new system could consist of an expanded number of primary care doctors often at remote sites, some of which might be small hospitals as well as the previously established clinics. It also could include more nursing homes; an intensified use of the UAB hospital as a place for the "very, very sick"; and an expanded version of UAB's youthful Office of Managed Care—health insurance.[96]

For all this to happen, however, large capitalization—an infusion of *new, big* money—was essential. And either the sale or the lease of the UAB hospital (not the sale of either the HSF or Kirklin Clinic) had to be considered

as an innovative possibility for acquiring the capital to make these investments. Academic health centers nationwide—for example, Tulane's—faced
with similar hospital problems were moving in the direction of sale or lease.
Moreover, if such a sale could deliver a fund approximating $700 million,
the proceeds could be placed in a massive endowment that could provide
substantial funds in interest which, over time, could be used to provide not
just capitalization for the UAB health system but predictable, steady budgets
for the School of Medicine and for some of the nonmedical programs.[97]

Then came concerted backpedaling. The following week, as this major
board presentation repeatedly found coverage in newspapers, Dale Allison, a
UAB media relations representative, did her best to defuse the implications
of the "strategic course correction." In concert with a carefully planned
fallback position, if necessary, developed by Jackson and others—"Our rationale is that until a buyer has the offering documents, we do not have
plans to sell"—she repeatedly stated to reporters that no decisions had been
made about placing the hospital on "the selling block." To the *Birmingham
News* she said simply, "It's premature to say that's going to happen or not
going to happen." Why did Allison, an experienced professional, choose
her words carefully? Besides the obvious matter of big and fast change,
what made this proposal so controversial? There is a complicated background story.[98]

In reports on Geheb's presentation, area hospitals found confirmation
that *public* UAB clearly sought to increase its "market share," at significant
cost to *private* competitors. They now had clarified perspective on UAB's
opening, as recently as March 1995, another satellite clinic at Roebuck, a
suburb some ten miles east of the city center. And in June that year UAB
had done its best in a bidding war to purchase the Shelby Medical Center
(SMC) in Pelham, south of the city center some twenty miles in an area
considered one of the fastest growing in the Southeast. SMC ultimately
went with the Baptist Health System. Still, in April 1995—six months before Geheb addressed the UA board—UAB's "threat" to the "market share"
of private sector health care intensified even more.[99] UAB struck a deal with
the entrepreneur James B. Little that gave UAB 75 percent of a start-up physician network, Triton Health Systems, permitting UAB to bring 200 of Alabama's primary care physicians into the UAB health system. Hence, around
the time of Geheb's presentation to the board, the local papers reported
that private hospitals in metropolitan Birmingham, fearful that the sale of
the UAB hospital indeed would provide massive funds that could lead to

an even more aggressive UAB health system, began to urge on members of the legislature that the hospital's proposed sale was not legal. The argument went that such a sale required constitutional amendment (nothing especially new to Alabama) because the University of Alabama—UAB hospital technically was University Hospital—had its organic origin in the Alabama Constitution.[100]

Tensions in metropolitan Birmingham found more fuel in another component of the plan Geheb articulated. Just as physician network expansion was well underway by the time Geheb spoke, so was UAB health insurance. When Bennett and Little connected their interests in the UAB-Triton arrangement of April 1995, an insurance program UAB had developed for its own employees, VIVA, became a more serious contender with the other two insurance programs UAB employees could choose from, Blue Cross/Blue Shield and Complete Health. Bennett and others of his team argued that in the name of fiscal responsibility UAB—like many other academic health centers—had little choice but to go down this road. Every UAB employee who elected to use VIVA was recirculating UAB money back into UAB, a crucial addition of funds during a developing financial crisis, rather than sending it out of the UAB economy.[101]

Others saw VIVA differently. Already deeply concerned about Bennett's articulated plan to invest monies generated by physicians and the hospital into nonmedical programs, some outspoken UAB physicians opposed VIVA. They urged that VIVA lacked points of flexibility for patients that Blue Cross/Blue Shield had. VIVA also reimbursed physicians at a lower rate than its competitors did. Bennett and Jackson countered that while less flexible on some points, VIVA allowed more people to be insured by offering lower premiums. Constantly worried about UAB physicians "talking down" VIVA with their patients, they urged Geheb to "deal with the problem." Even though VIVA continued to reflect "healthy market share" and soon represented the strongly preferred choice among most UAB employees, internal opposition continued and spilled over into the community where it merged with other criticisms of Bennett's "strategic course correction."[102]

And the spillover landed on fertile ground. Private business interests in Birmingham, already concerned about the implications of an expanding UAB health system, claimed serious foul. A UAB alumnus named Jerry A. Baker, Jr.—who happened to be the husband of the director of communications for Complete Health, a key competitor of VIVA—filed suit seeking to shut down UAB's entry into health insurance as well as the durable medical equipment business on grounds that such endeavors by a public sector entity were unconstitutional. Although the suit failed, such action clearly heightened public concern about the "strategic course correction."[103]

Finally, it was natural that some at UAB as well as citizens across Alabama had reservations about the big change explicit in any discussion of selling the hospital. On and off campus the UAB hospital enjoyed the image of being "the best public thing in Alabama, in a state that doesn't have too many good public things." No poll data were available to document the strength of this sentiment. Still, it found considerable reflection in "letters to the editor" and even in Bennett's personal correspondence. One longtime Birmingham citizen, Mrs. Maud Fowler, distilled her thoughts for Bennett in this way: "Could we not preserve . . . our hospital by giving Alabama citizens a chance to give donations? . . . We have come so far and have had devoted leaders who had a dream."[104]

Two undercurrents of history flowed beneath the whole story of the "strategic course correction," one close to the surface of daily routines, another far deeper in the life of the city. First, to be vilified for acting like a private sector operation was nothing new in UAB's experience. In a state that woefully underfunded all social services, including hospitals and education, for years political, corporate, and civic leaders, most recently including members of ACHE and certainly Governor James, had hammered away at UAB and other Alabama universities for not functioning with the "efficiency," "accountability," and "entrepreneurship" that many businesses supposedly displayed. Yet, time and again, when UAB sought to use private sector techniques to solve essentially *public* financial problems, problems often nonexistent in states with effective public policy, some other citizenry group screamed foul: UAB was "invading" private sector turf. The central point to remember about such "contradiction and hypocrisy," as Dick Hill recalled, is that had UAB over the years sat by passively and waited for appropriate state funding there would have been no UAB and hence no massive UAB economic benefits to the *private* sector of the state, not to mention the public life of Alabama.[105]

Second, a century-old irony coursed deeply beneath the plans. In anticipation of the intense point-counterpoint reaction that the Bennett-Jackson-Geheb plan was bound to engender, in August 1995 the three had contracted with the New York City–based marketing firm of Abernathy, MacGregor, Scanlon to assist with acquiring strong offers on the hospital. The Project Blazer task force, including board members and the chancellor, approved this action. Moreover, at the time Geheb addressed the board in October 1995, again with chancellor and board approval, through this firm they had hired the additional consultancy services of the prestigious J. P. Morgan Company of New York City. Just two months after the October board meeting, indeed, the Morgan Company changed the name of the plan from "Project Blazer" to something with a more sophisticated business management ring, "Project Capital." Here was the House of Morgan—the old Leviathan himself—lined up for some $600,000 to study the feasibility of "the strategic course correction," including the sale of the hospital. None could have predicted that the very East Coast banking house that virtually colonized Birmingham in the early 1900s, and through its U.S. Steel took much of Alabama's economics and public policy down the road to "third worlddom," would by 1995 become the very agent to which UAB turned for help. None could have predicted that UAB would want the assistance of the Morgan Company in continued efforts to deliver quality health care in a complex fiscal environment. Yet in the process, unknowingly but still with irony and poignancy, UAB sought to use Morgan to advance Birmingham's modernization and to deliver it from the insidious residuals left by the Leviathan himself—the Morgan Company—almost a century before. But so it was.[106]

After going public at the end of the October 1995 board meeting, Project Capital moved forward more than expeditiously. By early December 1995, one month after Geheb's board presentation, J. P. Morgan representatives were in Birmingham managing exploratory offers from the five top potential buyers or leasors: the Baptist Health System "and a group of voluntary not-for-profit hospitals," based in Birmingham; Quorum Health Group, Inc., based in Brentwood, Tennessee; Columbia/HCA Healthcare Corporation based in Nashville; Tenet Healthcare Corporation based in Santa Monica, California; and Birmingham's own well-known HealthSouth, Inc. UAB leadership carefully studied the Morgan group analysis and, as promised to the board, made plans to share this information with board members no later than the end of January 1996.[107]

Before the month was out, however, Bennett's cautious optimism about Project Capital turned to disappointment. The combination of advice from J. P. Morgan and the amounts of the various bids made Bennett, Jackson, and Geheb realize that the approximately $700 million they needed to garner from a possible sale was not to be unless the UAB doctors' practice (HSF) and the Kirklin Clinic were part of the deal, and they definitely were not. With far less enthusiasm but at least publicly not giving up, the three now turned briefly to a lease approach to advancing Project Capital, which did not seem to go far. As late as March 1996 Bennett again was convening his Project Capital task force at the Woodward House, bravely seeking to charge the group with still another approach: "The past several months . . . have been challenging, frustrating and enlightening. Our recent decision to postpone a 'sales option' in favor of improved internal governance and selective external alliance is a milestone."[108] For a while this crucial issue continued to spin downward, giving the impression to Edwards, Drummond, and Flaherty-Goldsmith that hospital finances were not just in bad shape but out of control from the perspective of presidential leadership. Indeed, here was only the most recent expression from board members that they had serious questions about "medical money" at UAB, including the inner workings of the foundation—an attitude that certainly preceded Bennett's presidency. Moreover, the continuing issue of "the hospital sale" led to what some longtime medical center leaders had been quietly lobbying for at least a decade and to what real and proposed "internal transfers" to enhance programs at the west end had so perversely punctuated. Finally, in October 1996 all this came to a head and a type of resolution. Acting on a proposal jointly drafted by HSF president John Whitaker and Geheb, the UA board decided to act on what it had been considering for over five years, well before the current crisis. There was a need for a joint operating agreement, whereby a Health System Managing Board would have authority over hospital finances. Trustee John Russell Thomas accepted the role of chairing the new board. Years later, reflecting on the whole episode, Bennett was concise: "I was moving too fast and understandably many were nervous."[109]

The Health System Managing Board consisted of eleven voting members: five non-HSF/university employees appointed by the HSF (three-year terms); five non-HSF/university employees appointed by the UA trustees (three-year terms); and one individual appointed by the HSF to serve as chair (one-year term). There also would be six ex officio (nonvoting) members: the chancellor of the UA system; the financial vice chancellor of the UA system; the president of UAB; the dean of the School of Medicine; the chair of the Department of Medicine; and the chair of the Department of Surgery. Of crucial importance, the largest financial components of UAB no longer reported to the UAB president. In some ways there now were two UABs: one managed by the Health System Managing Board, the other by the president and UAB's central administration.[110]

Final Turbulence: The Woodward House,
Still More Than a House

As complex and crucial as were the issues behind Project Capital, one of the results of its failure—its ushering in something different from "one university"—came about in part from happenings about as far removed from health care finances as anything could be. While Project Capital rose and fell between roughly July 1995 and March 1996, President Bennett's ability to lead came under question as a result of financial affairs related to the Woodward House. In its vigorous youth UAB had found the home to be symbolic of a modernizing Birmingham. At least in the short run, however, as the institution continued to reach for maturity, the Woodward House became a liability for the university much as such facilities had for older universities.

In October 1995 the Bennetts moved out of the Woodward House and back into their own home in Mountain Brook because of Nancy Bennett's continual problems with allergies as a result of the air in the Woodward House. Three months later, the Montgomery-based writer for the *Birmingham News*, Michael Sznajderman, began a series of award-winning stories, published during 1995 and 1996, suggesting that Bennett had mishandled public funds in connection with his tenure in the Woodward House (April 1994–October 1995) and in connection with the upkeep of his home in Mountain Brook. At times the allegations appeared months apart, each new report seemingly "another revelation of personal wrong-doing" at a time when Bennett took fire from other sources: from those critical of his seriously considering the sale of the hospital; from board members and some faculty concerned about Roozen's management style; and from those who feared the financial implications of Bennett's seeming conversion to the philosophy of "one university."

In January Sznajderman began with the story that while the Bennetts lived in the Woodward House, two maids normally assigned to housekeeping duties in the house also provided similar duties in the Bennetts' private residence at the university's expense.[111] On the heels of this story, and significant public criticism including strong remarks from Alabama attorney general Jeff Sessions, Bennett personally repaid the university $4,000 for the additional maid services. Moreover, to "clear the air and try to get the University beyond this development," on the advice of Jackson and UA system chief counsel Glenn Powell the board also authorized an internal investigation to determine what, if any, other financial malpractices might be involved, an investigation to be managed by independent counsel—the Montgomery attorney Thomas DeBray. In addition, on Jackson's advice, Bennett designated a task force to review the general financial status of the Woodward House, with the new vice president for development, Fred Brooke Lee, serving as chair and Jackson as cochair. The committee ultimately recommended philanthropy and cost cutting as ways for UAB to continue using the Woodward House.[112]

Despite these internal efforts, at the request of Attorney General Sessions, the State Ethics Commission soon launched its own investigation of possible wrong-doing out of the UAB president's office, and announced that DeBray would be cooperating with the commission—an announcement with which DeBray concurred. With Bennett retaining as his personal attorney his good friend Thomas E. Carruthers, the commission's work began to unfold in its standard confidential way; that is, the contents of the investigation both during and after the inquiry stayed confidential unless such information could be shown to be material to a civil suit.[113]

Meanwhile, Sznajderman dug deeper. He requested and ultimately received financial profiles of the Woodward House being assembled by the special task force, and reported that in the previous year Woodward House activities had cost some $340,000. When that hit the press, newspapers and politicians statewide, including longtime critic of higher education practices Governor Fob James, urged that such expenditures at UAB and for similar housing costs associated with Chancellor Austin's home in Tuscaloosa (and his condominium in Mountain Brook) documented the amount of money that all of higher education in Alabama *really* had. University presidents statewide stared at the floor: this was the background against which they entered the 1996 legislative session seeking badly needed budgetary support. Leaders of K–12 and the two-year system in public remained relatively quiet but undoubtedly shared some private smiles.[114] By mid-April 1996, indeed, the Bennett administration had a lot on its plate: not only the broad negative impact of certain Woodward House expenditures and the ongoing Ethics Commission investigation at a time when Bennett was pressing Vice President Lee for groundwork leading to a capital campaign, but the massive reverberations from the decision in March that the proposed cornerstone of Project Capital, the sale of the hospital, would not work. Bennett sought to reassert public confidence and momentum by sending out a form letter to numerous "public opinion makers" on the campus and in the community at large. First, it addressed the Woodward House issue with the news that the task force had completed a report indicating that although some Alabamians thought the estate should be sold and others wanted to lease it from UAB, as a university and community asset it was too great to lose. Instead, "I [now have] accepted the task force's report which called for halving the state support by reducing the operating costs and raising private support . . . [through the creation of] 'Friends of the Woodward House.'" Second, the letter announced that UAB soon would be participating in a more energized version of the Urban 13, recently renamed "The Great Cities-University Compact," and that he, President Bennett, "early next month [would be] off to Washington to explore innovative partnerships with the Federal government" to help make Birmingham an even better place to live and work. The letter concluded with an invitation: "I would encourage you to drop me a note with any thoughts you may have on these items of community interest."[115]

Dick Hill applauded the plans as far as they went. Yet, as one who had given an extensive newspaper interview in 1978 on the important community value of the Woodward House, he urged that a group such as Friends of the Woodward House should not be chaired by a community leader, as he had heard might happen; rather, "since this is still viewed as the UAB President's Mansion, I believe such leadership, at least initially, should be provided either by you [Bennett] or Fred [Lee]." Don Logan, former Birmingham civic leader and now CEO at Time, Inc., wrote from New York City that Bennett "seemed to have handled the situation concerning the Woodward House perfectly." Similar shows of support, either in letters to the editor in the *Birmingham News* or to Bennett personally, came from community leaders such as Charles Collatt, Barbara Ingalls Shook, and Jack O. Paden, and from campus leaders such as J. Russell Lindsey in comparative medicine and Robert Stanley in radiology. Not all, however, were positive. A written "anonymous suggestion" urged that Woodward House be converted to a faculty club funded essentially out of membership dues, perhaps with an initial bank loan up front to get it started. The UAB philosopher George Graham had a similar reaction: increase the amount of conferencing and structured "*academic* programs and events" that occurred in the facility. The Birmingham corporate leader Morris Hackney, whose brother Sheldon Hackney had been president of the University of Pennsylvania as it recently discovered its own role in urban outreach, "really [did] like [the] 'Great Cities-University Compact.' . . . I believe that those are the things that an Urban University should do and Birmingham needs it very badly." Still, he was a self-professed "Philistine" on the Woodward House: "Everyone would be better off if UAB could sell it to a developer." On political implications of the current Woodward House financial scandal, Hackney reacted pragmatically: "I do not believe that you could have done much else under the circumstances. It all may look a little different in another year."[116]

There was some truth in Hackney's prophecy. Much like an automobile mired in mud, its wheels spinning downward yet at times catching just enough to inch the automobile forward, in late April UAB had to deal with another "revelation" in the *Birmingham News*. According to the writer Jeff Hansen, Bennett's vice president for finance and administration, Samuel Jackson, had authorized the expenditure of $2,700 on a helicopter lease to move two of his financial managers, Mary Lee Rice and Fern Tomisek, from a snowed-in Atlanta airport to an equally snowed-in Birmingham for a meeting with attorney DeBray—a meeting that ultimately had to be canceled because DeBray could not drive from Montgomery to Birmingham because of the snow.[117] Of all those in the Bennett leadership team, it is ironic that Jackson was the one who needed to step forward on this incident. Over the previous three years he had been seeking to tighten the budgetary practices of the administration across numerous fronts. Confidentially and futilely he had urged Bennett to enforce his own presidential statements regarding limits on salary raises for physicians. Confidentially and futilely he had written Bennett about using the university housekeepers in his Mountain Brook home. Confidentially and for a while futilely he had written Bennett that his using university funds to pay for private social functions at the Woodward House was highly questionable from the perspective of the Internal Revenue Service and also in the context of strong accounting procedures (Jackson to Bennett, August 2, 1994: "I feel it is necessary for you to be aware of this situation and to be prepared in the event this becomes an issue in future years"; Jackson to Bennett, December 8, 1995: "I hope you will understand . . . [that] it is necessary sometimes to review and revise a transaction to assure its compliance with state and federal laws [which] our procedures were established to uphold. We will work harder to see that these things are accomplished in the most convenient and least offensive manner possible to you"). It was Jackson who, upon seeing the emergent crisis of the university's leadership, wrote Bennett that UAB's attorney, Ina Leonard, should be included in weekly inner-circle presidential staff meetings involving Roozen, Geheb, Lewis, and himself. It also was Jackson who advised his staff that any requests that he provide financial information to Vice Chancellor Linda Flaherty-Goldsmith needed to be handled by him, not others in the office, in accordance with Flaherty-Goldsmith's explicit request.[118]

Hence, acutely aware of how the "chopper flight" could be perceived in the current environment of virtual siege for alleged financial malpractices, Jackson quickly gave direct answers to an interrogating press: no state money paid for the flight; and "I decided the meeting was critical [for the integrity of the investigation regarding Woodward House expenditures] and approved the flight." No doubt because Jackson had turned to the UAB Education Foundation funds to cover the $2,700 tab, not to state funds, however, the issue received little further press coverage and, to Jackson's relief, never figured substantively into the various investigations related to financial practices within UAB leadership.[119]

Still, by July 1996—the same month that Chancellor Austin announced his resignation to assume the presidency of the University of Connecticut—and with the Ethics Commission not scheduled to rule on the case until September, the situation worsened. The state's Board of Examiners of Public Accounts decided to undertake its own analysis of UAB's management of the Woodward House. And, unlike materials submitted to the Ethics Commission, materials gathered by the Board of Examiners were indeed subject to public scrutiny. Hence, out of the collection of information gathered from UAB and deposited with the board, Sznajderman and other journalists found something else of concern. The contract for redecorating the Woodward House during the fall and winter of 1994—a contract for new furnishings and design initially thought to be worth $250,000—had gone to Bennett's neighbor, Betty Warnock, the wife of UAB's chair of nephrology, David Warnock. Despite nuances in the press statewide about such an arrangement possibly representing a violation of the state bid law, Sznajderman emphasized that the law gave universities leeway on retaining the services of lawyers and artists, including interior designers, and later cited a state officer's opinion that Warnock's personal design fee of $41,000 was anything but excessive considering the scale of the job.[120]

On the other hand, from these same files Sznajderman and others found clear evidence that Bennett, after a major storm, had used university employees paid out of university funds to clear brush from his Mountain Brook home and had given parties for private friends at the Woodward House, such as the "blessing of the house" occasion, charging the events to university accounts. Bennett, however, had recently repaid the university. Asked about these new borderline developments, UA board chair Jack Edwards gave Sznajderman a cautious response: "I think my position at this time is to wait and see what turns out. I must say Claude Bennett is a fine man. I don't think he has done anything intentionally wrong."[121]

Finally, as scheduled, on Wednesday, September 19, 1996, the Ethics Commission concluded its investigation with hearings, then rendered a judgment. This was no easy experience for Bennett or those around him, including Carruthers and Jackson (who provided the board with documentation of his own internal warnings to Bennett). After all the press coverage, however, the decision seemed relatively anticlimactic. By a 4–0 vote, the commission found Bennett to have committed a "minor violation of a non-criminal nature." The decision carried with it a $1,000 fine and the requirement that Bennett pay back to UAB $8,700 for additional personal "social functions," which he covered immediately.[122]

Before the conclusive meeting, Trustee Edwards had said to reporters that Bennett "had made a mistake of judgment. He made no secret of that." Before the committee had rendered its ruling, however, according to Sznajderman, Edwards also said that if the ethics panel "sanctioned Bennett, the board would have to meet to discuss the matter," and in fact the board already was scheduled to meet in Birmingham the next week. The next day Bennett released a statement that he "would never do anything to harm or discredit this great institution"; that he had "self-reported" crucial matters to the Ethics Commission; and that "I've acknowledged that I made a mistake and I have done what I can to right the situation." A decade later he stood by that analysis but added that his imprudent pursuit of "rapid change" led him to "misjudge other matters" of his presidency.[123]

Still, the board met as planned, and in mid-November Bennett announced that he would return to the Department of Medicine on January 1, 1997. As early as December 18, 1996, however, he had a signed commitment to be named chief executive officer of Biocryst Pharmaceuticals, Inc., then led by his longtime Birmingham protégé, Charles Bugg. With Trustee John Oliver serving as acting chancellor in the wake of Austin's move and spending considerable time at the UAB campus, on the same day Bennett resigned the board announced that the recently retired chancellor (chief campus officer) of the University of North Carolina–Chapel Hill, Paul Hardin, would assume the UAB presidency on an interim basis on January 1, 1997.[124]

Several months prior to Bennett's announcement, Oliver and other trustees had been heavily courting Hardin to fill the UA chancellor's position left vacant by Austin's move. This savvy attorney and academic administrator, however, had no intention of significantly postponing his retirement plans of "more family time and more golf time." In several intense conversations with Oliver, the offer evolved: if he were not interested in the chancellorship, how about the presidency of UAB? Hardin stood firm on his personal plans. He was happy to serve at UAB on an interim basis only until a regular presidential appointment could be made.[125]

Before Hardin's arrival in January 1997 other changes also occurred as Oliver worked firmly with Bennett to clear the way not just for a new leader but a new leadership team. The executive assistant to the president, James Lewis, retired. The vice president of finance and administration, Samuel Jackson, offered to step down in the name of "assisting with a transition that any new president has a right to ask for" so long as his "separation package" was honored. When board members checked with Bennett about such a "package," Bennett said there was no such thing. Jackson then delivered a document providing for such an arrangement. Although Bennett lacked board authority to have established such a separation package for Jackson and had initialed it, not signed it, ultimately—after considerable tension—the board honored the commitment and Jackson immediately returned to private business life. UAB ceased its own independent-counsel investigation in view of conclusions found by the Ethics Commission, although the investigation of the Board of Examiners continued well into 1997. In this way, what *Birmingham News* writers Tom Gordon and Betsy Butgereit called "the . . . most turbulent presidency" in UAB's history came to a close.[126]

Although the hospital's finances needed serious overhaul during the Bennett presidency, other elements of UAB continued to mature as an increasingly vital economic and social force for its city and state. Statistics tell some of the story. Between 1993 and 1996 UAB's total revenues moved from $872 million to $996 million; the payroll moved from $400 million to $438 million; and the physical plant went from 7.5 million to 8.4 million gross square feet. Although general faculty size slightly declined (as did overall enrollment), endowed faculty positions grew from forty-six to fifty-five as a result of major gifts targeted at the health sciences. Perhaps more important, with the continued instability of state funding during the Bennett presidency, it was all the more significant for UAB's historic growth in grants and contracts to hold firm. When Bennett became president UAB's extramural funds—not including state grants, as some universities do—had moved to just over $150 million. When he left office this support had grown to $182 million. In short, these numbers reveal many elements of significant qualitative development inside the institution during the Bennett presidency, especially in funded research. Moreover, from an economic impact perspective this financial dynamism allowed UAB, by the late 1990s, to use a full-time workforce of about 10,000 to deliver a multiplier effect, according to the historian Wayne Flynt, of "creating 53,000 jobs—one out of every three in Alabama"—and few indeed in heavy industry.[127] In short, despite the turbulence, in important ways UAB remained a crucial force of social progress.

Coda

Prospect

From Hardin to Reynolds

Swiftly, but through careful consultation with board members, interim president Paul Hardin filled administrative openings with equally interim appointments. Most notably, while continuing as the UA system's financial vice chancellor, Linda Flaherty-Goldsmith took the UAB job of interim vice president of finance and administration; and, upon Kenneth Roozen's announcement that he was moving to the University of South Carolina Medical Center, Peter O'Neil—longtime dean of the Department of Natural Sciences and Mathematics—assumed the role of interim provost. Convinced, however, that "certain things you do after a new president is named, if you can wait," Hardin quietly shut down plans for Fred Lee's capital campaign and suspended the active search for a medical dean, with Will Deal continuing as the interim in that position. Hardin also took a careful look at the Woodward House. Although it represented short-lived difficulties, he concluded that over the long term the house still could provide a vital symbol for UAB's civic engagement—if a symbol in need of reassertion. Accordingly, he and his wife, Barbara, launched the interim presidency with a series of social gatherings at the Woodward House, mixing campus and community at elegantly simple seated dinners.[1]

In other ways, too, UAB life moved forward. Against a January 1997 background of the board's approving the longstanding proposal that Gene Bartow's name be added to the front of the UAB Arena, the board named a search committee to select a new UAB president.[2] Those most curious about Alabama higher education wondered if this search would culminate before another crucial search, the search for a new chancellor of the UA system, reached fruition: a vital point in that the new president would be reporting to the chancellor. Even though the searches seemed to be moving parallel during the winter and spring of 1997, by April the board settled on Thomas E. Meredith, president of Western Kentucky University, to replace Austin. Meredith was onboard and functioning for the final crucial stages of the UAB president's search. And the search had some interesting twists and turns for the new chancellor to manage.[3]

African American faculty and staff of UAB, led by management professor George Munchus, went to the press with their concerns about the fact that there were no African Americans on the final short list, although soon to be former mayor Richard Arrington had been nominated but he declined. They urged that an institution such as UAB in a city such as Birmingham needed more diversity at the top. Now was the time to get that diversity. Several members of the board were known to agree with this criticism, documented with a look back at former presidents of UAB: if for the most part highly effective by any university's standards, there was an obvious lack of diversity in terms of both race and gender.[4] Nevertheless, as the search moved into its final stages in July 1997 the most visible candidate was not someone who fit with this call for generic diversity. Bernard Machen was a white man from Alabama, a former dean of dentistry at the University of North Carolina–Chapel Hill (who also had a doctorate in psychology), and currently the provost at the University of Michigan—major credentials for a major job. On July 14, however, the board released information on those who would undergo final interviews in Birmingham on July 16 and 17. There was Machen. But there also was a late entry into the search, a white woman named W. Ann Reynolds, a biologist who was currently chancellor of the City University of New York, formerly chancellor of the California State University system. On the heels of an intense and lengthy executive session, on July 17 the board went with Reynolds. Machen subsequently became president of the University of Utah and later the University of Florida.[5]

The coming of Ann Reynolds to Birmingham in September 1997 held the potential for a dramatic step in the further maturation of UAB. Granted, she represented a big change just in terms of her gender. She was UAB's first female president and, indeed, the first female president of any university in Alabama. But on a more subtle level she also represented significant change. All previous leaders of the institution arose out of that vital crucible— and the resultant personal bonding—of UAB's emerging in a time and at a place where many in Alabama and nationwide thought such development simply could not happen. Reynolds obviously was different. Indeed, it is commonplace in assessing organizations, including universities, to assume that the success of leadership from outside the original "magic circle"—in UAB's case, leadership by one never even secondarily touched by the spirit of the Dutchman—stands as a sign that infrastructure has institutionalized sufficient mission and values and is no longer dependent on historically legitimated intonation from the top. Yet, if Reynolds was known nationally for her heavy-handed administrative style,[6] she brought with her a reputation for scholarly attainments in science and for liberal activism, that is, for using universities to foster social progress, not just knowledge. Clearly, then, if from outside the "magic circle," she nevertheless had a philosophical kinship with UAB leaders preceding her, which offered possibilities for two important developments: appropriate continuity and appropriate change. Time would tell.

The Inheritance circa 1997

Regardless of her offering a social kinship with the past, Reynolds faced three daunting problems. First, she needed to show that she could *employ* her extensive national experiences and social philosophy to help shape a city in need of an actualized "next stage." Much as her predecessors had played pivotal roles in helping create the progressive Arrington era of Birmingham, which in turn energized the developing institution, she needed to be a pivotal player in the extraordinarily difficult task of assisting Birmingham with a cohesive focus for its *post*-Arrington period. This era, while filled with exciting new social and economic realities in both the public and private sectors of Birmingham, also included—as Robert G. Corley has written—"a widening chasm" of education and wealth with overt racial implications, just as in much of America.[7] Likewise, the era held the risk of many in Birmingham looking to UAB (much as the previous generation had unfortunately looked to U.S. Steel) as the "sole provider." If UAB could be a vital source of social change, other entities—for example, other medical centers plus banks, law firms, and insurance companies—had to play crucial roles for the city to avoid another experience with one force at the top. Reynolds needed to help shape this future and, poignantly, without the strategic advantages of clearly defined national waves of social change, especially regarding race, which permitted earlier UAB leaders such civic influence. Not easy, but possible.

Second, she needed to guide UAB at a time when U.S. government agencies, corporate leaders, accrediting bodies, and state-level educational oversight groups urged research universities to function by an orthodox for "quality" emergent for some time but never more gelled than in the late 1990s. Motivated by the end of American abundance as much as the high technology revolution, this formula said that research universities *must* assume higher standards of accountability, strategic planning, and, as Eric Gould has asserted, a corporate-style management ostensibly emphasizing transparency, dollars, and data.[8] Given that she had little choice but to move the institution further in this direction, Reynolds had to be careful not to let this modern orthodoxy of management eradicate the key to the rise of UAB. What had been essential to the vigorous youth also had to be central to its maturity: its entrepreneurial, risk-taking nature made possible through personal bonding—perhaps trust—and a clearly articulated mission from the top. From a different perspective, she needed to practice this mode of management without doing it the way more than a few corporate leaders did: using it as camouflage for an unyielding arrogance and self-aggrandizement. A complicated inheritance.

Third, unless things changed, Reynolds faced crucial elements of realpolitik. Major portions of the institution no longer were planned for daily reporting up through the president, but to the Health System Managing Board—which had to act decisively to get hospital finances back on track. Had much of Chancellor Bartlett's preferred reorganization plan of 1983 actually occurred in the waning months of the Bennett presidency? If so, this could always change. Also, the state in which she was coming to work had an approach to public policy rated as one of the worst in America. This possibly could change, too. Both of these forces, one internal to the university and the other external, added immensely to an already challenging situation.

By the same token, the people of UAB—faculty, staff, students, administration, alumni, community supporters, retirees, and the UA board—needed to embrace new influences from the top that might address these complex matters. If seeing leadership, if seeing a crucial combination of vision, decisiveness, authentic personal concern, and diplomacy, UAB needed to have the self-confidence to be willing to embrace someone not originally of the UAB family and make her not just part of it but truly head of it. Inheritance worked both ways.

Finally, while genuine challenges lay ahead, the fifth president certainly inherited much that was dynamic and strong and good. She inherited what modern Alabama's foremost public intellectual, Wayne Flynt, describes as "the least traditional and hidebound of the state's major universities."[9] With the exception of hospital finances (which, it turned out, could be revitalized), all sectors of the institution still showed both qualitative and quantitative growth. The dual notion of "a university without walls" was firmly established as a guiding "value" of its intellectual and clinical life. But this value, so rooted in the still deeper value of new thought and innovation, also had produced one complex place: a Carnegie I Research institution, a civic university, a place for modern health care, and an increasingly traditional, if still urban, campus. Then there was the additional key element of UAB's local living community. Much like all cities in America, Birmingham still had hills to climb. Yet the old Leviathan's closed-off steel colony, the one dominated by grime and prejudice that Carl Carmer probed in 1934 and again in 1960, no longer existed. If only Carmer could come back. This time he would find a city growing less out of material capital and more out of *social* capital. Powered by dramatically fewer shovels but by far better-informed imaginations, circa 1997 he would find many new and enduring lights in the valley.

Abbreviations

Repositories

ADAH   Alabama Department of Archives and History, Montgomery
BPLA   Birmingham Public Library Archives
MHSL   Mervyn H. Sterne Library, University of Alabama at Birmingham
UABA   University of Alabama at Birmingham Archives, a unit of Lister Hill Library for the Health Sciences
USAA   University of South Alabama Archives, Mobile

Primary Sources

APBC   Alabama Physicians Biographic Collection, UABA
BOT   Minutes of the Board of Trustees of the University of Alabama, located in the UA system office, Tuscaloosa
C/UABA   Papers of Emmett Carmichael, a collection within UABA
GCWGP   George C. Wallace Governor's Papers, ADAH
HRMF   Computerized listing of all faculty "start" and "end" dates, through 1994, from UAB Human Resource Management, in MRP
MC   McWilliams Correspondence, a subset of MRP, written communications chiefly between Tennant S. McWilliams and various persons who served as sources
MI   McWilliams Interviews, notes and transcriptions of interviews completed by Tennant S. McWilliams, organized alphabetically (by interviewee) in four loose-leaf binders; e.g., B2 = book 2; a subset of MRP to be given to UABA

MRP	McWilliams Research Papers, in possession of Tennant S. McWilliams, Birmingham, Alabama, to be given to UABA
OHC	Oral History Collection, UABA
PCC	Papers of Carl Carmer, New York State Historical Society, Cooperstown NY
PFAR	Papers of Frank A. Rose, W. S. Hoole Special Collections, Gorgas Library, University of Alabama, Tuscaloosa
PFPG	Papers of Frank Porter Graham, Southern Historical Collection, Wilson Library, UNC at Chapel Hill
PJRD	Papers of J. Rudolph Davidson, MRP
PJS	Papers of John Sparkman, W. S. Hoole Special Collections, Gorgas Library, University of Alabama, Tuscaloosa
PLH	Papers of Lister Hill, W. S. Hoole Special Collections, Gorgas Library, University of Alabama, Tuscaloosa
PPLBJ	Presidential Papers of Lyndon B. Johnson, Johnson Presidential Library and Museum, Austin, Texas
PSWJ	Papers of Samuel W. Jackson, in his possession
SJR	Senate Journal Record
UA/UABA	Materials on Birmingham developments located in the W. Stanley Hoole Special Collections, Gorgas Library, University of Alabama, Tuscaloosa; photocopied during the 1990s and entered as a collection within the UABA

Secondary Sources

AHR	*American Historical Review*
AJMS	*Alabama Journal of Medical Science*
AR	*Alabama [Historical] Review*
BN	*Birmingham News*
BPH	*Birmingham Post Herald*
DAU	*Dictionary of Academic Units at UAB . . . 1945–1997*, ed. William A. Harris and Timothy L. Pennycuff, 4th ed. (Birmingham, AL, 1997)
FF	*Facts and Figures* (UAB institutional data compiled annually by the UAB Office of the Vice President for Planning and Information)
JAH	*Journal of American History*
JAMA	*Journal of the American Medical Association*
JBHS	*Journal of the Birmingham Historical Society*

JHE	*Journal of Higher Education*
JMASA	*Journal of the Medical Association of the State of Alabama*
JSH	*Journal of Southern History*
JUH	*Journal of Urban History*
NEJM	*New England Journal of Medicine*
NR	*New Republic*
NYT	*New York Times*
SF	*Social Forces*
UAMCB	*University of Alabama Medical Center Bulletin*

Notes

Preface

1. Blaine A. Brownell and David R. Goldfield, eds., *The City in Southern History: The Growth of Urban Civilization in the South* (Port Washington, NY, 1977); David R. Goldfield, *Cotton Fields and Skyscrapers: Southern City and Region, 1607–1980* (Baton Rouge, 1982); Goldfield, *Region, Race, and Cities: Interpreting the Urban South* (Baton Rouge, 1997); John B. Boles, ed., *A Companion to the American South* (Malden, MA, 2002), 474–93. Don H. Doyle, "The Urbanization of Dixie," *JUH* 7 (November 1980): 83–91, recounts much of this historiographical story.

2. I am using "social capital" literally as stated in the text. For more specific usages, see, e.g., Alejandro Portes, "Social Capital: Its Origins and Applications in Modern Sociology," *Annual Review of Sociology* 24 (1998): 1–24. I thank my UAB colleague, the sociologist Mark LaGory, for instruction on this complicated idea. An example of what can be gleaned from *monographic* study of a Southern city and a university is Catherine Amelia Conner's "Bringing New Life to Birmingham: The Economic and Physical Impact of the University of Alabama at Birmingham, 1944–1990" (M.A. thesis, Auburn University, 2001). On the Goldfield reference, see Boles, ed, Companion, 489.

3. William E. Leuchtenburg, "The Historian and the Public Realm," *AHR* 97 (February 1992): 18.

4. The name of the medical center, as well as several other departments and buildings, changed several times over the years, thus the different renderings given over the course of this book.

Overture

1. Ann McCorquodale Burkhardt, "The Town within a City: The Five Points South Neighborhood, 1880–1930," *JBHS* 7 (November 1982): 70, 89n10; *Birmingham City Directory, 1950–51, 1954*; interview with Charles Zukoski, September 23, 1993, MI:B4; interview with Roger Hanson, January 19, 2001, MI:

B2; interview with Charles A. McCallum, September 19, 1993, MI:B3; interview with Samuel Barker, April 30, 1995, MI:B1. (All interviews were conducted by the author unless otherwise noted.) Racial mixing around Magnolia Point most likely resulted from its proximity to both black and white neighborhoods, as expanded upon by Burkhardt. J. Mills Thornton III's *Dividing Lines: Municipal Politics and the Struggle for Civil Rights in Montgomery, Birmingham, and Selma* (Tuscaloosa, AL, 2002), 141–379, is the most recent detailed portrait of Birmingham's rigid Old Order and the coming of social change. See also Diane McWhorter, *Carry Me Home* (New York, 2001)

2. Barker interview, April 30, 1995; Zukoski interview, September 23, 1993; R. Hanson interview, January 19, 2001; interview with S. Richardson Hill, Jr., April 11, 1995, MI:B2; *BN,* October 23, 2005; Michael Swindle, *Slouching towards Birmingham* (Berkeley, CA, 2005), 163–70; Joseph F. Volker, *The University and the City* (New York, 1971); Arnold Grobman, *Urban State Universities* (New York, 1988), 116. Kip Hubbard, in 1999 a UAB graduate student, produced "The Hubbard Report" under my direction. This is a statistical analysis of Southern urban areas and their higher education opportunities, which allowed me to see context for Volker's thesis. Copy in MRP.

3. C. Vann Woodward, *The Burden of Southern History* (Baton Rouge, 1968). On metaphorical versus concrete uses of the Burden thesis, see Tennant S. McWilliams, *The New South Faces the World* (Baton Rouge, 1988), 1–15.

4. Virginia Gauld (UAB vice president for Student Affairs) to author, May 7, 2002, MC:MRP.

5. Interview with Ada White Long, February 10, 1990, MI:B2.

6. The reference to "family" is from an interview with Charles A. McCallum, September 15, 2001, MI:B3.

7. Long interview, February 10, 1990.

8. *NYT,* August 13, 1991.

9. *U.S. News & World Report,* September 22, 1992.

10. Hugh Davis Graham and Nancy Diamond, *The Rise of American Research Universities: Elites and Challengers in the Postwar Era* (Baltimore, 1997), 151–52.

11. *Wall Street Journal,* November 23, 1994.

12. Interview with unidentified employee of the Fish Market restaurant, January 7, 1993, MI:B4; interview with Nadim Shunnarah (owner of the Pita Stop), January 8, 1993, MI:B3.

13. Abraham Flexner, *Universities: American, English, German* (New York, 1930), 3.

Chapter 1

1. Hilde De Ridder-Symoens, ed., *A History of the University in Europe,* vol. 1, *Universities in the Middle Ages* (Cambridge [UK], 1992); Gordon Leff, *Paris and Oxford Universities in the Thirteenth and Fourteenth Centuries* (New York, 1968); John W. Baldwin, *The Scholastic Culture of the Middle Ages, 1000–1300* (Lexington, MA, 1971), 19–20, 55–57.

2. Lewis Mumford, *The City in History* (New York, 1961), 275–76.

3. Thomas Bender, ed., *The University and the City: From Medieval Origins to the Present* (New York, 1988), esp. 290–97.

4. Ibid.

5. Walter Ruegg, "Themes," in *A History of the University in Europe,* vol. 1, *Universities in the Middle Ages,* 3, 18–19; abstracts of the forty-six (institution-specific) papers presented before the conference, "The University in Its Urban Setting," University of Aberdeen, July 2–5, 1993, copy in MC:MRP.

6. Baldwin, *Scholastic Culture of the Middle Ages,* 55–57; Lewis Mumford, *The Culture of the Cities* (New York, 1938), 34.

7. Bender, ed., *The University and the City,* 7–9.

8. Interview with Jaime del Castillo, October 10, 1997, MI:B1; Castillo to author, January 30, 1997, MC:MRP.

9. Page Smith, *Killing the Spirit: Higher Education in America* (New York, 1990), 303.

10. Bender, ed., *The University and the City.*

11. Henry Nash Smith, *Virgin Land* (Cambridge, MA, 1950); Frederick Rudolph, *The American College and University: A History* (New York, 1968), 95.

12. Morton White and Lucia White, *Intellectual versus the City, from Thomas Jefferson to Frank Lloyd Wright* (Cambridge, MA, 1962); George Dunlap, *The City in the American Novel* (New York, 1962).

13. Rudolph, *The American College and University,* 91–95; Thomas Jefferson, "Notes on the State of Virginia," 291, in *Thomas Jefferson: Writings,* ed. Merrill D. Peterson (New York, 1984); Herbert Baxter Adams, *Thomas Jefferson and the University of Virginia* (Washington, DC, 1888), 86–87, where Adams describes Jefferson's plan to locate the University of Virginia "far from the turmoil of the city" and "in the center of white population."

14. Bender, ed., *The University and the City,* 150–77.

15. Ibid.

16. Martin Bulmer, *The Chicago School of Sociology* (Chicago, 1986), 1–44; Bender, ed., *The University and the City,* 210–30; Richard Hofstadter, "The Age of the University," in Richard Hofstadter and C. DeWitt Hardy, eds., *The Development and Scope of Higher Education in the United States* (New York, 1952), 29–48.

17. David R. Jones, *The Origins of Civic Universities: Manchester, Leeds and Liverpool* (London, 1988), 14; Sylvia Harrop, "Faith above Faction: The Role of Religious Affiliation in the Foundation and Growth of Liverpool's Higher Education Institutions in the Late Nineteenth Century" (25-page typescript, MRP); Sarah V. Barnes, "England's Civic Universities and the Triumph of the Oxbridge Ideal," *History of Education Quarterly* 36 (Fall 1996): 271–305; Sarah Virginia Barnes, "Defining the University: A Comparative Perspective on the Process of Creating Institutional Identity at the University of Manchester and Northwestern University" (Ph.D. diss., Northwestern University, 1995); interview with Sylvia Harrop, October 31, 2002, MI:B2.

18. Rudolph, *The American College and University,* 262–440; Robert Wiebe, *The Search for Order, 1877–1920* (New York, 1967), 121; Bulmer, *The Chicago*

School of Sociology; Lawrence A. Cremin, *The Transformation of the School* (New York, 1961), 161–76; Raymond A. Mohl, "City and Region: The Missing Link in U.S. Urban History," *JUH* 28 (November 1998): 5–6.

19. Allan Nevins, *The Origins of the Land-Grant Colleges and State Universities* (Washington, DC, 1962); P. Smith, *Killing the Spirit,* 61, 64; Earle D. Ross, *Democracy's College: The Land-Grant Movement in the Formative Stages* (Ames, IA, 1942).

20. Richard Franklin Bensel, *Yankee Leviathan: The Origins of Central State Authority in America, 1859–1877* (New York, 1990), 69, 316; Bensel, *Sectionalism and American Political Development, 1880–1980* (Madison, WI, 1984), 46, 49, 63. The brief literary tracing of *Leviathan* is mine, but see also Ronald Radosh and Murray N. Rothbard, eds., *A New History of the Leviathan: Essays on the Rise of the Corporate State* (New York, 1972). For the Job quote, and even more characterization of Leviathan, see Job 41:1–34.

21. Nevins, *Origins of the Land-Grant Colleges and State Universities,* 6–26; William Belmont Parker, *The Life and Public Service of Justin Smith Morrill* (New York, 1924), 262–75; Rudolph, *The American College and University,* 250; Edward Danforth Eddy, Jr., *Colleges for Our Time: The Land-Grant Idea in American Education* (New York, 1957), 27–33; John Y. Simon, "The Politics of the Morrill Act," *Agricultural History* 37 (April 1963): 103–11.

22. Bensel, *Yankee Leviathan,* 60–64; C. Vann Woodward, *Origins of the New South, 1877–1913* (Baton Rouge, 1951), 291–320; Richard Franklin Bensel, *The Political Economy of American Industrialization, 1877–1900* (New York, 2000), 222–28, 349–51. Cf. Joseph J. Persky, *The Burden of Dependency: Colonial Themes in Southern Economic Thought* (Baltimore, 1992), esp. ch. 4.

23. There is no "paper documentation" for the Thanksgiving Day quote; he who spoke the quoted words was T. Ray Schultz, the author's maternal grandfather. Shortly after Thanksgiving, I wrote an essay on what I thought of my grandfather's statement—I wrote it for a Basic Studies class at Indian Springs School taught by William E. Leverette, who later was a historian at Furman University. No copy of the essay remains. Interview with William E. Leverette, January 6, 1994, MI:B2.

24. George R. Leighton, "Birmingham, Alabama: The City of Perpetual Promise," *Harper's Magazine* 175 (August 1937): 225; *NYT,* March 25, 1966.

25. Leah Rawls Atkins, *The Valley and the Hills* (Woodland Hills, CA, 1981), 1–15; William Warren Rogers et al., *Alabama: The History of a Deep South State* (Tuscaloosa, AL, 1994), 3–17; Marjorie Longenecker White, *The Birmingham District: An Industrial History and Guide* (Birmingham, AL, 1981), 7–9; Charles Hudson, *The Southeastern Indians* (Nashville, 1976), 5.

26. Atkins, *The Valley and the Hills,* 24, 41; M. White, *The Birmingham District,* 15.

27. M. White, *The Birmingham District,* 45–46; cf. W. David Lewis, *Sloss Furnaces and the Rise of the Birmingham District* (Tuscaloosa, AL, 1994), 17, which uses the work of the historian Eugene Genovese to assert, correctly, that planter antipathy for industrialists was not monolithic.

28. Woodward, *Origins of the New South,* 44–49, 210–13; Allen Johnston Going, *Bourbon Democracy in Alabama* (Tuscaloosa, AL, 1951); Jonathan M. Weiner,

Social Origins of the New South: Alabama, 1860–1885 (Baton Rouge, 1978); Sheldon Hackney, *Populism to Progressivism in Alabama* (Princeton, 1969), 147–208.

29. Virginia Van der Veer Hamilton, *Alabama: A Bicentennial History* (New York, 1977), 92–96; Malcolm C. McMillan, *Constitutional Development in Alabama, 1798–1901* (Chapel Hill, NC, 1955), 300ff.; J. Wayne Flynt, "Alabama's Shame," *Alabama Law Review* 53 (Fall 2001): 67–76. On Woodward's "bedfellows" theme, see his *Origins of the New South,* 75–106, 291–320.

30. Atkins, *The Valley and the Hills,* 46–47; *BN,* December 6, 2000.

31. Rogers et al., *Alabama,* 277–88; Henry M. McKiven, Jr., *Iron and Steel: Race, Class, and Community in Birmingham, Alabama, 1875–1920* (Chapel Hill, NC, 1995); Carl V. Harris, *Political Power in Birmingham, 1871–1921* (Knoxville, TN, 1977), 19–38.

32. Rogers et al., *Alabama,* 281–84; M. White, *The Birmingham District,* 40ff.; Bensel, *The Political Economy of American Industrialization,* 40.

33. Samuel L. Webb, *Two-Party Politics in a One-Party South* (Tuscaloosa, AL, 1997), 75; Leighton, "Birmingham, Alabama," 233; and, the source of Rhoades's quote, Jean Strouse, *Morgan: American Financier* (New York, 1999), 592–93.

34. Leighton, "Birmingham, Alabama," 234.

35. Gabriel Kolko, *The Triumph of Conservatism* (New York, 1963), 1–158.

36. Herbert L. Satterlee, *J. Pierpont Morgan: An Intimate Portrait* (New York, 1940), 26–28, 341–42; John P. Dyer, *"Fight'n Joe" Wheeler* (Baton Rouge, 1941), 299–302, which is complimentary of Wheeler's New South boosterism.

37. Strouse, *Morgan,* 320–22, 362ff.

38. Interview with David Vann, September 10, 1995, MI:B4; Charles Morgan, Jr., *One Man, One Voice* (New York, 1979), 27. U.S. Steel has allowed no scholar full access to its archival records telling of the corporation's control over Birmingham. Marlene Hunt Rickard was permitted access to vital records related to health-care services provided by TCI: see Rickard, "An Experiment in Welfare Capitalism: The Health Care Services of the Tennessee Coal, Iron and Railroad Company" (Ph.D. diss., University of Alabama, 1983). Otherwise, scholars seeking access to U.S. Steel records, especially as related to the all-important Fairfield plant in Birmingham, have been turned away. Rickard to author, December 2, 2002, Henry McKiven to author, November 27, 2002, Judith Stein to author, December 4, 2002, Raymond Mohl to author, December 6, 2004, all in MC:MRP. Interview with James Baggett (archivist, Birmingham Public Library), September 29, 2005, MI:B1. Kenneth Warren's *Big Steel: The First Century of the United States Steel Corporation, 1901–2001* (Pittsburgh, 2001) reflects usage of U.S. Steel records but little on Birmingham.

39. Leighton, "Birmingham, Alabama," 227.

40. Ibid., 231; Edward Shannon LaMonte, *Politics and Welfare in Birmingham, 1900–1975* (Tuscaloosa, AL, 1995), 1–39; Lynne B. Feldman, *A Sense of Common Place: Birmingham's Black Middle Class Community, 1890–1930* (Tuscaloosa, AL, 1999); Robert J. Norrell, "Caste in Steel: Jim Crow Careers in Birmingham, Alabama," *JAH* 73 (December 1986): 669–94; Charles E. Connerly, "One Great City or Colonial Economy: Explaining Birmingham's Annexation Struggles, 1945–1990," *JUH* 26 (November 1999): 49, 51–53.

41. Blaine A. Brownell, *The Urban Ethos in the South* (Baton Rouge, 1975), 17–21; Howard Rabinowitz, *The First New South* (Arlington Heights, IL, 1992), 66–67; Marilyn Davis Barefield, *A History of Mountain Brook, Alabama, and Incidentally of Shades Valley* (Birmingham, AL, 1989), 152ff.; Catherine Greene Brown, *A History of Forest Park* (Birmingham, AL, 1992); Lyn Johns, "Early Highlands and the Magic City," *JBHS* 6 (July 1979): 33–43; Burkhardt, "Town within a City," 1–85.

42. Carl V. Harris, "Stability and Change in Discrimination against Black Public Schools: Birmingham, Alabama, 1871–1931," *JSH* (August 1985): 375–416; Rogers et al., *Alabama,* 325–28; Ruth Bradbury LaMonte, "The Origins of an Urban School System: Birmingham, Alabama, 1873–1900," *JBHS* 5 (July 1977): 5–17; James D. Anderson, *The Education of Blacks in the South, 1860–1935* (Chapel Hill, NC, 1988), 232ff.

43. Howell Raines, "Remarks to Leadership Birmingham," February 15, 1991 (12-page typescript [copy], MRP); Raines, "Reflections on Alabama: A History of Silence," October 20, 1992 (13-page typescript [copy], MRP).

44. Leighton, "Birmingham, Alabama," 236; Margaret Armbrester, "Samuel Ullman: Birmingham Progressive," *AR* 47 (January 1994): 29–43; Lewis, *Sloss Furnaces,* 214–15; E. LaMonte, *Politics and Welfare,* 17; Feldman, *A Sense of Common Place,* 19, 115, 117, 120, 136, 190; Anderson, *Education of Blacks,* 198.

45. Clarence Cason, *90 Degrees in the Shade,* introduction by Wayne Flynt (1935; Tuscaloosa, AL, 1983); James Saxon Childers, *A Novel about a White Man and a Black Man in the Deep South,* introduction by Tennant S. McWilliams (1936; Tuscaloosa, AL, 1988); Renwick C. Kennedy, "What's Happening in the Cotton Belt," *NR* 71 (August 10, 1932): 765–67, and "Black Belt Aristocrats," *SF* 13 (October 1934): 1–6; Charles Frederick Zukoski, Sr., "A Life Story" (550-page typescript, Special Collections of MHSL, [1980]), 330ff.

46. Morton Sosna, *In Search of the Silent South* (New York, 1977); Hamilton, *Alabama,* 147; Robert Gaines Corley, "The Quest for Racial Harmony: Race Relations in Birmingham, Alabama, 1947–1963" (Ph.D. diss., University of Virginia, 1979), 43–79.

47. U.S. Census 1920, 1930; C. Harris, *Political Power,* 19–38.

48. Quoted in C. Harris, *Political Power,* 33.

49. Jonathan Daniels, *A Southerner Discovers the South* (New York, 1938), 279 (source of "landlord" quote); Barefield, *A History of Mountain Brook,* 51–106; Marvin Yeomans Whiting, *Vestavia Hills, Alabama: A Place Apart* (Vestavia Hills, AL, 2000), 8–17; Edward S. LaMonte, *George B. Ward: Birmingham's Urban Statesman* (Birmingham, AL, 1974); Leighton, "Birmingham, Alabama," 226; Glenn T. Eskew, "Demagoguery in Birmingham and the Building of Vestavia," *AR* 42 (July 1989): 206–15.

50. E. LaMonte, *Politics and Welfare,* 89–112; Leighton, "Birmingham, Alabama," 238–40; Zukoski, "A Life Story," 103, 501; Robin D. G. Kelley, "The Black Poor and the Politics of Opposition in a New South City, 1929–1970," in Michael B. Katz, ed., *The "Underclass" Debate* (Princeton, 1993), 297–304; Goldfield, *Cotton Fields and Skyscrapers,* 180.

51. E. LaMonte, *Politics and Welfare*, 123ff.; Douglas L. Smith, *The New Deal in the Urban South* (Baton Rouge, 1988); Lewis, *Sloss Furnaces*, 271–75, 420–21.

52. Allen Cronenburg, *Forth to the Mighty Conflict* (Tuscaloosa, AL, 1995), 52–53; George Brown Tindall, *The Emergence of the New South, 1913–1945* (Baton Rouge, 1967), 694ff.; U.S. Census, 1930, 1940, 1950.

53. Interview with Reverend John Porter, November 14, 2001, MI:B3.

54. Whiting, *Vestavia Hills*, 7–60; Barefield, *A History of Mountain Brook*, 107–24.

55. Marilyn Davis Barefield, *A History of Hoover, Alabama and Its People* (Birmingham, AL, 1992), 7, 50–145; Kelley, "The Black Poor," 305–17; Bobby M. Wilson, *Race and Place in Birmingham* (New York, 2000); *BN*, July 4, 1999, April 7 and December 3, 2001. On developer William Hoover's personal racial conservatism, see, e.g., Christopher MacGregor Scribner, *Renewing Birmingham: Federal Funding and the Promise of Change, 1929–1979* (Athens, GA, 2002), 66.

56. Scribner, *Renewing Birmingham*, 74–77; Irving Beiman, "Birmingham: Steel Giant with a Glass Jaw," in *Our Fair City*, ed. Robert S. Allen (New York, 1947), 99–122.

57. James Cobb, *Industrialization and Southern Society, 1877–1984* (Lexington, KY, 1984), 112–13.

Chapter 2

1. Quoted from "First Extension Center Bulletin," in James Bosarge, "History of UAB" (62-page typescript, MRP), 7.

2. Jeanie Thompson, *The Widening Circle: Extension and Continuing Education at the University of Alabama, 1904–1992* (Tuscaloosa, AL, 1992), 6–7; Rae Wohl Rohfeld, ed., *Expanding Access to Knowledge: Continuing Higher Education* (Washington, DC, 1990), 17–19.

3. Cremin, *Transformation of the School*, 87, 165–68.

4. Thompson, *The Widening Circle*, 7–13; U.S. Bureau of Education, *An Educational Study of Alabama* (Washington, DC, 1919).

5. Thompson, *The Widening Circle*, 26–30.

6. Bosarge, "History of UAB," 8–9; Smith-Schultz-Hodo Realty sales document (copy), MRP. Bosarge gives $22,312.24 for the price; I go with what shows on the actual sales document.

7. D. Smith, *The New Deal in the Urban South*, 66, 137; Doak S. Campbell et al., *Educational Activities of the Works Progress Administration* (Washington, DC, 1939), 17, 38; and Bruce J. Schulman, *From Cotton Belt to Sunbelt: Federal Policy, Economic Development, and the Transformation of the South, 1938–1950* (Durham, NC, 1994), 194, emphasizing that such aid did not seek racial change as later federal projects indeed did.

8. Virginia Van der Veer Hamilton interview with Thad Holt (transcription), interview no. 1, October 1974, Oral History Collection, MHSL; "Thad Holt," *The Story of Alabama*, ed. Marie Bankhead Owen, 4 vols. (New York, 1949), 4:410–11.

9. Thad Holt, "UAB: Giant of the Depression" (6-page typescript, MRP), 1–3; nontranscribed tape/oral history interview with Thad Holt, Oral History Collection, MHSL; Thompson, *The Widening Circle,* 344.

10. Bosarge, "History of UAB," 6–7; Edward K. Austin to Richard C. Foster, September 13, 1941, and Foster to Austin, September 15, 1941, UA/UABA.

11. W. Harold Taylor to R. E. Tidwell, March 25, 1938, R. C. Foster to A. Key Foster, March 19, 1940, Tidwell to R. C. Foster, April 23, 1940, all in UA/UABA; Bosarge, "History of UAB," 6–7.

12. Bosarge, "History of UAB," 8–9; Thompson, *The Widening Circle,* 35; Geraldine Emerson interview with Kathryn Cramer Morgan, January 24, 1986, OHC.

13. W. H. Taylor to R. E. Tidwell, July 24, 1941, Tidwell to R. C. Foster, July 26, 1941, Foster to Tidwell, July 28, 1941, Tidwell to Raymond R. Paty, May 9, 1945, all in UA/UABA; Robert J. Norrell, *A Promising Field: Engineering at Alabama, 1837–1987* (Tuscaloosa, AL, 1990), 159–60; Thompson, *The Widening Circle,* 35–36.

14. Bosarge, "History of UAB," 6–7.

15. Ibid.; Carl Martin Hames, *Hill Ferguson: His Life and Works* (Tuscaloosa, AL, 1978), 72.

16. Judson C. Ward, "Raymond Ross Paty: Chancellor of the University of Georgia System, 1946–48" (11-page typescript, dated May 28, 1998, MRP); Judson C. Ward to author, May 28, 1998, November 14, 2000, MC:MRP; Robert E. Tidwell to Raymond Paty, March 9, 1945, April 17, 1946, UA/UABA; Robert G. Corley and Samuel N. Stayer, *View from the Hilltop* (Birmingham, AL, 1981), 51–56.

17. Thompson, *The Widening Circle,* 36–39, 53–54, 66.

18. Key Foster to R. C. Foster, March 7, 1941, R. C. Foster to K. Foster, March 19, 1941, Robert Jemison, Jr., to R. C. Foster, April 30, 1941, all in UA/UABA.

19. *BN,* October 24, 1939; Richard A. Storm, Jr., to author, August 24, 2000 (with enclosed photocopy of newspaper clippings), MC:MRP; Storm to R. C. Foster, January 18, 1940, Foster to Storm, January 25, 1940, UA/UABA.

20. Robert Tidwell to R. C. Foster, June 24, 1940, UA/UABA.

21. Robert Tidwell to R. C. Foster, July 8, 1941, UA/UABA; Norrell, *A Promising Field,* 158.

22. Robert E. Tidwell to Raymond Paty, October 12, 1943, November 17, 1944, January 22, 1945, Tidwell to Carey E. Haigler, February 8, 1945, Tidwell to M. Huntley, July 26, 1945, Huntley to Tidwell, July 27, 1945, W. E. Pickens to Tidwell, July 27, 1945, all in UA/UABA.

23. W. H. Taylor to Robert E. Tidwell, March 25, 1938 (which includes "Report . . . on Engineering . . . at Birmingham"), UA/UABA; Bosarge, "History of UAB," 13; Norrell, *A Promising Field,* 158.

24. B. C. Riley to R. C. Foster, March 8, 1940, Robert E. Tidwell to Foster, June 24, March 16, 1940, Foster to Riley, March 25, 1940, Tidwell to Raymond Paty, June 15, 1945, all in UA/UABA.

25. Robert E. Tidwell to Everett J. Soop, May 23, 1946, Soop to Tidwell, May 28, June 14, 1946, UA/UABA.

26. William H. Brantley, Jr., "The Alabama Doctor," *The Alabama Lawyer* 6 (July 1945): 262–63; Howard Holley, *A History of Medicine in Alabama* (Birmingham, AL, 1982), 244–45; *Dadeville (AL) Record,* May 13, 1973; *BN,* June 29, 1973.

27. Brantley, "The Alabama Doctor," 262–64; Harriet E. Amos, *Cotton City* (Tuscaloosa, AL, 1985), 161, 218–19; Holley, *History of Medicine in Alabama,* 81–89; Reginald Horsman, *Josiah Nott of Mobile* (Baton Rouge, 1987), 227, 237–39, 244–51.

28. Holley, *History of Medicine in Alabama,* 89–95; Weiner, *Social Origins of the New South,* 186ff.; Hamilton, *Alabama,* 103–48; Joseph H. Parks and Oliver C. Weaver, Jr., *Birmingham-Southern College, 1856–1957* (Nashville, TN, 1956), 5–179.

29. Holley, *History of Medicine in Alabama,* 54, 95–96, 375–76; Tennant S. McWilliams and Ferris Ritchey, "Southern Doctors: Physicians and Social Change in Birmingham, Alabama, 1871–1910" (44-page typescript, MRP), 22–23; Hill Ferguson, comp., "Montezuma University Medical College" (2-page typescript, Clip File on Medical Colleges of Alabama, BPLA).

30. Holley, *History of Medicine in Alabama,* 206, 224–25; John W. DuBose, *Jefferson County and Birmingham, Alabama* (Birmingham, AL, 1887), 381–84.

31. McWilliams and Ritchey, "Southern Doctors," 10–17.

32. Ibid., 15–16, 23–24; Holley, *History of Medicine in Alabama,* 61–63, 65–69. Thomas J. Ward's *Black Physicians in the Jim Crow South* (Fayetteville, AR, 2003) depicts the setting for black physicians on a regional basis but does not focus on these doctors per se.

33. Robert G. Corley et al., "History of Hillman Hospital" (166-page typescript, MRP), 1987, 1–13; *BN,* July 22, 2005.

34. Corley et al., "History of Hillman Hospital," 13–14; Holley, *History of Medicine in Alabama,* 54–56.

35. Holley, *History of Medicine in Alabama,* 157, 165, 228–32; McWilliams and Ritchey, "Southern Doctors," 16–17; A. McGehee Harvey, *A Model of Its Kind,* 2 vols. (Baltimore, 1989), 1:50; Roger K. Newman, *Hugo Black: A Biography* (New York, 1994), 17; Steve Stutts, *Hugo Black of Alabama* (Montgomery, AL, 2005), 96–97.

36. Paul K. Conkin, *Gone with the Ivy: A Biography of Vanderbilt University* (Knoxville, TN, 1985), 147–84; Thomas H. English, *Emory University, 1915–1965* (Atlanta, 1966), 12; Henry Morton Bullock, *A History of Emory University* (Nashville, TN, 1936), 283–94.

37. English, *Emory University,* 13–14; Phinizy Spaulding, *The History of the Medical College of Georgia* (Athens, GA, 1987), 123.

38. English, *Emory University,* 14–32.

39. Ibid. Paul Starr traces the emergence of "authoritative" and socially influential medicine in *The Transformation of American Medicine* (New York, 1982), ch. 3. The applications of his general themes to the Birmingham situation, however, are mine.

40. Kenneth M. Ludmerer, *A Time to Heal: American Medical Education from the Turn of the Century to the Era of Managed Care* (New York, 1999), 18–19ff.;

A. Harvey, *A Model of Its Kind*, 1:50; Federal Writers Project, "A History of Public Health in Jefferson County," ch. 3 in "Through the War and Its Aftermath," in Papers of the Jefferson County Medical Society, BPLA; Carey V. Stabler, "The History of the Alabama Public Health System" (Ph.D. diss., Duke University, 1944), 1–50; Holley, *History of Medicine in Alabama*, 278ff.

41. Abraham Flexner, *Medical Education in the United States and Canada* (New York, 1910), 126–42.

42. David Alsobrook, "Mobile v. Birmingham: The Medical College Controversy, 1912–1920," *AR* 36 (January 1983): 37–56; Scott M. Speagle, "By Process of Elimination: The Political Decisions behind Locating a Four-Year Medical School in Birmingham," *Vulcan Historical Review* 2 (Spring 1998): 51–52, which suggests that at least some of the physician-proprietors of the Birmingham Medical College had encouraged a UA connection in the face of their institution's fiscal problems.

43. Ludmerer, *A Time to Heal*, 14–16; Starr, *The Transformation of American Medicine*, 79–144; Lewis, *Sloss Furnaces*, 2; Hamilton, *Alabama*, 144.

44. Hamilton, *Alabama*, 103–8.

45. Starr, *The Transformation of American Medicine*, 79–144.

46. Abraham Flexner to Hopson Owen Murfee, April 29, 1938, in Murfree, comp., *Correspondence on the Alabama State Medical Center* [1943?], Ref. Coll., UABA; Brantley, "The Alabama Doctor," 266; Speagle, "By Process of Elimination," 52; *BN*, July 21, 1929; *Birmingham Age-Herald*, September 11, 1931; Stuart Graves, "Present Status [of Alabama Medical Education]," June 1945, 9–10, UA/UABA.

47. J. N. Baker, "What Significance Has Alabama's Declining Medical Population?" *Journal of the Alabama Medical Association* 7 (May 1938): 2–6; Graves, "Present Status," 10; Dewey W. Grantham, *Southern Progressivism: The Reconciliation of Progress and Tradition* (Knoxville, TN, 1983), 311–18; William A. Link, *The Paradox of Southern Progressivism, 1880–1930* (Chapel Hill, NC, 1992), 19–23.

48. Holley, *History of Medicine in Alabama*, 105–6; Stuart Graves, "University Plans for Medical Education in Alabama" (10-page typescript [copy], C/UABA); Graves, "Present Status," 10; Wayne Flynt, *Poor But Proud* (Tuscaloosa, AL, 1989), 282; *BPH*, October 16, 1929; *University of Alabama Alumni News*, December 1929.

49. Graves, "Present Status," 12–13; Brantley, "The Alabama Doctor," 247, 266–67; *BN*, February 17, 1929, April 21, 1930, May 17, 1937, February 7, December 11, 1938; *Montgomery Advertiser*, October 17, 1939; *University of Alabama Alumni News*, May and December 1929; Tinsley R. Harrison, "The Medical School of the University of Alabama: Some Reminiscences," 1971, ch. 2, p. 6 (copy of transcript in MRP).

50. William H. Brantley, Jr., "An Alabama Medical Review," *AJMS* 4 (April 1967): 203–6; Holley, *History of Medicine in Alabama*, 106; Link, *The Paradox of Southern Progressivism*, 22–23.

51. McWilliams, *The New South Faces the World*, 121–40; Flynt, *Poor But Proud*, 181.

52. Murfree, *Correspondence;* Graves, "Present Status," 13; Speagle, "By Process of Elimination," 54–57.

53. C.W.M. Paytner to William D. Partlow, November 19, 1943, Medical School Building Commission Records, Governor Chauncey Sparks Papers (State Institutional Files), ADAH; Stuart Graves to Joseph C. Hinsey, February 18, 1944, UA/UABA; Robert Russell Kracke and William Gunter Kracke, "The University of Alabama Medical Center," *The Alabama Lawyer* 28 (January 1967): 78.

54. "Rockefeller Foundation Report [on Alabama Medical Education]," UA/UABA; Corley et al., "History of Hillman Hospital," 58–61; Fred Zaphee to William D. Partlow, November 22, 1943, Medical School Building Commission Records, Sparks Papers; Kracke and Kracke, "The University of Alabama Medical Center," 7, citing an interview with Mrs. Raymond Paty, August 1966.

55. "American Medical Association Report [on Alabama Medical Education]," UA/UABA.

56. Victor Johnson to Mrs. Roy Kracke, August 20, 1965, C/UABA.

57. Alston Callahan, "The UAB School of Medicine," *JMASA* 62 (December 1992): 7.

58. Ibid., 1–12; interview with Alston Callahan, October 15, 2002, MI:B1; Graves, "Present Status," 11–18; Wayne Flynt discusses the general influence of the Capitol Hill delegation in *Alabama in the Twentieth Century* (Tuscaloosa, AL, 2004), 66–70.

59. Kracke and Kracke, "The University of Alabama Medical Center," 81, with list of those on the Birmingham committee.

60. Graves, "Present Status," 12–13; Emmett B. Carmichael, "Our Dean," *Quarterly of Phi Beta Pi* 45 (November 1948): 159; J. W. MacQueen, "Medical Center in Birmingham," *Hospitals* 19 (March 1945): 44; Brantley, "The Alabama Doctor," 266.

61. "Thomas Jefferson Jones," in *The Story of Alabama,* ch. 4, p. 381; 4-page typescript of "Jones Bill-S.35-1943," copy in Minutes of the Four Year College Building Commission, August 30, 1943, UABA; Harvey H. Jackson III, "Chauncey M. Sparks, 1943–47," in Samuel L. Webb and Margaret E. Armbrester, eds., *Alabama Governors* (Tuscaloosa, AL, 2001), 190–93.

62. *Alabama General Laws, Regular Session, 1943, Act No. 89,* copy in Dean Kracke Files (Administrative), UABA; *BN,* February 16 and 17, 1944; Graves, "Present Status," 15–17.

63. *BN,* February 16, 1944; Kracke and Kracke, "The University of Alabama Medical Center," 80.

64. Stuart Graves to Joseph C. Hinsey, February 18, 1944, UA/UABA; *BN,* February 17 and 18, 1944.

65. Graves, "Present Status," 16–22; E. Carmichael, "Our Dean," 159; Raymond Paty to Chauncey Sparks, July 14, 1944, UA/UABA.

66. Stuart Graves to Joseph C. Hinsey, February 18, 1944, UA/UABA.

67. Bosarge, "History of UAB," 67.

68. Roy Kracke to Dad, October 11, 1944, Ellis W. Bacon to Kracke, December 22, 1942, copies in C/UABA; Drennen interview by Fisher, January 16, 1990.

69. Buford Roberts, "Front Porch Tales and Backyard Gossip about the Kracke Family" (36-page typescript [n.d.], MRP), 10–11; Oliver D. Street to Whom It May Concern, March 8, 1920, Robert F. Barber to Whom It May Concern, March 8, 1920, T. W. Throckmorton to Whom It May Concern, March 3, 1920, Roy Kracke to Mother, September 11, 1920, John A. Lusk to Whom It May Concern, [March 1920?], copies in C/UABA; E. Carmichael, "Our Dean," 157–59; Virginia Fisher interview with Rachel Kracke Drennen, January 16, 1990, transcription in OHC.

70. Drennen interview by Fisher, January 16, 1990.

71. Ibid.

72. Ibid.; interview with Robert Kracke (son of Roy Kracke), November 19, 1993, MI:B2.

73. Roy Kracke to William Maloney, June 20, 1944, as quoted in Kracke and Kracke, "The University of Alabama Medical Center," 81n111.

74. Jack C. Norris to Roy Kracke, April 24, 1944, Kracke to Norris, May 2, 1944, copies in C/UABA.

75. Weiner, *Social Origins of the New South,* 9–22, 33–34.

Chapter 3

1. Drennen interview by Fisher, January 16, 1990; Kracke interview, November 19, 1993.

2. Kracke interview, November 19, 1993; E. LaMonte, *Politics and Welfare,* 44, 148–51; Dwain Waldrep, "Henry Edmonds and His Controversy with the Southern Presbyterian Church," *JBHS* 9 (December 1985): 40–49; Marvin Yeomans Whiting, *The Bearing Day Is Not Gone . . . History of Independent Presbyterian Church* (Birmingham, AL, 1990), 13–49.

3. Roy Kracke to R. H. Wharton, April 25, 1944, C. H. Penick to Ernest Lowe, April 19, 1946, Kracke Medical Dean Records, UA/UABA; Victor Johnson, "Report on the Survey of the Medical College of Alabama, August 30, 1946," 4–15, 17, C/UABA; Pat Boyd Rumore, *Lawyers in a New South City: A History of the Legal Profession in Birmingham* (Birmingham, AL, 2000), 117.

4. "Progress Report of the Medical College of Alabama [1945–46]," 2–4 (15-page typescript, Kracke Medical Dean Records, UA/UABA); *Birmingham Age-Herald,* May 21, 1944; *BN,* November 16, 1944; Ernest Lowe to William E. Pickens, August 16, 1946, Kracke Medical Dean Records, UA/UABA; Johnson, "Survey of Medical College of Alabama," 18; Hames, *Hill Ferguson,* 71–72.

5. "Progress Report," 2–4; Holley, *History of Medicine in Alabama,* 107; Kracke interview, November 19, 1993.

6. "Progress Report," exhibit A; Holley, *History of Medicine in Alabama,* 107–8.

7. Johnson, "Survey of the Medical College of Alabama," 7, 21; Alston Callahan, "The UAB Medical Deans," *Alabama Medicine* 61 (December 1991): 17–18; Holley, *History of Medicine in Alabama,* 106–8.

8. "Progress Report," exhibit A; Holley, *History of Medicine in Alabama,* 108; *BN,* March 17, 2006.

9. Roy Kracke, "Considerations in Favor of Locating a Medical School in a Metropolitan Area," 3 (10-page typescript, Dean Kracke Administrative Files, UABA); Drennen interview by Fisher, January 16, 1990.

10. "Progress Report," exhibit A; *Birmingham Age-Herald,* May 19, 1946.

11. "Biographical Sketch of Robert Fulmer Guthrie" (11-page typescript, MRP); Roy Kracke to Raymond Paty, July 6, 1945, J. M. Mason to John Gallalee, April 30, 1949, Kracke Medical Dean Records, UA/UABA; "Progress Report," exhibit A; Kracke, "Considerations," 3.

12. *BN,* May 28, 1973; 2-page typescript (press release-obituary) on Barfield-Carter, C/UABA; Starr, *The Transformation of American Medicine,* 50, 96, 117, 124, 391; Robert R. Kracke, "Racial and Gender Prejudice in Medical Training, 1938–1946, and the Response of Roy R. Kracke, M.D." (14-page typescript, MRP).

13. "Progress Report," exhibit A; interview with Alston Callahan, September 11, 2001, MI:B1; *UAB Synopsis* 24 (December 12, 2005): 1, 3.

14. Holley, *History of Medicine in Alabama,* 195–96; Kracke interview, November 19, 1993.

15. *BN,* June 3, 1945.

16. "Progress Report," 13; Johnson, "Survey of the Medical College of Alabama," 37.

17. "Progress Report," 4; anonymous interview, June 15, 1995 (under seal), MI; "Annual Report of the Medical College, June 9, 1947," 10, Kracke Medical Dean Records, UA/UABA; Hames, *Hill Ferguson,* 72.

18. Anonymous interview, June 15, 1995. The oral tradition regarding pre-UA activities is from an interview with Wayne Finley, October 21, 2002, MI:B1.

19. Stuart Graves to L. P. Hosnette, September 2, 1944, Graves to Roy Kracke, September 6, 1944, Kracke Medical Dean Records, UA/UABA; "Progress Report," 6–7; Johnson, "Survey of the Medical College of Alabama," 3, 15; Graves to Victor Johnson, March 29, 1945, C/UABA.

20. Starr, *The Transformation of American Medicine,* 348–51; Virginia Van der Veer Hamilton, *Lister Hill: Statesman from the South* (Chapel Hill, NC, 1987), 136ff.; Scribner, *Renewing Birmingham,* 33–49; Lister Hill to Roy Kracke, February 3, March 20, 1945, John H. Bankhead to Kracke, March 21, 1946, Kracke to Raymond Paty, May 28, 1946, John Sparkman to Kracke, December 19, 1947, Kracke to Hill, August 2, 1946, all in C/UABA.

21. Holley, *History of Medicine in Alabama,* 360.

22. Scribner, *Renewing Birmingham,* 40; Kracke interview, November 19, 1993.

23. *BN,* November 21, 2000; Roy Kracke, "The Medical Care of the Veteran," *JAMA* 143 (August 12, 1950): 1321–27. The quote is from Carl Carmer, *Stars Fell on Alabama* (New York, 1934), 81.

24. Kracke, "Considerations," 9; Kracke, "The Medical Care of the Veteran," 1322–25.

25. John Sparkman to Roy Kracke, August 4, 1949, Kracke to T. M. Arnett, August 9, 1949, Charles Mayo to Kracke, July 27, 1949, all in C/UABA; Kracke, "The Medical Care of the Veteran"; Hames, *Hill Ferguson,* 72; Max Heldman, *The First Forty Years: University of Alabama School of Medicine* (Birmingham, AL, 1988), 12.

26. *BN*, November 16, 1944, August 2, 1946.

27. *BN*, August 2, 1946.

28. McWilliams and Ritchey, "Southern Doctors," 11–13; Ward, *Black Physicians*, 154ff.

29. E. LaMonte, *Politics and Welfare*, 142.

30. William C. Berman, *The Politics of the Civil Rights Movement during the Truman Administration* (Columbus, OH, 1970).

31. Roberts, "Front Porch Tales," 2; Robert S. Davis, Jr., to author, July 17, 2001, MC:MRP; Kracke interview, November 19, 1993; Margaret M. Story, "Civil War Unionists and the Political Culture of Loyalty in Alabama, 1860–61," *JSH* 69 (February 2003): 40–69.

32. Drennen interview by Fisher, January 16, 1990; Kracke interview, November 19, 1993; Charles Zukoski to author, August 12, 1994, MC:MRP; E. Culpepper Clark, *The Schoolhouse Door: Segregation's Last Stand at the University of Alabama* (New York, 1993), 11.

33. Kracke interview, November 19, 1993.

34. Zukoski, "A Life Story"; *BN*, August 27, September 6, 1996.

35. Neither Kennedy nor Kracke shows as members of the Governor's Committee, though Zukoski does. According to Kennedy, both he and Kracke and "a few others" believed they could "get more done" if they "pragmatically did not appear as formal members." Papers of Governor's Committee on Higher Education for Negroes, UA/UABA; interview with Renwick C. Kennedy, November 11, 1981 (untranscribed tape recording), Renwick C. Kennedy Papers, in author's possession.

36. Kracke interview, November 19, 1993; Cynthia Wilson (Tuskegee University archivist) to author, October 21, 22, 2002, MC:MRP; Ward, *Black Physicians*, 203ff.; Charles E. Wynes, *Charles Richard Drew: The Man and the Myth* (Urbana, IL, 1988), esp. 103–13. Wynes shows that although still perceived as true in many quarters, it is pure myth that Drew died on the side of the highway because a white ambulance driver refused to transport a black person.

37. Kracke interview, November 19, 1993; Timothy Pennycuff to author, October 18, 1999 (including a list of all recognized graduates from the Jefferson-Hillman Nursing School, 1944–51, MC:MRP); Scribner, *Renewing Birmingham*, 43, 153n21; Anita Smith, *The First Fifty Years: From Tuscaloosa to Birmingham* (Birmingham, AL, 2000), 10–27; Kracke, "Racial and Gender Prejudice in Medical Training"; *BN*, September 18, 1946.

38. Scribner, *Renewing Birmingham*, 42; Charles Zukoski to author, August 12, 1993, MC:MRP; Hames, *Hill Ferguson*, 72.

39. Kracke interview, November 19, 1993; Zukoski interview, September 23, 1993; Corley, "The Quest for Racial Harmony," 66–67.

40. Corley, "The Quest for Racial Harmony," 66–69; Charlotte Borst, "The Rise of Infant Mortality and Massive Resistance to Civil Rights: Gender, Race, and Indigent Medical Care in Birmingham, Alabama, 1950–64" (18-page typescript [copy], MRP), 1–3.

41. Corley, "The Quest for Racial Harmony," 66–69; Borst, "The Rise of Infant Mortality and Massive Resistance to Civil Rights," 1–3; *BN*, March 17, 1946.

42. Clarke, *The Schoolhouse Door*, 11.

43. On Hill's racial views, see Hamilton, *Lister Hill*, 211ff.

44. *BN*, April 10, 1946; Zukoski interview, September 23, 1993.

45. Roy Kracke to B. G. Shaw, January 7, 1946 (copy), Kracke Medical Dean Records, UA/UABA.

46. Scribner, *Renewing Birmingham*, 42–45; E. LaMonte, *Politics and Welfare*, 142–43; Corley, "The Quest for Racial Harmony," 46ff.

47. Expansion Plan Map [1944] (copy), Kracke Medical Dean Records, UA/UABA; *BN*, December 30, 1945.

48. Judson C. Ward to author, May 28, 1998, November 14, 2000 (including 10-page typescript by Ward titled "Raymond Ross Paty, Chancellor, University of Georgia System, 1946–48," MC:MRP).

49. BOT, 12 (December 14, 1946), 482; Roy Kracke to the board, November 29, 1946, Kracke Medical Dean Records, UA/UABA; Clark, *The Schoolhouse Door*, 12–14.

50. Clark, *The Schoolhouse Door*, 14.

51. Ibid.

52. Kracke's Montgomery lobby is reflected, e.g., in Kracke to Chester M. Black, March 7, 1947, George C. Wallace to Kracke, June 18, July 14, 1947, Kracke to Wallace, July 17, 1947, all in Kracke Medical Dean Records, UA/UABA. Lowe's quote is from Lowe to Kracke, December 1, 1947, UABA.

53. Clip from *BN*, November [10?], 1947, Kracke Medical Dean Records, UA/UABA.

54. "Annual Report of the Medical College, 1946–47," UABA; clip from *BN*, November [10?], 1947.

55. Kracke, "Considerations," 6.

56. *BN*, June 27, 1950.

57. Virginia E. Fisher, *Building on a Vision: A Fifty-Year Retrospective of UAB's Academic Health Center* (Birmingham, AL, 1995), 181; interview with S. R. Hill, February 23, 1993, MI:B2.

58. Ernest Lowe to Roy Kracke, June 25, 1947, December 30, 1947, Kracke Medical Dean Records, UA/UABA; Kracke interview, November 19, 1993; Borst, "The Rise of Infant Mortality," 1–3; interview with Samuel Cohn, October 15, 2000, MI:B1; Corley et al., "History of Hillman Hospital," 108.

59. Roy Kracke to Ernest Lowe, November 25, 1947, Kracke Medical Dean Records, UA/UABA; "Address by Roy Kracke [on Indigent Care Costs] at Tuskegee Institute, 1950" (10-page typescript, MRP).

60. Ernest Lowe to Roy Kracke, December 1, 1947, Kracke Medical Dean Records, UA/UABA.

61. Ibid.

62. *BN*, February 21, 1950.

63. Ernest Lowe to Roy Kracke, October 15, 1947, Kracke Medical Dean Records, UA/UABA; Kracke interview, November 19, 1993; Harrison, "Reminiscences," ch. 4, p. 1.

64. Ralph E. Adams to John Brauer, October 13, 1947, John Gallalee to George Teuscher, February 2, 1948 (copies), Dental Dean Records, UA/UABA.

65. Roy Kracke to Ralph E. Adams, August 29, 1947, Adams to Paul K. Losch, October 13, 1947, Adams to George Easton, October 13, 1947, Adams to H. M. Fuller, Olin Kirkland, John D. Sullivan, and R. R. Moorer, October 17, 1947 (copy of telegram), Harlan R. Horner to Kracke, November 5, 1947, Ralph E. Adams to Thad Morrison, December 15, 1947, all in Dental Dean Records, UA/UABA.

66. Thad Morrison to Roy Kracke, December 10, 1947, Kracke to Morrison, December 11, 1947, H. M. Fuller to John Gallalee, January 31, 1948, Gallalee to George Teuscher, March 27, 1948, Gallalee to Olin Kirkland, April 29, 1948, all in Dental Dean Records, UA/UABA; Joseph F. Volker, "Report on Unitarian Service Mission to Germany, 1948" (20-page typescript [copy], Joseph F. Volker [pre-UAB] Papers, UABA); John H. Mosteller, *Joseph Frances Volker* (Birmingham, AL, 1988), 42–44; Alabama Act 678 (October 9, 1947).

67. Joseph Volker to H. M. Fuller, April 20, 1948, Dental Dean Records, UA/UABA.

68. Typescript of press release announcing Volker as Tufts dean, May 22, 1947, and Olin Kirkland to Joseph Volker, April 28, 1949, Dental Dean Records, UA/UABA.

69. The quote is from Joseph Volker to John Gallalee, May 25, 1948; see also Volker to Gallalee, May 19, 1948, Ralph E. Adams to Gallalee, May 20, 1948, Gallalee to Volker, May 21, 1948, Volker to Gallalee, June 15, 1948 (copy of telegram), Gallalee to Volker, June 16, 1948 (copy of telegram), John D. Sullivan to Gallalee, June 16, 1948 (copy of telegram), Roy Kracke to Gallalee, June 30, 1948, Gallalee to Lon W. Morrey, July 1, 1948, Gallalee to Volker, June 10, 1948, all in Dental Dean Records, UA/UABA.

70. John Gallalee to Joseph Volker, May 28, June 4, 1948 (copy of telegram), typescript of press release from Tufts University, June 9, 1948, Gallalee to A. J. Mills, June 14, 1948, Gallalee to John D. Sullivan, June 3, 1948, Volker to Gallalee, June 11, 1948, all in Dental Dean Records, UA/UABA.

71. Holley, *History of Medicine in Alabama,* 360–61; A. Smith, *The First Fifty Years,* 122–23.

72. Starr, *The Transformation of American Medicine,* 340–41; Hamilton, *Lister Hill,* 204–5ff.

73. Starr, *The Transformation of American Medicine,* 341–42; Vannevar Bush, *Science: The Endless Frontier* (Washington, DC, 1945); Robert L. Geiger, *Research and Relevant Knowledge: American Research Universities since World War II* (New York, 1993), 14–19; interview with Charles A. McCallum, November 22, 1993, MI:B3; Holley, *History of Medicine in Alabama,* 236.

74. John Gallalee to George Easton, March 18, 1948, Dental Dean Records, UA/UABA; interview with Charles A. McCallum, March 2, 1993, MI:B3.

75. Virginia Fisher interview with Kathryn Morgan, July 20, 1989 (transcription), OHC; Drennen interview by Fisher, January 16, 1990; Kracke interview, November 19, 1993; Ward, "Paty"; Judson C. Ward to author, November 28, 2000, MC:MRP; Ernest Lowe to Roy Kracke, February 16, 1950, Kracke Medical Dean Records, UA/UABA; Thomas G. Dyer, *The University of Georgia: A Bicentennial History, 1785–1985* (Athens, GA, 1985), 264.

76. Callahan, "The UAB School of Medicine," 8; Holley, *History of Medicine in Alabama,* 190–91; Flynt, *Poor But Proud,* 176.

77. William Niedermeier, "A Remembrance of Thomas D. Spies," May 1993 (4-page typescript, MRP); Linda Akenhead, "Conquest of 'Hidden Hunger': The Work of Thomas Douglas Spies," JCMS/UAB Health Sciences Archives, Occasional Paper No. 1, MRP.

78. Johnson, "Survey of the Medical College of Alabama," 64–65; Kracke interview, November 19, 1993.

79. Interview with Alston Callahan, January 4, 1994, September 11, 2002, MI:B2; Kracke interview, November 19, 1993; Corley et al., "History of Hillman Hospital," 90.

80. Akenhead, "Conquest of 'Hidden Hunger,'" 27–28; William J. Murray, *Thomas M. Martin: A Biography* (Birmingham, AL, 1978), 125, 151, 209; Callahan interview, September 11, 2002; *BN,* July 10, 1941.

81. Fisher, *Building on a Vision,* 71, 183; William Niedermeier, "The Tough Hidden Hunger Fighter from Texas" (8-page typescript, MRP); Callahan interview, September 11, 2002; Norrell, *A Promising Field,* 143; Harrison, "Reminiscences," ch. 4, pp. 7–10.

82. Kracke interview, November 19, 1993; Corley et al., "History of Hillman Hospital," 90–91; Harrison, "Reminiscences," ch. 4, p. 11.

83. Scribner, *Renewing Birmingham,* 39.

84. *The Crippled Children's Clinic and Hospital, 1929–54* (N.p., 1955), copy in MRP; E. E. Cavaleri, "The Hospital That Football Built," *Birmingham Magazine* 5 (August 1966): 13–14; E. E. Cavaleri to William Riser, September 29, 1950, Harrison Medical Dean Records, UABA; Scribner, *Renewing Birmingham,* 39–40.

85. *BN,* October 31, 1947; Ernest Lowe to Roy Kracke, November 7, 1947, Kracke to Lowe, November 11, 1947; Kracke to John Gallalee, August 9, 1949 (including a 9-page typescript titled "A Summary of the Problem of the Children's Hospital," by Kracke), Kracke Medical Dean Records, UA/UABA; Hames, *Hill Ferguson,* 72; Fisher, *Building on a Vision,* 58, 61.

86. John Gallalee to Warren, Knight, and Davis, December 20, 1948, Roy Kracke to William R. Beck (Speaker, Alabama House of Representatives), May 2, 1949; typed notes detailing plans for joint use of new facility, emphasizing auditorium, with Warren, Knight, and Davis "footprint" design [1949], John M. Bruhn to Gallalee, March 17, 1949, I. J. Browder to Gallalee, January 13, 1949, all in Kracke Medical Dean Records, UA/UABA. The quote on "two oral surgery beds" related to Hill-Burton monies is from C. McCallum interview, March 2, 1993.

87. John Gallalee to John M. Bruhn, March 27, 1949, Kracke Medical Dean Records, UA/UABA; Gallalee to Joseph Volker, July 8, 1949, Volker to Gallalee, July 11, 1949, C. H. Penick to Volker, July 29, 1949, Gallalee to Volker, October 13, 1949, Volker to Gallalee, October 17, 1949, Gallalee to Volker, October 29, 1949, Gallalee to Volker and Roy Kracke, January 6, 1950, all in Volker Dental Dean Records, UABA.

88. C. McCallum interview, March 2, 1993; Timothy Pennycuff to author,

July 11, 1994 (including chronology of Medical Center Buildings), MC:MRP. I found no indication that Gallalee reprimanded the two deans for not abiding strictly by his directives regarding the "sup store."

89. Harrison, "Reminiscences," ch. 4, pp. 12–14; Kracke interview, November 19, 1993.

90. *DAU*, 74, 125; Harrison, "Reminiscences," ch. 4, pp. 12–14.

91. Holley, *History of Medicine in Alabama*, 114–15; Harrison, "Reminiscences," ch. 9, pp. 1–6.

92. Roy Kracke to Ernest Lowe, February 13, 1950, Kracke Medical Dean Records, UA/UABA.

93. Ernest Lowe to Kracke, February 16, 1950, Kracke Medical Dean Records, UA/UABA; *BN*, February 21, 1950.

94. *BN*, June 27, 1950; Eugene "Bull" Connor to Mrs. Roy Kracke, June 28, 1950, copy in MRP; Kracke interview, November 19, 1993; Morgan interview by Emerson, January 24, 1986; Fisher, *Building on a Vision*, 69; Kracke, "The Medical Care of the Veteran," 1321–27.

95. Holley, *History of Medicine in Alabama*, 113–14; James A. Pittman, "Tinsley Randolph Harrison, 1900–1978," *Transactions of the Association of American Physicians* 92 (1979): 30–32.

96. Holley, *History of Medicine in Alabama*, 196.

97. *BN*, June 27, 1950.

98. Stuart Graves to Joseph C. Hinsey, February 15, 1944, C/UABA.

Chapter 4

1. Harrison, "Reminiscences," ch. 5, p. 15.

2. Corley et al., "History of Hillman Hospital," 90–91.

3. Charles Zukoski to Tinsley Harrison, October 11 and 23, 1950, Harrison to L. D. Green, October 20, 1950, Harrison to Zukoski, October 19, 1950, all in Harrison Medical Dean Records, UABA.

4. Mrs. Emil Hess to Tinsley Harrison, April 3, 1951, Edward M. Friend, Jr. to Harrison, April 17, 1951, Harrison to Hess, April 6, 1951, all in Harrison Medical Dean Records, UABA.

5. Tinsley Harrison to E. M. Friend, Jr., April 26, 1951, MC:MRP.

6. Ibid.; Tinsley Harrison to Brewer Dixon (Talladega attorney and UA board member), May 7, 1951, Harrison to John Gallalee, May 11, 1951, Gallalee to Harrison, May 13, 1951, Dixon to Harrison, May 17, 1951, all in Harrison Medical Dean Records, UABA; *DAU*, 89, 118; Clifton O. Dummett to Joseph Volker, March 28, 1962, Volker to Dummett, March 30, 1962, Volker Personal Papers, UABA.

7. Harrison, "Reminiscences," ch. 5, pp. 1–2.

8. Ibid., ch. 5, pp. 3, 6; Thomas Spies to Tinsley Harrison, October 23, 1950, Harrison Medical Dean Records, UABA.

9. Harrison, "Reminiscences," ch. 4, p. 20, ch. 5, pp. 3–6.

10. Ibid., ch. 9, p. 18; Heldman, *The First Forty Years*, 16; Richard J. Bing to Howard Holley, February 23, 1984, APBC.

11. *DAU,* 100; Harrison, "Reminiscences," ch. 5, p. 9.

12. Harrison, "Reminiscences," ch. 5, pp. 10–11.

13. Clarence L. Mohr and Joseph E. Gordon, *Tulane: The Emergence of a Modern University, 1945–1980* (Baton Rouge, 2001), 11; Clarence Mohr to author, July 24, 2001, MC:MRP; Harrison, "Reminiscences," ch. 3, pp. 8, 12, ch. 4, p. 15.

14. Harrison, "Reminiscences," ch. 5, p. 10.

15. Ibid., ch. 5, p. 14.

16. Ibid., ch. 5, p. 12.

17. Ibid., ch. 5, pp. 12–13; Conkin, *Gone with the Ivy,* 277; *Chicago Daily News,* November 9, 1965.

18. Harrison, "Reminiscences," ch. 5, p. 12.

19. Ibid., ch. 5, pp. 13–14; *DAU,* 100.

20. Callahan, "UAB Medical School Deans," 20–21; Harrison, "Reminiscences," ch. 6, p. 1; *The Crimson and White,* March 20, 1951.

21. Harrison, "Reminiscences," ch. 6, pp. 1–2.

22. *DAU,* 30.

23. Charles E. Connerly, *"The Most Segregated City in America": City Planning and Civil Rights in Birmingham, 1920–1980* (Charlottesville, VA, 2005), 102–28; Scribner, *Renewing Birmingham,* 56–58; Corley et al., "History of Hillman Hospital," 101; *BN,* March 23, 1953; Harrison, "Reminiscences," ch. 6, p. 11.

24. Callahan, "The UAB Medical School Deans," 21.

25. *BN,* January 11, 1953; Corley et al., "History of Hillman Hospital," 91–92.

26. Corley et al., "History of Hillman Hospital," 94–95.

27. James Durrett to Mervyn Sterne, January 17, 1953, Sterne to Durrett, February 3, 1953 (copy), Durrett to Sterne, February 4, 1953, all in Durrett Medical Dean Records, UABA.

28. Harrison, "Reminiscences," ch. 6, pp. 2–5; Scribner, *Renewing Birmingham,* 48.

29. Harrison, "Reminiscences," ch. 6, pp. 2–5.

30. Ibid., 6–7.

31. Ibid., 7–8; *BN,* October 28, 2001.

32. Harrison, "Reminiscences," 5–6; Leah Rawls Atkins, *"Developed for the Service of Alabama": The Centennial History of the Alabama Power Company, 1906–2006* (Birmingham, AL, 2006), 243–44, 305–6.

33. Norrell, *A Promising Field,* 143.

34. John L. Carmichael et al., *The Saga of an American Family* (Birmingham, AL, 1982), 240–307; Clark, *The Schoolhouse Door,* 24–26.

35. Conkin, *Gone with the Ivy,* 357–58, 383–84, 402–5; Norrell, *A Promising Field,* 142–43; Clark, *The Schoolhouse Door,* 24–26; Harrison, "Reminiscences," ch. 6, p. 10; correspondence between O. C. Carmichael and Frank P. Graham, between 1937 and 1941, PFPG.

36. Clark, *The Schoolhouse Door,* 23–24, 30; Norrell, *A Promising Field,* 143–44, 159; *BN,* May 4, 1953; *Anniston Star,* August 30, 1953; *NYT,* May 29, 1953.

37. Conkin, *Gone with the Ivy,* 417, 421–22.

38. Harrison, "Reminiscences," ch. 6, pp. 11–12.

39. Ibid., ch. 6, p. 9; Corley et al., "History of Hillman Hospital," 104–5.

40. Harrison, "Reminiscences," ch. 6, pp. 13–14.

41. Ibid., ch. 6, p. 15, ch. 7, pp. 1–2; T. Duckett Jones, Maxwell E. Lapham, and Jack Masur, "The Report of the Special Survey Committee [on the] University of Alabama Medical Center," August 1954 (copy in UABA).

42. Jones, Lapham, and Masur, "Report of the Special Survey Committee," 29–33; Corley et al., "History of Hillman Hospital," 105–6.

43. Harrison, "Reminiscences," ch. 6, p. 15.

44. Interview with Matthew McNulty, March 4, 1995, MI:B3; Harrison, "Reminiscences," ch. 6, p. 12.

45. McNulty interview, March 4, 1995; Corley et al., "History of Hillman Hospital," 109–11.

46. Harrison, "Reminiscences," ch. 7, p. 1; Corley et al., "History of Hillman Hospital," 111–14; McNulty interview, March 4, 1995.

47. McNulty interview, March 4, 1995.

48. Harrison, "Reminiscences," ch. 7, pp. 2–3; Clark, *The Schoolhouse Door,* 1–133; interview with Charles A. McCallum, March 3, 1993, MI:B3.

49. Harrison, "Reminiscences," ch. 7, pp. 3–4.

50. Ibid., ch. 7, pp. 3, 5; McNulty interview, March 4, 1995.

51. Clark, *The Schoolhouse Door,* 126–34; Harrison, "Reminiscences," ch. 7, p. 6; C. McCallum interview, March 3, 1993.

52. Harrison, "Reminiscences," ch. 7, pp. 6–8, 10.

53. *BN,* August 4, 2001; *DAU,* 31, 87, 93; interview with Samuel Barker, March 3, 1993, MI:B1.

54. *DAU,* 76; C. McCallum interview, March 3, 1993.

55. S. R. Hill interviews, February 23, 1993, April 11, 1995.

56. Ibid.; Harrison, "Reminiscences," ch. 10, p. 10.

57. Callahan, "The UAB Medical School Deans," 20–21; Harrison, "Reminiscences," ch. 7, p. 11; Bill Weaver and Mary Claire Britt, "Dr. Lawrence Reynolds and His Medical History Collection," *AJMS* 21 (October 1984): 441–47.

58. *DAU,* 38, 45–46; McNulty interview, March 4, 1995; Harrison, "Reminiscences," ch. 3, p. 9, ch. 9, p. 18; interview with S. R. Hill, March 25, 1993, MI: B3; Lister Hill to Raymond Kiser, September 27, 1954, Kiser to Hill, September 29, 1954, Robert Berson to Hill, May 28, 1955, Hill to Berson, July 2, 1955, all in Lister Hill Files, UA/UABA.

59. Harrison, "Reminiscences," ch. 7, pp. 11–12, ch. 9, p. 26; *DAU,* appendix 3, 105–6.

60. Connerly, *"The Most Segregated City in America,"* 120–28; Scribner, *Renewing Birmingham,* 80; Harrison, "Reminiscences," ch. 7, p. 12; *BN,* November 4, 1951. The ironies and tragedies of urban renewal are explored on a national level in Scott Greer, *Urban Renewal and American Cities: The Dilemma of Democratic Institutions* (New York, 1965). On the Alabama scene, e.g., see Flynt, *Alabama in the Twentieth Century,* 188.

61. Brownell, *The Urban Ethos in the South,* 47–48; Champ Lyons to Sen. Hill,

May 28, 1956, Hill to Lyons, June 1, 1956, Lister Hill Files, UA/UABA; Robert Berson to Hill, September 12, 1956, University of Alabama Medical Center File, PLH; Scribner, *Renewing Birmingham,* 85–93; Numan V. Bartley, *The New South, 1945–1980* (Baton Rouge, 1995), 143–44; Schulman, *From Cotton Belt to Sunbelt,* esp. ch. 5.

62. Harrison, "Reminiscences," ch. 7, p. 12; *DAU,* appendix 3, 106; Fisher, *Building on a Vision,* 182, 184–86; Scribner, *Renewing Birmingham,* 98; Holley, *History of Medicine in Alabama,* 59; Corley et al., "History of Hillman Hospital," 125, 131.

63. Timothy Pennycuff to author, July 11, 1994, MRP, including notes on chronology of early UAB buildings; C. McCallum interview, November 22, 1993.

64. Harrison, "Reminiscences," ch. 7, pp. 12–13, 8:11–12; Scribner, *Renewing Birmingham,* 90–91; Timothy Pennycuff to author, July 11, 1994; Fisher, *Building on a Vision,* 182.

65. Fisher, *Building on a Vision,* 179; Joseph F. Volker *Vita,* Curriculum Vitae Files, UABA (hereafter Volker *Vita*); interview with Jefferson J. Bennett, February 23, 1994, MI:B1.

66. Harrison, "Reminiscences," ch. 7, pp. 4, 13; McNulty interview, March 4, 1995; Joseph Volker to O. C. Carmichael, September 14 and 20, October 1, 1954, Thomas F. Paine, Jr., to Carmichael, November 30, 1954, Carmichael to Paine, December 3, 1954, all in UA/UABA.

67. Thomas F. Paine, Jr., to O. C. Carmichael, November 30, 1954, Carmichael to Paine, December 3, 1954, Joseph Volker to Carmichael, December 15, 1954 (accompanied by handwritten note by Blanche Alexander [n.d.]), all in Volker Dental Dean Records, UABA.

68. O. C. Carmichael to Joseph Volker, January 3, 1955, Volker Dental Dean Records, UABA; Harrison, "Reminiscences," ch. 7, p. 5; *DAU,* 32; C. McCallum interview, September 15, 2001.

69. Fisher, *Building on a Vision,* 197–98; Harrison, "Reminiscences," ch. 7, p. 5; Volker *Vita;* interview with Samuel Barker, March 9, 1993, MI:B1.

70. "Annual Report of UA Medical Center, 1962–63," Ref. Coll., UABA; interview with Wayne and Sara Finley, October 21, 2002, MI:B1.

71. Harrison, "Reminiscences," ch. 12, p. 4; interview with Alice McCallum, March 5, 1993, MI:B3; *BN,* September 15, 1998.

72. Harrison, "Reminiscences," ch. 3, p. 9; Samuel Barker *Vita,* Curriculum Vitae Files, UABA (hereafter Barker *Vita*); Barker interview, March 9, 1993; interview with Charles A. McCallum, September 19, 2002, MI:B3; *BN,* September 5, 2002.

73. Barker interview, March 9, 1993; Fisher, *Building on a Vision,* 199; Charles Kochakian *Vita,* Curriculum Vitae Files, UABA; *BN,* February 14, 1999.

74. Volker *Vita;* Harrison, "Reminiscences," ch. 3, p. 9, ch. 12, pp. 5–6.

75. Volker, *The University and the City;* C. McCallum interview, September 19, 2002; Barker interview, April 30, 1995; interview with Roger Hanson, October 29, 2001, MI:B2. See also, e.g., two Volker speeches, "The Role of Engi-

neering and the Redevelopment of Cities" and "The Interfacing Role of the University," Volker President Records, UABA.

76. Volker, *The University and the City.*

77. Volker's papers and speeches make no references to what had happened with Britain's "civic universities," nor with Britain's later "concrete universities," as chronicled, e.g., in D. Jones, *The Origins of Civic Universities,* and in Barnes, "England's Civic Universities and the Triumph of the Oxbridge Ideal." Extensive interviews with Volker's colleagues also delivered no references to these particular transatlantic parallels.

78. Harrop, "Faith above Faction"; Zukoski interview, September 23, 1993; Zukoski, "A Life Story," 496–97; Harrop interview, October 31, 2000; interview with Grady Nunn, December 6, 2002, MI:B3; Virginia Fisher interview with Frank Rose (transcription), September 21, 1989, OHC; Joseph Volker to O. C. Carmichael, August 21, 1961, copy in Volker Dental Dean Records, UABA; Conrad Wright, ed., *A Stream of Light: A Sesquicentennial History of American Unitarianism* (Boston, 1975), 97–101.

79. Barker interview, March 9, 1993.

80. Ibid.; H. Adams, *Thomas Jefferson and the University of Virginia,* 86–87; Joseph Volker, *The Way of the Administrator* (Birmingham, AL, 1966), Distinguished Faculty Lecture (in the medical center) for 1966, copy in Volker Vice President Records, UABA; S. R. Hill interview, April 11, 1995; David Robinson, *The Unitarians and the Universalists* (Westport, CT, 1985), 23, 156.

81. Barker interview, March 9, 1993; C. McCallum interview, November 22, 1993; Volker, *The University and the City,* 19.

82. McNulty interview, March 4, 1995; Barker interview, March 9, 1993.

83. Joseph Volker to O. C. Carmichael, December 31, 1954, Carmichael to Volker, January 4, 1955, Volker Dental Dean Records, UABA.

84. Barker interview, March 9, 1993; McNulty interview, March 4, 1995.

85. Harrison, "Reminiscences," ch. 11, pp. 3, 6–8; Clark, *The Schoolhouse Door,* 34.

86. I. J. Browder to John Gallalee, November 17, 1949, Robert E. Tidwell to Gallalee, June 20, 1950, Browder to Gallalee, May 30, 1950, C. H. Penick to Elbert S. Jemison, January 24, 1950, Browder to Gallalee, May 31, 1951, Gallalee to Browder, June 1, 1951, all in Extension Center Files, UA/UABA.

87. John Gallalee to Robert E. Tidwell, October 24, 1950; A. R. Meadows to Gallalee, June 16, 1950, Extension Center Files, UA/UABA.

88. A. V. Weibel to John Gallalee, January 31, 1952, William P. Engel to Gallalee, January 23, 1952, Richard J. Stockam to Gallalee, January 29, 1952, all in SRI Files/UABA; *BN,* August 18, 2002. The lengthy quote is from author's interview with Jefferson J. Bennett, September 23, 1994, MI:B1.

89. J. Bennett interview, September 23, 1994; interview with Jerome ("Buddy") Cooper, July 12, 2000, MI:B1; interview with John Patterson, October 12, 2005, MI:B3.

90. *University of Alabama Extension Center News* 10 (December 1952): 1; Robert E. Tidwell to John Gallalee, June 1, 1953, Albion W. Knight to Gallalee, June 2, 1953, Extension Center Files, UABA.

91. Richard Eastwood to Robert E. Tidwell, February 12, 1954, O. C. Carmichael to Tidwell, February 24, 1954, Extension Center Files, UABA; Thompson, *The Widening Circle,* 57; George W. Campbell, "Continuing Educational Experience Offered at University of Alabama Extension Center," *Birmingham Magazine* 5 (July 1966): 8.

92. Hill Ferguson to John Gallalee, September 24, 1948, I. J. Browder to Gallalee, September 24, 1948, Town & Gown Files/UABA; Don Ward Haarbauer, "A Critical History of Non-Academic Theater in Birmingham, Alabama" (Ph.D. diss., University of Wisconsin, Madison, 1973), ch. 4; Hames, *Hill Ferguson,* 54–55; James Hatcher to Gallalee, May 23, 1953, Town & Gown Files, UABA.

93. Hames, *Hill Ferguson,* 55.

94. *BN,* May 28, 30, 1990; Barker interview, March 9, 1993.

95. *NYT,* May 30, June 9, 1990 (obit. on Roberts).

96. R. Hanson interview, October 29, 2001.

97. Thomas W. Martin to O. C. Carmichael, August 12, 1953, James R. Cudworth to Lee Bidgood, August 28, 1953, Bidgood to Cudworth, August 24, 1953, Bidgood to William A. Murray (SRI), August 24, 1953, Carmichael to Bidgood, August 12, 1953, all in Extension Center Files, UABA; W. Murray, *Thomas W. Martin,* 218 (which incorrectly states that Martin *easily* facilitated a four-year engineering program in Birmingham); Norrell, *A Promising Field,* 160–61; J. Bennett interview, February 23, 1994.

98. J. Bennett interview, February 23, 1994; interview with Jerome ("Buddy") Cooper, May 21, 2001, MI:B1.

99. Judith Stein, *Running Steel, Running America* (Chapel Hill, NC, 1998).

100. Stein, *Running Steel,* 287–88; interview with David Vann, December 10, 1995, MI:B4; Patterson interview, October 12, 2005.

101. Cooper interview, May 21, 2001; *NYT,* October 25, 1963; Stein, *Running Steel,* 67; George W. Campbell, "In the Beginning," *UAB Magazine* 6 (Fall 1986): 3; G. Campbell, "Continuing Educational Experience," 8; Rose interview by Fisher, September 21, 1989.

102. Gessner McCorvey to Ferguson, September 1, 1955, President Carmichael Files, UA/UABA.

103. Clark, *The Schoolhouse Door,* 126–33; Nunn interview, December 6, 2002; Rose interview by Fisher, September 21, 1989; Carmichael et al., *Saga of an American Family,* 290–99; *NYT,* February 8, 16, 1956, September 26, 1966; O. C. Carmichael to Joseph Volker, December 7, 1962, Volker Personal Papers, UABA.

104. Clark, *The Schoolhouse Door,* 136–39.

105. Ibid., 142; *BN,* October 25, 2002; Ehney A. Camp, Jr., *A History of the Investment Division of the Liberty National Life Insurance Company* (Tuscaloosa, AL, 1978), i–x.

106. G. Campbell, "In the Beginning," 3–4; James F. Caldwell, "For My Children" (350-page typescript, USAA), 5–6; Virginia Fisher interview with Joseph F. Volker (transcription), May 15, 1986; Rose interview by Fisher, September 21, 1989; *BN,* July 24, 1999.

107. Norrell, *A Promising Field,* 158–61, 165.

108. Wayne Echols to author, May 15, 2002, MC:MRP; Katherine Johnson

Randall, "Kudzuing of Colleges: The Proliferation and Balkanization of Higher Education in Alabama" (Ph.D. diss., University of Alabama, 2000).

109. Norrell, *A Promising Field*, 161.

110. Bosarge, "History of UAB," 13–15; *DAU*, 39–40; J. Bennett interview, February 23, 1994.

111. Harrison, "Reminiscences," ch. 7, pp. 24–26.

112. *DAU*, 46; Fisher, *Building on a Vision*, 183; Basil Hirschowitz, "Fiberoptics: Retrospect and Prospect," Distinguished Faculty Lecture (in the medical center) for 1989, UABA; "Hirschowitz Honored by Swedish Academy," *UAB Synopsis* 23 (October 4, 2004): 1; Harrison, "Reminiscences," ch. 9, p. 29. For examples of others' development work especially related to Washington, D.C., funding, see Joseph Volker to Sen. Lister Hill, February 23, 1956 (copy), Hill to Volker, February 28, 1956, Volker to Hill, March 9, 1956 (copy), Hill to Volker, March 12, April 4, 1956, Congressman George Huddleston to Volker, July 6, 1956, Hill to Volker, July 10, 1961, all in Volker Central Dean Records, UABA; Hill to Champ Lyons, January 28, 1959 (copy), Lyons to Hill, February 3, 1959, Champ Lyons File, PLH.

113. Harrison, "Reminiscences," ch. 7, pp. 19–24, ch. 11, p. 10; Robert Berson to Frank Rose, December 11, 1961 (copy), Rose to Joseph Volker, January 24, 1962, Volker to Rose (copy), January 25, 1962, all in Volker Personal Papers, UABA.

114. Harrison, "Reminiscences," ch. 8, pp. 2–4, 6–10; Callahan interviews, January 4, 1994, September 11, 2002. Callahan's obituary (*BN*, October 29, 2005) is an appropriately lengthy discussion of this fascinating physician.

115. Rose interview by Fisher, September 21, 1989; Harrison, "Reminiscences," ch. 7, pp. 25–26.

116. Rose interview by Fisher, September 21, 1989; Harrison, "Reminiscences," ch. 7, pp. 25–26.

117. *DAU*, 140–41; C. McCallum interview, March 2, 1993; *BN*, March 25, 1962; *BPH*, March 26, 1962; Richard Eastwood to Frank Rose, March 26, 1962 (copy), Volker Personal Papers, UABA.

118. Interview with C. McCallum, March 2, 1993.

119. S. R. Hill interview, March 25, 1993.

120. Ibid.; Harrison, "Reminiscences," ch. 11, pp. 16–17; Rose interview by Fisher, September 21, 1989.

121. S. R. Hill to Frank Rose, May 14, 1962 (copy), Volker Personal Papers, UABA; Rose interview by Fisher, September 21, 1989; C. McCallum interview, March 2, 1993; McCallum to Mike Ellis, March 20, 1990 (copy), Charles McCallum President Records, UABA.

122. Interview with J. Rudolph Davidson, March 3, 1993, MI:B1; J. Bennett interview, February 23, 1994.

Chapter 5

1. Carmer, *Stars Fell on Alabama*; Howell Raines, "'The Strange Country,'" in *Stars Fell on Alabama* (Tuscaloosa, AL, 2000), xi–xxii; Carl Carmer, "Back to

Alabama," *Holiday* 27 (March 1960): 50–58; Carmer to Mrs. Ira Moody, May 25, 1959, Carmer to Earl McGowin, May 25, 1959, Carmer to Justice Robert Harwood, May 25, 1959, Elizabeth Christian to Carmer, December 2, 1959, C. B. Bickerstaff to Carmer, February 19, 1960, McGowin to Carmer, March 2, 1960, Carmer to McGowin, March 14, 1960, all in PCC.

2. C. J. Coley to Carl Carmer, February 21, 1960, PCC; "Carmer Falls on Alabama," *BN,* February 20, 1960.

3. Whiting, *Vestavia Hills,* 49, 69, 297.

4. Transcript of CBS Reports, "Who Speaks for Birmingham?" 2, 15–16 (copy in MRP); videotape copy of "Who Speaks for Birmingham?" in possession of Jonathan Bass, Birmingham, Alabama; *Washington Post,* April 12, 1962.

5. Interview with Kitty Robinson, September 15, 2001, MI:B4; Virginia Fisher interview with Blanche Alexander, September 30, 1989 (transcription) and with Jane F. Williams, May 24, 1995 (transcription), OHC; Paul Brann *Vita,* Curriculum Vitae Files, UABA; *DAU,* 79, 82.

6. *BN,* July 23, 1999; Davidson interview, March 3, 1993.

7. Barker interview, March 9, 1993.

8. Interview with C. McCallum, March 3, 1992, MI:B3.

9. Ibid.; Robinson interview, September 15, 2001; *DAU,* 18, 49, 50–54, 57–58, 63.

10. *DAU,* 92; C. McCallum interview, March 3, 1992.

11. C. McCallum interview, March 3, 1992; Morgan interview by Fisher, July 20, 1989.

12. E.g., see *BN,* March 2, 1963.

13. S. R. Hill interview, March 25, 1993.

14. Ibid.; McNulty interview, March 4, 1995; "Annual Report of UA Medical Center, 1962–63," Ref. Coll., UABA; *UAMCB* 6 (November 1962): 1, 8.

15. Faculty Council Minutes, 1964–65, "Medical College Annual Report, 1963," Ref. Coll., UABA.

16. Ibid.; S. R. Hill to Joseph Volker, April 11, 1963, Hill Dean Records, UABA.

17. "Medical College Annual Report, 1963"; S. R. Hill interview, March 25, 1993.

18. "Annual Reports of Medical College, 1962–64," Ref. Coll., UABA.

19. Ibid.; S. R. Hill interview, March 25, 1993.

20. Heldman, *The First Forty Years,* 73, 79; Fisher, *Building on a Vision,* 196.

21. Heldman, *The First Forty Years,* 65, 73–74; Fisher, *Building on a Vision,* 201; Virginia Fisher interview with James A. Pittman, April 1, 1990 (transcription), OHC.

22. Heldman, *The First Forty Years,* 60; Virginia Fisher interview with Jefferson J. Bennett, August 30, 1994 (transcription), OHC; Fisher, *Building on a Vision,* 195.

23. Edward O. Wilson, *Naturalist* (Washington, DC, 1994), ch. 12; interview with E. O. Wilson, March 5, 1998, MI:B4.

24. Fisher, *Building on a Vision,* 195; interview with S. R. Hill, July 17, 1998, MI:B2.

25. Rose interview by Fisher, September 21, 1989; Clark, *The Schoolhouse Door*, 149–51.

26. Caldwell, "For My Children," 3–38.

27. Ibid., 26.

28. Interview with Jefferson J. Bennett, August 23, 1994, MI:B1.

29. Caldwell, "For My Children," 5; Michael Thomason, ed., *Mobile: The New History of Alabama's First City* (Tuscaloosa, AL, 2001), 92, 316–19.

30. Weiner, *Social Origins of the New South*, 162–63, 222; Caldwell, "For My Children," 5.

31. Interview with Fred Whiddon, January 20, 1993, MI:B4.

32. Interview with Bill McDermott, February 19, 1996, MI:B3; interview with Mylan Engle, February 19, 1996, MI:B1.

33. Whiddon interview, January 20, 1993; Caldwell, "For My Children," 31–33; Thomason, *Mobile*, 292.

34. Davidson interview, March 3, 1993.

35. Taylor Branch, *Parting the Waters: America in the King Years, 1954–1963* (New York, 1988), 314, 516–18, 572, 684, 834–38; Branch, *Pillar of Fire: America in the King Years, 1963–65* (New York, 1998), 179–87, 210–232n34; Nick Kotz, *Judgement Days: Lyndon Baines Johnson, Martin Luther King, Jr., and the Laws That Changed America* (New York, 2005).

36. Glen T. Eskew, *But for Birmingham: The Local and National Movements in the Civil Rights Struggle* (Chapel Hill, NC, 1997), 23, 210–16; Vann interview, December 10, 1995; *Wall Street Journal,* June 19, 1964, as cited in Elizabeth Jacoway and David Colburn, eds., *Southern Businessmen and Desegregation* (Baton Rouge, 1982), 233.

37. Eskew, *But for Birmingham,* 108, 182–89; Cooper interview, July 12, 2000.

38. Eskew, *But for Birmingham,* 191ff.

39. McWhorter, *Carry Me Home,* 303ff; Andrew M. Manus, *A Fire You Can't Put Out: The Civil Rights Lights of Birmingham's Fred Shuttlesworth* (Tuscaloosa, AL, 1999), 162ff.

40. R. Hanson interview, January 19, 2001; Zukoski interview, September 23, 1993.

41. R. Hanson interview, January 19, 2001; Rose interview by Fisher, September 21, 1989; interview with Abraham Siegel, October 14, 2001, MI:B4; "A Friend" to Joseph Volker, July 2, 1962, Volker Personal Papers, UABA.

42. Clark, *The Schoolhouse Door,* 213ff.; interview with Alan Dimick, January 5, 2003; *BN,* September 16 and 17, 1963; Timothy Pennycuff, " 'In a Moment of Fury': Desegregation at the University Medical Center in Birmingham, Alabama" (9-page typescript completed in 2003, MRP).

43. Zukoski, "A Life Story," 330; Bosarge, "History of UAB," 16; interview with Louis Dale, April 12, 1995, MI:B1; interview with Odessa Woolfolk, March 1, 1999, January 3, 2002, MI:B4; *Southern School News* 10 (March 1964): 6, which incorrectly reports Lawler as entering in the fall of 1964 when the second black student in the center, Ruth B. Lewis, gained admittance.

44. Medical College Faculty Council Petition, September 1963, Volker Vice

President Records; Matthew McNulty to Abraham Siegel, September 25; Scribner, *Renewing Birmingham*, 127; R. Hanson interview, January 19, 2001; Corley et al., "History of Hillman Hospital," 134; *Cahaba Valley News*, October 30, 1963.

45. C. McCallum interview, November 22, 1993; McNulty interview, March 4, 1995.

46. McWhorter, *Carry Me Home*, 331; Manus, *A Fire You Can't Put Out*, 31–32; McNulty interview, March 4, 1995.

47. Manus, *A Fire You Can't Put Out*, 155, 322; McNulty interview, March 4, 1995; Ward, *Black Physicians*, 211–12.

48. "Integration of Birmingham Hospital Staffs and Medical Organizations [based on an interview with James T. Montgomery]," *The Consortium: Concise History of Blacks in Medicine* (1983–84), 18–22, copy in OHC; Virginia Fisher interview with James T. Montgomery, August 26, 1987 (transcription), OHC; Matthew McNulty to Joseph Volker, September 18 and 19, 1964, Volker Vice President Records; Faculty Council Minutes, September 23, 1965, Medical College, Reference Collection, UABA. The written institutional records that would allow for *definitive* documentation of Montgomery's academic appointment remain lost.

49. R. Hanson interview, October 29, 2001; McWhorter, *Carry Me Home*, 169–71; Clifton Meador to author, September 29, 2005, MC:MRP.

50. Interview with Albert Brewer, February 1, 2002, MI:B1; Siegel interview, October 14, 2001; R. Hanson interview, October 29, 2001.

51. Frederick W. Kraus to Roger Hanson et al., May 20, 1963, and "Minutes of [AAUP] Meeting," May 21, 1963, Siegel Papers, MRP; R. Hanson interview, October 29, 2001; carbon typed copy of "Nettles Bill" in Siegel Papers.

52. R. Hanson interview, October 29, 2001; "Minutes of Meeting [of AAUP]" for May 27, October 21, 1963, "Resolutions Adopted by the State Conference of the AAUP," March 27, 1965, carbon typed copy of Hawkins Bill, Siegel Papers; Brewer interview, February 1, 2002; Dan T. Carter, *The Politics of Rage: George Wallace, the Origins of the New Conservatism, and the Transformation of American Politics* (New York, 1995), 232–35.

53. Rose interview by Fisher, September 21, 1989.

54. McNulty interview, March 4, 1995.

55. Joseph Volker to Jefferson J. Bennett and Matthew McNulty, April 8, 1964 (copy), Oscar Adams to G. T. McCorveny, May 19, 1964 (copy), Volker to Bennett and McNulty, July 8, 1964 (copy), McNulty to Volker, July 10, 1964, all in Volker Vice President Records.

56. Interview with Louis J. Willie, May 4, 1993, MI:B4; Oscar Adams to University of Alabama Board of Trustees, April 19, 1964, Joseph Volker to Matthew McNulty, September 18, 1964, copies in Volker Vice President Records.

57. Willie interview, May 4, 1993, from which "summit" is taken; McNulty interview, March 4, 1995, from which "relatively soon" is taken; Rose interview by Fisher, September 21, 1989.

58. Interview with James H. White III, March 23, 2001, MI:B4; Tennant S. McWilliams, "James Saxon Childers and Southern Liberalism in the 1930s," xvi–xvii, in Childers, *A White Man and a Black Man in the Deep South*. Along with James H. White III, during the early 1970s I occasionally played tennis

with Hendon and Zukoski where I witnessed this quixotic "personalism" and "good manners" between virtually mortal enemies on matters of race, even to the extent that if one of them double-faulted the other graciously offered a third serve. Zukoski: "Oh, Fox, just take one more; it's on me." (Hendon's close friends called him by the nickname "Fox.") See also *Saturday Evening Post* (April 27, 1957), p. 57.

59. R. Hanson interview, January 19, 2001.

60. Corley and Stayer, *View from the Hilltop*, 88ff.

61. Henry King Stanford to author, May 24, 1997, April 27, 1998, MC:MRP; Stanford, "Commissioner Bull Connor of Birmingham, Alabama" (photocopy of 5-page typescript [1996?]), MC:MRP; *Washington Post*, November 29, 1962.

62. Interview with Henry King Stanford, April 15, 1998, MI:B4; Corley and Stayer, *View from the Hilltop*, 88ff.; interview with Roger Hanson, October 20, 2001, MI:B2; McWhorter, *Carry Me Home*, 151–55, 359; Raines, "Reflections on Alabama," 14; Margaret House Hankins to author, December 1, 2004 (including a 3-page typescript on the Methodist Student Movement at BSC), and House to author, December 2, 2004, MC:MRP.

63. Stanford, "Commissioner Bull Connor"; Stanford interview, April 15, 1998; *NYT*, April 12, 1960; Eskew, *But for Birmingham*, 149–51.

64. Raines, "Reflections on Alabama," 14; Corley and Stayer, *View from the Hilltop*, 96–106.

65. Zukoski interview, September 23, 1993; George Campbell to Joseph Volker, October 8, 1964, Matthew McNulty to Volker, October 8, 1964, Volker Vice President Records; Robert Maddox, "A Report on the Desegregation of Higher Education in the American South" [1997] (15-page typescript, MRP); *BN*, December 12, 2002; *The Beacon* 7 (October 1964): 6.

66. McNulty interview, March 4, 1995; *BPH*, June 5, 1970; *BN*, March 31, 2005.

67. C. McCallum interview, March 2, 1993.

68. Ibid.; briefing paper on Clifton O. Dummett, Volker President Records.

69. Bonnie Kachelhofer to author, January 2, 2003, MC:MRP; obituary on Bronetta L. Scott, *Proceedings of American Association of Anatomists* 180 (September 1974): 183–84.

70. *BN*, April 17, 2000.

71. Paul Brann to Joseph Volker, March 31, 1965, Joseph Volker to Matthew McNulty, Hill, March 11 and 12, 1965; Willie interview, May 4, 1993; Pennycuff, "'In A Moment of Fury,'" 5, which derives its title from the contents of Abraham Siegel to James Crank (of University Hospital), [September 24?, 1963], Hill Medical Dean Records, UABA.

72. R. Hanson interview, January 19, 2001; Willie interview, May 4, 1993; Porter interview, November 14, 2001; *BN*, November 24, 2005. Cf. Scribner, *Renewing Birmingham*, 130–31, on Frank Spain's criticism of Volker's liberalism.

73. McNulty interview, March 4, 1995; McNulty to Joseph Volker, April 25, 1965, Volker Vice President Records.

74. McNulty interview, March 4, 1995.

75. Ibid.; Willie interview, May 4, 1993.

76. McNulty interview, March 4, 1995; Yvonne Willie to author, April 29, 1996 (with enclosed typescript memoir), MRP; interview with Durwood Bradley, March 8, 1993, MI:B1; Clifton Meador to author, September 29, 2005, MC:MRP.

77. Willie interview, May 4, 1993; McNulty interview, March 4, 1995; interview with Durwood Bradley, March 18, 1993, MI:B1.

78. Louis J. Willie to Matthew F. McNulty, May 17, 1965; see also John J. Drew to McNulty, May 17, 1965, copies in MRP.

79. James M. Quigley to Matthew McNulty, May 18, 1965, McNulty to Quigley, May 18, 1965, Quigley to McNulty, May 26, 1965, all copies in Volker Vice President Records; Fred Woodress to Joseph Volker, October 26, 1967, copy in Media Relations Administrative Records, UABA.

Chapter 6

1. Woolfolk interview, March 1, 1999; *BN*, March 21, 1963; *BPH*, November 19, 1963; Connerly, *"The Most Segregated City in America,"* 208–9.

2. E. LaMonte, *Politics and Welfare,* 196–99; Scribner, *Renewing Birmingham,* 133; Zukoski interview, September 23, 1993.

3. Scribner, *Renewing Birmingham,* 121–22; undated [1964–65] clippings from *BN*, Media Relations Files, UABA; Camp, *A History of the Investment Division of Liberty National Life Insurance Company;* Joseph Volker to S. R. Hill et al., March 6, 1968, Annual Reports and Correspondence, UABA.

4. *BPH*, February 24, 1965, February 9, 1967; *BN*, February 25, 1965; copy of program for meeting on "Mayor's Committee for Expansion of the Medical Center," in Volker Vice President Records; Zukoski interview, September 23, 1993.

5. Zukoski interview, September 23, 1993.

6. *BN*, March 3, 1965; *BPH*, March 4, 1965.

7. *BPH*, October 20, 1966; *BN*, November 22, 1966.

8. *BPH*, April 19, 1965; *BN*, November 22, 1966; *UAMCB* 9 (December 1965): 1; Connerly, *"The Most Segregated City in America,"* 208–9.

9. G. Campbell, "In the Beginning," 4; J. Bennett interview, February 23, 1994.

10. G. Campbell, "In the Beginning," 4; J. Bennett interview, February 23, 1994.

11. G. Campbell, "In the Beginning," 4; J. Bennett interview, February 23, 1994; "Tentative Outline of Study Leading to Plan for Development of Birmingham Campus" (2-page typescript [copy]), Joseph Volker to Frank Rose, August 21, 1965 (copy), Rose to Volker, August 24, 1965, Volker Vice President Records.

12. G. Campbell, "In the Beginning," 4.

13. J. Bennett interview, February 23, 1994.

14. H. Brandt Ayers, "The Rolling Tide Campus," *Anniston Star,* September 20, 1965.

15. J. Bennett interview, February 23, 1994.

16. Joseph Volker to Frank Rose, May 16, 1964 (copy), Paul Brann to Volker, October 27, 1964, Volker Vice President Records; Charles Murray, "Looking Back," *Wilson Quarterly* 8 (Autumn 1984): 97–137; Betty Doak Sherman, "From the Mountains to the Cities: UAB's Use of Appalachia Funds" (25-page typescript, MRP), 13–14.

17. Joseph Volker to Frank Rose, May 16, 1964.

18. Ibid.

19. John Sparkman to Frank Rose, February 27, 1968 (copy), PJS; Douglass Cater to the President [Lyndon B. Johnson], May 24, 1965, PPLBJ, Diary Backup; Sherman, "From the Mountains to the Cities," 12.

20. Joseph Volker to John L. Sweeney, September 27, 1965 (copy), Sweeney to Volker, September 30, 1965, Volker to Sen. Lister Hill, October 2, 1965 (copy), Hill to Volker, October 6, 1965, Volker to Congressman Robert E. Jones, February 28, 1966 (copy), Volker to Frank Rose, January 29, 1966 (copy), Albert T. Billingslea to Volker, September 19, 1966, all in Volker Vice President Records; *BN*, September 16, 1995; J. Bennett interview, February 23, 1994; Douglass Cater to Matthew McNulty, August 29, 1966, copy in MRP; Douglass Cater, "How to Have Open-Heart Surgery (and Almost Love It)," *NYT*, May 14, 1978.

21. John Sparkman to Frank Rose, February 27, 1968 (copy), Robert C. Weaver to Sparkman, March 13, 1968, Frank Rose File, PJS; Rose to Douglass Cater, March 12, 1968 (copy), Sparkman File, PFAR; J. Bennett interview, February 23, 1994; Cater to George Bundy, October 21, 1966 (copy), Lyndon B. Johnson to Rose, May 26, 1965 (copy), White House: University of Alabama File, PPLBJ.

22. Joseph Volker to Frank Rose, January 29, 1966 (copy), Matthew McNulty to Volker, April 26, May 17, 1966, UABA; *DAU*, 11, 25; Sherman, "From the Mountains to the Cities," 13–14.

23. "Tentative Outline"; G. Campbell, "In the Beginning," 4; J. Bennett interview, February 23, 1994; Howell Raines, "Goodbye to The Bear," *NR* 188 (January 24, 1983): 10–11. "The time was right" is from J. Bennett interview, February 23, 1994.

24. J. Bennett interview, February 23, 1994; Raines, "Goodbye to The Bear"; Howell Raines to author, December 15, 2004, MC:MRP. Former UA president, David Mathews, does not recall Bryant's opposing future development of UAB athletics, with the major exception of football—where Bryant did not want more competition for recruiting in-state. Coach Gene Bartow agrees that Bryant opposed development of UAB football, but also recalls Bryant opposing UAB basketball on the theory that Bartow would not be able to build a big basketball program without having a significant football program. David Mathews to author, December 16, 2004, MI:B3; interview with Gene Bartow, May 10, 2000, MI:B1.

25. Davidson interview, March 3, 1993.

26. Ibid.; BOT, 16 (May 28, 1966), 336ff.

27. Davidson interview, March 3, 1993; BOT, 16 (May 28, 1966), 336ff.

28. BOT, 16 (May 28, 1966), 336ff.; J. Bennett interview, February 23, 1994; G. Campbell, "In the Beginning," 4. The quote, "You are now on your own," is from the Jeff Bennett interview (Bennett recalled he was in the room with

Rose when Rose called Volker and Campbell). Similarly, Campbell's memoir gives, "Dr. Rose called up one afternoon . . . and said that we were on our own [financially]."

29. "An Address by President Frank A. Rose to the Joint Faculties of the University of Alabama in Birmingham," September 15, 1966, copy in Media Relations Files, UABA; G. Campbell, "Continuing Education Experience," 7–8; R. Hanson interview, January 19, 2001.

30. "Support the UAB Blood Donation Campaign," *UAMCB* 10 (December 1966): 1; *BN,* January 6, 1967, November 17, 1966; *BPH,* April 10, 1967.

31. *BN,* January 6, 1967, November 17, 1966; *BPH,* April 10, 1967.

32. Davidson interview, March 3, 1993; *DAU,* 47.

33. George W. Campbell, "CGS: Shared Authority," *Birmingham Magazine* 10 (March 1970): 22–23, 54; Davidson interview, March 3, 1993.

34. *BPH,* November 8, 1990; *UAB Reporter,* June 7, 1999; G. Campbell, "In the Beginning," 4; Curriculum Vitae Files, UABA; College of General Studies, Faculty Annual Reports, 1967–68, Campbell Dean Records, UABA; *DAU,* 16, 39, 40, 41, 48, 59, 59, 69, 112, 121.

35. "College of General Studies Plans Expansion," *UAMCB* 10 (November 1966): 1, 5, and 10 (December 1966): 1, 3; Curriculum Vitae Files, UABA; *DAU,* 3, 17, 39, 35, 59, 78, 122; Davidson interview, March 3, 1993.

36. Davidson interview, March 3, 1993.

37. Ibid.; College of General Studies, Annual Reports, 1967–68, 1968–69, Campbell Dean Records, UABA.

38. College of General Studies, Office of Admissions and Records, Annual Report, 1967–68, Campbell Dean Records, UABA; interview with Paul Spence, April 28, 1993, MI:B4; Davidson interview, March 3, 1993.

39. Davidson interview, March 3, 1993; G. Campbell, "In the Beginning," 4–5; William A. Nunnelley, *Bull Connor* (Tuscaloosa, AL, 1991), 122, 182–84; William D. Barnard, *Dixiecrats and Democrats: Alabama Politics, 1942–1950* (Tuscaloosa, AL, 1974), 55–58, 166. On Simpson, compared to Nunnelley's and Barnard's treatment, see Leah Rawls Atkins, "Senator James A. Simpson and Birmingham Politics of the 1930s," *AR* 41 (January 1988): 3–29.

40. G. Campbell, "In the Beginning," 5; interview with J. Rudolph Davidson, July 19, 2005, MI:B1.

41. Atkins, "Senator James A. Simpson," 28; Davidson interview, March 3, 1993.

42. Interview with Albert Brewer, January 22, 2002, MI:B1; Gordon E. Harvey, *A Question of Justice: New South Governors and Education, 1968–1976* (Tuscaloosa, AL, 2002), 1–64, emphasizing the complex environment in which Brewer worked; G. Campbell, "In the Beginning," 5.

43. Davidson interview, March 3, 1993; Sherman, "From the Mountains to the Cities," 14.

44. Stephen G. Katsinas, "George C. Wallace and the Founding of Alabama's Public Two-Year Colleges," *JHE* 65 (July–August 1994): 447–72; Randall, "Kudzuing of Colleges," chs. 4 and 5; Flynt, "Alabama's Shame," 67–76; *BN,* December 9, 2004.

45. S. R. Hill to H. C. Shirkey, March 15, 1965 (copy), Paul Brann to Hill et al., July 17, 1965 (including the joint operating agreement), Charles McCallum to Brann, August 5, 1965 (copy), Herschell Paul Bentley and Shirkey to A. M. Shook, Hill, and Clark D. West, September 28, 1965, Hill to Shirkey, October 6, 1965 (copy), all in S. R. Hill Medical Dean Records, UABA; *DAU*, 100, 166.

46. *BPH*, November 6, 1967; Fisher, *Building on a Vision*, 195; *DAU*, 187.

47. "Dr. Champ Lyons," *UAMCB* 9 (November 1965): 1; Holley, *History of Medicine in Alabama*, 114–15; Fisher, *Building on a Vision*, 47, 99, 181, 198; Tinsley R. Harrison, "The Effect of Champ Lyons on Medical Education in Alabama," *JMASA* 35 (February 1966): 105; Dale Short, "Pathfinder: W. Sterling Edwards," *UAB Medicine* 31 (Spring 2005): 20.

48. Interview with S. R. Hill, February 2, 1993, MI:B2; S. R. Hill to Mrs. Faye Kerner, March 14, 1966 (copy), S. R. Hill Medical Dean Records, UABA.

49. S. R. Hill interview, February 2, 1993; John Kirklin to W. Paul Brann, May 13, 1966 (copy), Matthew McNulty to S. R. Hill, May 19, 1966 (copy), McNulty to Hill, May 17, 1966 (copy), Kirklin to Buris R. Boshell, October 18, 1966 (copy), Kirklin to Joe Reeves, April 26, 1966, Hill to Kirklin, May 12, 1966 (copy), Frank Rose to Kirklin, May 10, 1966 (copy), Kirklin to Hill, May 9, 1966, all in Volker Vice President Records; *BN*, June 10, October 24, 1966; "A Beginning: A Dialogue with John W. Kirklin," *Birmingham Magazine* 10 (March 1970): 16–21, 43–46.

50. Anonymous interview, March 18, 1993, MI:B4 (under seal).

51. "A Beginning: A Dialogue with John W. Kirklin," 16–21, 43–46; interview with Donald Kahn, August 26, 2001, MI:B2; interview with Roger Hanson, October 24, 2001, MI:B2; Fisher, *Building on a Vision*, 193, 198; Anita Smith, "John W. Kirklin, M.D.," *UAB Medicine* 31 (Spring 2005): 10–11.

52. Fisher, *Building on a Vision*, 193, 197; John W. Kirklin and Brian G. Barratt-Boyes, *Cardiac Surgery* (New York, 1986).

53. Harrison, "Reminiscences," ch. 11, p. 16; interview with Richard R. Arrington, April 13, 1993, MI:B1.

54. Fisher, *Building on a Vision*, 200; *DAU*, 56; McNulty interview, March 4, 1995.

55. "University Hospital's North Wing Dedicated," *UAMCB* 10 (September 1966): 1, 7. To no avail, Volker and Hill also had sought to get funds for this project from the Joseph P. Kennedy Foundation. Sen. Lister Hill to Sargent Shriver, July 19, 1966 (copy), University of Alabama Medical Center File, PLH; Frank A. Rose to Robert F. Kennedy, July 12, 1966 (copy), S. R. Hill Medical Dean Records.

56. "Lyons-Harrison Research Building to be Dedicated," *UAMCB* 10 (November 1966): 1, 4; "Lyons-Harrison Building Dedication Will Feature Address by Sen. Hill," *Alabama M.D.* 2 (November 1966): 1; "Medical Center Expands Research Facilities," *NIH Trends* 1 (December 1966): 1, 5; Matthew McNulty to Sen. Lister Hill, August 20, 1963, Joseph Volker to Hill, November 29, 1963, University of Alabama File, PLH.

57. "America's 10 Best Hospitals," *Ladies Home Journal* 84 (February 1967): 34, 134; "Medical Deans Rate South's School, Consistently Agree on Duke and

Alabama," *JAMA* 202 (October 30, 1967): 39, 43–44; *BN*, November 3, 1967; *BPH*, October 11, November 6, 1967.

58. Joseph Volker to Sen. Hill, September 11, 1962, Sen. Hill to Volker, September 15, 1962 (copy), Sen. Hill to S. R. Hill, September 15, 1962 (copy), Volker to Sen. Hill, September 25, 1962, Sen. Hill to Volker, September 25, 1962 (copy), all in University of Alabama File, PLH; S. R. Hill to Douglass Cater, November 2, 1967 (copy), White House: University of Alabama, PPLBJ; S. R. Hill interview, March 25, 1993; *DAU*, 190.

59. Interview with Sara and Wayne Finley, October 1, 2002, MI:B1; Fisher, *Building on a Vision*, 183; Heldman, *The First Forty Years*, 72.

60. Fisher, *Building on a Vision*, 193, 197; Faculty and Staff Personnel Research Records, MRP; *DAU*, 50–51, 62, 124.

61. Fisher, *Building on a Vision*, 196; *DAU*, 159; C. McCallum interview, March 2, 1993.

62. Interview with Charles E. Bugg, March 24, 1993, MI:B1.

63. *DAU*, 152; S. R. Hill interview, March 25, 1993; Fisher, *Building on a Vision*, 99, 132, 186, 181, 188, 197, 201; "Transplants Logical Growth," *Birmingham Magazine* 10 (March 1970): 35–36.

64. John Kirklin to Joseph Volker, August 2, 1966, Volker to Kirklin, August 11, 1966 (copy), Volker Vice President Records; Fisher, *Building on a Vision*, 148, 191; interview with Harold P. Jones, August 30, 2001, MI:B4.

65. Fisher, *Building on a Vision*, 109, 113; Heldman, *The First Forty Years*, 55; S. R. Hill interview, March 25, 1993; interview with George Seibels, February 22, 1999, MI:B4; "Mission: Defeat Diabetes," *Birmingham Magazine* 10 (March 1970): 38–40.

66. Heldman, *The First Forty Years*, 71; Fisher, *Building on a Vision*, 202; *BN*, August 17, 1972; *DAU*, 6, 87, 111, 155.

67. *DAU*, 166, 190.

68. *BN*, October 19, 1967; Heldman, *The First Forty Years*, 76; "Glaze to Serve as UAB Grant Coordinator," *UAMCB* 11 (December 1965): 1–2; *DAU*, 13, 15, 50, 102, 105–6, 190.

69. Fisher, *Building on a Vision*, 94; *DAU*, 14, 40, 62, 168; *Opelika-Auburn News*, August 30, 1971; *Tupelo (MS) Journal*, August 31, 1972; *Baltimore Sun*, October 4, 1972; "Computers and the Educator," *Birmingham Magazine* 10 (March 1970): 40.

70. Fisher, *Building on a Vision*, 144, 191; *DAU*, 13, 163–64.

71. *BPH*, December 19, 1968; *DAU*, 168; Fisher, *Building on a Vision*, 187–88.

72. Joseph Volker to Sen. Lister Hill, November 21, 1964 (copy), Hill to Volker, December 18, 1964, Volker to Hill, September 25, 1965 (copy), Hill to Volker, September 27, 1965, Volker to Hill, October 2, 1965 (copy), Hill to Volker, October 6, December 31, 1965, all in Volker Vice President Records; Fisher, *Building on a Vision*, 112–13; *Mobile Register*, July 1, 1968.

73. *BPH*, December 19, 1968; *DAU*, 141; *BPH*, October 10, 1967.

74. Heldman, *The First Forty Years*, 181; *DAU*, 71, 74, 155; *BN*, April 24, 1963, May 29, 1969; "More Isn't Enough" [interview with James A. Pittman], *UAB Magazine* 2 (Fall 1986): 18; S. R. Hill interview, March 25, 1993.

75. A. Smith, *The First Fifty Years*, 161–80; *DAU*, 82–83.

76. J. Bennett interview, February 23, 1994; S. R. Hill interview, March 25, 1993.

77. A. Smith, *The First Fifty Years*, 181–95; *BN*, November 28, 1967.

78. Callahan interview, January 4, 1994; S. R. Hill interview, July 17, 1998.

79. Henry B. Peters, *School of Optometry, University of Alabama at Birmingham* (Birmingham, AL, 1994), 1–6; interview with Donald Springer, November 9, 2001, MI:B4; interview with John Amos, November 9, 2001, MI:B1.

80. Springer interview, November 9, 2001; Peters, *School of Optometry*, 1–7; interview with Henry Peters, March 9, 1993, MI:B3; "Report Prepared for Optometric Association," GCWGP, RC2 (Alabama Medical College).

81. S. R. Hill interview, July 17, 1998; interview with Alston Callahan, September 11, 2002, MI:B2; Peters, *School of Optometry*, 2; James H. Allen to John Hall Nelson, November 17, 1969 (copy), Roger L. Hiatt to Nelson, November 17, 1969 (copy), N. T. Simmonds to Nelson, November 18, 1969 (copy), "Availability of Optometric Services in Alabama, 1967," Nelson to George C. Wallace, August 4, 1971, Joseph M. Dixon to Charley Boswell, August 9, 1971 (copy), all in RC2 (Alabama Medical College), GCWGP; Harrison, "Reminiscences," ch. 4, pp. 15, 17.

82. Peters, *School of Optometry*, 2–3; Harrison, "Reminiscences," ch. 4, pp. 14–15.

83. Peters, *School of Optometry*, 2–3; Harrison, "Reminiscences," ch. 4, pp. 14–15; *BPH*, December 19, 1968.

84. S. R. Hill to State Rep. Hugh D. Merrill, May 22, 1967 (copy), S. R. Hill Medical Dean Records, UABA; Peters, *School of Optometry*, 3; S. R. Hill interview, July 17, 1998.

85. S. R. Hill interview, July 17, 1998; John Amos to author, July 26, 2001, MC:MRP.

86. Peters, *School of Optometry*, 3; Peters interview, March 9, 1993; interview with John Amos, October 2, 2001; Fisher, *Building on a Vision*, 201; *The Kaleidoscope*, September 24, 1969.

87. *DAU*, 91–92, 170; "Annual Report, 1969–70" (for School of Optometry), Annual Reports, UABA; Peters interview, March 9, 1993.

88. Amos interview, November 9, 2001; *BN*, September 15, 1975.

89. *Alabama Official and Statistical Register 1967* (Montgomery, AL, 1967), 130; Clyde G. Huggins, "The First Decade [of the USA College of Medicine]," *JMASA* 52 (February 1983): 9–10; Elisa Baldwin (of USA Archives) to author, August 1, 2001, MC:MRP; V. Gordon Moulton to author, September 21, 2001, MC:MRP; Whiddon interview, January 20, 1993; *BPH*, August 24, 31, 1966, September 26, 1967.

90. G. Harvey, *A Question of Justice*, 45–64; S. R. Hill interview, July 17, 1998; Carter, *Politics of Rage*, 28off.

91. Rogers et al., *Alabama*, 575–76; S. R. Hill interview, July 17, 1998; Davidson interview, March 3, 1993.

92. Caldwell, "For My Children," 299; Engle interview, February 19, 1996; McDermott interview, February 19, 1996.

93. Interview with Albert Brewer, September 22, 2002, MI:B1; S. R. Hill interview, March 25, 1993; S. R. Hill, "The Development of a Second Medical School in the State of Alabama," March 15, 1967 (5-page typescript), Walter B. Frommeyer to S. R. Hill, March 28, 1967, Hill to David Mathews, September 12, 1968 (copy) and Address to the Alabama State House of Representatives by James O. Finney, president, the Medical Association of the State of Alabama, August 26, 1966 (3-page typescript, [copy]), all in S. R. Hill Medical Dean Records, UABA; *BN*, October 3, 1967; State Rep. Quinton R. Bowers to Joseph Volker, March 2, 1968, Volker Vice President Records; Booz, Allen, and Hamilton, Inc., "Expansion of Medical Education in Alabama Report," November 20, 1967 (48-page typescript, UABA).

94. Tinsley Harrison and E. Joseph Reeves, *Principles and Problems of Ischemic Heart Disease* (Chicago, 1968); Tinsley R. Harrison to S. R. Hill, March 27, 1967, S. R. Hill Medical Dean Records, UABA.

95. *Mobile Press Register,* September 3, 1967; *BN,* November 29, 1967; David Mathews to James O. Finney and S. R. Hill, August 25, 1967 (copy), S. R. Hill Medical Dean Records, UABA.

96. Rogers et al., *Alabama,* 576.

97. Fisher, *Building on a Vision,* 202; Brewer interview, January 22, 2002; J. Bennett interview, February 23, 1994.

98. Joseph Volker to Jefferson J. Bennett, April 24, 1968 (copy), John Monro to Edward LaMonte, January 6, 1969 (copy), Volker to LaMonte, January 7, 1969 (copy), Volker to John Dunbar, January 20, 1969, all in Volker Vice President Records; George Campbell to Dunbar, May 27, 1970, CGS Annual Reports and Correspondence (1968–72), UABA; *BN,* April 4, 2002; *DAU,* 169, 192.

99. *BN,* April 21, May 17, July 14, 1968; *Shades Valley (AL) Sun,* April 25, 1968; *DAU,* 193; Sherman, "From the Mountains to the Cities," 15–16ff., documenting initial ARC allocations (which require state matching) as follows: $400,000 for CGS Bldg. No. 1, later the Education Building; $738,809 for CGS Bldg. No. 2, Natural Sciences, later the Chemistry Building; $449,046 for CGS Bldg. No. 3, Humanities, later the Arts and Humanities Building; and $420,232 for CGS Bldg. No. 4, Sterne Library.

100. Joseph Volker to Sen. Lister Hill, May 17, 1967, Hill to Volker, May 19, 1967 (copy), Hill to Robert C. Weaver, May 19, 1967 (copy), all in University of Alabama Medical Center File, PLH; *BPH,* December 21, 1968.

101. *BPH,* December 19 and 21, 1968; *BN,* December 20, 1968.

102. Woolfolk interview, March 1, 1999; Porter interview, November 14, 2001; *BN,* February 6, 2002.

103. Porter interview, November 14, 2001; Ernest A. Hardy, "A Study of Urban School Desegregation with Implications for the City School System of Birmingham, Alabama" (Ph.D. diss., University of Alabama, 1977), 138–51, 254–59.

104. *Birmingham World,* October 9, 1968.

105. Porter interview, November 14, 2001; interview with Mary Cargle, January 3, 2002, MI:B1; Woolfolk interview, March 1, 1999; Hardy, "A Study of Urban School Desegregation," 257–59.

106. Woolfolk interview, January 3, 2002; interview with Richard Walker, February 14, 2002, MI:B4.

107. Woolfolk interview, January 3, 2002; Walker interview, February 14, 2002; interview with Curtis Patton, June 28, 2002, MI:B3; "Chronological Guide to UAB Buildings," UABA.

108. Burkhardt, "Town within a City," 86n36.

109. *BN*, July 25, 2001; Woolfolk interview, January 3, 2002.

110. Woolfolk interview, January 3, 2002; Flynt, *Alabama in the Twentieth Century*, 290–91.

111. G. Harvey, *A Question of Justice*, 58–61; *BN*, May 9, June 3, 25, 26, July 9, 16, 29, 1969; *BPH*, June 26 and 27, 1969.

112. Senators John Sparkman and James Allen to Joseph Volker, May 5, 1969, telegram (copy), Media Relations Chronological Files, UABA; *BN*, June 3, July 21, 22, 29, 1969; *BPH*, July 22 and 28, 1969.

113. Typescript (2-page) of Radio News Release from the University of Alabama, June 16, 1969 (copy), and typescript (4-page) UA News Bureau Release, June 16, 1969 (copy), Media Relations Chronological Files, UABA; Brewer interview, September 22, 2002.

114. Brewer interview, September 22, 2002; interview with Tom Rast, April 28, 1993, MI:B4; *The Kaleidoscope*, September 24, 1969.

115. UA News Bureau Release, June 16, 1969 (copy); Joseph Volker to Frank Rose, August 23, 1965, Volker Vice President Records; J. Bennett interview, February 23, 1994. Later, Brewer did not deny the possible influence of Carmichael; at the time he just "was going on what Frank [Rose] and Joe [Volker] told [him]." Brewer interview, September 22, 2002.

Chapter 7

1. Virginia Volker to author, March 16, 2001, MC:MRP; W. Paul Brann to Ehney A. Camp, July 28, 1969 (copy), Volker President Records; Ellen Cooper Erdreich, "The Red Mountain Residence of Mr. and Mrs. A. H. Woodward," *JBHS* 7 (November 1981): 3–22; *BN*, July 24, 1999; *Birmingham City Directory, 1968, 1969*.

2. Conkin, *Gone with the Ivy*, 452.

3. Virginia Volker to author, March 16, 2001; interview with Virginia Volker, March 17, 2001, MI:B4.

4. Erdreich, "The Red Mountain Residence," 9; A. McCallum interview, March 5, 1993; V. Volker interview, March 17, 2001.

5. Jack Rosenthal, "Face-Lifting Due for Birmingham," *NYT*, May 7, 1970.

6. Jimmie Lewis Franklin, *Back to Birmingham: Richard Arrington, Jr., and His Times* (Tuscaloosa, AL, 1989), 62–91; *Knoxville Journal*, October 17, 1974; *Christian Science Monitor*, November 25, 1969; *Over the Mountain Journal*, September 21, 2000; *BN*, March 25 and 30, April 2 and 13, 2000.

7. Franklin, *Back to Birmingham*, 216ff.; *BN*, July 11, 14, and 15, 1999, April 14, June 10 and 11, 2000; Scribner, *Renewing Birmingham*, 112–17; 133–38; Eskew, *But for Birmingham*, 256–78, 328, 334–40, 369.

8. Howell Raines, "Changes Costing Birmingham Its Feeling of Security," *NYT,* September 7, 1979.

9. Ibid.

10. *NYT,* May 30, June 9, 1990.

11. Paul Spence to John Anderson, March 28, 1979 (copy), MC:MRP; "The University of Alabama at Birmingham, 1969–1978" (50-page typescript, S. R. Hill President Records, UABA), 45–48 (hereafter cited as "UAB 1969–78"); *BN,* August 29, 1968, January 15, 1976.

12. "UAB 1969–78," 29.

13. Lionel C. Skaggs to author, August 8, 1999, MC:MRP.

14. White interview, March 23, 2001.

15. Ibid.; interview with John M. Lyons, April 13, 2002, MI:B2.

16. "UAB 1969–78."

17. Ibid., 26–27.

18. *The Kaleidoscope,* July 16, 1969; S. R. Hill interview, April 11, 1995.

19. Barker interview, March 9, 1993; *DAU,* 50.

20. Heldman, *The First Forty Years,* 76; R. Hanson interview, October 29, 2001.

21. R. Hanson interview, October 29, 2001; Dale interview, April 12, 1995; Faculty Data Files, MRP.

22. *BN,* December 3 and 5, 1970; Bosarge, "History of UAB," 23, 29.

23. "UAB, 1969–78," 1–8.

24. *Birmingham Times,* March 11, 1971; Bosarge, "History of UAB," 39.

25. Davidson interview, March 3, 1993.

26. Ibid.; "UAB, 1969–78," 5.

27. "UAB, 1969–78," 25–27; Faculty Data Files and Faculty Biographical Files, MRP.

28. *DAU,* 12–13, 20–21, 69, 78, 104–5.

29. *DAU,* 1, 8, 16–17, 34–40, 57–59, 107, 111–12, 121–22.

30. "The College" and "The Schools," *University College Review,* special issue (Spring 1973): 106 (copy in MRP; hereafter cited as *UC Review*).

31. Untitled remarks by Joseph F. Volker, *UC Review,* 1; Barker interview, March 9, 1993; Mohr and Gordon, *Tulane,* xxii; Flexner, *Universities,* 232–34; Gerald Grant and David Riesman, *Perpetual Dream: Reform and Experiment in the American College* (Chicago, 1978), 188–89; Thomas Kelley, *For the Advancement of Learning: The University of Liverpool, 1881–1981* (Liverpool, 1981), 12–14; Robert Bryan to author, May 13 and 14, 2003, MC:MRP; Buffy Lockette, "A History of the College," *Alumni ClasNotes* [of Arts and Sciences of the University of Florida] (Spring 2003): 4–6.

32. Faculty Data and Biographical Files, MRP; *DAU,* 47–48; interview with James H. Woodward, September 24, 1993, MI:B4; Bosarge, "History of UAB," 49.

33. *DAU,* 16–17, 35; M. Gene Newport, *Thirty and Thriving—UAB School of Business: First 30 Years* (Birmingham, AL, 2002), 3.

34. Virginia Fisher interview with Frederick W. Conner, August 4, 1989, OHC; *Gainesville (FL) Sun,* November 3, 1995; Faculty Data and Biographical Files, MRP; interview with Frederick W. Conner, January 5, 1993, MI:B1; Robert Bryan to author, May 13 and 14, 2003, MC:MRP; Frederick W. Conner, *Cos-*

mic Optimism: A Study of the Interpretation of Evolution by American Poets from Emerson to Robinson (Gainesville, FL, 1949).

35. *DAU*, 10; William A. Harris, "A School of Arts and Sciences for UAB" (26-page typescript, MRP), 10.

36. Frederick Conner to Joseph Volker, March 24, 1972, Volker President Records; Harris, "A School of Arts and Sciences for UAB," 18–19.

37. "A Proposal for Regrouping and Renaming Divisions within the College of General Studies or University College," by W. Paul Brann, George Campbell, and Robert French, 1971, Volker President Records; Robert W. French to Paul Brann, George Campbell, John Dunbar, and S. R. Hill, October 16, 1972 (copy), Campbell to Joseph Volker, March 21, 1972 (copy), S. R. Hill Vice President Records, UABA; Virginia Fisher interview with Roger Hanson, February 7, 1990, OHC; Conner interview by Fisher, August 4, 1989; Frederick Conner to Volker, March 24, 1972, Campbell to Volker, March 27, 1972, Volker to Campbell, Conner, Roger Hanson, and George Passey, May 24, 1973 (copy), all in Volker President Records; "School of Arts and Sciences Annual Report, 1971–1972," Ref. Coll., UABA.

38. Harris, "A School of Arts and Sciences for UAB," 26–27.

39. Barker interview, March 9, 1993.

40. Joseph Volker to George Campbell, Frederick Conner, Roger Hanson, and George Passey, May 24, 1973; *DAU*, 59, 78, 122; UAB press release (untitled), June 7, 1973, Media Relations Files, UABA.

41. Newport, *Thirty and Thriving,* 8–9, 38.

42. *DAU*, 9, 27, 44–45, 101, 124; UAB press release (untitled), October 11, 1973, Media Relations Files, UABA.

43. "School of Education Annual Report, 1974–75," Ref. Coll., UABA; *DAU*, 59, 103, 132; UAB press release (untitled), March 1, 1974, Media Relations Records, UABA.

44. *DAU*, 27, 34.

45. Ibid., 122; Norman Eggleston to George Passey, March 11, 1976 (copy), Passey to Joseph Volker, March 29, 1996 (copy), Passey to David E. Harrell, Jr., April 13, 1976 (copy), Samuel Barker to Eggleston, May 2, 1977 (copy), all in MC: MRP.

46. Barker interview, March 9, 1993.

47. There is no paper documentation for information on this paragraph. The author was the one counseled by Professor Hamilton, and the author is the individual who had the conversation with President Volker. These were riveting conversations I have pondered for some thirty years.

48. Barker interview, April 30, 1995.

49. Interview with Ernest Porterfield, September 16, 1999, MI:B3; *DAU*, 122; Ernest Porterfield, *Black and White Mixed Marriages: An Ethnographic Study of Black-White Families* (Chicago, 1978).

50. Dale interview, April 12, 1995; James C. Cobb, *Away Down South: A History of Southern Identity* (New York, 2005), 263.

51. Zukoski interview, September 23, 1993; Nunn interview, December 6, 2002.

52. "Minutes of Meeting of University College Senate," especially for October 20, 1971, Ref. Coll., UABA; Bosarge, "History of UAB," 32–33; Nunn interview, Dec. 6, 2002.

53. Interview with George E. Passey, September 19, 2003, MI:B3.

54. Ibid.; interview with David Sparks, September 3, 1993, MI:B4; interview with James H. Woodward, September 25, 2003, MI:B4; School of Social and Behavioral Sciences, *Faculty Policies and Procedures Manual,* 1st ed. [1974?], Passey Dean Records, UABA.

55. Paul Spence to John Anderson, March 28, 1979, including a report, "The Development of University College Libraries," MC:MRP.

56. Ibid.; *The Kaleidoscope,* September 24, 1969.

57. Spence interview, April 28, 1993; Bosarge, "History of UAB," 50.

58. Spence interview, April 28, 1993; interview with Jerry W. Stephens, March 3, 1993, MI:B4; interview with James H. Woodward, September 24, 2003, MI:B4; Paul Spence to author, August 9, 2005.

59. *The Kaleidoscope,* May 14, 1973; Davidson interview, March 3, 1993.

60. *The Kaleidoscope,* April 1, 1970; interview with Jack Bergstresser, September 24, 2003, MI:B1; Barker interview, March 9, 1993; Craig Vetter, "Against the Wind: Nothing Fails Like Success," *Playboy Magazine* 32 (May 1985): 49. The author is indebted to Mark Duran of *Playboy* for assistance in relocating this article.

61. Susan R. Komives, Dudley B. Woodward, Jr., et al., eds., *Student Services,* 3rd ed. (San Francisco, 1966), xvii; interview with John Jones, March 24, 1993, MI:B2; interview with Aaron Lamar, March 10, 1993, MI:B2.

62. *DAU,* 169; Lamar interview, March 10, 1993.

63. Jim Writtman, "A Student's Right to Apathy," *The Kaleidoscope,* January 29, 1969; Lamar interview, March 10, 1993.

64. Interview with Cameron Spain McDonald Vowell, November 21, 2005, MI:B4; interview with William J. Baxley, November 11 and 23, 2005, MI:B1; Cameron Spain McDonald Vowell to author, November 20, 2005, MC:MRP; Samuel P. Hays, in collaboration with Barbara D. Hays, *Beauty, Health, and Permanence: Environmental Politics in the United States, 1955–1985* (New York, 1987), 58, 74–75, 324; *BN,* December 16, 1969, April 20–27, May 14 and 18, 1971; *BPH,* April 22 and 27, May 7, 1971; Linda Long, "Alabama's Missed Moment," *Business Alabama* 20 (January 2005): 17–19.

65. *The Kaleidoscope,* October 29, 1969; R. Hanson interview, October 29, 2001; interview with Bette Lee Hanson, October 24, 2001, MI:B2; Baxley interview, November 11, 2005.

66. *UAB University College* 2 (Summer 1971): 3; Bosarge, "History of UAB," 43; Cargle interview, January 3, 2002; Bracie Watson to Joseph Volker, September 12, 1974, Volker President Records; interview with Louis Dale, May 2, 2003, MI: B1.

67. Davidson interview, March 3, 1993; McCallum interview, March 2, 1993; interview with Jerry W. Stephens, May 6, 2003, MI:B4; Bosarge, "History of UAB," 34–38.

68. "Interview with Rozelle Reynolds," *UAB Magazine* 2 (Fall 1987): 6–7; *BN,* April 18, 2002; interview with C. Roger Nance, March 7, 1993, MI:B3.

69. *The Kaleidoscope,* September 24, October 15, 1969; Bosarge, "History of UAB," 35; Davidson interview, March 3, 1993; Rozelle Reynolds interview, *UAB Magazine* 2 (Fall 1987): 6–7.

70. Lamar interview, March 10, 1993; Woolfolk interview, March 1, 1994.

71. Lamar interview, March 10, 1993.

72. Ibid.; Faculty Data Files, MRP.

73. J. Jones interview, March 24, 1993; Lamar interview, March 10, 1993; *UAB Facts and Figures, 1994–1995* (Birmingham, AL, 1995), 21.

74. Lamar interview, March 10, 1993.

75. Ibid.; Andrew J. Marsh to author, May 9 and 27, 2003, MC:MRP.

76. Andrew J. Marsh to author, May 9 and 27, 2003, MC:MRP; Bosarge, "History of UAB," 23, 31; Amy E. Kilpatrick to Andrew J. Marsh, July 23, 2003 (copy), MC:MRP.

77. *The Kaleidoscope,* September 24, 1969; Bosarge, "History of UAB," 23.

78. Bosarge, "History of UAB," 28, 44; interview with Ward Haarbauer, April 14, 1995, MI:B2.

79. Joe Van Matre to author, May 10, 2001, MC:MRP; Bosarge, "History of UAB," 30, 40, 44; *The [President's] Annual Report 1975–76,* Ref. Coll., UABA; Thomas L. Alexander, "A Report on Fraternity and Sorority Founding Dates, University of Alabama in Birmingham," included in Thomas L. Alexander to Michael Raczynski, June 7, 2001 (copy), MC:MRP; [Michael Raczynski], "The Evolution of the UAB Honors Program [i.e., Convocation]," *UAB Twenty-Fifth Annual Honors Convocation,* May 21, 2000, p. 4. A number of UAB sources refer to James Dickey as the "Poet Laureate of the United States." There was no such title at that time; however, Dickey's role as "Poet Consultant to the United States" was in some ways the same thing. See Christopher Dickey, *Summer of Deliverance* (New York, 1998).

80. Interview with Virginia Horns-Marsh, December 15, 2001, MI:B3.

81. Cooper interview, May 21, 2001; *The [President's] Annual Report, 1975–76.*

82. Bosarge, "History of UAB," 31–32; UAB press release: "CGS Major Events of 1969," [n.d.], and press release: "Groundbreaking for First Building," January [?], 1970, Media Relations Press Releases, UABA; Carson McCullers, *The Heart Is a Lonely Hunter* (Boston, 1940).

83. Hamilton, *Lister Hill,* 281–82; Flynt, *Alabama in the Twentieth Century,* 66–70ff.; *BN,* July 9, 1969; *NYT,* November 17, 1985.

84. Brewer interview, February 2, 2002; *BN,* June 25, 1969; *BPH,* June 26, 1969.

85. *BN,* July 16, 1969; Davidson interview, March 3, 1993; Brewer interview, February 2, 2002.

86. Huggins, "The First Decade," 10; Brewer interview, February 2, 2002; Engle interview, February 19, 1996; McDermott interview, February 19, 1996; *Mobile Register,* October 8, 1971; *BN,* September 14 and 15, 1971.

87. *Mobile Register,* August 2, 3, and 5, 1971; Huggins, "The First Decade," 11, 14.

88. Whiddon interview, January 20, 1993; J. Bennett interview, February 23, 1994.

89. *UAB Employee Intercom,* August 1972; interview with James A. Pittman, June 24, 2003, MI:B3.

90. *BPH,* November 10, 1972, December 5, 1973; *BN,* November 26, 1972, December 10, 1973, August 18, 1974; *American Optometric News* 63 (October 1972): 1022.

91. *UAB Bulletin: The Medical Center,* December 1969, p. 3, July 1970, pp. 1–2, and October 1971, p. 5; *BN,* October 17, 20, and 21, 1971, February 29, 1972; *BPH,* October 19, 1971, September 28, 1974; *The [UAB] President's Report 1972,* Ref. Coll., UABA.

92. *BN,* August 16, 1972.

93. *UAB Bulletin: The Medical Center,* July 1970, p. 8; *Bessemer Advertiser,* October 22, 1971; *BN,* February 2, March 25, 1972.

94. *UAB Beacon* 14 (August 1970), 1–2; Jim Reed, "UA's Medical Giant," *Southern Hospitals* 39 (July 1971): 10; *Tuscaloosa News,* September 14, 1972; *BN,* March 28, 1973, February 14, April 18, July 14 and 31, September 1, 1974, November 28, 1975, July 19, 1977; *Daily Sentinel* (Scottsboro, AL), April 27, 1973; *Anadalusia (AL) Star News,* November 14, 1973; Tim L. Pennycuff, "SOM Leadership in the American Heart Association," *UAB Medicine* 31 (Spring 2005): 40.

95. *Alabama Messenger,* December 16, 1972; *Sumter County (AL) Journal,* December 20, 1972; *BPH,* May 31, 1976; Carter, *Politics of Rage,* 437; S. R. Hill interview, February 23, 1993; *BN,* August 25, 1986.

96. Joseph A. Volker, "The University of Alabama in Birmingham, 1969–1976" (58-page typescript, MRP), 48–54; Scribner, *Renewing Birmingham,* 143ff.; *NYT,* May 7, 1970.

97. Volker, "The University of Alabama in Birmingham, 1969–1976," 32; Heldman, *The First Forty Years,* 44, 71, 73; Fisher, *Building on a Vision,* 138, 173, 190, 197; *DAU,* 11–12.

98. *DAU,* 24–25.

99. Ibid.; McNulty interview, March 4, 1995; *Leader Dispatch* (Boaz, AL), January 22, 1971.

100. *Leader Dispatch,* January 22, 1971; *DAU,* 130–31; *The Beacon* 15 (February 1971): 3; interview with James Moon, April 14, 2000, MI:B3.

101. *BN,* December 17, 1970, September 13, 1972; *BPH,* April 1, 1972; *Jefferson Advertiser* (Trussville, AL), December 15, 1975.

102. *DAU,* 71.

103. James A. Pittman, "Dean's Report . . . [on] Expansion of the System," *AJMS* 12 (Spring 1975): 124–31; "Recommended Policy on Medical Education Programs at the University of Alabama, Tuscaloosa, University of Alabama in Birmingham and University of Alabama in Huntsville," March 12, 1971 (copy), James H. White III to David Mathews and Benjamin Graves, March 16, 1971 (copy), Mathews to S. R. Hill, March 18, 1971, Hill to Mathews, March 25, 1971 (copy), Hill to Joseph Volker, March 25, 1971 (copy), all in S. R. Hill Vice President Records; BOT, January 15, April 16, 1971; Heldman, *The First Forty Years,* 63; American Medical Association, *Meeting the Challenge of Family Practice* (Chicago, 1966); Clifton K. Meador, "The Art and Science of Non-Disease," *NEJM* (June 14, 1965): 92–95; *The [UAB] President's Report, 1970,* p. 2, Ref. Coll., UABA.

104. Interview with James A. Pittman, May 23, 2003, MI:B3.

105. Patricia J. West with Wilmer J. Coggins, *A Special Kind of Doctor* (Tuscaloosa, AL, 2004), ch. 2; *The [President's] Annual Report 1975–76,* 24–25; Heldman, *The First Forty Years,* 63; interview with S. R. Hill, March 25, 1995, MI:B2; Pittman interview, June 24, 2003; interview with Clifton K. Meador, August 21, 2003, MI:B3; David Mathews to author, December 16, 2004, MC:MRP.

106. *UAB President's Report, 1974,* p. 11, Ref. Coll., UABA; interviews with Clifton K. Meador, August 21, 2003, March 29, 2005, MI:B3; "MIST in Alabama," *Time* 94 (October 10, 1969): 72. The Birmingham civil rights leader Chris McNair, a noted photographer, took the shot of Meador that appeared in *Time.*

107. "Report of the Special Committee of the Board for System Medical Programs" (The McCall Report), BOT, November 18, 1972. Cf. original concept paper, "Report to the University of Alabama Special Education Committee," April 1, 1969, authored by Wayne Finley and others and submitted to President Frank Rose, copy in S. R. Hill Vice President Records; S. R. Hill to Joseph Volker, March 2 and 5, 1971, Volker President Records. On "defensive expansion," see Herbert Eugene Bolton, *The Spanish Borderlands* (New Haven, CT, 1921); on "ideals and self-interest," see Robert E. Osgood, *Ideals and Self-Interest in American Foreign Relations* (Chicago, 1953).

108. I witnessed this exchange as I was leaving McCallum's office after interviewing him on February 2, 1993; it was reconfirmed in an interview with Kitty Robinson on September 15, 2001: "Of course I said that; I probably said the exact same words to him many, many times."

109. Fisher, *Building on a Vision,* 141, 201; *BN,* October 6, 1971; *Birmingham Times,* October 28, 1971.

110. "Annual Report of the Director of Research Training, 1977–78," Volker Vice President Records.

111. *The [President's] Annual Report 1975–76; North Jackson Community News* (Stevenson, AL), August 5, 1976; C. McCallum interview, March 2, 1993.

112. *BN,* September 27, 1973; *Wetumpka Herald,* December 14, 1972; *Alabama Messenger,* July 24, 1976.

113. *The [President's] Annual Report 1975–76;* "Annual Report of the School of Dentistry, 1976–77," Ref. Coll., UABA; Minutes of the School of Dentistry Clinical Meeting, December 18, 1974 (copy), S. R. Hill Vice President Records.

114. Interview with Wilson Wright, Jr., April 30, 1998, MI:B4; C. McCallum interview, March 2, 1993.

115. Wright interview, April 30, 1998; C. McCallum interview, March 2, 1993; Carolyn Maddox to author, August 13, 2001, MC:MRP.

116. Charles McCallum to C. E. Klapper, November 19, 1969, McCallum to Margaret Klapper, December 5, 1969, McCallum to Ernest Hausman, January 12, 1970, copies, all in McCallum Dean Records; McCallum to S. R. Hill, April 10, 1974, S. R. Hill President Records.

117. "Data Summary," UAB School of Dentistry Prepared for Office of Civil Rights Compliance, May 8, 1978 (copy), McCallum Vice President Records, UABA; interview with Charles A. McCallum, March 22, 1993, MI:B3.

118. Fisher, *Building on a Vision*, 33, 109; Virginia Fisher and William A. Harris, ed., *The University and the Universe: The Internationalism of Joseph F. Volker,* with "Perspective" by Jane Williams (Birmingham, AL, n.d.), copy on Ref. Coll., UABA; *International Symposium on the Immunoglobulin System* (1972), copy in Volker President Records; C. McCallum interview, November 22, 1993; "Annual Report of the School of Dentistry, 1976–77"; Charles McCallum to Joseph Volker, December 2, 1974, Volker President Records; McCallum to Samuel Barker, February 21, 1974 (copy), William Vann to Clinical Faculty, April 9, 1974 (copy), S. R. Hill to McCallum, June 23, 1975 (copy), McCallum to Hill, November 1, 1975, Margaret Klapper to Claude Bennett et al., February 11, 1977 (copy), all in S. R. Hill Vice President Records.

119. *The [President's] Annual Report 1975–76; Sumter County Journal,* November 1, 1972; *BPH,* November 3, 1972; *Hartford (AL) New Herald,* October 23, 1975; interview with Lewis Menaker, March 23, 1993, MI:B3; Charles McCallum to Gayle Stephens (copy), August 31, 1976 (copy), McCallum to S. R. Hill, December 22, 1976, Hill to McCallum, December 27, 1976 (copy), all in S. R. Hill President Records.

120. A. Smith, *The First Fifty Years,* 215–31; Rachel Z. Booth to author, August 3, 2001, MC:MRP; *BN,* September 15, 1998; Andy Wallace to author, July 31, 2006, MC:MRP.

121. *UAB Bulletin: The Medical Center,* July 1970, p. 3; *UAB President's Report, 1974;* Peters, *School of Optometry,* 29–30; Pittman interview, June 24, 2003.

122. *DAU,* 105, 170; Peters, *School of Optometry,* 29–30; Pittman interview, June 24, 2003.

123. Virginia Fisher interview with Max Cooper, October 27, 1994, OHC; Virginia Fisher interview with Sergio Stagno, November 9, 1994, OHC; Heldman, *The First Forty Years,* 44–45; *DAU,* 100.

124. Heldman, *The First Forty Years,* 67.

125. Ibid., 77; *DAU,* 117, 158, 160, 165.

126. *DAU,* 19, 74, 152; Heldman, *The First Forty Years,* 34–38, 49.

127. Starr, *The Transformation of American Medicine,* 370; *NYT,* October 23, 1972.

128. Fisher, *Building on a Vision,* 198; Heldman, *The First Forty Years,* 47; Virginia Fisher interview with John Durant, July 28, 1994, OHC.

129. Carter, *Politics of Rage,* 317–20; S. R. Hill interview, March 25, 1993; Brewer interview, September 22, 2002; Tom R. McDougal to Board of Directors of Lurleen B. Wallace Memorial Cancer Hospital Fund, Inc., December 4, 1972 (copy), Hill to Clifton Meador and Bradley, June 29, 1972 (copy), S. R. Hill President Records.

130. Davidson interview, March 3, 1993; interview with John Durant, February 18, 1993, MI:B1.

131. Fisher, *Building on a Vision,* 189; *DAU,* 153; *BN,* March 19, June 23, August 25, 1972, April 14, August 6, 1974, January 25, February 20, 1975, January 15, 1977; *BPH,* June 23, 1972; *Southern Star* (Ozark, AL), August 13, 1975; *Montgomery Advertiser,* January 11, 1977; George E. Jay (of the National Cancer Institute) to Robert P. Glaze, May 30, 1972 (copy), Glaze to Jay, July 7, 1972 (copy),

John Durant to Cancer Center Faculty, October 23, 1973 (copy), all in S. R. Vice President Records; *UAB Conquest,* December 1973 (cancer center newsletter, copy in Media Relations Files, UABA).

132. Fisher, *Building on a Vision,* 189.

133. Starr, *The Transformation of American Medicine,* 381–83; S. R. Hill interview, March 25, 1993; Bradley interview, March 18, 1993; Pittman interview, June 24, 2003; Meador interview, August 21, 2003; Clifton Meador, "Chaos in Medical Education and the Big Money Fight of 1972," an address given August 21, 2003 at UAB's Pittman Center for Advanced Medical Science (videotape in UABA).

134. *UAB President's Report, 1972,* Ref. Coll., UABA; Pittman interview, June 24, 2003; S. R. Hill interview, March 25, 1993.

135. Davidson interview, March 3, 1993; interview with John M. Lyons, April 24, 2003, MI:B2; Pittman interview, June 24, 2003.

136. J. Durwood Bradley to S. R. Hill, March 15, 1972 (copy), Joseph Volker to Paul Brann, March 21, 1972 (copy), John Kirklin to Brann, April 21, 1972 (copy), Brann to Kirklin, April 27, 1972 (copy), all in Volker President Records; interview with Charles W. Scott, March 18, 1993, MI:B4.

137. John Kirklin to Paul Brann, April 21, 1972 (copy), Volker President Records; Davidson interview, March 3, 1993; Meador interview, August 21, 2003.

138. Paul Brann to John Kirklin, April 27, 1972 (copy), Joseph Volker to Durwood Bradley, May 5, 1972 (copy), Volker President Records; Davidson interview, March 3, 1993; Lyons interview, April 24, 2003; interviews with Clifton J. Meador, August 24, 2003, and March 29, 2005, MI:B3.

139. Volker to S. R. Hill, May 5, 1972 (copy), Ehney Camp to Joseph Volker, May 12, 1972, Volker President Records; *BN,* May 5–9, 1972; Meador interview, August 21, 2003.

140. Joseph Volker to Clifton Meador, May 5, 1972 (copy), Volker to Durwood Bradley, May 5, 1972 (copy), Bradley to Volker and S. R. Hill, May 7, 1972, Hill to John Kirklin, May 8, 1972 (copy), Hill and Volker to John Benton, May 10, 1972 (copy), Ehney Camp to Kirklin, December 20, 1971 (copy), Kirklin to Meador, January 4, 1972 (copy), all in Volker President Records; *BN,* May 5–11, 1972; press release, "John W. Kirklin," March 30, 1973, Media Relations Files, UABA.

141. S. R. Hill to Joseph Volker, May 12, 1972, and press release (draft), May 12, 1972, Volker President Records; *BN,* May 14, 1975; *Montgomery Advertiser,* May 13, 1972. See also "The Fight," a scrapbook of clippings accumulated by Clifton Meador's family, in UABA.

142. John Kirklin to Paul Brann, July 21, 1971 (copy), Volker President Records; interview with J. Claude Bennett, September 26, 2006, MI:B1.

143. J. Rufus Bealle to S. R. Hill, May 25, 1972, with photocopy of board resolution, S. R. Hill Vice President Records; Joseph Volker to Paul Brann, May 20, 1970 (copy), Volker to Clifton Meador, June 5, 1972 (copy), Volker President Records.

144. Joseph Volker to Clifton Meador, November 6, 1972 (copy), Volker Presi-

dent Records; *Greenville (AL) Advocate,* November 9, 1972, which covered the Smith-Goldstein exchange; Meador interview, August 21, 2003.

145. S. R. Hill to James A. Pittman, February 23, 1973 (copy), Volker President Records; Fisher, *Building on a Vision,* 201; press release, "Pittman Named Dean," March 14, 1973, Media Relations Files, UABA; Pittman interview, June 24, 2003; Meador interview, August 21, 2003.

146. *DAU,* 79–80, 167; *BN,* October 6, 2005; Pittman interview, June 23, 2004.

147. *DAU,* 149–50; Lorin A. Baumhover to Norman Eggleston, July 13, 1981 (copy), Harold W. Schnaper to Eggleston, December 8, 1981 (copy), MC:MRP.

148. *UAB President's Report, 1974; UAB President's Report, 1975,* Ref. Coll., UABA; *DAU,* 43, 47; Minutes of the School of Dentistry Clinical Faculty Meeting, November 27, 1974 (copy), Volker President Records; Pittman interview, May 23, 2003; G. Gayle Stephens, *The Intellectual Basis of Family Practice* (Tucson, AZ, 1982); J. J. Kirschenfeld, *No Greater Privilege: The Making of a Physician* (Montgomery, AL, 1992); James Pittman to T. Michael Harrington, May 26, 2003 (copy), MRP; James A. Pittman, "Family Practice: Past, Present and Possible Future" (38-page typescript, originally delivered before a Mercer University medical audience, January 2003), copy in MRP; Thomas S. Lawson to Benjamin B. Graves, David Mathews, Joseph F. Volker, and S. Richardson Hill, Jr., November 11, 1974, copy in S. R. Hill President Records.

149. West, 56–89; Pittman interview, May 23, 2003; James Pittman, "Dean's Report . . . on Expansion of the System," *AJMS* 12 (Spring 1975): 119–59; David Mathews to author, December 13, 2002, MC:MRP.

150. "Guide to UAB Buildings," Ref Coll., UABA; *BN,* August 17, 1975, February 8, 1978; *Alexander City (AL) Outlook,* February 3, 1978; *DAU,* 47; press release, "Kidney Dialysis," May 1976, Media Relations Records, UABA; *BN,* November 8, 2004, May 23, 2005; *UAB President's Report, 1975.*

151. Wilson interview, March 5, 1998; interview with Max Michael, May 16, 2003, MI:B3; David P. Adams, *American Board of Family Practice* (Lexington, KY, 1999); Larry A. Green et al., eds., *Keystone III: The Role of Family Practice in a Changing Health Care Environment* (Washington, DC, 2001).

Chapter 8

1. *BN,* June 16, 20, and 24, 1976; *Tuscaloosa News,* June 17, 1976; *Daily Mountain Eagle* (Jasper, AL), June 24, 1976; *Chronicle of Higher Education,* June 28, 1976.

2. Rast interview, April 28, 1993.

3. S. R. Hill interview, July 17, 1998.

4. Barker interview, March 9, 1993; Rast interview, April 28, 1993.

5. *Cullman (AL) Times,* May 30, 1976; *BN,* March 28, May 31, 1976; Barker interview, March 9, 1993.

6. Howard LaFay, "Alabama, Dixie with a Different Tune," *National Geo-*

graphic 148 (October 1975): 563; Karen J. Winkler, "Suddenly It's Birmingham," *Chronicle of Higher Education* 12 (April 19, 1976): 4.

7. Barker interview, March 9, 1993; *BN,* May 26, 1974, June 16, 1976.

8. *BPH,* December 17, 1975; *BN,* December 22, 1975; *Tuscaloosa News,* January 27, 1985.

9. Rast interview, April 28, 1993.

10. *Huntsville Times,* June 17, 1976; *BN,* June 16, 1976; *BPH,* May 19, 1976.

11. Davidson interview, March 3, 1993.

12. J. Bennett interview, February 23, 1994; Norrell, *A Promising Field,* 175, 187–88; *Huntsville Times,* June 17, 1976, May 11, 1980; interview with David Mathews, October 21, 2004, MI:B3, from which the assertion that "he never really liked the idea of a system" is taken.

13. *Alabama Journal,* February 13, 1978; *Tuscaloosa News,* November 19, December 10 and 11, 1978.

14. *BN,* June 17, 20, and 24, 1976; *Tuscaloosa News,* June 18, 1976, January 27, 1985; *Shades Valley (AL) Sun,* July 1, 1976; *Gadsden (AL) Times,* August 18, 1978.

15. *BPH,* December 29, 1976; "Hill Named President," *Alabama Medical Alumni Bulletin* 3 (Winter 1977): 1, 4; *Montgomery Advertiser,* January 15, 1977; *BN,* January 15, 1977; S. R. Hill interview, April 11, 1995: MI:B2.

16. "McCallum Appointed VP for Health Affairs," *Medical Center,* special issue (July–August 1977): 1; *DAU,* 16, 31, 50, 136, 138, 144–45; S. R. Hill interview, February 23, 1993.

17. White interview, March 23, 2001; S. R. Hill interview, March 25, 1993.

18. S. R. Hill interview, February 23, 1993; C. Bennett interview, September 26, 2006; White interview, March 23, 2001; Bugg interview, March 24, 1993; Wilson interview, March 5, 1998.

19. *Shades Valley (AL) Sun,* August 18, 1976; Lamar interview, March 10, 1995.

20. H. Jones interview, April 30, 2001; George C. Herring, *America's Longest War* (New York, 1986).

21. Peter H. Schuck, *Agent Orange on Trial: Mass Toxic Disasters in the Courts* (Cambridge, MA, 1986); interview with Mark LaGory, October 23, 2001, MI:B2; *BN,* March 2, 1984; author to Judge Jack B. Weinstein, February 2, 1999 (copy), Deborah E. Greenspan (Special [Court Appointed] Master in the Agent Orange Case) to author, May 11, 1999, MC:MRP.

22. Lamar interview, March 10, 1995; *DAU,* 54, 55; Bosarge, "History of UAB," 35–36.

23. Bosarge, "History of UAB," 52; Lamar interview, March 10, 1995.

24. S. R. Hill interview, February 23, 1993; Bartow interview, May 10, 2000; Lamar interview, March 10, 1995; "The University of North Carolina at Charlotte, 1965–Present," Special Collections, Web page of the University of North Carolina at Charlotte; *BN,* June 19, 1977; *Rocky Mountain News* (Denver), June 15, 1977.

25. S. R. Hill interview, February 23, 1993; "To Encourage the University of Alabama in Birmingham to Consider Fielding a Major Basketball Team," SJR

350, May 3, 1997 (copy), MRP; S. R. Hill to Ernest G. Williams, June 14, 1977 (copy), Winton M. Blount to Williams, June 16, 1977 (copy), Lillyan H. Fahy to S. R. Hill and Ehney A. Camp, May 12, 1977, all in S. R. Hill President Records.

26. S. R. Hill interview, February 23, 1993; *BN*, June 15, 1977.

27. Bartow interview, May 10, 2000; Gene Bartow to Jerry Young, April 27, 1977 (copy), MRP; S. R. Hill to Bartow, May 2, 1977 (copy), Bartow to Young, May 18, 1977 (copy), S. R. Hill President Papers, UABA; Young to Bartow, Mailgram, May 25, 1977 (copy), MRP; *BPH*, June 10 and 11, 1977; *BN*, June 10, 1977, October 19, 1994; *Chicago Tribune*, June 10, 1977; *Los Angeles Times*, December 8, 1978; Bartow to J. D. Morgan, June 14, 1977 (copy), MRP. From a different perspective, the *Los Angeles Times* (June 11, 1977) confirms Bartow's difficulties with fans and others loyal to Wooden.

28. *BN*, June 14, 1977; *Memphis Commercial Appeal*, June 14, 1977; *Los Angeles Times*, June 14, 1977.

29. *BN*, June 14, 1977; *BPH*, June 15, 1977.

30. *Montgomery Advertiser*, July 10, 1977.

31. *UAB Report*, July 22, 1977; *BPH*, July 15, 1977, February 14, 1978; *BN*, July 14, August 28, 1977, February 2, 1978; Shirley Whitacre (Membership Secretary, NCAA) to Gene Bartow, October 19, 1977 (copy), MRP; *The Kaleidoscope*, November 11, 1977.

32. *BN*, February 2, March 6, April 15, May 30 and 31, June 21, 1978; *BPH*, February 14, March 21, 1978.

33. *BN*, May 31, 1978; "Name Our Team" Winning Forms (copies), MRP; Bartow interview, May 10, 2000.

34. Lamar interview, March 10, 1995; Bartow interview, May 10, 2000; J. Jones interview, March 24, 1993.

35. Lamar interview, March 10, 1995; Bartow interview, May 10, 2000; J. Jones interview, March 24, 1993; *DAU*, 146.

36. J. Jones interview, March 24, 1993; S. R. Hill interview, March 25, 1993.

37. J. Jones interview, March 24, 1993; *The Kaleidoscope*, September 18, 1978.

38. *BN*, October 13, November 19, 21, 22, 23, 24, 25, and 26, 1978; *The Kaleidoscope*, November 22 and 28, 1978; *UAB Report*, November 17, December 1, 1978; *BPH*, November 25, 1978.

39. *UAB Report*, December 26 and 29, 1978; *BN*, December 29, 1978, January 5, 6, 7, 8, 10, 14, 20, and 21, 1979; Shirley Whitacre to Gene Bartow, March 7, 1979 (copy), MRP.

40. Homecoming Invitation [1979] (copy), MRP; *BN*, January 28, 1979.

41. *BN*, January 25 and 26, February 1, 4, 8, 18, 19, and 22, March 2, 1979; *BPH*, January 26, 1979; Barton interview, May 10, 2000.

42. Homecoming Invitation (copy), MRP; Tamika Dunning to author, October 19, 2001, MC:MRP; *The Kaleidoscope*, October 16, 2001.

43. *BN*, November 26, 1982, December 12, March 18, 1993.

44. *The Kaleidoscope*, January 22, 1979.

45. *UAB Baseball 2004 Media Guide*, 4; *BN*, June 8, 1999.

46. *BPH*, April 18 and 19, 1985.

47. *UAB Reporter,* November 20, 2000; interviews with James A. Garland, March 3, 1993, and May 7, 2001, MI:B2; *BN,* April 22, 1979, May 2, June 1, 1982, March 2, 3, and 21, July 6 and 7, August 8 and 17, December 9, 1983, August 9, 1984, December 11 and 12, 1984, January 20 and 23, 1985, January 15, 1986; *Birmingham Times,* December 15, 1983; *BPH,* December 16, 1983, August 25, December 10 and 12, 1984, January 22, 1985; *Montgomery Advertiser,* July 8, 1986 (an excellent overview of "the plan" and its problems). "Green space"—trees, shrubs, and grass—would be a key element in the Fine Arts Plaza, emergent "green space" informally known as "Salloway Gardens" in honor of Shirley Salloway, the assistant vice president in University College who worked closely with Garland on this project.

48. Interviews with Garland, March 3, 1993, and May 7, 2001.

49. *BPH,* October 28, 1983; *BN,* April 30, 1984; J. Jones interview, March 24, 1993; "Guide to UAB Buildings," MRP.

50. *BN,* April 26, 1976.

51. Ibid.; *DAU,* 40, 124, 147; interview with Cindy Holmes, March 13, 2001, MI:B2; undated press release on Hearn (1978), Media Relations Records, UABA.

52. *DAU,* 59, 103; Woodward interview, September 24, 2003.

53. E.g., see James C. Collins and Jerry I. Porras, *Built to Last* (New York, 2002), 169–84, on strategic advantages of "home-grown management."

54. Interview with Philip E. Austin, March 10, 1995, MI:B1.

55. *BN,* February 25 and 26, 1980; "The University of Alabama School of Medicine—the McCall Report—1980 [approved by BOT, February 23, 1981], copy in S. R. Hill President Records.

56. Pittman interview, June 24, 2003; *BPH,* January 12, 1980; *BN,* February 27, 1980, February 16 and 27, 1981; *Huntsville Times,* January 30, 1981, February 3, 1983; *Tuscaloosa News,* February 27, 1981.

57. *FF,* 1985–86 and 1986–87; *DAU,* 20, 31, 48, 80, 106; Fisher, *Building on a Vision,* 169, 193, 201; Pittman interview, June 24, 2003; Margaret A. Roser to author, August 25, 2003, Jennifer M. Long to author, August 27, 2003, MC:MRP.

58. *DAU,* 28, 31, 44, 92, 110, 117.

59. Starr, *The Transformation of American Medicine,* 187–89; *Cherokee County Herald* (Centre, AL), December 24, 1986; *DAU,* 41–42, 53, 113; *BN,* August 26, 2006.

60. *DAU,* 158–60; Bugg interview, March 24, 1993.

61. *DAU,* 79, 157–59, 162, 164.

62. Glenna Brown to author, July 23, 2003, MC:MRP.

63. *DAU,* 19, 73–74, 76, 125; Fisher, *Building on a Vision,* 195, 197, 193, 199.

64. Fisher, *Building on a Vision,* 163, 169, 191, 193, 197.

65. *FF,* 1985–86 and 1986–87; James Pittman, "The History of the [UAB] School of Medicine," Grand Rounds, UAB School of Medicine, February 5, 2000 (videotape in UABA); *BN,* November 20, 2005.

66. *DAU,* 9, 14, 21, 27, 34–35, 54, 59, 103, 122–23.

67. Ibid., 14, 36–37, 21, 40.

68. Ibid., 27, 29, 35, 37, 58.

69. Ibid., 59, 77, 103, 101, 127, 147.

70. Ibid., 1, 16–17, 67, 160; Newport, *Thirty and Thriving,* 7–8.

71. *DAU*, 108, 132; "School of Social and Behavioral Sciences Annual Report, 1979–80" (copy), MRP.

72. *DAU*, 112; Sparks interview, September 3, 1998; Meador interview, August 21, 2003; Passey interview, September 19, 2003.

73. Gerald Jonas, "Profile [of Dr. Neal Miller: Visceral Learning]," *The New Yorker* 48 (August 19 1972): 34–57, and 48 (August 26, 1972): 34–57; Edward Taub to author, July 23, 2003, MC:MRP; Neal E. Miller, "Behavioral Medicine: Symbiosis between Laboratory and Clinic," *Annual Reviews in Psychology* 34 (1983): 1–31.

74. Wilbert Fordyce, "Comment on the History and Origins of Division 38," *Health Psychologist* 25 (Summer 2003): 1, 15; Lewis Lipsitt to Edward Taub, July 23, 2003 (copy), MC:MRP; Meador interview, August 21, 2003.

75. J. Claude Bennett to S. R. Hill, March 31, 1981, Hill to Bennett, April 2, 1981 (copy), S. R. Hill President Records.

76. Sparks interview, September 3, 1998.

77. Ibid.

78. Passey interview, September 19, 2003.

79. Ibid.; Sparks interview, September 3, 1998; George E. Passey to Robert E. Levitt, May 13, 1977 (copy), Levitt to Passey, May 19, 1977 (copy), Passey Dean Records, UABA.

80. Passey interview, September 19, 2003; Sparks interview, September 3, 1998; Thomas K. Hearn to David L. Sparks, December 9, 1980 (copy), Hearn Vice President Records, UABA; George E. Passey to Sparks, November 24, 1980 (copy), S. R. Hill President Records.

81. Sparks interview, September 3, 1998; Passey interview, September 19, 2003; *DAU*, 112.

82. Robert E. Levitt to Carl E. McFarland, December 10, 1982, August 8, July 15, 1983 (copies), George E. Passey to McFarland, October 18, 1983 (copy), Sister Margaret McManus to McFarland, December 22, 1983 (copy), all in Passey Dean Records, UABA; Blaine A. Brownell to McFarland, August 17, 1987 (copy), Brownell Dean Records, UABA; *DAU*, 112.

83. McFarland to author, October 3, 2003, MC:MRP.

84. School of Social and Behavioral Sciences Annual Reports, 1985–2000, copies in MRP; Janice Lambert to author, October 1, 2001, Mary Frances Blanton to author, October 17, 2001, MC:MRP.

85. Ada Long to author, July 27, 1993, including copy of Long's ms., "Origins and Philosophy of the UAB Honors Program," MC:MRP; "A Proposal for an Honors Program in University College" (the "Benditt Report"), copy in MRP.

86. Ada Long to author, July 27, 1993; "A Proposal for an Honors Program in University College."

87. Ada Long to author, July 27, 1993; "A Proposal for an Honors Program in University College"; *BN*, November 16, 1983.

88. Ada Long to author, July 27, 1993; "A Proposal for an Honors Program in University College"; *BN*, November 16, 1983.

89. "Guide to UAB Buildings," MRP; "Honors Program Annual Report/Plan [for] 1992–93," copy in MRP.

90. *Urban Grant Act of 1978*, House of Representatives, Subcommittee on

Postsecondary Education [meeting in Birmingham, Alabama], 42nd Cong., 2nd sess., *Congressional Record,* March 23, 1978 (copy in Ref. Coll., UABA); S. R. Hill to Robert Glaze, March 24, 1978, forwarding to Congressman Ford and Commissioner Erdreich the ms. "Planning in an Urban University," by Herbert Garfinkel and Ronald W. Roskens, copy in S. R. Hill President Records; Grobman, *Urban State Universities,* 6, 87, 106–7.

91. S. R. Hill interview, April 11, 1995; Grobman, *Urban State Universities,* 106–7; Martin D. Jenkins and Bernard H. Ross, "The Urban Involvement in Higher Education: An Analysis of Selected Trends and Issues," *JHE* 46 (July–August 1975): 399–401; Arnold B. Grobman and Janet S. Sanders, *Interactions between Public Urban Universities and Their Cities* (Washington, DC, 1984); Southern Regional Education Board, *Urban Universities in the Eighties* (Atlanta, 1981).

92. Nevin Brown to author, December 8, 2004, MC:MRP; Geiger, *Research and Relevant Knowledge,* 176ff.; Graham and Diamond, *American Research Universities,* 72ff.

93. Grobman, *Urban State Universities,* 107; Geiger, *Research and Relevant Knowledge;* Daniel M. Johnson and David A. Bell, eds., *Metropolitan Universities: An Emerging Model in American Higher Education* (Denton, TX, 1995), 16, 178.

94. Thomas K. Hearn to author, December 17, 1998, MC:MRP; William M. Kimmelman, "Survey of Jefferson County Residents on Attitudes toward the University of Alabama in Birmingham," January 1977 (copy in MRP); S. R. Hill, Jr., "Urban Universities: Twentieth-Century Phenomenon," *Phi Kappa Phi Journal* 61 (Summer 1981): 38–39; S. R. Hill interview, February 23, 1993. On UAB's name change, see *UAB Report,* November 23, 1984.

95. S. R. Hill to George C. Wallace, January 17, 1983 (copy), and February 2, 1984 (copy), both with attached reports, S. R. Hill President Records; *Alabama Journal,* January 18, 1983.

96. S. R. Hill to George C. Wallace, January 17, 1983, and February 8, 1984 (copies), S. R. Hill Vice President Records; Ira W. Harvey, *A History of Educational Finance in Alabama, 1819–1986* (University, AL, 1989), 307–8.

97. George C. Wallace to S. R. Hill, February 10, 1984, S. R. Hill President Records; Carter, *Politics of Rage,* 344–45, 467.

98. S. R. Hill interview, February 23, 1993.

99. S. R. Hill interview, March 25, 1993.

100. *DAU,* 124, 147; Woodward interview, September 24, 2003.

101. *DAU,* 40, 50, 122, 147; S. R. Hill interview, March 25, 1993; *BN,* September 6, 2003.

102. *BPH,* May 29, 1983; *UAB Report,* January 18, 1985.

103. *FF,* 1979–80 through 1986–87.

104. Faye Holtzclaw to author, August 21, 2003, Joan Davis to author, August 18, 2003, MC:MRP; interview with Jerry W. Stephens, May 5, 2003, MI:B4.

105. Woodward interview, September 24, 2003.

106. Ibid.; "The City School: A UAB Professor [Daniel Lesnick] Looks Objectively at 'Back to Basics,'" *UAB Magazine* 6 (Fall 1986): 22–23.

107. Woodward interview, September 24, 2003. I served as Woodward's key staff officer (ex officio) on these committees. In the interview he confirmed the accuracy of my recollection of the strains and the arguments that unfolded in committee meetings.

108. Woodward interview, September 24, 2003; State of Alabama, ACT 94–202, March 17, 1994.

109. Interview with James H. Woodward, September 23, 2003, MI:B4.

110. Ibid.; "Department of History, Annual Report, 1979–80" (copy), MRP; *FF,* 1983–84 through 1989–90.

111. Stella Cocoris to author, August 6, 2003, MC:MRP; interview with James Garland, September 20, 2003, MI:B2. Cf. ch. 1, n. 17; *FF,* 1984–85 through 1988–89.

112. *FF,* 1988–89 through 1992–93.

113. *BN,* March 3, 2001; Flynt, *Alabama in the Twentieth Century,* 246; interview with J. Rudolph Davidson, October 18, 2005, MI:B1; interview with Bill O'Connor, November 19, 2005, MI:B3; Constitution of the State of Alabama, Amendment 399 (proposed March 1982, ratified April 1982), ACT Document No. 81-124.

114. Alabama State Senate, Rules of Order and Procedure, Rule No. 32; interview with William J. Baxley, October 26, 2005, and November 11, 2005, MI:B1; Davidson interview, October 18, 2005.

115. BOT, November 10, 1982; "Press Release: Announcement of Election of Seven New Members of the Board of Trustees of the University of Alabama," November 10, 1982, UAB Media Relations Records, UABA; Alabama Business Hall of Fame—Louis J. Willie, Jr., Web site of Culverhouse College of Commerce and Business Administration, University of Alabama; *BN,* July 3, 1983; *Tuscaloosa News,* July 1, 2, and 3, 1983; interview with J. Rudolph Davidson, February 3, 2004, MI:B1.

116. S. R. Hill to UAB Deans, Directors, and Department Heads, July 21, 1983 (copy), which has an attachment of a copy of Dalton E. McFarland to S. R. Hill, July 18, 1983, S. R. Hill President Records; Samuel Earle Hobbs to William J. Baxley, July 11, 1983 (copy), PJRD; Baxley interview, November 11, 2005; Davidson interview, October 18, 2005; *Tuscaloosa News,* January 27, 1985.

117. *FF,* 1979–80 through 1986–87.

118. Harvey, *A History of Educational Finance in Alabama,* 144ff.

119. S. R. Hill to Faculty and Staff, April 30, 1981 (copy), S. R. Hill President Records; *BN,* March 3, 2001.

120. Harvey, *A History of Educational Finance in Alabama,* 283–85, 294–95, 323, 411–12, 420; Wayne Echols to author, September 4, 2001, MC:MRP; Rogers et al., *Alabama,* 324. Cf. Don Eddins, *AEA: Head of the Class in Alabama Politics* (Montgomery, AL, 1997).

121. *FF,* 1978–79 through 1985–86; *Alabama Journal,* January 17, 1981; *Huntsville Times,* February 4, 1981; *BN,* February 16, 1981; Davidson interview, March 3, 1993; Pittman interview, June 24, 2003.

122. Davidson interview, March 3, 1993; Woodward interview, September 24, 2003.

123. *BN,* January 3, 1985; *BPH,* October 25, 1986; *FF,* 1979–80, pp. 75–76, 1988–89, pp. 101–2.

124. Joseph Volker to S. R. Hill, October 21, 1980 (copy), S. R. Hill President Records; *BPH,* July 12, 1986; Moon interview, April 14, 2000.

125. *FF,* 1979–80 through 1986–87.

126. Honors Program Annual Report, 1985–86 and 1986–87, Ref. Coll., UABA.

127. Jerry W. Stephens, "An Analysis of the Perceptions of Library Administrators Concerning the Allocation of Resources to Academic Departments" (Ph D. diss., University of Alabama, 1982); *BPH,* December 1, 1983; interview with Jerry W. Stephens, March 19, 1993, MI:B4; Spence interview, April 28, 1993.

128. Spence interview, April 28, 1993; Stephens interview, March 18, 1993.

129. Ibid.; Woodward interview, September 24, 2003; The suggestion for start-up funds (library acquisition funds) for arts and sciences faculty came from me in a May 1982 meeting of the Faculty-President Liaison Committee. I only have my calendar from that year to date the meeting—no written record of the actual discussion.

130. Claude Bennett to S. R. Hill, December 29, 1975, S. R. Hill Vice President Records; *BPH,* November 23 and 30, December 8, 14, and 16, 1983, December 10 and 12, 1984, January 21 and 22, 1985; *BN,* December 9 and 20, 1983, August 9, December 11 and 12, 1984, January 20 and 23, 1985, January 15, 1986, December 2, 2000; *Birmingham Times,* December 15, 1983.

131. *BPH,* March 1, 1980; *BN,* March 2, 1980; Pittman interview, May 23, 2003.

132. George C. Wallace to S. R. Hill, September 26, 1984, S. R. Hill President Records; *BN,* October 19, 1980, October 16 and 18, 1983, April 13 and 30, May 2, September 30, 1984, March 25, May 5 and 10, 1985, July 8 and 10, August 25, 1986; *BPH,* January 26, June 20, 1980, May 13, November 26, 1984, July 9, 1986; *Shades Valley (AL) Sun,* October 3, 1984, July 16, 1986; *Montgomery Advertiser,* July 6, 1986; *Birmingham Times,* July 10, 1986; *Mobile Press,* July 14, 1986.

133. *BN,* November 26, 1985.

134. *BPH,* January 23, 1984; Fob James to S. R. Hill, December 3, 1980, Hill to James, December 4, 1980 (copy), S. R. Hill President Records; Garland interview, September 20, 2003.

135. *Shades Valley (AL) Sun,* November 20, 1985; *BN,* July 19, 1983, November 26, December 23, 1985, June 2, 1986.

136. *BN,* July 22, 2000, November 18, 2005; Susan Matlock to author, October 21, 2005, Carolyn Garrity to author, October 25, 2005, MC:MRP.

137. S. R. Hill to Friends, July 1986 (copy), S. R. Hill President Records; *FF,* 1977–78 through 1986–87; untitled press release, May 6, 1986, UAB Media Relations Records, UABA. Katherine Bouma's "A Change in the Air" (*BN,* November 6, 2005) analyzes Birmingham's hard-won gains in getting enforcement of the 1970 Clean Air Act.

Chapter 9

1. "Time . . . the Changing of the Guard," *Medical Center Magazine* 30 (Winter 1986–87): 14–20; *DAU*, 141; Durwood Bradley to Charles McCallum, September 27, 1987, McCallum President Records.

2. *DAU*, 141–43; Timothy L. Pennycuff to author, January 25, 1999, MC: MRP; *BPH*, April 3, 1987.

3. Interview with Charles A. McCallum, September 19, 2002, MI:B3; S. R. Hill interview, February 23, 1993.

4. "Review of Administrative Structure of the University of Alabama at Birmingham—Confidential" (6-page typescript [copy], MRP).

5. C. McCallum interview, September 19, 2002; S. R. Hill interview, July 17, 1998.

6. C. McCallum interview, September 19, 2002; Davidson interview, February 3, 2004; S. R. Hill interview, July 17, 1998; Thomas A. Bartlett to Joab L. Thomas, Charles A. McCallum, and John C. Wright, November 6, 1986, Bartlett to McCallum, April 13, 1987, S. R. Hill to McCallum, September 16, 1987, McCallum to J. Rudolph Davidson, February 3, 1988, Davidson to McCallum, February 11, 1988, McCallum to Bartlett, March 24, 1988 (copy), all in McCallum President Records; Joe C. McCorquodale to Bartlett, December 9, 1987 (copy), PJRD. On advocacy of safeguards against excessive malpractice suits versus advocacy of general tort reform, see *BN*, August 25, 1986, March 22, 1987; and Edward L. Hardin, Jr., to author, March 16, 2004, MC:MRP. As president of the Alabama Trial Lawyers Association when Davidson was engaged in the complex issue of restrictions on malpractice awards, Hardin writes, "Ultimately, it's all about money. . . . the lawyer representing a client in a personal injury claim is dependent upon a doctor's cooperation to support his client's claim. Some physicians are good referral sources for the lawyers. The unwritten rule no. 1—for many years—has been: trial lawyers do not sue doctors who work with them."

7. John B. Hicks to C. A. McCallum, Joab L. Thomas, and John C. Wright, May 11, 1987 (copy), PJRD, transmitting the culminating and confidential document, "Remarks of President *Pro Tem* [John] Oliver," on why the three campus budgets should be unified as they emerged from the Legislature. Davidson interview, February 3, 2004.

8. C. McCallum interview, September 19, 2002; Jaroslav Pelikan, *The Idea of the University Reexamined* (New Haven, CT, 1992), 95–96; Henry Rosovsky, *The University: An Owner's Manual* (New York, 1990), 94–95; *Tuscaloosa News*, January 27, 1985.

9. C. McCallum interview, September 19, 2002; *BPH*, April 3, 1987; BOT, April 2, 1987; *BN*, July 20, 2006; BOT, April 2–4, 1987.

10. A. McCallum interview, March 5, 1993.

11. *BN*, July 11, 1985; James H. Woodward to Tom Coburn, September 3, 1985 (copy), PJRD; Woodward to Henry C. Goodrich, August 25, 1985 (copy), Charles McCallum to Guy Hunt, December 1, 1986 (copy), Woodward to George C. Wallace, June 19, 1987 (copy), McCallum to Hunt, June 25, August 26, 1987

(copies), Woodward to McCallum, June 5, 1987, author to McCallum, May 16, August 21, 1989, all in McCallum President Records; *FF,* 1987–88 through 1994–95. Hunt's Educational Advisory Committee consisted of Winton M. Blount (chairman), Eugene Gwaltney, Charles Webb, Sid McDonald, Carl Bailey, Al F. Delchamps, Joe Farley, John Woods, and Sid Nutting. I was a member of the task force along with Auburn's Wayne Flynt, Birmingham civic leader Caldwell Marks, and Birmingham school superintendent Cleveland Hammonds. S. R. Hill to McCallum, December 15, 1987, McCallum President Records.

12. *FF,* 1987–88 through 1993–94; Flynt, "Alabama's Shame," 67–76.

13. Woodward interview, September 24, 2003; C. McCallum interview, September 19, 2002.

14. Stella Cocoris to author, May 9, 2001, MC:MRP; Woodward interview, September 24, 2003.

15. James H. Woodward to James Pittman, December 9, 1987 (copy), McCallum President Records; Kathy Angus to author, May 17, 2000, MC:MRP.

16. Kathy Angus to author, May 17, 2000.

17. James Pittman to James H. Woodward, December 14, 1987 (copy), Woodward to Pittman, January 19, 1988 (copy), Kathy Angus to Woodward, January 22, 1988 (copy), Pittman to C. W. Scott, February 2, 1988 (copy), all in McCallum President Records; Woodward to J. Durwood Bradley, February 3, 1988 (copy), Pittman Dean Records, UABA.

18. *DAU,* 74; James H. Woodward to C. W. Scott, May 6, 1988 (copy), MRP; Scott to John R. Durant, May 12, 1988, with attached prospectus (copy), MRP.

19. *BN,* September 11, 1988.

20. George Hand to author, May 17, 2000, Virginia Gauld to author, June 27, 2000, Kathy Angus to author, June 29, 2000, all in MC:MRP; undated clipping, with photograph, from *UAB Reporter,* copy in MRP.

21. Virginia Gauld to EMSAP Committee, May 16, 1989 (copy), MRP.

22. See, e.g., "EMSAP Newsletter, 1999–2000," June 1, 2000 (15-page typescript, MRP); author to Kathy Angus, January 29, 1992 (copy), George S. Hand to James R. Boyce, April 21, 1992 (copy), MRP; *USA Today,* February 16, 2001.

23. Melody Izard to author, February 19, 1999, MC:MRP; Woodward to Charles McCallum, February 9, 1987, McCallum to Woodward, February 16, 1987 (copy), McCallum President Records.

24. J. Jones interview, March 24, 1993.

25. Fred L. Drake to Jerry Young, January 16, 1978 (copy), PJRD; Rast interview, April 28, 1993; "Guide to UAB Buildings," Ref. Coll., UABA; *Tuscaloosa News,* May 8, June 18, 1987; *Alabama Messenger,* September 22, 1990; *BN,* February 15, 1991.

26. *BPH,* May 4, November 14, 1989, September 25, 1990; *BN,* April 15, September 23, 1990; *National Library of Medicine News* 44 (May 1989): 1; *Tuscaloosa News,* May 4, 1989; *UAB Reporter,* November 20, 2000; Woodward interview, September 24, 2003; Charles McCallum to Frank Varga, September 25, 1990 (copy), McCallum to James Garland, May 13, October 21, 1991 (copy), McCallum President Records.

27. *FF,* 1987–88 through 1993–94; Ada W. Long to Committee on Qualifi-

cations [of] Phi Beta Kappa, September 16, 1985 (copy), Kenneth M. Greene to Long, March 13, 1986 (copy), Long to Charles McCallum, June 29, 1988 (copy), Douglas W. Fouard to McCallum, April 11, 1990 (copy), Phi Beta Kappa File, all in MRP; Kenneth M. Greene to Long, April 14, 1990 (copy), McCallum to Long, May 21, 1990 (copy), McCallum President Records; *NYT,* May 26, 1996.

28. Interview with Kitty Robinson, March 2, 1993, MI:B4.

29. Ibid.; *DAU,* 35, 143; Katherine Howard to Charles McCallum, August 21, 1989, Torrey Smitherman to McCallum, November 28, December 11, 1989, John M. Lyons to McCallum, March 2, 1989, McCallum to Samuel Earle Hobbs, March 1, 1989 (copy), all in McCallum President Records.

30. *FF,* 1986–87 through 1990–91; HRMF, 51, 137, 167, 174, 191, 200, 205, 259–60, 263, 275, 295; Roger L. Payne (U.S. Board of Geographic Names) to James L. McClintock, October 6, 1998 (copy), MRP.

31. Charles McCallum to Theodore M. Benditt, September 10, 1990, McCallum President Records.

32. William F. Raub (U.S. Dept. of Health and Human Services) to Charles A. McCallum, April 21, 1990, Patricia Goldman-Rakic (Society for Neuroscience) to McCallum, April 11, 1990, McCallum President Records; HRMF, 275; McCallum interview, September 19, 2002; see ch. 8, n. 73 above. For the M.D. versus Ph.D. tension with specific regard to psychosocial approaches to health care, see, e.g., Wilbert Fordyce to Frank Keefe, [2003?], reprinted in *Health Psychologist* 25 (Summer 2003): 15; Edward Taub to author, July 25, 2003, Lewis Lipsitt to Taub, July 23, 2003 (copy), MC:MRP.

33. *NYT,* June 13, 2000; *BN,* February 2, 2004. See also Norman Doidge, *The Brain That Changed Itself: Stories of Personal Triumph from the Frontiers of Brain Science* (New York, 2007), 132–63 being devoted to Taub.

34. *DAU,* 57, 82, 132, 141, 153; press release, March 9, 1990, Media Relations Files, UABA; A. Smith, *The First Fifty Years,* 312; Charles McCallum to Thomas A. Bartlett, October 13, 1986 (copy), McCallum to Bradford Wild (copy), March 5, 1987, Wild to McCallum, May 4, 1987, all in McCallum President Records.

35. Press release, October 14, 1988, Media Relations Files; *DAU,* 132; James E. Moon resume, Resume Files, UABA.

36. Clark Taylor to Charles McCallum, December 20, 1991, McCallum to Taylor, January 2 and 6, 1992 (copies), Taylor to McCallum, January 8, 1992, McCallum to John Durant, January 14, 1992 (copy), McCallum to Philip Austin, January 13, 1992, and January 24, 1992 (copy), all in McCallum President Records; *BPH,* January 9, 1992; interview with Martin Nowak, June 4, 2001, MI:B3; *DAU,* 132; C. McCallum interview, September 19, 2002; Durant interview, February 18, 1993.

37. Press release, July 15, 1992, Media Relations Files; *DAU,* 149–50; C. McCallum interview, November 22, 1993.

38. *DAU,* 43, 53, 98; *UAB Reporter,* July 17, 2000; HRMF, 184.

39. Charles McCallum to author, May 16, 1989 (copy), McCallum to James H. Woodward, May 16, 1989 (copy), McCallum President Records. The "Tennant S. McWilliams" mentioned in the text is the author.

40. C. McCallum interview, September 15, 2001; McCallum to Emil Hess,

July 20, 1989 (copy), McCallum to William Edmonds, July 18, 1989 (copy), McCallum President Records; *DAU,* 147–48; Rosovsky, *The University,* 77–98; Ralph D. Gray, *IUPUI—The Making of an Urban University* (Bloomington, 2003), 262–63.

41. Lydia Lewis Alexander et al., *Wearing Purple* (New York, 1996); press release, July 24, 1990, Media Relations Files; *DAU,* 122, 136; Stella Cocoris to author, May 9, 2001, MC:MRP; Charles McCallum to William A. Sibley, April 11, 1990, McCallum President Records.

42. Press release, August 27, 1991, Media Relations Files; *DAU,* 146, 156; Stella Cocoris to author, August 6, 2003, MC:MRP; *BPH,* August 21, 1991.

43. *BN,* November 16 and 17, 1989, October 5, 2000; *DAU,* 31; *BPH,* September 19, 1989.

44. *BN,* December 23, 1986; press releases, October 14, 1988, October 2, December 5, 1990, August 5, 1991; *DAU,* 91, 112–13, 136–37; Peters, *School of Optometry,* 28, 41, 47; *UAB Report,* October 5, 1990; "A Fond Farewell—Henry B. Peters: 1916–2000," *Focal Point* 6 (Spring/Summer 2000): 4–5.

45. Press releases, October 25, 1990, April 25, 1991, June 2, 1992, Media Relations Files, UABA; *DAU,* 55; HRMF, 70.

46. *DAU,* 74–75; press release, July 14, 1992, Media Relations Files, UABA; *DAU,* 55; HRMF, 70.

47. HRMF, 28, 32, 86, 106, 132, 140, 211, 230, 293; *DAU,* 79, 111; *BPH,* August 30, 1989; *Huntsville Times,* October 5, 1989; *FF,* 1987–88 through 1993–94.

48. *DAU,* 111; *Atlanta Constitution,* January 19, 1989; press release, March 30, 1990, December 17, 1991, Media Relations Files, UABA; S. R. Hill to Charles McCallum, December 5, 1989, McCallum President Records (including detailed analyses of Capital Campaign plans).

49. Charles McCallum to Mrs. Charles W. Ireland, December 20, 1991 (copy), December 1, 1992 (copy), McCallum to Carl Sagan, November 30, 1992 (copy), McCallum to Stephen Ambrose, November 9, 1992 (copy), McCallum to James L. Penick, February 6, 1992 (copy), all in McCallum President Records; James McClintock to author, November 17, 2001, MC:MRP.

50. Charles McCallum to Sanders Murell, October 2, 1987 (copy), June 19, 1990 (copy), McCallum to John Durant and William A. Sibley, November 26, 1990 (copy), all in McCallum President Records.

51. James H. Woodward to Charles McCallum, December 16, 1987, McCallum President Records; *BN,* June 6, 1988; press releases, October 27, 1989, March 30, 1990, Media Relations Files, UABA; "Moody's Municipal Credit Report [on University of Alabama at Birmingham Bond Issue]" (copy), MRP.

52. *BPH,* May 20, 1988; *BN,* May 20, 1988.

53. *BN,* February 5, 1987, May 19, August 14, September 28, 1988; Dudley Pewitt to Charles McCallum, February 4, 1987, McCallum to Selection Committee, Alabama Sports Hall of Fame, June 3, 1988 (copy), McCallum to Alf Van Hoose, August 18, 1988 (copy), Karl B. Friedman to McCallum, January 17, 1990, Winton M. Blount to Larry Striplin, June 17, 1988 (copy), Thomas E. Rast to Sylvester Croom, August 16, 1988 (copy), Mac Parsons to Striplin, May 24, 1988 (copy), all in McCallum President Records.

54. *DAU*, 158.

55. *BN*, July 7, 1987; *UAB Report*, October 2, 1987; Nunn interview, December 6, 2002; Virginia E. Fisher and William A. Harris, *The University and the Universe: The Internationalism of Joseph H. Volker* (Birmingham, AL, 1993).

56. Charles McCallum to Volker, September 9, 1987 (copy), McCallum President Records; *BN*, April 26, 1992; J. Jones interview, March 24, 1993.

57. *NYT*, October 8, 1991; *San Diego Union*, October 13, 1991; *Washington Post*, September 17, 1990; Armbrester, *Samuel Ullman*.

58. Margaret Armbrester to author, May 8, 2001, MC:MRP; Charles McCallum to Osamu Uno and Munehisa Sakuyama, June 18, 1990 (copy), McCallum to Sakuyama, June 3, 1991 (copy), McCallum President Records; Jiro Miyazawa to Armbrester, June 1, 1992 (copy), author to McCallum, February 19, 1993 (copy), McCallum to author, February 25, May 31, 1993, McCallum to Kiyoshi Miyazawa, May 31, 1993 (copy), McCallum to Branko Medenica, May 31, 1993 (copy), McCallum to Kenyu Akiba, May 31, 1993 (copy), Wyatt Haskell to Richard N. Friedman, May 1, 1993 (copy), Sanders Murell to James Garland, July 9, 1993 (copy), Murell to Armbrester et al., February 6, 1995 (copy), all in Samuel Ullman File, MRP.

59. *BN*, October 8, November 22, 1988; *NYT*, May 30, June 9, 1990; Haarbauer interview, April 14, 1995.

60. *DAU*, 9–10.

61. James H. Woodward to Morris Sirote, March 10, 1986 (copy), McCallum President Records; Shirley Salloway Kahn to author, April 21, 2004, MC:MRP; press release, October 7, 1992, Media Relations Files.

62. *BN*, October 4, 1992; press release, October 12, December 8, 1992, Media Relations Files; McCallum interview, September 15, 2001; Benditt interview, December 15, 2004.

63. M. Sanders Murell to Charles McCallum, November 28, 1989, July 13, 1990 (copy), McCallum to Alys R. Stephens, December 18, 1991 (copy), McCallum to Morris Sirote, November 15, 1990 (copy), August 14, 1991 (copy), McCallum to James Garland, August 15, 1991 (copy), McCallum to Stephens, December 18, 1991 (copy), all in McCallum President Records; *BN*, October 4 and 31, 1992, June 13 and 20, August 17, 1993; *BPH*, September 23, 1996; "Home Is Where the Heart Is," *Portico* 1 (March/April 2002): 60–63.

64. "Guide to UAB Buildings," Ref. Coll., UABA.

65. Margaret E. Armbrester, *The Civitan Story, 1917–1922* (Birmingham, AL, 1992); interview with Kenneth Roozen, May 25, 1993, MI:B4; *Chronicle of Higher Education* 13 (July 26, 1989): 25; Kenneth J. Roozen to author, February 9, 2004, MC:MRP; *BPH*, July 7, 1989; Charles McCallum to Philip Austin, July 24, 1989 (copy), Roozen to Doug Edgeton, October 4, 1989 (copy), McCallum to Linda Flaherty-Goldsmith, October 26, 1989 (copy), all in McCallum President Records.

66. *DAU*, 152, 166; Kenneth Roozen to author, February 9, 2004, MC:MRP; Sharon and Craig Ramey to Terry Hickey, April 2, 1990 (copy), McCallum to the Rameys, May 2, 1990 (copy), McCallum President Records.

67. *BN*, January 30, 2002; Sharon Landsmon Ramey and Craig T. Ramey,

"The Role of Universities in Child Development," in *Children and Youth*, ed. Herbert J. Walberg et al. (New York, 1997), 13–44.

68. *BPH*, November 23, 1988, October 14, 1991; *BN*, November 23, 1988, October 14, 1991; *Mobile Press Register*, November 24, 1988; *Tuscaloosa News*, November 24, 1988; "Guide to UAB Buildings," Ref. Coll., UABA.

69. *BPH*, August 30, 1989; *DAU*, 163; *Standard and Times* (Sheffield, AL), October 11, 1989; *Huntsville Times*, October 5, 1989, September 10, 1990; *BN*, March 25, 1988; "Guide to UAB Buildings," Ref. Coll., UABA.

70. Paul F. Griner, "President's Address: Academic Medicine's Changes and Challenges," *Transactions of the American Clinical and Climatological Association* 109 (1998): 1–18; Dwight E. Monson, "Managing and Improving Faculty Productivity," *Academic Clinical Practice* 11 (Winter 1998): 1–9; Stuart A. Capper and Crayton A. Fargason, Jr., "A Way to Approach Strategic Decisions Facing Academic Health Centers," *Academic Medicine* 71 (April 1996): 337–42.

71. *BN*, October 18, 1987; John Kirklin, "Training Horses, Quarterbacks, Pilots and Surgeons," (14-page typescript [copy], MRP); interview with Samuel W. Jackson, July 24, 2001, MI:B2; S. R. Hill interview, February 23, 1993; Durant interview, February 18, 1993.

72. S. R. Hill interview, February 23, 1993; *BPH*, October 16, 1989, June 13, 1992; *BN*, October 27, 1989; *Birmingham Business Journal* 9 (November 1991): 31, and 10 (December 1992): 24–27; *Tuscaloosa News*, November 3, 1991; Virginia Fisher interview with John Kirklin, June 12, 1990, OHC; Charles McCallum to John Durant, September 28, 1992 (copy), James H. Pittman to I. M. Pei, May 18, 1992 (copy), McCallum President Records.

73. Interview with Mike Ellis, February 19, 2004, MI:B1; *Montgomery Advertiser*, October 21, 1984; *Huntsville Times*, November 11, 1984; *BN*, February 24, 1991, May 31, 1992; *BPH*, March 26, 1991, June 13, 1992; Charles McCallum to Durant, March 30, 1992, (copy), McCallum President Records.

74. Charles McCallum to Philip Austin (with attachments), August 16, 1991 (copy), McCallum President Records; *BPH*, June 23, 1990; *BN*, November 13, 1992; *Huntsville Times*, February 10, 1992; "Guide to UAB Buildings," Ref. Coll., UABA; *Newsweek*, "How the Plague Began," Feb. 8, 1999.

75. Bugg interview, March 24, 1993; Fisher, *Building on a Vision*, 196; *DAU*, 159.

76. Fisher, *Building on a Vision*, 197; *BPH*, December 20, 1988, August 7, 1990, June 26, July 10, 1992; *Houston Chronicle*, August 7, 1990; *BN*, October 14, 1990, May 3, October 27, 1991, May 18, 1992; *Mobile Register*, May 13, 1992.

77. Fisher, *Building on a Vision*, 200; *DAU*, 156; *BN*, July 30, 1992; David Freedman, "Geographic Medicine: A Small World," *UAB Magazine*, no. 4 (Summer 1993): 10.

78. *BN*, October 3, 1990, February 28, 2002; *UAB Report*, October 5, 1990; McCallum interview, September 19, 2002; interview with David Rowland, March 10, 2004, MI:B4.

79. Rowland interview, March 10, 2004; McCallum interview, September 19, 2002.

80. McCallum interview, September 19, 2002; Charles McCallum to Charles Joiner, October 19, 1990 (copy), McCallum to Virginia Gauld et al., August 29,

1990 (copy), McCallum President Records; press release, October 2, 1990, Media Relations Files, UABA; *Montgomery Advertiser,* October 5, 1990. For a view of the Alabama two-year college system that is more positive than McCallum's, see, e.g., Fred Gainous, "Op-Ed Essays: Sharing the Perspective of Alabama's Two-Year Colleges," July 9, 1999 (19-page typescript, MRP).

81. BOT, September 28, 1990, p. 1127; press release, October 2, 1990, Media Relations Files, UABA; BOT [December]; *BN,* December 7, 1990; Charles McCallum to Jack Mott, December 21, 1990 (copy), McCallum President Records; Ellis interview, February 19, 2004.

82. BOT, December 7, 1990, p. 1488.

83. Charles McCallum to Samuel Earle Hobbs, March 1, 1989, Fred Gainous to Yetta G. Samford, November 16, 1990 (copy), McCallum to Vice Presidents and Deans, August 11, 1993 (copy), McCallum to John Walker, August 25, 1993 (copy), all in McCallum President Records; BOT, September 22, 1993, pp. 2455, 2458, 2475, and October 29, 1993, pp. 2508, 2509; C. McCallum interview, September 19, 2002; *BN,* March 26, 1993.

84. J. Steven Picou, "Football," *Encyclopedia of Southern Culture* (Chapel Hill, NC, 1989), 1221–24; Raines, "Goodbye to The Bear," 11; Richmond F. Brown, "'Football IS Life': The Battle for Football and Sanity at the University of South Alabama," *Gulf South Historical Review* 17 (Spring 2002): 6–39; Ira Berkow, "Alabama's Bryant and the Racial Issue," *NYT,* February 2, 1983, p. 87.

85. Bennett interview, February 23, 1994; *Wall Street Journal,* October 7, 1998; *BPH,* July 11, 2000; Bartow interview, May 10, 2000.

86. S. R. Hill to Joseph Volker, January 2, 1979 (copy), PJRD; *BN,* October 28; *Wall Street Journal,* October 7, 1998; *BPH,* July 11, 2000, August 5, 1987; *BN,* September 26, October 17, 1986, January 16, 1987; Gene Bartow to Charles McCallum, January 28, 1987, McCallum President Records; Bartow interview, May 10, 2000; George Graham to author, September 12, 2006, MC:MRP.

87. C. McCallum interview, September 15, 2001; Ellis interview, February 19, 2004; McCallum to Marvin Engle, December 12, 1989, McCallum President Records.

88. *UAB Report,* December 16, 1994; Reid Adair to author, April 21, 2004, MC: MRP.

89. Dudley Pewitt to David Knopp, January 29, 1991 (copy), Pewitt to Charles McCallum, January 29, 1991, McCallum President Records; "Statement on UAB Division III Football," March 13, 1991 (2-page typescript [copy], McCallum President Records); press release, March 13, 1991 (copy), Media Relations Files, UABA.

90. Press release, March 13, 1991 (copy), Media Relations Files, UABA; Charles McCallum to T. Michael Goodrich, September 19, 1991 (copy), Virginia Gauld to McCallum, November 7, 1991, McCallum to Kenneth J. Roozen, November 11, 1991 (copy), May 27, 1992 (copy), all in McCallum President Records; Davidson interview, February 3, 2004.

91. Charles McCallum to Philip Austin, November 12, 1992 (copy), McCallum President Records.

92. Charles McCallum to Gene Bartow, January 22, 1993 (copy), McCallum

to Philip Austin, January 22, 1993 (copy), McCallum President Records. Cf. Michael Sokolove, "Football Is a Sucker's Game," *New York Times Magazine,* December 22, 2002, p. 36.

93. C. McCallum interview, September 15, 2001; Arrington interview, May 13, 1993.

94. *BN,* March 17, 18, and 19, 1993, which includes a detailed narrative of UAB-UA basketball tensions; McCallum to Larry Striplin, January 27, 1989 (copy), McCallum President Records.

95. Charles McCallum, "The Challenge of Service," Distinguished Faculty Lecture, April 1972 (copy), James H. Woodward to McCallum, May 29, 1987, author to McCallum, June 2, 1987, Sheila Barons to McCallum, January 4, 1991, all in McCallum President Records; Woolfolk interview, March 1, 1999.

96. Consent Decree, in *Perry Woods et al. v. Board of Trustees of the University of Alabama et al.* (Civil Action Number 87-C-2182S), in the U.S. District Court for the Northern District of Alabama, Southern Division, November 9, 1990 (copy), Ina B. Leonard to John Walker, December 11, 1990 (copy), Brooks Baker to Richard Farrell, March 14, 1991 (copy), Farrell to Baker, March 19, 1991 (copy), files of UAB Legal Office.

97. *Knight v. Alabama,* 787 F. Supp. 1030 (N.D. Ala. 1991); "Chronology of *Knight v. Alabama*" (copy), 5-page typescript prepared by UA System Legal Office, MRP; *Tuscaloosa News,* January 31, 1980, April 2, 1991; *BN,* February 21, 1993; *The Kaleidoscope,* November 15, 1994; *UAB Reporter,* August 21, 1995; *BPH,* August 25, 1998; *NYT,* September 20, 1998; *Huntsville Times,* February 6, 1991, August 3, 1995; *Black Issues in Higher Education,* April 17, 1997. In September 2006, the Knight case appeared to be moving to final resolution. *BN,* September 30, 2006.

98. Ina Leonard to author, February 3, 2004, MC:MRP; interview with Glenn Powell, September 4, 2000, MI:B3; interview with Charles R. Clark, December 29, 2004, MI:B1. Copies of Clark's reports are in MRP.

99. Kenneth J. Roozen to author, February 9, 2004, MC:MRP; Dale interview, April 12, 1995; C. McCallum interview, November 22, 1993; Flynt, *Alabama in the Twentieth Century,* 367.

100. Kenneth J. Roozen to author, February 9, 2004; Dale interview, April 12, 1995; C. McCallum interview, November 22, 1993; Flynt, *Alabama in the Twentieth Century,* 367; *Los Angeles Sentinel,* December 8, 1988; Dale interview, Apr. 12, 1995.

101. C. McCallum interview, September 19, 2002.

102. *UAB Reporter,* September 18, 2000; *Birmingham World,* July 27, August 2, 1995; Charles McCallum to Crawford T. Johnson III, September 14, 1990 (copy), Diane Gray to Kenneth J. Roozen, November 12, 1990 (copy), McCallum President Records.

103. Cynthia Scott to author, March 3, 2000 (including report on Comprehensive Minority Faculty Development Program [CMFDP] through 1994), and "[UAB] Minority Participation Report . . . June 1995," 2–5, MRP; *BN,* May 24, 1995.

104. "Minority Participation Report," 2, 6; George Munchus to Black Faculty, December 2, 1991 (copy), MRP.

105. "Minority Participation Report," 2–5, exhibit 4.

106. Robert Glaze to Charles McCallum, September 10, 1987, Dudley Pewitt to McCallum, March 7, 1988, McCallum to Pewitt, March 21, 1988 (copy), McCallum to George Perdue, November 7, 1988 (copy), all in McCallum President Records; Perdue to Kenneth J. Roozen et al., April 25, 1995, with attachments, especially exhibits A–F, included in "Minority Participation Report"; press release, August 14, 2000, Media Relations Files, UABA; *UAB Reporter,* August 21, 2000.

107. Press release, February 14, 1991, Media Relations Files, UABA; G. Perdue interview, May 8, 2001, MI:B2.

108. Clint E. Bruess to author, February 14, 2000, author to Ira Harkavy, April 22, 2004, Harkavy to author, April 25, 2004, MC:MRP.

109. Charlene McKaig press release, October 25, 1991, Media Relations Files, UABA; Woolfolk interview, March 1, 1999; C. McCallum interview, November 22, 1993.

110. "Results of the Vision and Auditory Screening," February 28, 1991, Titusville 2000 Notes—A Summary of Activities" (July 1991), Charles McCallum to Pinnie H. Yarbrough, August 2, 1991 (copy), McCallum to Kenneth J. Roozen and Bill Croker, December 9, 1991 (copy), Odessa Woolfolk to McCallum, December 10, 191, McCallum to Richard Arrington, December 16, 1991 (copy), all in McCallum President Records; *UAB Reporter,* July 17, 2000.

111. Barbara Lewis to author, May 6, 2004, MC:MRP; interview with Barbara Lewis, May 7, 2004; Charles McCallum to author, December 12, 1991 (copy), McCallum President Records.

112. S. R. Hill to Houston Blount, May 14, 1992 (copy), McCallum President Records; Karen DeWitt, "Universities Become Full Partners in Cities in the South," *NYT,* August 13, 1991; *BN,* August 14, 1991; Charles McCallum, "The Bottom Line: Broadening the Faculty Reward System," *Teachers College Record* 95 (Spring 1994): 1–5; U.S. House of Representatives, Committee on Banking, Finance, and Urban Affairs, "The Role of Urban Universities in Economic and Community Development," Serial No. 102-40, October 28, 1991 (Washington, DC, 1992), 1–84.

113. *New Choices for Retirement Living* [a publication of *Reader's Digest*] 32 (September 1992): 61–70; *U.S. News & World Report* 113 (September 28, 1992): 113; *Rochester Post Bulletin,* September 3, 1992; Orbie Medders, "Why Go to Minnesota?" *Business Alabama Monthly* 7 (December 1992): 24–27; Dean Anason, "Atlanta's Neighbor Is Racing to Be the South's Health Hub," *Atlanta Business Chronicle,* November 13–19, 1992, pp. 1, 18B; *Eastern Shore Courier* (Fairhope, AL), February 10, 1993.

114. "Introduction," *[UAB] Dictionary of Academic Units,* ii–iii; Virginia Fisher and William Harris, "UAB Archives Annual Report, July 22, 1992–June 1993" (11-page typescript [copy], MRP).

115. Timothy Pennycuff to author, May 21, September 21, 2001, MC:MRP;

Fisher, *Building on a Vision,* 202; S. R. Hill to Charles McCallum, August 27, 1987, McCallum to Jeffrey Cohn, July 16, 1990 (copy), Edwin G. Waldrop to McCallum, August 20, 1990 (copy), McCallum to author, March 8, 1990 (copy), James Pittman to Edwin C. Bridges, June 22, 1992 (copy), McCallum to Jerry W. Stephens, November 1992 (copy), McCallum to John Durant, November 16, 1992 (copy), all in McCallum President Records.

116. *UAB Report,* December 11, 1992; *BPH,* July 24, August 11, 1990; *BN,* August 8, 1990, December 20, 1992; press release, December 8, 1992, Media Relations Files, UABA; "UAB's Economic Impact, [1985–1993]," a report prepared annually by the Business and Economic Services unit of the UAB Department of Economics (copy in MRP); Jerri Beck, "Scotty McCallum: UAB's Third President," *UAB Magazine* no. 4 (Summer 1993): 4–5.

117. *BN,* December 9, 1992, July 20, August 25, 1996, May 24, September 15, 1998; *BPH,* February 10, 1999.

Chapter 10

1. *BPH,* December 9, 1992; *BN,* February 13, 1993; C. McCallum interview, March 3, 1993; interview with J. Rudolph Davidson, March 15, 2004, MI:B1; S. R. Hill interview, July 17, 1998; Flynt, *Alabama in the Twentieth Century,* 246.

2. S. R. Hill interview, April 11, 1995; interview with Linda Flaherty-Goldsmith, October 23, 2001, MI:B2; *BN,* February 23, 1995.

3. S. R. Hill interview, April 11, 1995; Goldsmith interview, October 23, 2001; J. Claude Bennett to S. R. Hill, March 31, 1981, Hill to Bennett, April 2, 1981 (copy), S. R. Hill President Records; J. Claude Bennett to George C. Wallace, April 19, 1985 (copy), MRP.

4. Philip E. Austin, "Report to the Board of Trustees," July 20, 1993 (copy), MRP; *UAB Reporter,* June 12, 2001; Mark LaGory to author, September 21, 2004, MC:MRP; UAB/HRM Faculty Data, copy in MRP; Kenneth L. Wilson to author, June 18, 1991, Bennett to author, June 7, 1991, MC:MRP

5. *BPH,* December 10, 1992; P. Austin interview, March 10, 1995; Goldsmith interview, October 23, 2001. The "real academia" quote comes from the author's conversation with Bennett in May 1993; but see also *BPH,* December 10, 1992.

6. *BN,* July 20, 1993; *Birmingham World,* July 19, 22–28, 1993; Austin, "Report to the Board of Trustees"; BOT, 48 (June 28, 1993), 1595.

7. *BN,* July 21, 1993; *BPH,* July 22, 1993.

8. *BPH,* July 22, 1993; P. Austin interview, March 10, 1995; Graham and Diamond, *American Research Universities,* 151–52. In *Built to Last,* Collins and Porras probe growth stages and inculcation of values in all types of organizations.

9. *The Kaleidoscope,* January 12, 1993; *BN,* July 21 and 25, 1993.

10. Mike Ellis, "Special Meeting Notice," July 19, 1993, copy in MRP; "Comments by Dr. J. Claude Bennett upon His Appointment as President of the University of Alabama at Birmingham," July 20, 1993, Media Relations Files, UABA; *BN,* July 21, 1993.

11. *BN,* July 21, 1993.

12. Ibid.; Bugg interview, March 24, 1993; interview with Mark LaGory, September 23, 2004, MI:B2.

13. "Guest List" and diagram, with individual names, of seating arrangement for blessing of the house occasion, Bennett President Records, UABA; C. Bennett interview, Sept. 26, 2006.

14. S. R. Hill to Jarvis D. Ryals, April 19, 1994 (copy), Ryals to Sanders Murell, May 8, 1994 (copy), Ryals to Hill, May 25, 1994 (copy), all in S. R. Hill Post-President Records, UABA; Claude Bennett to Philip Austin, May 12, 1994 (copy), Bennett President Records.

15. Graham and Diamond, *American Research Universities,* 152; S. R. Hill to J. Claude Bennett, August 17, 1994 (copy), MC:MRP.

16. Virginia D. Gauld to Charles McCallum, November 20, 1995 (copy), David J. Rowland to Kenneth Roozen, January 9 and 18, 1996 (copy), Roozen to author, January 10, 1996, Rowland to Roozen, January 9, 1996 (copy), Thomas C. Meredith to Elected Members of the Board of Trustees et al., May 21, 1998 (copy), MC:MRP; *BN,* June 10, 2001; *BPH,* December 10, 1996; *Daily Mountain Eagle* (Jasper, AL), August 30, 1996; John M. Lyons to Henry Hector (of ACHE), December 6, 1993 (copy), Hector to Charles Nash (UA system Vice Chancellor for Academic Affairs), December 17, 1993 (copy), Rowland to Claude Bennett, January 11, 1994, Lyons to Bennett, February 21, 1994, Bennett to Philip E. Austin, September 3, 1996 (copy), all in Bennett President Records.

17. *DAU,* 138.

18. Ibid., 139; anonymous interview with author, July 24, 2003, MI:B3 (under seal); Jackson interview, July 24, 2001.

19. Samuel Jackson to Claude Bennett, May 25, 1995 (copy), Bennett President Records; Richard Berliner to author, September 23, 2004, Ann Bradberry to author, September 23, 2004 (with data from UAB Oracle and HURS personnel systems), MC:MRP; *BPH,* February 24, 2003.

20. *DAU,* 132; Ellen Jackson to author, March 2, 2001, MC:MRP; Claude Bennett to Tom Trasher, December 7, 1993 (copy), Bennett President Records.

21. Claude Bennett to Vice President and Deans, December 5, 1994 (copy), Bennett President Records; *DAU,* 141.

22. *DAU,* 142; Jackson interview, July 24, 2001.

23. Ibid., 65, 74; *BN,* July 16, 2003; Marlene Ricker, "William J. Koopman, M.D.," *UAB Medicine* 31 (Spring 2005): 14.

24. "President's Column," *UAB Report,* December 16, 1994, February 3, 1995; *BN,* February 3, March 15, 1995.

25. Interview with Charles A. McCallum, September 12, 2003, MI:B3.

26. Mark LaGory to author, September 21, 2004, MC:MRP.

27. C. McCallum interview, September 19, 2002; S. Jackson interview, July 24, 2001; anonymous interview (physician) with author, July 24, 2003.

28. LaGory interview, October 23, 2001; anonymous interview with author, July 24, 2003, MI:B3 (under seal); S. Jackson interview, July 24, 2002. The Hugo Black "conversion" is detailed in Newman, *Hugo Black,* 94–96ff.

29. *BN,* February 14, 2001; interview with Ada W. Long, May [15?], 2004, MI: B2.

30. Christina Bemrich to author, May 22, 2001 (which includes an analysis of UAB's printed [catalog] mission statements from 1967 through 1996), MC: MRP; Long interview, May [15?], 2004; interview with Edward LaMonte, June 9, 2001, MI:B2.

31. C. McCallum interview, September 15, 2001; Ira Harkavy (Penn Center for Community Partnerships) to author, April 7, 1993, October 2, 2004, MC: MRP.

32. J. Russell Lindsey to Bennett, April 22, 1996, Bennett President Records; *DAU,* 26.

33. *BN,* September 18, 1996.

34. *UAB Report,* February 3, 1995.

35. James E. Lewis to author, July 6, 1995; "Urban Affairs," November 4, 1994 (4-page typescript), summarizing recent national-level funding for cities and urban universities, and Robert G. Corley to William A. Sibley (copy), Bennett President Records; Nevin Brown to author, September 14, 2004, MC:MRP; Bender, ed., *The University and the City,* 290–97.

36. *DAU,* 138, 144.

37. Ibid.; *BN,* April 14, 1996.

38. *DAU,* 142–43; C. McCallum interview, September 19, 2002; Virginia Gauld to author, September 21, 2004, Lyons to author, September 21, 2004, MC: MRP; interview with Lyons, April 13, 2002, MI:B2.

39. S. Jackson interview, July 24, 2001; *DAU,* 142–43.

40. *DAU,* 124, 142–43.

41. *DAU,* 146; *BPH,* August 31, 1995; *Birmingham World,* November 3–4, 1994.

42. *DAU,* 112.

43. "Guide to UAB Buildings," General Reference, UABA; *DAU,* 91; *The Kaleidoscope,* November 19, 1996; Harry C. Marzette and Adriane C. Burks, "UAB Police Department," 35-page typescript completed in December 2000 (copy in MRP); Traci Fuller to author, October 5, 2000, MC:MRP; *The Kaleidoscope,* April 25, August 15, 2000; *BPH,* April 19, 1996; *Birmingham World,* May 11–17, 1995.

44. Jerry W. Stephens to James Woodward, July 13, 1987 (copy), Woodward to Charles McCallum, July 14, 1987 (copy), McCallum President Records; Stephens to author, October 7, 2004, MC:MRP.

45. *BN,* February 14, 1999.

46. Edward D. Whalen, *Responsibility Centered Management* (Bloomington, 1991); John M. Lyons to author, June 21, 2001, MC:MRP.

47. *DAU,* 16, 40; *BN,* May 2, 1996.

48. Jack Duncan to author, September 23, 2004, MI:B1; Warren S. Martin to author, September 27, 2004, MI:B3.

49. Anonymous interview with author, November 7, 2001, MI:B3 (under seal); Kenneth J. Roozen to author, November 5, 2004, MC:MRP.

50. Kenneth J. Roozen to author, November 5, 2004; C. Bennett interview, September 26, 2006.

51. Mark LaGory to author, September 16 and 25, 2001, MC:MRP; *UAB Report,* February 3 and 10, 1995.

52. Mary E. Guy to author, December 6, 2004, MC:MRP; *DAU,* 107–8; *Tusca-*

loosa News, December 15, 1995; *Huntsville Times,* November 18, 1996; *UAB Reporter,* May 19, July 14, 1997; LaGory interview, September 23, 2004.

53. Louis Dale to Deans, Directors, and Department Heads, November 13, 1995, MC:MRP; Marianne Merrill Moates, "Tanya McMillan Smoot," *UAB Magazine* 14 (Summer 1994): 24–27.

54. James Lal Penick to author, September 27, 2004, MC:MRP; *Birmingham World,* February 9–15, April 27–May 3, 1995.

55. "UAB Black Faculty Information, 1986–97," a report developed by UAB Human Resource Management, September 26, 1997; *DAU,* 41, 49, 57.

56. Kitty Collier to author, May 8, 2001, MC:MRP; photocopy of ACT 94-202 (providing for "a statewide general studies curriculum"), enacted March 17, 1994, MRP.

57. Woodward interview, September 24, 2003.

58. *BN,* October 26, December 9, 2004; *BPH,* May 26, 2001; Joseph L. Marks, *SREB Fact Book on Higher Education; Alabama Highlights, 1994/1995* (Atlanta, 1995); Samuel L. Webb to author, November 2, 2004, MC:MRP.

59. Glenna G. Brown to author, April 27, 2001, MC:MRP.

60. *FF,* 1993–1994 and 1996–97.

61. Linda H. Aiken et al., "The Nurse Shortage: Myth or Reality," *NEJM* 317 (September 2, 1987): 641–46; Robert Steinbrook, "Nursing the Crossfire," *NEJM* 346 (May 30, 2002): 1757–66; Starr, *The Transformation of American Medicine,* 364; A. Smith, *The First Fifty Years,* 329ff.; *NYT,* January 6, 2004; interview with Rachel Booth, April 27, 2001, MI:B1.

62. "Nursing Schools: How They Are Ranked," *Nurse Educator* 20 (January–February 1995): 16–19, *BN,* September 15, 1998; Booth interview, April 27, 2001.

63. *FF,* 1993–1994 and 1996–97.

64. Marilyn J. Field, ed., *Dental Education at the Crossroads: Challenges and Change* (Washington, DC, 1995); V. Matukas interview, Mar. 3, 1994, MI:B3.

65. Mary Lynne Capiluoto to author, October [22?], 2001, MC:MRP; interview with Victor Matukas, March 3, 1994, MI:B3; "Remembering Dr. Matukas," *Synopsis* 19 (November 13, 2000): 3.

66. *Birmingham Times,* December 16, 1993; *Birmingham World,* March 2, December 8–15, 1993; *BPH,* September 4, 19, and 23, 1996; *BN,* June 14, 1996, September 8 and 26, 1999.

67. Glenna G. Brown to author, April 28, 2001, MC:MRP.

68. *DAU,* 12, 37, 65, 68, 76, 152, 154–58, 160, 162, 165–66.

69. *BN,* November 9, 1995; *UAB Synopsis* 24 (December 5, 2005): 1–2; Richard B. Marchase to author, December 10, 2005, MC:MRP.

70. Graham and Diamond, *American Research Universities,* 151–52.

71. *BPH,* March 23, April 6, 1994, May 26, 1995; *BN,* May 26, 1995, December 3, 1996; "Plagiarism Suit Wins," *Science* 268 (May 26, 1995): 1125; *NYT,* May 19, 1995.

72. Interview with Virginia Gauld, December 29, 2004, MI:B2; *FF,* 1993–94 through 1996–97.

73. Gauld interview, December 29, 2004; U.S. Department of Labor, "Majority of Students Work for Pay," *Monthly Labor Review,* July 20, 1999, pp. 1–2.

74. *BN*, June 28, 1993; C. Roger Nance to author, December 12, 1994 (copy), MC:MRP; interview with Christopher Taylor, September 23, 2004, MI:B4.

75. *BPH*, March 4, 1996; *Dothan (AL) Eagle*, February 22, 1996.

76. UAB Institutional Studies and Services, "Enrollment by Race, Fall Terms, 1992–2003" (copy in MRP); *FF*, 1992–93 and 1996–97; Debbie Daily to author, November 21, 1994, containing report titled "UAB Student Demographics," MRP; Raymond Mohl, "Globalization, Latinization and the Nuevo New South," *Journal of American Ethnic History* 22 (Summer 2003): 31–66; "College Attendance Rate Changes . . . 1984–1994," *Chronicle of Higher Education*, September 2, 1996, p. 18; Andrew Marsh to author, September 23, 2004, MC:MRP; *BN*, May 24, 1995.

77. *BN*, July 25, August 5, 6, and 7, 1996; *BPH*, December 9, 1996.

78. Michael L. Slive to Mike Ellis, August 26, 1994 (copy), Claude Bennett to Shirley Whitacre (NCAA), September 18, 1995 (copy), "Analysis of Proposed Upgrade from 1AA to 1A Football" (copy), all in Bennett President Records.

79. *UAB Media Guide: Football 2004;* interview with Joe Davidson, December 3, 2004, MI:B1; *BN*, November 11, 2005.

80. *UAB Alumni Gazette* 12 (Spring 1994): 1; *BN*, July 10, 1994, November 24, 1998.

81. *BN*, July 10 and 12, 1994; *BPH*, July 11 and 19, 1999; interview with Richard R. Arrington, October 31, 1999, MI:B1; Rebecca Gordon to author, November 3, 2004, MC:MRP.

82. *BPH*, July 11, 12, 13, and 19, August 3, 22, and 25, 1994, July 19, 1999; *BN*, July 12 and 14, 1994, September 1, 1997; *Birmingham Times*, July 28, 1994.

83. Claude Bennett to Philip E. Austin, August 17, 1994 (copy), Bennett President Records; *BPH*, July 13, 14, and 15, 1994; *BN*, July 14, 1994; *Wall Street Journal*, November 23, 1994, October 7, 1998; "Remarks by President J. Claude Bennett . . . Concerning NCAA Division I-A Football at UAB," UAB press release, August 23, 1994, Media Relations Files, UABA.

84. *UAB Report*, December 16, 1994; Mike Ellis to Michael L. Slive, August 26, 1994 (copy), Joe Davidson to Brian Teter (Conference USA), May 29, 1995, MRP; Claude Bennett to Shirley Whitacre (NCAA), September 18, 1995 (copy), and "Analysis of Proposed Upgrade from 1AA to 1A Football" (5-page typescript), Bennett President Records; "Watson Brown: Profile," UAB Web site, Athletics/ Men's Football; Ron Clemmons to author, September 28, 2004, MC:MRP.

85. *BPH*, August 29, 1997; *BN*, August 27, September 21, 1997; Jeremy Bearden to author, April 23, 2001, MC:MRP.

86. *BPH*, July 12, 1994; Henry C. Randall to Claude Bennett, September 16, 1996, Diane Bradley to Bennett, September 15, 1996, Samuel W. Jackson to Bennett, July [25?], 1995, all in Bennett President Records; Kenneth Roozen to Virginia Gauld, Mike Ellis, and Joe Davidson, August 21, 1995, Roozen to Robert Staub, August 21, 1995, Tim McMinn to Bennett, August 1, 1995, Roozen to Mike Ellis, August 1, 1995, copies in MRP.

87. Interview with Alice McSpadden Williams, December 1, 2004, MI:B4; interview with Terry C. Cannon, November 16, 2004, MI:B2; Keith Hutcheson

to Robert Staub, November 2, 1994 (copy), MRP; interview with Charles A. McCallum, September 19, 2002, MI:B3.

88. *BPH*, March 26, 1996; interview with C. McCallum, September 19, 2000, MI:B3.

89. Kenneth Roozen to Gene Bartow, undated [1994] (copy), MRP.

90. C. McCallum interview, September 19, 2002; *BPH*, March 26, 1996.

91. Interview with Joe Davidson, December 3, 2004, MI:B1; *BPH*, March 26 and 27, 1996; *BN*, March 27, 1996.

92. *BPH*, March 29, 1996, December 15, 2000; *BN*, March 28, 1996; *Birmingham Business Journal*, February 8, 2001; *Birmingham Times*, May 30, 1996; interview with George Graham, March 26, 1996, MI:B2.

93. *BPH*, February 6, 1995; *BN*, March 27, 1996.

94. *BN*, February 3, March 15, July 21, 1995; *UAB Report*, December 16, 1994.

95. S. Jackson interview, July 24, 2001; S. Jackson to Philip E. Austin et al., September 11, 1995 (copy), Claude Bennett to Mary M. Buckelew, November 3, 1995 (copy), Bennett President Records; Neal A. Vanselow, "The Physician Workforce: Issues for Academic Medical Centers" (paper presented at Forum on the Future of Academic Medicine, New Orleans, December 6, 1996), copy in MRP.

96. *BN*, October 4, 1995; BOT, 47 (October 6, 1995), 1659.

97. *BN*, October 4, 1995; BOT, 47 (October 6, 1995), 1659; *BPH*, October 9, 1995; S. Jackson interview, July 24, 2001.

98. *BPH*, October 7, 1995; Andy Brimmer to Samuel W. Jackson, August 2, 1995 (copy), Bennett President Records.

99. *BN*, March 27, 1995; *Shelby County Reporter*, May 31, 1995; S. Jackson interview, July 24, 2001.

100. *BN*, October 4, 1995.

101. "UAB Enters Partnership to Form Health Care Network," press release, UAB Media Relations, April 21, 1995 (copy), Claude Bennett to James B. Little III, January 2, 1995 (copy), Ina Leonard to Bennett, March 23, 1995, Leonard to Thomas N. Caruthers, February 20, 1995 (copy), Samuel W. Jackson to Bennett, May 17, 1995, all in Bennett President Records; *BN*, April 21, 20, and 22, July 23, 1995.

102. *Huntsville News*, August 2, 1995; *DAU*, 225; S. Jackson interview, July 24, 2001.

103. *Birmingham Business Journal*, January 15, 1996; *BN*, January 3, 20, and 31, 1996.

104. Maud Fowler to Claude Bennett, November 10, 1995 (copy), Bennett to Fowler, December 6, 1995 (copy), Bennett President Records.

105. S. R. Hill interview, March 25, 1993; C. McCallum interview, September 15, 2001.

106. Samuel W. Jackson to Philip E. Austin et al., September 11, 1995 (copy), Bennett President Records; BOT, 47 (October 6, 1995), 1659; *BN*, April 25, 1996; Lauren L. Wainwright (of Sullivan and Cromwell law firm, New York) to author, August 10, 2005. On Morgan as Leviathan, see ch. 1, nn. 20, 32–37 above.

107. *BPH*, December 2, 1995.

108. Claude Bennett to Project Capital Committee, March 12, 1996 (copy), Bennett President Records; Samuel W. Jackson to Linda Flaherty-Goldsmith, April 15, 1996 (copy), PSWJ.

109. Kathleen Kaufman to author, October 1, 2001, MC:MRP; BOT, 48 (September 27, 1996), 1203, and 48 (December 14, 1996), 1043; C. Bennett interview, September 26, 2006.

110. Kathleen Kaufman to author, October 1, 2001; Kevin Lofton to author, August 19, 2001, Samuel Jackson to author, July 25, 2001, MC:MRP; C. McCallum interview, September 19, 2002.

111. Claude Bennett to Samuel W. Jackson, April 2, 1996 (copy), Philip Austin to Bennett, May 27, 1996 (copy), Bennett President Records; *BN*, January 15 and 26, 1996, March 2, 1997, May 18, 1999.

112. Claude Bennett to Philip Austin, February 26, 1996 (copy), Fred Brooke Lee to Luis O. Vasconez, May 1, 1996 (copy), S. R. Hill to Dale Allison and Mike Ellis, February 22, 1996 (copy), Samuel W. Jackson to Bennett, March 11, 1996 (copy), Lee to Task Force Membership (with attached membership list), February 27, 1996 (copy), Jackson to Lee, October 21, 1996, Lee to Jackson, October 21, 1996 (copy), Bennett to Jackson, November 12, 1996, all in Bennett President Records; *BN*, January 26, 1996; *Montgomery Advertiser*, January 28, March 2, 1996; *Tuscaloosa News*, March 4, 1996; *BN*, March 3, 5, 21, 22, and 25, April 10, December 1, 1996; *BPH*, April 16, 1996; "The University of Alabama at Birmingham Special Events Facilities Task Force," April 15, 1996 (10-page typescript), Bennett President Records.

113. *BN*, February 6 and 22, April 6, 1996, March 2, 1997.

114. *BPH*, February 24, 1996; *Montgomery Advertiser*, February 25, March 2 and 8, 1996; *Huntsville Times*, March 3, 1996; *Opelika-Auburn News*, February 26, 1996.

115. J. Claude Bennett to [form letter sent to on- and off-campus individuals, with attached list of 325 recipients], April 16, 1996 (copy), Bennett President Papers, UABA.

116. *BPH*, August 15, 1978; S. R. Hill to Claude Bennett, April 26, 1996, Alfred Bartolucci to Bennett, April 19, 1996 (copy), Don Logan to Bennett, May 23, 1996 (copy), Louis Boackle, Jr., to Bennett, March 11, 1996 (copy), Elton B. Stephens to Bennett, May 9, 1996 (copy), Jack O. Paden to Bennett, May 1, 1996 (copy), T. Morris Hackney to Bennett, April 26, 1996, Robert J. Stanley to Bennett, April 26, 1996 (copy), George Graham to Bennett, April 26, 1996, Barbara Ingalls Shook and Robert P. Shook to Fred Brooke Lee, April 3, 1996 (copy), all in Bennett President Records.

117. *BN*, April 25, 1996.

118. Samuel Jackson to Richard Telkamp, October 28, 1994 (copy), Jackson to Bennett, August 2, 1994, October 19, 1995 (copy), November 6, 1995 (copy), December 8, 1995 (copy), all in Bennett President Records.

119. *Tuscaloosa News*, November 14, 1996.

120. *BN*, July 21 and 30, 1996; *Tuscaloosa News*, July 31, 1996.

121. *BN*, September 15 and 21, 1996, March 2, 1997; Samuel W. Jackson to the

file, February 17, 1996 (copy), 4-page typescript titled "Sequence of Events at the Woodward House," accompanied by videotape, PSWJ.

122. *BN*, September 20, October 10 and 18, November 8, 1996, March 2, 1997; Samuel Jackson to Mac McArthur, September 18, 1996 (copy), PSWF, MRP.

123. *Tuscaloosa News*, November 14, 1996; C. Bennett interview, September 26, 2006.

124. BOT, 48 (September 27, 1996), 1110–11; Claude Bennett to the University of Alabama system, attn. Mr. John Oliver, Interim Chancellor, December 18, 1996, copy in MRP; *DAU*, 143–44; *BPH*, November 14, 1996; *BN*, November 15, 1996, January 2, 12, and 29, 1997; *UAB Reporter*, November 18, 1996; *The Kaleidoscope*, November 19, 1996; *Tuscaloosa News*, November 14, 1996; Mark LaGory to author, September 21, 2004, MC:MRP.

125. *UAB Reporter*, November 25, 1996; *BN*, November 14, 1996, January 28–29, 1997.

126. *BN*, November 14, 1996, March 2, 1997; *BPH*, January 25, 1997; Claude Bennett to John T. Oliver, October 15, 1996 (copy), James C. Pruett to the Board of Trustees of the University of Alabama at Birmingham, December 3, 1996 (copy), PSWJ.

127. *FF*, 1992–93 through 1995–96; Flynt, *Alabama in the Twentieth Century*, 248.

Coda

1. *DAU*, 74–75, 139–40; interview with Paul Hardin, May 19, 2001, MI:B2. An outline of these social gatherings, with guest lists, is located in the active files of the UAB Office of Special Events, in the Administration Building of UAB, some on the twelfth floor and some in the basement.

2. *BN*, March 24, 1997.

3. *BN*, April 17, 1997.

4. *BN*, April 3 and 17, 1997; *BPH*, July 16, 1997.

5. *BPH*, July 16, 1997; *DAU*, 143; Cinnamon Bair, "Wheels of Change," *Florida* 2 (Winter 2004): 10–13; Bair to author, September 28, 2004, MC:MRP; *NYT*, July 2, 17, and 18, 1997; "Ann Reynolds: A Pioneering President for UAB," *UAB Magazine* 18 (Winter 1998): 2–7.

6. Reynolds's difficulties as an administrator in New York are described in *NYT*, June 5, 24, and 29, 1997.

7. Robert G. Corley, "A Widening Chasm," *BN*, November 13, 2005.

8. Eric Gould, *The University in a Corporate Culture* (New Haven, CT, 2003), esp. ch. 3; Derek Bok, *Universities and the Future of America* (Durham and London, 1990).

9. Flynt, *Alabama in the Twentieth Century*, 285.

A Brief Essay on Sources

As shown in the Notes, the UAB Archives, which is a component of the Lister Hill Library of the Health Sciences at the University of Alabama at Birmingham, provides the overwhelming amount of "primary material" employed in this book. For all UAB presidents, and some of the vice presidents and deans, such holdings are carefully curated. Within this facility, too, are archival holdings related to the emergence of UAB, which are photocopies of materials in the W. S. Hoole Special Collections Library, University of Alabama. Likewise, the UAB Archives includes an Oral History Collection pertaining to many of the lead characters—not just administrators—in the UAB story. UA board of trustees minutes are available at the UA system office in Tuscaloosa. Manuscript materials collected by the author are to be given, some under seal, to the UAB Archives. These include McWilliams Research Correspondence, McWilliams Research Papers, McWilliams Interview Notes, and Papers of J. Rudolph Davidson. I completed other key archival research (see the notes) at the Archives of the University of South Alabama, the Birmingham Public Library Archives, the Alabama Department of Archives and History, and the Mervyn H. Sterne Library of the University of Alabama at Birmingham.

Although this book is not offered as a monograph in urban history, but rather as a narrative story about a university and its connections with a city, the role of research universities in the development of Southern cities underpins the book. Hence the slender, powerful volume, *The City in Southern History* (1977), edited by Blaine A. Brownell and David R. Goldfield, while in some ways superseded by recent works, remains a path-breaking classic and helped significantly in establishing the framework for this study. Still, the need remains for a general scholarly monograph treating the impact of research universities on post-1945 urban development in the American South. In this context, the short work written by Catherine Amelia Conner, "Bringing New Life to Birmingham: The Economic and Physical Impact of the University of Alabama at Birmingham, 1944–1990" (M.A. thesis, Auburn University, 2001), is most instructive. Yet I disagree with her assertion that UAB in many ways replaced U.S. Steel as a colonial force in Birmingham. Much of the money generated by U.S. Steel operations in Birmingham went back to banking houses and stockholders of the Northeast, while the money generated by UAB for the most part remained in Birmingham, recirculating with dramatic positive impact—the opposite of extractive economics.

As for cities and universities in general, Thomas E. Bender's *The University and the City: From Medieval Origins to the Present* (1988) guides one toward rich literature regarding both sides of the Atlantic. Even more, it delineates the notions of "international disciplinary community" and "local living community" so vital to examining the history of all universities, especially those connected to the emergence (or reemergence) of cities. Sylvia Harrop's various studies of Unitarians in the development of civic universities in England added immeasurably to my understanding of what motivated Joseph F. Volker as a university leader. Sarah Barnes's article, "England's Civic Universities and the Triumph of the Oxbridge Ideal," in the *History of Education Quarterly* (1996), assisted in a similar way. Arnold Grobman's *Urban State Universities* (1988) is a seminal start at synthesizing the study of urban universities in the United States.

Among the plethora of analyses of universities and health science, much in article form prompted by the pressing need to change how such institutions operate, two books were of particular importance to me: Paul Starr's *The Transformation of American Medicine* (1982), for the way it integrates the emergent "authority" of the physician into higher education; and Edward O. Wilson's *Naturalist* (1994), which in just one chapter tells so much about the origins and the higher-education implications of the molecular biology revolution. There are many new works on the general impact of U.S. universities, but none proved more helpful in this project than *The Rise of American Research Universities: Elites and Challengers in the Postwar Era* (1997), by Hugh Davis Graham and Nancy Diamond.

Closer to home, *Building on a Vision: A Fifty-Year Retrospective of UAB's Academic Health Center* (1995), by Virginia E. Fisher, which includes detailed appendices by William Ashley Harris and Timothy L. Pennycuff, gives fundamental details and striking photographs related to health sciences at UAB. Max Heldman's *The First Forty Years: University of Alabama School of Medicine* (1988) also contains important biographical information and intriguing sketches. Likewise, Howard Holley's *A History of Medicine in Alabama* (1982) is filled with important biographical and institutional (hospitals) information. The unpublished "History of Hillman Hospital" (1987) by Robert G. Corley and others is more analytical than most earlier studies of the future UAB hospital, especially on the way Hillman emerged out of an era in which segregation so heavily influenced health science and clinical care. Also unpublished but filled with insights about UAB's emergent hospital and medical school is Tinsley Harrison's lengthy and analytical, "The Medical School of the University of Alabama, Some Reminiscences" (1971). Two sources produced by UAB give indispensable data and factual chronology: *Dictionary of Academic Units At UAB . . . 1945–1997* (1997), by William A. Harris (fourth edition revised by Timothy L. Pennycuff); and *Facts and Figures,* an annually updated collection of wide-ranging data on UAB dating back to the 1970s and produced most recently by Mary Beth Adams.

Among the rich published sources related to Birmingham and the civil rights movement, with specific pertinence to the UAB story, are Edward S. LaMonte, *Politics and Welfare in Birmingham, 1900–1975* (1995); Glen T. Eskew, *But for Birmingham: The Local and National Movements in the Civil Rights Struggle* (1997); Diane McWhorter, *Carry Me Home* (2001); J. Mills Thornton, *Dividing Lines: Municipal Politics and the Struggle for Civil Rights in Montgomery, Birmingham, and Selma* (2002); and Charles E. Connerly, *"The Most Segregated City in America": City Planning and Civil Rights in Birmingham, 1920–1980* (2005). E. Culpepper Clark's *The Schoolhouse Door: Segregation's Last Stand at the University of Alabama* (1993) provides a detailed backdrop for race and politics in Alabama just as UAB was coming into its own and analyzes many of the personalities fundamental to the seminal developments in Birmingham. For a detailed study of the physical growth (square miles) of the city of Birmingham and its difficult experience with annexation, in part because of U.S. Steel's colonial grip, and UAB's role in this story, see Charles E. Connerly, "One Great City or Colonial Economy: Explaining Birmingham's Annexation Struggles, 1945–1990," *JUH* 26 (November 1999): 44–73, although I disagree with his usage of the word *colonial* as applied to UAB as ultimately a controlling force in Birmingham.

That Northeastern entrepreneurs "colonized" portions of the South in the years following the Civil War, making considerable use of cheap labor, is a central theme of this telling of the UAB story. General studies of such extractive economics and social control date back to scholarship of the 1930s, but certainly the most recognized is C. Vann Woodward's *Origins of the New South, 1877–1913* (1951). Yet a recent study of nineteenth-century America by Richard Franklin Bensel, *Yankee Leviathan: The Origins of Central State Authority in America* (1990), gives a broader version than Woodward's. It also provides crucial underpinning for my thoughts about Birmingham's need to gain control of its own destiny—taking it away from "outside" corporations such as U.S. Steel—through such locally controlled institutions (private and public) as UAB. Ira Harvey does not overtly connect his findings about poor public policy to Alabama's historic experience with extractive economics led by U.S. Steel. But his *History of Educational Finance in Alabama* (1989) is a major, detailed contribution on how such social services as higher education had to struggle long and hard because they were conceived in an age of racism and greed, despite noble efforts to the contrary.

Among the recent spate of books about the evolution and practices of U.S. Steel, I found these the most helpful: Judith Stein's *Running Steel, Running America* (1998); Diane McWhorter's *Carry Me Home* (2001); Henry M. McKiven's *Iron and Steel: Class, Race, and Community in Birmingham, Alabama, 1875–1920* (1995); and Jean Strouse's *Morgan: American Financier* (1999). Of course, as those before them, none of these writers was permitted access to the key U.S. Steel archives that pertain to the extractive nature of the corporation's relationship with Birmingham. Birmingham as a "steel city" in need of change is depicted, with considerable use of metaphor, most notably in Carl Carmer's *Stars Fell on Alabama* (1934) and his less well-known "Back to Alabama," an article in *Holiday* (1960). A similarly literary approach to these needs for change, though more confrontational, is the speech-text (unpublished) by Howell Raines, "Reflections on Alabama: A History of Silence" (1992).

Finally, on how UAB's attraction of federal funds helped take the place of the U.S. Steel payroll, Christopher MacGregor Scribner's *Renewing Birmingham: Federal Funding and the Promise of Change, 1929–1979* (2002) is strong. Though not focused on the post-1979 period, it emphasizes that Birmingham as a whole has room aplenty for more progress. A similar theme for all of Alabama—certainly including Birmingham—pervades Wayne Flynt's *Alabama in the Twentieth Century* (2004), from which this narrative about UAB and Birmingham has significantly benefited.

Index